Early Praise for *A Scrum Book*

There's a lot of wisdom in this book that is applicable and useful outside of a Scrum context. The patterns are pragmatic, engaging, and very well executed—a true joy to read.

➤ **Adam Tornhill**
  Author of *Software Design X-Rays* and *Your Code as a Crime Scene*

A Scrum Book: The Spirit of the Game is a valuable, well-organized resource whether for team members in the early days of their Scrum journey, for journeymen ScrumMasters looking to add techniques and approaches to their toolkit as they unlock more complex improvement efforts, or for master coaches looking for a well-structured body of knowledge into which to integrate and evolve their own patterns. Practices, tools, and principles (the what) are surfaced for us as we go about our daily work, and Sutherland, Coplien, et al. lay bare the philosophy, thinking, and reasoning (the why) to facilitate our learning.

➤ **Mark Gillett**
  Managing Director at Silver Lake, former COO at Skype and CVP at Microsoft

Within minutes of opening *A Scrum Book: The Spirit of the Game*, I implemented my first Scrum pattern and raised the level of my team's software game. I've dabbled in Scrum practices for years, but after reading this book, I have gained a deeper appreciation for the nuances behind those practices and how they work in concert to create an elegant whole. This book is a must read for anyone who works on a team to build software.

➤ **Michael Keeling**
  Staff Software Engineer at LendingHome and author of *Design It!*

This is a book for all Scrum practitioners, veterans as well as newbies. Starting with the first pattern (The Spirit of the Game) and continuing throughout the book, it's about people. You will be able to use the book and its patterns as a source of inspiration when you create your way of working according to Scrum. The book and its patterns cover the what of Scrum as well as its whys. There is no need to wait. Get it! Read it! Use it! Improve!

➤ **Arne Åhlander**
   Certified Scrum Trainer and CEO, Aqqurite AB

The book's use of Zen principles and the lessons from Japanese industrial culture makes this an incredibly fun read. It's extremely informative and I'm sure I'll continue to pick it up frequently to review the wise recommendations contained within.

➤ **Dary Merckens**
   CTO, Gunner Technology

You hold in your hands a work of art that will inspire, support, and challenge you and your organization to be better for the greater good. And have lots of fun while doing it.

➤ **Portia Tung**
   Author of *The Dream Team Nightmare: Tools and Techniques to Boost Team Productivity*, Enterprise Agile Coach, and Executive and Personal Coach and Play Researcher at The School of Play

A Scrum Book: The Spirit of the Game is a magical well of wisdom and experience that empowers you to resolve everyday tension in and remove impediments from your daily workflows. I've just applied the Development Partnership pattern in an isolated client-agency context, in order to bridge a communications divide that has gradually been derailing marketing operations for a blockchain product. It worked like a charm.

➤ **Miloš Milosavljević**
   Senior Account Director, Four Dots

This book is a tool that will help you discover why and how Scrum works. It does not matter if you are new to Scrum or a long-time practitioner, you will be transported to a new understanding of your world of work and the organizations where you do work. The patterns in this book provide strategies and a mindset to transform your Scrum journey. Start with the pattern, The Spirit of the Game, and I guarantee your journey will never end.

➤ **Bob Sarni**
   Founder and Princpal, iOnAgility

A Scrum Book: The Spirit of the Game offers you stepwise improvement no matter what level you are currently on in your agile journey. So if you wonder, "How can we do even better?" I would recommend reading this book. It is both a guidebook and a reference that contains powerful tools (patterns) to start or upgrade your Scrum. I am sure I will grab this book many times in the future.

➤ **René van Hees**
   Chief Software Architect, Thales Nederland B.V.

A Scrum Book: The Spirit of the Game is one of the most competent books I have read. It has absorbed 20 years wisdom of the Scrum community and teaches a system approach to organizational- and team-level issues. Learn patterns, apply them in your workplace, and see the world differently through lenses of System and Lean Thinking.

➤ **Ilia Pavlichenko**
  ScrumMaster, AgiliX

Having the right book at your side is key to success. *A Scrum Book: The Spirit of the Game* is designed to help a multitude of readers in search of a priceless Scrum reference book, whether it is used for studies, work, or to just get inspired. It has a scientific touch, making it a valuable and timeless reference. I truly enjoyed reading this book, and now it is part of my travel library.

➤ **Ralph Jocham**
  Founder/CEO, effective agile, GmbH

A Scrum Book

The Spirit of the Game

Jeff Sutherland
James O. Coplien

Lachlan Heasman
Mark den Hollander
Cesário Oliveira Ramos

and The Scrum Patterns Group:

Esther Vervloed, Neil Harrison, Kiro Harada, Joseph Yoder,
June Kim, Alan O'Callaghan, Mike Beedle, Gertrud Bjørnvig,
Dina Friis, Ville Reijonen, Gabrielle Benefield, Jens Østergaard,
Veli-Pekka Eloranta, Evan Leonard, and Ademar Aguiar

The Pragmatic Bookshelf

Raleigh, North Carolina

Many of the designations used by manufacturers and sellers to distinguish their products are claimed as trademarks. Where those designations appear in this book, and The Pragmatic Programmers, LLC was aware of a trademark claim, the designations have been printed in initial capital letters or in all capitals. The Pragmatic Starter Kit, The Pragmatic Programmer, Pragmatic Programming, Pragmatic Bookshelf, PragProg and the linking *g* device are trademarks of The Pragmatic Programmers, LLC.

Every precaution was taken in the preparation of this book. However, the publisher assumes no responsibility for errors or omissions, or for damages that may result from the use of information (including program listings) contained herein.

Our Pragmatic books, screencasts, and audio books can help you and your team create better software and have more fun. Visit us at *https://pragprog.com*.

The team that produced this book includes:

Publisher: Andy Hunt
VP of Operations: Janet Furlow
Managing Editor: Susan Conant
Development Editor: Adaobi Obi Tulton
Copy Editor: Sean Dennis
Indexing: Potomac Indexing, LLC
Layout: Gilson Graphics

For sales, volume licensing, and support, please contact *support@pragprog.com*.

For international rights, please contact *rights@pragprog.com*.

ISBN-13: 978-1-68050-671-6
Book version: P1.0—August 2019

In memory of Mike Beedle

11 October 1962 — 23 March 2018

Contents

Dedications xiii
Product Owner's Note xv
Preface xvii

Acknowledgments xxi
Introduction xxiii

1. **The Scrum Core as Patterns** 1
   ¶1 The Spirit of the Game   3
   The Core Patterns in Brief   7
   Beyond the Core   10

2. **Product Organization Pattern Language** 11
   Product Organization Sequence   12
   ¶2 The Mist   17
   ¶3 Fertile Soil   20
   ¶4 Conway's Law   23
   ¶5 Birds of a Feather   31
   ¶6 Involve the Managers   35
   ¶7 Scrum Team   45
   ¶8 Collocated Team   50
   ¶9 Small Teams   55
   ¶10 Cross-Functional Team   60
   ¶11 Product Owner   65
   ¶12 Product Owner Team   70
   ¶13 Development Partnership   73
   ¶14 Development Team   78
   ¶15 Stable Teams   82
   ¶16 Autonomous Team   86
   ¶17 Self-Organizing Team   91

A Scaling Sequence   94

¶18 Mitosis   97

Kaizen and Kaikaku   101

¶19 ScrumMaster   104

¶20 Oyatsu Jinja (Snack Shrine)   110

¶21 Small Red Phone   113

¶22 Scrum (Master) Coach   115

¶23 Fixed Work   119

¶24 Sprint Planning   123

¶25 Swarming: One-Piece Continuous Flow   127

¶26 Kaizen Pulse   132

¶27 Remove the Shade   136

¶28 Pop the Happy Bubble   139

¶29 Daily Scrum   143

¶30 ScrumMaster Incognito   148

¶31 Norms of Conduct   150

¶32 Emergency Procedure   152

¶33 Illegitimus Non Interruptus   157

¶34 Scrum of Scrums   161

¶35 Sprint Review   165

¶36 Sprint Retrospective   170

¶37 MetaScrum   176

¶38 Product Pride   181

3.   **Value Stream Pattern Language** **185**

Value Stream Sequence   187

¶39 Vision   191

¶40 Impediment List   195

¶41 Value Stream   198

¶42 Set-Based Design   203

¶43 Sprint Burndown Chart   210

¶44 Scrum Board   215

¶45 Product Roadmap   220

Rhythms: Patterns of Time   225

¶46 Sprint   228

¶47 Organizational Sprint Pulse   234

¶48 Release Plan   237

¶49 Release Range   241

Value and ROI   246

¶50 ROI-Ordered Backlog   248

¶51 High Value First 251

¶52 Change for Free 255

¶53 Money for Nothing 258

Product Backlog Sequence 261

¶54 Product Backlog 263

¶55 Product Backlog Item 268

¶56 Information Radiator 274

¶57 Pigs Estimate 280

¶58 Small Items 283

¶59 Granularity Gradient 288

¶60 Estimation Points 292

¶61 Fixed-Date PBI 297

¶62 Vacation PBI 300

¶63 Enabling Specification 306

¶64 Refined Product Backlog 311

¶65 Definition of Ready 316

Notes on Velocity 320

¶66 Yesterday's Weather 324

¶67 Running Average Velocity 326

¶68 Aggregate Velocity 329

¶69 Specialized Velocities 334

¶70 Updated Velocity 337

¶71 Sprint Goal 340

¶72 Sprint Backlog 345

¶73 Sprint Backlog Item 348

¶74 Teams That Finish Early Accelerate Faster 351

¶75 Production Episode 353

¶76 Developer-Ordered Work Plan 358

¶77 Follow the Moon 363

¶78 Visible Status 366

¶79 Dependencies First 371

¶80 Good Housekeeping 374

¶81 Whack the Mole 377

¶82 Definition of Done 382

¶83 Team Sprint 387

¶84 Responsive Deployment 391

¶85 Regular Product Increment 397

¶86 Release Staging Layers 401

¶87 Testable Improvements 405

¶88 One Step at a Time 410

¶89 Value Areas   415
¶90 Value Stream Fork   419
¶91 Happiness Metric   426
¶92 Scrumming the Scrum   440
¶93 Greatest Value   445
¶94 Product Wake   448

4.   **Composing Your Own Pattern Language**   451
     Project Languages   452
     A Project Language of Highly Effective Teams   452
     Your Own Pattern Language   453

A1. **Patlets**   457
     Patterns in the Product Organization Pattern Language   457
     Patterns in the Value Stream Pattern Language   461
     Patterns from the Organizational Patterns Book   466
     Patterns from Fearless Change   470

A2. **Picture Credits**   471

     Bibliography   485
     Index   499

Dedications

Cesário Ramos: *To Jacqueline for smiling all those times I told her I had to go away to "work" on the book; to Ken Schwaber for letting me join the Scrum.org trainers and to all of you using Scrum to improve the world.*

Mark den Hollander: *To Esther who always supports me in the endeavors I take.*

Veli-Pekka Eloranta: *To Aija for endless support and to all of you in the trenches who have less than one week since last commit.*

Esther Vervloed: *To Mark who asked me to join him in this journey.*

Evan Leonard: *To Joy, who continues to support my endless curiosity. And my parents who taught me to love what I do.*

Jim Coplien: *To Gertrud, who gave me new life, and to Bob Warfield, pioneer of the ¶29 Daily Scrum. SDG.*

Lachlan Heasman: *To Jen and my kids for accepting me travelling to the other side of the planet to work on these patterns. And my friend Jens for getting me involved in this work.*

Neil Harrison: *To Jesus Christ, my Lord and Savior, and the author and finisher of my faith.*

Ville Reijonen: *To Ewa.*

Ademar Aguiar: *To Quitéria and my daughters, Mariana and Leonor, for being always with me, even when I am out. To my friends Richard and Joe, for keeping on challenging me, despite of my "cousins."*

Jens Østergaard: *To all Scrum Teams building good products.*

Jeff Sutherland: *To Hiro Takeuchi and Ikujiro Nonaka who gave us the name Scrum and as the grandfathers of "scrum" continue to support and guide us in this work.*

Kiro Harada: *To all Kaizen practitioners sharing their wisdom and experience to make work easier and safer.*

Joseph Yoder: *To all those doing the right things for the right reasons. Also to the Scrum PLoP team for continuing to work hard all of these years to finish this project.*

June Kim: *To my late mother, who showed me curiosity and adventure, and to the authors of the Agile Manifesto who left a trail for me to follow.*

Alan O'Callaghan: *To my gorgeous wife, Ria, for her love, and for reminding sometimes when I need to laugh at myself. And to my grandchildren Tyler, Freya, Finnlay and Shay—who never seem to need reminding to laugh at me.*

Gertrud Bjørnvig: *To Cope for his endless passion and persistence—a huge factor for getting this book out.*

Dina Friis: *To Jim who prods me into thinking and to Jens who spurs me to act.*

Gabrielle Benefield: *To my amazing family, Robert, Aidan and Talia, for the never-ending adventure of life. To the amazing Agile community, for the never-ending adventure of learning.*

Product Owner's Note

The genesis of this book traces back to the summer of 2008 when Jens Østergaard, Gertrud Bjørnvig, and I were exploring dreams of how we could better share the message of Scrum with the world, while we were together at Stora Nyteboda—Jens' country house in Sweden. Knowing that patterns had already been used to describe organizational practices, we realized that they would also be a good match for the framework nature of Scrum. In May 2010, the first group of eight authors came together at Stora Nyteboda to start mining the patterns that would nurture this book's effort.

We steadily made progress over ten years marked by many moments of fellowship, anticipation, progress, struggle, joy, and occasional frustration. These patterns emerged from the collective hearts and souls of our twenty authors over that time. We all "have" all of them. So this is not so much a compendium of separate ideas from separate authors, but rather the result of nearly a decade of people supporting each other in learning and reflection, and synthesizing and annealing the patterns into a body of hard-won, practical, and authoritative insights. I wanted to take the opportunity in this note to first thank my nineteen friends and colleagues who were the wellspring of the work you hold in your hands (or are reading on your screen).

But the main message I want to convey in this note is to recognize the core editorial team within the author ranks who pulled this book together into a cogent Whole during the last three years of its development. That group meticulously undertook all the thankless work of refining the grammar, of securing permission for the artwork, of making the tough decisions of what's in and what's out, and a thousand other details. Christopher Alexander teaches us that beauty in architecture owes to attentiveness to structure down to the granularity of one-sixtieth of an inch as much as it does to the urban-scale patterns. Our editors adeptly traversed this entire range of manuscript detail to bring the book as close as we could to our vision of Wholeness and beauty. So I would like to especially thank Mark den Hollander, Cesário Ramos, and Lachlan Heasman, each of whom invested hundreds and sometimes thousands of hours doing the meticulous, tedious, and sometimes weighty work that aspires to a result that is a piece of literature rather than just a good technical book. Dina Friis joined this editorial effort as she could and also stands out in her thoughtful contributions and her challenges to the rest of us. Together, we fought the good that drives out the perfect—and while a pattern is never perfect, I feel that this team in particular helped move us a great distance along this spectrum. Friends, you have my very deepest and heartfelt appreciation.

Yet, in a broader sense, we all are only the messengers and editors of the great ideas from that broader Scrum community of which you are a part. On behalf of all the authors, I'd like to thank you for reading and using the patterns in this book, and for thereby improving your own world of work, and in turn making the whole world just a little bit better for all of us.

— James O. Coplien, Product Owner, *A Scrum Book.*

Preface

Welcome to the start of your new journey into Scrum, and perhaps even into yourself. The patterns you'll find here are tools that can help you not only to discover Scrum, but help you gain deeper insight into how and why it works. Much of that discovery will take you deep inside the practices and beliefs of your organization. It may challenge much of your current worldview, while at the same time making you feel at home.

Some of Scrum's origins lie in Japanese culture and Buddhism. Driving even more deeply, those who view Scrum as a way of work life rather than just as a method are more likely to find fulfillment in their Scrum journey. Zen Buddhists used the story of the Ten Bulls as a metaphor for the Zen journey into one's self. The bull has long been a symbol of reflection that predates its appearance in Chinese Buddhism in the eleventh century. The story metaphorically connects the pragmatic with the idealistic through pictures originally drawn by the twelfth-century Zen master Kaku-an Shu-en, where a simple person grows from a reductionist world of bulls, whips and effort to melt into nature and the world, ultimately to emerge like Putai—the laughing Buddha.

尋牛

The Search for the Bull

I am able to develop product. It's a job. It's often tiring. I've heard of this thing called Scrum but am not really sure whether people are actually using it or whether it works. I am exhausted from looking for it. It feels intuitive, but it's so different from anything we've done before that I'm not sure it's right.

見跡

Discovering the Footprints

I saw a Scrum book in the bookstore. I had heard stories of great men and women called ScrumMasters and Product Owners, and of a world of prosperity, of software in thirty days and two times the output in half of the time. Yet before they were only dreams and stories. Now it is as obvious as the nose on my face: there is something here that intrigues me, and it is real.

見牛

Perceiving the Bull

I have joined a Scrum Team, with great hopes and aspirations—Scrum must be here. I am in wonder of the many orders of magnitude claims and of Toyota-like quality. Others describe it differently, but it seems as though we are talking about the same thing. It fills my imagination and lifts my expectations.

得牛

Catching the Bull

I try Scrum with my team. It is a struggle between me and Scrum, and I am determined that I shall become master over this thing called Scrum. The effort is high to align it with my direction: it is like a wild animal. The harder I try to bend it to my will, the more problems that surface. This is not what I wanted, and it is not the Scrum I learned about at the agile conferences.

牧牛

Taming the Bull

I am still trying to use Scrum, but with more success. I am in harmony with *The Scrum Guide*. Scrum seems to do something useful. It wraps my old practices but makes obvious where I have strayed from a good path. Setbacks become more of a game than a struggle. There is no conflict with the way I used to do things. I grow happy. Or is it complacency?

騎牛帰家

Riding the Bull Home

Scrum now works for us! We are running Sprints, and life joins Sprints' cycles. Others follow along to join the Sprint rhythm, and a great team emerges. Is this Scrum? Whose Scrum? Jeff Sutherland's? Ken Schwaber's? Mine?

忘牛存人

The Bull Transcended

All the parts work in harmony: Product Owner and team, Scrum Team and customers: they all work together. Scrum mastered *me*. It is natural and it is obvious how to work. Its intuitiveness obviates the rule book called *The Scrum Guide*. There is no Scrum. What *is* there? Do I care?

人牛倶忘

Both Bull and Self Transcended

There is now an even broader Wholeness where there are no "parts working together." There is no boundary between parts, between self and how the self and others do work. We are a Whole. There is no Team and Customer, no Us and Them. I am not sure this is Scrum any more.

返本還源
Reaching the Source

It's obvious. I get it. Crap. It was part of me all along. I knew it—but did not know that I knew it. Why did I spend all that money on training and certification?

入鄽垂手
In the World

Now I can help my organization, and organizations everywhere, increase in the wisdom of development. I am happy—so happy that people call me crazy, every day listening to others and sharing the stories of my patterns with them.

Scrum is not an endpoint, but rather a journey in which team members join each other as they embark into new ways of organizing work. The principles that underlie this way of organizing work come from thinking *beyond* one's self. We must consider how the team works as a Whole and how the team and organization form an even greater Whole. Even beyond that we should ponder our connection to the market and the whole of our broader day-to-day work life.

However, it starts—and continues—as a journey *into* one's self. In Scrum, we take it that we must put aside our ego and our drive to control an outcome, and should instead harmonize with our market, colleagues, and work. All of this book's practical advice harkens back to these reflective foundations. So we start here with a playful adaptation of the story of the Ten Bulls as a metaphor for your Scrum journey. It is a journey intended to lead you to master Scrum knowledge and to broaden its contribution to your team and your own daily life —and then, beyond, to your world. Reaching that point will free you to grow into your next stage of mastery in the world of work and beyond.

You may be surprised to find such a story on the first pages of a Scrum book. Maybe you even find it a bit off-putting. That's O.K.: the rest of the book is much more soundly pragmatic. In our work we find most Scrum practice to align with the first few steps of the journey described here in the Preface. However, the current Self of some of you, and the future Self of others, may find that something here touches something deep within you or your team: a taste of the deeper Spirit of the Game.

Acknowledgments

In the same sense that it takes the proverbial village to raise a child, it takes a community to capture the patterns of a powerful discipline like Scrum. The authors have drawn insights from the thousands and thousands of Scrum practitioners worldwide with whom we have worked for many years. These are the folks on the front line, in the trenches, whose work bears out what works well and what doesn't work well in complex system development. We first and foremost acknowledge them—or perhaps we should say "you"—as those of our community who have contributed both directly and indirectly to the hard-won insights here. Thanks to all of you out there.

We also thank the Hillside Group, our umbrella "chartering" organization for sending its representatives to give us an outside perspective on how we were doing things, in spite of the fact that we kidnapped just about everyone they sent.

We very much appreciate those of the group who, with their selfless and often anonymous gifts, made it possible for many of the rest of the team to attend the annual event. You know who you are.

A special thanks to our co-author Jens Østergaard, the Lord of Stora Nyteboda, to the management and staff of Helenekilde Badhotel in Tisvildeleje, Denmark (2011–2014), of the Odawara Resort in Odawara, Japan (October 2015), and of Quinta da Pacheca in Régua, Portugal (2015–2019), all of whom warmly hosted us for our annual events and intensive editorial sessions. They were each homes away from home for our gatherings. And thanks to all who helped out at these venues: Sandra Dias and her team, as well as Christine Hegarty, Espen Suenson, and Mette Jaquet. In the same vein, we'd like to thank Neil Harrison, Jim Coplien, Cesário Ramos and, again, Jens Østergaard, who opened their homes to us for intensive editorial sessions. And we appreciate Kiro Harada, who arranged the session in Odawara; Ademar Aguiar, who arranged the author events at Pacheca; and Gertrud Bjørnvig, who coordinated the author gatherings at Helenekilde.

A very special thanks to our manuscript reviewers outside the Scrum Patterns Group, who patiently scoured the volume of material to give us feedback. We want to give a special mention to Mark Gillett, whose comments added a dimension of experience that complemented ours very well, and whose excruciatingly thorough review, detailed comments, and concrete suggestions almost give him the stature of an honorary co-author. Other relentless and thorough reviewers included Steve Berczuk, Paul Mock, Adam Tornhill, Dary Merckens, Joe Fair, Michael Keeling, Yvette Backer, John Pagonis, Marcelo R. Lopez, Jr., Jamie Collins, Portia Tung and Boško Majdanac, who spent countless hours poring over the manuscript to point out mistakes and opportunities for improvement. There were also great comments from Martin de Liefde, Chris Johnson, Al J. Simons, Jowen Mei, Peter Gfader, Kenny Munck, Nis Holst, Michiel Sival, Marko Leppänen, Johannes Koskinen, Jari Rauhamäki, Philipp Bachmann, Bob Sarni, and Rune Funch Søltoft. Many thanks, folks!

Many warm thanks to the Pragmatic Bookshelf editor who got us started, Brian MacDonald. But our warmest thanks goes to Adaobi Obi Tulton who worked patiently and tirelessly with us—especially with the editorial team of Jim Coplien, Cesário Ramos, Mark den Hollander and Lachlan Heasman—to bring the book through its final year of ascent to realization. It was a real pleasure to work with you, Adaobi!

The authors would like to warmly thank Joe Bergin for his own pattern which was the inspiration for our own pattern of the same name, ¶51 *High Value First.*

Many thanks to John Hayes for relating the experience of his Scrum Team as they tracked happiness and velocity, and for sharing the data we used for the graphs in *Happiness Metric.*

At Scrum PLoP 2015 Richard Gabriel was our guest, and led us in a workshop on effective writing. Thanks for caring and sharing, Dick.

Tsutomo Yasui and Yasunobu Kawaguchi contributed at the Sashimi Scrum Blitz in Odawara, Japan in October 2015.

Thanks to the people at autotracer.org and at inkscape.org for some raster-to-vector image conversions.

A great thanks to Nofoprint in Helsingør, Denmark, and to Søren Mikkelsen, for their support and responsiveness in producing the alpha versions of the book manuscript—great quality work, folks!

And, last, thanks to the many who helped review and refine the book through their presence at our Writers' Workshops and through correspondence, including Dan Greening, Doug Shimp, Paul DuPuy, Martien van Steenbergen, and Adrian Lander.

Introduction

This is a book about Scrum—a simple but powerful way for people to work together. Scrum is about helping small teams create, build, and evolve a product, one slice at a time. Scrum is as much about people as it is about the products they build and use. It defines a work environment where teams can challenge themselves to become better and better at their work over time. Its simplicity is much of its power: *The Scrum Guide*[1] is a succinct definition of Scrum fundamentals and it's only 19 pages long.

Scrum is not a development method, but rather a product development framework. A method prescribes steps that transform a problem definition into a solution. Scrum, on the other hand, is a framework for the team to continuously evaluate its product and evolve it into a *better* solution. More than that, Scrum also guides the team to continuously evaluate *how* it builds the product, and to creatively adapt its process to work more efficiently, deliver ever more responsively, and to grow product quality. Scrum defines how a self-managing team might best structure its work to deliver product increments to create the highest possible value for all stakeholders. Scrum focuses outward on the product that will add value to the community and to the end user, while also reflecting on how to make the development process ever more powerful, and the workplace a fulfilling and happy place. Scrum shines in complex domains where product requirements are unclear. It dissolves this uncertainty with frequent feedback, short iterations, time-boxing, and continuous workflow. Scrum is certainly the most widely adopted of all agile approaches: journalism, advertising, software development, and automobile construction are all examples of industries and professions where Scrum has made inroads.

---

1. Jeff Sutherland and Ken Schwaber. *The Scrum Guide*. ScrumGuides.org, http://www.scrumguides.org (accessed 5 January 2017).

Scrum—Through the Lens of Experience

Scrum has its roots in Japanese manufacturing. It takes its foundations broadly from the Toyota Product Development System, and in particular, from the Toyota Production System. Scrum adoption has grown rapidly since its inception in 1993 and its introduction to the public in 1995. Yet, it is still new to many organizations. For those new to Scrum, it may be a mystery to identify where to start. For organizations already using Scrum, it can be a challenge to find out where to focus improvement. Over the time that we, the book's authors, have been using Scrum (and we have been using Scrum since its inception), we have come to understand the networks of patterns that make it work: *how* Scrum works, *why* it works, and *how* best to apply it in daily practice.

We have several person-centuries of combined experience with Scrum. This book gathers that collective experience into proven solutions called *patterns* that we have distilled from observing many Scrum Teams—both their successes and failures. These solutions will help you implement and improve your use of Scrum, whether you are a beginner or an experienced practitioner. Though pragmatic and grounded in experience, this book also stands on Scrum's deepest foundations and reflects contributions from many early shapers of Scrum, including its inventor. As a rationalized oracle, this book hopes to help dispel many of the widespread myths about Scrum and its practices.

The solutions in this book not only draw on prior art and publication but also tap into the vast experience of a broad international community of product developers. The patterns come from our work with Scrum Teams worldwide, from our home bases in Japan, the Nordics, the U.K., Portugal, Canada, U.S., Netherlands, and Australia—and from our experiences on every continent except Antarctica. We have observed these patterns in many contexts, from organizations with thousands of staff members to small teams of three people; and in dozens of industries: telecommunications, banking, education, machine automation, and countless others. Each pattern has been through a process of detailed review by up to a dozen people, each of whom applied their collective dirty-hands experience with Scrum to relentlessly refine each one. Dozens of candidate patterns didn't make it to the book, as they rose only to the level of anecdotal experience, or lacked empirical validation, or were just precursors to greater patterns. We believe that the patterns in this book have something special. The pattern community calls it "the Quality without a name," or sometimes just "the Quality," a kind of Wholeness that aspires to day-to-day excellence.

Adaptive Problems, Adaptive Solutions

The Scrum Guide defines Scrum as "a framework within which people can address complex adaptive problems, while productively and creatively delivering products of the highest possible value."[2] This definition describes both Scrum's assumptions and the perspectives we develop from using it. One way to recognize a complex problem is to recognize it as one that you don't fully understand until seeing its solution, and that you can't derive the solution from first principles ahead of time. Solving the problem begs exploration and feedback. The problem's dynamic element demands adaptive solutions that change over time and with our engagement. Our current solution meets our current needs—but these will change. An example of this kind of problem is new product development: it may be easy to see why the product was a success after it is successful, but to be certain beforehand is impossible.

Beyond the Rulebook

Speaking of *The Scrum Guide*, we view it just as the rulebook for Scrum. It's important to understand the rules, and it's even useful to follow them most of the time. But reading the rulebook of chess won't make you a great chess player. After learning the rules, the player then learns about common strategies for the game; the player may also learn basic techniques at this level. Next is learning how to combine strategies you learn from others while maybe adding some of your own. Ultimately, one can transcend any formalism and proceed from the cues one receives from one's center, from one's instinct. This book is for those who want to understand the rules more clearly; for those who want to grow by combining ideas and by evolving the fundamental structure of the system, rather than by merely refining technique. Jeff Sutherland points this out:

> In recent years the Scrum Patterns Group has evolved a comprehensive set of patterns for Scrum that allow teams to try proven approaches that have worked in many companies. While *The Scrum Guide* describes the basic rules of Scrum, the patterns amplify the guide by showing teams how to solve problems in a specific context.

So *The Scrum Guide* is the rulebook, and the patterns look beyond the rules. These patterns shape the on-the-job-training of making Scrum work for you on your way up the ladder of ongoing improvement. Some day, long from now, you may even outgrow these patterns as you evolve them and define your own. There are no points for doing Scrum, and these patterns are the gate through which

---

2. Jeff Sutherland and Ken Schwaber. *The Scrum Guide*. ScrumGuides.org, http://www.scrumguides.org (accessed 5 January 2017).

a highly driven team passes on the road to the top echelons of performance. Patterns do their job when they help people honestly and critically search within themselves on their path to excellence. One ignores the patterns at one's peril, but only an unthinking organization follows them slavishly.

Patterns of Scrum

We describe elements of the Scrum framework using a form called *patterns*. What is a pattern? One simple definition is that a pattern is a repeatably applicable solution to a problem that arises in a specific context. Christopher Alexander, a building architect, popularized the modern notion of patterns as a way for communities to celebrate, socialize, and refine the design norms of their built world, in *The Timeless Way of Building [Ale79]*. The pattern-writing form (see Pattern Form on page xxviii later in this chapter) structures the written insights that describe how people build things—things that aspire to a quality of Wholeness which pattern folks call "the Quality without a name." You might have experienced the feeling of this Quality if you have seen some result in an area in which you have deep experience, that just "feels right" or gives you a deep sense of warmth, contentment, and confidence.

Alexander's work focused on constructing towns, neighborhoods, and buildings, but the underlying theory extends to anything built in a community. Beyond that, patterns structure broad solutions to recurring general problems, while each one unveils a concrete, proven solution in the reader's mind. Patterns in general describe forms and how designers compose them as they create and evolve structure in their worlds. This book focuses on the two main structures that organizations build to realize Scrum: the organization with its roles, relationships, and periodic gatherings of people, and the Value Stream that choreographs these gatherings over time and connects them to their wellsprings and to their effluent out to the market. Scrum patterns are the forms we create and compose when we structure both the development organization and the development process.

Each pattern helps you focus your thinking on a single, well-contextualized problem at a time. Working in small steps reduces risk and helps teams move forward with confidence in "process improvement." Each pattern describes the solution in enough detail to bring you to the point of that "aha" where you recognize the solution deep within yourself. Beyond that, the pattern suggests how it might change the organization, and it looks ahead to both negative and positive consequences of doing so. Patterns also draw on experience to suggest a set of next steps that are likely to make the system yet more Whole. A carefully chosen *sequence* of such patterns—a listing of the canonical order in which the organization designer introduces change—can resolve product development issues and, importantly, help the organization understand Scrum more in depth.

The Birth of a Pattern

Patterns come from our reflective observations about our hands-on interactions to solve problems in the world. We have the first inkling of a pattern when we see a problem and hear the small voice within us pointing us toward a solution. We try the solution to see if it works in our situation. If it does, then we keep using it and move on to the next challenge. And if it doesn't, we back out the change and try something else. (Sounds agile, doesn't it?) Repeated substantiated experiences with such solutions crystallize them and give them stature as patterns. We may eventually write them down and share them within our community.

Patterns in general come out of community, and the patterns here are no exception. The patterns have their roots in our collective experience. The authors have worked together to choose only the best from a much larger set of candidate patterns that arose along the way. Each pattern has earned its position here because it represents something singular, fundamental, or important, or because it communicates otherwise elusive common sense. The authors have supported each other in reshaping and polishing these patterns to incorporate perspectives from across the whole Scrum community. They reflect input and engagement from a broad constituency and, in particular, from people who carry the foundational insights of Scrum from its inception and early practice.

These patterns go beyond descriptions of vernacular practice to capture the deep nuggets of insight that often elude everyday practitioners. For example, most people believe the purpose of the *¶29 Daily Scrum* is to answer the Three Questions; in fact, the Wikipedia article for stand-up meetings until recently said that the main focus of the *Daily Scrum* was to answer the Three Questions. (Notice that we refer to patterns using a notation that starts with a "¶" semaphore followed by the pattern number and the pattern name. The section Book Notations on page xxxvii later in this chapter describes such notations and naming conventions in some detail.) To set the record straight, the *Daily Scrum* instead exists as an event where the *¶14 Development Team* replans the *¶46 Sprint*: answering the questions takes only a small fraction of the time and is done just to provide context for the replanning. There are also widespread misunderstandings about what it means to fail a *Sprint*, about the *¶71 Sprint Goal*, and about the role of specification in Scrum. In this book, we tap into longstanding experience, timeless origins, and the most authoritative sources to set the record straight. Each pattern has been through a long journey of review and refinement so you can enjoy a powerful synthesis of informed and authoritative views on those Scrum elements that they explain and clarify.

Beyond being just a "solution to a problem in a context," each pattern explores the forces at play in the complex contexts of organizational development and workflow. These forces are the *why* behind the pattern. Through these patterns, you can understand the problem in depth and better appreciate *why* the solution might work. However, if you find something in your deepest self, whispering in your ear to try something other than what the pattern suggests, you are probably best to follow that instinct. You know your situation and problem better than we can ever encode in writing. If the pattern awakens your instinct and opens a path towards higher ground, it has done its job. A pattern is not always a goal, but a gate through which you pass on the way to seeing and acting more clearly. And in the agile spirit, the proof is in the tasting. Patterns are often small changes that you can implement provisionally. After inspecting and adapting, you may either go on to the next pattern or may in some cases decide to take one step backwards, undo the pattern, and try something else. Scrum is an empirical framework and each pattern should offer empirical evidence that it works, to validate your decision to apply it.

Pattern Form

We divide written patterns into sections that lead the reader on a literary journey into understanding why the pattern works. A pattern always starts with a picture that serves as a kind of visual mnemonic for the pattern. The first section of text generally describes the situation in which this pattern occurs; this is called the *context* of the pattern. Three stars delimit the end of the context. The second section is a statement of a problem that occurs in this context, usually highlighted in **bold**. Then follow the trade-offs that play in the problem. We call these *forces*, after the metaphor of the forces of gravity and wind that an architect or builder must balance in the built world. However, Scrum patterns, like Alexander's patterns, view forces in a much more inclusive way that includes our vulgar instincts, our aspirations, and our fears. Now we can tie together our context, problem, and forces with a solution. The solution is a simple, direct action in **bold** text, couched in a short explanation to make the solution clear. Then come the three stars again to delimit the end of the solution. In most complex domains there are always loose ends after applying even the best of solutions, so we usually add more descriptive text detailing how to introduce the solution. This text also describes *how* and *why* the pattern works, so the reader can build on his or her own insight to build the most Whole result. The application of the solution results in a new situation with a new context, with new problems to solve, leading to new patterns.

At the beginning of each pattern, we have annotated the pattern name with zero, one, or two stars. If a pattern has two stars, we believe that you ultimately will need this solution to resolve the forces to move forward in Scrum. If it has one star, we still believe that the pattern is the core of a good solution; however, we cannot argue that it is the *only* way. If the pattern has zero stars we still feel it works as a solution and that it is the best solution much of the time—though other good solutions exist as well.

No Pattern Stands Alone

It's tempting to cherry-pick patterns and try to apply them to solve problems in isolation. In simple systems, we can tire-patch individual problems without being distracted by adjacent concerns. However, in a complex system such as a workplace organization, changes we make in one place may have unintended side effects elsewhere. Though each pattern helps us focus on the problem at hand, context is everything. Applying each pattern in the broader context of the patterns that are already there helps us avoid unintentional setbacks from side effects. A pattern language strives to order patterns in a way that minimizes such setbacks. We have worked hard to do that for you here.

For example, consider the patterns *¶16 Autonomous Team* and *¶10 Cross-Functional Team*. You might decide that team autonomy is such a central agile principle that you want to put it in place early, so you try to apply that pattern first. But then you find that the team really can't be autonomous, as it shows signs of depending on external workers to fill gaps in their expertise as work calls for specific competencies. The commitment to becoming cross-functional needs to be in place before a team can achieve autonomy, so it will be suboptimal to consider one without considering the other.

When you apply a pattern, the solution will itself create new forces that you must resolve at the next level of detail, so it's also important to have hints about what to do next. As much as each pattern describes a single solution to a problem, interdependencies of complex system components imply that no pattern stands alone. We must think of each pattern like the bumper sticker from the 1960s: "Think globally, act locally." Alexander tells us:

> Each pattern can exist in the world, only to the extent that is supported by other patterns: the larger patterns in which it is embedded, the patterns of the same

size that surround it, and the smaller patterns which are embedded in it. (From *A Pattern Language: Towns, Buildings, Construction* [AIS77], p. xii.)

We share this fundamental view of the world, that says when you build something you must also repair and make better the world around it. The world at large then gradually improves, becomes more coherent and more Whole. A set of patterns that work together to this end is called a *pattern language*. A language has a grammar that defines "legal" sequences of "parts." In a pattern language, the parts are patterns, but the relationships between the parts are as much or more part of the language than the parts themselves. Each pattern describes the context of those patterns that are prerequisites for the current one. And each pattern also advises us about what other patterns might further refine our Whole to help complete this one. These relationships, or connections, form a structure, a grammar, a language. This book presents two such languages: the Product Organization Pattern Language on page 11, and the Value Stream Pattern Language on page 185.

Sometimes, you just need patience. Fixing an organization often has more of the complexity of a train wreck than that of putting on tire patches. While acting locally, think globally. Sometimes you will need to apply several patterns —maybe over several months—to solve a complex problem in the organization. Together, these patterns will resolve the forces in the organization in a way that allows the solution to emerge. We say that the patterns *generate* the solution, indirectly, rather than subdue the system by force. It might take some mental discipline to subdue your instincts to try to coerce the system into providing immediate gratification. In the end, you can't control a complex system, and it may require several individually small nudges to turn the ship. But remember: apply a single pattern at a time (¶88 *One Step at a Time*).

Patterns Are About People

Most importantly, patterns are about people. Some of our clients want us to tell them what to do in Scrum transformations, or to answer pointed questions about a particular decision in their journey. Those who use patterns in this way are missing the core of their power. It is true that these Scrum patterns encode centuries of hard-won experience. Nonetheless, your particular situation usually brings its own forces, trade-offs, and opportunities—and if you're really in touch with your team and your business, the ability to recognize a great solution already lies deep within you. Rather than creating patterns as instruction manuals, we wrote these to inspire you to carefully consider the forces at play in a particular situation, to draw you into wrestling with problems at a deeper level than business dialectic usually affords, and to lead you to discover those gems of collective insight that lie latent in the collective experience and spirit of your Scrum Team. They may remind you of what you once knew before you learned the modern techniques of your trade or the practices of current fashion in your industry. Like Scrum, patterns provide no final answers. Both of them are ways to engage our instinct to refine the day-to-day processes by which we build great things that add value to our community.

Kaizen Spirit

Lastly, it will be a long time before you run out of patterns for improving your organization. Scrum, like patterns, is based on a passionate and ever-present spirit of improvement that the Japanese call *kaizen* (カイゼン). A good Scrum Team celebrates the discovery of a new shortcoming, carefully ponders what allowed such a failure to arise, and then looks within itself, perhaps guided by friends and patterns, to seek solutions to the problem. Even when things are going well, great Scrum Teams constantly have the question on their mind: *How can we do even better?* This attitude is the heart of Scrum, and it shows up in events that range from the *Daily Scrum* where the team replans the *Sprint* to squeeze the absolute maximum value from their work, to the ¶36 *Sprint Retrospective* where the team collectively reflects on problems and improvement. Both the Value Stream and Product Organization Structure languages offer patterns to make problems visible and effect frequent improvements so the team gets better and better. Value increases accordingly —whether "value" means higher quality product to an end user, or whether it means a better work environment and a happier team.

Getting Started

New Scrum Teams can use pattern languages as a kind of roadmap to introduce Scrum into their organizations, one pattern at a time. Dependencies between patterns form a complex graph, albeit a directed graph with no backtracking. Knowing where to start can be overwhelming. This section will help you get started with pattern languages and pattern sequences.

This book contains two pattern languages. We call them "languages" because they define constraints on the combination and ordering of the parts (the patterns) in the same way that a grammar does (for example, for words). As mentioned earlier, one pattern language (in Chapter 2) deals with the organizational structure and another (Chapter 3) deals with the structure of the Value Stream. Don't let the titles scare you: we'll introduce you to anything you need to know about Value Streams if it's important for moving ahead.

Both pattern languages are broadly about organizational *design*, at a level above the implementation concerns germane to your organization. You can implement each pattern in a million different ways. One language describes the design of the Scrum organization; the other describes the metaphorical stream along which the product flows, turning the raw materials of its tributaries into products that flow into the market. There is usually one Scrum organization per Value Stream.

We split these patterns into two languages because the patterns of each language tend to be highly coupled to each other, but loosely coupled to patterns in the other language. We find that this structuring helps newcomers more readily understand the big picture of Scrum. The connections between patterns became more clear as we added new patterns, and they started to fit together like puzzle pieces that belonged in two separate puzzles. Then we fine-tuned the languages' structure and content by evaluating sequences that they generated, to form a more rigorous "grammar" of ordering. By synchronicity, our overall result matches the division of organizational design patterns found in earlier research such as in *Organizational Patterns of Agile Software Development [CH04]*. As you design your new organization, you should freely pick and choose patterns from both chapters.

To get started, get together as a Scrum Team. Start with the book in one hand and a pad of small stickies in the other. Read through the patterns that catch your eye and put a sticky note on the first page of each pattern that excites you, or makes you nod, or that intrigues you as being able to make your Scrum more whole. Then create a totally ordered list of the patterns you have selected in the order you choose to implement them. Don't get too serious about it; you can follow your intuition and change the ordering at any time. There can be a few patterns from the Product Organization Structure language and then a few from the Value Stream language according to your team's collective insight. To order your patterns, place ones that have more extensive scope (larger context) before those with a more refined scope. For example, if you are a Product Owner and already have a vision for your product, you might start with a Product Roadmap and then introduce a Product Backlog and Product Backlog Items. Maybe you decide to hire someone to help you through the Scrum process from this point on so you bring a ScrumMaster on board. Alternatively, you may hire a Development Team and let it take the lead to hire a ScrumMaster. Eventually you start working towards a Refined Product Backlog. Ordering your list of patterns is always a matter of common sense.

Pattern Sequences

We call this ordered list of candidate patterns a *sequence*, or sometimes a *project language* (which is unrelated to the field of traditional project management, and that the same word is used is merely an accident of history). We present five example sequences in the book: the Product Organization Sequence on page 12, the Value Stream Sequence on page 187, a Product Backlog Sequence on page 261, a A Scaling Sequence on page 94, and a sequence called A Project Language of Highly Effective Teams on page 452. Each sequence describes one typical path through the language, and you can use them as inspiration for your own project language. Most example sequences start at the beginning, assuming you have absolutely no Scrum structure in place; if you have already started, find your existing context in the language and start there. Start with the biggest pattern where you can create something, then move to the patterns that refine it by selecting the smaller patterns you think will apply in your situation; then work through the even smaller patterns that refine these even further, and select the ones that help you fix your particular problem. And thus starts your journey of improvement. Agile is as agile does, and implementing Scrum is itself a process of inspecting and adapting. Implement one pattern at a time so you can unambiguously assess afterwards whether it worked (see ¶88 *One Step at a Time*). You'll adjust the patterns in your sequence now and again, reordering, taking some patterns out, and putting others in.

Piecemeal Progress Toward Wholeness

Deciding where to start can be important to gain traction and influence in an organization. But instead of finding "the right starting point" as described earlier, you can simply start anywhere. Taking a pattern from the book and working out how it fits in your organization and implementing the solution will take you on a path to more patterns and more change. Progress will be piecemeal as you move from one pattern to the next. You will find implementing the solution in one pattern will make a change in your situation—in the world—and thus creates a new context and the opportunity to apply another pattern to further improve it. This will be a piecemeal process of changing your team or organization.

Maybe you find that something is missing. We took the patterns to as high a level of excellence as our experience could afford. Maybe you need to finish the job for us, in your particular context. A pattern is always a work in progress. As Paul Valery asserted for his poems, a pattern is never finished by its author: it is only abandoned. We have abandoned them into your hands, and they will again take up vivacity only when you make them your own. Take the liberty of evolving these patterns in your own direction. Assemble the community and write your *own* patterns, and add them to your own pattern language. We have offered a starting point, and in spite of our experience, we can't foresee every problem that will arise. We certainly don't have an exhaustive knowledge of solutions specific to your situation. Especially in local contexts, you will be able to recall broad prior experience to know what has worked for you before. Such knowledge too often gets lost, and one can often find it hidden among the neurons of the gray-haired folk in your organization. Build a community around this pattern-writing activity and evolve *your* pattern language. You need to build *the* pattern language for your group: each of the book's two major chapters comprises only *a* pattern language. We feel we have roughed out the big picture. We hope you take this accumulated knowledge seriously, but in the end, it's your show.

We want to take this opportunity to implore you to attend to the links each pattern offers: both to the patterns it refines, and to the patterns that further refine it. Although you may be acting locally, everything you do is in the context of the global organization. Always think about the wholeness of the Whole you are striving to improve; about your entire organization inside and outside the Scrum parts; and about all the people whose lives you touch in your world of work.

The Fundamental Process

In the spirit of "build the right process and you'll build the right product," the most basic process is what the agile folk call "inspect and adapt." Deming called it *plan-do-check-act* (PDCA) and later renamed it *plan-do-study-act* (PDSA) to emphasize the importance of analysis over mere inspection. Christopher Alexander calls it *the fundamental process*. This is the heart of Scrum, and the cycle of process improvement is Scrum's heartbeat. The ¶46 *Sprint* in Scrum is first a cycle of process improvement and second, a cycle of regular delivery.

The early work of Christopher Alexander (the building pattern guy) on patterns had strong links to Japanese culture and some of its philosophical literature. In the same way, Scrum finds its roots in Japanese industrial culture and its deeper philosophy. In recent years, Alexander expanded his vision of pattern theory, of how to apply patterns, and of how patterns work. In a series of works collectively called *The Nature of Order* (*The Nature of Order: An Essay on the Art of Building and the Nature of the Universe—Book 1, The Phenomenon of Life [Ale04], Book 2, The Process of Creating Life [Ale04a], Book 3, A Vision of a Living World [Ale04b], Book 4, The Luminous Ground [Ale04c]*), Alexander describes the process by which people interact with the built world using their fullest humanity, striving to increase the Quality in all they do. This process well applies to your Scrum journey. We offer his "fundamental process" as follows as a guideline that might inspire you in your application of these patterns. We include it here as much for the sake of what it says about the importance of the human element as for its steps. For "centers" in the following, you can substitute "patterns." Note that the patterns themselves help guide the intuition of the designer and the steps that the process follows, as Alexander describes in *Book 2, The Process of Creating Life [Ale04a]* (p. 216):

1. At any given moment in a process, we have a certain partially evolved state of a structure. This state is described by the wholeness: the system of centers, and their relative nesting and degrees of life.

2. We pay attention as profoundly as possible to this WHOLENESS—its global, large-scale order, both actual and latent.

3. We try to identify the sense in which this structure is weakest as a whole, weakest in its coherence as a whole, most deeply lacking in feeling.

4. We look for the latent centers in the whole. These are not those centers which are robust and exist strongly already; rather, they are centers which are dimly present in a weak form, but which seem to us to contribute to or cause the current absence of life in the whole.

5. We then choose one of these latent centers to work on. It may be a large center, or middle-sized, or small.

6. We use one or more of the fifteen structure-preserving transformations [simple structures], singly or in combination, to differentiate and strengthen the structure in its wholeness.

7. As a result of the differentiation which occurs, new centers are born. The extent of the fifteen properties which accompany creation of new centers will also take place.

8. In particular we shall have increased the strength of certain larger centers; we shall also have increased the strength of parallel centers; and we shall also have increased the strength of smaller centers. As a whole, the structure will now, as a result of this differentiation, be stronger and have more coherence and definition as a living structure.

9. We test to make sure that this is actually so, and that the presumed increase of life has actually taken place.

10. We also test that what we have done is the simplest differentiation possible, to accomplish this goal in respect of the center that is under development.

11. When complete, we go back to the beginning of the cycle, and apply the same process again.

Sometimes a pattern won't resolve the forces you have in your context. Remember that there are no silver bullets; these patterns are based on the experiences we've collected, and your situation may be different. You *will* need to locally adapt each pattern to *your* situation. You can implement each pattern a million different ways without it ever being the same twice.

A Quick Tour of the Book

This is probably not a book you will read cover to cover. We're glad you're starting with the introduction. A good next step might be to read the very first pattern, ¶1 *The Spirit of the Game*: it may help you ponder how high your aspirations should reach when applying these patterns. Then, you might take a day to skim the patterns in the book, reading just the **boldface** text, which we use to help you internalize how the pieces integrate into an overall concept. That's why the boldface bits are there.

The book weaves together two intertwined narratives. The patterns are the heart of the book, and in some sense the rest of the text is secondary supporting material. In accordance with broad convention, each pattern has a number (see Book Notations on page xxxvii, which follows), and the patterns appear in the book in numerical order. The order of the patterns within Chapter 2 and Chapter 3 reflect a typical order in which one might apply the patterns, the canonical sequence for applying them. We explored this in more detail in Patterns of Scrum on page xxvi. Patterns also refer to each other by number, and the links between them form a graph which reflects the structure of the pattern language that contains them. We have woven the second narrative into spaces between the patterns. It includes chapters such as this one that describe the book's approach, philosophy, and history; a minimal pattern-based exposition of the Scrum Core in Chapter 1; and other small sections that clarify or amplify special topics. Many of these topics, while important to Scrum, are not patterns per se, but instead describe broad concepts or principles on which the patterns stand. So, for example, the section Notes on Velocity on page 320 appears right before a group of patterns that focus on velocity. Also among these interludes you will find example sequences that describe how the patterns link to each other in an idealized order of application.

At the heart of the book are the two pattern languages in Chapters 2 and 3. Each of these pattern languages offers one perspective on the multiple forms cutting across your organization. Chapter 2 focuses on the roles, relationships, and gatherings of people, and Chapter 3 on the organization of the workflow. You may certainly pick and choose from both chapters as described earlier. Each pattern is numbered, and patterns refer to each other by pattern number rather than by page number, in accord with the convention that Alexander used in his work. After reading *The Spirit of the Game*, you might read the main sequences: the Product Organization Sequence on page 12, and the Value Stream Sequence on page 187. Those sequences will give you an overview of the Wholes that the pattern languages represent and may draw you into more deeply reading individual patterns that speak to you.

Chapter 4 talks about how to bring the pattern languages into your own space, and gives an example sequence (project language) to build a high-performing team.

This book builds on past work which itself contributed much to agile foundations, and which itself has a wealth of insight into making Scrum work. Rather than reiterating those patterns here, we refer to the original source. However, we want you to be able to recognize those patterns within yourself when you come across them, and we include short descriptions of each one to help jog your memory. Chapter 5 provides *patlets* (small, one-sentence pattern summaries) for patterns from other sources, particularly from *Organizational Patterns of Agile Software Development [CH04]*. The same chapter contains patlets for the patterns in this book—we tend to use it as an annotated topical index when we are seeking how to solve a particular problem.

Book Notations

Good patterns not only work together as elements of a grammar or language that can generate countless system variants, but their names also enrich the design vocabulary in the everyday spoken and written language of organization design discourse. So the term *Sprint Review* is three things. First, the *Sprint Review* is the name we give to a group of people who assemble for a time-boxed interval each ¶46 *Sprint* to assess the state of the product increment. We can point to that group of people and say, "Oh, look, they're having their *Sprint Review* over there right now." You can see it, point to it, and refer to any instance of it by name. Second, it describes the process one uses to create such a gathering, and the process can be found in writing under the name ¶35 *Sprint Review* in this book. You notice that the name begins with the curious prefix ¶35, to be read: *Pattern 35*. The patterns appear in the book in numerical order according to this prefix. Lastly, *Sprint Review* becomes a term that we use in our everyday language as we discuss our Scrum implementation, how it is going, and how to improve it.

This book frequently uses pattern names in this latter sense, as though they were ordinary English phrases. We try to introduce patterns in the book before referring to them in this way. But, still, we call out each use of such terms as a pattern, so as to distinguish the words from vernacular English. The traditional pattern literature dating back to the late 1970s has always distinguished pattern names in a small caps typeface. However, since there were technical issues that prevented us from using the preferred typeface, our work-around is to distinguish patterns with a prefix that includes a ¶ character and the pattern number as described earlier. But since a page full of such prefixes (and for those using electronic books or reading this on the web, a page full of hyperlinks) could potentially be too distracting, only the first reference to a given pattern within a given section will appear this way; subsequent references appear in a *distinguished typeface*. The book often refers to organizational patterns from other sources, though the section Patlets on page 457 includes a synopsis of each one called a *patlet*. When we reference one of those patterns, we give its name, its pattern number (with the perfunctory ¶) and a reference (page number or hyperlink) to the patlet text within the book. For example, we would refer to *Community of Trust* as *¶95 Community of Trust* on page 466.

What Now?

We've covered a lot of ground in this introduction; congratulations for getting this far. Next up is the first chapter of the book, The Scrum Core as Patterns on page 1. In this chapter, you get better acquainted with Scrum, starting with our first pattern (*¶1 The Spirit of the Game*) which is followed by a definition of Scrum using the patterns in this book.

As we wrote earlier, you do not have to read the book cover to cover but we do recommend you read the first chapter. *The Scrum Core as Patterns* helps to familiarize you with what may be new to you (patterns) through something familiar (Scrum). However, you don't have to start there. Here are some other options you might like to try.

- Read through one of the sequences. They give you an overview of the patterns in the language and one way to order their use.

- Skim all the patterns by reading just those parts of the patterns that appear in boldface.

- Start with an element of Scrum your team is struggling with, read that pattern and the patterns that refine it, then use these to improve how you are working.

- Find a pattern that matches where your teams are and see what refines this position in the pattern languages.

- Read through the Patlets on page 457, which are short summaries of all the patterns in the book (and in a few other books).

- Flip through the book and stop at a pattern that looks interesting or has an interesting title (*¶20 Oyatsu Jinja (Snack Shrine)* usually grabs attention).

- After you have spent time reading, reflecting, and trying the patterns, we invite you to read Composing Your Own Pattern Language on page 451.

No matter how you start, we do recommend having a pencil and some sticky notes at hand. Take advantage of the whitespace in the book to write your thoughts. Use the sticky notes to mark pages you want to come back to. We know when a book has had an impact on us because it is worn from many readings; we hope that is the case for your copy.

CHAPTER 1

The Scrum Core as Patterns

This chapter will set you on your path in three ways:

1. We give a succinct overview of Scrum that helps you see the big picture.

2. We tie the main elements of Scrum to patterns, to hone your intuition of how they work together.

3. We introduce the most fundamental rules of the game called "People Building Something Together."

We will help you broaden your understanding of Scrum in a way that will attune your intuition as to what patterns are. It will also make clear that this is a book about broad experience with people and about how *you* can benefit by tailoring those organizational building blocks to your situation. It's not a book of rules and absolutes that you can follow blindly.

We will describe Scrum in terms of its two large-scale structures: the organization that builds a product, and the Value Stream along which the product flows. Each of these is a *Whole*, a designed thing in its own right. A pattern language guides us one step at a time as we build such a Whole. This book presents two pattern languages, one for each of two conceptual Wholes, that provide expert and proven guidance as you build your Scrum organization.

This chapter introduces you to the very first pattern, ¶1 *The Spirit of the Game*, which stands at the head of each pattern language. It sets the stage for all remaining patterns. Even more important, we hope that this chapter and *The Spirit of the Game* will give you newfound insight on how to think about this book, how to use it, and on how to use Scrum.

Think of Scrum as a game we play. As with most games, it can be a wonderful form of engagement if its players appreciate both the discipline and freedom that help them create value. Most of the patterns in the book suggest organizational changes that work that way. But at a deeper level, you should approach the art of building or growing your organization as a game as well. We find that one does well to approach patterns somewhat playfully, with hope of realizing each pattern's benefit and with a degree of comfort to adopt each pattern's disciplines. Your exploration is more like serious play than a regimented game, and much of your inquiry will relate more to common sense than to following the rules. You may explore what *Done* means to you (see *¶82 Definition of Done*), how long a *Sprint* should be, how many people should be on your team, and a thousand other considerations. Engagement with the game is about trying things out, assessing the result, and proceeding accordingly. It may mean saying "no" to some patterns. But if you say "no" out of fear or discomfort rather than from a posture of great expectation, or if you say "no" to stay in line with what some rule book says, you may not yet have the proper grounding to take such work forward. We're going to try to help you start off on the right foot.

When poorly played, "People Building Something Together" is a game that our team or our company tries to win. In the larger scheme of things, Scrum is a game that never ends. Our company and our competitors may take turns in the lead as each one innovates new features, paths to market, or other increments of value to society. Played this way in the long term, we lift the quality of life of the entire community. Getting there in a complex world is about being in touch with that world, inspecting at every step and innovating as a community to do the right thing in the moment. That's where we start, and it is in that sense that the first pattern underlies the rest. A good pattern stands on its own, and we'll let the pattern explain itself.

¶1 The Spirit of the Game

Confidence stars: **

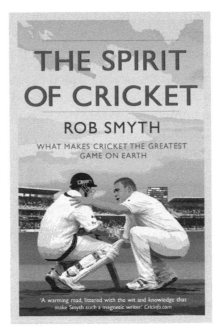

...the Scrum framework does not have all the answers, which means that the team cannot look to Scrum for direction when it does not give a final answer.

❖ ❖ ❖

Written rules might give concrete guidance for how to work together, but *spirit* is part of culture that guides interactions and may be discerned only when ignored or violated.

Cricket is a game that owes much of its unique appeal to the fact that it should be played not only within its laws but also within the Spirit of the Game. If the players do anything to abuse this spirit it injures the game itself. The major responsibility for ensuring the spirit of fair play rests with the captains.[1]

> On 16 May 1999 the actions of the captain in a world cup cricket game caused the umpire to intervene even in the absence of any violation of an explicit cricket law. The captain of the Indian team complained to the umpire that the South African captain was using an earpiece to communicate with the coach. The

---

1. Marylebone Cricket Club. "The Laws of Cricket." Lords.org, http://www.lords.org/mcc/laws-of-cricket/preamble-to-the-laws/, 2012 (accessed 13 August 2013).

earpiece, though not in violation of a stated law of cricket, was in violation of the spirit of the game and was removed for breaking this spirit.[2]

Scrum requires a spirit of interaction between people, and that spirit can be difficult to define. This spirit is part of the culture of the organization and may be indiscernible for the people within the culture. Though it may be difficult to define, the spirit is easy to recognize when it is broken.

Scrum is a lightweight process framework which is simple to understand but difficult to master.[3] Because it is easy to understand, people tend to fill in their blind spots with assumptions. It's easy to assume that Scrum requires only simple changes in work practices, while missing its core spirit. Consequently, some treat Scrum as instructions rather than as guiding principles. Scrum itself does not give any answers but creates transparency on a daily basis, so team members can start to gain insights into how they work together. With this insight, they can start to improve.

Culture plays out in habits, and changing habits is difficult. Moving from a command-and-control organization to *¶16 Autonomous Team*s might feel uncomfortable for developers as they are faced with the need to think more for themselves. It might make managers feel that they are losing power as the teams can make decisions without their approval. Individuals in the organization might balk at changing behavior with the excuse that "we have always done it like this." We may take comfort in the fact that what we are doing now works in some known way. We don't want to mess with that success —just tweak it a bit. Thus can an organization sabotage Scrum by holding on to old ways of working. The standing organizational design can be at odds with Scrum principles. For example, a Vice President might demand a fixed date and scope, creating constraints that the team cannot satisfy. This will likely lead to unintended consequences such as poor quality or burnout. Another example is when a project manager requests daily reports from the *¶14 Development Team*: it telegraphs suspicion instead of trust, wasted time instead of efficiency, and an expectation of control instead of autonomy.

In Scrum, the *Development Team* should be an *Autonomous Team* and also a *¶17 Self-Organizing Team.* There is no hierarchy within the team. This is easier said than done because prior hierarchy might persist. One example on

---

2. "SA Captain told to remove hearing device that's 'against spirit of game.'" ESPNCricInfo.com, http://www.espncricinfo.com/page2/content/story/82603.html, 1999 (accessed 13 August 2013).

3. Jeff Sutherland and Ken Schwaber. *The Scrum Guide.* ScrumGuides.org, http://www.scrumguides.org (accessed 5 January 2017).

an organizational level is when a manager "tries to improve" the Scrum implementation by using the team's development tracking tool for individual performance assessment. The focus turns from teams to individuals, and such metrics are at best second- or third-hand measurements that abstract away crucial contributions beyond the number of bricks they have laid that day. This thwarts team autonomy and self-organization, and may constrain the way the team works (individuals act in accordance with measurements instead of their own effectiveness, perhaps to optimize their financial compensation) so it falls short of its potential effectiveness. Another example is when a resource manager changes the team composition every *¶46 Sprint* trying to optimize the knowledge needed for each *Sprint*: this of course robs the team of self-organization opportunities and destroys their autonomy.

Scrum is about teamwork, but some prefer to pursue personal success instead of team success, or even broader definitions of success.

In the land of the blind, the one-eyed man is king. Anyone in the organization can assert their authority by claiming they can see what others don't. A team member, a Vice President, or a manager can assert any outlandish measure, using the excuse that it does not violate any rules in *The Scrum Guide*. Some misunderstand the spirit, ignore the spirit, or are coerced to break the spirit. That the question of "compliance" even arises is itself outside the spirit.

The examples from the earlier paragraph are not literally in contradiction with *The Scrum Guide*, but neither are they in the spirit of the Agile Manifesto and its sixteen principles, which are mainly about people, their interactions, and change.[4] As Scrum is under the umbrella of these values, it stands against what these examples say about their organizations, based on at least one of the principles: "Build projects around motivated individuals. Give them the environment and support their needs, and trust them to get the job done."

Therefore:

When using Scrum, the product community must focus on explicitly creating a culture in the organization where people know and follow the spirit of Scrum.

Everyone working in or with a *¶7 Scrum Team* needs to help develop this culture by leading by example.

❖ ❖ ❖

4. *Manifesto for Agile Software Development: Principles.* Agilemanifesto.org, http://agilemanifesto.org/principles.html, 2001, accessed 23 January 2017.

To create the culture you must be the culture. This involves deliberately breaking from old ways of thinking and acting (which themselves may be imperceptible; see *Organizational Culture and Leadership, 3rd ed. [Sch06]*). In the previous examples, everyone's goal should be to work within the spirit of Scrum to resolve the problems. When starting to use the Scrum framework, the team will find it challenging to work within the spirit. It will feel uncomfortable for people, and will be arduous—again, it's about habits. To overcome this challenge, it is essential to start with good ¶119 *ScrumMasters* and ¶11 *Product Owners*, and it is necessary for everyone on the team to support each other to work within the spirit. A new culture emerges, where the spirit will be inherent in the ways of working and interacting.

In Scrum and cricket there are clear rules for the game; in both, it is essential that the spirit is a guide for the people using these rules.

The Spirit of the Game plays out in ¶119 *Patron Role* on page 469, ¶95 *Community of Trust* on page 466, and ¶3 *Fertile Soil*.

The pattern header picture is from the cover of *The Spirit of Cricket: What makes cricket the greatest game on Earth [Smy10]*; a special thanks to the publisher, Elliot & Thompson, for permission.

The Core Patterns in Brief

We can describe Scrum in terms of three *roles*, five *events*, and three *artifacts*. In this book we view each of these, as well as many more fine-grained elements of Scrum, as *patterns*—solutions to organizational, process, and business problems. At a higher level, an organization views Scrum as a way to structure the workforce, as well as a way to organize how work flows through that organizational structure. We have structured much of this book around these two ways of looking at Scrum in the large. The roles, events, and artifacts are patterns that contribute to one or the other, or both, of these larger structures. In fact, it is a bit artificial to separate Scrum into these two parts: Scrum is a quite simple, integrated worldview. However, to some degree, the organizational concerns belong with each other and reinforce each other, as do the process concerns, so it will likely be easier for you to grasp the whole if the book can help you first grasp these two focused concerns.

But before we dive more deeply into Scrum, here we present it in a nutshell, as a single Whole, perhaps in the simplest possible terms. The core of Scrum stands on these twelve patterns. We will of course dive into each of these in more depth, each in its own turn—as well as many smaller patterns that refine them and help tie them together.

We can succinctly define Scrum in terms of its roles, its events, and its artifacts. We start with a list that defines terms for Scrum's roles. Each term is both an ordinary word phrase describing the role, and also the name of a pattern describing the role. The terms for events and artifacts work the same way. There are three roles in Scrum:

- the ¶11 *Product Owner*, who owns the vision of the product direction and its rollout;

- the ¶14 *Development Team*, which builds product increments to the *Product Owner*'s specification; and

- the ¶19 *ScrumMaster*, who owns the process and leads incremental improvement efforts.

Each one of these is both the name of a role and a pattern that describes that role. We use pattern names the same way in the text ahead for the *events* and *artifacts* of Scrum. These roles work in a product team called a ¶7 *Scrum Team*. They interact with each other in five main events:

- the ¶46 *Sprint*, a time-boxed interval that is typically two weeks long and sets development cadence;

- ¶24 *Sprint Planning*, an event where stakeholders (mainly the *Scrum Team* members) together plan upcoming development, focusing on the work ahead of them in the current *Sprint*;

- the ¶29 *Daily Scrum*, an event at which the *Development Team* adjusts the *Sprint* plan, focusing on the next 24 hours;

- the ¶35 *Sprint Review*, an event where stakeholders overview the product status; and

- the ¶36 *Sprint Retrospective*, where the *Scrum Team* members assess how the process is working for them.

Underlying the framework are three artifacts:

- the ¶54 *Product Backlog*, which the *Scrum Team* uses to plan upcoming deliveries;

- the ¶72 *Sprint Backlog*, which the *Development Team* uses as its work plan for the current *Sprint*; and

- the ¶85 *Regular Product Increment*, which the team delivers to end users.

Each one of these is a pattern: something that the organization builds to add to or refine either the organization or its development process. What we "build" may take the shape of a role or of a temporary gathering of people or of a list of items or the product itself—any fruit of human innovation and design.

As an organization introduces Scrum, it might introduce these elements one at a time, as is the usual practice for patterns. The roadmap for introducing patterns one at a time is called a *sequence*. Here is a typical or canonical sequence by which these patterns fit together to introduce Scrum in a development effort. This is probably the minimal set of patterns which together could be called Scrum.

¶7 *Scrum Team* The *Scrum Team* emerges from the broader organization or culture. It is both a ¶8 *Collocated Team* and a ¶10 *Cross-Functional Team* that operates as a small business, making independent decisions to respond to stakeholders and the market. The first member of the *Scrum Team* is usually the...

¶11 *Product Owner* ...who leads the newly formed team to realize his or her ¶39 *Vision* to create value. The *Product Owner* is the single person accountable to realize the *Vision*, to create value through that *Vision*, and to concretely communicate the vision through the *Product Backlog*. The *Product Owner* is the voice of value to rest of the *Scrum Team*.

¶14 *Development Team* The *Product Owner* hires a team to implement the product as a series of *Regular Product Increment*s, to realize the *Vision*. (By "hire" we mean to associate a committed group to the effort, whether in the formal sense of employment for wages or through some other form of organizational commitment.) The *Development Team* is a team within the *Scrum Team*.

¶19 *ScrumMaster* The *Scrum Team* identifies (chooses or hires, as previously described) a *ScrumMaster* as the team's servant leader to guide them in the Scrum process, and in continuous improvement.

¶54 *Product Backlog* Foresight, experience, and circumstances guide decisions about what to build and deliver now, next week, and next month. The *Product Owner* builds an ordered list of *Regular Product Increment*s called the *Product Backlog*, based on today's best estimate of business conditions. The *Product Backlog* makes the likely trajectory of long-term delivery visible to all stakeholders. The *Product Owner* builds the initial *Product Backlog* and leads the *Scrum Team* to refine, break down, and update its content over subsequent iterations.

¶46 *Sprint* The team starts its first iteration, called a *Sprint*, to plan and develop a *Regular Product Increment*. *Sprint*s have a consistent length of typically one, two, or four workweeks, establishing a fixed cadence of work, delivery, review, and process improvement done together.

¶24 *Sprint Planning* The *Scrum Team*—the *Product Owner*, *Development Team*, and the *ScrumMaster*—assembles to plan the development part of the *Sprint*, to build a potentially releasable *Regular Product Increment*.

¶72 *Sprint Backlog* The *Development Team* plans how it will achieve the *Sprint*'s objective, called the *¶71 Sprint Goal*, and how it will develop the *¶55 Product Backlog Item*s to deliver the *Regular Product Increment*. The *Development Team* creates a work plan called a *Sprint Backlog*.

¶29 *Daily Scrum* Once development starts in the *Sprint*, the *Development Team* assembles every day in an event called the *Daily Scrum* to adjust their work plan to optimize its chances of meeting the *Sprint Goal* and of delivering the *Product Backlog Item*s they forecast that they would deliver.

¶35 *Sprint Review* At the end of the *Sprint*, development stops, and the *Scrum Team* together evaluates progress on the product. The *Product Owner* decides what changes to incorporate into the imminent release.

¶85 *Regular Product Increment* *Product Backlog Item*s that the *Product Owner* has decided to incorporate compose into a cohesive *Regular Product*

Increment which the *Product Owner* may choose to make available for use by stakeholders. The items in the *Regular Product Increment* must comply to a predefined ¶*182 Definition of Done.*

¶*36 Sprint Retrospective* As the last gathering of the *Sprint*, the *Scrum Team* assembles to contemplate how best to make incremental process improvements, and commits to make one such improvement during the next *Sprint*.

Beyond the Core

Now you know all of Scrum—albeit only to a somewhat shallow level. We're just getting started. The patterns that follow take you beyond the *what* of Scrum into its *whys*. We wanted to start you off gently with this chapter to help you understand the big picture of Scrum if you are new to Scrum, and to make it clear that your success with Scrum depends as much on how these patterns inform your insight and experience as it does on fully "doing Scrum." There are no Scrum police. But the patterns capture broad experience with a strong track record, and while no one will keep score of how many patterns you use, our ambition and hope is that the patterns' history and the persuasion of their rationale should give you confidence to use them. The key is to get the whole team to self-organize, to take charge together, and to move forward together.

The next two chapters build on what you know so far, both through the patterns we have introduced here and by introducing additional patterns that add texture and refinement to this foundation. In particular, the next chapter, Product Organization Pattern Language on page 11 talks about you as a person, and your colleagues, and how you come together in different settings and groups to take work forward. Take your time to browse the patterns and to follow the links from one to another. Reflect on how they touch on your own past experiences, and look for them within yourself. If one speaks to you, tailor it to your organization and get your team to try it. Now your exploration starts: do great things, and enjoy the journey!

CHAPTER 2

Product Organization Pattern Language

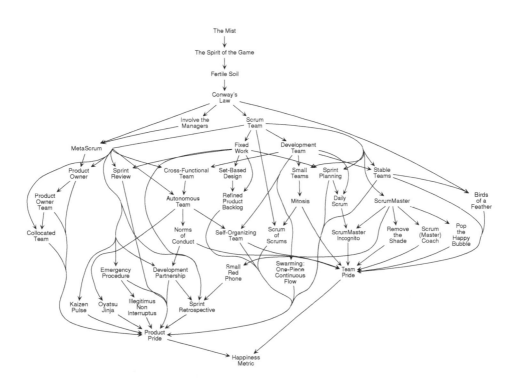

This chapter describes a set of patterns you can use to build your ¶7 *Scrum Team* and the other associations of people and loci of relationships that are common to Scrum practice. The Product Organization is one major Whole to which you must attend when introducing Scrum; the other one is the Value Stream Pattern Language on page 185. You build your organization and your process in parallel, each a little at a time, weaving together patterns from both chapters.

The preceding figure shows the relationships between the patterns in this chapter. We apply patterns one at a time. The figure is a guide for the order in which we should apply them. This structure is called a *pattern language*, because just as a language like English describes how we can sequence words in meaningful ways, this graph describes meaningful pattern sequences. More precisely, it is called a *generative pattern language* because it *generates* "sentences" that are combinations of patterns that powerfully reinforce each other.

Each node of the graph is a pattern, and the lines between patterns depict ordering dependencies between them. The graph therefore shows, for each pattern, the patterns above it, which you should already have considered before applying any given pattern—and the ones below it, which are candidates for next steps once you have put the current one in place. Of course, instead of just forging ahead, you can jump to another place in the graph and add a pattern that refines some other pattern you had applied earlier. One pattern is said to *refine* another (or to refine several other patterns), or the other way around, one pattern is said to *contain* one or more other patterns. So *The Spirit of the Game* refines ¶2 *The Mist*, and ¶4 *Conway's Law* contains *Scrum Team*.

There are, of course, almost countless ways to sequence the patterns, each sequence giving rise to a Scrum organization with a slightly different character. Though you should challenge yourself by considering most of the patterns in this book over time, you don't have to use all of them. You will usually pick the patterns that catch your eye and then organize them into a sequence using the graph as a guide. But the dependencies aren't strict and we encourage you to engage your insight and intuition as you apply the patterns. Of course, it is O.K. to change your mind along the way.

In the next section, we present a kind of canonical or default sequence for the major patterns in the Product Organization Pattern Language. But, again, use your insight and intuition rather than following the sequence as a mandate. You know more about your organization and your situation than we do.

Product Organization Sequence

A *pattern* is an instruction to shape something we build to increase the Wholeness of the Whole. *Organizational patterns*—such as those in this section —are networks of people that an organization builds, restructures, or incrementally refines with an eye to overall improvement (see Kaizen and Kaikaku on page 101). The organization applies these patterns according to a *sequence*, trying only one pattern at a time to assess its contribution to organizational quality. Occasionally a pattern doesn't work as expected, and it makes sense to try another pattern or to try patterns in a different order. Many different sequences can work, with as many or as few patterns as the organization sees fit, applied in what the organization feels is the best order. If a pattern is like a word, the sequences are like sentences.

A *pattern language* is the set of rules for combining the patterns in meaningful orders; as a "language" it has a grammar that can generate all sequences that are meaningful "sentences." While the number of combinations of patterns is large, not all orderings make sense. In the pattern language for a house one usually builds the foundations before the walls, and a pattern language for a house would probably *constrain* that the foundation be built before the walls.

Here we offer an archetypical sequence for the Product Organization Pattern Language. It starts with the "largest" pattern, i.e., that which metaphorically covers the largest area. Subsequent patterns subdivide that space or add small increments to it according to the precedence given in the sequence. Each pattern describes some configuration of people in relationship who have come together to pursue some interest of the organization. Some, like ¶7 *Scrum Team*, are long-term configurations of membership while others like the ¶29 *Daily Scrum* are short-lived in any particular incarnation. You will not be able to find all the groups (configurations of people) on the organizational chart. Some, like ¶24 *Sprint Planning*, form periodically, and while there is some stability to this group's constituency, it also has some ad hoc membership. Some may happen only occasionally or perhaps not at all, such as the association of folks to enact an ¶32 *Emergency Procedure*. Some, like ¶1 *The Spirit of the Game* or ¶38 *Product Pride*, describe qualities taken on by some of those groups of people.

It is useful to think of the patterns as building the spaces, or the identities, for groups of people who gather occasionally or periodically to exchange ideas, build things, solve problems, and to grow together. Any single individual may have a place in many of these configurations of group interaction, though usually engaging in only one at a time, and perhaps several over the course of a day. The Product Organization Pattern Language builds the "organization chart" for these sometimes tacit and usually dynamic configurations of human interaction that each come together around some purpose.

The sequence presented below doesn't catalog all the book's Product Organization patterns, but rather features a core subset of patterns that give an organization its most salient features. The ensuing pages present all the patterns we have chosen to include in this pattern language. We present them more or less in the order of a meaningful sequence of unfolding.

A sequence is more structural than temporal, and it may take a small bit of mental training to think of it in other than the terms we normally use for development processes. For example, the ¶11 *Product Owner* is probably the first on the scene—the seed around which the organization will grow. After he or she does some up-front work, a ¶14 *Development Team* may join, and then a ¶19 *ScrumMaster*. Thus assembled, we now have a *Scrum Team.* Yet if the initial intent is to create a *Scrum Team* and that's what we set out to do, maybe in fact it is instead seeded with members of a *Development Team* to which we later add the other roles. So if the *Product Owner* is the first on the scene, we kind of pretend that he or she *is* the entire, primordial *Scrum Team*, which we later differentiate by adding *ScrumMaster* and *Development Team* roles. The same slight fiction works if the effort grows out of a *Development Team*.

¶1 *The Spirit of the Game* The environment is animated by an agile spirit that can handle novel and unusual situations as well as respond to the continual changes facing most organizations, while working within a framework of discipline for the orderly engagement of all players.

¶2 *The Mist* There is a vague longing across some community which sparks attempts by groups to solve great problems locally or individually, and while aspiring to do great things, stops at small, local benefits for want of effective cooperation.

¶95 *Community of Trust on page 466* Team members create an environment where they consider themselves as a team (a community), with sufficient trust to feel safe interacting with each other. They take explicit, obvious, and consistent actions to demonstrate trust. They set up working procedures by mutual agreement, rather than by unilateral edicts.

¶3 *Fertile Soil* Interaction qualities both reflect and define organization qualities. Create cultural foundations for the values of Commitment, Focus, Openness, Respect and Courage in the teams' day-to-day behaviors and interactions.

¶4 *Conway's Law* Product groups form around opportunities to serve some constituency by creating a product that serves some segment of society, as a precursor to aligning the work, the organization and business, and the market.

¶5 *Birds of a Feather* Additional cross-cutting groups form around internal areas of interest such as technology or other core competencies that support the work.

¶6 *Involve the Managers* The effort may grow to the point where it can benefit from business administration support, broad coordination, and a locus of responsibility to initiate discontinuous change. The enterprise adds a small management staff as "über ScrumMasters" who can initiate radical change, remove impediments, provide administration and coordinate from a "big picture" position.

¶7 *Scrum Team* The Scrum Team emerges from the broader organization: a ¶8 *Collocated Team* and ¶10 *Cross-Functional Team* that operates as a small business within the context of the organization, making independent decisions to respond to stakeholders and the market. It is brought into existence and led by the...

¶11 *Product Owner* who leads the newly formed team to realize his or her ¶39 *Vision* for creating value. The Product Owner is the single person who takes accountability for realizing the Vision, for the value that emanates from the delivery of that Vision, and for the contents of the Product Backlog. The Product Owner is the voice of value to rest of the Scrum Team.

¶13 *Development Partnership* The Product Owner leads an effort to forge a partnership with the constituency that will be served by the organization's product.

¶14 *Development Team* The Product Owner hires a team to implement the product as a series of product increments that realize the Vision. (As previously described, by "hire" we mean to associate a committed group to the effort, whether through formal employment or some other form of organizational commitment.)

¶19 *ScrumMaster* The new team hires a ScrumMaster as their "servant leader" to guide the team in using the Scrum process, and in continuous improvement.

¶24 *Sprint Planning* The Scrum Team—the Product Owner, Development Team, and the ScrumMaster—assembles to plan a Production Episode and build a potentially shippable product increment.

¶25 *Swarming: One-Piece Continuous Flow* During production, the team works as one mind, minimizing inventory and work in progress by taking each Product Increment continuously through its development tasks from beginning to end.

¶29 *Daily Scrum* The Development Team assembles every day to replan their work and to optimize their chances of meeting the Sprint Goal.

¶32 *Emergency Procedure* If the team faces serious trouble that threatens the team's ability to meet the Sprint Goal, the team assembles to discuss escalation strategies that may entail replanning, getting outside help, decreasing the scope of the deliverable, or aborting the current Sprint and doing more fundamental replanning.

¶33 *Illegitimus Non Interruptus* Scrum Teams develop the discipline to notice when product churn falls outside statistical norms, such that they abort the Sprint, take corrective action, and replan.

¶34 *Scrum of Scrums* Each day, all the Development Teams for a given product synchronize with each other and work together to solve problems and move the teams towards the Sprint Goal.

¶35 *Sprint Review* At the end of the Sprint, the Scrum Team evaluates progress on the product; the Product Owner decides what changes to incorporate into the imminent release.

¶36 *Sprint Retrospective* As the last gathering of the Sprint, the Scrum Team assembles to contemplate how best to make incremental process improvements, and commits to one such improvement during the next Sprint.

¶37 *MetaScrum* If management is interfering with the teams, you should create a regular encounter between management and the Product Owners where management has a chance to influence product direction.

¶38 *Product Pride* The team grows to identify with the product they build and are proud to be in the business of producing it.

¶118 *Team Pride on page 469* The team has a "team spirit" and is proud of who they are.

¶2 The Mist

Confidence stars: *

...great works start with a vague longing across some community. Individual tinkerers and craftsmen strive to solve great problems locally or individually, often from the limited perspective of their trade. Though they aspire to do great things, they stop at small, local benefits for want of effective cooperation. The culture has already gained a sense of the need to explore improvements together, toward the greater good—*¶1 The Spirit of the Game.*

❖ ❖ ❖

Innovation has enjoyed its greatest days when humankind has come together in groups. Earliest humankind lived together in small groups able to live from a small subsistence economy. The author Steve Johnson credits cities with being the cradle of innovation as people with diverse skill sets and backgrounds were able to freely trade notes, in *Where Good Ideas Come From: The Natural History of Innovation [Joh11]* (Chapter 2, "Liquid Networks"). As people came together in groups, production supplemented subsistence. In the same sense that cities grew, production institutions similarly became the new engines of innovation. The innovations that came from groups of workers and their colleagues inspired market enthusiasm and allowed them to reap the resulting economic rewards.

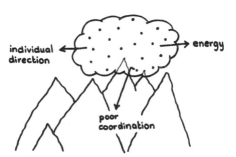

Yet such communities have perhaps always been limited from achieving their full potential as they stayed beneath the shadow of hierarchy. There have always been strong patterns of human nature that elicit conformance from individuals' social, professional, and economic behavior. Indeed, conformance has usually been the standard by which one is accepted into a society, and there was usually some authority defining the rules of acceptance—a ruler, a religion, labor unions, or academic standards. Feudal lords proposed and serfs disposed. Humanity's most rapid period of economic growth, during the industrial revolution, saw the hands of many carrying out the designs of a few. The good drove out the perfect. Variety and progress languished through saws which we today view as humorous, such as: "You can have any color of car as long as it's black," or "I think there is a world market for maybe five computers."

Therefore,

An individual, or a collective mind of several individuals, together create an environment where the necessary pre-work and evaluation can establish the primordial soup from which Scrum teams emerge. The core of this pre-work follows an emerging vision to improve quality of life. That vision is based in a product that will add value both for those who build it and those who use it. That vision breaks with the servitude habits of past work practices and foresees a more undifferentiated world of give-and-take between those who conceive it, those who build it, and those who use it. Scrum, as Jeff Sutherland conceived it, foresees the ability—even for those who have nothing —to have hope of being able to build something from nothing.

associated interests

❖ ❖ ❖

Ideas start to come together about a product that can contribute to quality of life, and about how to excite and engage people to realize such a product and evolve it with the involvement of some community of stakeholders. People start to come together in groups of common interest, bound together as much by *The Spirit of the Game* as by their passion for the product or for the purpose it serves. Over time these collections of people cultivate *¶3 Fertile Soil* while aspiring to build something great, something cool, something exciting—with a shared purpose, to realize a *¶39 Vision*.

The first step is the growing synthesis of ideas about the artifact as well as the processes to realize it, culminating in some consciousness about such a constellation of ideas as a *Vision*.

¶3 Fertile Soil

Confidence stars: *

...people are coming together out of *¶2 The Mist* to make something great, and want to collaborate in the spirit of Scrum (*¶1 The Spirit of the Game*).

❖   ❖   ❖

It is the moment-by-moment interactions of people working together on a product that build and sustain product organizations. Interaction qualities both reflect and define organization qualities.

We often conceive of organizations in terms of the artifacts that their people create, such as legal documents, buildings, logos, policies and procedures. With respect to the all-important role of process, it is more useful to view an organization as a patterning of human interactions. If we understand these interactions well, we gain great insight into the workings of the organization as a whole (see *Complexity and the Experience of Leading Organizations [GS05]*, p. 208). To realize any of Scrum's benefits in a traditional organization, the nature of these interactions must change. If groups mechanically follow Scrum rules while holding on to their usual patterns of interaction, they will not realize the framework's real value.

Organizational values are the bedrock of the processes, structure, and atmosphere of the workplace (see "Values, spirituality and organisations: a complex responsive process perspective" in *Complexity and the Experience of Leading Organizations [GS05]*, p. 208). They are the framework within which organizational interactions unfold. In many cases, an organization's articulated values are just corporate wall decorations, and the real values lie deeper and may long remain implicit. But if the values have teeth, the corporate culture might employ them to extract conformance in staff behavior. Good values are intrinsic and come from within. They enable team members to do their jobs. For example, if the team values transparency, problems will more likely surface earlier than if the team has learned to not "make waves." Good values both reflect how members of the organization see themselves working and motivate people to work towards an agreed goal. Lesser values are extrinsic and strive to control people to do what might be against their will. Values must be a touchstone by which the team can both evaluate and justify their actions.

Whenever our own work depends on the work of others, there is a non-zero probability that the other people won't complete what everyone expected they would complete. As a consequence, the team as a whole may fail. While the chances of such failure may be extremely small, the possibility of failure still creates a level of uneasiness. If the uneasiness is sufficiently large, even if it is unwarranted, people take defensive measures such as frequently checking on progress or limiting the freedom with which people may innovate or carry out their work. People may even try to commandeer others' work.

People in general want to succeed and do their best at work so they can feel good about it. It might be reasonable to presume on everyone's goodwill to find how to best work with each other; much of this is common sense. But in the heat of battle, as team members are working hard to a goal, it can be easy to forget the human element. Forcing the team to adhere to some external imposed set of values—particularly those for which the team does not feel ownership—may build resentment. But a *laissez-faire* approach too easily results in casual violations, even of common sense. People need to be reminded of the basics now and then.

To build a product of the *¶93 Greatest Value* requires that producers work in a way that allows the team to recognize such value when they achieve it, and to support decisions that carry the team in that direction. Where our interactions focus on our own concerns or controlling others, we limit the opportunity for growth: for others, ourselves, and the organization we are working in.

Therefore:

Demonstrate the values of Commitment, Focus, Openness, Respect and Courage in your day-to-day behaviors and interactions (*Agile Software Development with Scrum (Series in Agile Software Development) [SB01]*). **This helps create a virtuous circle that supports transparency, and that makes it possible to build on the inspection and adaptation at the core of effective Scrum efforts.** Explicitly enacting these values encourages others to improve their qualities of behavior and interaction as well. *Fertile Soil* nourishes both the incremental and momentous change (see Kaizen and Kaikaku on page 101) to carry you towards the *Greatest Value*.

❖ ❖ ❖

The quality of the plant depends on the quality of the soil it grows in. The quality of the organization is dependent on the interactions between individuals in the organization; see *Tools and Techniques of Leadership and Management: Meeting the Challenge of Complexity [Sta12]*, p. 180. Where the organization requires transparency to inspect and adapt there needs to be transparency, inspection and adaptation demonstrated by the people in the organization. It is only by acting in this way that you can create the interactions needed to create and sustain your Scrum organization. Transparency also supports objectivity and can accelerate trust building. Within Toyota they say, "build people, not just cars" (*The Toyota Way Fieldbook: A Practical Guide for Implementing Toyota's 4Ps [LM05]*, p. 242). To describe their belief in people, they use the analogy of a garden:

> The soil is tended and prepared, the seeds are watered, and when the seeds grow, the soil is maintained, weeded, and watered again until finally the fruit is ready — (*The Toyota Way Fieldbook: A Practical Guide for Implementing Toyota's 4Ps [LM05]*, p. 242).

The first statement in the values of the Agile Manifesto underscores the importance of people and their interactions: "Individuals and interactions over processes and tools."[1]

The *Fertile Soil* for Scrum requires you to commit to a goal, which may range from something as small as your immediate work to something as large as a ¶41 *Value Stream*. Show your commitment to be complete and encompassing: commitment is all or nothing. Focus your efforts to meet your commitments. Be open about your work, show the successes, the failures and the impediments. Respect the people who work with you. Have the courage to do all this; see Chapter 9 in *Agile Software Development with Scrum (Series in Agile Software Development) [SB01]*.

This pattern provides the medium in which to grow the organization's structure. The structures that grows from *Fertile Soil* will be your implementation of Scrum. ¶4 *Conway's Law* will give you guidance on how to create an adaptable organization where teams are decoupled from product architecture to allow crucial communication at the right time, between the right people, about the right thing. Other patterns that follow will help you structure and further refine your organization.

---

1. *Manifesto for Agile Software Development: Principles.* Agilemanifesto.org, http://agilemanifesto.org/principles.html, 2001, accessed 23 January 2017.

¶4 Conway's Law

Confidence stars: **

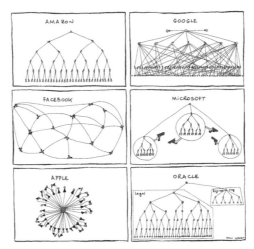

Picture credit: Manu Cornet / www.bonkersworld.net

...things are working well as everyone just does what needs to be done out of pure passion, so seamlessly that an observer might conclude that everyone has the ability to read each other's mind. However, as the organization and product grow, so does the amount of information that teams must master, manage, and share to get their job done. Decisions are becoming more sensitive to the context (of both the teams and the products), with complexity that begs some kind of structure to keep things running smoothly as the organization matures. You are seeking an organizational structure that will optimize the team's ability to get things done to create the *¶93 Greatest Value*.

❖   ❖   ❖

Effective communication and feedback are at the heart of effective complex system development, and the organization structure should be optimized for the most crucial paths of communication. Communication and regular feedback, together with self-organization, are the agile heart. The interaction of people with diverse, cross-cutting concerns lies at the heart of innovation (*Where Good Ideas Come From [Joh11]*).

*¶14 Development Team*s working on complex products continuously struggle with the dual nature of function and form. We tend to create boundaries between development activities and organizational units along these lines. Yet function and form are just socially constructed and somewhat arbitrary categories: reliability might be just as compelling a concern for a given system, while beauty, backwards compatibility, or some other concern might dominate

a given development effort. In each case, the business will be best served if the *Development Team* organizes itself around the most crucial business concerns—whatever they may be.

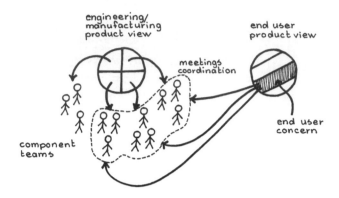

As your team just starts to mature in its early days and starts moving towards building a ¶7 *Scrum Team*, you have more people who can conveniently work as one organizational unit to cover all the functions of a business (release planning, development, and professional growth). But growth and maturity also cause discomfort, as teams yearn for the unstructured effectiveness of the simple days of informal work. Yet to grow and to properly manage the product in the market requires a somewhat disciplined organizational structure and some lightweight governance.

Cultures have an intrinsic need for structure for the efficient functioning of the whole. The most effective communication always happens locally within the realm of the familiar, so it's crucial to localize the decision-making process around the most crucial organizational concerns. It's important in any non-trivial social organization that people quickly be able to associate any given domain of interest with the most efficient "place to go" when they need information about that area or need to take action in that area.

A simple organizational partitioning (i.e., a hierarchy) is enough in simple domains that must deal with only one set of separable concerns. But the hierarchical approach breaks down in the more typical case of development efforts with multiple overlapping concerns. This pushes toward larger, more complex organizational units that try to correct the problem with economies of scope. Yet the most effective work teams are ¶9 *Small Teams*, and you need to partition the work somehow.

However, no team is an island, and a development nation is more than a collection of islands. Teams individually develop their own identity, where a natural sense of xenophobia (need for the familiar) causes teams to give only secondary stature to concerns coming from outside their social circle. If you limit the enterprise to one set of social interactions, based on a single simple partitioning, you shut down the out-of-bounds ideas that fuel innovation.

The speed of decision-making is paramount. Some issues are urgent ("We are being attacked by another tribe and must mount a defense against them,") while others, though important, tolerate or even beg longer deliberation ("What is the best location for the new meeting hall?"). The term *shearing layers* describes related processes that move at different speeds, after the notion of tectonic plates that move across each other, and as such lead up to an earthquake. Both building architects (*How Buildings Learn: What Happens After They're Built [Bra95]*) and the field of software architecture (see *Pattern Languages of Program Design 4 [FHR00]*) have adopted the phrase to describe structures or concerns with differing rates of change in a tightly coupled system. A company should structure its organization to be able to quickly respond to issues in the first category without destroying its effectiveness for issues in the second.

Another agile principle is that we are outward facing: that is, our focus and concern are on the end user, market, and customers rather than on the tools and technologies we use to do our work. The organization should reflect this concern as well, as it's key to the value proposition and the construction of the entire *¶41 Value Stream* of development.

In the end, the structure of the organization should have as much to do with the structure of the process as the structure of the product.

Therefore,

Organize the workforce into *Small Teams* of more or less five people, partitioned according to the most important concerns for the creation of value by the enterprise. Supplement this structure with a small number of cross-cutting structures for secondary but important concerns, never forgetting that these structures are only optimizations in what is otherwise an open environment of unconstrained cooperation.

Consider an enterprise that is building a mobile phone. They might organize their *Scrum Team*s around the major deliverables or purchasable options. So there may be one team for the address book, another for the calendar, and another for the more traditional phone functionality: see *¶89 Value Areas*. Those are the primary concerns of the business. But there may be groups that come together to define practices, policies, and corporate standards (e.g., the user interface look and feel), comprising representatives from each *Scrum*

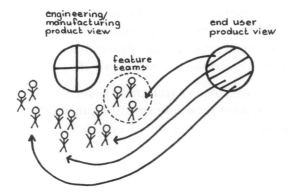

Team. Those groups don't build product but serve as information exchanges and as sources of standards that guide development. In healthy organizations there is nearly complete overlap between the membership of these latter groups and development team membership.

In most environments, the primary organizing structure reflects the primary stakeholder structure, which is usually the market. For this reason, we don't organize *Scrum Team*s along the partitioning of internal artifacts, nor according to the loci of domain expertise, but rather along the lines of market deliverables such as features. Organizing around features or other market deliverables is also a boon to market responsiveness and reduced time-to-market because the team is the locus of *all* work necessary to implement a feature. This keeps coordination within an organizational boundary. If work subassemblies or core competencies drive the organizational structure, then changes in the market or in the nature of the deliverable will likely entail coordination between multiple teams or organizations—reducing responsiveness and increasing decision-making time.

If this is the only structure, it supports only the market view, and it marginalizes a host of other valid business concerns. For this structure to work, it must be supplemented by cross-cutting structures that support a second level of communication efficiency, e.g., those related to the core competencies. So this pattern almost always appears together with a pattern like ¶5 *Birds of a Feather* and the pattern described in ¶122 *Domain Expertise in Roles* on page 469. The organizational role structure cuts through the walls that naturally form between teams. Engage product efforts within an enterprise to connect with each other and with executive management through the ¶37 *MetaScrum*. Teams that have developed a degree of team pride (see ¶118 *Team Pride* on page 469) will be more effective, as this or some other equivalent force will encourage responsibility. This helps ensure that these structures remain in play in spite of the xenophobic effects of team membership.

Tie it all together with an open environment with no walls and no doors. *Development Team*s are units only of development commitment, and there should be no interference limiting the free interworking between developers across teams. Add small rooms nearby for short periods of quiet, serious reflection and small meetings.

Any component of value is fair game as an organizing criterion. For example, Scrum highly values the collocation of team members, so the most basic organizational boundaries are likely to correspond to *¶8 Collocated Team*s.

❖   ❖   ❖

Note that there are two levels of *Conway's Law* in a good Scrum: one driven by a focus on the product, and another driven by a focus on competency areas. At the surface level we organize the team according to the process; that is the primary concern for both the inward- and outward-facing aspects of process. So the three spheres of process dominion are:

- the *Development Team* who owns decisions about the suitable use of technology and technique in building the product;

- the *¶11 Product Owner*, who owns the definition and direction of the product; and,

- the *¶19 ScrumMaster* who is accountable that the process supports the *Development Team*'s regular delivery.

Scrum *Development Team*s are feature (product) teams. That is, the primary organizing principle of a *Scrum Team* is that it aligns with a train of feature deliveries along a *Value Stream*. There is a weak, shallow hierarchical organization within Scrum that accommodates multiple *Development Team*s within each product development, sharing a common *Product Owner*, in an organization called a *¶34 Scrum of Scrums*. Each *Development Team* within a single product development builds one set of features at a time. Over time, key business drivers, shared business knowledge, and *Value Stream* artifacts will tie these features together. There are no recognized titles or subdivisions within the *Development Team*.

There are many ways to divide work into feature teams. A *Development Team* may deliver features to a given market (see *¶129 Organization Follows Market* on page 470), or develop product for some subset of the enterprise technology spectrum (one team for phones and another for tablets, though both share much of the same software). In general, each team should be formed around some product that accounts for a component of enterprise value: see also *¶90 Value Stream Fork*. However, Scrum discourages a *Development Team* structure where each team owns one *part* of the product, or just a product subassembly. If the members of any single team can develop only one part of the system, then they will need to coordinate more development decisions with other teams. It becomes hard for teams to make decisions locally, and the results include delayed feedback and handoffs.

At the second level of *Conway's Law* within Scrum, people organize around competency areas in which proficiency drives value. These *Birds of a Feather* help members deepen their facility in some professional or technical area as they share ideas or take training. Most people have an innate desire to improve (see *Drive: The Surprising Truth About What Motivates Us [Pin11]*), and these groups feed individual pride as team members learn and grow. But again, these groups do not form a reporting structure, and any team member may belong to several *Birds of a Feather* as well as to their own *Scrum Team*. See also *Domain Expertise in Roles* on page 469.

Development Team boundaries, and identity, as well as *Scrum Team* boundaries and identity, are explicit. The notion of team identity is key to *Team Pride* on page 469 and to the efficient operation of the organization, since team identity brings the social context that helps optimize decision-making. Any notion of organizational identity beyond these two should be tacit rather than explicit or administered. Again, there are no formal titles within the *Development Team* other than "Developer." If there is only one inviolate rule, it's that no individual can use their tacit station of expertise to override a team consensus or in any other way diminish a spirit of teamwork, as in *¶1 The Spirit of the Game*. A jointly developed *¶31 Norms of Conduct* is a strong harbinger of team identity.

There can be expertise in roles at the individual level, but it's important to complete this pattern with *¶10 Cross-Functional Teams* wherever possible to optimize the possibility of local decision-making.

The original Conway's Law came out of software (see *Datamation 14 [Con68]*, pp. 28–31). There are many myths associated with the origin and practice of Conway's Law. It was long held that object orientation supported Conway's Law by localizing market concerns inside of classes. That's half-true; classes tend to encapsulate the long-term concerns of organizational core competency. Yet, object orientation seems to focus on the connection between developers' expertise and the artifacts they develop rather than on any connection to the market or to use cases. Concerns for alignment with market structure should trump concerns for the developers' worldview of their process and product.

The waterfall style of development had its heyday. In waterfall organizations, the primary organizational structure followed process stages: requirements analysis, design, implementation, and test (*Proceedings of IEEE WESCON [Roy70]*, pp. 1–9). Per Conway's Law, the *organization* structure reflected those *process* concerns. The software might very well reflect those phases as well: for example, a Service-Oriented Architecture (SOA) will evidence most of the value-added requirements in the service integration layer, while the individual services are found in another layer. Waterfall puts all the features into the developers' hands at once, which supports reasoning about interactions between features. While the software design approaches of the waterfall era tried to bring market concerns (use cases) in line with the architecture, the organizational structure cut across that taxonomy. The same can be said about assembly line organization in factories.

Because *Development Team*s are feature teams, they should focus on one feature at a time (as in *¶25 Swarming: One-Piece Continuous Flow*). Scrum's primary market deliverable is a feature, and in this sense, there is good alignment between the team structure and the market. Scrum is silent on the form of the product architecture, but in the spirit of agile it tends to discourage individual code ownership. Every *Development Team* has license to work on any part of the product. We can say that Scrum balances the organizational benefits of encapsulation with the benefits of aligning the team with the market deliverable. The *Product Owner*, with support from the *Development Team*, manages how to handle feature interactions that emerge over time.

Consider, for example, that one team may implement the Call Waiting feature for a telecom system while another implements Call Forwarding. Because of emergence, you can't always foresee the cost of resolving dependencies between any two given *¶55 Product Backlog Item*s (*PBI*s) so it is, in general, impossible to overcome this problem by assigning *PBI*s to teams. In any case, prematurely assigning work to teams may make it impossible for people to work effectively on the hard parts (especially those related to the interaction between the parts) and limits self-organization at the *Scrum Team* level. The two features may be highly interdependent, but the Scrum structure doesn't give first-class stature to those interactions. In this case, it probably would be better if a single team developed both features. How to allocate work to teams builds on ongoing planning and shared decision-making, starting with *¶24 Sprint Planning*. A good *Scrum Team* strives to partition the work across *Development Team*s through intimate, but time-boxed, interactions between the *Product Owner* and the *Development Team*, as in events to continually reestablish a *¶64 Refined Product Backlog* as well as through *Sprint Planning*.

Management is usually a component of the organizational mix, although there are some Scrum developments that run without any managers (e.g., see the recent video about the agile transformation at Bosch Software Innovations.[2]) The Scrum ethos tends to focus on the people and the product, and the focus is embodied in the Scrum roles and the organizations (like the *Development Team* and *¶12 Product Owner Team*) that they represent. If an organization with pre-existing managers sets out to introduce Scrum, it is too easy for the Scrum effort to dismiss the management part of the organization as other-worldly. In such situations where a management-free organization is not an option, it is crucial to *¶6 Involve the Managers.*

---

2. Bosch Software Innovations. "Lessons learned: Agile organization at Bosch Software Innovations." YouTube.com, 15 June 2018, https://www.youtube.com/watch?v=CwodQs7D8BY.

¶5 Birds of a Feather

Confidence stars: *

Monarch butterflies have periodic get-togethers in Central America.

...the Scrum organization and its roles are in place. *¶14 Development Teams* are working effectively as *¶16 Autonomous Teams* to build product. They are *¶10 Cross-Functional Teams*, and the expertise in individual teams grows only through the insights that each team gains from its own work.

❖ ❖ ❖

Core competencies are a crucial element of enterprise value that cuts across development organization boundaries. While Scrum focuses on improving the process and improving the product, it's crucial to invest in the people who do this work and in their skill sets that support enterprise needs in both of those areas.

"Empowerment" and "self-managing teams" are often rallying cries for organizations transitioning to agile approaches. But empowering a team can insulate it, and cause it to form its own boundaries and to decrease sharing of information, including long-term insights that may contribute to enterprise-wide domain knowledge, business acumen, or strategy (see "The Limits of Participatory Management" in *Across the Board 54* [Hec95]).

Knowledge relationships form a lattice structure in any non-trivial human organization. Yet most formal organization structures (including organization into Scrum products and organization of Scrum products into Scrum *Development Teams*) are hierarchical. Peter Senge quotes Bohm, noting that hierarchy is antithetical to the dialogue that lies at the foundation of organizational learning (*The Fifth Discipline* [Sen06], p. 288).

People enjoy mastering their skills as individuals, but such skill development can go only so far for individuals working in isolation. Cross-fertilization and

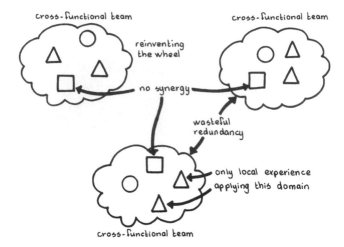

broad diversity in ideas, technologies, and cultures lie at the root of innovation (see "Liquid Networks" in *Where Good Ideas Come From [Joh11]*).

Therefore: **Create ad hoc "birds of a feather" groups for each area of significant enterprise core competency or developer interest, where interested parties can trade notes on technologies, domain knowledge, and processes that are key to enterprise advancement.**

In the spirit of self-organization, each team—or maybe each team member— makes an autonomous decision about whether to join the community or not. However, a team does not get a voice in the community without also agreeing to abide by the decisions of the community.

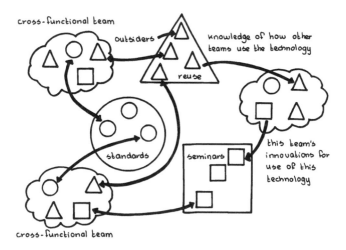

❖ ❖ ❖

Such groups can also be good loci of personal and career development, and can provide an outlet for the people-management talents of a traditional management-heavy organization that transitions to Scrum. Managers manage people; *¶7 Scrum Team*s manage product.

Along with autonomy and a sense of transcendent purpose, Pink (in *Drive: The Surprising Truth About What Motivates Us [Pin11]*) has highlighted research showing that a sense of mastery is a key enabler for team achievement and well-being. *Birds of a Feather* are local communities to hone organizational excellence, with the potential byproduct of increasing *individual* effectiveness. Such teams become loci of *¶118 Team Pride* on page 469 and the potential for feeding the sense of mastery that motivates team players. Such fora have taken on many forms under many names over the years: birds of a feather, guilds, quality circles, communities of practice, and others.

This is not matrix management. The "birds of a feather" organizations are not loci of product control nor, in fact, should they be entwined in any kind of externally applied control. All such organizations are self-managing. The best of these organizations form spontaneously around the enthusiasm for some core competency. In some cases, for the formation of such groups, encouragement from *¶19 ScrumMaster*s or *¶11 Product Owner*s may be necessary. In all cases, these groups should agree to an informal charter that supports their existence and should periodically review whether they are adding value to their constituency, to the company, or to the community. Leverage managers (*¶6 Involve the Managers*) who can provide support and organizational commitment to broaden the scope of influence of such groups across development teams, products, or entire organizations and companies.

As in a neighborhood, our actions affect one another by virtue of our common location and resources—so too with *Birds of a Feather* groups. However, it should be emphasized that *Birds of a Feather* groups normally have no mandate to implement proposed improvements; their main roles are to help everyone become better informed and to remain better aware of improvement ideas, experience, expertise, suggestions, and efforts across the enterprise. Individual *Scrum Team*s retain the mandate to try new *kaizen* (see Kaizen and Kaikaku on page 101) and to assess their effectiveness.

Don't neglect business-domain knowledge as a key opportunity for professional growth among developers. Technical knowledge is often available as a commodity, but key business competencies may be hard-won and often are available only through scarce resources. What's more, the payoff is high from developers being able to understand the business. Richard Gabriel reports that at his company, Lucid, the engineers were better able to relate their work to a corporate balance sheet than the business people could.

If your organization is too small for separate *Birds of a Feather* groups to make sense, join some local meet-up groups instead. Do that anyhow.

In 1991, Lave and Wenger introduced the concept of Communities of Practice[3] to describe the theory of situated learning which, in short, is about individuals acquiring professional skills through social co-participation (from Wikipedia[4]). Spotify has several structures in place called *tribes*, *chapters*, and *guilds* that provide a natural place for various flavors of cross-team fertilization (as related by Henrik Kniberg[5]). Siili Solutions in Helsinki calls such groups *tribes*. Progress Software in the United States used such a group to select a single defect-tracking tool for all teams to use, so that everyone in the whole organization knew where to find and report defects.

3. "Community of Practice." Wikipedia. https://en.wikipedia.org/wiki/Community_of_practice (accessed 5 June 2018).
4. "Situated learning." Wikipedia. https://en.wikipedia.org/wiki/Situated_learning (accessed 5 June 2018).
5. Henrik Kniberg. "Spotify Engineering Culture Part 1 (Agile Enterprise Transition with Scrum and Kanban)." YouTube.com, https://www.youtube.com/watch?v=4GK1NDTWbkY (accessed 28 January 2019).

¶6 Involve the Managers

Confidence stars: *

...the organization has committed to adopting Scrum and is now starting to use Scrum to guide the conception and realization of its products. But Scrum is considerably different than traditional organizational structures, and questions arise about the place of traditional organizational roles. Those who were comfortable with management roles in traditional product development now seek analogues in the Scrum culture. Management has a particularly visible presence in large organizations that produce multiple products, but also carries influence in traditional organizations of all sizes. Management responsibilities overlap with those of Scrum roles. An imminent dilemma becomes clear as the organization deliberates the extent of management control, or whether there should be management at all.

❖   ❖   ❖

There are no managers in the Scrum framework. Scrum *¶14 Development Team*s are *¶16 Autonomous Team*s, and the *¶11 Product Owner*, while accountable to stakeholders and investors, isn't subject to control by any higher power within the enterprise. So managers in an agile transformation have difficulty finding an outlet for their contribution except as an otherwise undifferentiated support role.

A development manager in a traditional organization coordinates work and may actually give work assignments in a *Development Team*. But the need for responsiveness, and for making rapid decisions close to the work, suggest that developers instead manage their own day-to-day development activities. This is how Scrum product development works. Yet the traditional management skill set and identity may still make sense in a complex product development organization. This skill set falls outside of day-to-day development and outside of what Scrum brings to the organization.

The position of "manager" often carries distinguished standing under the law in terms of being able to speak for the company, and in terms of carrying liability for corporate activities. Managers have the station and power to restructure the organization while *Product Owners* do not. While individual ¶7 *Scrum Team*s can navigate daily interruptions and exigencies, they individually cannot adeptly deal with issues beyond the scope of a single team. For example, it is awkward for any single *Product Owner* to bear the contractual responsibility for a relationship with an external vendor that supplies multiple product developments (i.e., the development efforts of multiple *Product Owners*).

In the usual English language sense of the term, *management* is fundamentally about control and responsibility, according to the dictionary definition (*New Oxford American Dictionary [SLJA17]*). Responsibility means willingness to take accountability. One reason there is no management in Scrum is that control of the development process is decentralized across members of the *Autonomous Team*. Because development is complex, development leadership moves dynamically from team member to team member. Efficient work languishes under any locus of centralized control or management. Yet, there are functions other than development per se necessary to sustain a product development effort. The fact that the *Product Owner* controls (has the final say over) the direction of the product is indeed a form of control, so the sentiment that Scrum is without any loci of control is a myth.

There are yet other facets of operating a production organization that, as with the *Product Owner* case, may be better suited to centralized decision-making than to collective consensus. For example, some crucial business decisions may owe more to "gut feeling" than can be substantiated by caucusing or empirical grounding alone. When considering whether to transition from analog to digital telecommunications, AT&T justified that the existing analog technology was economically superior, and decided to not pursue the local digital switching market. Northern Telecom started developing the DMS-100 digital switch in the late 1970s and caught AT&T off-guard, as digital had become fashionable in the age when digital watches were emerging. The market *perception* of value trumped the engineering analysis. Evolving an existing product wasn't enough: it was a matter of launching a new product line. Though there were intense discussions of these issues at the engineering level in Northern Telecom, it was ultimately a management decision for them to pursue digital switching out of a hunch and vision. They beat AT&T to that market in 1979.[6]

In an enterprise that develops multiple products, it is awkward for existing *Scrum Team*s to deal with strategic issues related to the lifetime or very existence of a team or product. For example, decisions in a scaled organization (producing multiple products) include collective considerations, such as responsible distribution of risk-taking across different products at different times. While *Product Owner*s can take responsibility for a product, they cannot levy accountability on themselves. They are unlikely to have an adequately objective view to defund their own product when business sense dictates that they should. So individual products may themselves not have the scope, resources, or fallback ability to take major risks.

*Scrum Team*s emphasize ongoing kaizen, but kaizen emphasizes ongoing, local, incremental change. Sometimes a product or even an enterprise must go through discontinuous changes to survive. Extreme cases include Sun Microsystems slimming down its hardware business, Nokia going from making rubber boots to making cellular phones, and Toyota going from making weaving machines to making cars. IBM went from 1985 hardware sales accounting for almost three quarters of their income (in which software was a bundled component: see *InfoWorld 9 [Wei87]*), to a services organization where 2015 hardware sales were less than 10 percent of the income.[7] In 1986, management decided to boost its services business from 25 percent of its income to 40 percent of its income within six years (*Computerworld XIX [Gal85]*, p. 52).

*Product Owner*s and *Scrum Team*s may be blind to such opportunities because they usually focus on managing risk through the incremental changes of kaizen. They may not want to mitigate risk by killing a product—namely, their own product. Team members may view radical change—called *kaikaku* in Japanese (see Kaizen and Kaikaku on page 101)—as a threat. Any single product organization may feel that great leaps such as those of the above examples exceed their risk appetite. If an organization pushes all responsibility for improvement into individual products or onto the lowest-level team,

---

6. "Overview & Background on Electronic & Digital Switching Systems." Telephone World, http://www.phworld.org/switch/overview.htm, January 2013 (accessed 5 December 2017).
7. "How IBM Makes Money? Understanding IBM Business Model." R&P Research, http://web.archive.org/web/20180121141146/http://revenuesandprofits.com/how-ibm-makes-money/, n.d. (accessed 27 January 2019).

the result can be several locally optimized products that ignore opportunities for broader product or business synergy.

Managers are often present in the organization at the outset of an agile transformation; they may even initiate it. And they want to help. Teams that have been taught they are self-managing often view such management help as unwelcome. A manager keeps meddling in the affairs of the Scrum team, distracting the team, and generally becoming a nuisance. In extreme cases, the manager might even take on technical work or tell team members how to do their job. Wayne Rosing disposed of all such managers when taking the reins of vice president of engineering at Google in 2001, and had all 160 or so of them report directly to him, as he tells in *Fast Company 69 [Ham03]*. Yet Rosing took this decision as a manager himself: *somebody* has to ignite discontinuous changes if an organization is to move forward on more than just local optimization.

Therefore:

Sustain a management function that can act from a position of power to initiate, and take responsibility for, radical changes in the organization, and deal with impediments that may be too weighty for the ¶19 ScrumMaster or *Product Owner* **in the Scrum Team**. *Scrum Team*s manage themselves in all matters of tactical and most strategic *product* direction, functioning largely as *Autonomous Teams*. *Scrum Team*s interface with managers in a weekly ¶37 *MetaScrum* event (typically through their *Product Owner*s), but managers do not take part in other Scrum events.

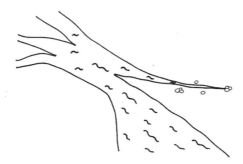

While *Scrum Team*s manage themselves to chart their own kaizen direction, management will seek opportunities to challenge them with more radical *kaikaku* changes (*Lean Magazine 15 [Cop17]*). As such, managers can play a key role in innovation: of thinking in directions that product management (the *Product Owner*) might find threatening to its own existence.

Great managers fill a servant leader role, yet they carry more power than a *ScrumMaster* by virtue of their position. A manager might intervene to resolve conflicts between *Product Owner*s of different products. And managers can use their power to set policy that charts an organization on a strategy to achieve the *¶93 Greatest Value*. For example, management might remove the accountability for a given product direction from an existing steering board and assign it to a *Product Owner* willing to take on that responsibility. On a day-to-day basis, management may serve as the last escalation step for impediments that stand in the way of delivering product; their station of power and resources can often resolve problems in ways inaccessible to the *Scrum Team*.

Managers can powerfully fill a facilitating and coordinating role in large organizations supporting multiple products. They can also use the power of their position, and potentially their access to corporate resources, to serve the *¶34 Scrum of Scrums* and *MetaScrum* in resolving urgent impediments. If an impediment such as friction with an external supplier is holding up the *¶46 Sprint*, the *MetaScrum* may escalate to management to ask their support in resolving the issue.

A manager can also fill the role of a Firewall (see *¶114 Firewall* on page 468) to run interference against stakeholders who would interfere with the team. Again, this is traditionally a *ScrumMaster* responsibility, but managers might be more effective at managing this problem when it involves parties outside the organization.

A handful of additional management roles may take stations leading *¶5 Birds of a Feather* groups, particularly with respect to the traditional activity of career growth. Such managers close to the teams may deal with personnel development and administration.

❖ ❖ ❖

The enterprise can now manage risk from a perspective of broader oversight and objectivity greater than any single *Product Owner* brings to the table. Overall corporate-level innovation and efficiency can more readily improve. *Product Owner*s retain responsibility for risk management and decision-making at a level commensurate with their scope of influence and of product content control: that of their own product. Management can nonetheless raise the risk appetite for the enterprise with radical redirection, recombination, or other action whose scope is broader than a single product. If a product is languishing, there may be a need to kill it (see *¶94 Product Wake*) and to free its people to work on other, perhaps new, products. This may offer an opportunity for global improvements that might otherwise stop at local optimizations within the kaizen scope of a *Product Owner*. For example, the broader view might discover that one product is cannibalizing the market of another, and that the net benefit to the market and realization of the highest value (see Value and ROI on page 246) will result from stopping production on one of the two products.

One reason that management can take the risk to strike out in radical new directions derives in part from their oversight of a broad portfolio of products that can take up the slack for each other, and in part from their intangible talent for having "great hunches" that have propelled them into their position (see "Liquid Networks" in *Where Good Ideas Come From: The Natural History of Innovation [Joh11]*, and *Gut Feelings: The Intelligence of the Unconscious [Gig08]*). The higher management are in the organization, the more they augment rationality with decisions from the gut, as Gerd Gigerenzer notes in "Leadership and Intuition" (*Risk Savvy: How to Make Good Decisions [Gig14]*). They can remove organizational impediments and bring the organizational structure in line with Scrum goals. For example, management may initiate a policy to remove product direction decisions from a sales and marketing organization that has become powerful, and shift the responsibility to the *Product Owner*. Again, drawing on the Nortel experience, we find this:

> What was different about Nortel was that even managers and directors at the most senior levels were prepared to, and indeed were used to, thinking in an open and challenging manner about ways of working and ways of organizing and were far more willing to question the continuing relevance of current portfolios of products and services. At all levels they took a much more playful and expansive approach to thinking about organizations.
>
> ...They recognized a number of paradoxes and seemed prepared not only to live with but to apply these paradoxes to the management of organisation [sic] and innovation.
>
> ...They suggested that incremental innovation could be achieved by traditional organisational structures but that radical innovation required an organisation that was capable of moving beyond current structures. (From *Managers of Innovation: Insights into Making Innovation Happen [SS04]*, ff. 46.)

Also, managers provide a locus of both strategic and tactical coordination and support in large organizations. *Empowerment* was a buzzword of the 1980s—a kind of cult of *Autonomous Teams*. Whereas managers originally supported teams with coordination and facilitation, research at DuPont, AT&T, and other large companies found that empowerment destroyed valuable connections between teams (*The Limits of Participatory Management [Hec95]*). Management served a valuable function that *Autonomous Teams*, *taken to the extreme*, destroy. However, keep the management population small: remember that Rosing from the earlier Google story had 160 direct reports with no intervening managers. As in Rosing's case, this likely means that much of the existing management population may need to find new roles within the organization.

In fact, Project Oxygen at Google reinterpreted the role played by those titled as managers so that they functioned more as coaches than managers (*How Google Sold Its Engineers on Management [Gar13]*). Google recognized that good managers do not micromanage, that they communicate effectively, are caring yet productive, and that they focus on growing their people's careers. While these traits characterize great managers in a traditional environment, a great *ScrumMaster* fills this coaching role on a *Scrum Team*.

On a day-by-day basis, the *Scrum Team* can invite managers to remove obstacles that stand in the way of delivery. This prevents the team from having to create work-arounds and helps resolve structural problems instead of leaving it to development to fight symptoms.

Note that management should be seeking synergy between *products* that each already have their own *¶41 Value Stream*. This pattern is not an excuse for management to subcontract parts of a product development to multiple vendors, unless each component already has market standing (e.g., as a commodity) in its own right. Unless there are economies of scope for the company as a whole, whereby several development efforts might share the intake from an external vendor, individual *Product Owner*s should manage such subcontracting arrangements.

Management may decide that a particular business strategy (like IBM's dominance in selling iron and copper) has come to the end of its useful life, and may decide to stop work on such products except for warranty replacement and minimal maintenance. That frees the business to move in a new direction (i.e., selling services, consulting, outsourcing, the Cloud). It is unlikely that the hardware *Product Owner* would himself or herself take the business in what he or she perceived as a suicidal direction, even though a broader business perspective may view it as for the greater corporate good. Management can start a new replacement business, driven by a *Product Owner* who brings a *¶39 Vision* suitable to the new direction. This is a radical, *kaikaku* change.

Of course, managers work closely with *Product Owner*s on all such initiatives. The main difference between *Product Owner* and manager influence and activity lies in the scope and extent of a change: largely, the split between *kaizen* and *kaikaku*. Managers interface with the *Scrum Teams* in the *MetaScrum*, so managers interface primarily with the *Product Owner* role in Scrum. The *MetaScrum* is one forum that helps the manager keep in touch with what is going on in the organization (transparency and sharing information), and vice versa. It gives regular formal management access to the *Scrum Teams*. Managers should not otherwise intervene in Scrum events.

Managers become the focal point of scaling. Rather than scaling a product, managers scale the enterprise and facilitate the interactions between parts of the corporation. A *Product Owner*, and not a manager, heads each product, with a very thin and narrow veneer of management at the next level up. It is an impediment if managers come to need management from other managers. Again, going back to the role Northern Telecom managers played in innovation:

> Nortel is very flat. You won't see much hierarchy in the place... you will find champions all over the place at all sorts of levels. (*Computerworld XIX [Gal85]*, p. 50.)

In a large organization, managers can help fill a so-called "human resources" function that looks beyond matching the talents of individual candidates to an immediate need, focusing on broad competencies and an aptitude for learning. Good companies hire for the broad talent and hunger to learn that could benefit any one of a number of products over time and over a long career, rather than desperately hiring the talent that will enable any current product to meet its delivery goals. Closer to production, other management functions can support ongoing career development, knowledge management, and competency development, perhaps by leading *Birds of a Feather* organizations. Spotify has Chapter Lead managers who, while still being squad (*Development Team*) members, act as line managers within their Chapter. Some of their responsibilities include personnel development and salary administration.[8] Each Chapter is topically focused. This works well as long as the manager is not managing production; otherwise, the group reporting to the manager is likely to reflect that area of expertise rather than being a *¶10 Cross-Functional Team*.

Eric Ries says in *Lean Startup [Rie11]* (pp. 2–3) that our belief in entrepreneurial success is often tied to the myth of "perseverance, creative genius, and hard work," whereas in reality he has found "that it's the boring stuff that matters the most... Entrepreneurship is a kind of management." We often stereotype the *ScrumMaster* as being the chief cook and bottle washer that handles the

---

8. Ashley Hardy. "Agile Team Organisation: Squads, Chapters, Tribes and Guilds." medium.com, https://medium.com/@achardypm/agile-team-organisation-squads-chapters-tribes-and-guilds-80932ace0fdc, 14 February 2016 (accessed 4 December 2017).

dirty work, but everyone chips in on the daily chores in a great team. The *ScrumMaster* and Manager bear a bit more of this burden. Letting the *Development Team* do their thing builds the foundation to create great value. The unglamorous stuff is a distraction.

We relate the story of a Dutch company called Tony's Chocolonely as an example. Some journalists discovered that most chocolate was produced by slavery and child labor (think: *¶2 The Mist*). They pondered how they could improve the world: "We lead by example and prove that commercially successful chocolate can be made without slavery and exploitation"[9] (think: *Vision*). "And not just our chocolate. No. All chocolate worldwide. When there is no more slavery in the chocolate industry, then we will have achieved our goal"[10] (think: *Greatest Value*). The business grew. With the growth of the firm came the distractions of finance, purchasing, and a host of other management concerns. They were not able to focus on their goal anymore. They reluctantly started a search for a manager who knew how to handle such concerns, but the founder felt those they interviewed were opportunists just in it for the money, like "used car salesmen." Part of the problem is that one of the founders, Maurice Dekker, was looking for someone just like himself, but he realized the ultimate irony was that his very skill set—or lack of a management skill set—was the root of the problem that the manager might solve. Eventually they started a collaboration with the person who is now their CEO, Henk Jan, and have since grown to be the largest chocolate producer in the Netherlands.[11] And the company produces chocolate in a slave-free value stream, as recognized by a 2007 Dutch court ruling.[12]

Some would-be management responsibilities often fall to the *ScrumMaster*, such as "managing" the *¶82 Definition of Done*. And the *ScrumMaster* can challenge the *Scrum Team* to *kaikaku* within the team's realm of control. It is important

9. Api Podder. Amsterdam-based Tony's Chocolonely Brings Mission of 100 Percent Slave-Free Chocolate to the U.S. My Social Good News, https://mysocialgoodnews.com/amsterdam-based-tonys-chocolonely-brings-mission-100-percent-slave-free-chocolate-u-s/ (accessed 28 January 2019).

10. Tonys Chocolonely Annual Report. https://tonyschocolonely.com/storage/configurations/tonyschocolonelycom.app/files/jaarfairslag/2017-2017/tc_jaarfairslag_2016_en_totaal_01.pdf, 2017 (no longer accessible; accessed 6 June 2018).

11. "Z Doc: TONY, Van Chocoladecrimineel Tot Wereldverbeteraar." Documentary on Dutch television RTLZ, 20:30–22:00, 11 December 2017, https://tonyschocolonely.com/nl/nl/doe-mee/tony-de-film (accessed 28 January 2019).

12. "Tony's Chocolonely." Wikipedia, https://en.wikipedia.org/wiki/Tony's_Chocolonely (accessed 17 December 2017).

to recognize that, unlike management, the *ScrumMaster* has no direct control over the team, but must work through persuasion and exhortation.

In the literature, one will find admonitions such as "management should create a good (safe, supportive, etc.) environment in which the team can work." Maybe. Managers have less ability to improve a team's sense of safety than they have to destroy it. Pointing to such a responsibility implies that the *Scrum Team* has lost control over its environment, or perhaps that it never had such control. There is a balance to be struck here, but it is better to err on the side of recognizing the team's autonomy over things it can control, and for management to focus on issues largely outside the reach of the team's sphere of influence.

Traditional managers must take care not to fall back into their former activities once they start evolving their role under Scrum, particularly if they interfere with the ordinary course of work of *Product Owner*s or of the *Development Team*. Managers must, in particular, respect the *Product Owner*'s authority over product content and release. They must also respect the *Development Team*'s self-direction as to the *how*, the *who*, and sometimes the *when* of feature development. It is the *ScrumMaster*'s job to make such a situation visible when it arises and to initiate the conversations towards removing such an impediment. And though managers may have control over the team, such control is never at the level of individual product or release strategy. The strongest foundation of management power is the reluctance to use it, and using it sparingly.

The pattern ¶133 *Smoke-Filled Room* on page 470 foreshadows this pattern. *Smoke-Filled Room* on page 470 testified to the fact that sometimes management has to make decisions without first broadly engaging everyone who would be affected by those decisions, but it wrongly equated exigency with secrecy. Managers can be a powerful force that can respond to precipitous emergencies and can sometimes more ably steer the big ship than a consensus process can. But, they should operate in trust and openness instead of acting as the kind of shadowy cabal implied by the earlier pattern.

¶7 Scrum Team

Confidence stars: **

A team (producers and supporters) working closely together to achieve a vision—complete with a guard to protect the team.

...you have a *¶39 Vision* of a product for your customers. You have started to record the ideas your customers are going to love and you need to start to make these ideas a reality. You don't know how to make the product or whether the ideas are correct, but what you do know is there will be new ideas as you learn more.

❖　❖　❖

Many great *Vision*s are beyond the reach of solo efforts, and to achieve such a *Vision* you need to build the complex product, bring it to the market and leverage feedback

Some products simply cannot realize greatness at the hands of a single individual; it's too easy to develop a low-value product in a feedback vacuum. Experience shows that person for person, teams outperform individuals: Many hands make light work.

History, experience, and inclination will draw individuals to particular areas of focus (e.g., eliciting needs from the market as opposed to production), but too much specialization (e.g., wanting to be in production without dealing with other development tasks like documentation or testing) can lead to expertise starvation as development needs vary from delivery to delivery. Role differentiation should primarily follow from variations in the long-term rhythms of those roles' primary activity. For example, one set of roles may deal with the market on a release cadence while another set of roles may deal with day-to-day production issues.

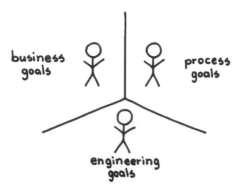

The work rhythms of business and development are different with good reason, and letting them work separately increases autonomy and lets each focus on what it does best. The good part is that this gives the business the freedom to work on other things while development readies the product for delivery. The bad part is the handoff that happens if the business gives the order to develop a product and transfers the responsibility of product delivery to a separate development organization. The handoff may include a deadline and, because the business and development organizations are decoupled, the deadline may be arbitrary with respect to what development can actually deliver. The only thing that development can do is increase their rate of production.

Focus on the whole product is a state of mind. It is hard to develop that mindset as an assembly line worker producing some small part of a product. Being decoupled from any whole-product focus makes work feel less meaningful and robs people of a sense of ownership for the Vision, or being able to identify with the purpose of the product.

A team should be a locus of learning and improvement, and the team structure should support learning. Solving a complex problem means that you will learn a lot during development and use that learning to let the solution emerge. Both the business and development could respectively elicit and act on feedback relevant to their own worldviews. A solution that works well from the perspective of the business might not yield the ¶93 *Greatest Value*. The same is true of development perspective. The frenetic pace of development and the intellectual demands of building a product work together to draw our focus to only the problem at hand. We're so busy building a product that we can't be bothered to do it better. And neither development nor the business are attendant to the more transcendent issue of process, which is very worrisome from the perspective of the Japanese roots of Scrum that advise us "build the right process and you'll build the right product."

Fast feedback makes learning timely and effective. Learning is even more effective when people with different expertise and perspectives work together during development. People that focus on the activities of developing the product often have less time to think about how to improve.

Therefore:

Form a team that has all the necessary competencies: the people who can make and deliver the product (a ¶14 Development Team), a ¶11 Product Owner who guides product direction, and a ¶19 ScrumMaster who facilitates learning.

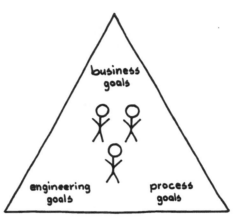

A *Development Team* has the skill and knowledge to implement products and to do all the work necessary to put them in the hands of end users. A *Product Owner* is the manifestation of the business within the *Scrum Team* (connecting it with the customer). A *ScrumMaster* has the skill and knowledge to coach a *Scrum Team*, help it continuously improve its development process, and address Impediments.

Usually, the *Product Owner* brings the *Scrum Team* into existence to realize his or her *Vision* to achieve value, and in many contexts the *Product Owner* will work within an enterprise to create the *Scrum Team* as a small, autonomous enterprise within the larger entity. The *Product Owner* will lead the team toward the *Vision*. Teams may add small numbers of Developers and may grow over time, but never beyond ¶9 *Small Teams* of no more than about seven developers in any *Development Team*.

The developers have their own identity as a *Development Team* that manages itself to its forecasts and commitments. The *Product Owner* and Developers together hire or appoint the *ScrumMaster*; the *ScrumMaster* takes ownership of the process and supports the team in ongoing improvement.

The *Scrum Team* is more than a wrapper for including the *Product Owner* in a team. The *Scrum Team* is a small business that can work within the context of the organization and make independent decisions to respond to the customer. This change in structure has a significant effect in the development of products when using Scrum.

❖ ❖ ❖

The *Scrum Team* provides an organizational home for the *Product Owner*'s *Vision*. Each *Scrum Team* runs like a small enterprise, as an *¶16 Autonomous Team*. Each team comes together around shared values and is conscious of, and may even articulate, its *¶31 Norms of Conduct*.

A small and interactive *Scrum Team* creates opportunities for feedback from the development of the product (as a *¶85 Regular Product Increment*) into the *¶54 Product Backlog*. Because the *Development Team* spends a lot of time with the *Product Owner*—building a strong working relationship—the *Development Team* can come to understand the product direction well. The *Product Owner* will also gain a deeper understanding of the implementation of the product, leading to other joint decisions between the *Development Team* and *Product Owner* that may increase ROI or other value.

The *Scrum Team* creates a structure that supports alignment for the team around the product direction and goals. The team meets regularly to attend to fixed work such as periodic review and planning (*¶23 Fixed Work*), and other central events like *¶24 Sprint Planning*. Teams have a purpose and, without the explicit link to the product direction via the *Scrum Team*, the purpose of the team can become fractured. Functional subgroups each have their own independent purpose: there are no such groups within a *Scrum Team*. The climate for product development can also be established via the *Scrum Team*. Whether a product needs to be highly secure, delivered very quickly, or be extremely robust, the *Scrum Team* can quickly establish that these might be so by its connection to the product market. The close connection between the *Development Team* with the *Product Owner* fosters a climate that steers overall development in the right direction. Multiple *Scrum Teams* align informally as needed, and more formally through the overarching *¶37 MetaScrum*.

True teams are almost always *¶8 Collocated Teams*. Size the team according to *Small Teams*, ensure that it is a *¶10 Cross-Functional Team* and let the team manage the *Development Team* membership over time according to *¶15 Stable Teams*. This creates the opportunity for the team to become autonomous and self-organizing as well as aligned with the product.

*Development Team*s within a common product development work on the same cadence (*¶47 Organizational Sprint Pulse*). They coordinate freely with each other as needed, with a daily opportunity for formal coordination in the *¶34 Scrum of Scrums* as well as once per *¶46 Sprint* in each of the *¶35 Sprint Review* and *¶36 Sprint Retrospective*. Great teams work in a rhythm of alternating focus on process improvement and production (*¶26 Kaizen Pulse*).

Emergency situations may cause the team to take exceptional action to break cadence; see *¶32 Emergency Procedure*.

For outsourcing, or other co-development programs, consider using *¶13 Development Partnership* to staff the *Scrum Team* roles, with particular attentiveness to keeping the *Product Owner* close to the business drivers.

While multiple people working together can produce more than the sum of what they could do independently, a group setting leads to coordination and communication overhead that have a cost called *process loss*. Counter this process loss with *Small Teams*.

Jeff Sutherland evolved the *Scrum Team* concept from the organization of the Toyota Production System work cell, which normally comprises workers and a Chief Engineer. Jeff split the Chief Engineer role in two, with the business focus going to the *Product Owner* and the process focus going to the *ScrumMaster*.

¶8 Collocated Team

Confidence stars: **

...you have set up one or more *¶9 Small Teams* that are *¶10 Cross-Functional Teams*, working together on a product.

❖ ❖ ❖

Complex collaborative development such as knowledge work requires high-quality communication to be effective. It is difficult to predict the timing, frequency, and duration of this communication necessary for success.

Some people like to work in solitude, and having cubicles can help people have some space of their own to concentrate. Or having your own office may be a sign of career success. In either case, the little telltale signs of their progress—like a cheer on the arrival of an awaited parcel, or the updates on their personal status board—are out of sight and out of mind. We try to compensate by booking meeting spaces for people to get together. It seems like the number of meeting spaces in all buildings is under-engineered, leading to increased overhead for having time together. The result is to discourage people to make the effort to meet, and reduced interpersonal communication. People often resort to using a lower-fidelity method of communication—IM, email, phone, fax, telegraph, Jira ticket, carrier pigeon, or post, instead.

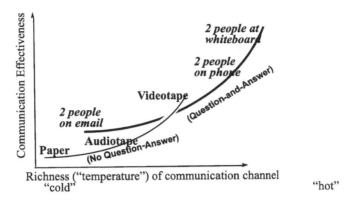

The graph shows two sets of situations: those in which question and answer are available and those in which they are not. "Warmer" indicates that more emotional and informational richness gets conveyed (Agile Software Development [Coc06], pp. 90–100).

Communication depends on more than being able to send and receive messages: the receiver must also understand message. A rich communication channel supports the nuances of interpersonal communication including verbal and nonverbal attributes. There must be rapid feedback to confirm understanding while the message is still "fresh" for both the sender and the receiver. nonverbal communication is important "to express emotions, communicate interpersonal relationships, support verbal interaction" (*Bodily Communication [Arg10]*, p. 303).

The Allen Curve from 1977 shows that when people separate to a distance of 10 meters their probability of communicating at least once a week is less than 10 percent (*Managing the Flow of Technology [All77]*). Despite recent developments in communication technology, Allen has said this has not improved:

> In his seminal 1977 book, Managing the Flow of Technology, Thomas J. Allen was the first to measure the strong negative correlation between physical distance and frequency of communication. The "Allen curve" estimates that we are four times as likely to communicate regularly with someone sitting six feet away from us as with someone 60 feet away, and that we almost never communicate with colleagues on separate floors or in separate buildings.

> But the office is no longer just a physical place; we can enter it by logging on, attend meetings from anywhere, and collaborate on documents without ever seeing one another. It would seem that distance-shrinking technologies break the Allen curve, and that communication no longer correlates to distance.

Wrong. The Allen curve holds. In fact, as distance-shrinking technology accelerates, proximity is apparently becoming more important. Studies by Ben Waber show that both face-to-face and digital communications follow the Allen curve. In one study, engineers who shared a physical office were 20% more likely to stay in touch digitally than those who worked elsewhere. When they needed to collaborate closely, co-located coworkers e-mailed four times as frequently as colleagues in different locations, which led to 32% faster project completion times. (From *Harvard Business Review 92 [WML14]*.)

Even more powerful than distance are features of the building architecture; being in different offices is a liability, in different hallways a serious liability, on different building levels an extreme liability, and in separate buildings a disaster. We have heard the CEO of one of the world's largest telecommunications companies say that their popular telecommunications product is not a tool suitable to supporting multisite software development.

Distance Effects on Communications

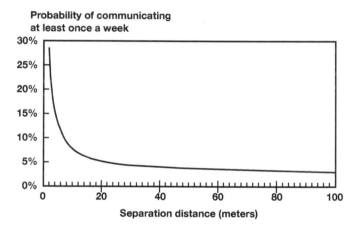

Probability of people communicating with each other once a week decreases when the distance between them increases. Managing the Flow of Technology [All77]

Team members that are physically separated cannot function together effectively, and sometimes not at all. Even the New Zealand All Blacks can't win if they play on three rugby pitches simultaneously. (Well, maybe there are a few teams they could beat even then.)

Therefore:

Collocate the team members, ideally in a room of their own, within *talking* distance. Alistair Cockburn suggests that the entire team sit within the length of one school bus (*Agile Software Development [Coc06]*, p. 102).

Collocation allows for people working together to have ad hoc conversations with ease. People share information regularly and rapidly. Collocated staff can also enjoy casual conversations about non-work topics that increase team cohesion.

Reinertsen admonishes us that "[c]ollocation is the closest thing to fairy dust that we have to improve communications on the development team" (*Managing the Design Factory: A Product Developer's Toolkit [Rei98]*, p. 113).

However, there is still an occasional need for quiet uninterrupted thinking, phone calls, or pair discussions. Therefore, the work environment should provide quiet rooms such as small offices that can be used as needed. If collocated team members spend most of their time working in isolation in such spaces, or if they wear headphones most of the time, or if the bulk of their communication takes place via Slack or some other electronic media, it seriously limits the benefits of collocation. The *¶19 ScrumMaster* should explore the reasons behind such behavior and confront the team.

❖ ❖ ❖

Some people may find this awkward, especially people with a preference for solitary work. Working in teams and working in *Collocated Teams* are not for everyone and these people may need to be helped out of the organization to work for an institution more suitable to their preferences—or maybe Scrum is not for them. While some people may find that frequent broad social contact takes them out of their comfort zone, most people can adapt their actions to the broader needs of the team. It takes more energy for some people than others to do so, but such communication is necessary for effective teamwork.

For organizations that like to have large teams—or think they must have large teams—collocation can be very difficult. There may be a lack of space or a significant moving cost to have people shift locations. This will be an important moment for the organization, deciding to deal with this situation as an impediment or to accept this suboptimal state. See *Small Teams*, *Cross-Functional Teams*, and *¶4 Conway's Law*.

Infants learn to recognize the phonemes of their native language through repeated exposure to them. Studies have shown that physical presence is crucial. Infants exposed to foreign language phonemes learned to recognize them as if they had heard them from a physically present person. However, the infants showed no learning if they were exposed to the phonemes through either audio or audiovisual media (*Nature Reviews Neuroscience 5 [Kuh04]*). Communication is a social process, and communication becomes less effective when technology limits the naturalness of the communication channel. This tends to substantiate the inadequacy of teleconferences *and* videoconferences for effective communication. In your next tele- or videoconference, observe the differences between that session and face-to-face interaction. Note the differences in the amount of time someone speaks in a single turn; in the amount of interruptions, overlaps, and backchannels; and in the degree of formality when switching speakers. The studies have shown that the tele- or videoconference does not replicate face-to-face interaction (*Human-Computer Interaction 8 [OWW93]*).

Members of a collocated team are likely to exhibit pride in their identity and in the product they build; see *¶38 Product Pride*:

> Collocated team members' development of trust is also significantly identified with perceptions regarding equitable decision-making, and may affect team pride and self-respect, further affecting processes of vulnerability and self-disclosure (*Trust in Virtual Teams: Organization, Strategies and Assurance for Successful Projects [Wis13]*, p. 116).

¶9 Small Teams

Confidence stars: **

Every Monday morning the CEO of our 5000 person company would send out an email starting with the words "Hello Team." We all knew we were not One Team.

...complex product development is a collaborative activity that requires people working together to build it. When people are working together with a common goal, having these people work as a team is usually the best way to optimize the work.

There is an emerging *¶39 Vision* and energy to pursue it is gathering as the stakeholders come out of *¶2 The Mist*.

❖ ❖ ❖

When there's a ton of work ahead, you are tempted to throw the world at it. But complex work demands a high degree of shared knowledge and coordination, such as product design and development. This kind of work defies such an approach.

There are clear advantages to having more than one person carry out difficult work. With many eyes and voices, the team can avoid the biases that might arise in solo efforts. And everyone learns firsthand from exploring the new frontiers that a team encounters during complex development. This can lead to large groups of people trying to work together. Such teams tend to attract specialists and that tends to make the team grow.

Deadlines may push you to allocate as many people as you can to work in parallel to get it done. But unless the work is decomposable into independent parts, any time savings will be more than eaten up by communication and coordination overhead.

When status within an organization is proportional to team size, large teams can emerge as a part of the politics of the organization.

Having large teams of people working together means having fewer small teams. It is tempting to think that having large teams reduces the hassles of having numerous small teams. But there is no such thing as a large team. Large organizations self-organize into small (sub-)teams that can get things done. You may think having one big team is going to be easy, but then you end up with a heap of smaller ones anyway. So why not start with what works and the structure to which groups of people naturally evolve?

Having a large group of people working together on interdependent tasks unfortunately leads to unexpected problems.

The more people working together, the greater the overhead of communication. Good communication is essential for effective teamwork; however, this overhead has a harmful effect on communication quality. As the group grows, there is proportionally less information transferred within the group, yet there needs to be more information transferred with the increased number of people. Taken to extreme, communication and coordination overhead consumes nearly all the resources of the group, leaving almost no time to do productive work. This is like the problem in computers called "thrashing" where a lot of energy is expended without actually accomplishing anything. Alternatively, the organization may designate communication clearinghouses such as management roles, decision forums, and committees that are organizational structures in their own right. These extra communication links create communication bottlenecks, impair communication fidelity, or both.

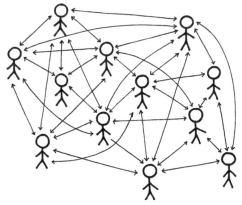

With larger groups of people, the relative contribution of everyone diminishes. This can have a non-negligible motivational effect, as free riding and social loafing (where the individuals contribute less in the group than they would working on their own) increases as the size of the team increases. The result can be that large groups produce less than small groups, or that large groups produce lower-quality outcomes than small groups.

When there are large groups of people working together, there is a greater need to coordinate these individuals. This coordination effort is called *process loss*. As Steiner described in 1972, the actual productivity of a team is the potential productivity minus the process loss (*Group Process and Productivity* [Ste72], p. 9). As team size increases so does the process loss, effectively limiting the growth of productivity with increasing team size. In these situations, teams add more and more roles to support coordination that do not add value and effectively reduce the productivity of the team (the number of roles like this in a team is the Wally Number, named after Scott Adam's character in *Dilbert*).

Christopher Alexander cites a study that shows communication effectiveness drops with an increase in group size. In his pattern, "Small Meeting Rooms," he notes that during meetings, "[i]n a group of 12, one person never talks. In a group of 24, there are 6 people who never talk" ("Small Meeting Rooms" in *A Pattern Language* [AIS77], pattern 151).

Despite the conjecturally legitimate forces that lead to having larger teams, these large groups of people come with significant problems.

Therefore:

Use *Small Teams* of people working on serialized work rather than striving for false parallelism.

Consider ¶7 *Scrum Team*s to be around five or so people. They need the appropriate expertise and the ability to work together, which can lead to a ¶10 *Cross-Functional Team*.

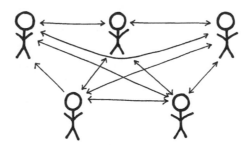

People working in *Small Teams* have a greater sense of attachment to the team and the goals of the team, have better communication within the team with more opportunities to be heard, and are generally more productive. *Small Teams* help overcome negative teamwork effects such as social loafing and process loss as well as facilitate more positive effects like the Kohler effect (motivation to not be the worst-performing member of a team).

❖ ❖ ❖

In a Small, *Cross-Functional Team*, it may be challenging to work out who needs to be on the team to create the *¶85 Regular Product Increment*. Rather than incurring the overhead of an oracle (such as a manager) or other additional role to work this out, try using *¶116 Self-Selecting Team* on page 468. Where the team size starts to grow, an opportunity exists for exploring more deeply the organizational problems for which growth tries to compensate. For example, an overly complex architecture may lead to a team that depends on many specialists working together to complete the increment. It is a good investment to resolve these issues by striving to keep the team small while still being able to deliver a product increment. Both the product and process can benefit from such tidiness.

Broad research efforts have shown small teams to be more effective than larger teams in many dimensions, and that people prefer being in small teams to being in a larger organization. In 1958, participants in research by Slater preferred being in a team of five rather than larger teams (*Group Process and Productivity [Ste72]*, p. 86). The team members found that larger teams were less coordinated, more difficult to share ideas in, and were not as effective in using the team member's time. Members of smaller teams (two to four members) also preferred to be in teams of five, showing a preference for small team size. Research conducted by Kameda et al. in 1992 shows increasing performance with larger team size, then decreasing performance above a certain point. The experiment used team sizes of two, four, six, and twelve people. The conclusion was that the performance of members in a team of four people was highest (*Social Psychology Quarterly 55 [KSDP92]*). In more recent research on software development, teams with nine or more people were found to be less productive than teams with fewer than nine members (*Journal of Systems and Software 85 [RSBH12]*). Other studies have shown that a critical mass of three people was both necessary and sufficient to perform better than the best individuals. So, though small is beautiful, three is probably a lower bound on effective team size (*Journal of Personality and Social Psychology 90 [LHSB06]*).

Experiment to find the best size for your team: we will not give you an optimal number here. Most efforts start with one or two people and then grow when they receive official funding. Remember that great teams grow from small teams that work. Add new team members with great trepidation. Cross-training and broadening expertise across the team is almost always better in the long term than growing the team to compensate for missing expertise. Cutting people from an overly large team to achieve the right size can lead people to grieve over the broken relationship. It is better to look for natural opportunities to move people out of the group such as attrition, promotion, or a team member's initiative to seek career opportunities in another team.

Larger teams (statistically) experience more churn than smaller teams, so the larger a team is, the less likely it is that its membership will be stable over time. *Small Teams* therefore support *¶15 Stable Teams.*

If a team starts to grow too large, consider *¶18 Mitosis.*

¶10 Cross-Functional Team

Confidence stars: **

The team as a whole should embody all the talent necessary to deliver product.

...the *¶7 Scrum Team* is organizing its development effort, and are choosing team members, or are assessing how to grow the team skill set.

❖ ❖ ❖

The *Scrum Team* is not able to work autonomously because it does not have all the skills required to complete a complex network of tasks. By depending on skills from people outside the team, the team cannot take ownership for finishing their tasks. It reduces the team's influence on the time it takes to finish and can tarnish the quality of the end result. The core lean principles of consistency and reduced rework depend on short feedback loops. Most complex development requires people with numerous talents from areas as diverse as human factors, engineering excellence, and quality assurance. It is rare that one finds all these talents in members of a single team, let alone in any given individual. Teams often organize around areas of competence: birds of a feather flock together. This is sometimes called a functional organization. Yet, it is costly to coordinate these functions across team boundaries because efficient communications take place between those who share the context of the current work—and that is usually the team members.

A complex product might require that the team has mastered numerous skills to develop *Done* functionality (see *¶82 Definition of Done*). When work calls for an additional individual for each required skill, the team will become too big to be effective. You might be tempted to not extend the skill set in the team and to instead introduce external dependencies. On the other hand, you might choose to give the work to the team so they can develop and learn the required skill. But learning takes time.

Local learning can become local optimization, where a group of specialists develop practices and processes that optimize their work. Specialization, local practices and processes can all be sources of efficiency in an organization, but can also create problems at the group boundary. To attack these problems, an organization can define "contracts" outlining how to work with each other (e.g., service requests). Such contracts might specify the nature of the work that an organization is willing to do along with expected durations for responses to requests. Anyone needing the group's specialization would have to use these contracts. However, this can slow development of the product as a whole even though it increases the efficiency of the local department. Again, there may be a need for additional coordination groups within the organization to manage these boundary contracts, to negotiate exceptions or ensure all parties understand what is required, and to make sure each team meets its obligations to other teams—and to the customer, according to the obligations of these contracts.

New products—or new versions of existing products—each create a new world for their customers. Because you cannot know in advance what this new world will be like, you must focus on learning and experimentation as the product evolves. The team must find lessons in its experience with actual customer use of each product increment rather than according to some pre-arranged plan. And the team must integrate these lessons across the product development process. Everyone recognizes the advantages of local flow, autonomy, and control that come from working as an individual within a step of the process or within a functional area. However, such a work structure moves everyone (except the person doing the last step) further from the end user and the broad insights that come from interactions at that boundary. This may result in suboptimal local functions but greater optimization across the entire product development process.

Therefore:

Each *Scrum Team* should include all talent necessary to deliver *Done* functionality.

It's good to pay attention to skill set coverage when initially creating the team, but it's more important that the charter team members share enthusiasm for the *¶39 Vision* and that they have a track record of learning new things. Because things change over time, it is unlikely that the team will be able to foresee all its long-term skill needs from the beginning.

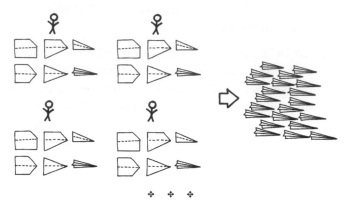

❖   ❖   ❖

Instead of changing team membership as the need for new skills emerges, grow the people internally and strive for *¶9 Small Teams* and *¶15 Stable Teams*. Over time, cross-train team members so they grow their skill sets to accommodate more and more competency areas (see *¶123 Moderate Truck Number* on page 469). This will increase the ability of the team to work as an *¶16 Autonomous Team*. With *Cross-Functional Teams* it becomes easier to *¶131 Distribute Work Evenly* on page 470.

The team members now have all the opportunities to learn secondary skills. They can swarm (see *¶25 Swarming: One-Piece Continuous Flow*) on *¶55 Product Backlog Items* (*PBIs*), which increases learning opportunities and optimizes flow to help get functionality to *Done* fast. The development of secondary skills makes the team more flexible so any member can stand in for another that has become unavailable. The team always makes progress and is autonomous.

Scrum is silent on how to handle a missing competency. Let common sense prevail; for example, ask for help from another team, or subcontract large work increments that might surprise the team. It is understandable if the team needs such help now and then. But if the team finds they frequently depend on external help, then they should view this as an impediment and take measures (such as training, reorganization, or hiring) to remedy the situation.

For example, a team of software programmers may find themselves building a product in an area outside their native expertise, such as pharmaceuticals or aerospace. It is tempting to appoint a person on the team for each of the underrepresented competencies, perhaps by consulting with an external domain expert. However, the team representative may not know how much they don't know, and may not even know what questions to ask the domain experts. Most domain experts carry domain expertise as tacit knowledge, so they are not in a position to recover the right insights to support the software person in a proper implementation. It is crucial that team members understand the implications of domain considerations on the implementation and have a thorough knowledge of both the business and solution space. In a recent article, Jesse Watson of Amazon noted that it's crucial that both of these factors co-exist "within one skull."[13] It is better to bring the expert on board to the team and to broaden the knowledge with cross-training. But remember *Small Teams*: adding specialists may grow the team to a point where teamwork diminishes to almost nothing.

These teams naturally act like "feature teams" (see *¶4 Conway's Law*) because most *PBI*s are feature-shaped: marketable elements of revenue-generating functional product increment. If *Cross-Functional Team*s develop the product, then handoffs naturally disappear from the *¶41 Value Stream*: the team itself can develop any feature without outside support or intervention. Involving multiple teams introduces delays in feedback loops, increases the waste (*muda*) of rework, and creates inconsistency (*mura*) between development stages in the *Value Stream*.

A study published in the Harvard Business Review of two corporations, one organized functionally and the other by product, suggests that cross-functional teams offer the best features of both organizational structures (see "Organizational Choice: Product vs. Function" in *Harvard Business Review 46 [WL68]*).

¶42 Set-Based Design is a technique that keeps developers engaged in many disciplines and domains that may be relevant to the business, even if they ultimately don't make it through to the current product. Such practice broadens the expertise base of the team and enterprise and reduces the probability that the team will be surprised by the need to master some new discipline.

As the team integrates new lessons there will be new product ideas. Change will proceed quickly (and must be allowed to proceed quickly). Change will be the norm rather than the exception. This requires small organizations where everyone knows what is happening: organizations that can embrace change, work across specializations, regularly deliver value and are, for want of another term: agile.

---

13. Jesse Watson. "The Hard Thing about Software Development." LinkedIn.com, https://www.linkedin.com/pulse/hard-thing-software-development-jesse-watson, 12 July 2017 (accessed 4 July 2018).

A Game

Assemble several small teams who will compete in a game to make and fly paper airplanes. Each team member may make only one fold at a time, and then must switch to work on another plane. No plane may have more than 15 folds. It must be at least 15 centimeters long and 8 centimeters wide. It must have a blunt tip at least 2 centimeters wide. To qualify as a quality product the plane must fly 3 meters horizontally when the tester tests it. The tester may test each plane only once.

Try the game, and apply Scrum patterns (hint: *Swarming: One-Piece Continuous Flow*) to optimize the number of quality planes produced in a one-minute Sprint.

¶11 Product Owner

Confidence stars: **

Henry Ford testing a car he envisioned (by hitting it with an ax), and which his company built—from hemp

...while everyone holds their own broad notion of the *¶39 Vision* and of possible good outcomes, the community seeks a leader around whom they can rally their passion and enthusiasm.

❖ ❖ ❖

One person needs to be responsible for the *¶54 Product Backlog*. This person needs deep domain knowledge, business insight, understanding of product technology, technical dependencies, and the authority to force rank the backlog to maximize business value.

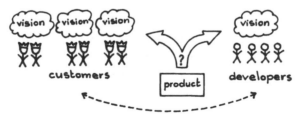

¶7 Scrum Team members need a single, well-formed, sequenced list of *¶55 Product Backlog Item*s to help focus on delivering value. Without this list, the team may generate features that the market will never or rarely use (though the team still bears the effort to maintain them). They may deliver features at the wrong time (suboptimizing revenue) or deliver nothing. The *Scrum Team* needs the backlog in a timely manner to support and maximize the team's velocity; a committee cannot achieve this timeliness. Committees are also

likely to encapsulate compromise and to come to somewhat incoherent conclusions.

Too many organizations put several people or groups in charge of charting product rollout, with staff members from multiple departments all bringing their perspective to the product rollout planning process. This is a good idea to the extent that multiple perspectives broaden insight into how to most effectively deliver the product to the consumer. However, these committees too often represent internal corporate functions, disconnected from market concerns where the real value lies. Further, these groups often lack authority to make decisions and need "sponsorship," with yet another group being the arbiter of the important decisions for the product. The decisions are further away from both the work on the product and the people doing the work, which can be de-motivating for the developers when they are not part of this process (or even when they are). Discussions often degrade into political considerations and competitions to retain control or to increase benefits for a given constituency, rather than benefit those at the end of the ¶41 *Value Stream*s. These negotiations slow the process, delay product delivery, reduce quality and erode the coherence of the backlog.

Some organizations put rollout planning in the hands of a committee of bosses or managers. Sometimes they can't even agree to what the product is. It's almost impossible to make this work without a single focal point. You need someone to explicitly lead product development.

One common approach is to hire a project manager to oversee the team's day-to-day work. The project manager does the work that management may feel is too important to ignore but not important enough to distract from their own pressing agendas. Though this is very common—almost ubiquitous—the approach in fact slows product delivery and may reduce quality and profitability. First, the organization is building a *product* rather than carrying out a *project*. When project development completes, the product is still in the field and questions of maintenance and added feature development find only awkward answers. Organizationally separating product creation from ongoing development ("maintenance") creates many problems. Secondly, the company rarely gives the project manager responsibility for value such as ROI or net present value (see Value and ROI on page 246), so his or her incentive is to deliver as fast as possible within the financial constraints. Without this responsibility, the project manager is more likely to make short-term decisions with long-term consequences, and short-term decisions tend not to have positive long-term consequences.

You can maximize revenue by continuously engaging your users as beta sites to refine the product (where the deliverables are the beta deliveries), but customers are much more comfortable if a person on the vendor side instead takes responsibility for up-front planning and thinking. Lean says that it is important to line up the decisions early on, so that the decisions are easy to make once the time comes to make them.

Therefore:

Get a *Product Owner* to order the *Product Backlog* and take responsibility for the vision of the product, and for the value that emanates from the delivery of that vision.

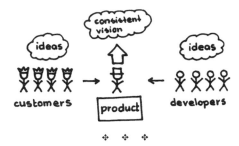

❖   ❖   ❖

*Product Owner*s own their products: they have the final say over product content and delivery ordering. The *Product Owner* role is not just to "manage" the product; it's that, too, but more so, the product is their baby, their passion. True *Product Owner*s are driven by ¶38 *Product Pride.*

The *Product Owner* becomes the single point of contact for issues related to product content, delivery, and scheduling. The *Product Owner* has final control over the rollout of the product that he or she owns, and is accountable for the resulting ROI. While this role takes up a staff position, and therefore a cost, a good *Product Owner* can dramatically grow a product revenue stream and increase delivered value.

The best *Product Owner* is as close to value delivery as possible. There are multiple stakeholders—the end user; the organization deriving revenue from end-user use of the product; persons concerned with regulatory authorities, legal issues, or standards bodies; and potentially many others. Stakeholders often cannot be *Product Owner*s because they have limited knowledge, a conflict of interest, or lack of authority to make decisions. One of the *Product Owner*'s primary measures of success is value generation from the product —the business plan.

There is no customer in Scrum. The customer role is present in many real-world value streams. Scrum tends to reflect the Lean vision of partnership between the business and end user, rather than a relationship of animosity or of at-arms-length or over-the-wall communication; see ¶13 *Development Partnership*. Customers can realize paths to market, but the enterprise should be mindful that customers are an added handoff that can introduce delay and waste. These often are impediments for the *Product Owner* to remove. In Scrum, the *Product Owner* represents the interests of all stakeholders, including customers (see ¶113 *Surrogate Customer* on page 468). The *Product Owner* manages all business relationships external to the team, which eliminates handoffs between the business vision and the development effort.

The *Scrum Team* needs to tune into the *Product Owner* and ignore other voices within the organization so that the team can stay focused. The ¶14 *Development Team* should refer those with a wish to redirect or re-prioritize the team's work to the *Product Owner*. The ¶19 *ScrumMaster* should help in these cases to protect the *Development Team* from interruptions.

The *Product Backlog* documents the decisions around all the conversations of how to achieve the *Product Owner*'s *Vision*. Ideally, it reflects a consensus view (particularly with respect to the *Development Team*'s perspective) but the *Product Owner* has the final word on its content and ordering. Each *Scrum Team* needs one *Product Owner* to develop one *Product Backlog* for its *Development Teams*. If multiple teams are developing a single product together, there should be a single *Product Backlog* that drives these teams' work.

> We bring together a team of people who are really passionate about [a] subject. If you write a 70-page document that says this is the product you're supposed to build, you actually push the creativity out with process. The engineer who says, you know what, there's a feature here that you forgot that I would really like to add. You don't want to push that creativity out of the product.
>
> The consensus-driven approach where the team works together to build a vision around what they're building and still leaves enough room for each member of the team to participate creatively, is really inspiring and yields us some of the best outcomes we've had.[14]

If the creation of the *Product Backlog* takes too much time or more expertise that one person can provide, the *Product Owner* should form a ¶12 *Product Owner Team* that works with him or her as Chief *Product Owner*, retaining the final say over the sequencing of the *Product Backlog*.

---

14. Marissa Mayer. "Inside Google's New-Product Process." *BusinessWeek.com*, http://www.businessweek.com/technology/content/jun2006/tc20060629_411177.htm, 30 June 2006 (accessed 23 June 2010).

Anyone can offer anything as content for the *Product Backlog*. The contributor owns the item in as much that they must provide support for fully forming the *Product Backlog Item*. The *Product Owner Team* sequences that item in the global *Product Backlog*—again, with the *Product Owner* having final say over the sequencing.

Great *Product Owner*s have a sound user experience (UX) skill set or at least can tap into such expertise on the *Product Owner Team*. Gentle persuasion, care, and attentiveness on the part of team members with UX skills can lead a *Product Owner* to pick up many of these skills over time.

The *Product Owner* is also responsible for the ¶45 *Product Roadmap* and the ¶48 *Release Plan*.

It is often difficult to fill the *Product Owner* position. The business passion and knowledge may exist in a business expert (sometimes the CEO) who does not have enough time to fully manage the *Product Backlog*, especially in small or young development organizations. Any *Development Team* member may take on any *Product Owner* work in consultation with the existing *Product Owner*, or can temporarily fill the *Product Owner* role in his or her absence. The *Development Team* and *ScrumMaster* should ensure that such a situation does not persist indefinitely.

¶12 Product Owner Team

Confidence stars: *

Toyota Motor Corporation president Akio Toyoda and his team presenting the new Toyota GR sports car.

...the *¶11 Product Owner* wants to improve the effectiveness of the *¶41 Value Stream.*

A single *Product Owner* is accountable for all value such as return on investment and should handle market analysis, product discovery, stakeholder management, customer feedback, and most other market-facing work, while also enabling the team to build the right thing.

❖ ❖ ❖

The *Product Owner* has more to do than a single person can handle well (see, for example, *Proceedings of the Agile Development Conference [MBN04]*).

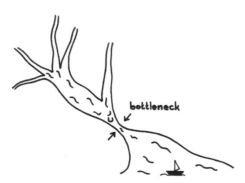

The *Product Owner* may ask the *¶14 Development Team* for help, but that would only shift the burden to the developers. It would also take away capacity from actual development. There is no incentive for the *Product Owner* to improve and learn how to become a better *Product Owner*.

Not getting the *¶55 Product Backlog Items Ready* (see *¶65 Definition of Ready*) may result in the *Development Team* building the wrong things. It will also increase communication with the *Product Owner*, which slows the *Development Team* down.

Development Teams that do not have enough *Product Backlog Items* waste capacity. If the team doesn't receive enough *¶63 Enabling Specifications* for the market window targeted by the upcoming *¶46 Sprint*, it invites the *Development Team* to work on lower value *Product Backlog Items* or start working on *Product Backlog Items* that are not *Ready*. By adding delay, it might decrease the overall value that the team might otherwise produce.

Having enough time to reflect on *Product Backlog Items* helps to understand their relative value, identify dependencies, and gives possibility to capitalize on market opportunities.

One way to help a *Product Owner* to perform many tasks is by hiring a team of specialists. However, this leads to problems of handoff and communication. This can result in reduced understanding of customer problems and inadequate solutions.

The developers can help by clarifying details with other stakeholders as long as it does not contradict the *Product Owner*'s direction. It is important to maintain the single point of accountability for success and failure: the *Product Owner* should not be a committee.

Therefore:

Create a *Product Owner Team*, led by the Chief Product Owner, whose members together carry out product ownership.

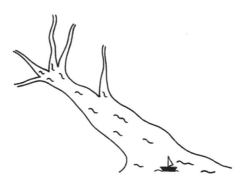

A *Product Owner Team* gathers several people responsible for guiding the teams in creating the *¶54 Product Backlog*. When creating a *Product Owner Team*, it is important that there be a Chief Product Owner (*CPO*) who has final authority over the ordering of the *Product Backlog*. The CPO plus the other people that support the CPO is what we call the *Product Owner Team*. Some may call the *Product Owner Team* members the 'Product Owners'—but these people do not own anything. The CPO is the single *Product Owner* and the "single wringable neck" accountable for the success of the product.

The CPO clearly communicates the strategy and the *Product Backlog Item*s. The CPO works with the *Product Owner Team* members to select and order backlog items for the teams. The *Product Owner Team* members can help the CPO work with the *Development Team*s to break the backlog into small *Product Backlog Item*s for execution.

Experience suggests that the *Product Owner Team* should be a *¶8 Collocated Team*. Splitting the *Product Owner* function across organizational boundaries (particularly across corporate boundaries) may make things worse than just having a single *Product Owner* on one side or the other.

❖ ❖ ❖

The *Product Owner Team* carries out the product ownership for large products.

The *Product Owner Team* realizes the *¶39 Vision* by ordering the *Product Backlog Item*s through a single *Product Backlog*.

Most *Product Owner Team* members come from a business background. However, product ownership means more than owning just the *Value Stream*s. The *Product Owner Team* also produces *Enabling Specification*s for the *Development Team* (often in collaboration with the *Development Team* as they work together toward a *¶64 Refined Product Backlog*), which sometimes requires research into user-experience issues as well as low-level technologies and development approaches that are key to the product strategy. The *Product Owner Team* may explore these areas through *¶42 Set-Based Design*s to support an *Enabling Specification* for the *Development Team*.

Like the *Product Owner*, the entire *Product Owner Team* should be energized by an attitude of *¶38 Product Pride*.

¶13 Development Partnership

Confidence stars: *

Multiple parties in the ¶41 Value Stream should strive to work as harmoniously as possible.

...an enterprise may lack development staff with competencies to develop a product for a new market, so they outsource some or all development to another organization. Such engagements are "partnerships," or "contracted" or "outsourced" work. (Third-party *commodity* goods and services are outside the focus of this pattern.)

❖ ❖ ❖

Partnerships are beautiful when they work, but corporate and organizational boundaries are often arbitrary with respect to how the organizational units develop products together. Though business needs may span several disciplines, an organization may choose to focus on its core competencies while going to more capable providers to fill in the gaps. For example, a manufacturer is unlikely to have the in-house expertise to develop its own personnel management software, yet has special needs that cannot be met by off-the-shelf software. Or a business may get caught by surprise as it finds itself in a market that needs expertise that is unavailable in-house. So, the enterprise adapts by engaging an outside firm to meet the need. Here, "outside" usually means another company, but the walls can be equally high between the client and another internal department.

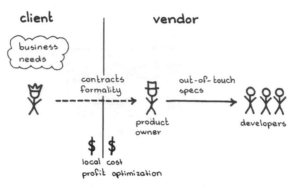

This sets up a vendor-client dichotomy. It's natural for each side to keep many of their processes—processes that connect their own people together well, but don't naturally integrate outsiders. Handoffs—particularly of requirements —start becoming more frequent. Developers face a crisis of allegiance split between their employer (or boss) and the client. The ¶14 *Development Team* may face difficulty obtaining requirements or context from the client organization due to political firewalls or lack of knowledge about whom to approach. The lack of trust built into such an approach may be at the root of fixed-scope contracts, which usually leave someone unhappy when applied in a complex domain. Nobody wins.

Who should employ the ¶11 *Product Owner*: the vendor or the client? The client has the domain knowledge and should be in control of product content. Yet it is in the client's interest to reap the highest possible value (see Value and ROI on page 246) which means the client has an interest in minimizing the vendor's profits. On the other hand, perhaps the vendor should manage *its* own profitability from the engagement. This suggests that the *Product Owner* live on the vendor side. The usual solution is to place a Proxy *Product Owner* with the *Development Team* on the vendor side. The Proxy *Product Owner* becomes the first line of defense for questions of clarification from the team, and may even represent the *Product Owner* at activities as important as the ¶64 *Refined Product Backlog* event or ¶24 *Sprint Planning*. If the Proxy *Product Owner* on the vendor side does not work in the same office as the actual *Product Owner*, all the problems of a multisite setup ensue; development becomes two one-way communications instead of one two-way communication.

Even worse, the client may just propose that the vendor draw on its own staff for the *Product Owner* role. However, this usually reduces the *Product Owner* to a product manager or project manager who in fact doesn't own anything, who cannot speak authoritatively to the content of the product, and who usually cannot make product decisions unilaterally. The usual result is delays in requirements clarification, or in *¶85 Regular Product Increment*s that simply don't meet client expectations.

Therefore:

Create a partnership between clients and vendors that breaks down walls between the organizations. The initial agreement makes the rules of engagement clear, and these rules should include consideration for collocated development, equitable risk sharing, and ongoing adjustment to the definition of the deliverable, with a vision of a continued long-term engagement after the initial business goals are met.

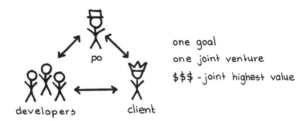

Because the best *Product Owner*s are as close to value delivery as possible, the *Product Owner* works for the client. The *Product Owner* will of course be attentive to maximizing value for his or her employer but will also honor the spirit and letter of the agreement according to how the vendor will realize benefit from the engagement.

It is best if the *Development Team* be physically situated on the client site. There's much to be said about picking up cues about the culture and the implied product needs by just noting how the client works, or by hearing the talk around the water cooler. This also has the benefit of making domain experts more readily available to the *Development Team*.

In the absence of full-time collocation, the *Product Owner* should strive to be around the vendor *Development Team* members much of the time. One must inspect and adapt to find what "much of the time" means, but successful examples are at least six hours a day, four days a week, or four hours a day full-time—not one or two days a week or an appearance at a daily teleconference meeting. If there is a *¶12 Product Owner Team*, the Chief Product Owner should nonetheless engage with the *Development Team* to this degree. Again, it is tempting to solve this problem with a proxy, but experience suggests that arrangement causes too much loss in requirement communication. (In reality, it may make transparent that the titled *Product Owner* doesn't actually own the product or is disengaged.)

The business model should share risk between the vendor and client. There are many ways to do this; see *¶52 Change for Free* and *¶53 Money for Nothing*. In the best case, the vendor shares both the risk and the benefit. For example, the agreement may stipulate some long-term sharing of the profit (and maybe loss as well) from the vendor-built product.

In short, though outsourcing splits the work across multiple political organizations, this does not excuse the development from following the principles of Scrum. Embrace the same principles as though the same boss signed everyone's paycheck.

❖ ❖ ❖

The vendor and client can work together to reduce the most waste and to achieve the *¶93 Greatest Value* for the joint scope, rather than optimizing locally and individually.

Cultural alignment is more important than technical expertise as regards product governance. The loyalty of all team members—*Product Owner*, *¶19 ScrumMaster*, and *Development Team* members—is to the product rather than to their organization. All allegiance is to the *Product Owner*.

Things go much more smoothly when you synchronize the partners' cadences: see *¶47 Organizational Sprint Pulse*.

The *ScrumMaster* must be particularly attentive to interference from remote managers who want to "help" the team and to local managers who want to pressure the team to meet contractual obligations.

It is difficult to fully plan out these engagements: what may look good on paper may fail miserably in practice. Inspect and adapt, and expect to learn how to correct many bad decisions during the first few months. Aggressively use the *¶36 Sprint Retrospective* to adjust and fix problems rapidly.

Over time, the *Development Team* may become more and more part of the client culture. A seasoned agile vendor can help lead the client into a more agile way of doing things. Having a long-term engagement means that both sides can avoid the cost of renewed contract negotiations when considering new business needs, or the untenable overhead on the client to engage a new vendor and integrate them into the overall business processes. Maintaining *¶15 Stable Teams* requires particular attention in these arrangements.

All parties in such a partnership should share a sense of *¶38 Product Pride.* An imbalance in this attitude across partners may signal that one partner has an overly controlling influence over the other, more unwitting party.

See also *¶8 Collocated Team,* and the Federation Pattern of Terunobu Fujino (*Federation Pattern [Fuj99]*). Furthermore, there is a curious overlap between this pattern and the foundations of *¶130 Face-to-Face Before Working Remotely* on page 470.

¶14 Development Team

Alias: Development/Delivery Team

Confidence stars: **

...coming out of *¶2 The Mist*, the *¶11 Product Owner* has a product *¶39 Vision* whose realization is beyond the reach of any individual. The *Product Owner* is either working alone at the forefront of a new venture or working in the company of people who share passion for the same *Vision*. The fledgling effort might have formed in *The Mist* and needs to come together. The effort is at a point of taking steps to turn the *Vision* into a reality, both by coordinating the work of the longstanding members of the group and by potentially involving new people. Together, they seek a way to balance their collective identity with individual development responsibilities: to connect to each other under a framework that manages time and talent to support the business and create a rewarding workplace.

❖ ❖ ❖

Many great endeavors cannot achieve excellence through individual effort alone; the greatest power in production comes from teamwork. Great individuals can produce great products, but starting with a single individual makes it difficult to scale later. Each new person detracts from the effectiveness of everyone else on the team by about 25 percent for about 6 months (rule of thumb from James Coplien). Some products simply cannot realize greatness at the hands of a single individual, and without good feedback it is easy to get blindsided. Experience shows that person for person, teams outperform individuals: many hands make light work. While industry data show a range of 10 to 1 in *individual* programmer to *teams* output (*Making Software [OW10]*, pp. 567–574), other data show that some teams outperformed others by a factor of 2000 to 1 (*Scrum: The Art of Doing Twice the Work in Half the Time [SS14]*, p. 42).

On the other hand, it's difficult to form a consensus direction across an overly large group—too many cooks spoil the broth. A development department composed of handfuls of people *can* eventually achieve consensus, but usually can do so only with long mutual deliberation and socialization. Such delay is intolerable in a responsive business.

In the lean startup model, everybody does everything, whether related to business, process, or production. The problem is that market shearing layers (different segments of the market whose needs evolve at different rates) and rates of change can be different than those of development. Market analysis and planning can play out over several months, while development for the market typically follows a monthly rhythm (*¶77 Follow the Moon*) and can be as short as a day, or even hours or minutes for live customer emergencies. So putting both functions in one tightly coupled organizational unit puts stress on people and on schedules. Such a model is not sustainable as the enterprise grows.

Organizations need to run on multiple cadences. One cadence may be the day-to-day work of creating a product; another may be the longer cycles of working with the market. Role differentiation should primarily follow from variations in these cadences, according to the "Role Theory" chapter in *The Handbook of Social Psychology [LA68]* (pp. 488–567). History, experience, and inclination draws individuals to particular roles, which may lead to problems for organizations because roles may not work to the needed cadences. The organization needs to work coherently.

Therefore:

Building on *¶15 Stable Teams*, create a *Development Team* that rallies around a product inspired by the *Product Owner*'s *Vision*, to deliver successive increments of that product through the *¶41 Value Stream* to its end users. The team is a bonding of approximately five collocated individuals (see

¶8 *Collocated Team* and ¶9 *Small Teams*) committed to working with each other towards a common goal.

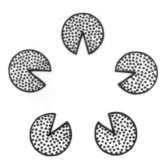

The team is autonomous: self-selected, self-organizing, and self-managing. Give the individuals a collective identity to realize the *Product Owner*'s *Vision*. The *Product Owner* can tell them: "This is your product—do it."

❖ ❖ ❖

The individuals forge a new identity tied to the product's *Vision* while honoring each other's identity within the new organizational unit. It's not about scaling individual potential to raise productivity to some production level. It is about changing the paradigm of development to that of a collective mind, a Whole that can achieve more than the sum of the individuals.

You can build the team either top-down or bottom-up, but in either case you need a *Vision* to seed the team. In the top-down approach, the *Product Owner* hires the team after securing funding for the effort. The bottom-up approach arises from a setting like that of a lean startup: *We are a bunch of nerds and we struggle to respond to the market and we want to be identified as the development team. Who do we respond to? The Product Owner. How do we work? From the top of the* ¶54 *Product Backlog*. The team can further evolve according to the Scrum framework with the introduction of other patterns, as described in the rest of this pattern.

If you don't yet have a stable candidate team in place, then strongly consider building a ¶116 *Self-Selecting Team* on page 468 from available personnel, from scratch, and/or from the market. Look for a community of trust (see ¶95 *Community of Trust* on page 466): if the trust doesn't yet exist in the current set of individuals, it will be the first thing the group will need to take care of.

We generically call the team members *Developers* to avoid any labeling or compartmentalization that might violate the not-separateness of the Whole. A *Developer* works as a member of only a single *Development Team*. The team minimizes specialization and has no internal subteams but rather has undifferentiated membership. Scrum avoids any kind of assembly line structure within teams or across teams, with *all* work for each deliverable taking place within a single *Development Team*. This means that, for example, there is no separate testing team, and no separate team to bridge development with operational aspects of development such as product configuration. As early as possible, strive to build a *¶10 Cross-Functional Team* that has the skill set and talent, or the appetite to develop the skills and talents necessary to building a succession of complete, *Done* product increments (see *¶82 Definition of Done*).

Though Scrum tradition recommends team sizes of seven plus or minus two, effective teams tend to be smaller. The pattern *¶110 Size the Organization* on page 468 (from *Organizational Patterns of Agile Software Development [CH04]*, Section 4.2.2) recommends a membership closer to five. Our experience suggests that the best *Development Team*s may comprise as few as three developers.

A *Development Team* should work as one mind, focused on the *¶71 Sprint Goal* and *swarming* together around individual increments of development, rather than individually "putting in their time at their station" (see *¶25 Swarming: One-Piece Continuous Flow*). The team convenes a daily event to replan work in progress, called The *¶29 Daily Scrum*.

Small efforts sometimes arise to meet isolated, short-term business needs. In such cases it might be overkill to build a team; consider *¶112 Solo Virtuoso* on page 468.

As mentioned earlier, the team can differentiate itself by evolving according to the Scrum framework with other patterns. The *Product Backlog* guides the team's work to produce *¶85 Regular Product Increment*s in time-boxed development intervals called *¶46 Sprint*s. Team members create their own work plan (*¶72 Sprint Backlog*) for each *Sprint* and manage themselves during the production part of a *Sprint*. During the production part of a *Sprint*, protect the *Development Team* so its members can work as an *¶16 Autonomous Team* and manage their work as a *¶17 Self-Organizing Team*. The *Product Owner* and a *¶19 ScrumMaster* provide such protection, as well as encouragement, support, and process guidance.

¶15 Stable Teams

Confidence stars: **

...teams have been producing product for some time. An ever-changing business landscape raises questions about staff adjustment, growth, and optimal team composition.

✧   ✧   ✧

Stakeholders are happiest with teams who can meet their expectations in a timely fashion, so the team wants to do what is necessary to reduce variance in its predictions.

In project management there is a tendency to confuse human beings with human resources. It leads to "resource management," lining up demand with each team's capacity (or, sometimes, each team member's capacity) to contribute to the deliverable.

It often results in moving people from team to team when starting projects, or crisis to crisis during delivery, and leads to an unstable environment with added costs of:

- administration to keep track of what people are working on,

- reduced efficiency, as teams need to integrate a new member (effectively creating a new team) and the new member needs to learn about the team and its product,

- exposure to Brooks' Law ("adding manpower to a late software project makes it later" (*The Mythical Man-Month: Essays on Software Engineering* [Bro95], p. 25)).

When teams are formed from a resource pool, the resource utilization often leads to multitasking with people distributed across several teams and often on several products. Add in changing requirements and the instability becomes unbearable. So we need to fix something—the stable and unstable parts must be balanced. For years the response has been to freeze the requirements so our ever-changing resources are able to deliver at a (hopefully) predictable time. Locking down the requirements of our products prevents us from learning, and ignores product changes that could create the *¶93 Greatest Value*, so this is not a good solution.

Therefore,

Keep teams stable and avoid shuffling people around between teams. *Stable Teams* **tend to get to know their capacity, which makes it possible for the business to have some predictability.** Dedicate team members to a single team whenever possible.

❖   ❖   ❖

Members of *Stable Teams* get to know each other. The team members experience each other's work style and learn how much work they can do together. A *Stable Team* grows in familiarity and consistency of meeting mutual expectations and starts developing a community of trust (see *¶95 Community of Trust* on page 466).

Research has shown that fatigued NASA crews that had worked extensively together made about half as many mistakes as teams of rested pilots with no prior joint work experience (*Harvard Business Review 87* [Cou09]). This is because many of the factors that relate to effective teamwork (such as shared mental models, cohesion, climate, and psychological safety) come about only in teams that have consistently worked together (see *Psychological Science in the Public Interest 7* [KI06], pp. 77–124 and *Personnel Psychology 70* [FFKP17]).

People that work together for only a short period of time will probably not invest much energy in improving their work processes or social interactions with each other—in a couple of months (or less) they will be working with other people. On the other hand, if people understand that they will stay with the same colleagues for longer periods of time, they are more likely to invest energy in creating an enjoyable team environment and improving their work processes.

A team can use its velocity (see Notes on Velocity on page 320) to measure improvement in its capacity for work. Many ¶7 *Scrum Teams* use velocity as a key to predictability. Velocity is currently the most-proven praxis to increase the level of predictability. But what is often forgotten, when measuring a team's velocity, is that the only way a team can get to know its velocity is by having the same team members over a longer period of time.

¶10 *Cross-Functional Teams* will benefit the most from long-term stability because there are more opportunities to share knowledge and experience. Specialized teams (e.g., that provide services for specialized skill sets or technologies) will also yield some benefits but have broader negative consequences for the organization—for example, creating queues and requiring extra administrative overhead for work.

Stable Teams will create pressure on the work pipeline. The workflow now must structure work to fit with the teams, rather than restructuring teams to fit with work—or to handle crises. This will, in turn, highlight capability issues that the organization must address. For example, constantly reshuffling a specialist between teams will make it visible that some skill set is missing across several teams. As you transition to *Stable Teams*, temporarily assign specialists where they are needed with the stipulation that they cross-train team members in their area of expertise, to reduce risk in the long term.

Start using *Stable Teams* by committing to keeping teams together, potentially using self-selecting teams (see ¶116 *Self-Selecting Team* on page 468). Then follow up by managing the work to fit this structure, and make an effort to accommodate gaps in capability in the teams. Let the teams self-organize to spread competencies and to explore the best team compositions; you will find that a structure converges quickly.

The organization replaces the "flexibility" of shifting people from crisis to crisis with flexible work assignment. Such flexibility lets teams take on work in accordance within their current capability and capacity, which in turn leads to more accurate forecasting. Moving people between teams to be "flexible" instead leads to higher cost and uncertainty.

This pattern helps the team grow and share its expertise over time to reduce the risk of losing a team member; see *¶123 Moderate Truck Number* on page 469.

A stable team that uses *¶60 Estimation Points* and lets the *¶57 Pigs Estimate* can get a realistic number for their velocity after a few *¶46 Sprints*; see *¶67 Running Average Velocity*.

Having *Stable Teams* allows an individual to master the work of the team. When there are multiple *¶14 Development Teams* or multiple *Scrum Teams*, using *¶5 Birds of a Feather* can support team members in furthering their mastery.

A *Stable Team* builds a collective identity that can be a foundation of a shared sense of pride, both in the product and in belonging to the team (see *¶38 Product Pride* and *¶118 Team Pride* on page 469).

¶16 Autonomous Team

Alias: Self-Managing Team

Confidence stars: **

...a new team is coming together to work in Scrum, or an existing team is adopting Scrum. In either case, it is necessary for the team to establish how to work together.

❖   ❖   ❖

When it comes to policies and procedures, one size does not fit all. Different teams have different people and dynamics unique to themselves. Also, a team with a given responsibility and the expertise necessary to fulfill it knows best how to go about doing it.

By definition, a stakeholder has a vested interest in the success of a Scrum endeavor. As such, it is natural to want to have some control over the development effort. Stakeholders with product responsibility feel safer if they have the authority to direct details of the work. However, stakeholders outside the *¶14 Development Team* are likely not to know the details of development work, so the policies and procedures they may want may not suit the team's needs nor contribute to the *¶93 Greatest Value*. And if a *¶7 Scrum Team* finds itself doing its work within a larger corporate structure, that structure may want to impose business goals or steer development direction out of concern for its own return on investment, even from a superficial base of knowledge about the product or its rollout. At the very least, these interventions send the subtle but unmistakable message that the corporation does not trust the team to act on its own. This sets up an "us versus them" mentality; it erodes trust (see *¶95 Community of Trust* on page 466).

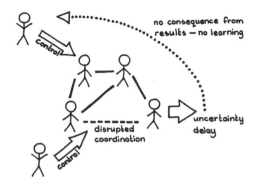

Too often a well-meaning organization strives for economies of scope by defining "best practices" designed for the greater good. Management and administrative bodies often stipulate such practices as standards. In the spirit of the lean canon, standards *can* be enabling. However, one team's Best Practice can be another team's poison, and teams should consider adopting these of their own initiative—either individually or collectively—rather than following an external mandate.

Decisions made locally are more efficient than decisions imposed from outside a team.

Therefore:

The *Scrum Team* makes its decisions free from external control, and while it is an open system attentive to external considerations, the team charts its own direction according to its pursuit of value without undue external influence. Similarly, at the next level the *Development Team* governs itself during the ¶75 Production Episode without outside intervention.

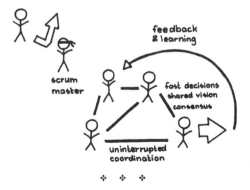

❖ ❖ ❖

Teams keep control over actions that lead to results for which they are accountable. While making decisions that affect their own processes, the teams are still open to interaction with other development and delivery teams, they still keep their internal work visible through *¶56 Information Radiator*s, and they seek input on how to improve from groups such as *¶5 Birds of a Feather*.

Autonomy includes establishment of one's own culture, including any *¶31 Norms of Conduct* as well as reward systems. It also includes how the team carries out work; see *¶17 Self-Organizing Team*.

This does not mean that the *Development Team* has the authority to simply do whatever it wants (and maybe not accomplish anything): if the organization has adopted Scrum, the *Development Team* follows Scrum. Effective autonomy always lies within the constraints of the organization's values and goals—in this case, the team has a common commitment to evolve toward the *¶39 Vision* and to create value through the *¶41 Value Stream*.

An important part of autonomy is the authority to set up the team's organization (*Self-Organizing Team*). While a team that is autonomous is more likely to be able to manage itself over time, these two patterns incrementally build on each other, and either may initially precede the other. An *Autonomous Team* can define and execute its own processes: it decides how it works. It includes the organizational pattern, *¶101 Developer Controls Process* on page 467, but goes beyond process to the creation of the team's own culture.

Much of the *¶19 ScrumMaster*'s work, largely as a *¶114 Firewall* on page 468, entails maintaining the autonomy of the *Development Team* and occasionally of the broader *Scrum Team*. Organizational norms and rituals also help protect the autonomy of the team; see *¶20 Oyatsu Jinja (Snack Shrine)* as an example.

It is important to understand the link between autonomy and accountability: if a team is autonomous, people trust that they will do what they set out to do, and the team is accountable to those who trust them. The team has the responsibility and the authority to meet the *¶71 Sprint Goal*.

A possible danger in an *Autonomous Team* is that the team may become blind to its own weaknesses. Therefore, temper *Autonomous Team*s with *¶28 Pop the Happy Bubble*, as well as having the *ScrumMaster* working along with the teams to give them feedback, to convey feedback from outside the team, and to keep them open to feedback from other sources. The teams remain part of the larger open systems in which they are embedded and are subject to reviews (such as the *¶35 Sprint Review* and *¶36 Sprint Retrospective*) and external feedback.

A team that is autonomous is best able to examine and increase its own velocity (see Notes on Velocity on page 320) to optimize value creation. Extending the *Value Stream* metaphor, water flowing downhill can cut its own channel to find the fastest and most efficient path down the mountain.

People are generally most motivated and engaged when they have autonomy (*Drive: The Surprising Truth About What Motivates Us [Pin11]*). When successful, this sets up a virtuous circle: *Autonomous Team*s that prove their accountability gain more autonomy, allowing them to be more successful. This is an important success factor in highly effective organizations.

Note that while this pattern as written focuses on the *Development Team* and on the complete *Scrum Team*, it extends even to pairs of Developers (see *¶126 Developing in Pairs* on page 469) working together. Autonomy extends all the way to the level of individual team members, who are trusted to do their best to report successes, failures, and willful process compliance (or not) on their own rather than being externally monitored. In fact, research shows that a decrease in what is usually called "transparency" helps surface and resolve impediments. Workers felt that being seen fixing a defect would invite external interference; left unobserved, workers were willing to make things right and quality improved. Respecting individual autonomy means respecting privacy (see "The Transparency Paradox" in *Administrative Science Quarterly 57 [Ber12]*). Think twice before adopting a tool that allows management to track defects.

Autonomy should extend in the opposite direction in the long term as well, so the whole *Value Stream* becomes an autonomous entity. Toyota has gathered the production of virtually every conceivable automotive component under a single confederation umbrella. Supply-chain management across the entire enterprise ties it together as an autonomous unit.

Scaling can be the enemy of autonomy, and it is often difficult to sustain team autonomy while growing. It may take much effort to avoid adding control structures with more teams. There is also a longstanding organizational principle that a manager's power is a function of that manager's scope of *control*, so organizations with latent management structures run the risk of management flexing its muscle in the interest of keeping development coordinated and on-track. A good *ScrumMaster* will intervene and may challenge the teams to better self-organize.

Jens Østergaard observes that *Development Team* autonomy is the "heart of Scrum." It is central to Scrum's effectiveness; without it, it is hard to argue that it is even possible to do Scrum. And Jeff Sutherland writes (with emphasis on "pillars of Scrum" and "dramatic") (*The Scrum Handbook [Sut10]*, pp. 23–24):

> One of the pillars of Scrum is that once the Team makes its commitment, any additions or changes must be deferred until the next Sprint. This means that if halfway through the Sprint the Product Owner decides there is a new item he or she would like the Team to work on, he cannot make the change until the start of the next Sprint. If an external circumstance appears that significantly changes priorities, and means the Team would be wasting its time if it continued working, the Product Owner or the team can terminate the Sprint. The Team stops, and a new Sprint Planning meeting initiates a new Sprint. The disruption of doing this is usually great; this serves as a disincentive for the Product Owner or team to resort to this dramatic decision.

The structure of a product and its development process often make the difference of whether teams can develop that product together while retaining a modicum of autonomy. In multi-team Scrums, it's important to structure the product to support partitioning the work between several loosely coupled teams. See ¶4 *Conway's Law* and ¶129 *Organization Follows Market* on page 470.

Counter the potential myopia and inbreeding of an *Autonomous Team* with ¶34 *Scrum of Scrums*, *Birds of a Feather*, ¶24 *Sprint Planning*, *Sprint Review*, and the *Sprint Retrospective*. See also ¶115 *Gatekeeper* on page 468.

¶17 Self-Organizing Team

Confidence stars: **

Birds organize themselves into formation and continually reorganize their formation.

...an organization has established a community of trust (see *¶95 Community of Trust* on page 466) and tills the *¶3 Fertile Soil*. The *¶14 Development Team* is running as an *¶16 Autonomous Team*.

❖ ❖ ❖

There is no one way to structure a team or work that is correct for all situations and all work, and thus unchanging over time.

For any multi-person work, you must organize tasks and people to work together in a coherent, coordinated manner. Otherwise, you risk falling into chaos. But this organization can be complex.

To reduce complexity, organizations will standardize structures and processes. This may be through adoption of a best practice or through historical development of the organization's culture. Best practices develop in a specific context to achieve specific objectives, and these may not suit a given organization (*Managing the Design Factory: A Product Developer's Toolkit [Rei98]*, p. 184). In any complex endeavor, you can rarely forecast ahead of time which of several shared foundations will be the optimal one: you need only something that is "good enough," and let emergence guide you from there. An organization may develop its own best practice structures and processes at certain times, as situations demand; they become established practices. However, though these approaches usually work for a while, they will not continue to be the best practices as time goes on. The business situation changes as management approaches advance and technology improves. The team may become stuck at a new plateau.

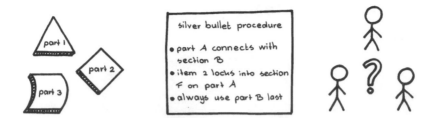

People can be comfortable when someone else leads and tells them what to do. This direction and control has some consequences. Motivation and workplace factors such as turnover rate and job satisfaction can suffer when people are working for controlling managers (see "The impact of work design, autonomy support, and strategy on employee outcomes: A differentiated perspective on self-determination at work" in *Motivation and Emotion 39 [Gün15]*). Moreover, the people doing the work are the ones who understand how to do their jobs the best. When workers don't have control of their work, valuable opportunities for efficiency, effectiveness, and for quality results are missed. For example, a factory worker may take the initiative to improve the efficiency or safety of a task. This improvement might never come were we to expect it from a manager who is too out of touch with the situation to appreciate the need for a solution, let alone conceive of a solution.

Development Team members often have specialized skills; it is beneficial to take advantage of their differences to work efficiently. But if everyone works only within his or her own expertise, tasks may get delayed instead of being spread more evenly.

Therefore:

The *Development Team* organizes itself to get its work *Done* (see ¶82 Definition of Done). The *Development Team* is solely responsible for how it does its work.

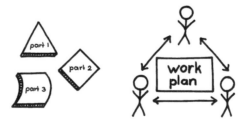

The *Development Team* controls all aspects of its day-to-day work. For example, they run the *¶29 Daily Scrum* meetings, and decide who works on what. They decide the order of work, and decide how to organize *¶25 Swarming: One-Piece*

Continuous Flow. The team decides how to take advantage of the *Development Team* members' special skills and areas of expertise. It may include deciding who pairs with whom, and so forth.

❖　❖　❖

Note that self-organization requires maturity and discipline. Some people are uncomfortable with self-organization. Stakeholders such as the *¶11 Product Owner* may be tempted to jump in to help, or the *¶19 ScrumMaster* might think they know who should work on what (at no time does the *ScrumMaster* assign people to work on tasks or tell Developers how to work). But people outside of the *Development Team* need to let the team learn through self-organization, even if it is initially difficult. A *¶22 Scrum (Master) Coach* can help.

One danger in removing an explicit supervisory role is that another individual (on the team) may fill that same role, forcing his or her will on the team through charisma, bullying, or dominating the conversation. This leaves the team with exactly the same dynamics as it had previously. The *ScrumMaster* needs to understand this may happen and prepare the team by modeling behaviors that ensure everyone on the *Development Team* can contribute. This will help establish norms for the team. If this type of behavior does appear (or anything else that inhibits self-organization) it is the responsibility of the *ScrumMaster* to help the team identify and resolve the impediment.

Naturally, self-organization is easiest with *¶9 Small Teams* and *¶8 Collocated Teams*, because the logistics are easier in both cases.

This pattern is one of the practices at the heart of Scrum. It allows the work in a *¶46 Sprint* to move forward in the most efficient manner. It improves the morale of the *Development Team* (and there is evidence of improved performance; see *Small Group Research 48 [JTAL16]*). It allows the *Development Team* to examine itself and improve (see *¶36 Sprint Retrospective*, *¶92 Scrumming the Scrum*, and *¶91 Happiness Metric*, for example.) With it, the *Development Team* becomes self-healing—it can see its faults and has the power to fix them. This is one of the most important patterns for a Scrum organization to master.

When the business allows *Development Team*s to self-organize, the teams gain both freedom and commensurate responsibility: it is the gate to a *Community of Trust* on page 466. A team that has its own say over how it builds the product is likely to become more proud both of itself and of the product; see *Team Pride* (patlet for *¶118 Team Pride* on page 469) and *¶38 Product Pride*, respectively.

See also *¶76 Developer-Ordered Work Plan*, *Swarming*, and *¶100 Informal Labor Plan* on page 467.

A Scaling Sequence

The next pattern, *¶18 Mitosis*, is a *scaling pattern*. We often see *¶7 Scrum Teams* with a desire to scale, with the primary reason to increase output. However, market consumption must rise to match any production increase; otherwise, the excess productivity is just waste. In any case, the best way to grow a team's output is by removing impediments and by improving the process.

Scaling legitimately occurs under just one circumstance: when the product grows organically to the point where the demand for new features outstrips even a high-performing *Scrum Team*'s capacity to deliver in a timely fashion. A "high-performing" team is one that has been a *Stable Team* for some time (see *¶15 Stable Teams*), maintains a consistent velocity, and continually delivers on business outcomes. If such a team, using *¶26 Kaizen Pulse*, has diminishing returns on its self-improvement efforts relative to the market's required rate of delivery of business value, then it may be an option to add *¶14 Development Teams*.

Scaling is not about transforming an existing micromanaged organization to an Agile one (that is a quite different question; see *¶6 Involve the Managers*). When someone asks, "We have over 500 developers: how do we scale to Scrum?" is an example of someone asking the wrong question. How do they know they need 500 developers? Nor is "scaling" a proper response to a product that is late in delivery. Brook's Law (*The Mythical Man-Month: Essays on Software Engineering [Bro95]*, Chapter 2)—that adding people to a late project makes it later—still applies at team level. Scaling is about the piecemeal growth of the *Development Teams* in response to the growth of the product itself. Scrum has always scaled in that sense. Jeff Sutherland started the first multi-team Scrum at IDX in 1994. Exactly how Scrum scales is in large part situational, but the following patterns are common. Most of them fall within the scope of the Product Organization Pattern Language on page 11.

Reacting with the old muscle memory of waterfall, management's knee-jerk reaction to a need for greater productivity is to add new people to existing teams, or to add new teams. In the big majority of cases this is a misstep. Scrum has its roots in the Toyota Production System (TPS), and one of its architects wrote a whole book based on the contrast between its approach and "large-scale production" (*Toyota Production System: Beyond Large-Scale Production [Ohn88]*). The best approach is to:

- Coach the *¶11 Product Owner* to focus the *Scrum Team* on the most important work;

- Help the *¶19 ScrumMaster* to remove impediments; and,

- Grow the *Development Team*'s ability to deliver quality-assured product.

In a minority of cases, the prescribed approach may be insufficient. But it is still necessary to first improve the *Scrum Team* to its maximum. Large organizations grow piecemeal from small organizations that work. That's what this sequence is about. One may need to scale across geographically remote markets to meet diverse market needs (extensive localization or dependence on local laws, customs, or usage patterns). One may need to scale simply because of the intellectual mass of a single product. Examples include systems such as those that track and identify military threats and guide missiles to intercept them, or telecommunications products that must provide all telecommunication needs—local phone, toll calls, data, video, emergency services, billing, CRM, mobile, voice messaging, text messaging, Centrex, and business services—to a single market.

The following patterns focus on scaling a development effort. The underlying message is that it is best to scale Scrum using Scrum itself. The alignment of multiple teams behind a single product *¶39 Vision* requires that they work from a single *¶54 Product Backlog* managed by a *Product Owner* supported by an appropriately-sized *¶12 Product Owner Team*. Other patterns (like *¶82 Definition of Done*) are about the same as for single teams, with the change being only in unified scope of application (i.e., all teams share a common *Definition of Done*). Above all, the *Development Teams*' self-organization and autonomy are preconditions for success. We present the patterns in a typical sequence of application that you may want to consider following if you plan to grow your organization.

¶7 Scrum Team The starting point is always the single *Scrum Team*. Most organizations are tempted to "scale" as a shortcut to fixing the team. In the absence of a high-performing team you will only be scaling your dysfunctions and adding complexity to your organization.

¶12 Product Owner Team A *Product Owner Team* works under the leadership of a single Chief Product Owner to help with *Product Backlog* management across *¶89 Value Areas*.

¶18 Mitosis If the product grows beyond the capacity of a single, high-performing *Scrum Team* to deliver, the team may hire additional developers. With too many people in the *Development Team*, the team splits into two

smaller *Development Team*s. Organize the teams so that they remain ¶*10 Cross-Functional Team*s and work across all parts of the product. The teams must keep delivering end-user functionality from a single *Product Backlog*. Organize development so that the *Cross-Functional Team*s can keep delivering end-user functionality, following ¶*4 Conway's Law*.

¶*34 Scrum of Scrums* With multiple teams working from the same *Product Backlog*, it is crucial to keep them all aligned with the product *Vision*. The self-organizing *Development Team*s collaborate to deliver common ¶*71 Sprint Goal*s, and coordinate with each other to resolve emergent issues and dependencies.

¶*37 MetaScrum* Regularly coordinate among multiple products within an enterprise, and entertain management input through a forum that includes the *Product Owner*s and executive management, which works on aligning the expectations of management stakeholders.

¶*47 Organizational Sprint Pulse* All the teams work in the same ¶*46 Sprint* cadence and schedule to maintain a consistent view on progress. All teams together deliver an integrated single ¶*85 Regular Product Increment* at the end of each *Sprint* that is a *Done* contribution to furthering the *Vision* (in the sense of *Definition of Done*).

¶*89 Value Areas* The product domains become too broad for all teams to understand, yet it is not possible to divide the product into separate sub-products in the market. The teams specialize according to areas of customer value, each one continuing to be cross-functional across its value area. This is a temporary organization, put in place until teams again grow to be cross-functional teams.

¶*90 Value Stream Fork* Successful ¶*41 Value Stream*s may grow in scope. One problem with success is that the result can outstrip the original *Vision*. If so, split the *Value Stream* into multiple streams, each with its own *Product Backlog*, bringing focus and a refined *Vision* to each one.

¶18 Mitosis

Confidence stars: *

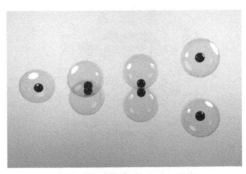

...you've been adding people to the team to keep up with stakeholder demand. However, the team is starting to work more as two teams than one, and team members have difficulty tracking everything that's going on.

❖   ❖   ❖

One should grow a *¶7 Scrum Team* in an incremental, piecemeal fashion, but eventually the team just becomes too large to remain efficient. *¶9 Small Teams* are the most efficient, but sometimes you need to grow. You could grow the organization large enough to be able to meet market demands for an increased breadth or volume of features, but large teams tend to be inefficient. Fred Brooks said that two programmers can do in two months what one programmer can do in one month (as in *The Mythical Man-Month: Essays on Software Engineering [Bro95]*): one realizes little benefit by adding more people to an existing development effort. Adding team members incrementally smooths out the "ramp-up cost" of transition but results in a crowd rather than a team.

One team for one product is the most efficient way to work. All team members will know exactly how their work fits into the past, present, and future. They can change direction quickly if the work of other team members requires it. The learning you get from working flows more naturally in one team than in two. It is easier for the *¶11 Product Owner* to coordinate with one *¶14 Development Team* than with two. Handling two teams creates more work for the *¶19 ScrumMaster*; having a *ScrumMaster* per team adds another line of coordination.

We can distinguish between the terms *formal team* and *instrumental team*. A formal team is what you see on the org chart, and corresponds to titled positions like *ScrumMaster* and *Product Owner*. However, instrumental teams come from the empirical loci of social interactions between individuals. It is

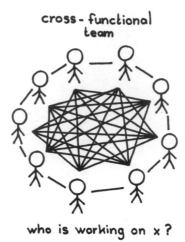

cross - functional
team

who is working on x ?

a good thing to align the informal and formal structures. And while it's also good to have one team as described earlier, it's folly to pretend that two empirical teams are in fact one team.

You could hire a new team on the side, but the effort to bring a group of new people up to speed on the product, culture, and technology is awkward. As a rule of thumb, every person you add to a product development organization detracts 25 percent from the effectiveness of everyone in that organization for about six months. In any case, there is "ramp-up" time associated with each new staff member, and that time and its corresponding overhead grow larger as the organization grows larger (Brooks' Law[15]). Furthermore, you need substantial cash on hand or a strong cash flow to realize a large staff increment. As organizations move from just being successful to a stage of growth, the management of most companies "consolidates the company and marshals resources for growth. The owner takes the cash and the established borrowing power of the company and risks it all in financing growth" (from *Harvard Business Review 61 [CL83]*). If loaded annual technical head count cost is $100,000, and you bring on a team of five from outside the organization —knowing that it takes about six months for new hires to fully become integrated into the effort—it will take $300,000 just to get started. Additional time is likely to pass before revenues grow to cover the incremental staff cost. You can reduce the six-month interval if the teams are in-house, but an organization must be large to sustain a pool of teams that are available on demand. And scaling experts suggest that such a team needs experience in

15. "Brooks's [sic.] Law," https://en.wikipedia.org/wiki/Brooks's_law, April 2018 (accessed 5 June 2018).

the domain of application and needs to already be working as a "high-performance team," which further restricts the possibility that any available team might be a match for the work.[16]

Further, some national labor laws often make it very costly for firms to dismiss employees who have worked past their "probationary period" (usually six months). This means it is not cost-effective for firms to hire and fire teams at will unless they can easily assign the people to other internal efforts. That implies that the firm is large. According to the U.S. Census Bureau, companies with annual revenues of $1.2 million or less do 85 percent of all software development, which suggests they have five to eight employees.[17] They rarely have the in-house resources to "consolidate the company and marshal resources for growth."

Therefore:

Differentiate a single large *Development Team* into two small teams after it gradually grows to the point of inefficiency—about seven people in the old team. Carry over the experience, domain and product knowledge, and culture of the original team into each new team.

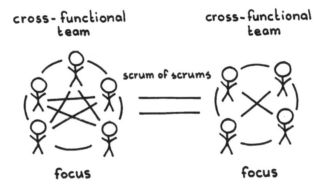

It is important that each resulting team remain a *¶10 Cross-Functional Team* after the split, with broad enough coverage of disciplines to be able to autonomously deliver a *¶85 Regular Product Increment* (see *¶16 Autonomous Team*). Each new team should have the authority to work on all parts of the product.

16. Carl Erickson. "Small Teams Are Dramatically More Efficient than Large Teams." https://spin.atomicobject.com/2012/01/11/small-teams-are-dramatically-more-efficient-than-large-teams/, 11 January 2012 (accessed 13 April 2017).
17. Carl Erickson. "Small Teams Are Dramatically More Efficient than Large Teams." https://spin.atomicobject.com/2012/01/11/small-teams-are-dramatically-more-efficient-than-large-teams/, 11 January 2012 (accessed 13 April 2017).

❖ ❖ ❖

Each new *Development Team* should have its own *ScrumMaster* and developers. The new team works from the same *¶54 Product Backlog* as the original team, and works with the same *Product Owner*. The teams working on any given product still coordinate with each other and should share the same work environment (see *¶8 Collocated Team*), but each team should have autonomy to deliver each of the *¶55 Product Backlog Item*s it takes into a *¶75 Production Episode*.

Members of separate teams should continue to coordinate with each other informally, and as necessary, through the daily rhythm of *¶34 Scrum of Scrums* events.

Sometimes the original team has a person who is the only specialist in some area necessary to the team's success, which implies that the corresponding knowledge may be lacking in one of the resulting teams. Use *¶42 Set-Based Design*, *¶5 Birds of a Feather*, and *¶111 Apprenticeship* on page 468 to remove the impediment as soon as possible; in the interim, the team just does its best to cover the missing area.

Growing from one team to two teams is hard. A rule of thumb is that you take about a 40 percent hit in velocity (see Notes on Velocity on page 320) to support the coordination necessary for two teams to do the work of a single team made up of the same team members. The percentage may decrease as the number of teams increases, which suggests that it may make sense to scale only if one plans to scale big.

If it feels natural that one of the new teams supports its own stakeholder community, then consider *¶90 Value Stream Fork* or *¶89 Value Areas*.

Incremental growth, and ultimate differentiation into parts, is the fundamental process that underlies Christopher Alexander's Theory of Centers and lies at the core of how he views harmonious growth of structure. He articulates the general principles in *The Nature of Order: An Essay on the Art of Building and the Nature of the Universe—Book 1, The Phenomenon of Life [Ale04a]*, and explores them more explicitly in Chapter 24 ("The Process of Repair") of *The Timeless Way of Building [Ale79]*.

Keeping the team small helps to concentrate its sense of identity, which in turn fuels a positive sense of team membership (see *¶118 Team Pride* on page 469).

Kaizen and Kaikaku

Scrum is a framework not only for producing product, but also for constantly advancing the abilities of the team creating that product. From a process perspective, Scrum is all about improvement, which, in Japanese, is just "改善." In its own process improvement effort, Toyota took *kaizen* as a slogan, usually written as "カイゼン." The international community picked up the term and started using it in the sense they projected from Toyota's programs: continued, relentless improvement. The next pattern, *¶19 ScrumMaster*, describes the role that owns the Scrum process in a Scrum team and which often leads the charge for kaizen. However, it's important to remember that kaizen is everyone's job: the *ScrumMaster* is just the team's kaizen conscience.

> **Kaizen** *(改善) is the Japanese word for "improvement." In business, kaizen refers to activities that continuously improve all functions and involve all employees from the CEO to the assembly line workers. It also applies to processes, such as purchasing and logistics, that cross organizational boundaries into the supply chain. It has been applied in healthcare, psychotherapy, life-coaching, government, and banking.*
>
> . . .
>
> *Kaizen is a daily process, the purpose of which goes beyond simple productivity improvement. It is also a process that, when done correctly, humanizes the workplace, eliminates overly hard work ("muri"), and teaches people how to perform experiments on their work using the scientific method and how to learn to spot and eliminate waste in business processes.*[18]

The team can use kaizen opportunistically or to remedy known shortcomings. It is a Japanese workplace tradition that upon noticing a personal or team shortcoming, the team *does hansei*: that is, they take a posture of individual or collective regret for the shortfall. Here, kaizen is related to restoring self-worth and honor, and reflects the sense behind *¶93 Greatest Value*. There is a Toyota saying that "there is no kaizen without hansei." So you would usually approach kaizen not with celebration, slogans, and excitement, but with humility and resolve. See *¶28 Pop the Happy Bubble*.

The term *kaizen* usually implies *incremental improvement*. Much of agile is based on taking small steps, as in *¶88 One Step at a Time*. The problem with taking *only* incremental steps is that you can land in a local optimum. Occasionally taking greater risk and making a different kind of change—often a larger change—can take you to higher ground. This is a kind of radical change, which in Japanese is *kaikaku* (改革): an extreme kaizen.

---

18. "Kaizen." Wikipedia, https://en.wikipedia.org/wiki/Kaizen, 7 September 2018, (accessed 3 October 2018).

In fact, it is likely that most improvement comes from incremental change. The British bicycling team (Team Sky) popularized the notion of *marginal gains* in 2003, showing that many tiny improvements in bike design and training add up. Though marginal gains are overhyped, the approach certainly merits serious consideration in any improvement effort. *Financial Times* says:

> ...most productivity growth came from existing companies improving existing products, rather than new businesses or products. That was true in the 1980s and still is.[19]

Toyota's employee suggestion box has yielded over 1,800 kaizens for factory line efficiency—a form of marginal gains. But they can become a kind of diminishing return, begging more radical change to attain the next level of excellence.[20] To keep moving ahead requires occasional discontinuity, and *Financial Times* adds:

> Google may A/B test its way to greater profits [by fine-tuning web page color schemes—a small change that supported higher engagement and resulting higher profits] but the company's success has been built on a leap forward in search technology in the late 1990s, and even more fundamentally on the publicly funded efforts to develop the web and the internet.[21]

They add that kaizen is likely to take care of itself, and hint that more radical change may require an external disruption. Great Scrum teams alternate radical and incremental change to sustain what might be called *continuous discontinuity*. Kaikaku changes often originate with management, as they may entail change to the corporate governance or structure—changes at the enterprise or system level. See ¶6 *Involve the Managers*.

As an example of diminishing returns from kaizen, consider how Toyota treats poke-yoke (a "failsafe" mechanism that guides the work in a way that avoids errors; see ¶32 *Emergency Procedure*). Each failsafe brings with it overhead which over time may add up to unacceptable waste—especially if it leads to complacency that dulls the team members' awareness and prevents them

19. Tim Hartford. "Marginal gains matter but game changers transform." *Financial Times*, https://www.ft.com/content/6b5c046c-0fc0-11e7-a88c-50ba212dce4d, 24 March 2017 (accessed 17 December 2017).

20. "Challenging Marginal Gains Mathematics: 10 Myths about How Marginal Gains Add Up." https://www.youtube.com/watch?v=28E9IzSmFvI, 12 May 2017 (accessed 17 December 2017).

21. Tim Hartford. "Marginal gains matter but game changers transform." *Financial Times*, https://www.ft.com/content/6b5c046c-0fc0-11e7-a88c-50ba212dce4d, 24 March 2017 (accessed 17 December 2017).

from suffering the occasional priceless setback that leads them into learning. The team must be circumspect about this trade-off.

Some patterns that we might casually include in the set of incremental changes may in fact require kaikaku action. For example, it may be difficult to transition from functional teams or component teams to ¶10 Cross-Functional Teams in a piecemeal fashion. Organizations might best be advised to put the right structure in place up front with management support. Experience shows that it does not happen of its own accord, especially in large organizations. Other patterns may be the same; each organization can judge for itself.

Russ Ackoff, pioneer in the field of operations research, systems thinking and management science, admonishes us to look beyond "continuous improvement" to systems thinking that deals with the Whole. The alternative to continual improvement is discontinuous improvement, focusing on properties of the Whole, through creativity that breaks with what preceded it.[22]

---

22. Russ Ackoff. "If Russ Ackoff had given a TED Talk..." Video recording, https://www.youtube.com/watch?v=OqEeIG8aPPk, 1994 (accessed 25 December 2017).

¶19 ScrumMaster

Confidence stars: **

Sir Edmund Hillary, with Sherpa Tenzing Norgay following, in the British expedition led by John Hunt that conquered Everest for the first time in history (1953). Recognition goes to those who achieve the goal, supported by the facilitation of those playing less glorious, but core, roles in the mission. ScrumMasters often lead from behind.

...a *¶14 Development Team* and *¶11 Product Owner* have come together to develop a complex product for some market. The *Product Owner* is managing the business side and defining product content, while the *Development Team* focuses on the best tools and techniques to do its job. Neither role has the mandate to examine how they work together or how to implement the overall Scrum process.

❖ ❖ ❖

Development Teams, Product Owners, and organizations cannot get the benefits of Scrum without deep understanding and application of its principles and values.

Without deep understanding of Scrum theory and its principles, it is challenging for an organization to create the most valuable product using Scrum. And although an organization may understand how well it is performing, it doesn't always know how to improve. When we see ourselves accurately, it is sometimes clear what we can do to improve. But often it is hard to see what the problems could be if you are part of the problem yourself. A person with a detached view can make us aware of our own blocking behaviors and thinking, so that we can decide to do something about them.

Teams adopt Scrum as a kaizen and kaikaku (see Kaizen and Kaikaku on page 101) to improve quality, interval, and throughput. Scrum works because of an extensive, powerful, and profound system of principles, theories, values, and foundations that combine in complex ways to support complex development. "Articulated Scrum"—the level of artifacts, roles, and events at which a typical practitioner usually understands Scrum—are only a caricature of richer underlying principles. Team members rarely understand these richer principles, or may simply be inattentive to them, but these principles are fundamental to success with Scrum.

Removing organizational impediments, facilitating disagreements and discussions, organizing group events and courses, keeping the library current, bringing career opportunities to the group—all of these are activities of a healthy team. Some of this work is a response to inputs from outside the ¶7 *Scrum Team* about shortcomings in meeting stakeholder expectations; some is an opportunistic chance to improve from within. Many of these activities are time-consuming "distractions" that neither the *Product Owner* nor the *Development Team* are eager to add to their responsibilities. So these tasks often fall to other roles like administrative staff and managers. Managers bring with them a mantle of control, and a traditional administrator responds to the control and direction of the team member requesting some service. In both cases, it entangles those involved in the activity with the other role, and dilutes individual autonomy in bringing such work to completion.

There are deeper structural problems that owe to the focus that the *Product Owner* and *Development Team* roles respectively bring to their jobs. While focusing on delivering the most value (see Value and ROI on page 246) or on reaching a specific ¶71 *Sprint Goal* or on completing a ¶46 *Sprint*, it's easy to lose sight of the larger picture. It becomes difficult for individuals to separate their own interests from those of the team, or those of product development as a whole.

One of the common casualties of this myopia is the process. The Japanese roots of Scrum tell us, "build the right process and you'll build the right product." Yet if you focus exclusively on the product, whether from a business strategy or development perspective, it's easy to forget the rigor and attention that process improvement deserves. It takes discipline for a team to police itself instead of rationalizing away agreed process standards. For example, a *Development Team* may see no immediate consequences from failing to comply with a couple of minor development standards or from skipping a couple of tests or from letting that one minor defect reach the market. A *Product Owner* may interrupt development to impose his or her will just this once. The team might be so myopic as to never take the initiative to deepen their Scrum knowledge or to invest any time at all in process improvement. Such conduct might be in line with the usual rationalized responsibilities for these roles, but it can be destructive in the long term.

It's easy for an ingrown team to take ownership of its accomplishment and not wait to react to consequences. When implementation is done, it takes patience to wait for testing; when testing is done, it takes time to wait for market feedback. Even if the team has put feedback loops in place, it's too easy to be lulled into a sense of complacency if the feedback is constant. "The quality is O.K.; our defect backlog hasn't changed from 2,000 defects for 18 months." If each role is focused on its own job (e.g., setting product direction or delivering what was asked), it may receive no other feedback about product quality.

It's easy for a sense of autonomy to become a sense of isolation. A *Development Team* member may feel that his or her concerns are likely to fall on deaf ears even if others in the same role speak in concert. After all, they are *only Development Team* members and stakeholders often dismiss their insights on strategic issues. The *Product Owner* also needs an advocate.

And a team that is focused on pleasing the stakeholders or on doing a good job or on meeting a schedule can often lose sight of its own needs. Scrum has two products: the deliverable and the team. While everyone may be a good citizen and be attentive to doing his or her job, team health and growth are crucial to the wellbeing of the enterprise. Everybody could do this, but something that is everybody's responsibility is nobody's responsibility.

Therefore:

Introduce a *ScrumMaster* that guides and leads the *Product Owner*, *Development Team*, and broader organization in understanding the Scrum framework, its principles, and values. The *ScrumMaster* defends the Scrum process and nurtures the organization to successfully use Scrum. The *ScrumMaster* acts as a guide to explain the deeper underlying principles that might be at play when a given impediment arises, and can interpret these principles together with the team, to support them in identifying and implementing a solution.

The *ScrumMaster* guides the organization and *Scrum Team* to reflect and improve, and helps to resolve impediments and to improve the Scrum process-es. This is why even top performers in sports, music, entertainment, and

other fields usually have personal coaches. Interestingly, the coaches are not necessarily the top performers, but are particularly adept at teaching, observing, and challenging their protégés to reach ever greater heights.

The *ScrumMaster* helps *Product Owners* succeed by guiding them. For example, suppose the *Product Owner* does not order the *¶54 Product Backlog* properly. The *ScrumMaster* could simply ask the *Product Owner* to order it, but a better approach would be to give subtle guidance to the *Product Owner* on how to go about ordering *¶55 Product Backlog Items* on the backlog. The *ScrumMaster* might ask a question like this: "We will be planning our next *Sprint* in the next few days, and the *Development Team* is wondering what we should work on next. It appears that items A and B are both important, but we don't know which is most important. You have insight into the organization's vision, business model, and finances. You also have a good perspective on user needs and desires. Based on these, can you figure out which we should work on now?" (This approach has overtones of flattery, but that's not the purpose. Instead, it shows the *Product Owner* how and why they are valuable.)

The *ScrumMaster* is responsible for the team's enactment of Scrum but has no authority over the *Development Team* or *Product Owner*. The *ScrumMaster*'s primary activities are:

1. observing and asking questions;
2. facilitating;
3. teaching;
4. intervening and, most importantly;
5. actively doing nothing.

"Doing nothing" may be the most important activity because every time the *ScrumMaster* "solves" a problem or decides for the team, the team loses an opportunity to learn and grow.

An example at a Daily Scrum: As the one responsible for the Scrum process, it is the *ScrumMaster*'s job to motivate the team take ownership for the *¶29 Daily Scrum* (see *¶30 ScrumMaster Incognito*).

❖ ❖ ❖

The *ScrumMaster* is not the manager of the team and has no authority over the team's decisions or actions. The *ScrumMaster* may never direct the team about what to do or how to do its job, but must employ effective persuasion and motivation. One key job of the *ScrumMaster* is to fight complacency (see *¶28 Pop the Happy Bubble*). The only direct power that a *ScrumMaster* can wield is to remove a disruptive person from the team (see *¶27 Remove the Shade*).

A way to characterize the overall role of the *ScrumMaster* during the initial phase of Scrum adoption is as a coach for the *Development Team* and its members. The *ScrumMaster* is responsible for the Scrum process and particularly helps the *Development Team* to deliver a *¶85 Regular Product Increment* each *Sprint*, at a minimum. This is hard enough for teams starting with Scrum and is a good initial goal to strive for. Ideally, the *Scrum Team* selects the *ScrumMaster* itself—and selecting the *ScrumMaster* is often the team's first act of self-organization. The team may remove a *ScrumMaster* who is not getting the team to improve their process and certainly one who is not holding the team to their agreed-upon process standards. In any case, the *ScrumMaster* is a servant leader to the *Scrum Team*.

The pattern *¶128 Producer Roles* on page 469 explains that team members typically are either *producers* (people who directly contribute to the ROI of the organization) or *supporters* (people who help the producers do their jobs). The *ScrumMaster* is the quintessential supporter: everything the *ScrumMaster* does should focus on helping the rest of the team (who are typically all producers) be effective. The *ScrumMaster* may deal with external impediments that don't directly require the input or expertise of the *Development Team* or *Product Owner*. In an extreme case, the *ScrumMaster* may remove a disruptive team member from the team if the disruption is a serious, fundamental process impediment that the team cannot otherwise address (see *Remove the Shade*).

The *ScrumMaster* serves the team out of empathy and care for the team and its objectives, but should not be assimilated enough into the team to dull his or her edge of objectivity. It is a balance. The *ScrumMaster* should be within the social closure of the team enough to retain keen awareness of how things are going, but not lose external objectivity. One consequence of this perspective is that it may not even make sense for a single person to be part-time *ScrumMaster* and part-time *Development Team* member. Part of maintaining the balance is to avoid becoming aloof, or being perceived as aloof. The *ScrumMaster* should strive to be present to support and serve the team as unexpected impediments spontaneously pop up. See *¶21 Small Red Phone*.

The *ScrumMaster* is sometimes the face of the team to the rest of the world. In this capacity, the *ScrumMaster* can help protect the team against unwanted distractions (see *¶114 Firewall* on page 468). Anyone from outside the *Scrum Team* wanting to confront a team member or the team as a whole should go through the *ScrumMaster*. The *ScrumMaster* protects the team from unwarranted threats and criticisms while distilling what information is of use for the team to improve. And the *ScrumMaster* may in the end facilitate a direct communication between such outside parties and the team. However, in no way should this mean that the *ScrumMaster* is the communication channel for the team. On the contrary, team members should communicate freely and frequently with anybody they need to. But occasionally, a single contact point is expedient, and the team should inspect and adapt in having the *ScrumMaster* fill that role (see *¶115 Gatekeeper* on page 468).

Again, an important role of the *ScrumMaster* is to help the team understand the "whys" behind the elements of Scrum. The *ScrumMaster* is the standard-bearer for the *Scrum Team* and organization to guide them within the Spirit of Scrum (see *¶1 The Spirit of the Game*).

The nature of Scrum is that it can be a high-pressure environment. Each *Sprint* can feel fast-paced and even frantic. Over time, this can actually demotivate individuals and cause burnout. The *ScrumMaster* encourages team members, praises small successes, and ensures that the *Development Team* keeps operating at a sustainable pace. The *ScrumMaster* role itself can be a high-pressure job. To prevent burnout, the *ScrumMaster* should seek coaching; see *¶22 Scrum (Master) Coach*.

An important result is that Scrum at the team level impacts the organization as it expands from just tactical interventions within the *Development Team* to a more strategic role. Thus it can help change the culture of the entire organization. To help spread such strategic outreach across the organization, consider using a ScrumMaster *¶5 Birds of a Feather* where *ScrumMaster*s can share, socialize, and coordinate improvement initiatives.

¶20 Oyatsu Jinja (Snack Shrine)

Alias: Snack Shrine, Oyatsu Jinja (おやつ神社)

...a *¶14 Development Team* has been successfully delivering *¶85 Regular Product Increment*s at a sustainable pace. Both the team and its technical practices have been improving. Recently, more and more requests for help are coming into the team. Members from other teams come asking for technical advice. Managers and other stakeholders frequently come to the team to learn how they work and discuss their new business ideas. Team members often feel interrupted and have less time to concentrate on product development.

❖ ❖ ❖

A *Development Team* needs an environment free from interruptions. At the same time, the team members need to interact with one another and the *¶11 Product Owner*. Additionally, the team needs to interact with people outside the team, like stakeholders and other teams, to continuously improve and share information.

Having the team isolated can impede communication, whereas making the environment fully open to visitors can damage the team's effectiveness (*X-teams: How to Build Teams that Lead, Innovate and Succeed [AB07]*).

Therefore:

Create an *Oyatsu Jinja* (Snack Shrine) near the team area, with some candies, snacks, and drinks (coffee or tea). The shrine needs to be located far enough from the team's work area so that chatting at the shrine does not disturb the team. However, the shrine needs to be close enough to the team so that people at the shrine and in the team area can recognize one another. *Oyatsu Jinja* is not a secret place as activities at the shrine need to be observable by the team. It is important that people using the shrine do not interrupt the team.

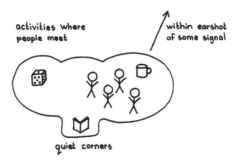

From A Pattern Language [AIS77], "A Place to Wait".

Team members can visit the shrine to take breaks. Snacks help people to relax and give people an opportunity to interact. The shrine creates a place for team members to chat and get help without disturbing the rest of the team.

Stakeholders can visit the shrine. Rather than directly going to the team and interrupting them, they meet team members at the shrine. In many cases, chatting at the shrine is good enough. If the visitors need help from a team member not at the shrine, they will wait for him or her at the shrine until the team member takes a break. If the team members see the visitors at the shrine, they can adjust when to take a break. If the *Development Team* is concentrating and no team member is at the shrine, the visitor will notice this and come back to the shrine again sometime later.

Oyatsu Jinja also works as a good communication place after Scrum events. For example, after finishing a *¶29 Daily Scrum*, *¶35 Sprint Review*, and/or *¶36 Sprint Retrospective*, members can use the shrine for quick follow-up chatting, if necessary.

The shrine can also be an experimental place for kaizen (see Kaizen and Kaikaku on page 101) and self-organization. Anyone is welcome to contribute some snacks to the shrine and to help keep the shrine a clean and nice place to meet. For example, some teams develop their own process to keep the coffee fresh. This shrine becomes a locus for self-organization.

Oyatsu Jinja can also work in multiple-team environments. A single shrine can work like a town square for the teams. In this case it is important to locate the shrine in a place easily accessible and visible to the teams.

❖ ❖ ❖

This pattern relates to ¶132 *The Water Cooler* on page 470 as it is a common area people can go to chat. *The Water Cooler* (or coffee machine or employee lounge) is a place that reinforces the informal communication network that helps information flow quickly between people that might otherwise be disconnected by issues of location or organization structure. *Oyatsu Jinja* differs from *The Water Cooler* in the sense that *Oyatsu Jinja* is highly visible and located close enough to the team to facilitate a sustainable communication environment (or *ba* (場)). While the *Oyatsu Jinja* can serve as a locus of some *Water Cooler* encounters, its main focus is more intentional communication between the *Development Team* and those outside that team.

This pattern is also related to ¶135 *Do Food* on page 470 (*Fearless Change [RM05]*). There is something social about breaking bread that can lower barriers and encourage good communication.

There are similarities between this pattern and ¶115 *Gatekeeper* on page 468. In this pattern, the gatekeeper is the *Oyatsu Jinja* rather than an individual.

A team can be motivated to defend its own focus if the members believe in themselves and in their product; see ¶38 *Product Pride*.

The sketch as shown in the solution is inspired by the pattern, *A Place to Wait* from Christopher Alexander, that "creates a situation which makes the waiting positive" (*A Pattern Language [AIS77]*, "A Place to Wait", pattern 150). You can also conceive of *Oyatsu Jinja* as a key waypoint in an implementation of Alexander's *Intimacy Gradient* (*A Pattern Language [AIS77]*, pattern 127).

Editor's note: This pattern bore the longstanding name Oyatsu Jinja (おやつ神社). However, technical issues during production prevented kanji characters from appearing in pattern names.

¶21 Small Red Phone

...key roles are in place and you want to sustain the dynamics of a *¶7 Scrum Team* that is collocated and accessible.

❖   ❖   ❖

Scrum depends on second-by-second feedback. If individuals are remote or not around, then the team can become blocked waiting for their input. On the other hand, *¶11 Product Owner*s and *¶19 ScrumMaster*s cannot and should not hand-hold the team. They are sometimes—rightly—elsewhere, albeit working hard to support the team's work. Yet occasions arise when it is crucial that they be immediately accessible to the *¶14 Development Team*, which is the goose that lays the golden egg. And even though development may not stop if they are unavailable for a few seconds, strategic problems can waylay the team if these roles stay inaccessible for just a few hours, or sometimes minutes. An example of such a situation is when the *Development Team* comes to an emergent understanding that it fundamentally misunderstands some *¶55 Product Backlog Item.* Another example is when the *Development Team* needs information from some external stakeholder who has been interacting with the team through the *Product Owner* or *ScrumMaster* but doesn't know how to get in touch.

We could just make key roles' individual work phone numbers available to the team, but then they are likely to be distracted continuously as they are working to build support for the team or to mitigate problems on the *Development Team*'s behalf (see *¶109 Don't Interrupt an Interrupt* on page 468).

Therefore:

Issue a red cellular phone, with its own number, to each critical staff member, to be used to reach these key players only in critical situations. Likely targets for such a phone include the *Product Owner* and the *ScrumMaster*. Publish the phone number to members of the *Scrum Team* with the understanding that it is to be used only in the most urgent situations.

Create some kind of humorous or light disincentive that encourages members to keep its use to a minimum. Such a disincentive can include an activity reminiscent of the Abnormal Termination of Sprint Ceremony that helps memorialize the incident and bring focus to it for the *¶36 Sprint Retrospective* (see *¶32 Emergency Procedure*).

❖   ❖   ❖

Richard Gabriel reflects on his years working with software development teams, where developers may be working at odd hours and weekends. Inevitably they would need access to some physically secured resource, such as a computer server, which required physically present action to be restored to service. Richard insisted that there always be someone present during off-hours who knew how to pick locks, so that a dead machine or network router didn't become a showstopper.

Small Red Phone is an interruption-based style of communication. Contrast this with the much preferred protocol of *¶20 Oyatsu Jinja (Snack Shrine)*.

In many instances, this pattern is a compensation for a faulty bureaucracy. If you feel like you need this pattern frequently, you should consider trying *¶8 Collocated Team* instead. For example, neither *Small Red Phone*, nor anything else, can be a long-term work-around for multisite development.

Thanks to Kenny Munck of ID4Real.

¶22 Scrum (Master) Coach

Confidence stars: *

...your *¶19 ScrumMaster* is serving the *¶14 Development Team* and helping the team to continually improve.

❖ ❖ ❖

The *ScrumMaster* is sometimes the source of the *¶7 Scrum Team*'s problems, or might not be performing up to par, or otherwise simply wants to improve.

The world *ScrumMaster* population is growing, which means that many *ScrumMaster*s are new at their jobs. There are many facets to the *ScrumMaster* role, and it is easy to overlook some of them. Also, no single person has encountered every possible challenge, and unfamiliar circumstances require new thinking. Conversely, even the most experienced *ScrumMaster* can easily fall into routines; being "experienced" implies some kind of reuse of prior successes.

While one of the *ScrumMaster*'s functions is to *¶28 Pop the Happy Bubble* of the *Development Team*, a *ScrumMaster* may become content with the current state of the *Scrum Team* and lose kaizen mind as well. Additionally, the *ScrumMaster* may come to accept some organizational impediments to be just business as usual, as familiarity dulls their sense of excellence—or the

ScrumMaster may come to assume that some situations cannot be changed. This is against kaizen mind (see Kaizen and Kaikaku on page 101).

In the extreme, a *ScrumMaster* may be personally limited and may be at risk of seeming unfit for the role. Or circumstances in the team may trigger memories that the *ScrumMaster* projects onto others.

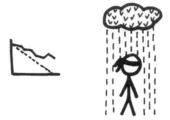

Without help, the *ScrumMaster*'s actions may damage relationships within the *Scrum Team* and with the team's stakeholders.

Therefore:

The *ScrumMaster* should periodically seek opportunities for reflection and growth with a sparring partner or coach.

The coach may be another *ScrumMaster* in the organization or someone external to the organization. In either case, the person should have enough distance from the *ScrumMaster*'s situation to be able to dispassionately engage with the issues at play. It is essential that whoever the ScrumMaster is working with is not caught in the same situation as the ScrumMaster.

The coach need not have prior experience (or certification) in the subject matter at hand. Sometimes a good question is better than a definitive answer because it can unlock one's thinking. As with ¶126 *Developing in Pairs* on page 469, sometimes it is the novice that teaches the master.

There are many forms of coaching. The interaction may be cathartic, challenging, or transformational as the situation requires, as long as the goal is to help the ScrumMaster to better serve the team.

Trust is essential between the *ScrumMaster* and coach. Real progress comes faster when the *ScrumMaster* is able to fully disclose both the details of the situation and their reactions to it. And then, the *ScrumMaster* must actually be willing to change.

The coach may observe the *Development Team* and the *ScrumMaster*'s interactions with the team, but should not intervene. Any intervention would confuse the *ScrumMaster*'s relationship with the team and the relationship between the coach and *ScrumMaster*. The focus of the coach must be to improve the team by helping the *ScrumMaster* better serve the team.

❖ ❖ ❖

A *ScrumMaster* who continues to develop kaizen mind in herself will be better able to serve and develop kaizen within the team. As with a priest, who does not minister to his or her own struggles and seeks the counsel of another, so should the *ScrumMaster* not try to resolve his or her struggles alone. As the *ScrumMaster* increases his or her awareness and becomes ever better in helping the team, the team can grow in confidence, ability, and its own sense of wellbeing (see *¶118 Team Pride* on page 469).

Ideally, a *ScrumMaster* will seek a coach not just as an opportunity for continuous improvement, but also when he or she discovers specific shortcomings in carrying out the job. In some larger organizations there may be support for *ScrumMasters* through *¶5 Birds of a Feather* structures. In smaller organizations, the *ScrumMaster* will need to look outside the organization for help. In other situations, someone may recommend the *ScrumMaster* work with a coach. This recommendation may come as a surprise for the *ScrumMaster*, but we suggest that this is taken as a positive opportunity to grow and improve, with the *ScrumMaster* trying to be as open and trusting of the coach as he or she feels comfortable.

When one person serves as coach to many *ScrumMaster*s in a single organization, there is risk that the coach's biases may rub off on the organization. The *ScrumMaster* should be conscious of this possibility when selecting a coach.

Coaching is a subtle activity. It almost always leads to changes in behaviors, and change may be upsetting in its own right. Further, these new behaviors can too easily create an impression that is akin to disingenuousness; that is, the change can be perceived as happening for its own sake. For the coachee, such change might be progress, for others interacting with the coachee it can be upsetting as they need to accommodate the change. For example, a *ScrumMaster* who starts using an active listening style in conflict situations might be viewed as disingenuously out of character. While *Scrum Team* members may intellectually understand that active listening is a good tool, it may be off-putting to them to see such out-of-character behavior in the *ScrumMaster* who previously was less finessed in his or her interactions. It takes time both for the coached individual to assimilate the new behaviors naturally and for the team to accommodate the new interaction style, and these two changes can happen at different rates. This problem is further detailed in "The Coaching Ripple Effect" in *Psychology of Well-Being: Theory, Research and Practice [OC13]* (p. 2). The first author of this work elaborated:

> In other words, a leader's capacity to conduct new, more challenging conversations in an elegant and competent manner, might lag behind their initiative in commencing such conversations. Significant changes of style are rarely born fully formed.

¶23 Fixed Work

Mechanics account the time spent tuning a race car engine separately from the estimated race completion time. Engine tuning is routine; race times should get shorter and shorter.

...you are organizing the work that needs to be done to deliver the product, and the *¶11 Product Owner* is looking for ways to get help from the team to prepare requirements and the *¶54 Product Backlog*.

Scrum divides time in two. There is a continuous timeline for analysis and the business, and a cyclic *¶46 Sprint* timeline for production. Time for analysis and innovation is impossible to estimate and may unfold over long intervals, because it arises unpredictably in a process that Steve Johnson calls "the slow hunch" in *Where Good Ideas Come From [Joh11]*.

❖ ❖ ❖

All work must be accounted for if the *Product Owner* is to use team velocity (see Notes on Velocity on page 320) for release planning, yet not all development work can be time-boxed. For example, the team cannot foreordain the moment at which they will have progressed enough toward creating a *¶64 Refined Product Backlog* to pronounce any single *¶55 Product Backlog Item* as being *Ready* (see *¶65 Definition of Ready*). There is always fixed, recurring work that is not accounted for in *¶14 Development Team* estimates.

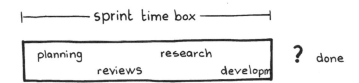

The *Product Backlog* is the primary tool for budgeting product development work. The *Product Owner* orders *Product Backlog Items* (*PBIs*) in consideration of development estimates and anticipated value. Teams commit to the ¶71 *Sprint Goal*, and the *Development Team* is confident about their estimates. That work takes time. *Development Team* members are responsible for fitting all work within the bounds of a ¶75 *Production Episode*.

Usually, *Development Team* members can forecast only the development tasks related to their skill set, experience, and area of responsibility—usually, those that involve building the product. Other work may be difficult, or impossible, for the developers to estimate. For example, some analysis tasks require open-ended research to evaluate development feasibility, cost, and trade-offs. While analysis is usually the *Product Owner*'s job, such analysis often requires input from or work by the *Development Team*. You can try to time-box such research, but that can lead to repeated extensions of the research time. And while research activities produce insights, they rarely produce the kind of ¶85 *Regular Product Increment* expected from work done during the *Production Episode*—the development part of a *Sprint*. This raises doubts about doing such work within the *Sprint*, and about budgeting it on the *Product Backlog*: if it is not producing product, it may be some form of waste.

This wouldn't be a problem if the ¶12 *Product Owner Team* alone could do the research because the *Product Owner*s can manage their own time. However, it is often the case that *Product Owner*s have a strong business skill set but a weaker skill set to actually build the artifacts necessary to support their research. Yet, issues of technology and production often arise as key elements of business risk and, as such, fall within the *Product Owner*'s purview.

The *Product Backlog* documents only some of the work that broadly falls under the heading of product development, let alone time that the team spends outside development activities. Examples include the time spent on ¶24 *Sprint Planning*, ¶35 *Sprint Review*, drag (e.g., the time we spend drinking coffee or networking in the office), the ¶36 *Sprint Retrospective*, and time focused on maintaining a *Refined Product Backlog*.

Therefore:

Divide all *Development Team* work into that whose duration they estimate (namely, work on the product) and that which they cannot estimate (such as the work to understand requirements as the team moves *PBI*s to Ready). In each *Sprint*, plan to work on just enough estimated tasks to fill the *Production Episode* time box. Set aside periodic time boxes for non-estimable work, outside the *Production Episode* budget, and complete as much of each kind of such work as time-boxing allows. Each *Sprint*, the ¶7 *Scrum Team* does only as much of a given kind of work (e.g., analysis work, business planning, review activities) as will fit inside the corresponding time box for such work. Move this work into events such as *Sprint Planning*, the *Sprint Review*, the *Sprint Retrospective*, and time boxes where the whole *Scrum Team* works to continuously maintain a *Refined Product Backlog*.

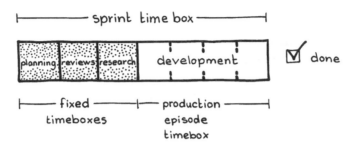

If the team feels that work on any set of non-estimable tasks is complete for the time being, there is no need to fill out the corresponding time box with work. For example, if the team finishes *Sprint Planning* before its time box is up, the *Development Team* can immediately move on to the *Production Episode*.

❖   ❖   ❖

Now, the *Development Team* can sustain work on items that are difficult to estimate, such as tasks that require fundamental innovation or which otherwise entail high uncertainty. Removing such work from the *Product Backlog*, and therefore from *Production Episode* time, allows the work to proceed at its own pace. Tasks that require fundamental innovation or breakthroughs, such as work that the *Development Team* does in support of the *Product Owner*, can now proceed at their own pace without time-boxing work within the *Production Episode*. The time allotted to *Refined Product Backlog* and *Sprint Planning* accommodates an unbounded amount of such work without affecting the *Production Episode* budget or diminishing development time.

The *total* time per *Sprint* for *Fixed Work*, and further, for each kind of *Fixed Work* in a *Sprint*, is nonetheless time-boxed. For example, the team may decide to explore alternatives for a high-performance network routing algorithm, and while one can neither time-box the overall effort for that particular task nor schedule its completion, it is possible to time-box the work on that effort per *Sprint* by restricting it to time-boxed events. So all such work may take place within *Sprint Planning*, which is time-boxed, or within the time-boxed work of an ongoing (across *Sprint*s) ¶42 *Set-Based Design* effort.

Additionally, the *Product Owner* may still fund the team to work on well-contained (i.e., finitely estimable) *PBIs* within the *Sprint*, even though they may not contribute directly to the product. If the *Product Owner Team* lacks the expertise necessary to assess the business consequences of some technology concern (e.g., product performance analysis, prototype construction) then the *Product Owner* can fund the *Development Team* to do such analysis work in a *Set-Based Design* exercise during the *Sprint*. Such work applies to activities that the *Development Team* can estimate with a reasonably small margin of error, or for which the *Product Owner* and *Development Team* together set a pre-determined time box. For example, if the *Product Owner* needs a prototyping tool and can use it to create an *¶63 Enabling Specification* that helps the team understand what deliverable to build, it is fine to use a *PBI* to direct the team to do this work. Such a tool feeds the *¶41 Value Stream* and has demonstrable return on investment.

However, the *Scrum Team* should recognize that such work is often waste as it detracts from the *Development Team*'s focus on the current product increment. Having the *Product Owner Team* instead handle analysis work avoids reducing valuable development time. The prototype-building tool mentioned above is a good example because it is a one-time cost with ongoing return on investment. If the *Product Owner* repeatedly asks the team to actually do the analysis instead of delivering an *Enabling Specification*, it may point to a lack of expertise on the part of the *Product Owner Team* and the team should deal with it as an impediment. The variance in this work across *Sprints* directly creates variance in the *Development Team*'s work capacity, which makes prediction difficult. In this latter case, the *Product Owner Team* should train or hire team members to fill out the skill set or achieve the right staffing level to ensure more consistent delivery of *Enabling Specification*s to the developers.

As an alternative, consider a compromise approach that can manage the *Development Team*'s time contribution to analysis (and, by extension, to other activities) as *PBI*s: Design Sprints as in *Set-Based Design*.

¶24 Sprint Planning

Confidence stars: **

...now that the team has defined and refined the *¶54 Product Backlog*, the *¶55 Product Backlog Item*s (*PBIs*) still represent only potential value. They can produce value (i.e., move to the end of the *¶41 Value Stream*) only when development makes them real. You are ready to embark on a *¶46 Sprint* to develop one or more *PBIs* to create a *¶85 Regular Product Increment*.

❖ ❖ ❖

A *Sprint* should produce a *Regular Product Increment*. Yet simply pulling *PBIs* off the top of the *Product Backlog* does not necessarily result in work that creates the *¶93 Greatest Value* or work that fits into the *Sprint*'s time box to produce the product increment.

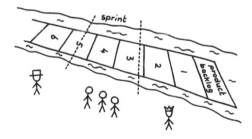

It would be nice to just work from the top of the *Product Backlog* without worrying about the work ordering, but there are several reasons that doesn't usually happen. *PBIs* are not of uniform size and the team has to create a deliverable product increment within the time box of a *Sprint*. So the team has to figure out what will fit and they may have to juggle the *PBI* ordering, and maybe even adjust some *PBI* content.

Tasks are often interdependent, and given the team's knowledge of the current product state and of the domain, it might realize that it can save time by developing feature P before feature Q, or by doing task X before task Y.

The *¶7 Scrum Team* as a whole typically does not understand *PBIs* in enough detail to completely prescribe how the *¶14 Development Team* will implement them. In fact, design of *PBIs* to that level is waste because *PBIs* might queue up undeveloped for some time, and the business and team context may change over time, making all the work you have put into the *PBIs* irrelevant. Or other *PBIs* may find their way onto the *Product Backlog*, possibly deferring some *PBIs* indefinitely. But some design thinking is in order for the *Development Team* to consider how they will implement a given *PBI*. If they do this too early, then such plans may become out-of-date, and they don't want to plan too late.

Development Team members may need to adjust their work plan during the *Sprint* as they come to understand more about business needs and technical constraints. This is difficult when working with large, monolithic *PBIs*.

Therefore:

At the beginning of every *Sprint*, the *Scrum Team* (or all the teams that together deliver a jointly developed product increment) meets to plan how it will create value during the *Sprint*. The team agrees to a *¶71 Sprint Goal* and creates a plan for what the *Development Team* will develop and how the team will develop it. This requires that the *Scrum Team* do a detailed enough design of the solution to have a high degree of confidence about how to build the product, and requires that team members feel they can complete their work plan during the *Sprint* (see *¶59 Granularity Gradient*).

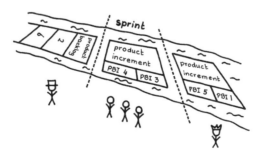

Sprint Planning is the initial activity in a *Sprint*. It is the transition along the *Value Stream* between the *Product Backlog* and the *Development Team*'s work plan.

During *Sprint Planning*, the *Scrum Team* creates the *Sprint Goal* and produces the initial version of the *¶72 Sprint Backlog*. An incidental output is an updated *Product Backlog*. If the *Product Backlog* is not yet a totally refined backlog at the beginning of *Sprint Planning* (perhaps because the *¶11 Product Owner* has added new items near the top of the backlog since last meeting with the *Development Team*), then the *Scrum Team* discusses, estimates, breaks down, and orders the new *Product Backlog Item*s to prepare for the work plan of the imminent *Sprint*.

The main activities of *Sprint Planning* are for the team to ensure the *Product Backlog* is *ready* (see *¶65 Definition of Ready*); to come to a consensus on a *Sprint Goal*; to select the *PBI*s the team forecasts it can deliver this *Sprint*; and to plan how to do that work and achieve the *Sprint Goal*. Most teams find it best to do these activities concurrently—for example, figuring out how to do work helps you understand its scope and effort required (velocity can be effective for forecasting the amount of work that the *Development Team* can complete in a *Sprint*; see Notes on Velocity on page 320). That, of course, influences how much the *Development Team* can complete in a *Sprint*.

It is important that *Sprint Planning* allow time for enough design to create a well-understood *Sprint Backlog*. But the planning should be time-boxed. A rule of thumb is that the event should take no more than four hours for a two-week *Sprint* and proportionally less for shorter *Sprint*s. If it takes longer, it takes longer—but seek kaizen opportunities to reduce the amount of time to plan and to correspondingly increase the time spent on building product.

If the *Product Owner* has not sufficiently specified a *PBI* for the *Development Team* to design its associated *¶73 Sprint Backlog Item*s, the *Development Team* should not accept it for the *Sprint* (see *¶63 Enabling Specification* or *Definition of Ready*). Inadequately specified *PBI*s are a major cause of effort bloat and subsequent *Sprint* failure. Jeff Sutherland reports on one *Scrum Team* that had a standing rule that if *PBI*s were not sufficiently specified, the team would all go to the beach. (This sent a clear message to the *Product Owner* about the *Product Backlog*!)

A key output of *Sprint Planning* is that the *Development Team* should be able to explain how it can accomplish the *Sprint Goal*. If they can explain their work, it's a good sign that they have discussed it to a good level of understanding, which raises the probability that the team actually can do it in the amount of time they estimate. A team might consider this as a measure of the effectiveness of the meeting.

As noted above, *Sprint Planning* produces the initial version of the *Sprint Backlog*. This is the initial plan the *Development Team* works from in the

Sprint, which it refines and adjusts every day at the *¶29 Daily Scrum*. The *Daily Scrum* is primarily a daily replanning event.

❖   ❖   ❖

The quality of *Sprint Planning* strongly influences the success of subsequent *Daily Scrum* events. If the *Sprint Goal* and *Sprint Backlog* are well-defined and understood, the *Development Team* is likely to have effective *Daily Scrums*, and any required replanning will be clear. A poor *Sprint Planning* activity may increase the burden on recurring *¶34 Scrum of Scrums* doing multi-team development.

The obvious outputs of *Sprint Planning* are the *Sprint Backlog* and the *Sprint Goal*. But *Sprint Planning* also strengthens the *¶117 Unity of Purpose* on page 468, and helps the *Development Team* and the *Product Owner* better understand each other's needs and motivations. This strengthens the *¶95 Community of Trust* on page 466, and cultivates *¶3 Fertile Soil*.

The team polishes the backlog not only to strive for the *Greatest Value* but out of sheer *¶38 Product Pride*.

¶25 Swarming: One-Piece Continuous Flow

Confidence stars: *

...organizations, teams, and individuals bring things to *Done* (see *¶82 Definition of Done*) by working together on them. While it is the *¶11 Product Owner*'s responsibility to order the *¶54 Product Backlog* to maximize value delivery, it is the responsibility of the *¶14 Development Team* to order the implementation of the *¶72 Sprint Backlog* to maximize flow of production. (See *¶76 Developer-Ordered Work Plan.*)

❖ ❖ ❖

Working on too many things at once can radically reduce individual effectiveness, team velocity, or enterprise well-being. It can cripple velocity and can sometimes reduce it to zero. If everyone is working on their own thing individually, they are unlikely to help each other and, in the long term, learn from each other.

The personal preferences of a team member and impediments in the work environment often cause scattered effort. A team working on multiple items at once results in excessive work in process, low process efficiency and associated delays.

> Work in process (WIP), work in progress (WIP), goods in process, or in-process inventory are a company's partially finished goods waiting for completion and eventual sale or the value of these items. These items are either just being fabricated or waiting for further processing in a queue or a buffer storage. The term is used in production and supply-chain management.

> Optimal production management aims to minimize work in process. Work in process requires storage space, represents bound capital not available for investment and carries an inherent risk of earlier expiration of shelf life of the products. A queue leading to a production step shows that the step is well buffered

for shortage in supplies from preceding steps, but may also indicate insufficient capacity to process the output from these preceding steps.[23]

Consider a team that attempts to improve throughput with parallelism, with each person working on a single ¶55 *Product Backlog Item* (*PBI*) at a time. Working alone, *Development Team* members are more likely to focus on building the item than on testing it, partly because both the expertise and appetite for testing are small relative to the creative tasks of designing and building. If multiple work items are delayed during a ¶46 *Sprint*, there is an increased risk of not bringing the *PBI*s to *Done* by the end of the *Sprint*. Even worse, in Silicon Valley and in Europe, some teams working on complex software find that not identifying and fixing a bug in a *Sprint* can turn one hour of testing at code complete to 24 hours of testing three weeks later. If the team defers testing instead of *Swarming*, something that could be delivered in a month can take two years to deliver.

Compounding the problem, Jerry Weinberg offers this rule-of-thumb model on how multitasking delays getting things done (*Quality Software Management: Volume 1, Systems Thinking [Wei92]*, p. 284):

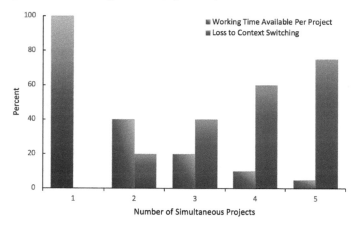

Even worse, recent brain research shows that multitasking makes you stupid as well as slow, while increasing stress and accelerating aging (*Proceedings of Agile 2007 [RL07]*).

Working on many things at once gives the illusion that things are going faster and plays on management's desire for efficiency of the individual worker. Yet, this increases the number of defects that the team must fix and test later, escalates development costs, and slips release dates.

---

23. "Work in Process." Wikipedia, https://en.wikipedia.org/wiki/Work_in_process (accessed 27 January 2019).

The team can divide work across subgroups, but each subgroup can work autonomously only to the degree that the work items are mutually independent. Items tend to be mutually coupled in a complex system, and dealing with these dependencies can block progress and add delay, though *circular* dependencies are rarely necessary when ordering work items. *Development Team* members often want to work independently to avoid stepping on each other's code, a symptom of a dysfunctional team with poor process and engineering practices. Google solved this problem by implementing a daily meeting and *Swarming* to get things *Done* (*Proceedings of Agile 2006 [Str06]*).

Therefore:

Focus maximum team effort on one item in the *Product Backlog* and complete all known work as soon as possible. Whoever takes this item is Captain of the team. Everyone must help the Captain if they can and no one can interrupt the Captain. As soon as the Captain is *Done*, whoever takes responsibility for the next backlog item is Captain.

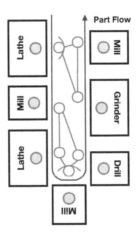

In 1947, we arranged machines in parallel lines or in an L shape and tried having one worker operate three or four machines along the processing route. We encountered strong resistance among the production workers, however, even though there was no increase in work or hours. Our craftsmen did not like the new arrangement that required them to function as multi-skilled operators. They did not like changing from "one operator, one machine" to a system of "one operator, many machines in different processes." Taiichi Ohno, The Toyota Production System, *1988, Chapter 1. Toyota Production System: Beyond Large-Scale Production [Ohn88] — Figure from Liker, The Toyota Way: 14 Management Principles from the World's Greatest Manufacturer [Lik04], 2004, Chapter 8, Figure 8–4.*

This pattern is about maximizing velocity to deliver business value by getting the team to work together. It requires a mind shift to focus on flow of production by swarming on the backlog items instead of on the efficiency of a given task. Individual efficiency does not optimize production while slack can speed things up.

Paradoxically, while *Swarming* means that the team is focusing on one *PBI* at a time, it also implies a rapid interleaving of many development activities on the item in progress. The team may do a few minutes of implementation, followed by a short increment of testing, which may actually lead to additional analysis and subsequent eddies of development until the *PBI* becomes *Done*. Carrying out one development phase at a time is another way to avoid teamwork, and *Swarming* works best when all team members bring all their talents to bear all the time.

This is a fractal pattern and applies at the enterprise level, portfolio level, team level, and the individual level; see Covey (*The 7 Habits of Highly Effective People [Cov94]*). It leads to happier teams and cultural success.

❖   ❖   ❖

You can encourage a team to Swarm by keeping the team's identity focused on the team as a whole rather than individuals. Limit or eliminate rewards for outstanding individual accomplishment. Work against a "hero culture" by eliminating overtime, overtime pay, and a work ethic that values working harder. Working together as a team on one *PBI* at a time will broaden team members into new skill sets and result in more multi-skilled individuals. It can also motivate the team to do something great every *Sprint* with a well-articulated ¶71 *Sprint Goal*.

Working the highest-priority *PBI* on the ¶44 *Scrum Board* will tend to cause individuals and teams to self-organize to maximize flow in a *Sprint*. Systematic A/S in Denmark showed how implementing this pattern doubled the productivity of every team in the company (*Proceedings of Agile 2007 [SJJ07]*). Citrix Online applied this pattern at the enterprise level and reduced release cycles from 42 months to less than 10 months resulting in substantial gains in market share for its products (*Proceedings of 43rd Hawaii International Conference on System Sciences [Gre10]*).

Implementing this pattern moves the team toward one-piece continuous flow. Toyota demonstrated that this optimizes production capacity:

> *In its ideal, one-piece flow means that parts move from one value-adding processing step directly to the next value-adding processing step, and then to the customer, without any waiting time or batching between those steps. For many*

years we called this "continuous flow production." Toyota now refers to it as "one-by-one production," perhaps because many manufacturers will point to a moving production line with parts in queue between the value-adding steps and erroneously say, "We have continuous flow, because everything is moving." Such a misinterpretation is more difficult to make when we use the phrase "one-by-one production" (Toyota Kata: Managing People for Improvement, Adaptiveness and Superior Results [Rot10], p. 45).

Working on one *Product Backlog Item* at a time makes it unnecessary to coordinate between work items in progress. Instead, the team can work on the least dependent items first.

The team continuously adjusts its tack in a *Developer-Ordered Work Plan*. They come together as one mind to modulate this direction every day in the *¶29 Daily Scrum*. However, all direction adjustments happen within the terms of the *Sprint Goal*, which itself is a rallying point that can help channel the flow of the team. Mark Gillett, an experienced executive manager and technology investor, remarks, "Teams that behave as if there is a series of tasks (and perhaps handoffs) for individuals will see less value than those who identify needs for and dynamically partner to work a *PBI* to *Done*." A team that works closely together builds a shared vision of what the product is and is able to grow pride in the product and in their achievement; see *¶38 Product Pride*.

Members of the Scrum community have also been talking about *Swarming* for many years. See, for example, Dan Rawsthorne's work (*Exploring Scrum: The Fundamentals, 2nd ed.* [RS11]).

¶26 Kaizen Pulse

Confidence stars: *

...the *¶14 Development Team* has shown sustainable performance as indicated by a dependable level of velocity (see Notes on Velocity on page 320), quality, or other measure, and now wants to go to the next level. The team's measures of capacity and quality are transparent (*¶3 Fertile Soil*), and the team wishes them to remain so, and to take pride in improving them. The team is doing kaizen and introducing improvements *¶88 One Step at a Time*.

❖ ❖ ❖

Because it takes time to establish a statistically sound baseline, it's difficult to show improvement from minute to minute, hour to hour, or even from *¶46 Sprint* to *Sprint*. Further, *Sprint*s are usually the granularity of the most popular measures of *Development Team* effectiveness, and particularly of velocity. The same is true for other noble desirables such as, for example, product value, value per estimation point, product quality, or team passion (see *¶91 Happiness Metric*).

In the end, Scrum—like the Toyota Production System—is fundamentally about only two things: kaizen mind and people. Improvement is important and the phrase "continuous improvement" emerges frequently from pundits' lips. Yet truly continuous improvement has a paradoxical problem. It's important to be able to measure an improvement, at least to know if a given change made things better or worse. We always measure improvement relative to some baseline, and any single process measurement we take at any point in time is subject to the vagaries of process variation. That means that we need a statistical baseline as a reference for improvement.

More importantly, there is a crucial human side to process improvement: people, as groups, take time to absorb change. It's O.K. to carry an ongoing consciousness of the need to improve, but you can't continually focus on improving everything. Internalizing improved development approaches and adapting new techniques takes time. In the end, good production is a matter of practices of habit, and habit formation itself takes time. So at the *¶29 Daily Scrum*, the *Development Team* members make tactical adjustments toward the *¶71 Sprint Goal* more than they dwell on changing long-term practices, habits, or behaviors.

If the velocity (or other measure) is varying wildly anyhow, you'll never be able to measure the benefit or damage done by a kaizen program. If you make multiple changes at once, you can't know which ones contributed to changing the velocity—or value, defect reduction, or any other measure of value.

Therefore:

Alternate periods of controlled velocity with spikes of process improvement. We might call this *continual improvement* instead of *continuous improvement*. Start by establishing a velocity baseline and bringing it into statistical control (a rule of thumb for the velocity is to reduce its variance to within 20 percent). Then introduce a single new improvement into product development. The *Development Team*—or, as suitable, the *¶11 Product Owner* or *¶19 ScrumMaster*—commit to Intentional Practice as Jon Jagger describes in *97 Things Every Programmer Should Know [Hen10]*, pp. 44–45. Practice the improvement and make it routine through tireless repetition.

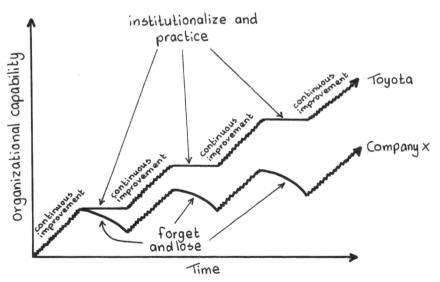

From Takeuchi et al., *Extreme Toyota: Radical Contradictions That Drive Success at the World's Best Manufacturer [OSTD08 TOS08]*, p. 84.

Constant reflection is important as the *¶7 Scrum Team* members together introduce changes and evaluate their potential for long-term improvement.

Some changes have unforeseeable liabilities and, of course, the team should reverse any decision to adopt practices which experience proves detrimental to velocity or to long-term value.

❖   ❖   ❖

The *Sprint* is the major instrument of strategic kaizen in Scrum. When the velocity stabilizes during the period of Intentional Practice, the team can either enjoy a subsequent period of predictable *Sprint* delivery or can prepare for another velocity-increasing kaizen. There will be turbulence as the team climbs to a new level by improving the process and team dynamics, or by improving the product. Both the ¶36 *Sprint Retrospective* and the ¶35 *Sprint Review* offer opportunities to evaluate the team's convergence on a new plateau; however, such evaluations need to take place over several successive reviews to increase confidence in the stability of the results (i.e., to ensure that they aren't temporary). While the *Daily Scrum* can effect *change*, *Sprint Retrospective*s and *Sprint Review*s effect *transition*—and strategic changes are lasting changes. For a change to be discontinuous is neither sufficient nor necessary to qualify it as a strategic change.

We can talk about two kinds of velocity kaizen: those that reduce variance in velocity, and those that increase velocity. The same principle applies to any measured value indicator. Many kaizens are more appropriate to bringing the process into statistical control than to increasing performance or value. These kinds of kaizens are not only appropriate, but also important, when the *Scrum Team* is trying to reduce variance in velocity. Some of the most common reasons for variance in velocity include lack of ¶10 *Cross-Functional Team*s, management interference with production, and poor requirements. Kaizens that mitigate these problems can help bring a team to a good baseline.

Complex systems are full of surprises. Change is rarely good for its own sake, and the best-intentioned changes often have negative consequences when reality comes home to roost. Strive to measure the value of the change (value, velocity, consistency, defect density), and be prepared to retrench if the change actually makes things worse. Go beyond single-dimensional measures: your efforts may increase velocity and decrease value (such as ROI; see *Value and ROI*) at the same time, and you'll never notice the decrease in overall value if you measure only velocity. So while Piagetian learning provides a model that is monotonically increasing over time, moving from ever higher plateaus to the next level, the learning models of Keegan (*Higher Psychology: Approaches and Methods, 2nd ed. [Kee09]*) are more realistic and recognize that learning is a complex process rich with setbacks. To reiterate: The *Scrum Team* should continuously monitor ¶50 *ROI-Ordered Backlog* and other value throughout improvement cycles, because velocity alone is not an indicator of increased value. It is important to remember that velocity is a tool for prediction rather than for value, and that value is the end goal.

The pattern *¶70 Updated Velocity* is about establishing a new velocity baseline.

Contrast with *¶92 Scrumming the Scrum.*

In terms of pattern theory, this is more of a "meta-pattern" than a proper pattern. It tempers the way that the team uses the fundamental process (make local change, review, reflect; or the plan-do-check-act (PDCA) or plan-do-study-act (PDSA) cycle) on which the whole of incremental pattern practice is based. This pattern combines the structural improvements of organizational change with the time dimension of progress by introducing statistical variation. It adds a dimension of statistical control to the "check" part of PDCA, which is too easy to consider as being a static analysis of the system state. It is more in line with Deming's updating of the term to PDSA, which begs the intellectual investment of *study* rather than just honoring the formality of an inspection.

A team that improves its processes is likely to improve its product, and combined with ongoing product advances, *Kaizen Pulse* is a major contributor to *¶38 Product Pride* and helps the team achieve the *¶93 Greatest Value* in the long term.

Related to the *Kaizen Pulse* cycle is the need to alternate between more radical, structure-changing improvements (sometimes called *kaikaku*) and the subsequent refinements on those changes, which are usually more incremental in nature (for which the term *kaizen* (カイゼン) is invoked more narrowly than for its usual Japanese use and meaning (改善)). See Kaizen and Kaikaku on page 101.

The basic pattern comes from *Extreme Toyota: Radical Contradictions That Drive Success at the World's Best Manufacturer [OSTD08 TOS08].*

¶27 Remove the Shade

Alias: Let the Light In

Confidence stars: *

...you have *¶15 Stable Teams* and have tried to balance the workload across team members (see *¶131 Distribute Work Evenly* on page 470), develop in pairs (*¶126 Developing in Pairs* on page 469), and have a good apprenticeship program (see *¶111 Apprenticeship* on page 468).

❖ ❖ ❖

You notice that team members always postpone decisions and important work until one especially skilled *¶14 Development Team* member is present, but as the *¶19 ScrumMaster* you want all team members to perform optimally according to their abilities.

The skilled team member is always the one the organization calls for when particularly important work looms, because everyone knows that individual will likely drive such decisions in the end. This team member often ends up playing a Hero role, being the one called in when the business needs a fast solution. The other *Development Team* members tend to give up on complicated assignments because they know the Hero can do it better and the organization will ask for the Hero's opinion anyway.

Sometimes a Hero can act like a busy parent who finds it easier to do things alone instead of helping others to learn. So the Hero will be very productive while the other team members work in the shade without the necessary light to grow. At the same time the Hero risks burning out.

These scenarios create a lack of courage and motivation in the *Development Team* members. They will stop growing and the team becomes more like a one-man army with supporters than a self-organizing team where everyone contributes something of value.

Therefore:

Remove the Hero from the team so the rest of the team can grow, like flowers getting light after a big tree falls in the storm. Find another outlet for the Hero's talents, perhaps elsewhere in the company or organization.

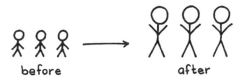

before   after

development team

✧ ✧ ✧

It is not an easy solution to implement. Management can be upset if they are close to the Hero. The Hero could be upset by the removal because it could feel like a degradation. Productivity will go down while the team is learning to take over.

We can relate an experience from a Danish company where a team had a Scrum team member that did five times more work than any other team member—and didn't have time to go to the *¶29 Daily Scrum*. After the *ScrumMaster* removed this productive team member from the team, the team's velocity doubled. This is just one example out of many where the overall velocity in a *¶7 Scrum Team* increases after removing "a hero."

It may be unpopular, and therefore harder, to remove the shading team member if the *¶11 Product Owner* has come to depend too much on that individual. That makes it harder to remove him or her. On the other hand, it also exposes that the team is vulnerable to losing a single individual, and that perhaps the team should work harder on raising its *truck number* to reduce the risk of dependency on a single individual (see *¶123 Moderate Truck Number* on page 469).

Normally it is the *ScrumMaster*, as owner of process issues, who owns this issue. Good *ScrumMaster*s will try to mitigate the problem by coaching the individual or by taking other measures short of removing the person from the team. However, in the end, it is the *ScrumMaster* who has the authority to remove a shading member from the team. A good *ScrumMaster* may decide what course of action to take after consultation with all team members. If the individual causing the shade is the *ScrumMaster*, the rest of the *Scrum Team* has the power to dismiss the individual.

The *ScrumMaster* of a team that shrank from 20 to 5 said in an interview:

> Those who wanted to try something else were allowed to leave the team. But sometimes there was an outcry when I presented it for the team. "Now we will die, we can't do it. If he leaves we will have to give up" they said. I told them that I believed that the rest of the team will grow. If there is a strong architect then there will be a small flower behind him. When we cut down this tree just wait and see I believe that you will grow. And that is what I have seen happening.

This pattern goes along with *Moderate Truck Number* on page 469.

Letting everyone on the team share the work and have a sense of key contribution elevates the team's sense of self-worth (see *¶118 Team Pride* on page 469). Giving the key jobs to just one person, or having a team member who otherwise demoralizes the rest of the team, can destroy it.

In some cases, there may be room elsewhere for the Hero to add value, perhaps as an individual contributor (see *¶112 Solo Virtuoso* on page 468).

A lighter-weight version of this pattern is to limit the work of the Hero to only within his or her realm of expertise. The *ScrumMaster* can agree with the Hero that the Hero will avoid the kind of work at which he or she typically excels or in areas where the team has come to depend on the Hero, and to take on other work instead. The Hero can still be valuable as a coach or resource to others in areas of expertise provided that the role is limited to advising. *Developing in Pairs* on page 469 is often a good transition.

¶28 Pop the Happy Bubble

Alias: Beyond the Happy Bubble

...the *¶7 Scrum Team* has overcome some impediments and is working more effectively than before.

❖ ❖ ❖

Teams can get into a state where they are satisfied with the improvements they have made. However, this allows dysfunctions to persist. It is like a bubble of happiness surrounds them and insulates them from unpleasant but true information.

Many organizations adopt Scrum in a crisis where the time they need to develop a new version of their product is far longer than the market is willing to wait. After the initial adjustments to Scrum, the team delivers *¶85 Regular Product Increment*s. The transition from no product to any product is such a significant success that it inhibits removing any other impediments because none of the observed impediments are of the magnitude of the previous state. The team does not feel it is worth putting the effort into resolving such comparatively small problems.

In environments where there is support for ongoing improvement, a successful team often cannot see how to improve. Over time, it gets harder and harder to improve. The team has harvested all the low-hanging fruit. It may be the team has reached the limit of its knowledge or experience and cannot see there is an alternative to how it is working.

The *¶36 Sprint Retrospective*s can become self-congratulatory affairs that produce few (if any) process changes, or that produce superficial changes with no real impact on the team. Eventually the team ceases to hold *Sprint Retrospective*s because it sees no way to improve—apart from stopping to perpetuate the shared myth of great performance.

Some teams may see no way to improve because all the impediments they have are "outside the team." When they fail to achieve the ¶71 *Sprint Goal*, they always ascribe it to one-time, exceptional events. And there is always some one-time event. They feel that if only some other "they" could do something about this, the team would improve.

Facing up to problems is aversive and resolving impediments can force teams to have uncomfortable conversations or to make difficult decisions. It is natural for people to avoid such unpleasant experiences. This can be the case in a team that is highly social cohesive where everyone likes to work with each other and just wants to get along. This makes it difficult to acknowledge problems. In cultures that teach people not to rock the boat, it becomes more and more difficult to acknowledge problems. Where there isn't the courage and determination to accept problems and change there can never be any improvement.

A team may be living in a Happy Bubble, but one of the biggest challenges is that bubbles are transparent—it is very hard for a team to see the Happy Bubble that surrounds it. It almost always takes an outside perspective to pick up on such behavior. The team needs to seek feedback from independent observers. This is something teams may not want to seek. The observers will need to have the courage to be honest with team members and deal with the unpleasantness of results of their feedback.

On the other hand, all teams have the capacity to improve. They just may not see it.

Therefore:

Jolt the team into awareness of its situation (pop the Happy Bubble): force the team to confront its happy-bubble-ness by showing the members important deficiencies. Then, together with the team, plan actions to improve. Create a culture in the team of relentless, continuous self-examination and improvement.

This is a pattern of repair—the best situation is to avoid getting in the Happy Bubble in the first place. When someone (like the ¶19 *ScrumMaster*) raises an issue that everyone is ignoring, challenge the team with the issue and ask them how they plan to resolve it. The key is getting the team to admit it has a problem in the first place.

The best person who can take the team beyond the Happy Bubble is someone who is on the *Scrum Team* and who is willing and able to bring up difficult issues. This person must be able to see the issues, raise the issues and instigate change. The person must have the respect and trust of the *Scrum Team* and maintain the team's autonomy and self-organization. The *Scrum-Master* is in a unique position to pop the Happy Bubble because of his or her perspective on the whole team, and because of the objectivity that owes to the *ScrumMaster* practice of removing him- or herself from development decisions. However, when the *ScrumMaster* confronts the team, the message must be that *we* (not *you*) are not performing well enough, and what will *we* do about it.

What if the *ScrumMaster* is part of the problem? If it is only the *ScrumMaster*, the team can take care of it internally. However, because the *ScrumMaster* has the broader process view, if the *ScrumMaster* is in the Happy Bubble, it is very likely the whole team is also in the Happy Bubble. In this case, the ¶11 *Product Owner* may have to take drastic measures, such as bringing in an outside perspective, either informally or formally. This is a last resort for times when the Happy Bubble is causing serious disruption and other measures have failed.

An external bubble-popper is inferior to someone within the *Scrum Team*, but may be necessary if the entire team is unaware of the Happy Bubble. Anyone in a leadership role can initiate the involvement of this external bubble-popper. It is crucial that there is hard data to back up claims of the team's performance and the existence of a Happy Bubble. The fact that the team is in a Happy Bubble means that they may be skeptical about even having a problem. Confront team members with data so they can't argue it away. The best role external to the team is probably a *ScrumMaster* from another team, particularly if the *ScrumMaster* is also blind to the dysfunction. This role is unique in that it is both objective and neutral and can see the whole picture. This provides a mirror to the team so it can understand the implications of its plateauing behavior. The *ScrumMaster* plays a questioning role. However, a *ScrumMaster* who is too strong and tries to force a specific solution can disrupt the team's self-organization. Where possible, use Socratic questioning.

❖   ❖   ❖

The hoped-for result is that the team becomes aware of its deficiencies, recommits to improve, and takes steps to improve. The most basic result is awareness, and that may be the most important. Popping the Happy Bubble raises awareness of problems that the team might address with ¶92 *Scrumming the Scrum*. Conversely, the patterns of *Scrumming the Scrum*, *Sprint Retrospectives* and ¶31 *Norms of Conduct* help prevent happy bubbles in the first place.

The ideal result is that the team learns why it got in the Happy Bubble in the first place and takes steps to prevent the formation of future Happy Bubbles.

Some people might not enjoy being jolted out of their Happy Bubble. They may perceive it as unreasonable pressure to perform at an unwarranted level. In extreme cases, people might leave the team. An effect of this pressure may be a sudden disruption that removes the euphoric feeling that the team has been under, resulting in a lack of motivation and potentially harming the team dynamics with people leaving the organization as a result.

The most possible positive long-term consequence of repeatedly popping the Happy Bubble is that the team gains an appreciation for its ability to reflect and improve. This is a rightful source of *Team Pride* (see *¶118 Team Pride* on page 469).

¶29 Daily Scrum

Confidence stars: **

...a *¶7 Scrum Team* has come together and it is ready to start, or has started a *¶46 Sprint*. As such, the *¶14 Development Team* has created a *¶72 Sprint Backlog* and is working to achieve the *¶71 Sprint Goal*. Yet, in the words of German Field Marshall Helmuth von Moltke, "no plan of operations extends with any certainty beyond the first contact with the main hostile force." In short, plans created during *¶24 Sprint Planning* become almost immediately obsolete.

❖ ❖ ❖

The team makes progress in a *Sprint* by finishing *¶73 Sprint Backlog Items*, but given the complexity of the work, the characteristics, size, and quantity of tasks change frequently—sometimes minute by minute.

For example, alternative solutions, needed but unknown knowledge, hidden tasks, misunderstood requirements, requirements requiring further elaboration, dependencies among developers, or problems in the form of blockages may emerge in the team's day-to-day work. The problem is how to cope with these issues in an effective way.

There are 9×10^{157} ways to order 100 tasks, yet only a few of these ways will put the team "in the zone" where work becomes effortless and velocity significantly increases (see Notes on Velocity on page 320). Because of the changing nature of the work, the team needs to adopt a new ordering at least once a day to move beyond mediocrity.

In addition to the work, team member absences (such as a sick day) may force the team to reconsider its work plan.

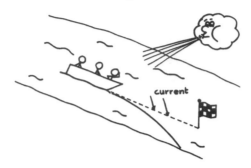

On the other hand, too much replanning and reestimating wastes time and suffocates developers. But too little replanning and reestimating leads to blockages that cause delays or obsolete plans that no longer represent reality.

Individuals can make decisions very quickly, but in a team environment it is impossible for individuals to take decisions in isolation. You need engagement with everyone who might be affected by the decision. It takes time to get agreement from all such parties.

An individual may need to bring up an issue to the whole team. But it may be difficult to find an opportunity to do so. In particular, issues continue to be impediments until the team fixes them.

Therefore:

Have a short event every day to replan the *Sprint*, to optimize the chances first of meeting the *Sprint Goal* and second of completing all *Sprint Backlog Items*. Strictly time-box the meeting to keep focus on the daily plan and to avoid robbing time from development. Focus on the next day's work but keep the remainder of the *Sprint* in mind.

Keep the meeting to 15 minutes or less. The team manages itself to its time box, and the *¶19 ScrumMaster* will enforce this aspect of the process if necessary. Many teams stand during the meeting to emphasize the short duration of the meeting. The team can continue afterward to take care of business unfinished in the *Daily Scrum*, but to spend more than 15 minutes a day on such replanning is a sign of need for Kaizen and Kaikaku on page 101.

It is vital that every member of the *Development Team* attend. In the rare occasion that a developer needs to be absent because of illness or conflict, it probably doesn't make sense to send a substitute; the team will bring the developer up to date at the next *Daily Scrum*, at the latest.

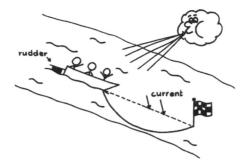

In order to plan, you must know where you are, as well as what problems are standing in the way. And you need a complete picture. One popular technique is for each person in the *Development Team* to answer the following three questions:

- What did I do yesterday that helped the *Development Team* meet the *Sprint Goal*?

- What will I do today to help the *Development Team* meet the *Sprint Goal*?

- Do I see any impediment that hinders me or the *Development Team* from meeting the *Sprint Goal*?

Note that as developers voice impediments, there is a natural tendency to delve into them and explore possible solutions. But this meeting is for replanning and decision-making, not for problem-solving. Instead, a few members of the *Development Team* might agree to meet during the day to work out the solution—thus not wasting everyone else's time. They will report what they have done at the next day's *Daily Scrum*.

Of course, impediments often force changes to the plan. So the team adjusts its plan for the day to get around the blockages. That is one thing this meeting is all about.

This is the *Development Team*'s meeting. People outside the *Development Team* may attend the *Daily Scrum* at the invitation of the *Development Team*. The *Development Team* may wish to consider that there is a spirit of transparency in Scrum. But on the other hand, outsiders may influence the meeting by their very presence. In any case, only the *Development Team* actively participates in the meeting. This applies to the *¶11 Product Owner* as well as any other person not a member of the *Development Team*.

The *ScrumMaster* may attend the meeting at any time, especially in the early days of Scrum in the organization, mainly to enforce time-boxing and other aspects of the process. But too often the *Development Team* will start treating the *ScrumMaster* as a manager at these meetings. In that case it is better that *ScrumMaster*s excuse themselves from these meetings, or that they take on the role of a *¶30 ScrumMaster Incognito* when they do attend.

The *Daily Scrum* results in an updated *Sprint Backlog*, as well as associated *¶56 Information Radiator*s. However, it is crucial to understand that the *Daily Scrum* is a replanning meeting and not a status meeting. Radiated information is a byproduct of rather than the aim of the meeting.

❖   ❖   ❖

The ethos of the *Daily Scrum* is a reality check: will we meet the *Sprint Goal*? The result of the *Daily Scrum* is a new daily plan grounded in reality, and generates a team that is more prone to cooperate and that has a better shared vision and understanding of what they are doing together. The team becomes better attuned to the landscape of impediments in which it is working.

The ritual of *Daily Scrum*s helps a sense of team identity emerge from a group of people. It brings them together to refocus on their shared purpose and common identity. It reinforces team morale (see *¶118 Team Pride* on page 469). In some way, it is a daily version of an earlier published pattern that advises team members to first coordinate the broad issues over the table before drilling down into work tasks individually: see *¶130 Face-to-Face Before Working Remotely* on page 470.

Special activities such as *¶32 Emergency Procedure* will likely originate from discussions in the *Daily Scrum*.

*Daily Scrum*s have additional benefits as well:

- Reduces time wasted because the team makes impediments visible daily;
- Helps find opportunities for coordination because everyone knows what everyone else is working on;
- Reinforces a shared vision of the *Sprint Goal*;
- Promotes team jelling by ensuring at least one global interaction every day;
- Promotes knowledge sharing and the identification of knowledge gaps;
- Increases the overall sense of urgency;
- Encourages trust and honesty among developers through a verifiable daily status; and,
- Strengthens the culture of the *Development Team* through shared rituals and encouragement of active participation.

The idea of *stand-up meetings* has a long tradition, and was reportedly used at events where Queen Victoria of England was present: it was necessary to stand in the presence of the queen. The Scrum practice has its roots in Coplien's analysis of the Borland Quattro Pro for Windows (QPW) project (*Dr. Dobb's Journal of Software Tools 19 [CE94]*, pp. 88–97), which had a remarkable track record in rapidly producing value and quality. Bob Warfield was running the project at the time and offers the following reflection:

> It was a crucial part of our productivity, and today it is a cornerstone of Agile/Scrum where it is called a "Standing" meeting or a "Stand Up" meeting. Apparently some folks took it a bit literally and started doing the meeting without chairs. That's fine, I think I'll keep the chairs in my meetings, but they're short enough that not having chairs shouldn't be a problem. I used to tell people to get them to the meeting on time that there'd be two fewer chairs than attendees, but that was just my lame joke and I don't recall actually ever doing that.[24]

The first Scrum team implemented the daily meeting in February 1994 based on the QPW initiative. The Scrum team concluded that the daily meetings at Borland were instrumental in achieving extraordinary performance. The Scrum team implemented daily meetings during its second monthly *Sprint*. In March 1994, the team pulled the same amount of work into the *Sprint* as the previous month, and completed it already during the first week. Since then, effective daily meetings have significantly improved the velocity of Scrum teams worldwide.

One last note: Laypersons often equate "doing Scrum" with having the *Daily Scrum*. While the *Daily Scrum*, at the ¶44 *Scrum Board*, is one of the most noticeable events of Scrum organizations, there is much more to Scrum than can be characterized by the use of any set of tools. By analogy, kicking a football around in a park can look a lot like playing football, but it isn't football. This pattern refers to many other patterns that represent crucial components of the Scrum framework, and yet those, too, are only a starting point.

This pattern is an evolution of the previously published ¶134 *Stand-Up Meeting* on page 470.

---

24. Robert Warfield. "How I Helped Start the Agile/Scrum Movement 20 Years Ago." Smoothspan Blog, 2 October 2014, https://smoothspan.com/2014/10/02/how-i-helped-start-the-agilescrum-movement-20-years-ago/ (accessed 14 February 2019).

¶30 ScrumMaster Incognito

Confidence stars: *

Find the ScrumMaster in this picture.

...you have a *¶19 ScrumMaster* who is serving a *¶14 Development Team*. The *Development Team* is supposed to use the *¶29 Daily Scrum* to share information on progress and to adjust the direction of the *¶72 Sprint Backlog*, to coordinate remaining work in the *¶46 Sprint*.

❖   ❖   ❖

At the *Daily Scrum*, the *Development Team* members address the *ScrumMaster* instead of discussing issues with each other. The *Development Team* members repeatedly await direction or approval before acting. This implies that they are neither taking ownership of the event nor acting as a team.

Scrum *Development Team* members are in the best position to know the details of implementation planning. Far too often, developers play it safe by just using the meeting to report current status to the *ScrumMaster* instead of taking decisions to replan the *Sprint*. This may be a habit from a former Project Manager relationship, or it may reflect the team's misunderstanding of the *ScrumMaster* role. If I am a developer at the *Daily Scrum* and I say something, I probably will focus my words on the one person who I am pretty sure is listening (because they insisted on having the meeting), so the tendency in a weak team might be to address the *ScrumMaster*. The dysfunction may go so far that the team expects explicit direction from the *ScrumMaster*.

Therefore:

As the owner of the Scrum process, it is the *ScrumMaster*'s job to ensure the team takes ownership of the *Daily Scrum*.

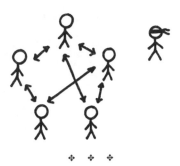

❖ ❖ ❖

One way to remove this problem is for the *ScrumMaster* to become invisible. For example the *ScrumMaster* can move to stand behind a person who persists in reporting status, or can just quietly leave the room. Another way is to educate the *Development Team* members on why it is important that they take responsibility.

The *Daily Scrum* is about inspecting the progress in the current *Sprint* and adapting the work plan to reach the *¶71 Sprint Goal*. The *Development Team* therefore owns the *Daily Scrum*. The *ScrumMaster* may still attend, but will not intervene in the *Development Team*'s planning unless asked—and then never by directing them or prejudicing their judgment on organizing the work. (The *ScrumMaster* may intervene on issues of process, such as time-boxing, but it is still best that the developers handle even these issues themselves.)

This relationship between the *Development Team* and the *ScrumMaster* of course extends beyond the *Daily Scrum* to all aspects of *how* the team builds the product.

Building the intrinsic motivation to take responsibility to plan their own work requires that the team is confident and that its members be invested in the results. Both of these are preconditions for cutting the apron strings to the *ScrumMaster*, and each of these grows as the team becomes more autonomous (see *¶16 Autonomous Team*) and boosts its self-esteem (see *¶118 Team Pride* on page 469).

The *ScrumMaster* need not be present at the *Daily Scrum*. The *ScrumMaster* makes the benefit of the *Daily Scrum* clear to the team members so that they themselves take ownership of its result.

¶31 Norms of Conduct

...a new *¶7 Scrum Team* has come together and is working as an *¶16 Autonomous Team.*

❖   ❖   ❖

A *Scrum Team* benefits from a common agreement among its members about what they aspire to become, how they will make decisions, how they will provide feedback to each other, and what they collectively value.

Every member of a *Scrum Team* has preconceived notions about how to behave, rooted in their previous experience and their understanding of the present culture. Such notions generally go unspoken, either because people just assume that everyone else shares the same notions, or because they aren't even aware that they have them. But different peoples' norms of behavior can conflict, leading to misunderstandings and distrust.

A team will rapidly (within minutes: *Academy of Management Journal 32 [Ger89]*) develop norms whether this is done explicitly or not. When the team does not *explicitly* develop norms it is only by luck that the team norms will support effective teamwork.

A *¶17 Self-Organizing Team* that is unable to get all issues out on the table will leave things unsaid. Questions will remain unanswered and the team will miss the opportunity to evaluate possible solutions.

Therefore:

The *Scrum Team* agrees to norms of conduct (expectations about acceptable behaviors; see *Annual Review of Psychology 41 [LM90]*) to enable it to grow into high performance.

As a example, we can relate the experience of a team comprising people from several hierarchical levels. There were, for example, professors that were part of the team. Because of the hierarchical relationship nobody felt safe enough to challenge the professors when promises were broken, or even during team discussions. After a Norms of Conduct session, the team became a safe environment and now knew how to engage in productive conflict. The team came up with the following Norms of Conduct:

OPENNESS

We see it as professionalism to hold each other accountable when we do not follow up on our promises.

We believe that proactively informing the team of possible delays is our duty.

COURAGE

We see asking for help as a sign of strength and professional behavior.

RESPECT

We expect that every team member is accountable to all others.

We value and are thankful for remarks and criticism from all team members.

The ideal time to create Norms of Conduct is the moment the team first comes together, as the *Scrum Team* forms. A group can best express its norms in terms of what people can and should do rather than in terms of behaviors they should avoid. The norms provide safety because people can refer to them in *¶36 Sprint Retrospective*s when tension rises in the team.

❖　❖　❖

With the safety to engage in productive conflict, the *Scrum Team* is ready to grow into high performance. This will result in an increasing *¶91 Happiness Metric*. Taking ownership of the norms of local culture, and honoring them, is a fundamental source of *Team Pride* (see *¶118 Team Pride* on page 469).

Try to broaden the scope of the most fundamental principles of work and community, as in *¶13 Development Partnership*. See also *¶95 Community of Trust* on page 466.

Many organizations have *working agreements* which tend to address team operations, while Norms of Conduct is more about values and human behavior. The two may exist side by side in any organization.

¶32 Emergency Procedure

Alias: Stop the Line

Jeff Sutherland's colleague Ed Atterbury getting shot down over Hanoi by a SAM Missile. You can see him bailing out!

...companies, teams, and individuals often find their efforts are failing to deliver on time and the *¶43 Sprint Burndown Chart* shows failure is virtually certain. Rapid identification of problems and quick response is fundamental to the spirit of agility.

❖   ❖   ❖

Problems arise in the middle of a *¶46 Sprint* due to emergent requirements or unanticipated changes. By mid-*Sprint*, it may be obvious that the *¶14 Development Team* cannot complete the *¶72 Sprint Backlog* successfully. The team is high on the *Sprint Burndown Chart* and sees that it cannot achieve the *¶71 Sprint Goal* at the current rate of getting things done.

Causes of *Sprint* dysfunction are legion and this pattern focuses primarily on the top three of these common problems:

- Emergent requirements
- Technical problems
- Loss of critical people or capabilities
- Overestimated capacity (use *¶66 Yesterday's Weather*)
- Unplanned interruptions (use *¶33 Illegitimus Non Interruptus*)
- Previous work not *Done* (use *¶82 Definition of Done*)
- *¶11 Product Owner* changes backlog (use *Product Owner*)
- Management interference (use *¶6 Involve the Managers* and *¶37 MetaScrum*)

Agility requires rapid response to change, and that means making problems visible as early as possible. Unfortunately, new teams and average teams often do not want problems to become visible. In particular, they do not want to stop work, fix problems, and risk criticism. At the first NUMMI (New United Motor Manufacturing, Inc) Toyota plant in America, Japanese management visited the plant after six months and saw that employees were afraid to pull the *andon* (lamp) cord—the cord that causes a trouble lamp to turn on and that starts a countdown timer to stop the production line. Workers had not stopped the line enough to fix their impediments. The management pulled the *andon* cord to stop the production line then and there, to communicate to the workers that their biggest impediment was their reluctance to stop the line. Stopping the line makes problems visible so they are fixed properly. "No problem is a problem" is the Japanese management mantra (*MIT Sloan Management Review 51 [Sho10]*, pp. 63–68).

The team must consult the *Product Owner* when things are not going well. Not only that, the *Development Team* should agree with the *Product Owner* on how to quickly address major problems that affect reaching the *Sprint Goal*.

Therefore:

When high on the burndown, try a technique used routinely by pilots. When bad things happen, execute the *Emergency Procedure* designed specifically for the problem.

Do not delay execution while trying to figure out what is wrong or what to do. In a fighter aircraft, you could be dead in less time than it takes to figure out what is going on. It is the responsibility of the *¶19 ScrumMaster* to make sure the team immediately executes the Scrum *Emergency Procedure*, preferably by mid-*Sprint*, when things are going off-track. This will require careful coordination with the *Product Owner*, yet kaizen mind requires execution of this pattern even when the *Product Owner* is not available. Great teams act without permission and ask for forgiveness later (see *¶95 Community of Trust* on page 466).

Scrum Emergency Procedure: (do only as much as necessary)

1. Change the way the team does the work. Do something different.
2. Get help, usually by offloading backlog to someone else.
3. Reduce scope.
4. Abort the *Sprint* and replan.
5. Inform management how the emergency affects release dates.

Teams often want to reduce scope when they encounter difficulty. Great teams find a way to instead execute a different strategy to achieve the *Sprint Goal*. In the 2005–6 football (soccer) season, John Terry, Chelsea's captain and center back, had to take over as goalkeeper in a game against Reading after

Petr Cech suffered a fractured skull, and then the substitute goalkeeper who replaced him, Carlo Cuddicini, was carried off unconscious before halftime. Terry made two fine saves and Chelsea won the game 2–0. Similarly in software, adopting new practices that remove waste can multiply performance while drastically cutting effort.

When multiple teams are working on the same products, one team can often pass backlog to another team who has slack. The company PatientKeeper, a pioneer in agile development in the medical sector, automated this strategy (*Proceedings of Agile Development Conference (ADC'05) [Sut05]*). If a team was behind, it could assign *¶73 Sprint Backlog Item*s to another team. If the second team could not take them, they passed it to a third team. If the third team could not take them, all three met to decide what to do. This automatically leveled the loading of backlog across teams so they could all finish together.

Reducing scope early so the team can finish planned work is better than coasting into failure. The organization can inspect and adapt to problems rather than be surprised. See *¶74 Teams That Finish Early Accelerate Faster*.

Aborting the *Sprint* (stop the line) may be the best option, particularly if the team consistently fails to deliver. Only the *Product Owner* may decide whether to abort the *Sprint*: as bad as things may be, the *Product Owner* may judge that the business payoff may not be worth it, or that aborting the *Sprint* may otherwise have long-term negative consequences in the market or the business.

After terminating the *Sprint* the team typically convenes a brief *¶24 Sprint Planning* for an abbreviated *Sprint* (to stay on cadence as per *¶47 Organizational Sprint Pulse*; see also *¶77 Follow the Moon*) to achieve the *Sprint Goal*, if possible, and to deliver as much value as possible. Alternatively, the team may convene a more protracted *¶36 Sprint Retrospective* to explore and rectify problems in the environment and the team's Scrum implementation, and then replan and move on to the next *Sprint*. But, again, much of the value in *Sprint* termination comes in making it publicly visible that there are fundamental impediments that keep the team from doing its job. A visible problem is one that the team can fix.

Sprint termination sends a strong message throughout the organization that something is wrong and increases the capability of removing impediments that cause failure. One playful Scrum tradition (or at least metaphor) is the "Abnormal Termination of Sprint Ceremony" which is ostensibly carried out in the lobby of corporate headquarters, where the *Development Team* members gather to lay on their backs, scream, and flail their arms and legs in the air to let off steam. The intent is to make it visible that the *Product Owner* has abrogated the team's commitment.

The *¶7 Scrum Team* executes this pattern, and it is particularly useful for high-performing teams. For teams that are serious about kaizen (see Kaizen and Kaikaku on page 101), Scrum is an extreme sport and they enter into a *Sprint* with some risk in order to go faster. Their primary risk is emergent requirements or unexpected technical problems as the team has addressed most other causes of failure. The team may need to use this pattern every third or fourth *Sprint*, particularly when implementing new technologies and pushing the state of the art. However, for most emergencies, great teams will recover and meet *Sprint Goal*s. And if they stop the line (abort the *Sprint*) they will poka-yoke (*Toyota Kata: Managing People for Improvement, Adaptiveness and Superior Results [Rot10]*) their process so the same problem does not recur.

> *Poka-yoke (ポカヨケ) [poka joke] is a Japanese term that means "fail-safing" or "mistake-proofing." A poka-yoke is any mechanism in a lean manufacturing process that helps an equipment operator avoid (yokeru) mistakes (poka). Its purpose is to eliminate product defects by preventing, correcting, or drawing attention to human errors as they occur.* [25]

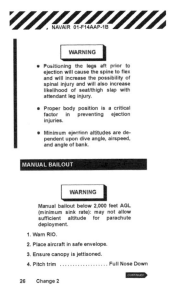

Making problems visible is part of kaizen mind; see *Kaizen and Kaikaku*.

❖ ❖ ❖

---

25. "Poke-yoke." Wikipedia, https://en.wikipedia.org/wiki/Poka-yoke, 19 May 2018 (accessed 6 June 2018).

The team will learn to rapidly respond to change in a disciplined way and overcome challenges. In many organizations, when things are not going well, teams are not thinking clearly and are frustrated and demotivated. They fail to understand the cause of their problems and the way to fix them. Executing the *Emergency Procedure* will train the team to focus on success and systematically remove impediments. Great teams will surprise themselves with their ability to overcome adversity and move from strength to strength. It increases chances for successfully delivering a *¶85 Regular Product Increment* both in the short term and long term. The team will feel it is doing all it can when using *Emergency Procedure* to get back on the right track, out of both professional pride (see *¶118 Team Pride* on page 469) and *¶38 Product Pride*.

You can use *Emergency Procedure* in a more disciplined way to raise transparency into unmanaged requirements with the pattern *Illegitimus Non Interruptus*.

See also *¶97 Take No Small Slips* on page 467.

This pattern anticipates use by highly disciplined teams. If a team is using this too often (e.g., more often than once every four *Sprint*s) and is not improving its value, quality, and rate of delivery, then the team might reflect about whether something is fundamentally wrong in the environment or in the team's use of Scrum. It is usually better for young teams to do their best to deliver, to take the *Sprint* to the end, then fail the *Sprint*. Away from the heat of battle in the *Sprint Retrospective*, the team can explore the drivers for failure and plan kaizen. Some process improvements may help the team resort to *Emergency Procedure* in analogous future situations.

¶33 Illegitimus Non Interruptus

Confidence stars: *

Cows on Gower Commons.

...the *¶7 Scrum Team* is serving many stakeholders, all of whom are competing for attention from the team. Requests and demands come to the team from management, from Customer A through Customer Z, and from sales and marketing. In addition, work in progress may uncover surprise shortcomings in the product itself that require attention. The frequency and importance of these requests varies over time, and occasionally their volume and urgency are overwhelming.

❖ ❖ ❖

Changing priorities or problems in the field often interrupt the work of *Scrum Team*s during a *¶46 Sprint*. Sales and marketing demands, combined with management interference, can cause chronic dysfunction in a team, repeated failure of *Sprint*s, failure to meet release dates, and even company failure.

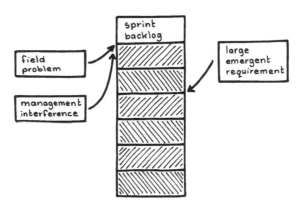

In many ways, the *Scrum Team* is a community resource that meets the needs of many stakeholders. The **tragedy of the commons** is a dilemma arising from the situation in which multiple individuals, acting independently and rationally consulting their own self-interest, will ultimately deplete a shared limited resource even when it is clear that it is not in anyone's long-term interest for this to happen. American ecologist and philosopher Garret Hardin first described this dilemma in an influential article titled "The Tragedy of the Commons," which was first published in the journal *Science* in 1968.[26]

The *Scrum Team* is a critical resource for creating new software and maintaining old software. This makes it a central resource for solving problems that arise during both development and product use, for technical communications with customers, for marketing demos, and for special projects to serve the needs of everyone in the organization. See ¶102 *Work Flows Inward* on page 467.

Often poor product ownership allows competing priorities in a company to reach a *Scrum Team*. Some teams have even been bribed to work on features not in the ¶54 *Product Backlog*.

In almost all cases, it is desirable to have the *Scrum Team* "eat their own dog food." If they produce a defect that gets into the field, they need to fix it as soon as possible. Setting up special maintenance teams to fix defects incentivizes the *Scrum Team* to not be attentive to latent defects.

For these, and many other reasons, a *Scrum Team* is always exposed to interrupts that disrupt production.

Therefore:

Explicitly allot time for interrupts and do not allow more work than fits within the allotment. If work exceeds the allotment, abort the *Sprint*.

Set up three simple rules that will cause the organization to self-organize to avoid disrupting production.

This strategy will help the team replan during the *Sprint* to raise the chances of delivering the complete ¶85 *Regular Product Increment*.

1. The team creates a buffer for unexpected items based on historical data. For example, let's say that a third of the team's work on average comes from unplanned work coming into the *Sprint* unexpectedly. If the team Notes on Velocity on page 320 averages 60 points, the team reserves 20 points for the interrupt buffer.

---

26. "The Tragedy of the Commons." Wikipedia, https://en.wikipedia.org/wiki/Tragedy_of_the_commons, June 2018 (accessed 6 June 2018).

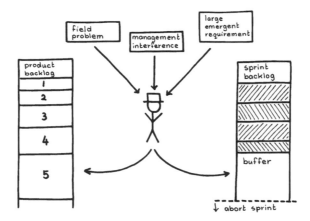

2. All non-trivial requests must go through the *¶11 Product Owner* for triage. (Web page spelling errors and compilation errors are examples of trivial errors where the fix is so obvious that there is no benefit from additional business insight. Developers may spend some small, time-boxed amount of time addressing even non-trivial defects before escalating to the *Product Owner*.) The *Product Owner* will give some items low priority if there is no perceived value relative to the business plan. The *Product Owner* will push many other items to subsequent *Sprint*s even if they have immediate value. A few items are critical and the team must complete them in the current *Sprint*, so the *Product Owner* puts them into the interrupt buffer.

3. If the buffer starts to overflow, that is, the *Product Owner* puts one point more than 20 points into the *Sprint*, the *Scrum Team* must automatically abort, the *Sprint* must be replanned, and the *Product Owner* notifies management that dates will slip.

It is essential to get management agreement on these rules and to enforce them. The *Product Owner* must always be available to the team and other stakeholders. In the *Product Owner*'s absence, the *Scrum Team* should designate one of its own to temporarily fill that role.

The *Product Owner* balances the buffer size to balance short-term customer satisfaction with future revenue generation. Often, a *Product Owner* has third-party metrics on customer satisfaction that he or she can adjust up or down with buffer size.

This strategy is independent of the focus on fixing all defects that arise in the *Sprint* from backlog items worked on during the *Sprint* (see *¶80 Good Housekeeping*). It is also independent of *¶55 Product Backlog Item*s assigned to a *Sprint* by the *Product Owner* as part of *¶24 Sprint Planning* to reduce technical debt. Low defect tolerance increases velocity in general, but exceeding the buffer typically generates at least a 50 percent reduction in velocity. The *Product Owner* must use common sense to balance these forces. See *¶81 Whack the Mole*.

❖ ❖ ❖

These rules will invariably cause individuals to self-organize to avoid blowing up a *Sprint*, as no individual wants to be seen as the direct cause of *Sprint* failure.

Even better, the buffer will tend to never be full, allowing the team to finish early and pull forward from the backlog and/or work on removing impediments. This is important because *¶74 Teams That Finish Early Accelerate Faster*. Furthermore, if the team uses *¶66 Yesterday's Weather* to size the buffer and the buffer almost never fills up, the buffer size continuously gets smaller, making the interrupt problem go away.

Counterintuitively, this does not cause critical problems to be hidden or unresolved. The *Product Owner* will put any critical items on the *Product Backlog*. This helps the team increase its velocity and increase the output of future *Sprint*s. This typically allows more than enough time to address critical items and often with spare capacity.

A team exhibits a high degree of *¶38 Product Pride* to pause in its work for the good of the product quality and reputation. Other related patterns include: *Product Owner*, *Product Backlog*, *Teams That Finish Early Accelerate Faster*, *Work Flows Inward* on page 467, and *¶98 Completion Headroom* on page 467.

¶34 Scrum of Scrums

Confidence stars: *

...a *¶7 Scrum Team* is working on a single product with multiple *¶14 Development Teams*. The *Development Team*s need to coordinate dependencies and shared work. Unresolved dependencies within individual teams are a shared challenge of all teams.

❖ ❖ ❖

When multiple teams work independently of each other they tend to focus myopically on their own concerns and lose sight of any common goals.

Organizations might revert to a command-and-control approach in the false belief that agility only works at the scale of one team, but complexity has grown, not diminished, in this circumstance. Hierarchical control increases delays and reduces the responsiveness of the teams and the wider organization to business and technology changes.

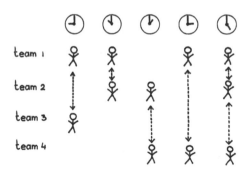

The *Scrum Team* could break the problem into smaller pieces so each *Development Team* could work separately on part of the deliverable. However, the Taylorist idea *Principles of Scientific Management [Tay4]* that optimizing the whole follows from optimizing each local part does not work in complex environments (*International Journal of Operations and Production Management 14*

[Bur94], and *International Journal of Operations and Production Management 17 [DLP97]*). Unexpected dependencies arise between the work efforts, slowing delivery, and reducing the ability of the organization to respond to change.

The separate teams could coalesce into a single, undifferentiated team but the communication and coordination overhead would grow exponentially, causing informal subgroups to appear, probably along demarcation lines that would mean they were less than cross-functional.

The multiple teams could report to a common manager or management function responsible to resolve dependencies, blockers and other inter-team issues as they arise. That manager would create a master plan to coordinate the *Development Teams*' work. However, this approach surrenders the autonomy of the teams, lowers their investment in the product (their sense of having "skin in the game"), reduces responsiveness and flexibility, and limits the learning opportunities that arise during development. Richard Hackman, in his book, *Leading Teams [Hac02]*, claims that successful teams are aware of and handle their surroundings themselves, which includes coordinating with other teams. Rosabeth Moss Kanter of the Harvard Business School, in her study of empowerment in the workplace, has written that as the world becomes more disruptive "the number of 'exceptions' and change requirements go up, and companies must rely on more and more of their people to make decisions on matters for which a routine response may not exist..." (*Change Masters: Innovation and Entrepreneurship in the American Corporation [Kan84]*, p. 18). At the same time, experience shows there is genuine autonomy only when teams and individuals accept responsibility—and accountability—for their decision-making. While directions "from above" may create the space for autonomous decision-making, self-governance becomes a reality only when those "below" intend to occupy that space and act on that intention (*The Social Psychology of Organizations [KK66]*, p. 398).

Self-governing teams are not only more responsive and adaptive to change, they are the only sustainable source of job satisfaction (*A Pattern Language: Towns, Buildings, Construction [AIS77]*, p. 398). On the other hand, autonomy without alignment can result in each team moving off in its own direction, to the detriment of both the product and the organization (*Across the Board 54 [Hec95]*).

Therefore: **Give the right and the responsibility to collaborate on delivering common goals identified by the ¶11 Product Owner to the Development Teams themselves. Permit the teams to figure out the best way to coordinate their efforts.**

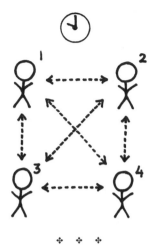

❖ ❖ ❖

Successful alignment requires that everyone involved in the development, in every team, must have visibility of the product as a whole, its *Vision* (see Vision on page 191) and its goals. This will typically involve expansion of the *¶12 Product Owner Team* to a level judged by the *Scrum Team* to be appropriate. *Development Team*s will use some of their capacity to support the *Product Owner*.

Scaling, when it does occur, is always situational, so the exact forms of collaboration will be determined by the *Development Team*s, but typical tactics include:

- Sprinting together—at the same cadence, at the same time, using *¶47 Organizational Sprint Pulse*

- Maintaining a common *¶82 Definition of Done*

- Common *¶24 Sprint Planning*, *¶35 Sprint Review*s and other mandatory Scrum events

- Holding *¶64 Refined Product Backlog* events in common

- Creating semi-formal optimizing networks of *¶5 Birds of a Feather*, utilizing common competencies such as architecture across the teams to proactively handle issues that are known in advance

- Establish a regular *Scrum of Scrums* event,[27] perhaps daily, after the teams' *¶29 Daily Scrum* events, to resolve emergent dependencies and issues, and to get things to *Done* (see *Definition of Done*).

---

27. The *Scrum of Scrums* as a daily meeting of 'ambassadors' from multiple teams is described on the Agile Alliance website. https://www.agilealliance.org/glossary/scrum-of-scrums/.

Whatever the formal arrangements for coordinating dependencies and discussing impediments, the teams should not postpone resolving them to the *Scrum of Scrums*. The teams work on the impediments as they emerge. When teams need to coordinate, the teams can just talk to each other without waiting for the next meeting on the schedule. *Development Team*s organize themselves to get their work Done and minimize dependency risk using *¶79 Dependencies First*. The *¶19 ScrumMaster*s help to remove impediments to the *Development Team*'s progress, and teams can invoke the *¶32 Emergency Procedure* as a last resort. It is the level of spontaneous interaction and unscripted collaboration between teams and their members that is the true measure of the effectiveness of the *Scrum of Scrums*.

Teams and their members should bring issues to the *Scrum of Scrums* out of *¶38 Product Pride* rather than out of fear or even duty.

The *Scrum of Scrums* is a well-established pattern, first implemented at IDX Systems (now GE Healthcare) in 1996. Jeff Sutherland was Senior Vice-President of Engineering, with Ken Schwaber on board as a consultant to help roll out Scrum. There were eight business units, each with multiple product lines. Each product had its own *Scrum of Scrums*. Some products had multiple *Scrum of Scrums* with a higher level *Scrum of Scrums*. Every product had to deliver to the market with a release cycle of three months or less and all products had to be fully integrated, upgraded, and deployed every six months to support regional healthcare providers like the Stanford Health System. It is clear from this example that there may be multiple, even parallel *Scrum of Scrums* and even that a daily *Scrum of Scrums* (considered as an event) can split into sub-meetings with separate foci. The first publication mentioning *Scrum of Scrums* was in 2001 (*Cutter IT Journal: The Great Methodology Debate [Sut01]*) and it also appeared in the Scrum Papers[28] in 2011.

---

28. Jeff Sutherland. *The Scrum Papers*, http://scruminc.com/scrumpapers.pdf (accessed 11 January 2017), no permalink, draft, 29 January, 2011.

¶35 Sprint Review

Confidence stars: **

...the *¶75 Production Episode* is over.

❖   ❖   ❖

There must be closure on the state of a product after development is over; having completed a checklist of anticipated outcomes doesn't alone ensure that the product has come as far as necessary, or that the team will take the appropriate next steps in development. A *¶14 Development Team* works as an *¶16 Autonomous Team* and a *¶17 Self-Organizing Team*, producing *¶85 Regular Product Increment*s, completing *¶55 Product Backlog Item*s (*PBIs*) as they understand them, in light of a *¶71 Sprint Goal* that provides context and focus.

The *¶11 Product Owner* and the *Development Team* work together to deliver value to the organization by creating a *Regular Product Increment*. *Development Team* members generally work among themselves during the *Production Episode*, but they are accountable to the *Product Owner* and other stakeholders to make sure they have developed the right thing. Left to their own impressions for too long, they may stray from the intent of the *¶39 Vision*.

Good *Product Owners* can concretely envision the *Regular Product Increment* that they ask the team to build during *¶24 Sprint Planning*. Even though this vision stands on thorough planning and discussion with the *Development Team*, to the level of being an *¶63 Enabling Specification*, one can't have perfect foresight when building a complex product. Concrete implementations almost always raise questions beyond those that arise while envisioning the product or while discussing it with the team. And there is always the possibility that communications between the *Product Owner* and the team loses information, or that *Product Owners* don't communicate all of their tacit assumptions and aspirations for the product.

To inspect what is really going on you need transparency, and the only way to get that is by inspecting working product—rather than by just checking off items on the *¶72 Sprint Backlog*, for example (*Agile Project Management with Scrum [Sch01]*, p. 56). Even checking off a list of stipulations for the *Regular Product Increment* isn't enough, because such lists are always necessarily incomplete because of the possibility of latent and emergent requirements—that is, of unknown unknowns. It is also necessary to establish a *¶95 Community of Trust* on page 466.

Therefore:

End the *Production Episode* with an event to assess the status of the product and to learn about end-user needs, risks, opportunities, problems, and likely completion dates to ensure product is moving in the direction of *¶93 Greatest Value*. The *Development Team*, the *Product Owner*, and other invited stakeholders attend the event. They work together both to discuss what parts of the *Regular Product Increment* are and are not ready for deployment, about lessons learned about the product during the *¶46 Sprint*, and about tentative future product plans. The group ideally achieves consensus about deployment decisions and future plans, but the *Product Owner* has the final say in these matters.

A good way to address problems in complex development is with short feedback loops that let stakeholders assess the solution so the team can adapt quickly without going too far astray. The *Sprint Review* is the focal point of deliberation and feedback during the *Sprint* cycle. The *Product Owner* can invite any stakeholder to the *Sprint Review* and is well-advised to invite key end users and elicit their feedback.

The participants inspect the product not only to learn about the suitability of the current product increment for delivery, but to provide information to shape future work (such as reordering the *¶54 Product Backlog*).

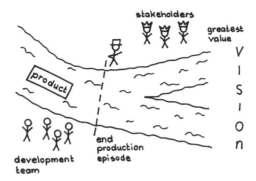

The event should be time-boxed to a maximum of three hours. The focus is on assessing the product. The *Development Team* should not spend more than about 30 minutes specifically preparing for this event. Too often a team will prop up the product with temporary supporting structures to make it work well for the *Sprint Review*, or will spend time trying to "impress" the stakeholders with a sophisticated presentation. There is very little opportunity to be convincing here: the product stands on its own. The team demonstrates the product in an environment approximating that of an end user, without any special "demo support," and without any props that could make the product appear better than it is. A good rule of thumb is: *No PowerPoint*® (unless your product is PowerPoint).

Typical activities for this event may include:

- Hands-on exploration of the product by users.

- Discussing whether the team achieved the *Sprint Goal*, or not.

- The *Product Owner* identifies which *PBI*s are *Done* and which are not (see ¶82 *Definition of Done*).

- The *Development Team* demonstrates the functionality that was Done.

- The *Product Owner* evaluates the product and determines whether to accept the *PBI*(s).

- The *Product Owner* typically specifies acceptance tests, usually at *Sprint Planning*. The *Product Owner* might run them during the *Sprint Review*.

- Occasionally the *Product Owner* might accept a *PBI* before the end of the *Sprint* (see ¶84 *Responsive Deployment*); however, the team should still hold the *Sprint Review*, and they and other pertinent stakeholders should review partial product increments released during the *Sprint*.

- The participants discuss the direction of the product, and possible ordering of the *Product Backlog*. The focus is on *learning*.

- The discussions should consider indicators of *product* health including the *Development Team*'s velocity, the conjectural (and real) level of technical debt, the current status of bugs and builds, and progress on the ¶45 *Product Roadmap*.

- The team should review progress on actions identified at the previous *Sprint Review*. Many such action items may have been cast as *PBI*s, but others may require specific attention outside the usual focus given to *PBI*s during review. For example, the team may have identified an issue with unclarity or conflict in requirements across two key customers. The team should continue to bring focus to that product issue until it is resolved, though it is not itself part of a product increment.

It is good for the *Product Owner* to adopt a vulnerable posture and to hear whether the team endorses and trusts the decisions and directions by which he or she is directing the team, particularly with respect to the product direction and dealing with technical debt and product quality. This helps reinforce the *Community of Trust*.

Note that this meeting is all about the product. Discussions about the ¶7 *Scrum Team*'s performance and processes happen in the ¶36 *Sprint Retrospective*.

❖   ❖   ❖

A *Sprint Review* creates information for all parties: the *Product Owner* and stakeholders learn about the status of the product concerning possible shipment and future direction. The *Development Team* learns how well they met the expectations of the stakeholders, giving them more information for their *Sprint Retrospective*.

A good way to validate status and get feedback on the *PBI*(s) is by having users explore them hands-on (*Harvard Business Review 93 [Kol15]*, ff. 66). For example, members of user focus groups who support the team with different market perspectives can offer on-the-ground insights. Another example is that of a game studio that has gamers play their game to get feedback. Such assessment during the *Sprint Review* is not a substitute for, say, a full acceptance test; however, *Enabling Specifications* can sometimes reduce the need for such extensive testing. (Scrum's iterative development is not an excuse to omit long-running stability or endurance tests, if the *Product Owner* can empirically justify the need for them.) Thoughtful users nonetheless appreciate the opportunity to be listened to, and engaging them in this review builds trust. End users may indeed notice lapses between the product and their expectations, and in any case can provide great input as the group discusses future product directions.

Many Scrum adherents view the *Sprint Review* as the main mechanism of agile feedback in Scrum, bringing to mind the usual forces of emergent requirements and market changes, change in business conditions, and so forth. There may be a bit of that. But a *Product Owner* and other stakeholders are unlikely to always be able to assess, in a three-hour meeting, whether a complex product increment really does meet the intended need or not. More realistic and honest insight comes from trying to use the product in a more realistic application setting, over a more protracted period of time. However, the *Product Owner* and other stakeholders *can* and *will* notice misaligned assumptions and perspectives between what people believed they agreed to at *Sprint Planning*, and what the *Development Team* delivers. Such discrepancies come less often from emergence or evolution, or from a change in the mind of the customer, than from problems in the process. One of the main functions of the *Sprint Review* is for the team to note what process lapses allowed them to deliver something the customer did not expect, and to carry this knowledge forward into the *Sprint Retrospective*.

A *Sprint Review* is an opportunity for the team to reflect on their accomplishments during the past *Sprint*, which contributes to growth in *¶38 Product Pride*. A *Sprint Review* can be a form of celebration if the team reaches a particularly noteworthy goal, or just for the sake of celebrating now and then. A company in Finland would occasionally have a *Sprint Review* in a sauna, with good food and drink, going late into the evening. The event covered the perfunctory agenda items but the real focus was for the team to celebrate its work together. (Thanks to Jukka Järvelä for this story!)

¶36 Sprint Retrospective

Confidence stars: **

...you are reaching the end of a *¶46 Sprint*, and are getting ready for the next one. Naturally, no matter how well it went, you would like to improve.

❖ ❖ ❖

Over time, without explicit attention, processes and discipline tend to decay. People get sloppy. Making isolated process changes without due focus feeds entropy, but without periodic change the team misses opportunities to increase value.

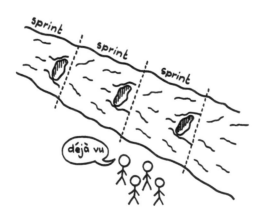

You want to continually improve. The *¶29 Daily Scrum* gives the team a chance to examine itself and improve the product direction on a daily basis. However, it is not a forum appropriate to re-chart the process for several reasons.

First of all, there is daily variation in performance, and it is pointless to make adjustments in response to what are just normal process variations. A single day (from one *Daily Scrum* to the next) is often too short to see whether a change really results in the desired improvement, and changing processes in the middle of the Sprint is disruptive at best. Second, the focus of the *Daily Scrum* is inspection and adaptation to achieve the *¶71 Sprint Goal*. Thus, the horizon is very short-term, and the *¶14 Development Team* is focusing on completing its work rather than on systematic team issues. A third reason is that in the heat of battle (in the middle of a *Sprint*), you are likely to get only one or two perspectives on a problem, rather than a full appreciation of most contributing factors. It is dangerous and inappropriate for the team to draw conclusions from incomplete information.

At the *¶35 Sprint Review*, the team reviews the product with the stakeholders. This event is not the place to analyze problems and to propose improvements, but to rather focus on the product. The *Development Team* and the *¶11 Product Owner* should take ownership of these problems as a *¶17 Self-Organizing Team* and determine how to deal with them outside the *Sprint Review*, without the stakeholders. The product focus of the *Sprint Review* rallies the team and stakeholders around one-time problems. Yet, it is even more crucial in Scrum to explore the recurring process patterns that contribute to problems that seem independent and unrelated, but rarely are.

Since *Sprints* come one after another, there is a tendency to rush from one *Sprint* right into the next, with little or no thought about *how* the team completed (or not) the work. This leads to doing the same things over and over, making the same mistakes.

Having made several improvements over previous *Sprints* the *¶7 Scrum Team* might become convinced they are doing a good job and that there are no new improvements to be found ("This is just the way how we work!"). The added value of improving seems to decline and the team may therefore view it as a waste of time ("We are already very busy doing real work!").

When a team examines itself, it makes its members vulnerable to criticism. Individuals might feel embarrassed, threatened, or incompetent. This can lead to defensive behavior in which team members can deny their own responsibility, both individually and collectively, and externalize the problem (*Teaching smart people how to learn* [Arg91]).

Therefore:

At the end of each *Sprint*, have an event where the *Scrum Team* can assess how it performed its work during the *Sprint*.

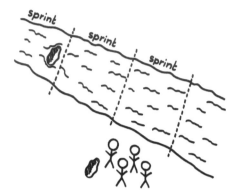

Hold a *Sprint Retrospective* at the end of the *Sprint*. This is a natural time for reflection. Examining completed work unveils a full system perspective (where the system is the team and its processes). Taking stock of how one is doing while in the middle of a process gives only a partial picture, and from a very limited perspective. So we align retrospectives with completion of work—at *Sprint* boundaries. In addition, the challenges and triumphs of the *Sprint* are still fresh in everyone's minds.

The team proposes process changes in the interest of achieving ¶93 *Greatest Value*. A process change can relate to people, relationships, process, environment, or tools.

❖   ❖   ❖

Scrum has its roots in the Toyota Production System (TPS), which has process improvement at its heart. In the TPS manual we find the instruction, "Checking is about *hansei*." *Hansei* is a deep form of personal or collective regret for having failed. A good *Scrum Team* does *hansei* over its failures, and then redirects the energy of regret for the failure into positive energy for fixing the problem; see ¶92 *Scrumming the Scrum*. The *Sprint Retrospective* is therefore also a time of healing and renewal for the team. The lean community considers Taiichi Ohno to be the founder of the TPS. A famous quote commonly attributed to him is:

> No one has more trouble than the person who claims to have no trouble. (Having no problems is the biggest problem of all.)[29]

---

29. Taiichi Ohno. AZQuotes, Taiichi Ohno Quotes, http://www.azquotes.com/author/44597-Taiichi_Ohno, n.d., (accessed 11 July 2018).

Focus on developing a culture where the *Sprint Retrospective* becomes an integral part of every *Sprint*. Build it into the regular cadence of the team. Avoid the temptation to skip it because you feel you need the time to complete the last of the *Sprint*'s work. This would reinforce a cultural belief that Retrospectives are not really important.

Time-box the meeting. Allow enough time to explore issues in some depth, but don't make it so long that people get bored. Scrum recommends no longer than a three-hour meeting for a one-month *Sprint*. The meeting is usually shorter when the *Sprint* is shorter.

Normally, the entire *Scrum Team* should attend, including the *Product Owner*. On rare occasions, if the *Development Team* members feel that the *Product Owner* dominates the conversation or otherwise suppresses frank and open discussion, they might ask the *Product Owner* not to attend. Note that this is likely a sign of larger problems. Because Scrum is a framework that helps remove problems to achieve ever greater value, and since the *Product Owner* is at the heart of the value proposition, trusted participation of the *Product Owner* in these meetings is key to long-term success beyond any superficial measure.

One principle of the Agile Manifesto[30] is to have regular Retrospectives:

> At regular intervals, the team reflects on how to become more effective, then tunes and adjusts its behavior accordingly.

Retrospectives, especially regularly scheduled ones, can easily become superficial meetings that explore no substantive issues. To deal with this, use known effective methods of Retrospectives, such as cataloged in *Agile Retrospectives: Making Good Teams Great [DL06]*. For example, one method is to identify things that went well, ongoing problems, and specific things to do (*Agile Software Development, 2nd ed. [Coc06]*, *Project Retrospectives: A Handbook for Team Reviews [Ker01]*). Consider varying the method from time to time. Base the discussion on empirical insight. In particular, examine such concrete indicators as percent of the *¶72 Sprint Backlog* completed and team velocity. Furthermore, identify specific process changes that the team will make during the next *Sprint*.

Priority-order the planned changes in the *¶40 Impediment List*. The pattern *¶88 One Step at a Time* recommends that the team make a single change at a time, so they can understand how each change contributes to improvement;

---

30. *Manifesto for Agile Software Development: Principles.* Agilemanifesto.org, http://agilemanifesto.org/principles.html, 2001, accessed 23 January 2017.

see also *Scrumming the Scrum*. The pattern *¶91 Happiness Metric* suggests embracing the change that would most increase the team's passion and sense of engagement. Also, be sure that you can measure the benefits and liabilities that the change brings about: its cost, benefits, and disadvantages (see *¶87 Testable Improvements*).

Consistent use of a *Sprint Retrospective* does not guarantee process improvement or even process stability. Though it's not sufficient to just do Retrospectives, it's probably necessary to regularly bring the issue of kaizen mind to a focus (see Kaizen and Kaikaku on page 101). Done right, *Sprint Retrospective*s encourage the team and give them pride in being able to improve over time; see *¶38 Product Pride*.

Retrospectives can easily degenerate into whining sessions. In order to combat this problem, go into the Retrospective following Norm Kerth's prime directive: "Regardless of what we discover, we understand and truly believe that everyone did the best job they could, given what they knew at the time, their skills and abilities, the resources available, and the situation at hand" ("Retrospective Exercises," Chapter Six of *Project Retrospectives: A Handbook for Team Reviews [Ker01]*). This requires a community such as the one described in *¶95 Community of Trust* on page 466. Also, make the team aware of what they themselves can change and what they cannot change in the short term, or maybe not at all (*The 7 Habits of Highly Effective People [Cov94]*). Furthermore, identify both good things ("nuggets") and problems. Don't just look at the bad. Some of the good things may be worth writing down. For example, a written *¶82 Definition of Done* should grow as the team discovers and learns new techniques for getting to *Done* (see *Definition of Done*). Whining can also indicate deeper issues, and the *¶19 ScrumMaster* should be attentive for cues of deeper problems in the overall tone of the Retrospective event.

Note that Retrospectives of just two or three hours are typically insufficient to explore deep issues. *Sprint Retrospective*s are therefore somewhat of a compromise between depth of discussion and length of the meeting. A problem found during the *Sprint Retrospective* might owe to deeper, complex relationships that the group cannot properly surface and explore in just three hours. An experience report from Jeff Sutherland based on a communication he had with the Investment Group notes the following:

> Impediments are like mosquitos. You swat one and 25 come back. So, you need to get the root-cause. What you have to do is drain the swamp to get those mosquitos to stop coming.

In order to "drain the swamp" you can consider working at the level of double- or even triple-loop learning as described by Swieringa and Wierdsma (*Becoming a Learning Organization: Beyond the Learning Curve [SW92]*, pp. 37–42). In short: single-loop learning is about changing the rules and double-loop learning changes the underlying structure. Triple-loop learning deals with the essential principles and values at the organization's foundations and history. Norm Kerth suggests taking three days to explore the deep structural issues in an organization, and he has proposed a framework for three-day, off-site Retrospectives that drive to this level of improvement (*Project Retrospectives: A Handbook for Team Reviews [Ker01]*). The extensive Retrospective of Kerth is more suitable for dealing with deep vulnerabilities of the team because it invests more time to create trust between team members than in the relatively short *Sprint Retrospectives*. It also enables deeper kaikaku (discontinuous) changes beyond the incremental changes which are usually the focus of a *Sprint Retrospective*.

The Skype audiovisual engineering team, responsible for Skype's high-quality audio and video at the time and also for codec development, held occasional two- to three-day off-site meetings in conjunction with their ¶83 *Team Sprint*s. These events led to new inventions, redesign of their own workspace, and development process innovations. — *[Gil19]*

¶37 MetaScrum

The National Advisory Committee for Aeronautics in session at Washington to discuss plans to place America foremost in the development of aviation.

...the enterprise has introduced Scrum into its development organizations, which were formerly using traditional management practices. Development organizations are in place and the *¶41 Value Stream*s are set to develop product. The enterprise has additional functions and organs, such as management and operations, which lack a good connection to the development organizations—the *¶7 Scrum Team*s. Further, organizations for different products have no recognized way to interact with each other.

❖ ❖ ❖

Scrum Teams are in place, but direction (or the threat of interference) from legacy management structures causes confusion about the locus of control over product content and direction. Managers may be messing with the backlog or interfering with the *¶14 Development Team* during the *¶46 Sprint*, causing the team to fail *Sprint*s or to trigger *¶32 Emergency Procedure*. Repeated violations of the *¶11 Product Owner*s' authority may make it difficult for teams to do their job to optimize value. It is possible that some *Scrum Team*s are failing to deliver valuable *¶85 Regular Product Increment*s towards the *¶39 Vision* because a rough relationship between the *Scrum Team*s and management leads to noise in the requirements. Or management may be too passive in supporting the team—for example, by being lax in its responsibility to hold customers to business and contractual agreements at the corporate level.

Nonetheless, markets regularly present conflicting and changing needs, and stakeholders (such as those with corporate shares, and managers with a stake in the corporate direction) will occasionally raise concerns or desires with respect to how the organization works. It's important to make those concerns transparent. But just because management expresses such concerns doesn't necessarily imply that it's helpful for them to intervene in development

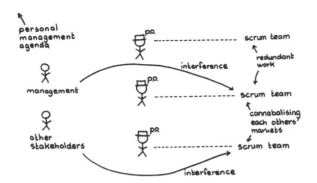

work. A healthy *Scrum Team* that honors the authority of the *Product Owner* will treat management mandates much differently than market requests; to mix both of these discussions in the same forum can lead to confusion. The enterprise may need to change individual or collective product directions because of competitive issues, market changes, sales contracts, or technical challenges and opportunities in development. Each *¶12 Product Owner Team* needs to meet regularly with stakeholders to align perspectives and expectations across products and *Value Stream*s.

Therefore:

Create a *MetaScrum* as a forum where the entire enterprise can align behind the *Product Owner*s' backlogs at every level of Scrum in the organization. The *MetaScrum* meets regularly and comprises the *Product Owner*s and executive corporate management. The CEO attends. The *MetaScrum* has a *MetaScrum Product Owner* who facilitates the alignment between management, the *Scrum Team*s, and other stakeholders. This *MetaScrum Product Owner* usually runs the meetings and leads the alignment between *Product Owner*s, senior management, and development management.

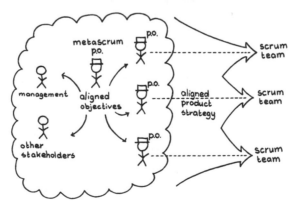

The *MetaScrum* has a cadence that corresponds to a kind of corporate-level *¶47 Organizational Sprint Pulse*. It meets once during each such interval in an event that is a kind of *¶24 Sprint Planning* that encompasses what *Scrum Team Sprint*s will deliver during that interval.

At this meeting, *Scrum Team*s can request support, funding, information, or even products—anything they are lacking to complete their delivery—from stakeholders outside the *Scrum Team*. The *MetaScrum* can be the venue to raise such requests and to make decisions to support them. Management and other *Product Owner*s can argue for changes to *¶54 Product Backlog*s at this regular meeting. At the end of this meeting, the *Product Backlog*s are locked down for management input until the next *MetaScrum* meeting.

❖ ❖ ❖

The *MetaScrum* offers a forum where *Product Owner*s can socialize their own plans and resolve portfolio-level concerns. The *Product Owner*s, potentially with input from management, shift emphasis and priority between products, marketing initiatives, and other product programs. The *MetaScrum* can sensitize *Product Owner*s to executive management directions and can inform management on how product plans support corporate goals. Between *MetaScrum* meetings, *Scrum Team*s work without management interference. A healthy organization does not violate the *Product Owner*s' authority, and good *Product Owner*s carefully consider input from all stakeholders, including management. See *¶6 Involve the Managers*.

The *MetaScrum* is *not* a body through which management controls product direction, but rather a forum for coordination between products and between products and management. Management can propose product changes through the *MetaScrum* but *Product Owner*s still own the direction of their respective products. One highly popularized *MetaScrum* instance was in fact used to impose management will on product development. It's important that, as regards product development, *Scrum Team*s remain autonomous.

A common thing that happened at PatientKeeper (a company that provides healthcare applications for physicians), where the product organization was fully Scrum, was that they needed to delay certain hospital live dates and accelerate others because of market factors, sales contracts, and development issues. If there were major commitment changes, the *MetaScrum* had to decide who would talk to the CIO at each client (hospital) by the end of the day of the *MetaScrum* meeting. Also at PatientKeeper, the *MetaScrum* Product Owner ran the *MetaScrum* and brought about alignment with senior management and the department heads. The CEO was in the *MetaScrum* and would usually not intervene in the *MetaScrum* itself except to facilitate as needed. However, he aggressively removed organizational impediments that the *MetaScrum* identified—including changing management. People said he was like the *¶19 ScrumMaster* of the *MetaScrum*—a sort of über *ScrumMaster*— but he left operations to the *¶34 Scrum of Scrums* Master.

At 3M, the chief executive of a division runs the *MetaScrum* by assuming the role of *MetaScrum Product Owner* for her organization. The *MetaScrum* focuses on alignment around the backlog, meeting twice per week. Here she wants to get the priorities clear and addressed. A separate leadership team focuses on removing organizational impediments.

Systematic (a company that develops software and systems solutions) in Denmark and Saab Defense in Sweden run the whole organization as a Scrum. They have a forum at the top of the management hierarchy which functions like a high-level *Scrum of Scrums*.

The *MetaScrum* is the focal point of enterprise-level change. The organization as a whole has a strategic vision, a backlog, a roadmap, *Regular Product Increment* (reorganizations, new market initiatives, etc.), and such other Scrum components necessary to make the enterprise run smoothly and accelerate well. Stakeholders may change the direction of the organization, change staffing, or change budget allocations to remove impediments, so people with authority to do this must be part of this body.

Each *Value Stream* and product makes its impediments visible at the *MetaScrum* level. It may be that the resources of individual products are inadequate to address such impediments, while the corporation as a whole can provide the horsepower to resolve such issues. It may also be that the problem has tacit links across products that will become visible only by making the issue transparent in a joint forum. Good *MetaScrum Product Owner*s will recognize problems that surface in the *MetaScrum* meeting and will resolve them that same day if possible, and as soon as possible otherwise.

A good *MetaScrum* is the locus of all inter-product decisions. All who have a voice in product decisions should be invited to the meeting. The *MetaScrum* meets on a regular schedule so that everyone knows where and when they will take product decisions. Strong support and presence of the CEO is important to make the *MetaScrum* work. Steve Jobs raised all strategic product decisions to a meeting every two weeks at Apple—an example of a *MetaScrum* implementation. For smaller companies, a *MetaScrum* often meets every week to keep pace with the cycle of change in the organization.

While each *Product Owner* has final authority over their *Product Backlog*, they need to work within an approved budget. The *MetaScrum* is the forum for budget changes at the corporate level. Management and the *Product Owner*s make small changes on the spot; if the decision involves weighty issues, such as the need to seek additional investment, management and the *Product Owner*s take action immediately after the meeting to pursue a decision path.

In the best implementations, the *MetaScrum* is a powerful force in the organization. If the *Product Owner*s agree to a management proposal at a *MetaScrum* event, that decision is final until the next *MetaScrum*. Managers may not approach the *Scrum Team*s with additional talking points until the next *MetaScrum* event, so the *Scrum Team*s can work without interruption from management. Even the customers and sales force learn that after the *MetaScrum* event is over, it is futile to try to alter agreements until the next one.

The *MetaScrum* is accountable to all the stakeholders of the organization to steer a viable business that creates value for every stakeholder group. This includes the organization's employees, the customers, and the investors. Use common sense in being more or less inclusive, but keep *MetaScrum* workings and decisions transparent.

In good time, good corporations may find that management plays a diminishing role in product management and corporate power slowly shifts from executive management to the *Product Owner*s. The organization becomes flatter. Executive managers and heads of department may relinquish what has become an antiquated role to become *Product Owner*s, closer to where the action is.

See also *Involve the Managers*.

The first published reference to the *MetaScrum* (*Proceedings of Agile Development Conference (ADC'05) [Sut05]*) describes the PatientKeeper *MetaScrum* that started in 2003.

¶38 Product Pride

Confidence stars: *

A man came upon a construction site where three people were working. He asked the first, "What are you doing?" and the man replied: "I am laying bricks." He asked the second, "What are you doing?" and the man replied: "I am building a wall." As he approached the third, he heard him humming a tune as he worked, and asked, "What are you doing?" The man stood, looked up at the sky, and smiled, "I am building a cathedral!" [31]

...you have a *Community of Trust* (see *¶95 Community of Trust* on page 466) and have a common *¶39 Vision*. The *¶7 Scrum Team* is working towards that *Vision*.

❖　❖　❖

Team members need to know their work matters and have a say in how it's done.

The *Scrum Team* should build a product to the best of their abilities. However, market conditions or organizational concerns can put pressure on the *Scrum Team* to deliver *something* as soon as possible. This can tempt the *Scrum Team* to take shortcuts, which will result in lower quality of the product, technical debt, and wasteful rework. Such pressure on the *Scrum Team* reduces its autonomy. Not meeting your own expectation on quality degrades the pride you take in your work and in the result—the product.

---

31. Attributed to Christopher Wren, Wikiquotes.org, https://en.wikiquote.org/wiki/Christopher_Wren, 5 June 2018 (accessed 6 June 2018).

A *¶11 Product Owner* should have a deep appreciation of stakeholder wants and needs, and should understand exactly how product increments will increase product value (see Value and ROI on page 246) by meeting and exceeding the expectations of the market and other stakeholders. Impediments, such as lack of direct customer contact or authority to make decisions, may create an environment where there is a lack of clarity about the product *Vision* and result in a meandering *¶54 Product Backlog* that does not create the *¶93 Greatest Value*. Consequently, the team may have low energy or low enthusiasm for the product, and they may instead turn their energy to side projects.

Therefore:

Create a climate that enables Autonomy, Mastery, and Purpose.

No one can either impose or bestow *Product Pride*. Instead it is an outcome that emerges when mastery, autonomy, and purpose converge (*Drive: The Surprising Truth About What Motivates Us [Pin11]*). Climate is "the shared perception of the way things are around here" and "can be locally created by what leaders do, what circumstances apply, and what environments afford" (*The Handbook of Organizational Culture and Climate [AWP10]*). The *Scrum Team* controls its own destiny, so this work belongs to the *Scrum Team*.

For example, the *Scrum Team* has a hand in creating the *¶71 Sprint Goal*. The team should be a *¶10 Cross-Functional Team* to ensure that it is capable in all product development areas. If developers voluntarily sign up to join teams whose work or membership attracts them, it creates a foundation to align shared purpose with individual values (see *¶116 Self-Selecting Team* on page 468). See also *¶16 Autonomous Team*.

A *Scrum Team* takes pride in building the product right and in the recognition of good craftsmanship. The *¶19 ScrumMaster* will help the team to excel in its skills and in how it works (see *¶26 Kaizen Pulse* and *¶92 Scrumming the Scrum*). Everyone takes pride when the right *¶85 Regular Product Increments* appear. The feedback from the market gives recognition of the *Scrum Team*'s effort, furthering the team's pride.

Building the right product creates *Product Pride*. A great team has *ba* (場)— the potential for doing great things starts by aligning around a shared purpose. It is less so that purpose brings teams together; instead it emerges from great latent teams. *Product Owners* will be the initial carriers of this enthusiasm as part of the *Vision*, and part of their job is to make it infectious.

❖   ❖   ❖

When a Product comes to its end, the organization should recognize and honor the *Scrum Team* for its effort and contributions. Therefore, hold a *¶94 Product Wake*. It magnifies *Product Pride* to embrace the fact that someday the product will dissolve into *¶2 The Mist*. The effect of *Product Pride* is, however, much larger than the product itself.

> Two big evils in our world are our readiness to be herded along with the crowd and apparent indifference to destruction of all kinds. (From *The Irish Monthly 79* [Bir51])

Having pride means working to your own standard of quality and taking ownership of the results. This opens the doorway to freedom in service of the world, and leads to a team that feels it is doing morally profound work, as in *¶91 Happiness Metric*.

CHAPTER 3

Value Stream Pattern Language

Whereas the Product Organization Pattern Language on page 11 builds the relationships between the people and teams in a Scrum organization, the Value Stream Pattern Language builds relationships between steps of product construction, and the artifacts that represent parts of the process. The *Scrum Team* builds the Value Stream to frame out the overall rhythms and activities of development. Value generally flows from the *¶39 Vision* into the *¶54 Product Backlog*, and from there into the *¶72 Sprint Backlog* and eventually into the *¶85 Regular Product Increment*. Many other patterns refine these larger *Value Stream* components along the way.

The following picture is the pattern-language graph for the Value Stream Pattern Language, and shows the dependencies between the language's patterns. We described how to use a pattern language graph in the first section of the *Product Organization Pattern Language*.

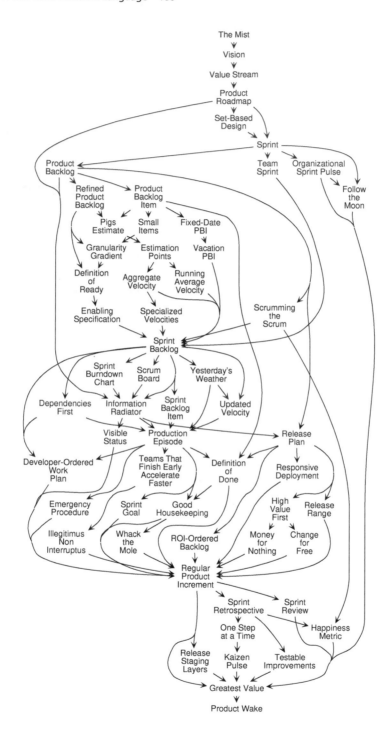

Value Stream Sequence

Scrum is as much about crafting the process as it is about building the product. There is a saw in Lean that advises: "Build the right process, and you'll build the right product." The most fundamental process is that of "inspect and adapt," which organizations can use to steer both the product *and* the process. We use the metaphor of a streambed that is the path through which the product travels on its journey from the *¶39 Vision* to its end users. We think of the *Vision*, *¶54 Product Backlog*, and *¶72 Sprint Backlog* as the lining of this stream—these are Scrum artifacts. But they are also demarcations of time that reflect how development flows from conception to delivery.

A *value stream* is just a sequence of activities that produce value. An enterprise can design a *Value Stream* to build a product, offer a service, or to otherwise create value. The core Scrum *Value Stream* focuses on delivering a *¶85 Regular Product Increment* for end users. These activities that produce value for the end users also create value for shareholders, for the *¶14 Development Team* (e.g., pride in building something great, an enhanced opportunity for professional development), and others. We think of each of these as a *Value Stream* in its own right, even though they may all emanate from the same broader product development effort.

This is one sequence (intended to be an archetypical one) that highlights the main patterns along the main waypoints of building and refining a *Value Stream*. We omitted some smaller patterns to help maintain the big picture perspective. Again, the sequence is only archetypical, and you may find it useful to apply the patterns in an order that differs from that which we describe here.

¶2 *The Mist* Great works start with a vague longing across some community, and with its attempts to solve great problems locally or individually, and while aspiring to do great things, stops at small, local benefits for want of effective cooperation.

¶39 *Vision* These longings come together in an articulated vision of the desired future state—the great thing that the *Scrum Team* will build. Everyone involved in realizing the problem shares this *Vision*. One person, the *Product Owner*, comes to embody the *Vision* by taking responsibility for it, and for the value that emanates from building the product.

¶41 *Value Stream* An organization congeals around these longings with a passion to build something great and generate value, with a vision not only of the end results but of the means for achieving those ideas and to drive an evolving stream of deliverables to a growing notion of collective self. The sweat and bricks and mortar of design and product realization flow into the *Value Stream* at points that complement each other and support a harmonious flow of work.

¶45 Product Roadmap With ever a playful eye to the possibility of change and new ideas, a direction that may attain the greater good starts to congeal out of *The Mist*. There are several potential paths to building something great and generating value as led by the *Vision*. The *Vision* becomes a collection of dreams, of product increments, organized to facilitate early decisions that will guide the best-known path to Wholeness at any given time.

¶46 Sprint The *Value Stream* develops deliverable product increments in uniformly time-boxed episodes of product development called *Sprints*. Each increment is a *Done* contribution to furthering the vision. Uniform episodes also give the opportunity for meaningful improvement of *Value Stream* development processes. A natural cycle of *Sprint*s might *¶77 Follow the Moon*.

¶54 Product Backlog Foresight, experience, and circumstances lend insight on what the best decisions might be at imminent forks in the roadmap. A vision of a specific path through the roadmap emerges to add value at every step, based on today's best guess of business conditions. The *Product Backlog* makes the immediate likely trajectory of long-term delivery visible to all stakeholders. See the Product Backlog Sequence on page 261.

¶55 Product Backlog Item The *Scrum Team* breaks down the product into individual deliverables called *Product Backlog Item*s (*PBI*s), which are the focus of the effort to build deliverables. Developers accept those *PBI*s into development that meet the *¶65 Definition of Ready*, and which the developers have estimated, as in *¶57 Pigs Estimate*.

¶71 Sprint Goal The Team commits to a *Sprint Goal*, the "must do" of the *Sprint*, which will result when the work of the *Sprint* is complete. The *Sprint Goal* creates a focus for teamwork, helping the team work together instead of focusing on multiple independent efforts.

¶72 Sprint Backlog The *Development Team* plans how it will achieve the *Sprint Goal* and develop the *Product Backlog Item*s that will allow them to deliver the Product Increment, and creates a work plan called a *Sprint Backlog*.

¶175 *Production Episode* The *Development Team* works toward the *Sprint Goal* and the delivery of the *Product Increment*. The developers update the *Sprint Backlog* every day in the ¶29 *Daily Scrum*. The team works largely uninterrupted, ¶25 *Swarming: One-Piece Continuous Flow* as a team to develop one *PBI* at a time.

¶184 *Responsive Deployment* As development progresses, there are small deliveries inside the larger *Sprint* cycles to address emergencies and fix bugs, or to generate value as opportunistically as possible, without waiting for the end of the *Sprint*.

¶35 *Sprint Review* After development for the *Sprint* is over, the *Product Owner* and invited stakeholders assess the current state of the product and what parts of it are ready for inclusion in a *Product Increment*. Work from the most recent *Sprint* must meet the ¶82 *Definition of Done* before the *Scrum Team* deploys the *Product Increment*.

¶36 *Sprint Retrospective* The team also assesses the current state of its process and seeks opportunities for improvement, choosing one key improvement that the team together will realize in the next *Sprint*, and making it a *PBI* so that Scrum becomes the vehicle for improving the process: ¶92 *Scrumming the Scrum*.

¶185 *Regular Product Increment* Approved *Product Backlog Item*s compose into a cohesive *Product Increment* which the *Product Owner* may choose to make available for use.

¶186 *Release Staging Layers* The scope of delivery and application of *Product Increment*s expands and contracts as experience testifies to the soundness of a given increment, while weaker increments die off.

¶189 *Value Areas* *Value Stream*s may have independent tributaries that distinct teams can develop separately, but which the market chooses to use together as an integrated Whole. The enterprise can internally partition such work into *Value Areas*, each of which works like a small, self-contained entity to develop a product part for which there is no market alternative. All such *Value Areas* lie behind a market perception of a single product with potentially multiple *Value Stream*s.

¶190 *Value Stream Fork* Successful *Value Stream*s may grow in scope, and one problem with success is that the result can outstrip the original vision. If so, the original single *Value Stream* may become multiple streams, each with its own *Product Backlog* and *Product Owner*, bringing focus and a refined *Vision* to each one.

¶93 *Greatest Value* While it remains in use, the product produces the greatest value possible; and while development is still active, the product direction changes to provide the highest value.

¶94 *Product Wake* The cycles of life and nature ultimately bring products to the end of their useful lives, and they should be brought to an end in a way that returns their resources to nature and that recognizes the dignity of all stakeholders.

¶39 Vision

Alias: Product Vision

Confidence stars: **

The moon landing program started with a vision.

...having come out of *¶2 The Mist*, some core visionary individual or group must make their passion concrete, in a conceptualization that can be shared, and excite a group of people to work as one mind to build something that will increase the quality of life for their constituency.

❖   ❖   ❖

People thrive within constraints that channel their creativity and work towards a common good, but it's also true that overly specific constraints can turn contributors into subservient robots who blindly follow orders rather than following with their heart.

To achieve a great vision usually requires the work of an aligned team, as well as alignment between that team and its stakeholders. Teams comprise individuals with opinions and feelings, and though they all may be well-meaning, each may conceptualize and express their anticipated contributions in different ways. This creates the appearance of a conflict between team members. Yet if one strips off such noise that can dominate how team members view each other, one can usually tap into shared feelings and conceptualizations that draw deeply on the shared culture of the stakeholders.

This diversity in perspective within a team brings great value, because it raises the probability that the team will overlook no great idea. Admitting multiple perspectives and soliciting the input of people with different backgrounds and experiences helps the effort explore a wide variety of options. The different experiences and ideas open additional, innovative perspectives that can be valuable. Unchecked, these differences can fracture the team by taking the team in multiple directions.

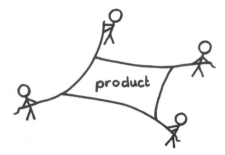

For a team to be truly effective, all members need to be pulling in the same direction.

The team works in the direction of a shared goal. When the shared goal is too broadly defined or vague, the team risks exploring too many lower-value directions. The effort can lose energy and momentum in the false starts of unnecessary experimentation. If the shared goal is too narrow, it overly constrains the team and they may leave valuable directions unexplored—a waste of intellect and creativity.

A goal becomes shared when the team takes ownership of it. The team takes ownership of the goal when it co-creates it: It becomes *their* goal.

The future is inherently unknowable; committing to a final result or plan over a long time frame is fraught with danger. There are too many external forces to consider. Yet teams need a shared goal to create cohesion and direct performance.

Therefore:

The individual who embodies the passion for this new product effort takes on the role of ¶11 *Product Owner*, around whom stakeholders and potential future coworkers rally to articulate and together to define and refine a *Vision*. The *Vision* is a description of how the product supports a desired future toward which an envisioned future *Product Organization* advances (as described in the Product Organization Pattern Language on page 11).

✣ ✣ ✣

We can think of the *Vision* as having two components. The first—which we just refer to just as the *Vision*—is a broad future direction, while the *Product Vision* breaks down that broad direction into more specific business components. The *Vision* provides a flexible, explicit rallying point to guide the emergent group forward as a team. It supports systems-thinking understanding of how the envisioned product effort will benefit their own lives and those of their end users and of other stakeholders. One key aspect of the *Vision* pertains to the product itself. The *Product Vision* goes beyond being a vague motherhood statement and is quite concrete. The *Product Vision* lies at the intersection of the passion behind the idea, the demand for the idea, and the feasibility of building something great. Typically, the *Product Vision* (*Agile Product Management With Scrum: Creating Products That Customers Love, 1st ed.* [Pic10], p. 24) covers these considerations:

- Key features of the product
- Who is going to use the product
- Customer needs the product will address
- How the vendor will benefit

The *Product Owner* owns the *Vision* and sets out to realize it by creating a *Product Organization Pattern Language* as well as by defining a *¶41 Value Stream*. The *Product Owner* articulates a path toward the *Vision* as a *¶45 Product Roadmap*, and works with stakeholders to reduce it to a concrete, specific *¶54 Product Backlog*. Each of these helps clarify the *Vision*, in varying forms and degrees, to the *Product Organization* and particularly to the *¶7 Scrum Team*s. The *Vision* gives everyone a greater sense of direction and collective purpose (see *¶117 Unity of Purpose* on page 468). The *Product Organization* and the teams can in turn vet deliverables in terms of their support for the *Vision*. Teams can measure their progress against bringing this *Vision* to reality.

Having an effective *Vision* can help set direction, help inspire and unify the *Scrum Team*, and help shape the behavior of the team without constraining its creativity. A great *Vision* is one that gets you out of bed in the morning and charges you up for the day. The *Vision* guides the creation and enactment of a *Value Stream* to realize the *Vision* and deliver a series of product increments to stakeholders.

*Vision*s evolve over time, and some product efforts bring a quick discovery that the original *Vision* was off the mark, but the basic ideas can carry through to support what is sometimes an even grander *Vision*. Because we are agile, we can adjust our progress towards the *Vision*, or can even adjust the *Vision* itself over time.

Katsuaki Watanabe, then CEO of Toyota, believed in setting "impossible goals" as visions that drove Toyota's strategic direction:

> Many of Toyota's goals are purposely vague, allowing employees to channel their energies in different directions and forcing specialists from different functions to collaborate across the rigid silos in which they usually work. For example, Watanabe has said that his goal is to build a car that makes the air cleaner, prevents accidents, makes people healthier and happier when they drive it, and gets you from coast to coast on one tank of gas... *Harvard Business Review* 86 [OSTD08 TOS08]

At the end of the 1970s, Bill Gates and Paul Allen had a vision of "a computer on every desk and in every home." The *Vision* became reality when "there was kind of a magical breakthrough when the computer became cheap, and we could see that everyone could afford a computer."[1] Now in the twenty-first century, Elon Musk is working on his vision "to make humanity a multi-planet species."[2] He has already taken successful steps in accomplishing his vision by making reusable rockets to lower the cost of launches.[3]

A great *Vision* aspires to some, perhaps transcendent, ¶93 *Greatest Value*. For example, journalists in the Netherlands started a new chocolate company, Tony's Chocolonely, out of a vision of creating chocolate bars made with slave-free labor.[4]

1. Bill Gates. Interview. Academy of Achievement. http://www.achievement.org/autodoc/page/gat0int-1, 2010 (accessed 27 August 2016).
2. Carl Hofman. "Elon Musk Is Betting His Fortune on a Mission Beyond Earth's Orbit." Wired.com, http://www.wired.com/2007/05/ff-space-musk, 22 May 2007 (accessed 27 August 2016).
3. Julie Johnson and Dana Hull. "Musk's SpaceX returns rocket for perfect upright landing." In *The Seattle Times*, http://www.seattletimes.com/business/boeing-aerospace/musks-spacex-returns-rocket-for-perfect-upright-landing/, 22 December 2015 (accessed 27 August 2016).
4. Tonys Chocolonely Annual Report. https://tonyschocolonely.com/storage/configurations/tonyschocolonelycom.app/files/jaarfairslag/2017-2017/tc_jaarfairslag_2016_en_totaal_01.pdf, 2017 (no longer accessible; accessed 6 June 2018).

¶40 Impediment List

Alias: Impediment Backlog

Confidence stars: *

...the *¶7 Scrum Team* is trying to make progress on the product.

❖ ❖ ❖

Team members often run into problems that hinder their progress. Fixing them in the moment may not be possible, practical, and/or in the best interest of the organization or team.

Internal or external events can slow the *¶14 Development Team*'s work. Team members might want to fix the problem immediately, but that takes effort away from making progress toward the *¶71 Sprint Goal.*

On the other hand, if you don't resolve an impediment immediately, it can shift from being an acute problem to a chronic problem; something you just live with and kind of ignore.

An impediment often prevents the *Development Team* from doing its work. It may also prevent it from improving its performance. For example, team interaction issues can get in the way of making progress, and slow or outdated equipment may prevent the team from working at its best.

Therefore:

Make all non-trivial issues visible with an *Impediment List*; **raise them up to the right people in the organization for resolution.** The *¶19 ScrumMaster* orders the list by relative severity and value.

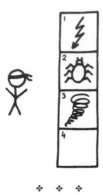

❖   ❖   ❖

Any *Scrum Team* member may add an impediment to the list to make it visible. This presupposes that the *Scrum Team* is a *Community of Trust* (see *¶95 Community of Trust* on page 466), because some impediments may be difficult to raise, such as personal ones relating to health, family situation, or team conflict. A team member should always be able to confide in the *ScrumMaster* regarding such impediments. In the interest of preserving the dignity of individuals, the *ScrumMaster* may choose to resolve some impediments discretely.

The *Development Team* members themselves resolve most items on the *Impediment List*, but they also may find help from others outside the *Scrum Team*. *ScrumMaster*s may personally attend to impediments that would otherwise be a distraction for the rest of the team, and which do not require their expertise to resolve. Alternatively, the *Development Team* may work with the *¶11 Product Owner* to add work to the *¶54 Product Backlog* to resolve an impediment.

During the *¶36 Sprint Retrospective*, the *Scrum Team* is likely to add new impediments to the list. This is also a good opportunity to refine the *Impediment List*.

The *Impediment List* is a manifestation of kaizen mind (see Kaizen and Kaikaku on page 101). An empty *Impediment List* means that you aren't looking hard enough for ways to improve. ("No problem is a problem.") On the other hand, the team must address impediments in a timely manner; otherwise improvement stops. Impediments on the list must not become stale.

True story: A team was complaining about their manager who wasn't removing impediments for them. I asked if the manager knew what the impediments were and they said they assumed he did. I had the team write the impediments on fluorescent sticky notes with the word "Block" in bold at the top, and took them to the manager. As he wasn't there I plastered them around his monitor so he couldn't miss them. Half an hour later he called out looking for me. He came up and asked if these were blockers from the team. I responded: Yes, and he smiled saying it was great as he now knew what he needed to be working on.

¶41 Value Stream

Confidence stars: **

...the *¶11 Product Owner* has defined a *¶39 Vision* and is now seeking ways for it to create *value*, where we define *value* as something of worth to some person or set of people whom we wish to serve.

❖ ❖ ❖

The development process and the path from conception to market are as important to product success as the product idea itself. In simple development, as in agrarian societies, the raw materials were close at hand and the vendor (the owner of the grape vines) could relay them to the consumer (a hungry traveler). As production became more advanced, the processes behind the product also became more complex (such as making wine). Unlike the workforce skills required for simple agrarian products, the innovation and wherewithal to support complex endeavors requires teamwork. Intellectual endeavors beg a more open system, where the inputs and connections between development networks form a dense network.

Building a complex product like a car or a software program may require many teams and a deep understanding of how to coordinate their work. However, execution alone—good processes and good people—won't carry the day.

Therefore:

The *Product Owner* creates an ecosystem whose elements build on each other to deliver ever-increasing value in an evolving product. At the center of this ecosystem, there is a process to deliver ongoing and evolving streams of product increments to stakeholders: the *Value Stream*.

Value Stream building blocks include the artifacts (backlogs, product components) and processes that guide and coordinate the creation of these artifacts (through events and joint work). The people involved in the Value Stream are instrumental in building, enacting, and evolving the processes that guide the creation of these artifacts.

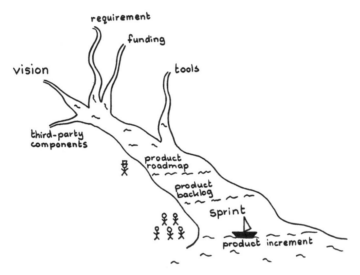

The *Value Stream* structure is dynamic and the *Product Owner* may tailor it to changing business conditions, stakeholder relationships, or even product increment content. However, from an organizational perspective, the development component of the Scrum *Value Stream* comprises one organization: the ¶7 *Scrum Team*. The *Scrum Team* carries out all development activity without significant handoffs to or from other teams.

Toyota manages to build many cars with a lot of variety and high quality by applying the Toyota Production System (TPS) (*Toyota Production System: Beyond Large-Scale Production [Ohn88]*). This production system consists of world-class processes, good employee training, and elimination of waste. Yet, the processes don't emerge from thin air; many of them reflect the structure of the path from the raw materials to a sales lot. This raises crucial questions: Who designs the assembly line or its robots? Who decides what is written on the process instruction cards at each work cell? Such activities fall within the scope of building a *Value Stream*. The retailer Tesco analyzed their *Value Stream* (from supplier to store sales) and discovered significant improvement opportunities. As a result of making the improvements in their *Value Stream*, the "supplied items began to flow more quickly," which resulted in "lower costs and growing sales for Tesco and its suppliers" (*Seeing the Whole Value Stream, 2nd ed. [JWBL13]*). "Their success in redesigning their grocery supply network helped them grow from being a mid-sized grocery retailer in the U.K. markets to being the third largest retailer in the world within a decade" (the same source).

❖ ❖ ❖

The ¶54 *Product Backlog*, ¶72 *Sprint Backlog*s, and ¶44 *Scrum Board*s, together with many other following patterns, help form a Whole through which work flows as it progresses to delivery. The *Value Stream* is, in part, the organizational structures and processes that provide cradle-to-cradle support for the product. It is also a structuring of time that defines the life stages of value from conception through analysis, design, delivery, and ongoing product care. ¶85 *Regular Product Increment*s flow in time through the *Product Backlog*, *Sprint Backlog*s, and *Scrum Board*s. These are the artifacts that reflect the workflow through the *Product Owner* and the ¶14 *Development Team*.

The rationale behind a single *Scrum Team* per *Value Stream* is to eliminate handoffs. Handoffs lead to feedback delay, which in turn causes rework— a particularly pernicious form of waste (*muda*). To be effective, the *Scrum Team* needs both the business solution insight of the *Product Owner* and the development capabilities of a ¶10 *Cross-Functional Team*. Though commodity goods and services may come from other sources and flow through the *Scrum Team*, a *Value Stream* does not split value-adding development across multiple teams.

While product and value flow downstream, there is also a corresponding upstream flow. New requirements, defect reports, and product ideas emerge from the market and from the development process itself and can affect subsequent work along the stream. Much upstream flow happens during the structured feedback events of the Scrum framework, and particularly during ¶35 *Sprint Review* and ¶24 *Sprint Planning*; however, defect reports and other feedback may come at any time. To deliver the ¶93 *Greatest Value*, the team may disrupt the ¶75 *Production Episode* to remediate defects and foster ¶38 *Product Pride*. Most *Value Stream*s field requests from end users and customers with a customer support function which, among other things, does triage on such requests to separate operational issues and user errors from defect reports and requests for product extension. That is the first "line of defense," with the *Product Owner* being the next stage who filters and organizes such requests. Most of the corresponding downstream flow happens in discrete deliveries called *Regular Product Increment*s, but high-performing *Value Stream*s can use the more incremental *¶84 Responsive Deployment* to deliver off-cadence.

Any given product can support multiple *Value Stream*s, so a given *Scrum Team* may manage several *Value Stream*s. Any given *Scrum Team* usually creates value for several stakeholders, and this implies that there are often several *Value Stream*s at play. The client, end user, and customers are obvious stakeholders, but the *Scrum Team* should maintain a *Value Stream* that makes work ever less stressful, more fun, and more fulfilling for itself.

There are a small number of key patterns that describe smaller Wholes within the *Value Stream*. Much of the remainder of this chapter comprises those patterns. Some of these patterns reflect processes related to production. Typical of such patterns are:

- *¶45 Product Roadmap*—the map of alternative paths to value

- *¶46 Sprint* and *Sprint Backlog*—the time and content dimensions of a product increment

- *Regular Product Increment*—the realization of *Vision* components

Beyond focusing on the product for its own sake, it is important to remember that the *Value Stream* is a living system that is ever getting better, and that there are patterns around the processes for such improvement work. Typical of these patterns are:

- *¶26 Kaizen Pulse*—running a development as an alternation between base-lining and attempts to improve

- *¶36 Sprint Retrospective*—explicitly focusing on process improvement as much or more than on product improvement

- *¶92 Scrumming the Scrum*—using the Scrum framework itself as a tool to manage the work of process improvement

The pattern you are reading describes the *Value Stream* only as a generic construct that goes hand-in-hand with Scrum's nature as a generic framework. Individual products each have their own *Value Stream*s whose roots lie in the raw materials or sources of innovation and that contribute to the respective products' value. A *Scrum Team* might want to use *Value Stream* Mapping to explore the particulars of its own *Value Stream*. You can learn details of *Value Stream* Mapping from Mike Rother's *Toyota Kata* (*Toyota Kata: Managing*

People for Improvement, Adaptiveness and Superior Results [Rot10]). Such an analysis may help a *Scrum Team* refine the existing Scrum patterns or to add new patterns germane to the needs of a particular business.

¶42 Set-Based Design

Confidence stars: **

As a young Toyota engineer, you attack a problem with relish. You carefully identify the cause of the problem, taking care to do a thorough five-why analysis. You then think and think and come up with a brilliant solution. You detail the solution and run in to share it with your mentor. Instead of evaluating the idea on its merits and congratulating you, he asks, "What other alternatives have you considered? How does this solution compare with those alternatives?" You are stopped dead in your tracks, as you were convinced you had the best approach. (From The Toyota Way: 14 Management Principles from the World's Greatest Manufacturer [Lik04], p. 263.)

...a *¶7 Scrum Team* has come together as a *Community of Trust* (see *¶95 Community of Trust* on page 466). The *Scrum Team* is working from a *¶54 Product Backlog* that they refine continuously. Some *¶55 Product Backlog Items* (*PBIs*) near the top of the *Product Backlog* are *Ready* (see *¶65 Definition of Ready*) to go into a *¶75 Production Episode*, while others nearer the bottom of the backlog are far beyond the current horizon of concern. In between we find *PBIs* that may be likely candidates for *¶85 Regular Product Increments*. Several of them may be alternatives for other *PBIs* on the backlog. Sometimes the *Scrum Team* may have alternative *PBIs* in mind for those listed on the backlog. Yet other *PBIs* are *Ready* (see *Definition of Ready*), and the team is confident of what to build, but is exploring the "how" of building those *PBIs* with several ideas in mind for each of them.

❖   ❖   ❖

There may be many possible solutions to a complex problem. It is often impossible to predict which is best.

Selecting a single option and developing it aggressively now adds additional work later when new information emerges that forces team members to reconsider their initial decision. In a large system, with many subsystems and many teams, this rework causes delays by forcing work to stop while the *Scrum Team* deliberates the new decision and works out consequences for other parts of the system.

While we value embracing change, we also value eliminating wasteful rework. It is easy to see in hindsight where we were stuck in analysis paralysis or how we initially lunged headstrong in the wrong direction. The challenge is to find the middle path.

Consider this graph from a classic article on Iterative User Interface Design by Jakob Nielsen, a father of UI and UX design (*IEEE Computer 26 [Nie93]*):

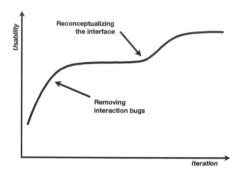

Interface quality as a function of the number of design iterations: Measured usability will normally go up for each additional iteration, until the design potentially reaches a point where it plateaus. IEEE Computer 26 [Nie93]

In this article, which makes a strong case for using iteration to improve product quality, Nielsen states, "we do not really know what leads to the creative insights necessary for a fundamentally novel and better interface design." Consequently, we can say that iteration is insufficient for innovation. Customer feedback on regular product increments will improve the product, but it will not fundamentally reshape the conception of the product itself. Development organizations need an alternative solution to guide them as they work to differentiate critical new business features from existing offerings.

Therefore: **develop many options in parallel, fixing only the critical constraints up front.**

To accomplish this, each development episode proceeds to develop a chosen set of design alternatives in parallel. Developers working on the feature continuously maintain current estimates for each alternative in the set. When all alternatives reach the halfway point, there is a meeting to trade notes and to evaluate which options to eliminate, and to discuss new options that they may have discovered. If a clear winner has emerged, the parallel work stops and the plan of record adopts the winner. If not, the team (always with input from the *¶11 Product Owner*) will budget itself an additional work increment to gain additional understanding. The process of reducing options over time looks like this:

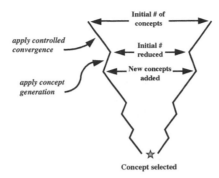

Intentional phases of convergence and divergence *Naval Engineers Journal 121 [SDB09]*.

As team members develop each option through successive iterations, they gradually increase the fidelity of the work output (*Naval Engineers Journal 121 [SDB09]*). An initial work increment may only produce a hand-wavy sketch, a second might produce a throw-away prototype, and a final work increment would produce an initial real implementation. So each time the *Product Owner* and ¶14 *Development Team* members decide to eliminate some options, they also increase the level of detail of the remaining options.

A single option will vary multiple parameters (e.g., algorithm selection, data structure, screen layout) to explore different design alternatives. The team should be particularly attentive to the number of parameters they vary across the multiple options. As the teams grows in understanding of how to run *Set-Based Design*, they can increase the number of parameters being varied. Be thoughtful about the degree of overlap between the options. Independent options will cover more of the design space, but fixing a parameter will increase robustness of the result. When done well, a team can minimize the lead time by reducing the number of experiments. The point here is that you can design your learning, rather than proceed from surprise to surprise.

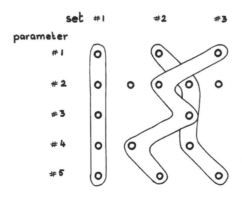

The number of options increases with each iteration, while the number of exploration sets decreases.

❖   ❖   ❖

Depending on the scope and the extent of the *Set-Based Design* exercise, the results can feed directly into a *¶46 Sprint* or their insights can inform decisions as the team builds a *¶64 Refined Product Backlog*.

With too many solution options before them, dependent teams cannot lock in their system designs. However, this does not mean that work must wait for a decision. By working within the critical constraints, the team can start work on the design of a subsystem while keeping in mind how it must fit within the overall solution space of the larger system. In fact, the team may leave some parameters open until production, never fixing them during design. In some cases it is even possible to offer the alternatives to the customer as options.

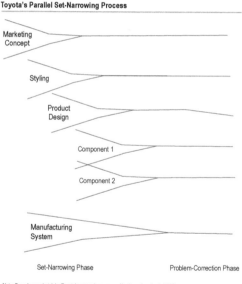

Toyota's Parallel Set-Narrowing Process

Marketing Concept

Styling

Product Design

Component 1

Component 2

Manufacturing System

Set-Narrowing Phase   Problem-Correction Phase

Note: Based on a sketch by Toyota's general manager of body engineering in 1993.

Converging interdependent components over time ("The Second Toyota Paradox: How Delaying Decisions Can Make Better Cars Faster," *Sloan Management Review 36* [WLCS95], p. 43).

A key consideration is when to begin converging toward the final solution. Ford and Sobek modeled Toyota's development process using real options and ran 100 simulations of a 900-day long project ("Adapting Real Options to New Product Development by Modeling the Second Toyota Paradox" in *IEEE Transactions on Engineering Management 52* [FS05]).

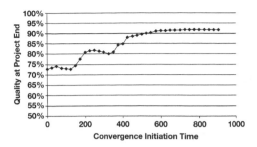

Expected quality of point-based and set-based development projects (*IEEE Transactions on Engineering Management 52 [FS05]*).

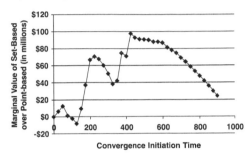

Expected values of flexibility in set-based development relative to point-based development (*IEEE Transactions on Engineering Management 52 [FS05]*).

These findings suggest that the optimal time for convergence is near the middle of the overall project span. However, the authors caution that if there are delays early in the project, it may be wise to push convergence even a little later than the midpoint. Therefore, the *Product Owner* must have visibility into the overall progress of the divergent work.

Toyota prefers to have the same people together develop all the options. This way the group develops a feeling for the problem space, which can guide the design of new options. They can accelerate the process by developing several options concurrently rather than sequentially. This rapid comparing of options as the team builds them creates the shared experience needed to develop one's intuition. It's also worth pointing out that *Set-Based Design* ensures people maintain competencies in areas that haven't been used in a product in a long time. This preserves corporate memory that may again become valuable for future products.

Google's Design Sprint is one approach for rapidly evaluating many design ideas. The authors claim it "gives teams a shortcut to learning without building and launching." The process begins with mapping out the problem and identifying an important area to focus on, and concludes with testing a high-fidelity proto-type with customers. The whole process takes 1 week or less.[5]

Lastly, at these key moments when the process eliminates an option that some team has passionately developed, we must consider the human dimension: it can hurt when others judge your work, and it is possible that a team member may take the decision as a personal slight. This loss creates the need for a "rite of passage" of sorts. Robert Heath, author of *Celebrating Failure*, recommends that leaders should "acknowledge failures with positive comments. Congratulate everyone on their efforts and remind them of the strengths and wisdom they gained from the experience. Put in perspective, a failure can do as much to motivate a team as a win" (*Celebrating Failure: The Power of Taking Risks, Making Mistakes, and Thinking Big [Hea09]*).

These in-the-moment comments, however, will mean nothing if they do not take place within a larger culture of continuous learning. Google's culture of "blameless postmortems" is one such example. It draws from experience in other areas like healthcare and avionics, where failure can be fatal. In these workplaces, the focus after a failure is not on the individuals involved but on the larger system, and uncovering the underlying reasons why people had partial or incorrect information which led to the undesirable result. Lunney and Lueder write (*Site Reliability Engineering: How Google Runs Production Systems [LL16]*) that "you can't 'fix' people, but you can fix systems and processes to better support people making the right choices when designing and maintaining complex systems." The team must fully own the idea of collective improvement for this pattern to succeed.

The *¶12 Product Owner Team* may apply this approach to evaluate which of several alternative *PBI*s to retain on the *Product Backlog*, or may use it to explore alternatives for a high-risk or high-uncertainty *PBI* or entire *Regular Product Increment*. Such a design exploration may cross several *Sprint* boundaries.

Alternatively, the *Development Team* may use this approach within a *Sprint* to evaluate risk across multiple implementation alternatives, and can use the resulting insight to select one alternative. When doing *Set-Based Design* within a *Sprint*, the *Development Team* should time-box the exploration. Because the process creates a high rate of emergent requirements (that's why they do it), it is difficult to estimate how much the team will accomplish in the time box. Therefore, when using this approach, the team must accept the

---

5.   Jake Knapp (Google Ventures) et al. "The Design Sprint." http://www.gv.com/sprint/, n.d., no permalink, accessed 2 November 2017.

fact that there is a risk that the exploration may not result in a potentially shippable *Regular Product Increment*, but it is nonetheless worth the time spent for the insight gained.

Whether the results of a given *Set-Based Design* make it to the market or not, the team gains confidence in such features' presence (or not) in the product, increasing *¶38 Product Pride.*

¶43 Sprint Burndown Chart

...*¶24 Sprint Planning* has ended, the *¶75 Production Episode* has started, and the *¶14 Development Team* is fully engaged.

Based on its understanding of its capacity, its *velocity* (see Notes on Velocity on page 320) and its estimate of the effort required to develop the top *¶55 Product Backlog Item*s (PBIs), the *Development Team* has agreed to a *¶71 Sprint Goal* and created its development and construction plan in the form of a *¶72 Sprint Backlog*.

The *Development Team* is committed to the *Sprint Goal*, and to doing everything it can to complete the *Product Backlog Item*s that it forecast it would complete in this *Production Episode* time box.

❖ ❖ ❖

The *Development Team* members focus most of their attention on technical, production, and engineering tasks, but they must also attend to business issues as a self-managing team (see *¶16 Autonomous Team*). It is important that team members have timely access to information about their progress towards meeting their forecast, so that they can pivot immediately if necessary.

There are too many unknowns for the team's delivery forecast to be a guarantee, and yet the statement of the *Sprint Goal* and the team's forecast delivery have raised stakeholders' expectations.

The *Development Team* needs a clear understanding of its estimated remaining work on a frequent, perhaps daily, basis so it can manage its progress during the *¶46 Sprint*.

If it turns out that the *Development Team* has overestimated its capacity for work, the *¶7 Scrum Team* needs to be able to communicate this to stakeholders (perhaps directly, perhaps through the *¶11 Product Owner*) as early as possible. It may even be necessary to escalate into *¶32 Emergency Procedure*, so that the *Scrum Team*, and possibly the business and customers, can collaborate to find a solution.

If, on the other hand, the *Development Team* turns out to have significantly overestimated the effort needed to turn *Product Backlog Item*s into a potentially shippable increment, then it will have spare capacity at the end of the *Sprint*. The *Scrum Team* as a whole needs to decide how best to use that capacity.

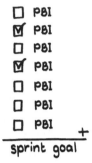

This might cause the *Product Owner* to pull forward *Product Backlog Item*s, originally slated for the next *Sprint*, for development in the current *Sprint* (or, by agreement, the *Development Team* can just continue working from the top of the *¶54 Product Backlog*). The *Development Team* can update its work plan accordingly in the *¶29 Daily Scrum.* (And the *Development Team* and *Product Owner* together probably have some work to do the next time they work toward a *¶64 Refined Product Backlog.*)

It would be very useful to forecast which of these fates await the *Development Team* at the end of the *Sprint*, and to make that information transparent to stakeholders.

Therefore:

Create a graph that plots estimated work remaining in the *Sprint* against the amount of time remaining in the time box. Plot the *Sprint*'s progress as a trend line on the graph so that its slope gives an immediately obvious and intuitive indicator as to likelihood of the *Development Team* meeting its target. Post the graph where all *Scrum Team* members have easy access to it. Update it regularly, at least on a daily basis.

The following graph is called a *Sprint Burndown Chart*, or *Sprint Burndown Graph.*

The concept of the *Sprint Burndown Chart* is an analogy drawn from the experiences of pilots trying to land high-performance fighter aircraft. It is

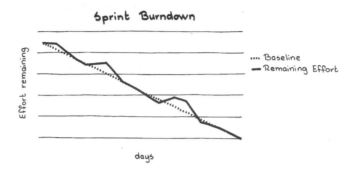

designed to detect when the plane is high on the glide path. It also shows distance to the end of the runway, rate of descent, and is an indirect indication of airspeed and direction. When the plane is high on the glide path it is often necessary to abort the landing. If the pilot tries to drop more quickly by pulling the nose up and reducing power, he or she can get behind the power curve, where going slower requires more power and causes a crash. (This is analogous to Brooks' Law in *The Mythical Man-Month: Essays on Software Engineering [Bro95]* that says adding people to a late project makes it later). However, a good pilot who detects the problem early enough can take safe and effective action to land the plane on the end of the runway. Poor pilots may try to land anyway and touch down beyond the end of the runway. On an aircraft carrier, this can destroy the airplane and often the pilot.

In a *Sprint Burndown Chart*, the Y-axis reflects the overall effort estimated to achieve the forecast. The unit of measurement should be the same as that used to estimate the *Product Backlog Items* (i.e., ¶*60 Estimation Points*).

The X-axis shows the number of working days left in the *Sprint*. The graph depict a countdown of working days to 0 (the last day of the *Sprint*), or calendar dates (i.e., January 4, March 5, etc.) or how many days have passed in the *Sprint*.

The *Development Team* owns the *Sprint Burndown Chart*. It is a tool originally intended for use by the *Development Team* rather than by external stakeholders—management included. However, in broad use it is a popular ¶*56 Information Radiator* that gives a wider audience transparency into what is happening inside the *Production Episode*: there is no need to hide anything in Scrum, and transparency can sometimes lead to early impediment detection and resolution. But it is there primarily to help the team manage itself, rather than to provide information to any other party managing development.

In developments using a *Sprint Burndown Chart*, the *¶19 ScrumMaster* may need to remind the *Development Team* to update it regularly, and to lead the team towards choosing a format that most clearly and easily expresses its intent.

Since value is directly associated with *Product Backlog Item*s rather than with *¶73 Sprint Backlog Item*s, the team should track work remaining at the level of the *Product Backlog Item*s to be delivered. As the team completes work items, they decrement the overall amount of work remaining, and plot the new total on the graph. Here, "completed" is best interpreted as *Done* (see *¶82 Definition of Done*), which implies that the team updates the chart only when a *Product Backlog Item* is brought to *Done*. Tracking *Done* keeps the team attentive to progress on delivering the *Sprint* value. If the graph were to instead depict completion of *Sprint Backlog Item*s, then it would display how much work remains. It is in theory possible to complete almost all work and deliver little or no value if the work on most *Product Backlog Item*s remains incomplete.

The team marks off the estimated work for completed items, rather than the actual expended effort; we do not want and do not need the tedium of measuring time taken by individual tasks or *Product Backlog Item*s. Update the *Sprint Burndown Chart* in only two cases. In the first case, the team updates the chart when a *Product Backlog Item* comes to *Done*, burning down by that *Product Backlog Item*'s original estimated effort. The second case relates to the discovery of emergent requirements and unplanned work. One might increase the *Product Backlog Item* estimate accordingly and adjust the chart upward by the delta of newly discovered work. Do not reduce the amount of remaining work for a partially completed *Product Backlog Item*. The job of the *Sprint Burndown Chart* is to focus the team forward on remaining work in the days left in the *Sprint* rather than looking back to the past, however recent. The accuracy of the estimate for any given item does not normally affect the estimates for the remaining items.

There is a strong benefit in maintaining the chart on a wall, as a hand-drawn poster, rather than outsourcing it to a tool. On the one hand, it strengthens the *Development Team*'s sense of ownership to physically draw the trend line, and on the other hand there is pressure to keep it simple, focusing on only the essential information the *Development Team* needs. It is not easy to hide a wall poster, either purposefully or by accident. The *Sprint Burndown Chart* becomes a powerful tool for reinforcing self-management in these circumstances. You can also easily annotate the *Sprint Burndown Chart* with important events and use those data during the *¶36 Sprint Retrospective*.

Most Burndown Charts include a reference line for the average burndown rate, drawn from the top of the Y-axis (effort) to the right-most calibration mark of the X-axis (time). The team can compare the trend line of the *Sprint*'s actual progress against the reference line. If the team finds its progress is significantly above the average burndown rate, then it may conclude it is likely to not deliver the entire *Sprint Backlog*. If, on the other hand, it is significantly below the average trend line, the *Development Team* may conclude it has spare capacity in the *Sprint*. A less simplistic approach would compare the current *Sprint*'s trajectory against the trajectory for recent *Sprint*s, because the burndown path is rarely linear.

❖ ❖ ❖

Some *Development Team*s use graphs that show the effort needed to complete tasks rather than *Product Backlog Item*s and some use a "double y-axis" with both *Product Backlog Item*s and tasks shown, with a different colored trend line for each on the same Burndown Chart.

The *Development Team* is free to choose whatever representation suits its needs best, but it should realize that most often not all development tasks are known at the end of *Sprint Planning*. New tasks emerge as the team learns more during the *Sprint*, meaning it should increase the amount of remaining work as described above. The *Development Team* should focus on how much they will deliver rather than on how much work they have done. Moreover, it is possible for the *Development Team* to have completed a great number of tasks without actually delivering much value.

This should never be true of *Product Backlog Item*s, assuming no new ones are allowed to enter the *Sprint* (unless the team has already achieved the *Sprint Goal*). Since the *Product Backlog Item*s represent the essential value propositions of the *Sprint Goal*, the trend line on a *Sprint Burndown Chart*— which focuses on the effort estimated to develop the *Product Backlog Items*— keeps the team centered on its delivery of business value.

Ken Schwaber was the first to describe the *Sprint Burndown Chart* in May 2001. He invented it during his period at Fidelity Investments.[6]

---

6.   Ken Schwaber. "Sprint Burndown." Web.archive.org, http://web.archive.org/web/20010503112119/www.controlchaos.com/sburndown.htm, May 2001 (accessed 2 November 2017).

¶44 Scrum Board

Confidence stars: **

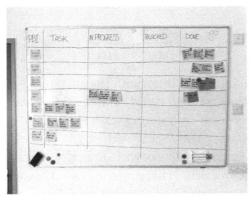

...¶24 Sprint Planning has ended with the ¶11 Product Owner and the ¶14 Development Team agreeing on a ¶71 Sprint Goal. The Development Team has forecast what ¶55 Product Backlog Items (PBIs) it believes it will deliver this ¶46 Sprint. The ¶75 Production Episode has started.

The Development Team has a plan expressed in the ¶72 Sprint Backlog, and members of the team are applying their skills in the way they think best to accomplish the tasks in the plan. New information is continually surfacing during development, and the Development Team members are struggling to replan accordingly.

❖   ❖   ❖

There is a danger that the Development Team collectively will lose sight of its construction and development goals. It needs to synchronize its efforts constantly, so as to inspect and adapt the plan as required.

The phrase "fog of war" was first defined in 1896 by a Colonel in the British Royal Engineers as "the state of ignorance in which commanders frequently find themselves as regards the real strength and position, not only of their foes, but also of their friends" (The Fog of War [HM96]). Typically, it is not so much a lack of information, but an overload of different intelligence reports, from different sources and in different formats, driven by a rapidly changing tactical situation that creates the fog. Background noise prevents a focus on the critical information in anything like a timely fashion. Information overload causes emotional overload that in turn leads to poor decision-making.

Compare the ¶16 *Autonomous Team* with the situation of a military comman-der. We can define the strategic direction in terms of the *Sprint Goal* and, to a lesser degree, in terms of completing work on the *PBI*s as per the *Develop-ment Team*'s forecast for this *Sprint*. The *PBI*s are often an approach to achieving the business imperative of the *Sprint Goal*, and tasks or work items are tactical objectives towards delivering the *PBI*s. They are the team's chosen path to completing the *PBI*s. The *Development Team* may plot this path at the beginning of the *Sprint Backlog*, but progress brings increased clarity that frustrates the best laid plans of mice and men. So the team must frequently revisit their tactics.

Collaboration between people with different functional backgrounds is much harder without transparency. Individual *Development Team* members need con-stant reminders of how their work relates to the bigger picture of the *Sprint Goal*, and the team as a whole needs to focus collectively on it on a regular basis.

Therefore:

Create a *Scrum Board* that represents the *Sprint Backlog* and its evolution during the *Sprint*. The *Development Team* maintains it, controls it, and owns it. Post it where all *Development Team* members have easy access to it as an ¶56 *Information Radiator*.

A *Scrum Board*, a.k.a. *Task Board*, is typically a big poster on a wall; it relates development tasks and other ¶73 *Sprint Backlog Item*s to *Product Backlog Item*s, and *PBI*s to the *Sprint Goal* to which they contribute.

PBIs	SBIs		
	To Do	In Progress	Done
A	▭ ▭ ▭ ▭ ▭	▭ ▭	▭ ▭
B	▭ ▭ ▭		
C	▭ ▭ ▭		

❖ ❖ ❖

The team can now visualize the state of tactical work on tasks together with *PBI* completion status, and can use specific task status to determine if they are still on track or if they need to update the work plan to complete *PBIs* or to meet the *Sprint Goal*. If the team can visualize progress on the *Sprint Backlog*, it makes such replanning easier.

The team can post a statement of the *Sprint Goal* and a *¶43 Sprint Burndown Chart* along with the *Scrum Board* (*Essential Scrum: A Practical Guide to the Most Popular Agile Process [Rub12]*, pp. 356–358).

The *Development Team* collectively owns the *Scrum Board*, and typically updates it as the team completes *Sprint Backlog Items*. However the *¶19 ScrumMaster* may want to remind the *Development Team* to keep the *Scrum Board* up to date, and will also help the team understand the significance of the data the Board is presenting. This is especially true when an incomplete or delayed development task or other *Sprint Backlog Item* threatens the *Development Team*'s ability to meet its forecast. The team can then take collective action to remove the impediment.

In short, the *Scrum Board* is a planning tool for action management, owned and controlled by the *Development Team* and, as such, can help build the necessary muscle memory needed for the *Development Team* to become truly self-managing. Used consistently, the *Scrum Board* lowers the communication cost of developers trying to find out what other *Development Team* members are doing, and of managing the dependencies between their various tasks. Above all, it helps everyone maintain their collective focus.

Where possible, it is a good idea to hold the *¶29 Daily Scrum* around the *Scrum Board* because then the *Development Team* can create the daily plan with the latest information available.

Scrum does not prescribe the format of a *Scrum Board* (*Proceedings of the 12th annual ACM symposium on User interface software and technology [MSNG99]*). It is for the team to decide the most useful way of presenting the information it needs. It should be possible for all developers to view and manipulate the board together as a team. A small computer screen works against this, and moving items with a keyboard or pointing device is awkward even if the screen is large. The best *Scrum Board*s are tactile and use simple "technologies" such as sticky notes or whiteboards. The following describes just one example:

- The board is a large poster displaying a matrix. Cards and sticky notes represent *PBIs* and *Sprint Backlog Items*, respectively. The team moves sticky notes across the board to represent its progress to *Done* (see *¶82 Definition of Done*).

- The board prominently displays the *Sprint Goal* as a named state, or as a short statement explaining how it benefits the end user.

- The chart has a row for each *PBI* in the current *Sprint*. There is one column each for *PBI*s; for *Sprint Backlog Item*s 'To Do'; for *Sprint Backlog Item*s 'In Progress'; for completed *Sprint Backlog Item*s; and 'Done' for *PBI*s that are *Done*.

- Cards representing the *PBI*s start in the *PBI* column and the team moves them to the 'Done' column only when it completes all the *Sprint Backlog Item*s for it, and it meets the *Definition of Done*. When *Development Team* members start a task, they move the sticky note that represents it to the 'In Progress' column. When they complete a *Sprint Backlog Item*, they move its sticky note to the 'Done' column and the developers who worked on it can now pick up a new one.

- The *Development Team* has met its forecast when all the *PBI* cards have reached the 'Done' column.

- Each *Scrum Board* lasts for the length of the *Sprint*. New *Sprint*s require that the team create a new *Scrum Board* or that an existing *Scrum Board* be reset.

This pattern is an *Information Radiator* and is related to the *Sprint Burndown Chart*.

However, the *Scrum Board* should not be confused with a Kanban Board, despite superficial similarities. While they both depict the progress of tickets as they move through various states, the purpose is not the same. A *Autonomous Team* owns and controls a *Scrum Board*: it does not control them. It is a tool that allows the team to plan, and replan as necessary, how to meet its objectives in a *Sprint*.

A Kanban Board, on the other hand, maps the life-cycle of a product or a feature as it moves from inception through its various states (and *multiple* teams may work on it), to the point where a team delivers the feature to the customer. Each state has a Work-In-Progress (WIP) limit associated with it. Advocates of Kanban (in software development; see *Kanban: Successful Evolutionary Change for Your Technology Business [And10]*) claim that it visualizes a "pull" system where each upstream state feeds its output into the next downstream state only when there is available capacity. Kanban, however, does not mandate that teams be either cross-functional or self-managing. It leaves open who controls the board and sets the WIP limits. In these circumstances it is easy for command-and-control managements to turn the Kanban Board into a tool for a "push" system by setting arbitrary WIP limits, and pressuring developers to work to full capacity

By contrast, in Scrum, the self-managing *Development Team* controls work in progress by pulling *PBI*s from the top of the Product Backlog on a *Sprint*-by-*Sprint* basis and through swarming on the individual *Sprint Backlog Item*s.

One last note: Laypersons often equate "doing Scrum" with the use of a *Scrum Board*. While a *Scrum Board* is one of the most noticeable tools of Scrum organizations (the other being the *Daily Scrum*), there is much more to Scrum than any set of tools can capture. By analogy, kicking a soccer ball around in the park can look a lot like playing soccer, but it is not soccer. This pattern refers to many other patterns that represent crucial components of the Scrum framework, and yet those, too, are only a starting point.

¶45 Product Roadmap

Confidence stars: *

There are many routes to your destination. Base your next step on the current situation and the best possible path.

...there is a product *¶39 Vision* for the organization. It is important for the *¶11 Product Owner* to share this vision with the team and the stakeholders. There are many potential paths to business success, and ever-emerging insights from the *Product Owner* and the developers affect the chosen path through the sequence of *¶85 Regular Product Increments*.

❖ ❖ ❖

The *Product Owner* is confident about a general product direction and might even be confident of the destination. Even so, there are many paths to reach a given market position, level of profitability, market penetration, and other product objectives. Unfortunately, it's usually impossible to know beforehand the best path to take. The *Product Owner* has a hunch for which *Regular Product Increment*s are good options for market success. Without foreseeing the experience that comes with a few releases and growing market knowledge, what looks good now may not look good later. And it's silly to blindly act on every initial hunch, so it's a good idea to keep options open. Holding too tightly to a false certainty about some exact plan can lead to a death march. So how can *Product Owner*s contemplate and communicate the big picture and overall goals to the teams and stakeholders, and also help maintain the right stuff on the *¶54 Product Backlog?*

When starting to develop a new product, product management often starts with brainstorming important features and ideas for key deliverables. To describe these features and ideas, it is tempting to fully detail how they will work and fully specify the steps needed to make these ideas real while they are fresh in your mind. You may even want to estimate them to specify a ¶48 *Release Plan* and fantasize about when you might finish the project. This is often referred to as waterfall development.

It can take a lot of time to understand the *Vision* and note how strategic business decisions will affect the direction of the product. There is a danger that many details of the *Product Owner*'s *Vision* can remain tacit. A good *Product Owner* may have an agile spirit, knowing that he or she can benefit the enterprise by changing the details of *Regular Product Increment*s when new information emerges. But good *Product Owner*s also have a "plan B" in their back pocket for dealing with some of the challenges and changes they can foresee. These may include some specific feature as an alternative to another, or just multiple different release sequences of the same *Regular Product Increment*s. The best *Product Owner*s make these alternatives visible.

Yet, these options don't have a proper place on the *Product Backlog*. The *Product Backlog* shows one delivery ordering of one set of *Regular Product Increment*s. It must reflect a committed ordering of deliverables by the *Product Owner* in light of the best current information. However, this information changes ¶46 *Sprint* by *Sprint* and hour by hour. It's important to have a place to remember the possible directions that the ¶7 *Scrum Team* has explored and which are still open to possible deployment—subject to business conditions and other criteria that might change. You want to keep all product direction decisions, all of the "known knowns," and all "known unknowns" visible to the entire *Scrum Team* and other stakeholders.

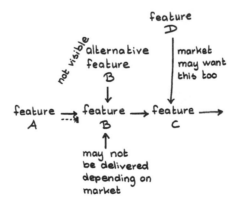

You could track all of these options on one *Product Backlog* and just move the unlikely ¶55 *Product Backlog Item*s to the bottom. However, that may lose information about the dependencies between *Product Backlog Item*s and timing information that is important to the *Release Plan*. In other words, a *Product Backlog* is one-dimensional and you would need to add complex annotations to express multiple deployment options; this would leave it less transparent.

As *Scrum Team*s are working through *Sprint*s (including both ¶24 *Sprint Planning* and development), they can often get lost in the details of current and short-term work, leading to local optimization and missing the big picture. It is important to sustain awareness of how current tasks and envisioned features fit into the big picture and to also demarcate important decision points which could lead to new directions and influence the *Product Backlog* ordering.

Therefore,

Create a *Product Roadmap* as a focal point to reflect the overall *Vision* and to drive the *Product Backlog*. The Roadmap presents options in two dimensions (alternative decision paths in time and sequence), while the *Product Backlog* depicts ordering in only one dimension (monotonically progressing time). The *Product Roadmap* outlines alternatives, and the opportunity to collectively make decisions at well-defined decision points: do we go right or left here? The *Product Backlog* is today's best guess of the path we will take through the *Product Roadmap*. The Roadmap may evolve to reflect changes to the business strategy.

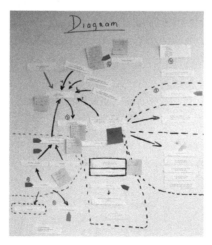

A *Product Roadmap* is a graph with intersection points. To get from A to B in the path, development must fulfill some requirement. To build a *Product*

Roadmap the *Product Owner* must identify the conditions for meeting the *Vision*. All stakeholders must contribute in identifying the conditions. Many paths can lead to implementation of the *Vision*. The *Product Roadmap* should be a plan for how to follow the road that yields the highest long-term value.

Each step in the *Product Roadmap* must create value as obtained from the *¶41 Value Stream*s. To help the *Product Owner* order the *Product Backlog*, he or she may benefit from a value estimate for each link in the Roadmap. Therefore, a good *Product Owner* annotates the *Product Roadmap* with available information about cost and value.

The *Product Roadmap* is based on current known conditions. Things will change. There are always surprises from many sources including competitive analysis, SWOT (strengths, weaknesses, opportunities, threats) analysis, stakeholder expectations, market conditions, projected velocities, and hard market deadlines. The *Product Owner* owns the *Product Roadmap* and is responsible for updating it when business conditions change or relevant information becomes available. The *Product Backlog* should reflect the best-known current path through the Roadmap, and the *Product Owner* derives the *Release Plan* from the *Product Backlog*.

❖ ❖ ❖

With an up-to-date Roadmap in hand, the team has guidance to maintain the *Product Backlog* in successive *Sprint*s. The *Scrum Team* and all stakeholders have a greater sense of direction and *Unity of Purpose* (see *¶117 Unity of Purpose* on page 468) as well as an understanding of the overall product *Vision*. Ensure that the Roadmap remains transparent to all stakeholders as an *¶56 Information Radiator*.

The *Product Backlog* will evolve from the *Product Roadmap* as the latter offers insight into the consequences of key decisions about the product direction.

Building a *Product Roadmap* as an explicit artifact might require a non-trivial effort, but the effort may be worthwhile when product delivery options become complex, or just to make tacit backup plans visible. The *Product Roadmap* also has a benefit of supporting the discussions at all Scrum events, giving important insight into the concrete aspects of the *Product Owner Vision*.

A Roadmap can never perfectly foresee the future of a changing landscape. Trying to foresee every contingency is futile; keep alternative product directions at the level of strategic, rather than tactical, decisions. The top of the *Product Backlog* should detail tactical changes prompted by new information.

A *Product Backlog* is not a *Product Roadmap*. A *Product Roadmap* communicates strategic information and makes visible the options that *Product Owner* has for the product. In contrast to this, the *¶72 Sprint Backlog* contains largely tactical information. The *Product Backlog* is intermediate to these two, abstracting away options that the *Product Owner* has currently decided not to roll out.

Any point in the *Product Roadmap* may list several alternative options, and the *Product Owner* may choose one or more of them at will, usually on a just-in-time basis. Use *¶42 Set-Based Design* to help qualify candidates for the *Product Backlog*.

Good *Product Roadmap*s are as simple as possible. Use simple and flexible technology, such as sticky notes on a board, rather than computerized tools. Use the roadmap to show deployment dependencies and alternatives rather than release plans; use the *Product Backlog* as a basis for release planning, and limit release planning to the current "plan of record" to avoid confusing stakeholders with too many alternative potential release dates.

Rhythms: Patterns of Time

To a first approximation, it is more important that we attend to some tasks regularly than it is that we attend to them often. For example, it's important to brush your teeth, and many people follow so-called proven recommendations of attending to it three times a day. Cope's dentist recommends that if he does it really well, he needs to do it only once a day. Dina has learned that it is twice a day. What is important is that all of these recommendations have a rhythm, and as such, they lead to habit formation in human beings. By making events such as eating, or brushing your teeth, or planning upcoming work habitual, we can relieve the team of focusing on *when*, so they can focus on *what*. Thus, in Scrum it is best to first establish a cadence, and then adjust the frequency and duration of each event as you inspect and adapt.

Rhythm is a strong and pervasive foundation of human existence. Renowned anthropologist Edward Hall, who specializes in cultural notions of *time*, writes, "I am convinced that it will ultimately be proved that almost every facet of human behavior is involved in the rhythmic process" (*The Dance of Life [Hal88]*, p. 153). Sociology professor Eviatar Zerubavel notes that we are governed on one hand by cycles of nature, such as going to bed every night, and on the other hand by cycles of the "machine," such as business and delivery schedules (*Everyday Revolutionaries: Working Women and the Transformation of American Life [Hel98]*, p. 140). Sometimes there is ambiguity between them, such as in the length of a ¶46 *Sprint*, which is about a month long by default (though most contemporary teams override the default with a Sprint length of one or two weeks)—*month* coming from the same root as the word *moon*. Natural rhythms tend to be periodic and happen of their own accord.

To the degree we can tie our Scrum production rhythms to other "natural" rhythms and their events, these natural rhythms can serve as sentinels and reminders of the associated impending Scrum activity. So ¶29 *Daily Scrums* happen daily, on the cycle of the Earth's rotation; *Sprints* tend to follow business cycles which, from a Scrum perspective, are part of what people accept as being the more natural ecosystem for the practice of Scrum. (Of course, those business cycles may loosely follow natural cycles in their own right: see ¶77 *Follow the Moon*.) In general, there is a strong interweaving of the time and process aspects of Scrum as emphasized here in the Value Stream Pattern Language on page 185, with the coming together of people that are the focus of the Product Organization Pattern Language on page 11. Scrum events are configurations of space (relationships between people) in some context of time (an event).

Scrum features many patterns that are based on rhythm. All Scrum events (the *Sprint* itself, *¶24 Sprint Planning*, *¶35 Sprint Review*, *¶36 Sprint Retrospective*, and the *Daily Scrum*) are based on rhythms. *¶47 Organizational Sprint Pulse* aligns multiple teams around a common rhythm. Having these events recur on a known cadence avoids the waste of having to repeatedly find time for them.

Rhythm and time-boxing are two sides of the same coin. *Sprint*s might start every two weeks; that means that a *Sprint*'s duration is no longer than two weeks.

Scrum's rhythms come from long experience and are to some degree prescribed: for example, *The Scrum Guide*[7] says that a *Sprint* may not be longer than one calendar month, and it typically is no shorter than a week. A great *¶7 Scrum Team* matches the actual duration of a cadence to yield the most output, or comfort, or predictability, or other desirable trait. In most Western cultures, when we sit together at lunch at work, some people finish consuming their food in 7 minutes and some take 25 minutes. But we sit there together for 30 minutes and then, as though on cue, we go back to work. We find built-in clocks that balance our social needs. The cadence serves that social need rather than vice versa. And different cultures have different social needs: these lunchtime synchronization intervals may change or nearly disappear the nearer a culture is to the equator. Scrum does not presume that one size fits all, and it is up to each team to find its place within the recommended range (or sometimes, outside that range) that works best.

Iterations are also fundamental to Scrum, and iterations work best if they follow a cadence.

Good kaizen (see Kaizen and Kaikaku on page 101) often has roots in sustaining a good rhythm. Just as daily cycles reinforce brushing your teeth, so the natural cycles of the day, business week, and month can reinforce good practices that align with them. This fits into the notion of *intentional practice* in *¶88 One Step at a Time*.

Hall invented the term *monochronic* to describe cultures that are attentive to linear time and rhythms. The Swiss are the stereotype of a monochronic culture. And Hall uses the word *polychronic* to describe cultures based on a shared model of multiple simultaneous time streams: the usual stereotype here is Mexican culture. So, in a monochronic culture, patients queue at the doctor's office and people take appointment times seriously. In a polychronic

---

7.   Jeff Sutherland and Ken Schwaber. *The Scrum Guide*. ScrumGuides.org, http://www.scrumguides.org (accessed 5 January 2017).

culture, the doctor may come into reception and spend a little bit of time with each patient before seeing them in the examining room. Monochronic cultures focus on the process of the whole, while polychronic cultures are more concerned with the individual. While the gross Scrum framework is monochronic and based on rhythms as described above, work within the *¶75 Production Episode* is highly polychronic: everyone doing everything all the time. Most development cultures, rooted in indigenous and corporate norms, may struggle a bit with adopting one or the other of these styles of working. Such adjustment is part of the deep learning necessary to mastering agile development while meeting market needs.

¶46 Sprint

Confidence stars: **

...you have a *¶41 Value Stream* with a *¶54 Product Backlog* that defines ten-tative deliverables and delivery order. In line with agile values, you are striving to deliver early and to get into a rhythm of *¶85 Regular Product Increment*s while managing production cost.

❖ ❖ ❖

The most fundamental human processes build on cadence. Human culture often realizes cycles in rituals and other visible events of its calendar. As a culture matures, the rituals and events become more overt and newcomers learn events as their introduction to the culture. The centerpiece of any product development effort should honor business expectations to deliver products regularly and punctually, with satisfying content and value.

Teams must manage many risks during complex product development. In spite of the best planning, there is still always a risk that the team inadvertently solves the wrong problem, and cost and schedule estimation are traditionally rife with uncertainty. Agile tells us to use frequent feedback to reduce risk and maximize the chances for success, inspecting and adapting. Using shorter development intervals produces more frequent feedback—and while that can help, substantial variance may remain and accumulate over time, even when delivering small work batches of non-uniform size (*The Principles of Product Development Flow: Second Generation Lean Product Development [Rei09]*, pp. 176–178).

In an ideal world, a team could produce anything on demand, but a team can't get into a long-term flow of regular delivery without some kind of cadence. Being agile requires the freedom to inspect and adapt, but benchmarks of improvement and accomplishment drive people in a business setting. Constraints enable innovation, and the *¶14 Development Team* wants to be assured that it is making progress toward business goals.

Individuals in complete isolation can choose to do what they want, but shared context can benefit groups of people working together. The *Product Backlog* provides some of that context but is better suited to the long-term business outlook than to delivery. A business wants to manage delivery expectations beyond a simple ordering of *Regular Product Increments*. And the business wants to manage risk: long-running complex projects too often deliver the wrong thing, or fail to deliver everything they set out to do. And while it's important that the *¶7 Scrum Team* consider the *Product Backlog* as a whole, the *Development Team* must eventually and repeatedly focus on slices of that backlog and get down to producing specific *Regular Product Increments* that are *Done* (see *¶82 Definition of Done*). While the Team members may eventually deliver everything in the *Product Backlog*, they need to deliver small increments often enough to support fast feedback and correction cycles; otherwise, the market can suffer for a long time when the product fails to meet end-user needs.

Therefore:

Organize development around recurring, frequent, fixed-length, time-boxed intervals called *Sprints*. The *Sprint* is both a single time-boxed period of product *delivery effort* (duration) as well as a unit demarcating *delivery interval* on the release calendar (cadence). The recurring nature of the *Sprint* supports the *iterative* nature of Scrum, enabling short feedback cycles that help reduce rework. The time-boxed nature of the *Sprint* corresponds to the effort behind the granularity of *Regular Product Increment* delivery, and supports the *incremental* nature of Scrum.

Regular cadence fundamentally scopes the effect of variance to one interval of iteration and short-circuits the long-term accumulation of variance (*The Principles of Product Development Flow: Second Generation Lean Product Development [Rei09]*).

The maximum *Sprint* length is one calendar month. Dominant practice seems to follow two-week *Sprints*, and one-week *Sprints* are not uncommon. The length of the *Sprint* needs to balance the forces of being long enough to deliver a valuable *Regular Product Increment* and short enough for the Scrum team to gain useful feedback. A *Sprint* may not take longer than four weeks because the feedback loops become too long. Teams just starting Scrum may use one-week *Sprints* to speed up the feedback they receive as they shape their initial process.

During the *Sprint*, the team focuses on the *¶71 Sprint Goal* and strives to achieve its *forecast* of completing all work on the *¶72 Sprint Backlog*.

The *Sprint* starts with a gathering of the entire *Scrum Team* in *¶24 Sprint Planning* to update the *Product Backlog*, after which the *Development Team* creates a work plan. After *Sprint Planning* comes a time-boxed work interval, the *¶75 Production Episode*, during which the *Development Team* builds the *Regular Product Increment*. In the meantime, the *¶11 Product Owner* continues to engage stakeholders and prepares the *Product Backlog* for the *next Sprint*. During this work interval, the *Development Team* assesses progress and replans the *Sprint* in a daily stand-up called the *¶29 Daily Scrum*. Every day, the *Development Team* updates the *Sprint Backlog* with a new *¶76 Developer-Ordered Work Plan* optimized to achieve the *Sprint Goal*. At the end of this work interval comes the *¶35 Sprint Review*, where the *Product Owner* reviews the *Regular Product Increment* and the team discusses the status of the product; and a *¶36 Sprint Retrospective* where *Scrum Team* members together assess how to improve their process.

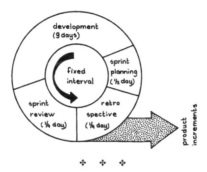

❖   ❖   ❖

Sprint rhythms apply to the *Development Team*. *Product Owners* work in a parallel process, and while they synchronize with the *Development Team* according to the *Sprint* time box, they can spread much of their work with stakeholders and with the *Product Backlog* across several *Sprints*.

We can regard a *Sprint* in three ways: as a unit of time, as a unit of *Regular Product Increment*, and as a unit of learning. It is first a unit of *time*: the implementation of regular delivery that we find in *Regular Product Increment*. It is a fixed time increment. It is a number of steps along the side of the *Value Stream*. In most professional organizations *time* translates into *cost*, so *Sprints* also translate into units of cost based on the time worked by developers (see *¶15 Stable Teams*). Originally, Scrum had one-month *Sprints* after the natural rhythm of *¶77 Follow the Moon*. The *Development Team* owns the development time box: they pull their workload for the development interval from the top of the *Product Backlog*, and they manage their own work during the development time box. The time box is not a constraint to push developers to finish, but a gift within which they self-manage. When the *Sprint* is over, it is over: in Scrum, we never extend a *Sprint* to accommodate undone work (or for any other reason). Knowing that the *Sprint* will end when it ends encourages the team to focus on best using the time it has.

Second, a *Sprint* is a representation of a *Regular Product Increment* at the usual granularity of market delivery. *Sprint*s provide frequent delivery to support both incremental and iterative development:

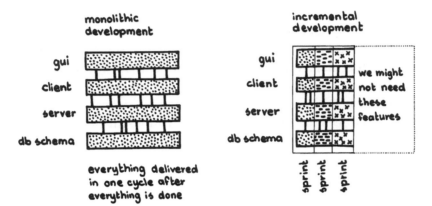

The *Sprint* schedule delineates delivery dates. However, *Sprint*s are units of *Regular Product Increment effort* rather than of *delivery* or *work*. Scrum calls its smallest units of delivery ¶55 *Product Backlog Items*, which combine into a *Product Increment*. By default, every *Sprint* encompasses the same amount of effort, but each may vary in the amount delivered because of emergent requirements, increases in velocity, variation in the quality of requirements, and other normal statistical variations.

Third, a *Sprint* is the major unit of learning in Scrum. Scrum is a minimal framework that puts people into a mindset of learning and feedback. It's important to have a learning cycle that builds on discipline, habit, and frames of reference of past accomplishment and future checkpoints. The *Sprint* itself —as a unit not just of time, but also of delivery of *Regular Product Increment* —provides a high-context frame of reference for deliberation and kaizen. But Sprint cadence also contributes powerfully to learning, just as having weekly piano lessons helps a pianist integrate great advances over periods longer than the week between sessions. The major ritual of *product* learning is the *Sprint Review*, and the major ritual of *process* learning is the *Sprint Retrospective*. Each *Sprint* has one instance of each of these events, one after the other, at the end of the time box.

We use the term *velocity* (see Notes on Velocity on page 320) for the amount of work that a team can complete in a single *Sprint*. It is a measure of each team's *demonstrated* capacity to do work in a *Sprint*. The current best practice is to measure velocity in units of relative time. See *Production Episode*.

Knowing that each *Sprint* has a constant cost, a *Product Owner* can do rough cost projections for the work of a *Development Team* over a period of time. The time-boxing also limits the number of working hours to avoid burnout and variations in production, and to encourage common working hours within which cooperation and teamwork can flourish.

The *Product Backlog Item*s that reach a state of *Done* during a *Sprint* become delivery candidates for that *Sprint* or a subsequent *Sprint*. We separate the decision of whether something is *Done* from the decision of shipping to market: the *Product Owner* makes the decision of when to release a *Product Backlog Item* to the market. However, early and frequent delivery leads to timely feedback and reduces the inventory of items with latent problems.

In exceptional cases, particularly when it becomes impossible to meet the *Sprint Goal*, the *Product Owner* may shorten a *Sprint*: see *¶32 Emergency Procedure*.

A *Development Team* within the product organization carries out production. A *Sprint* can best deliver high-quality product if the people working on it can sustain strong team dynamics (the alternative is to try to coordinate the work of individuals in multiple, dissociated organizations); therefore, make sure that a *¶10 Cross-Functional Team* develops the product increments within a *Sprint*.

Teams synchronize on a smaller scale using *¶80 Good Housekeeping* and *Daily Scrum*, and on a larger scale with *¶47 Organizational Sprint Pulse*. The *Product Owner* may elect to deliver a *Sprint* as a "friendly user," alpha or beta release, or to any subset of the market along the *¶86 Release Staging Layers*. The learning cycle also has a larger-scale rhythm as in *¶26 Kaizen Pulse*.

A *¶83 Team Sprint* is a Sprint where the *Development Team* drives the content of the *Sprint Backlog*. This gives the *Development Team* members a chance to be a bit selfish about their own agendas and to add value close to home for themselves, in areas that never quite make it to the top of the *Product Backlog* during normal *Sprint*s.

Regarding cadence and its relationship to deep human makeup and culture, see Hall's work on the anthropology of time (*The Dance of Life [Hal88]*). On how cadence leads to learning, and therefore predictability, see the work of Greville and Buehner on causal learning (*Journal of Experimental Psychology 139 [GB10]*). On the intrinsic human motivation to achieve and improve, see

Dan Pink's popular book on motivation (*Drive: The Surprising Truth About What Motivates Us [Pin11]*). On innovation and constraints, see Johnson's book on the contributing factors for innovation (*Where Good Ideas Come From: The Natural History of Innovation [Joh11]*, p. 84).

¶47 Organizational Sprint Pulse

Alias: Team Pulse, Sprint Pulse

Each group does it own dance, but as groups they synchronize to the same starting and ending of the song.

...the organization has one or more *¶10 Cross-Functional Team*s working in *¶46 Sprint*s.

❖ ❖ ❖

The *¶7 Scrum Team* and the rest of the organization are out-of-step, causing either waiting time or *Sprint* interruptions.

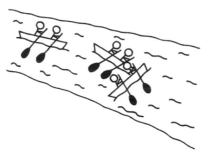

*Scrum Team*s depend on finances, sales and marketing, support, and other functions in an organization. Though we want *Scrum Team*s to be largely *¶16 Autonomous Team*s, they are rarely wholly independent units. A *Scrum Team* needs to coordinate with the rest of the organization and other teams. For example, when integrating a component from a supplier, doing integration test, or introducing new tools, the *Scrum Team* usually interacts with other departments or enterprises that feed its *¶41 Value Stream*. If the surrounding organizations have a monthly pulse owing to their business rhythm, and the *Scrum Team* has starting or ending dates for its *Sprint*s that clash with those of the partner teams, the organization as a whole risks being out-of-step. The same is true if the *Scrum Team*s have different *Sprint* lengths.

On one hand, we want the surrounding organization to respect the teams' *Sprint*s and to not disturb them arbitrarily. At the same time, we need to support the flow from the broader organization into the *Scrum Team*s so we avoid unnecessary waiting or untimely interrupts.

Sharing common *Sprint* lengths can take away some freedom from each team. On the other hand it's important to optimize flow by harmonizing *¶85 Regular Product Increment*s with the organization's rhythm.

Therefore:

Synchronize the rhythms of the *Scrum Team*s' *Sprint*s and the rhythms of the surrounding organization. Let the organization as a whole follow a monthly rhythm that can harmonize flow for *Scrum Team*s' *Sprint*s, as well as for the financial rhythm of the business. Allow teams and departments to choose shorter *Sprint*s. For example, use a *Sprint* length of 1, 2, or 4 weeks.

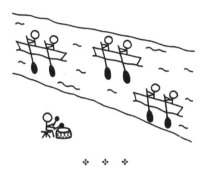

❖ ❖ ❖

As a manager from a Scrum organization with *Organizational Sprint Pulse* formulated it:

> Since things are done in Sprints of equal length, it is easier to synchronize. For example, if department A needs something from department B, it can be expected to be worked on in the near future. At least the progress can be followed.

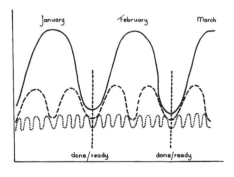

In other words, working at the same cadence reduces *mura* (inconsistency) by keeping the workflows in balance and aligning *Sprint* start and end dates. Cadence creates natural synchronization points across the enterprise, and without synchronization points, inventory can build up. Consistent cadence helps smooth out flow (*The Principles of Product Development Flow: Second Generation Lean Product Development [Rei09]*, pp. 176–178), reducing *muri* (stress). Being in sync makes it possible for all teams to work together to resolve dependencies immediately, in real time, instead of waiting for the next opportunity to align and to "get in step." Reducing both *mura* and *muri* contribute to reduced waste. *Organizational Sprint Pulse* makes it easier for teams to share goals and to work together, and makes it easier for all teams to share a single instance of each of the major *Sprint* events of *¶24 Sprint Planning*, the *¶35 Sprint Review*, and the *¶36 Sprint Retrospective*. These combined waste reductions contribute to achieving the *¶93 Greatest Value*.

Most Scrum organizations in the wild use *Organizational Sprint Pulse*—and the literature generally recommends using it (*Proceedings of XP 2012 [EB12]*). This is particularly important in large development efforts or when there are several firms working together on a product, as in *¶13 Development Partnership*.

Organizational Sprint Pulse can appear to compensate for lack of *Cross-Functional Teams* and *¶15 Stable Teams* in order to keep specialization and resource management reminiscent of pre-Scrum times. Explicit synchronization points can be (ab)used to move team members between teams or to coordinate between specialized teams. This is not the intention of the pattern. *Organizational Sprint Pulse* works best with *Cross-Functional Teams* and *Stable Teams*.

Organizational Sprint Pulse focuses on external coordination, while *¶34 Scrum of Scrums* focuses on internal (to the jointly developed product) coordination. For some deeper considerations about cadence, see *¶77 Follow the Moon*.

¶48 Release Plan

Confidence stars: *

A Royal Air Force C17 carrier aircraft bound for Nepal on 27 April, 2015, loaded with humanitarian aid and supplies. The velocity of the plane, the time it takes each pallet to exit the C17, and the ordering of the pallets define which pallet will land where.

...with the *¶39 Vision* in place you need to craft a plan to gather investment and resources to develop the product. You have a *¶54 Product Backlog* in place and you are using *¶55 Product Backlog Item*s (*PBIs*) that form *¶85 Regular Product Increment*s. You have estimated *Product Backlog Item*s in your *Product Backlog* and you know the velocities of all of your teams.

❖   ❖   ❖

The *¶11 Product Owner* needs to be able to communicate to stakeholders when the next release is coming out and which *Product Backlog Item*s the release contains. Sometimes, the release date is an important constraint, and other times the release contents are the main constraint. The risks inherent in an over-constrained problem arise when constraining both the date and contents, and the *Product Owner* must make such risk transparent.

If the *¶14 Development Team*s can see a committed long-term direction in terms of explicit *Regular Product Increment*s, they are more likely to expend the effort to get there, and are more likely to build the right things along the way toward the product *Vision*.

A lack of clear agreement on the content of the next release can give the stakeholders the impression that the scope is negotiable up until the release date. As a result, the release date can suffer from feature creep and the team ends up postponing delivery over and over again.

When the *Product Owner* has a history with the market, teams, and stakeholders with a high degree of trust, an overview plan and estimations alone may be adequate. If, on the other hand, the *Product Owner* is new to the teams, market, or

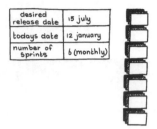

stakeholders and there is low trust, or the plan carries a higher-than-normal element of risk, you might need a more detailed plan and estimations.

Product Owners that create a release plan in isolation will miss out on the intelligence and insights of the *Development Teams*. Furthermore, the teams will not feel ownership of the plan and therefore they will be less likely to feel committed to any forecast.

Therefore:

Create an initial *Product Backlog* together with the *Development Teams* that communicates by which sequence of Increments you plan to realize the *Vision* and maximize value. That is, use the backlog to make a *Release Plan*. Use that plan to acquire the necessary investor commitment and team forecasts to develop your product.

The focus is always on progress at the product level. If you have multiple *Development Teams* working together from a single *Product Backlog*, then they can use their historic velocities (see Notes on Velocity on page 320) to forecast the *Regular Product Increments* that the teams working together will produce, given the current backlog ordering, but in a way that does not depend on pre-assigning specific *Product Backlog Items* to individual teams. Because velocities vary, there is also variance in the expected schedule for any set of *Regular Product Increments*, and a variation in the content of the *Regular Product Increments* for any given delivery date.

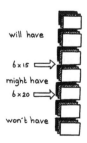

❖   ❖   ❖

The *Release Plan* is an ordered list of deliverables for the next few releases. Even with small variance in teams' velocities, the delivery schedule becomes unreasonably uncertain after just a few *¶46 Sprint*s. As a rule of thumb, looking beyond three *Sprint*s involves more guessing than statistically justifiable projection.

Together with *¶23 Fixed Work*, the *Release Plan* accounts for all work to bring the *PBI* to *Done* (see *¶82 Definition of Done*). The team may not separate "hardening" work or "quality work" from the rest of the work for any *PBI*. The *Product Owner* regularly updates the *Release Plan* with the latest insights from the market and the teams' velocities.

Starting at the top and working your way down the backlog, sum each *PBI*'s estimation units (e.g., *¶60 Estimation Points*) until you reach the sum of the known team velocities. The *Regular Product Increment* for the next release comprises these items at the top of the *Product Backlog*. Continue your way down the backlog to collect *PBI*s into *Regular Product Increment*s and to assign *Regular Product Increment*s to successive releases. Update the *¶45 Product Roadmap* based on this plan.

For example, assume that the team estimates each *PBI* in the preceding sketch requires 10 estimation points of work. The team has six *Sprint*s of time available to it before July 15, and we want to know what we will be able to deliver by then. The team has a history of sustaining a velocity between 15 and 20 points per *Sprint*. All other considerations equal, the team will deliver between 90 and 120 estimation points of work by July 15. We can count off *PBI* estimates from the top of the backlog, in this case at 10 points apiece, corresponding to the work we anticipate that the team will complete. In this case, they will complete between 9 and 12 *PBI*s, all other factors being equal.

One could, *in theory*, take a more rigorous approach to these calculations: for example, to stipulate that the velocity range between 15 and 20 covers two standard deviations of all velocities for the past five *Sprint*s or so. Then, in theory, one would pronounce that the forecast delivery for the next *Sprint* was 95% certain, and so on with less certainty for subsequent *Sprint*s. However, in reality, parameters like velocity, team constitution, *Product Backlog* content (it changes!), and market conditions vary enough that the contributions to variance from outside factors undermine any attempt even at statistical certainty. The approach is nonetheless a reasonable indicator and general predictor of the future, much in the same sense that we can more or less depend on the weatherman's forecast.

A common agile phrase is the recommendation to "defer decisions to the last responsible moment." Some *PBI*s may have a target date that constitutes such a "responsible moment" (a desired or mandated delivery date), but responsible lean practice pulls decisions forward instead of deferring them. Release planning uses the *Product Backlog* as a framework for pulling decisions as far forward as possible (e.g., considerations of dependencies between *PBI*s, or the alignment of *PBI*s or *Regular Product Increment* to a release date). All else being equal, it is important to initiate work as soon as possible, since design and implementation help make emergent requirements visible early, and give the team early data about risk. Deferring work, or the decisions that drive work, only delays the inevitable. See *Proceedings of the 8th Annual Conference on the International Group for Lean Construction [Bal00]*, and also *¶79 Dependencies First* and *¶64 Refined Product Backlog*.

Using this approach you can update estimated release dates according to team velocities. The approach enjoys broad contemporary Scrum practice worldwide. See "Planning a Release" (Chapter 9) in *User Stories Applied [Coh04]*; "Release Planning Essentials" (Chapter 13) in *Agile Estimating and Planning [Coh05]*; and, "Planning: Managing Scope" (Chapter 12) in *Extreme Programming Explained: Embrace Change [Bec04]*.

The *Product Owner* can either target long-term value (see Value and ROI on page 246 and ROI-Ordered Backlog on page 248) with a *Release Plan* that accounts for how *PBI*s reinforce each other, or can plan a project-styled series of releases based on *¶51 High Value First*. However, the team should not use such estimates as exact dates for any given *PBI*, and no delivery date should ever be interpreted as a binding commitment. The *Release Plan* is based on estimates and acknowledges flexibility rather than inevitability. Scrum keeps delivery dates fixed, so the *Sprint* end date is sacred, at which time the team delivers its best effort. The price of agility is some uncertainty. See the pattern *¶49 Release Range*.

It is also acceptable to release some *PBI*s before the end of the *Sprint*, releasing the *Regular Product Increment* a bit at a time to smooth out delivery flow and to minimize the inventory of completed work; see *¶84 Responsive Deployment*.

¶49 Release Range

Confidence stars: *

Cherry trees start to blossom on different dates every year. Over the centuries Japanese cultural traditions have evolved around this rhythm of nature. The season is so central to Japanese culture that efforts are taken on a national level to forecast the range of dates for the best cherry tree viewing (hanami).

...the *¶11 Product Owner* is building a *¶48 Release Plan* based on team velocities. The team takes work into its *¶46 Sprints* based on *¶66 Yesterday's Weather*.

❖　❖　❖

Stakeholders (e.g., managers or customers) tend to treat any single delivery date as definitive, and they tend to treat definitive feature lists as commitments.

Stakeholders want to know release dates, but you cannot forecast a delivery to fall on an exact date, as there might emerge new requirements or delays; in addition, team velocities might gradually change. The possibility of such uncertainty lies close to the foundations of agile development.

Estimates are almost always lacking in precision, or accuracy, or both. In general, the future is uncertain in any project and the *Product Owner* and other stakeholders must live with that. The delivery might be late because *¶14 Development Team* members leave the company or become sick; production machines may have unexpected down time; it's always impossible to know precisely how much work a thorny problem will take to resolve; and so forth. While taking all this into account, it is hard for the *Development Team* to give a precise release date for a *¶55 Product Backlog Item* (*PBI*). An estimate is just that: the best guess at the current time of how long it will take to do something. This fact runs afoul of the madness in business expectations that any complex development effort should be able to precisely predict completion and delivery dates ahead of time.

When a team estimates work effort on *PBI*s or *Sprint* tasks, they too often give a single number with no variance. One popular technique in this category, used for long-term "projects," is a Release Burndown. At best, the team estimates the total effort to retire a particular *PBI* about which a stakeholder inquires, and then charts a trajectory that spans several *Sprint*s. It's like a ¶43 *Sprint Burndown Chart* but it features per-*Sprint* tracking rather than day-by-day tracking:

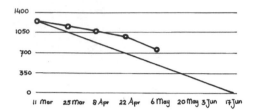

The ¶7 *Scrum Team* may create such a graph using the current velocity (see Notes on Velocity on page 320), with the best intentions of predicting when the "project" will be complete. However, because variance accumulates with time, because the list of anticipated *PBI*s may change over the *Sprint*s, and because velocity may change (even drop), the forecast completion date is likely to be inaccurate. Because stakeholders receive only a concrete completion estimate, they may hold this date as a given or even as a commitment, and there is likely to be disappointment all around in the likely event that the anticipated work is not complete on that date. Most use of the release burndown chart is a holdover from previous waterfall development.

An alternative is for the team to create a range of estimates for each item that range from pessimistic to optimistic. However, that is time consuming, is not based on an empirical history, and is difficult to fit within a consensus framework. The team spends more time discussing how confident they are about an estimate than raising their confidence by exploring uncertain issues. This meta-deliberation leads the team to accumulate an ever-growing list of concerns that feed a pessimistic estimate, and these become a cloud over the estimate that lowers the team's confidence in the estimate and increases their sense of risk of taking the item into a *Sprint*. The team should be confident about estimates for the upcoming *Sprint* (see ¶60 *Estimation Points*); a lack of confidence suggests that latent variance remains in the estimates. Reducing the variance of items in later *Sprint*s can't rescue the uncertainty from even a modest variance in velocity. Range estimation also begs the question: "What is the variance in the team's estimate of variance?" and it's too easy to get into numbers-driven project management hell. Further, this approach tends to weaken the team's sense of commitment: they will tend to be content with consistently meeting the least ambitious forecast.

Therefore:

Make pessimistic and optimistic estimates for release dates based on *Product Backlog Item* estimates and a range of historic team velocities. Use a high and low team velocity from the past several months to calculate, respectively, the most pessimistic and most optimistic dates for each given release. The *Scrum Team* should accept release ranges so they feel committed to them. Note that this range is empirically derived, in contrast to the team articulating its gut feelings about worst-case and best-case estimates.

In the following example, the business has asked the team when it will deliver a certain set of *PBI*s. The team always delivers starting at the top of the ¶54 *Product Backlog* and works its way deeper into the backlog during succeeding *Sprint*s. The team can compute its estimate for the total amount of effort required to accomplish such a delivery by summing the work estimates for all *PBI*s from the top of the backlog down to that desired point. Then the team divides that sum by the optimistic velocity, which suggests how many *Sprint*s it will take to deliver all these items in the best case. Then the team divides the same sum by the pessimistic velocity to compute what might be the worst-case number of *Sprint*s required to complete the work. A *Sprint* corresponds to a fixed time interval, so the team can directly map the results onto a development duration.

total estimation points desired	120
optimistic velocity	20
pessimistic velocity	15

120 ÷ 20 = ○ ○ ○ ○ ○ ○

120 ÷ 15 = ○ ○ ○ ○ ○ ○
○ ○

The team can define the velocity range by looking at the velocities of the last few (three to five) *Sprint*s, using the lowest among them as the pessimistic number, and the highest among them as the optimistic number. You can discard the top and bottom outliers first if you like. Remain consistent in your technique in the long term.

❖   ❖   ❖

The *Scrum Team* and the stakeholders can align their expectations about the timing of upcoming *¶85 Regular Product Increment*s, and of the delivery of individual *PBI*s.

This approach accommodates emerging requirements to arrive at a range of release dates. Then you can tell the customer that the release will very likely be within this range. The team, and particularly the *¶19 ScrumMaster*, should help stakeholders understand this as a benefit rather than as just an "unfortunate fuzziness." *¶6 Involve the Managers* when it is impractical for the *Product Owner* or *ScrumMaster* to do this, provided that management is also on board to agile principles.

The approach here is analogous to weather forecasts: *there is a 60 percent chance that it will rain today and a 40 percent change that it will not.* In the same way, the team can introduce the *Release Range* to stakeholders. *There is an 80 percent chance that the release will be ready on day X and a 20 percent chance that it will be delayed to day Y.*

However, sometimes stakeholders want an exact date: for example, if the organization needs to release the product at a trade show. This may tempt the team to use the pessimistic estimate. However, this sets up a fixed-cost, fixed-scope release plan and may limit the *Product Owner*'s ability to change the *Product Backlog* ordering to take advantage of emergent opportunities in the market. The pessimistic number does not in any case represent an exact guaranteed date, and sometimes it's as undesirable to deliver early as to deliver late. Such highballing of the estimates almost always signals the tacit desire for a commitment, and agile teams should avoid it. Such thinking kills kaizen mind (see Kaizen and Kaikaku on page 101).

Hard deadlines do exist in the real world, however. You may need to have that demo ready in time for that trade show. Impending legislation may force the enterprise to change its software to be compliant with the law (at this writing, investment banks are scrambling to meet a deadline for the implementation of United States IRS 871(M) for which the deadline has already passed). However, there are never hard guarantees in complex development. The *Product Owner* can manage risk by positioning items appropriately on the *Product Backlog* so they come to the top and enter a *Sprint* in time for timely deployment.

If there are no historic data of velocities of the teams, then the team can apply knowledge from previous similar developments in the same domain. Of course, in this case, the team should make it visible that the estimates are based on limited historic data and are likely to be unreliable. On the other hand, the *Product Owner* might want to be flexible with the release scope. It might make sense to drop features from the release to avoid delivering late. In all such cases, it is best to defer to the *Development Team* as the authority on these estimates and their reliability (see *¶57 Pigs Estimate*).

The *Scrum Team* should revisit *Release Range* estimates regularly. As development goes forward the ranges can become more focused.

You can do an analogous calculation for fixed-date planning, to report a range of *PBI*s that the team might deliver by a given deadline.

To improve its predictions, a good *Scrum Team* reduces the variance in its velocity. See the *Notes on Velocity*.

Value and ROI

We can argue that a *¶7 Scrum Team* exists to create value. Scrum has historically called this value *ROI*. However, the term *ROI* evokes an image of capitalized machinery that is atypical of software and other intellectually intensive businesses. But Scrum is best-suited for just these kinds of complex domains. Most Scrum products do not depend on intensive financial capitalization but tend to draw most of their value from "intellectual capital," and Jeff Sutherland has even said that he created Scrum to help people make something from nothing. In any case, there are other measures of financial value such as net present value (NPV), cash flow, and many more. Scrum applies to products seeking to optimize any and all of these.

Yet not all worthy businesses are in this for the money. Scrum is making ever deeper inroads into public service and government software, where the goal is to responsively develop public services. There, we might measure value in terms of citizen satisfaction with public services, or lives saved by first responders. So the term ROI appears nowhere in *The Scrum Guide*, but the term *value* recurs frequently. The *¶11 Product Owner* is accountable for optimizing value, yet value can founder if either *¶14 Development Team* members or the *¶19 ScrumMaster* are delinquent in their tasks.

As every *Scrum Team* serves several sets of stakeholders, each team should be attentive to multiple facets of value. We value that our team members have ample, quality vacation time, which is the main reason behind *¶62 Vacation PBI*. We value that the team has a challenging, humane, and reasonably stress-free environment, and the *ScrumMaster* has the mandate to sustain a healthy culture. We value that our end users have defect-free products, so we fix defects *now* with *¶81 Whack the Mole*. And we may value excellence, and improvement for its own sake, so we relentlessly focus on improving both the product and process (see Kaizen and Kaikaku on page 101).

Even on the economic front, the value question becomes more interesting in subcontracted product development. If a subcontractor develops a product for a corporate client, at a modest fixed cost, and the client makes a record profit from the product, it in some sense sets up an unfair economy. (The vendor may think twice before developing another product for the same client.) An equitable sharing of value is part of any sound *¶13 Development Partnership*. The same principle extends more broadly to all stakeholders that contribute to product development.

In the old days of system development, we found a role called *system engineer* whose job it was to *optimize value*. System engineers worked with three theories of value; an *economic* theory, a *psychological* theory, and a *casuistic* theory (*A Methodology for Systems Engineering [Hal62]*). The economic theory of value harkens back to where we started with ROI, NPV, and cash flow. The psychological theory of value relates to the mental health and contentment, and maybe even passion, of the team. And the casuistic theory of value relates to tradition and to "doing the right thing." In its most vulgar form, it may manifest itself as the Scrum Values; we find a more finessed version in *¶1 The Spirit of the Game*. Systems engineers previously used parameterized mathematical models to optimize value equations by adjusting coefficients for each of several kinds of value. While we are not recommending such a reductionist approach, to informally consider the trade-offs and to discuss them as a team will likely both leave the team with a greater legacy, and better leave it with a feeling of a job well done at the end of the day.

Value should be more than just a matter of locally optimizing the profitability of each *¶55 Product Backlog Item* (*PBI*) in isolation. reordering *PBIs* to hit the best market windows can increase the profitability of every item in the *Product Backlog Item*. The team might optimize different *PBIs* for different theories of value. Value emerges over time as a property of the entire backlog and its ordering (e.g., consider cost of delay as one exemplary consideration). The *¶39 Vision* plays a crucial role both in assessing value and adjusting work to increase value—and the team may adjust the *Vision* itself to recharter the team on a trajectory to higher value.

So when a *Scrum Team* aspires to create the *¶93 Greatest Value*, each team should consider what is really important to their end users but also to themselves, their colleagues, their loved ones, and their fellow world citizens all together. Scrum can help you optimize any theory of value.

The next pattern, *¶50 ROI-Ordered Backlog*, is explicitly about value. Most of the rest of the *¶54 Product Backlog* patterns also deal principally with value. *Product Owners* often annotate each *Product Backlog Item* with some measure of incremental value. While we usually think of this annotation as representing profitability, consider using another measure—such as the corporate image in the community—as a refreshing alternative. You may ultimately evolve to using two or three informal indicators of value to help guide *Product Backlog* ordering.

¶50 ROI-Ordered Backlog

Orienteering is a group of sports that requires navigational skills, using a map and compass to navigate from point to point in diverse and usually unfamiliar terrain while moving at speed. [8] Part of a winning strategy is to visit control points in an order that yields the highest value.

…you have a backlog of *¶55 Product Backlog Items* and need criteria to order them on the *¶54 Product Backlog*.

❖   ❖   ❖

The goal of a *¶7 Scrum Team* is to deliver value, and it is the responsibility of the *¶11 Product Owner* to optimize long-term value (see Value and ROI on page 246). The *Product Owner* achieves this in part by ordering the *Product Backlog*. The backlog must be a single, ordered list of *PBIs* (*Product Backlog Items*) that brings focus to the *¶14 Development Team*, and the entire enterprise, on the deliverables.

You could order *PBIs* by the priorities of your dominant customer. However, that might lock out other customers, and in any case tends to focus on revenues rather than costs. Since cost is also a key consideration in ROI, focusing on customers alone isn't enough.

You could order them by the priorities of the *Product Owner* in isolation. But the question arises: What criteria should the *Product Owner* use to set the priorities of the *Product Backlog Items*?

Most *Product Owners* annotate each *PBI* with a tentative ROI or other business value. It might seem obvious to order the *Product Backlog* with the highest ROI items first. However, the value of a *PBI* is in part a function of the features that previous *PBIs* already support, in part on the timing of delivery to the market, and in general on the item's position in the backlog. Simple dependencies between *PBIs* further constrain the ordering. And because we are

---

8. Wikipedia. Orienteering. https://en.wikipedia.org/wiki/Orienteering, July 2018, access 11 August 2018.

agile and the business is dynamic, *PBI* positions on the backlog may change frequently, even during a *¶46 Sprint*. So while a value annotation on a *PBI* may be a useful temporary convenience, it doesn't prescribe an ordering that will always ensure the best *Value and ROI*.

Proper ordering of the *Product Backlog Item*s to line up development dependencies foreseen by the *Development Team* can avoid rework and facilitate a smooth flow of products to market. So you could order *PBI*s solely according to the team's insight on dependencies, but that misses out on major revenue-generating opportunities that may arise for *PBI*s whose ordering is less constrained.

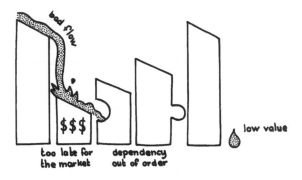

Therefore:

The *Product Owner* orders *PBI*s in a way that generates the largest long-term ROI. The *Product Owner* must account for both revenue and cost. If the *Product Owner* reorders *PBI*s, then he or she must account for the resulting value changes to the affected *¶85 Regular Product Increment*. The *Product Owner* has the mandate to make decisions on behalf of all the stakeholders, but would be wise to weigh the supplications and insights of all stakeholders in balancing the value equation.

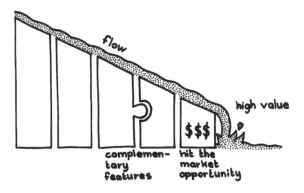

While the common Scrum measure is "ROI," a *Product Owner* may certainly choose to optimize Return on Equity (ROE), Net Present Value (NPV), or any other measure or indicator of value. In general, Scrum supports the enterprise in optimizing any value, including noneconomic values such as corporate reputation, staff esprit de corps, minimal turnover, number of clients served, etc. Most *Product Owner*s will want to optimize a combination of several such values. Note that this may result in a determination which is more relative that absolute in nature: see *¶60 Estimation Points*.

❖ ❖ ❖

The *¶41 Value Stream* will be set up to produce *Regular Product Increment*s with the best possibility of generating high long-term value.

This evaluation can rarely be reduced to a formula. Such ordering is always imperfect and benefits from good judgment, insight, and experience.

The notion of *priority* for *PBI*s is flawed. The term *priority* is an attribute of an individual element that defines an ordering of the collection. However, *Product Backlog* ordering focuses on overall, emergent value, which is often more complex than the sum of the values of individual *PBI*s. Overall value is the sum of individual *PBI* values only for a single given ordering: all else being equal, a different ordering may yield a higher overall value. You can't sit back and assign context-free priorities to *PBI*s and then sort the *Product Backlog*, because a *PBI*'s individual value is often a function of its position in the backlog. Some market offerings make sense only if they build on previous offerings; some market offerings are sensitive to market timing. Reordering items can change the value contribution of each one. In fact, Jeff Sutherland notes that you can as much as double your long-term value just by reordering the *PBI*s.

One point of the solution is worth reiterating: ROI needn't be just about money. In general, it is about value. Most value systems are rooted in the economic theory of value: the ability to exchange one artifact or token of value for another of equal value. However, an enterprise may also value employee retention, good customer relations, a good public image, or many other desiderata that fall outside the economic theory of value. It is possible to view many items of value as a return on some kind of investment. See, for example, *¶83 Team Sprint*.

To serve process improvement, ROI or other values need to be measurable—even if only in relative terms.

As an alternative approach, see *¶51 High Value First*, which can support the well-known patterns *¶52 Change for Free* and *¶53 Money for Nothing*. But if you order the *Product Backlog* by long-term value, you can't easily use *Change for Free* or *Money for Nothing*.

¶51 High Value First

In the game of "Supermarket Sweep," teams compete to fill shopping trolleys with the highest-value selection of goods in a fixed time. This event was the American 1 Supermarket Sweep at Polly's Supermarket in Jackson, Michigan, benefiting the Food Bank of South Central Michigan. Team in photo: American One Credit Union. Photo by JTV, Jackson, Michigan, USA.

...you are a client of a vendor that uses Scrum to develop its product and both are involved in *¶24 Sprint Planning*. You are trying to decide which *¶55 Product Backlog Item*s (*PBI*s) to schedule in the next few iterations or *¶46 Sprint*s. The Product Ownership role most likely lies on the client side.

The *¶14 Development Team* is working with just one client so the relative value of individual *Product Backlog Item*s is clear, using the client as an oracle. The *Development Team* can readily estimate the *PBI* at hand.

❖ ❖ ❖

One in the hand is worth two in the bush, and short-term developments should deliver value as early as possible. While an *¶50 ROI-Ordered Backlog* can deliver the highest overall lifetime value, enterprises with quarterly targets don't want to wait a lifetime to realize such value. It is sometimes more important to realize reasonable value now than to optimize net present value over the long term. Fixed-scope, fixed-cost projects are an example of when you want to realize value close to the time of client engagement.

In top-down (structured, hierarchically decomposed) development, the developers often don't get good guidance as to the relative business value of the features required. They may spend a lot of effort (time and money) on low-value features. Everyone wins if the enterprise achieves high value early.

From the client's standpoint, some features are essential and some "would be nice to have." By common economics (the Pareto Principle), 80 percent of the business value comes from 20 percent of the features. To the degree clients are engaged in ordering the backlog, they can get the highest value for their investment. If the client agreement is set up to pay the vendor for time and materials, or if it is a fixed-cost contract, the vendor loses little or nothing as a consequence of such reordering. Particularly in service-intensive businesses, the cost of a *Sprint* is constant.

It is reasonable to ask the client to express the value of each *Product Backlog Item*. The *Development Team* will assign each one a cost (the estimate). This can be difficult to get right as a one-time exercise. What's worse, the value is likely to change over time as business conditions and strategies change, and value changes with the ongoing delivery of *Product Backlog Item*s.

Therefore:

Build the high value, most essential *Product Backlog Item*s first. When the value curve and the cost curve cross, cancel the project. At any point, schedule the highest-value remaining *PBI* in the next available iterations. If the cost of a *PBI* starts higher than its value, you can often split the *PBI* into its essential and inessential parts. Once the *¶7 Scrum Team* and the client re-estimate these parts, you may be in a better position to proceed.

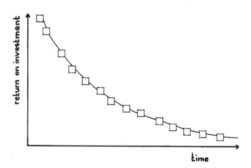

You can streamline the implementation of *High Value First* by letting the client, in person, direct (or at least propose) changes to the *¶54 Product Backlog* ordering at *Sprint Planning*. Clients can make on-the-spot adjustments based on the latest net present value (NPV) data or other available indicator of profitability of individual backlog items. A client can order the *Product Backlog* to optimize their own value; the most straightforward way to do this is to locate the *¶11 Product Owner* role on the client side. Rather than following the usual practice where the *Product Owner orders PBI*s to achieve the highest long-term value (see *Value and ROI*), the *Product Owner prioritizes PBI*s according to their incremental contribution to ROI or NPV.

❖   ❖   ❖

Having done *High Value First*, you can then follow with *¶52 Change for Free* and *¶53 Money for Nothing*. As an alternative, see the pattern *ROI-Ordered*

Backlog, which sacrifices short-term optimization of the ROI of individual elements to gain the highest ROI (or other value) in the long term.

The value of *PBI*s will generally decrease as *Sprint*s progress. The cost per *PBI* will generally increase, as it gets harder to incorporate new *PBI*s as you go along. In software, refactoring tries to keep this rising cost curve as flat as possible by keeping the design coherent, even as the product evolves. At some point, however, the remaining *PBI*s are probably not worth building. Note that this is one of the major ways that agile processes can save money over planned development: the development effort just drops the low-value requirements. You may also deliver the product sooner.

In extremely volatile situations, the crossing-curves effect may not occur. You might only learn of a high-value requirement late in the process so the value curve might take a sharp upward turn. But this ability to quickly retarget the project toward a different goal delivers value in a different way: you get a more suitable product.

High Value First assumes, of course, that your estimate of value is measurable, and you can optimize overall value only to the degree that it is accurate. This is often difficult to achieve. Errors in the estimates can quickly come to be larger than the differences in *PBI* value.

Short iterations force you to think in terms of small granularity features. (This is a problem that generally challenges incremental development, but the problem is even more pronounced when using *High Value First*.) This makes estimation easier, but partitioning harder. It can cause the team to focus too much on wasteful over-specifying and over-planning. If an important, valuable feature is more complex than the team can complete in one *Sprint*, the team may deliver part of it in the current *Sprint* with the rest in the next one (or more) *Sprint*s. If the client sees value only after the team has delivered all the parts, it becomes impossible to ascribe value to the *¶85 Regular Product Increment* of any single *Sprint*, and it becomes problematic to order the backlog by value.

There are often claims that it isn't at all possible to deliver a specific, valuable *PBI* piecemeal, *Sprint* by *Sprint*. In our experience, the *Scrum Team* can always break down a *PBI* so that the team can individually deliver small pieces. Google has 10,000 developers who make more than 5,500 commits daily on their mainline, without using any branching.[9] If you are considering resorting

---

9. John Thomas and Ashish Kumar. "Google's Scaled Trunk-Based Development." Paul-Hammant.com, https://paulhammant.com/2013/05/06/googles-scaled-trunk-based-development/ (accessed 2 November 2017).

to branching, please reconsider. If you reconsider and still feel branching is in order, reconsider again.

This pattern also assumes that the value is greater than the cost estimate from the *Development Team*. However, note that the team doesn't have to develop any extra scaffolding to support these low-value features since the team always focuses on developing only what is necessary to support an imminent delivery.

There is an additional cost here. Since the developers don't see every *Product Backlog Item* from the beginning, they cannot make certain optimizations that might lower cost. But these optimizations will waste money if requirements change and make the optimizations obsolete; deal with this using *Change for Free*. Whether the optimizations are worthwhile depends on the delivery horizon of the team: if the changes are more than two or three *Sprints* away, they are probably beyond the *Scrum Team*'s delivery horizon.

Complicating this approach is the fact that the first (and every) release needs to create an end-to-end version of the product. It may be that the team delivers some features in skeleton form only, or that it temporarily disables some features for a single release.

We derived this pattern from the original pattern by Joe Bergin, (*Agile Software: Patterns of Practice [Ber13]* "High Value First," pp. 35–36). Used with permission. Thanks, Joe!

¶52 Change for Free

Free tailoring with purchase.

...you have a *¶54 Product Backlog* ordered by *¶51 High Value First* under a fixed-cost, fixed-scope contract between a vendor and a client. You want to support the client with the freedom to change requirements after development has started. You are supporting a single client or a client base represented by a unified perspective. The *¶14 Development Team*'s velocity (see Notes on Velocity on page 320) has a low variance (on the order of 10 or 15 percent). Either the team has prior experience in this domain, or there is some other verifiable expectation of being able to create an initial set of *¶63 Enabling Specification*s for the product. The prospect for emergent requirements, and requirements changes, is small but non-negligible.

❖ ❖ ❖

Some *PBIs* (*¶55 Product Backlog Items*) are somewhat context-free and independently deliverable, and you want to respond to client changes driven by clients' desire to increase their profitability. You don't want to allow changes that lead to significant rework, as that can lower the vendor's ROI or other measure of value (see *Value and ROI*). On the other hand, it may take only a little investment to put a *PBI* on the *Product Backlog*, and it is very little work to remove the *PBI* or move it around.

Each *PBI* has an associated cost estimate that has been (or can be) provided by the *Development Team*. The *¶11 Product Owner* knows the ROI of each item, and the client is responsible for knowing how much value the item provides to them.

Even though you have fixed price and fixed scope, new requirements may still emerge. It serves the interests neither of the client nor of the vendor to stick to a fixed list of deliverables if there is something to gain, and nothing to lose, by renegotiating.

Anticipating that any up-front agreement of work on a complex product will not cover what clients really need, some firms have a business model based in large part on cornering the client into paying change fees for work they request after the initial delivery (see "Change for Free and Money for Nothing" in *Scrum: The Art of Doing Twice the Work in Half the Time [SS14]*, ff. 193). Such practices erode trust, which in turn can lead to a climate of adversarial checks and balances in the long term—and all the inefficiencies that go with them.

The bottom of the requirements list is rarely mission critical for clients. However, they can still benefit if they can receive those items within the originally negotiated budget.

Therefore: **Fix the price and the scope, and make a contractual agreement to commit to the top 80 percent of the *PBIs*, ordered according to their value to the client. The vendor might exceed that 80 percent target if it can complete the work within the contracted cost. Offer clients the option of exchanging an emergent requirement for any existing *PBI* of equal (or lower) value to them, as long as the development cost of the new item is no more than the cost of the original.**

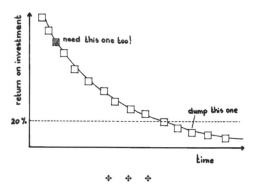

❖ ❖ ❖

The team orders the *Product Backlog* to create *¶85 Regular Product Increments* that can accommodate client changes and increase overall value (at least to the client, but preferably to both vendor and client) without increasing cost. With the cost capped, the vendor can establish a fixed price that yields fair profit. The focus is on *¶93 Greatest Value*, both for the vendor and client, in the time frame that each expects.

This pattern works best for highly experienced *¶7 Scrum Teams* that are longstanding *¶15 Stable Teams* and that are highly experienced in building products in the client domain. The *Development Team*(s) should estimate each item's cost before the *Product Owner* positions it in the *Product Backlog*. The success of this pattern depends on the team's ability to estimate all *PBIs* accurately up front. This in turn suggests that most *PBIs* should have the stature of an *Enabling Specification* early on, so this pattern works best in low-risk domains or domains very familiar to the team. Of course, this pattern doesn't apply to *PBI*s that the *Development Team* is working on in the current *¶46 Sprint*. Such *PBI*s are usually beyond the reach of negotiation.

In general, the vendor and client can work as a team to share these benefits instead of accounting them individually; *¶13 Development Partnership*. Jeff Sutherland describes how it works in *Scrum: The Art of Doing Twice the Work in Half the Time [SS14]*:

> That's why I came up with the idea of "Change for Free." In a standard fixed-price contract, just say changes are free. List all the functionality you expect; for example, if you're building a tank, you want one that can go seventy-five miles per hour and shoot ten rounds a minute, has seating for four, has AC, etc.— everything you think you need for that tank. The builder looks at that description and says, "Hmm, making that engine, I'll call that 100 points, the loading mechanism, let's call that 50, the seating, 5..." on down the list. At the end there is a set number of points for each feature. Then every Sprint, the customer, who in this scenario is contractually obligated to work closely with the Product Owner, can change priorities completely. Any item or feature in the Backlog can be moved anywhere else. And new features? No problem: just drop equivalently sized features from the deliverables. "Oh, you want a laser-guided system now? Well, that's 50 points of work—to compensate for that addition, let's drop 50 points of low-priority features from the bottom of the Backlog."

This approach can become unwieldy if you are supporting multiple clients, since one client's request will affect everyone's schedule, and this approach to *Product Backlog* management sets an expectation that successive deliveries will follow each other closely in order of business value.

See also *¶53 Money for Nothing*.

The *Money for Nothing* and *Change for Free* concepts originated in a class Jeff Sutherland conducted in the Netherlands in 2006.

¶53 Money for Nothing

...the *¶7 Scrum Team* is acting as a vendor to develop and deliver the content of a *¶54 Product Backlog* that they ordered using *¶51 High Value First.* The *Scrum Team* realizes its value through a fixed-price agreement or perhaps a shared-risk *¶13 Development Partnership* whereby it receives a share of the client's profit. There is usually a short-term profitability horizon, as is typical with fixed-scope agreements.

❖ ❖ ❖

It doesn't make sense to spend time developing increments that cost more than they're worth. The client is the next link down from the *Scrum Team* in the *¶41 Value Stream,* and it is interested in realizing value for itself from an accumulated, fixed number of *¶85 Regular Product Increment*s delivered from the *Scrum Team* as vendor.

The big picture is this: many agreements between vendors and clients need to look far beyond the horizon of certainty into the future. That Scrum works in *¶46 Sprint*s and has a flexible *Product Backlog* adds the possibility of a flexible pay-as-you-go engagement in addition to traditional fixed-price, fixed-scope agreements. Dealing with the far future can be risky business, but sometimes decision criteria become more crisp and clear closer to the point of delivery than when drafting an agreement far in advance. Both the vendor and the client want the best value from such an engagement. The vendor's value comes primarily from the engagement income, and more subtly from the goodwill and reputation that it can develop both for its own sake and for securing future engagements. The client's value comes through the product that the vendor builds for it, whether from services the product offers to the client's end users or from sale of the product to customers further downstream. The agreed-upon price that the client pays the vendor reduces the client's value. There are several approaches to such an engagement that reduce risk or increase profitability more or less to the vendor and the client. Perhaps the dominant consideration is whether both sides hold the agreement to be *fair*: that is, neither side has knowingly gained value at the expense of the other.

Because of *High Value First*, we know that value (such as net present value) to the client of each delivered *Regular Product Increment* drops monotonically over time. With perfect foresight it might be possible to identify the exact *Sprint* that corresponds to the point of diminishing returns: any development beyond that point would amount to overproduction and would create waste for the client. However, it is difficult to predict that point at the beginning of development. On the other hand, we can identify the decision points up front: they are the *Sprint*s, which can be continuously evaluated for their *Regular Product Increment*s' profitability.

While an early termination penalty in lieu of full payment could reduce both the client's gross expenditure and net vendor income as well, forcing the vendor to take delivery of and pay for the full feature set also creates ill will. And while a pure pay-as-you go arrangement could optimize the client's value for cost, it also reduces potential net income to the vendor. However, it also frees the vendor for other engagements whose profitability may be higher than what they could gain by forcing the current client to pay an early termination penalty. The vendor still suffers a small opportunity cost from being idle between the termination of the current agreement and the start of work with a new client. If it is a fixed-cost, fixed-scope agreement, the vendor saves nothing by early termination and is likely to take delivery on those *Sprint*s yielding marginal value, "just in case." However, the client may ultimately feel the value recovered from the product wasn't worth the price. The vendor receives full price in this case, but the client may view the vendor as having taken unfair advantage of the imperfect foresight (i.e., that the late product increments would be of low value).

Therefore: **Stop development when the cost of continuing exceeds the benefit that the client enterprise will receive from the development.**

❖ ❖ ❖

The vendor works to deliver to the client as long as ongoing work continues to increase the overall value (such as net present value) of all *Regular Product Increment*s.

In addition to ensuring that value to the client doesn't decrease, also make sure that stopping development at these points won't cripple the vendor's profitability or value. The client may agree to pay a termination fee to the vendor in the event that it terminates the agreement early, but the client still pays much less than if it had pursued the agreement to the end. One can

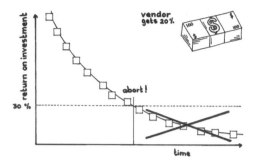

argue in all fairness that such a fee covers the vendor's opportunity costs while lining up new business. It is best that the vendor ensures, from the beginning, that each deliverable (*Sprint*) has positive value to the client, so that the client doesn't put the vendor at risk over the life-cycle development.

For an example, see "Change for Free and Money for Nothing" in *Scrum: The Art of Doing Twice the Work in Half the Time [SS14]* (Chapter 8, ff. 193), that describes a pay-as-you-go contract where the client negotiated the right to terminate the contract at the end of any *Sprint*—as long as they paid 20 percent of the cost of remaining development. The client paid $3.2 million for a product bid at $10 million and got it 17 months early, thanks to incremental delivery and being able to stop development when the feature set was complete. Furthermore, the client also used ¶52 *Change for Free* to redirect some of the work into areas of higher value. In the meantime, the vendor, who had set up the contract to give a profit margin of 15 percent, ended with a net profit margin of 60 percent. Released from the contract early, the vendor was able to pursue additional contracts instead of having to wait 17 months to do so.

This pattern focuses on the benefits from the ever-growing insight over time into the profitability of a previously agreed feature set in a *Regular Product Increment*. See also *Change for Free*, which capitalizes on the enterprise's ability to better define *Regular Product Increment* functionality as time goes on.

Having gained confidence from the success of short-term engagements with this safety net, both vendors and clients are more likely to take higher risk through a *Development Partnership*.

The *Money for Nothing* and *Change for Free* concepts originated in a class Jeff Sutherland conducted in the Netherlands in 2006.

Product Backlog Sequence

The ¶54 *Product Backlog* is a built artifact: an internal product used by the ¶7 *Scrum Team* to order its work and to assemble the outward-facing ¶85 *Regular Product Increment*. It is "owned" by the ¶11 *Product Owner* who has the final say on its content. The *Product Owner* continually manages the *Product Backlog* to help the team manage its work toward achieving the ¶93 *Greatest Value*.

The *Product Backlog* is just one segment of the ¶41 *Value Stream*. Ideas flow into it from stakeholders upstream, and specifications flow out of it into the ¶72 *Sprint Backlog* for realization during a ¶46 *Sprint*.

The *Product Backlog* is a Whole which the team can build. The team can develop the *Product Backlog* according to a sequence that suggests an ordering for the patterns it comprises. The team can weave this sequence together with the Value Stream Sequence on page 187 to elaborate those steps pertinent to developing the backlog itself. What follows is a typical sequence for starting up and maintaining a *Product Backlog*. Individual products may find other orderings equally useful: inspect and adapt.

¶50 *ROI-Ordered Backlog* Normally the *Product Owner* orders the *Product Backlog* to achieve the highest ROI based on current knowledge, with the goal being the *Greatest Value*. The initial backlog comprises a list of ¶71 *Sprint Goal*s, each designed to characterize a single release in a sequence of *Regular Product Increment*.

¶51 *High Value First* Alternatively, the organization can choose to work with a fixed-scope, fixed-cost client to take advantage of approaches like ¶52 *Change for Free* and ¶53 *Money for Nothing*.

¶55 *Product Backlog Item* The *Product Owner*, perhaps with the help of the rest of the *Scrum Team*, breaks down the envisioned *Regular Product Increment*s into ¶55 *Product Backlog Item*s (PBIs).

¶56 *Information Radiator* The team posts the backlog and other key team artifacts visibly, both for its own reference and to inform other stakeholders.

¶59 *Granularity Gradient* As part of breaking down the backlog, the *Product Owner* and the ¶14 *Development Team* reduce the *Product Backlog Item*s near the top of the backlog to ¶58 *Small Items*, leaving later *Product Backlog Item*s intact.

¶63 *Enabling Specification* The *Product Owner* ensures that the *Development Team* members perfectly understand each *Product Backlog Item* scheduled for the next *Sprint*.

¶64 *Refined Product Backlog* The *Product Owner* and the *Development Team* meet regularly to ensure the *Product Backlog* stays up to date.

¶65 *Definition of Ready* Right before the ¶75 *Production Episode*, at ¶24 *Sprint Planning*, the *Product Owner* and the *Development Team* together ensure the *Product Backlog* is ordered properly with respect to dependencies and market considerations, and developers estimate every imminent *Product Backlog Item*. At *Sprint Planning*, the *Development Team* pulls ¶65 *Definition of Ready* items from the top of the *Product Backlog* to achieve the *Sprint Goal*. These *Product Backlog Item*s will drive their *Production Episode* work plan.

¶54 Product Backlog

Confidence stars: **

Barrels of whiskey lined up by vintage year which, after aging, will determine the delivery order.

...you have defined a *¶41 Value Stream* by which the *¶11 Product Owner*'s *¶39 Vision* flows to the market. You envision a product development effort in the organization, supported by one or more *¶14 Development Team*s that seek strategic direction. Many stakeholders, including Team members, have different ideas on how to achieve the *Vision*. The *Development Team* needs guidance on how to interact with the *Product Owner* to support the best implementation of the *Vision*, and to ultimately have a foundation for a good tactical direction for each *¶46 Sprint*.

❖ ❖ ❖

At any given time, it is important that the whole team is aligned about what it needs to deliver next, and that the direction be transparent. The *Development Team* can't do everything at once—in fact, you can't even do two things well at the same time. It's important to maintain focus.

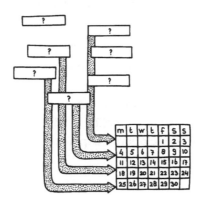

While it's good to have a *¶45 Product Roadmap*, it's also important to pull decisions forward to order them properly as soon as enough supporting information is available. The *Product Roadmap* consciously leaves options open and decisions unbound. It's important to force the exercise of binding the ordering and even near-term scheduling based on best current information so that stakeholders can be on notice for what is *likely* to transpire, with the acknowledgment that, as an agile enterprise, a *¶7 Scrum Team* works with stakeholders to sacrifice stability of schedule in the interest of increasing value.

It's important to make product direction decisions transparent to stakeholders. The delivery order must reflect dependencies between deliverables, as well as coordination with project calendar events: deliveries from suppliers, marketing campaigns, releases by partners or competitors, and so forth. Each *Development Team* needs its own direction, yet coordination becomes difficult if the *Scrum Team* has multiple *Development Team*s, each of which maintains its own long-term list of *¶85 Regular Product Increment*s. It is impossible to easily see the order of delivery if each team keeps its own list.

Therefore: **For each product, create a single ordered list called the *Product Backlog*—a list of *Regular Product Increment* contributions called *¶55 Product Backlog Item*s (PBIs), arranged in their expected delivery order.** The *Product Backlog* details the *Product Owner*'s *Vision* for the product as informed by the expectations of all stakeholders, with each *PBI* describing a contribution to a deliverable *Regular Product Increment*. The *Product Owner* has final authority over the content of the *Product Backlog*; however, the *Product Owner* usually develops the *Product Backlog* in a joint effort with the *Development Team* during regular events convened to maintain a *¶64 Refined Product Backlog*, as well as during *¶24 Sprint Planning*.

The Team should make the *Product Backlog* transparent to all stakeholders as an *¶56 Information Radiator*.

Scrum calls a *Product Backlog Ready* (see *¶65 Definition of Ready*) if it is a *Refined Product Backlog* and if the *Development Team* feels confident enough about the top items to take them into a *Sprint*. The work at the top of the *Product Backlog* drives the *Development Team*s, and each *Development Team* works from only a single *Product Backlog*. The *Product Backlog* drives *all Development Team* work—developers respond to no other source of work requests external to their team.

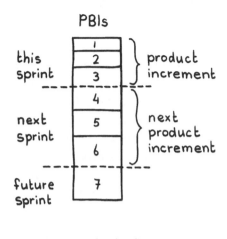

❖ ❖ ❖

The *Product Backlog* makes the current likely trajectory of long-term delivery transparent to all stakeholders. The *Product Owner* typically derives the *Product Backlog* from a *Vision* or some other strategic document that captures value drivers. If the *Product Owner* has a *Product Roadmap*, it too can guide the *Product Backlog* contents. A good initial *Product Backlog* is a list of ¶71 *Sprint Goal*s that takes the product in the direction of the *Vision*, where each *Sprint Goal* becomes the core of the corresponding *Regular Product Increment*.

This list typically corresponds to a single product or product line; however, it can be any list of deliverables over which a single *Product Owner* has authority. We give the *Product Owner* authority over the *Product Backlog* because he or she is accountable for value (¶50 *ROI-Ordered Backlog*), and the *Product Backlog* is the sole instrument reflecting the *Product Owner*'s control over the *Development Team*'s sprint towards value. The *Product Backlog* details the *Product Owner Vision* to drive the downstream activities of the *Value Stream*.

The *Product Backlog* provides an opportunity for feedback from stakeholders early in the journey of a *Regular Product Increment* through the *Value Stream*. It is visible to all stakeholders including end users, partners, Team members, and any managers in the organization. It is dynamic and can change whenever the *Product Owner* gains new information about the market, business conditions, new estimates from the *Development Team* or anything else that may affect the *Vision* or *ROI-Ordered Backlog*. At any given time it represents the *Product Owner*'s best possible path to value through the *Product Roadmap*, and best possible realization of the *Vision*.

Having a single *Product Backlog* per product can put an end to the thrashing that can occur between groups with differences in perspective within a company.

Note that it is a *Product Backlog* and not a Requirements Backlog. The *Product Owner* uses the *Product Backlog* to describe *Regular Product Increment*s that implement whatever requirements are necessary for customers to realize a value increment in the corresponding *Sprint*. As such, the *Product Backlog* records the *joint planning decisions* of the *Scrum Team*, rather than serving as a vehicle to communicate requirements between stakeholders, the *Product Owner*, and the *Development Team*. The *Product Owner* discusses the details of *PBI*s face-to-face with the *Development Team* during Backlog Refinement (see *Refined Product Backlog*) and *Sprint Planning* to help the team internalize an ¶63 *Enabling Specification*.

That said, the *Product Backlog* can describe contributions that increase value indirectly, rather than as a direct increment to the product itself. Faster or more easily maintained machines on the manufacturing line might be an example, or better office space for workers. An occasional process improvement may also appear on the *Product Backlog*: see ¶92 *Scrumming the Scrum*. In this sense it is useful to think of the *Product Backlog* as a *value backlog*. See "The Backlog: What to Do When" in *Scrum: The Art of Doing Twice the Work in Half the Time [SS14]*, pp. 173–175.

The *Product Backlog* may contain more or less information about dependencies between *PBI*s, market timing constraints, or any other structuring of the requirements. A lean mindset suggests keeping it simple. Annotating each *PBI* with a cost or estimate of effort, as well as that *PBI*'s contribution to value (see *Value and ROI*) can help the *Product Owner* optimize value during business planning. The *Product Owner* may of course need to adjust the value annotation of a *PBI* over time as its position in the backlog changes, since an earlier or later delivery, or changes in the external environment, might change the *PBI*'s alignment to market need.

The team usually annotates the *Product Backlog* with forecast *Sprint* boundaries, which are the units of granularity of the product delivery schedule. Based on the *Development Team* estimates of *PBI*s, the *Scrum Team* can derive a rough ¶48 *Release Plan*. Such plans might be meaningful for only two to five *Sprint*s in the future; extrapolating further pretends being able to know more than one should presume for agile development.

Within a *Sprint*, a *Development Team* may work on *PBI*s in any order to optimize the chances of meeting the *Sprint Goal*; see ¶76 *Developer-Ordered Work Plan*.

Break down the topmost *PBI*s according to a *¶59 Granularity Gradient* and refine them to be *Enabling Specifications*. The team should strive never to be more than a week away from having a *Refined Product Backlog*. Spreading the backlog refinement work across short daily meetings (the Backlog Refinement Meetings) helps smooth out flow and minimize the inventory of stale requirements. The *Product Owner* and the *Development Team* together should continuously be striving to meet the *Definition of Ready* for the topmost items when working together on the backlog.

Historically, Jeff Sutherland split Toyota's Chief Engineer into the *Product Owner* and *¶19 ScrumMaster* roles, reflecting business and development concerns respectively. The *Product Backlog* is the main Scrum artifact for the business half of that split while the *¶72 Sprint Backlog* reflects the development part.

The *Product Backlog* makes *¶102 Work Flows Inward* on page 467 possible.

¶55 Product Backlog Item

Confidence stars: **

...you are building a *¶54 Product Backlog* from items that will drive your business. The *¶39 Vision* is in place and the *Product Backlog* may contain early informal notions of market releases or *¶71 Sprint Goals*.

❖ ❖ ❖

You want to best organize work to optimize the product's value (Return on Investment, Net Present Value, etc.; see *Value and ROI*). Scrum focuses a lot on how to organize work, and it's obvious that "doing things right" contributes to solid value. However, *Value and ROI* may relate even more strongly to stakeholders and to "doing the right thing."

More broadly, value comes from delivering something of worth to stakeholders. An enterprise has many stakeholders: customers, end users, shareholders, marketing and sales, support, designers, architects, developers, and testers, each of whom contributes to an overall sense of value and stands to benefit from the ongoing creation of *¶85 Regular Product Increments*.

An ideal system increases value for all of the stakeholders, rather than benefiting one at the expense of the other. While everyone may have to give something (time, money, work), we want to achieve the paradox that everyone

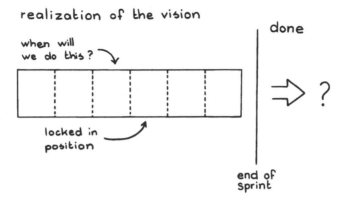

gets more than they give—or, at least as reduced to cynical terms, that everyone gets as much as they give.

Therefore:

Create distinct specifications of changes and additions to the product, called *Product Backlog Item*s (*PBIs*), that together form the *Product Backlog*. Each *PBI* describes something that the *¶14 Development Team* can develop and deliver to add value to relevant stakeholders when *Done* (see *¶82 Definition of Done*). The most common stakeholder is the market, or its representative —the *¶11 Product Owner*. However, a *PBI* may describe work that reduces cost to the enterprise or reduces effort for the *Development Team*, or a tool that helps the *¶12 Product Owner Team* better do its work. A *PBI* can describe anything that has potential value to a stakeholder.

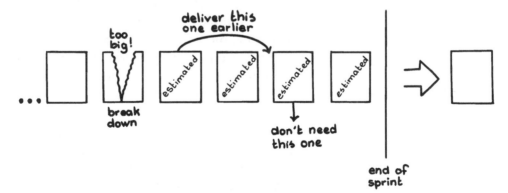

A *PBI* should have a name or other designation that helps relevant stakeholders crisply recall what the deliverable encompasses. A good *PBI* captures the stakeholder-facing decisions that the *Product Owner* has taken, or agreements between the *Product Owner* and *Development Team*—the things they should write down to help them together remember. A good *PBI* has development estimates provided by the *Development Team* that will implement it, as well as notes about the *PBI*'s contribution to *Value and ROI*.

The *PBI* is the focal point of Scrum deliverables. The lifetime of a Scrum deliverable starts with the *Vision*, which the *Product Owner* breaks down into *Sprint Goal*s that correspond to *Regular Product Increment*s. The *¶7 Scrum Team* breaks down those *Regular Product Increment*s into *PBI*s, which are the most granular unit of delivery in Scrum, working with the *Product Owner* as required (see *¶64 Refined Product Backlog*). The *Product Owner*, with support from the rest of the team, brings *PBI*s to a status of *Ready* (see *¶65 Definition of Ready*)—clearly specified, valuable, and worthy of development. The *PBI*s together drive the implementation of the solution described in the *Development Team*'s work plan, the *¶72 Sprint Backlog*. *PBI*s that achieve the stature of *Done* are delivery-ready.

❖ ❖ ❖

A *PBI* is usually one piece of a larger *Regular Product Increment*, and the focus of the best *PBI*s is on a product *solution* that lies in the *Vision* rather than on the requirements behind that contribution to the increment. The *Scrum Team* and the *Product Owner* discuss the requirements behind each deliverable face-to-face as they together make the backlog *Ready*. The team and other stakeholders can employ user stories, story boards, interaction diagrams, prototypes, user narratives, and whatever tools they choose to shape a *Product Backlog Item*, but these artifacts in general are not themselves effective *PBI*s. For example, there may be many user stories for a single deliverable, each from a different stakeholder, that expresses the need and motivation of that stakeholder with respect to that deliverable. Yet it is the deliverable, and not its facilities, that should stand as the unit of administration, estimation, and delivery in Scrum—and the *PBI* represents that deliverable. The *Scrum Team* discusses requirement details face-to-face as they build a *Refined Product Backlog* and as they prepare for the *¶46 Sprint* at hand in *¶24 Sprint Planning*. So a good *PBI represents* a set of requirements rather than being a mechanism to communicate requirements. A good *PBI* memorializes one or more rich interactions between and among the *Development Team* and the *Product Owner*, rather than itself being the vehicle by which the *Development Team* learn requirements. That said, the *PBI* can serve as a home for details about scenarios, properties of size or weight or speed or time, that the team might forget: development decisions have more detail than a group of people can retain in their heads for two weeks. And though a good *Product Backlog Item* lives in the solution space rather than in the problem space, it falls short of specifying *how* to implement and deploy the solution. That is up to the *Development Team*.

While a *PBI* is a written artifact that appears on the *Product Backlog*, much of the information passed from the *Product Owner* to the *Development Team* occurs verbally and interactively in Scrum planning events. A question-and-answer form of exchange, after an initial presentation by the *Product Owner*, is totally appropriate. A common pitfall is for the *Product Owner* to instead turn a *PBI* into a *comprehensive* document that developers can read to minimize the amount of interaction the *Product Owner* will need with the *Development Team*. As a rule of thumb, *PBI*s should start lightweight and grow in detail and specificity as time progresses. The *PBI* may nonetheless carry detailed market information that will be important to realize the *PBI* (such as detailed response time requirements, or limitations on size or weight), because such information reflects a *Product Owner* or team decision on the nature of the deliverable.

The team should give special attention to *PBI*s near the top of the *Product Backlog*, which will soon go into a *¶75 Production Episode*. The *Product Owner* and *Development Team* should discuss these to the point where *Development Team* members view them as *¶63 Enabling Specification*s.

Make sure that the *PBI*s reflect any and all business and development dependencies between the work tasks necessary to deliver them. Use *¶61 Fixed-Date PBI* for *PBI*s that depend on a particular calendar date (for example, because they are awaiting delivery of a previously ordered part with a promised delivery date).

While Scrum does not stipulate any format for *PBI*s, apply caution in relying on using user stories. User stories present a quick summary of some *what* for a *PBI*, but much of their value comes in identifying the stakeholder (*who*) and the stakeholder's motivation (*why*). User stories are in the requirements space. One *PBI* may satisfy the requirements germane to several user stories. From the perspective of release management, the elements of the *Product Backlog* are deliverables awaiting development rather than the requirements that these deliverables satisfy. The team may use any format by which stakeholders can easily recognize or envision a deliverable to which they can relate.

*PBI*s that are smaller than about 10 percent of a *Sprint* delivery usually yield the best estimates. Get to *¶58 Small Items* with approaches such as *¶59 Granularity Gradient* to avoid the waste of breaking down the entire backlog. The *Development Team* should collectively estimate all *PBI*s (*¶57 Pigs Estimate*), with a best practice being *¶60 Estimation Points*.

The team should generally not use *PBIs* to direct inwardly focused work items or tasks: that confuses the value delivered with the mechanisms used to create that value. Such confusion can cause the business to lose its external market focus. *PBIs* tend to add value for the stakeholders, rather than to the work environment, manufacturing plant, or workspace. Use the *Sprint Backlog* for items like these if they support development of some *PBI*, and use the *¶40 Impediment List* to log process issues and to keep them visible.

The *Development Team* should manage its own work plan, or *Sprint Backlog*, without undue meddling from the *Product Owner*. Some items, like cleaning the shop floor, daily machine maintenance, or refactoring code, are so routine that they are not even explicit in the work plan let alone directed at the business level. Other internal-facing work items such as testing and writing purchase orders might be explicit in the work plan, but are unlikely to explicitly appear as *PBIs*. Sometimes, these items loom large enough to threaten long term value: for example, cumulative effects of ignoring daily machine maintenance, or *¶80 Good Housekeeping*, may leave a work environment that is unsafe or inefficient and which begs a sizable cleanup effort. In these exceptional situations, the *Product Owner* may include bugs, overdue machine maintenance, technical debt reduction, and other traditionally inwardly facing items in *PBIs* because they have become large enough to merit business-level oversight.

On the other hand, while most *PBIs* relate to the *Regular Product Increment*, a *PBI* can certainly describe any deliverable that increases stakeholder value. Advanced teams might use the concept of "stakeholder" in a broad sense. The team might even use *PBIs* for internal documents such as engineering diagrams because they add value for the team, which in this case we treat as a stakeholder; there will certainly be a *PBI* for any external user manuals. (An alternative is to treat internal documentation as part of the *Definition of Done*. As a rule of thumb, use *PBIs* for large units of internal work so they remain visible, and use the *Definition of Done* for small recurring units of work that would clutter the work plan.)

PBIs should nonetheless focus on *what*, *when* and for *whom* rather than *how*. If the *Product Owner* is spending much time dealing with the *how* of development rather than the *what*, *when* and *who*, then the team should seek out and address the underlying impediments. See also *¶33 Illegitimus Non Interruptus* for a description of an advanced approach for using *PBIs* to bring important concerns outside the *Regular Product Increment* itself into sharp focus.

An advanced use of *PBIs* is to elicit process improvement work that requires work by the *Development Team* during the *Sprint*. See *¶92 Scrumming the Scrum*.

When completed at the end of the *Sprint*, the product contribution driven by a *Product Backlog Item* must meet the *Definition of Done*.

You can order *PBI*s on the basis of cost and value aspirations (for what *value* means here, see *Value and ROI*). Even with all other things being equal, changing the position of a *PBI* in the backlog can change its contribution to value (e.g., because of market timing issues, such as a season or competitive dynamic). You can order the *Product Backlog* either on the basis of the individual value estimates for relatively independent *PBI*s (as in *¶51 High Value First*) or on the basis of overall, long-term, integrative *¶50 ROI-Ordered Backlog*.

¶56 Information Radiator

Confidence stars: **

The Release Train (the plan of how parts integrate into the product as a whole) is visible to everyone, facilitating planning and awareness of where things are.

...information drives product development, and it is essential for everyone involved in developing a product to have the right information and the same information whenever they need it. *¶14 Development Team*s and the organizations in which they work comprise individuals who capture, interpret, and distribute this information, but may not distribute the information broadly enough or as often as needed.

❖　❖　❖

Without valuable and timely information, the organization dies.

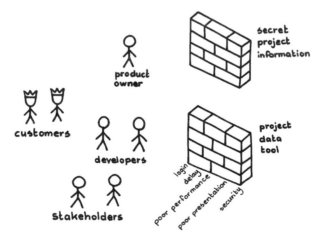

On January 28, 1986, the American space shuttle orbiter Challenger broke up 73 seconds after takeoff, killing all crew members aboard. The commission that investigated the accident found lapses in communication of vital information:

The commission also found that Morton Thiokol, the company that designed the solid rocket boosters, had ignored warnings about potential issues. NASA managers were aware of these design problems but also failed to take action. Famously, scientist Richard Feynman, a member of the commission, demonstrated the O-ring flaw to the public using a simple glass of ice water. (From a *History Channel* article on the Challenger explosion.[10])

Data are just meaningless bits; it is only when a human being interprets the data, in the context of his or her memory and knowledge, that data become useful—that they become information. Disagreements about context, such as what value the Team is creating or what the organization values about how it works, result in vague, unfocused discussions about the interpretation of events, or interpretations based on the single, loudest perspective. Dangerous assumptions and hopes often fill the vacuum left by lack of good information.

It is easy to keep information to yourself or only share it with a few peers whereas many other people need to know what you know. As sharing information can take a lot of time, there can be a temptation not to do it at all. Busy developers might view communication efforts as overhead or management crap (e.g., "I'm paid to make products, not reports.").

Too much data, untimely information and irrelevant information can be as bad as no information. People may eventually tune out and miss the important bits. Information needs to come to the right people at the right time to support the best possible decisions, but it is very easy for people to keep information to themselves. It may be that someone is intentionally withholding information—where the person with the information uses it for control or assumes that others do not need to know it. Or someone may unintentionally withhold information, forgetting to pass information on or not being in the habit of sharing information.

Information also loses value with time. Knowing what a competitor will do next month is more valuable at the beginning of the month than at the end. When information surfaces late it can be costly, as the team may have made decisions based on incorrect or missing information. "If I knew that before" is a common utterance in modern workplaces and sums up the problem of not sharing information.

It is easy to put formal processes in place to elicit data and socialize it into information (for example project status meetings). Such processes are cumbersome, intrusive, waste the time of most people involved and come with a discouraging overhead (e.g., "I'm paid to make products, not attend meetings").

---

10. "Challenger Explosion." The History Channel. http://www.history.com/topics/challenger-disaster, n.d. (viewed 14 August 2018).

Even small organizations can generate an enormous volume of information. Individuals may have to discover the information they need in the abyss of data, which may be a daunting exercise that acts as a deterrent. Even using digital search tools, people may find the cost of the effort to be too high when seeking information vital to their work.

Therefore:

Collaboratively maintain physical artifacts that keep information visible to all stakeholders.

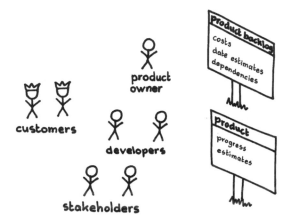

Collaboratively develop *Information Radiator*s with the people who need the information. Accept that the first version will not be correct and instead review and revise what information it displays and how to display it. Be ruthless in discarding what has not worked—this may mean you will end up with a completely different *Information Radiator* than you first thought you needed, which is great if you are sharing the information in the best way.

Simple, handmade displays work best for sharing information. Digital tools may be attractive but can easily flood people with too much data. Ironically, they simultaneously limit the view of information to the size of the display. They constrain the way you interact with the information. In addition, they typically require more work to use and populate than simple charts. In summary, the goal is to achieve low cost in producing the information and high effectiveness in using the information.

Once they have been created, the team should probably evolve the *Information Radiator*s occasionally or they will become wallpaper. This means you will need to continually put effort into maintaining the information. This is a small price to pay.

The information will need to be as accurate as needed to support decision-making. This might mean you will have to share bad news. Be courageous and do this without fear of consequences. It is hard to correct an unacknowledged problem. Using an *Information Radiator* to passive-aggressively lay blame is never a good choice—it destroys the *¶95 Community of Trust* on page 466 and breaks *¶1 The Spirit of the Game*.

❖ ❖ ❖

Good information radiators both help the team organize their thinking and planning, and largely eliminate the need for formal status reporting meetings in an agile environment. Sometimes, however, just making information visible may itself uncover deeper issues:

> On a Scrum project the teams used a whiteboard that showed the chain of application-systems needed to produce features.
>
> The application-systems were managed by different departments and teams. At every Retrospective the board showed which features could not be completed and which application-system was blocking delivery. The teams used red magnets for "broken" application-systems, black magnets for "stubbed" application-systems, and blue magnets for "working" application-systems.
>
> After a while, people—and especially management of the blocking application-systems—became annoyed by the transparency and requested to not use the board anymore. The teams persisted and eventually this transparency led to important improvement efforts across the organization.

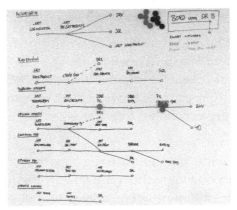

An *Information Radiator* needs to attract attention.[11] In the preceding example, the team acted to bring focus to blockers rather than trying to identify any locus of blame. Developing the radiator collaboratively with the consumers

11. Alistair Cockburn. "Origin of the term Information Radiator." Alistair.cockburn.us, https://staging.cockburn.us/origin-of-the-term-information-radiator/, August, 2017 (accessed 8 June 2018).

of the information can support this need for bringing focus to issues as they arise. It is crucial that the team display the *Information Radiators* where people can't miss seeing them. A simple indicator of summary information attracts attention and brings the workforce to an immediate recognition of the *implication* of a failure more than to its *cause*. For example, something as simple as a traffic light for the build status makes transparent (or at least translucent) what is happening, and it runs deep in Western culture that a red light implies trouble. But if the traffic light starts cueing people to ascribe blame, it is serving the wrong purpose.

Starting to use *Information Radiators* sometimes brings physical and political challenges. Some organizations have policies about the content, location, and means of affixing wall hangings (it may be to "avoid damaging the walls, paint, and design prints"). You may need to convince people that the cost of repainting a wall is far less than cost of making decisions without the correct information. There may also be a fear of radiating proprietary information; a simple encoding process can obviate this risk without being a deterrent to radiating information to the team (for example see bit-planner.com).

In corporate scale Scrum adoption there can be a desire for uniformity "so we all know what we're doing." Different teams need different information and will develop different work practices, so *Information Radiators* will vary from team to team. This situation can be uncomfortable for some people. Over time, the dialogue will nudge the organization to choose *Information Radiators* that optimize the overall happiness of the development ecosystem.

Many organizations have paid for expensive software to manage and organize information, and there may be a push to use this rather than anything hand crafted. Software tools make for information refrigerators instead of information radiators, and we need to be brave enough to admit to making bad decisions such as buying expensive software when we could have used some sticky notes.

A healthy organization might embrace the opportunity to remodel the development space to accommodate the trade-offs between livable working space, protection of proprietary information, adequate wall space (e.g., glass walls) for sticky notes, and room lighting (putting stickies on the windows might darken the room).

With the *Information Radiators* set up, the team is ready to manage releases (see ¶48 *Release Plan*) and ¶75 *Production Episodes* with the benefit of insight into recent history and current status.

Information from an *Information Radiator* is often also consumed by the producers of that information. One important benefit of *Information Radiator*s is that they send the message that the team has nothing to hide from itself (or others). Good *Information Radiator*s digest raw data into higher-order information.

Here are examples of *Information Radiator*s used in Scrum:

- *¶44 Scrum Board*, owned by the *Development Team*s
- *¶40 Impediment List*, owned by the *¶19 ScrumMaster*
- *¶43 Sprint Burndown Chart*s (when on walls), also owned by the *Development Team*s

While *Information Radiator*s inform the day's work, they are not a call to action. If a particular status warrants immediate attention, go beyond just *Information Radiator*s to use *¶78 Visible Status*.

Toyota Production System's "visual control" in the 1980s is one foundation of *Information Radiator*s. Alistair Cockburn coined the term *information radiator* in the year 2001 (*Agile Software Development: The Cooperative Game, 2nd ed. [Coc06]*, p. 504).

An *Information Radiator* culture can facilitate both improved collaboration with other Scrum teams and other parts of the organization, and can as well facilitate the team to adopt broader ownership of its processes, of its decisions, and of the product.

¶57 Pigs Estimate

Confidence stars: **

...the team has a *¶54 Product Backlog* or *¶72 Sprint Backlog* in hand. The team uses effort estimates, both for *¶55 Product Backlog Item*s (*PBI*s) and tasks (or other Sprint Backlog Items), to forecast, plan, and schedule work and deliveries. The *¶14 Development Team* manages itself as an *¶16 Autonomous Team*.

❖ ❖ ❖

The team should ground its estimates in reality rather than assumptions or wishful thinking.

Sometimes when new work comes in, a caring manager may want to protect the team from the work of estimating it, and may take the initiative to estimate it him- or herself. It will take the team some energy to undo a standing estimate, particularly if a manager, the *¶11 Product Owner*, or someone else in authority or with power over the team, imposes the estimate on the team.

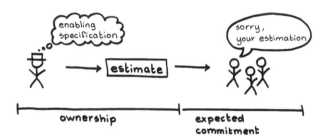

Development efforts tend to rely on experienced people and experts to do estimation. But maybe the people who are going to do the work are less experienced, or the team has forgotten to involve an important area (for example, Testing) in making the estimates.

A team might not feel responsible for the backlog when others determine the estimates. If the expert is within the team, a hierarchy might emerge and the team as a whole might not take ownership of the estimates.

Therefore:

Let the people who are committed to do the actual work do the estimation. In the Scrum sense, it is pigs that estimate—not chickens (*Agile Software Development with Scrum (Series in Agile Software Development) [SB01]*, p. 31; *Agile Estimating and Planning, 1 edition [Coh05]*, p. 51; and *Essential Scrum: A Practical Guide to the Most Popular Agile Process [Rub12]*, p. 123).

The terms Pigs (*Development Team* members) and Chickens (everyone else) finds its roots in the following joke:

> *A chicken and a pig are together when the chicken says, "Let's start a restaurant!" The Pig thinks it over and says, "What would we call the restaurant?" The chicken says, "Ham n' Eggs!" The pig says, "No thanks, I'd be committed, but you'd only be involved!"* (From *Agile Software Development with Scrum (Series in Agile Software Development) [SB01]*, p. 42)

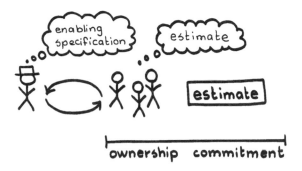

The estimate should be a consensus generated from the perspectives of all relevant development areas. Research shows that estimates are much better when combining independent estimates, with iteration and feedback, from everyone who participates in development. Since *Development Team*s are cross-functional, it's possible for the *Development Team* to create very good estimates together (*IEEE Software 31 [Jør14a]*).

❖ ❖ ❖

The team feels committed to ownership for its work. This is good in its own right but will also increase the focus that the team brings to its estimation efforts. Oh, and one gets better estimates in the long term if they come from the *Development Team*.

In particular, the *Product Owner* (perhaps together with the *¶12 Product Owner Team*) estimates the Business Value, and the *Development Team* estimates the cost or effort necessary to complete the *PBIs*. Each of these groups can use Wideband Delphi [12] or any other technique to build a consensus view (see *¶60 Estimation Points*). It is particularly important to capture the perspectives of all members of the cross-functional *Development Team*.

The *Development Team* should continuously revise estimates as new information emerges. The team can estimate newly created *Product Backlog Item*s as it works with the *Product Owner* toward creating a *¶64 Refined Product Backlog*, and it is natural to review estimates at *¶24 Sprint Planning*. The *Development Team* can follow its intuition about which estimates to revisit in light of new information. Estimates also come up for renewal as the *¶7 Scrum Team* restructures the *Product Backlog* while building a *Refined Product Backlog* or striving for a *¶59 Granularity Gradient*.

In most applications of this pattern in Scrum, the estimate is only a forecast, and stakeholders should never view it as implying a commitment. On the other hand, no one other than "the pigs" is allowed to speak to estimation. There should never be a ground for challenging an estimate a priori. For example, *Product Owner*s cannot impose their wishes for delivery on the team's grounded forecast about how long work will take. Empirical insights from experience over time will help the team adjust its estimates to be more accurate.

---

12. Wikipedia, "Wideband Delphi." Wikipedia, https://en.wikipedia.org/wiki/Wideband_delphi, September 2017 (accessed 2 November 2017).

¶58 Small Items

Confidence stars: *

...a *¶7 Scrum Team* is regularly creating product increments where many factors influence the ordering of the *¶54 Product Backlog*, and the team may not perfectly understand these factors when ordering the backlog. For example, the *¶14 Development Team* doesn't know the *exact* amount of work required to complete a *¶55 Product Backlog Item* (*PBI*) until they complete it. In addition, the *¶11 Product Owner* cannot pinpoint how much value a new *Product Backlog Item* will create over its lifetime.

❖ ❖ ❖

Big ideas are great to have but the devil is in the details.

It can be very easy to have big ideas and use these to make up a *Product Backlog*. Big ideas have their place in Scrum (as a *¶39 Vision*) and to some extent in the *Product Backlog* (*¶59 Granularity Gradient*). However, it is more difficult for the entire team to concisely conceptualize large *Product Backlog Items*, which can limit the *Product Owner*'s ability to relate them as an *¶63 Enabling Specification* to the *Development Team*. Communication and understanding are key for the *Product Owner* and *Development Team* to be able to work together. The *Product Backlog* is the nexus for this work, so it must comprise items that support communication and building shared understanding.

Whether a large item has too much information or too little detail, it carries high risk. If the item is a big and vague idea, successful implementation is almost impossible, which may lead to endless rework by the *Development Team*. This is obviously wasteful. If the large item conveys a large amount of information (such as scenarios or acceptance criteria), the *Development Team* risks not completing the work for all the specified requirements within a *¶46 Sprint*. Both of these are common scenarios for *Scrum Teams*. The *Development*

Team may be starved for information if it interacts with the *Product Owner* too infrequently or too superficially. Circumstances may force the *Development Team* to "wing it" with whatever information it has.

Increasing the size of work items increases variance and errors in their estimates (*Software Project Effort Estimation: Foundations and Best Practice Guidelines for Success [TJ14]*, p. 142.) By definition, an estimate is a guess, so it is imperfect. We know when we measure anything that the measurement we obtain is a combination of the actual value and some error amount. For estimates (which are not measured), we can expect the error component to be large and wildly varying for different items. If this error is 20 percent (probably a relatively small error value), then for a large item this error is proportionally larger than for a small item. For example, an estimate of a large item at 20 days has an error of four days, whereas an estimate of a smaller item at five days has an error of only one day. It is unlikely that the error of an estimate will be the same between larger and smaller items or between any two items we have in a *Product Backlog* or *¶72 Sprint Backlog*. As described above, it is more difficult for developers to thoroughly understand larger items, which may result in a larger *percentage* error in the estimate. If we add up the estimates across the *Product Backlog* (for a *¶48 Release Plan*), then we are adding these errors together. We can always correct this with some kind of padding or other contingency, and we can complicate the estimation regimen to reduce the risk of missing deadlines—at the expense of precision. A better tack may be to deliver a version of the product rather than spend all the time planning.

Feedback is an essential part of Scrum; the *¶35 Sprint Review* is a formal opportunity for the *Scrum Team* to gain feedback on progress of the product. The *Sprint Review* is most effective at providing this feedback when there is a potentially shippable *¶85 Regular Product Increment*. Working with large items can limit the opportunity for the *Development Team* to finish this *Regular Product Increment*, giving the *Scrum Team* nothing to review. This greatly limits feedback, which is the lifeblood of an agile team, because the product is in a state between planning and delivery—a nowhere land. Moreover, apart from feedback, this state gives no visibility about progress because the *Scrum Team* cannot really know where the product is with respect to the *Product Backlog* or *¶45 Product Roadmap*; the position is a guess until deployment.

The habit of hoarding work or defending one's ability to finish it can be strong and difficult to change in many organizational cultures. These cultures may not view the effort to make smaller *¶73 Sprint Backlog Items* (*SBIs*) as worth the benefit. If a *Development Team* creates *SBIs* that are so large that each one takes many days to complete during the *Sprint*, the *¶29 Daily Scrum* becomes a pointless ritual. With no visibility of progress or changes in direction, the *Daily Scrum* may as well become a daily group hug (except that a hug may be a better use of the time).

When the team fails to deliver *SBI*s (not bringing them to *Done*: see *¶82 Definition of Done*), even if the team is "almost Done," it will struggle to meet the *¶71 Sprint Goal* and to deliver value. The team finds that its small incompletions have large consequences. This symptom most often points to the deeper problem of the *Scrum Team*'s misunderstanding of the *PBI*s/*SBI*s. The team might not understand the magnitude of the work required or the risks involved. In addition, the team might not understand the *PBI* itself.

Teams generally estimate required work in terms of detailed sizing of individual tasks. However, the *Scrum Team* needs reasonably accurate aggregate estimates for release planning. If the team cannot rely on estimates, it cannot rely on the plans either. Actually, estimates are a gauge of how well the *Development Team* understands a given item: if estimates are wildly inaccurate, it is an indicator that the team doesn't understand the item well enough to develop it. An inaccurately estimated *PBI* may be difficult to order against other *PBI*s, as estimated value and ROI (see Value and ROI on page 246) reflect the union of both the commercial value and the estimate effort to deliver.

Rindfleischetikierungsüberwachungsaufgabenübertragungsgesetz

Large items are by nature hard to understand, estimate, and reliably deliver.

Therefore:

Break work down into *Small Items* that are steps to deliver the big ideas, so the *Development Team* can master its understanding of each small item individually. Large items cloud understanding of important details, and misunderstanding causes surprises. The team can reduce schedule surprises by administering and working on *Small Items*.

A *Small Item* is a *Product Backlog Item* (*PBI*) or *Sprint Backlog Item* (*SBI*) the *Development Team* can easily understand and quickly (in the case of *PBI*) take to *Done*. "Quickly" for an *SBI* means within two days of work from start to *Done*; the time frame is arbitrary and depends on your planning horizon, but for sound implementation of this pattern, two days is a recommended maximum. Though we strongly recommend using relative estimation (see ¶60 *Estimation Points*) for *PBI*s, rather than time-based estimation, a *Development Team* will develop a feel for what it can achieve in a given time frame; setting the two-day limit taps into that experience.

Estimating smaller items benefits from the law of large numbers and is better-suited to complex and uncertain work than is top-down estimation (*Software Project Effort Estimation: Foundations and Best Practice Guidelines for Success* *[TJ14]*, p. 142). Estimation expert Magne Jørgensen recommends that for new projects developed by experts in the field, bottom-up estimation works best (*Information Software Technology [Jør14]*).

Breaking items down helps us understand dependencies between items. For example, if you have two items that depend on each other, you can decompose each into smaller items that break the circular dependency. This can give the *Product Owner* more freedom in ordering the *Product Backlog*, and can allow more flexible ordering of *SBI*s in a *Sprint*.

law for the delegation of monitoring beef labelling

Having smaller and better understood items to estimate will increase overall estimation accuracy and precision. However, the goal of this pattern is *not* to produce highly precise estimates. One must still play the game of estimating for the process to work: namely, to understand the item well enough to implement it correctly. The major output of this pattern is that team members understand the items thoroughly so they can deliver them reliably first and improve forecasting second. The aggregate estimate is useful in making a *Release Plan* and also during ¶24 *Sprint Planning*.

We are more interested in combined estimates of items and trends over time than in estimates of individual items.

To have *Small Items*, a *Scrum Team* needs to spend more time on refinement of the *Product Backlog* with an increased focus on design of the product. As a consequence there will be less time on estimation. *Scrum Team*s and organizations new to Scrum will find this unnerving as estimates—particularly of cost—drive traditional product development practice. With greater flow that can come with *Small Items* there is a significantly lower risk of a *Development Team* not delivering a *PBI*, and this will stabilize cost (which becomes the cost of a *Sprint*), so the driving force for product development must be value or customer outcome rather than cost to deliver. This is a cultural change in product development that will require support for its implementation.

Breaking down large *PBI*s and *SBI*s helps developers understand them, because it necessarily involves design work. *Small Items* help the team increase the likelihood that it will achieve its forecast.

❖ ❖ ❖

Small Items in a *Product Backlog* allows for more regular delivery and better feedback on product direction. As well as creating opportunities to adjust the product to maximize value, the *Product Owner* must be actively engaged with the *Scrum Team* and the product to take full advantage of feedback. This level of engagement may require the *Product Owner*s to have support of a *¶12 Product Owner Team* to cover all required work, but the benefits of this situation should clearly outweigh the extra cost.

Using *Small Items* in the *Sprint Backlog* helps reduce the "leakage" that results from failing to deliver any particular *SBI*. Using *Small Items* in the *Product Backlog* gives insight into *PBI*s earlier so the team can bring them to *Ready* (see *¶65 Definition of Ready*), increasing the chance that they become truly *Enabling Specification*s. Focus on items at the top of the *Product Backlog* as described in *Granularity Gradient*.

Some teams that have adopted *Small Items* have found it takes more work to manage the larger number of items in the *Product Backlog* or *Sprint Backlog*. *Granularity Gradient* helps remedy this problem for *PBI*s. In the case of *SBI*s, the blame often lies with the tool teams have adopted to help manage their backlog. Using sticky notes for *SBI*s rather than an online tool seems to resolve this tool problem.

Jeff Sutherland reports observing a significant decrease in *Estimation Points* (story points) delivered as the size of the *PBI*s increased.

¶59 Granularity Gradient

Confidence stars: *

In the primordial pattern literature, Christopher Alexander recommends a granularity gradient for the size of windows along the story levels of a house (see the pattern "Natural Doors and Windows" in A Pattern Language [AIS77].)

...the *¶11 Product Owner* has laid out a release vision as a *¶54 Product Backlog*, taking the market value of each item into consideration, as well as cost estimates from the *¶14 Development Team*.

❖ ❖ ❖

¶58 Small Items **are easiest to estimate, but breaking down work items is a lot of work in itself.** The work estimates for small product increments and tasks have less error than for larger ones for three reasons:

1. The magnitude of the work (and therefore of the possible error) is smaller than for a larger increment or task.

2. The team can better understand smaller deliverables and tasks than larger ones.

3. The *percentage* error on smaller deliverables and tasks is less than for large ones because there is less of an element of guessing (and the maximum size of any error is implicitly mitigated.)

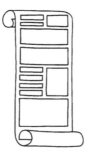

If the team has not broken down large *¶55 Product Backlog Items* (*PBIs*) into small ones, the estimate for each one will be coarse and imprecise. It is easy to believe that any estimates are better than no estimates—and that may be true. It is also easy to avoid the discipline of going the extra mile to estimate at a finer level. You can get into analysis paralysis if you spend too much time on estimation. Furthermore, those who want to manipulate schedules can too easily use detailed estimates to micromanage developers.

It is important that the *Development Team* reduce the estimation error as much as is reasonable so it is confident in meeting its forecast to the *Product Owner*, and so the *Product Owner* can in turn meet his or her commitment to the market. It takes work to break down large requirements into small ones. That work takes time, time that is waste in the *¶41 Value Stream*. Furthermore, a *Product Backlog* with many items is hard to manage.

For near-term items, the effort the team spends estimating work is worth the cost: the market will remember a schedule slip longer than it will remember how much it paid for an item.

However, emergent requirements can invalidate even the best estimates: changes in the market, in technology, or team staffing. The longer that time goes on, the higher the likelihood that such changes may emerge. The more distant a *PBI* is in time, the lower the confidence in the estimate. On the other hand, one can use lead time to one's advantage; long lead time means more time to reduce the uncertainty that comes with any new product increment idea. Boehm (*Software Engineering Economics [Boe81]*, p. 311) has shown empirically that estimates may be too large or too small by a factor of as much as four until the team is able to detail requirements, and such detailing takes place over time. But because of changes in the market and other factors in the environment, breaking down long-term requirements is not enough and, in general, there is nothing that one can do to estimate long-term requirements with certainty. And just the passage of time isn't enough (*Software Estimation: Demystifying the black art [McC06]*, p. 38). The team must be continuously incorporating new insights they gain: into the state of the market, into the team's own changing level of experience, and into the ongoing changes in the product itself. This is one reason that long-term waterfall development cycles miss the mark. Yet even in the short term, the best of estimates fall victim to emergent requirements. Such requirements may double the number of tasks or overall effort required to meet a market need.

Processing large batch sizes increases the variance in the process. To reduce variance, reduce batch size (*The Principles of Product Development Flow: Second Generation Lean Product Development [Rei09]*, p. 112).

Relatively worthless components of a development increment can easily hide in a larger *PBI*, but become visible when considered on their own merits after breaking down the larger *PBI*.

Therefore:

Break down the earliest *PBIs* into *Small Items* of half a ¶46 *Sprint* or less of work for an individual (about 10 percent of the total *Sprint* work) each. The team should break down later *PBIs* so that their size is proportional to their depth in the *Product Backlog*. A *PBI* that lies more than four or five *Sprints* in the future may be arbitrarily large and may be little more than a whim of what the feature should do.

Said another way, no *PBI* within the top two or three *Sprints* should take more than 10 percent of the total *PBI* effort for that *Sprint*, and keeping them below 5 percent of the total effort is even better. Even if emergent requirements cause the estimate to double during the *Sprint*, the team can still complete and deliver many *PBIs*.

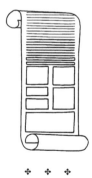

❖   ❖   ❖

Breaking down the *Product Backlog* this way lays a foundation for a more fully ¶64 *Refined Product Backlog* (towards ¶65 *Definition of Ready*). Small *PBIs* and small ¶73 *Sprint Backlog Items* both reduce risk by reducing the leakage cost if the team fails to take any single unit of delivery or work to completion. See *Small Items*.

With a gradient of size, the *Product Backlog* effectively offers a top-down view of the items that are closer to the bottom and a bottom-up view of those closer to the top. This is in line with the recommendation of (*Software Project Effort Estimation [TJ14]*, p. 143), which says to "[p]refer top-down estimation in the early (conceptual) phases of a project and switch to bottom-up estimation where specific development tasks and assignments are known."

Estimate all the *PBI*s including the ones for the distant future. Refresh those estimates less frequently than those whose release time is more imminent. Accept higher estimation uncertainty the further that work lies in the future. Do not waste the effort of breaking distant *PBI*s down, since unplanned changes are likely to overshadow the increased precision. But remember that perhaps the main purpose of estimation and backlog refinement is to get the team to start thinking about the forthcoming feature; see *Refined Product Backlog*.

Avoid estimating at a level of granularity that would lead to micromanagement. ¶60 *Estimation Points* are the preferred method, but with simple math even those can be converted to hours for any given *Sprint*. Some Scrum folklore recommends estimating to the granularity of two hours; in experience, we have found such fine estimates to be self-fulfilling prophecies in complex emergent projects, and estimating to the granularity of about a day is enough.

This is a broadly accepted practice.

¶60 Estimation Points

Planning Poker® Cards, Mountain Goat Software. Used with permission.

...you have *¶55 Product Backlog Items* on your *¶54 Product Backlog*, and you need an approach to estimate the effort required to implement those items.

❖   ❖   ❖

It is important to have reliable estimates. Customers are happiest when products meet or exceed their expectations. A team wants to size the work of a *¶46 Sprint* properly so it will deliver what the customer expects: too much work for the *Sprint* and stakeholder expectations suffer; too little work for the *Sprint* and the team has extra time on its hands for which work has not been planned or prepared. The same problems extend to longer time horizons, of delivering something several *Sprints* too late or several *Sprints* too early. However, if you spend a lot of effort estimating in days or hours, and your velocity changes (see Notes on Velocity on page 320), then the estimates are all wrong, anyhow.

Part of being reliable is being up to date: to ensure that the most current knowledge stands behind the team's estimates. It's hard to be up to date if it takes a long, boring exercise to torture estimates from the team.

The *¶11 Product Owner* wants to know the earliest potential release date for a set of features. The natural inclination is to ask people to estimate the number of hours required to finish each item, and then to add up the hours required to finish all desired features and to project that number onto a calendar, presuming a fixed team size and a work week of 37–40 hours. However, the estimates for work completion don't account for "in-between work" activities such as meetings, doing email, administration, the costs of context switching, and even of many business tasks, including work ordering and estimation itself. A typical work week is much shorter than 40 hours, with teams more typically spending about half that much on focused work. A

Harris Poll survey found that people spend only about 45 percent of their time on "primary job duties."[13] But the truth is, nobody *really* knows how many of those 40 hours are overhead and how many are real work. That makes it hard to know how many weeks it will take to accomplish a given number of hours of work.

An estimate is not a commitment, but rather a best guess of the work to complete a given *Product Backlog Item* (PBI) or *¶73 Sprint Backlog Item* (SBI). If the team is using absolute estimation units such as days or hours, it may suggest to stakeholders that the team can calculate a possible availability date for a given item assuming, say, a 40-hour work week for each team member, and to "prove" that the team can complete the item earlier. The problem, of course, is that the 40-hour week is a fiction. The difference between the stakeholders' naive calculation and the team's more informed calculation breaks down trust between them, and stakeholders may view any attempt to explain away the disparity as a difference between real hours and ideal hours with suspicion.

The *¶14 Development Team* needs to measure how process improvement affects its capacity for work. Removing impediments may cause velocity to increase. Without a velocity measure based on *Estimation Points*, it is difficult and often impossible to assess the results of an intended process improvement.

The *Development Team* and the *Product Owner* want to have a certain level of accuracy in the estimation. People have difficulty estimating in absolute units (e.g., meters, days) (see "Wedding Planning" in *Scrum: The Art of Doing Twice the Work in Half the Time [SS14]*, ff. 118, and also *Essential Scrum: A Practical Guide to the Most Popular Agile Process [Rub12]*, ff. 125). Research shows that estimating in relative units is a more accurate alternative.[14] When using absolute estimations, the units we use for estimation imply a corresponding duration. People can agree on the size of a thing like a 100-meter track but they will have a hard time agreeing on how fast it takes to run the 100 meters. We can agree that running 200 meters will probably take more than double the time as for 100 meters, though we may not be able to agree on the time for either. Experience will tell us how long it will take to run 100

---

13. Bourree Lam. "The Wasted Workday." In *The Atlantic*, 4 December 2014, https://www.theatlantic.com/business/archive/2014/12/the-wasted-workday/383380/ (accessed 2 November 2017).

14. James Grenning. "Planning Poker or How to avoid analysis paralysis while release planning." https://wingman-sw.com/papers/PlanningPoker-v1.1.pdf, 2002 (accessed 2 November 2017).

meters, which means that we should be able to project how long it would take to run twice as long.

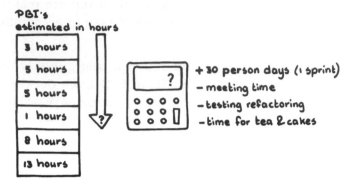

Therefore: **Use unitless numbers for effort estimation. Use relative estimation, starting with the *Estimation Points* for some simple work item that everyone understands well as a baseline for the rest.**

To estimate *Product Backlog Item*s, the initial baseline can be some *PBI* about which the team has consensus understanding. For the ¶72 *Sprint Backlog*, it can be some task, deliverable, or other unit of measure of the *Development Team*'s choice for which the team has consensus understanding of the likely effort involved.

In all cases, the team should consider *all* work necessary to bring the corresponding item (*PBI* or *Sprint Backlog Item*) to the equivalent of *Done* (see ¶82 *Definition of Done*).

The team can communicate its *velocity* (see *Notes on Velocity*) in units of *Estimation Points* per *Sprint*.

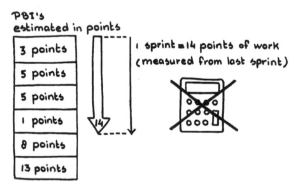

The estimation includes all work necessary for the *Development Team* to develop the *Product Backlog Item* to *Done*.

❖　❖　❖

Having a velocity "standard" in hand, the team can derive its velocity as a basis for prediction and improvement. See *¶67 Running Average Velocity* and *¶68 Aggregate Velocity* for common ways to apply velocity in the Scrum framework.

Poker-planning, as conceived by Grenning[15] and further elaborated and popularized by Cohn (*Agile Estimating and Planning [Coh05]*), is a modern implementation of the Delphi technique that has proven to be an excellent approach to generate *Estimation Points*. Poker-planning is based on a nonlinear scale (approximately the Fibonacci numbers) that helps break down linear thinking. The main idea behind the use of the Fibonacci series is that the distance between allowable estimates increases as the estimates increase, reflecting the increasing uncertainty with increasingly high estimates. To help weaken any faith that might remain in the precision of large estimates, the scale rounds down larger Fibonacci numbers (e.g., 21 becomes 20, because 21 has too many significant digits, etc.).

A team often anchors its poker-planning exercise with a baseline. The baseline is usually a small number (1, 2, or 3) and the team associates that number with some low-effort *¶58 Small Items*, with which the *Development Team* has high familiarity and confidence. After the first round of estimation, every item is a baseline, by transitive closure of relative estimation. This obviates the need for techniques like reference stories.

Some teams give a pessimistic and optimistic estimate for each item to caveat their forecasts. It is common Scrum practice to instead give a single consensus estimate for each item, and then separately derive confidence ranges empirically from historic data. This makes estimation go faster and provides a solid foundation for believing that the confidence range is something other than an arbitrary attempt to avoid blame. See *¶49 Release Range*.

A common practice in Scrum is to call *Estimation Points* "Gummi Bears." Ron Jeffries first mentions this name in 1999, and other references attribute it to an XP project led by Joseph Pelrine.[16]

---

15. James Grenning. "Planning Poker or How to avoid analysis paralysis while release planning." https://wingman-sw.com/papers/PlanningPoker-v1.1.pdf, 2002 (accessed 2 November 2017).
16. "Agile Practices Timeline." AgileAlliance.org, https://www.agilealliance.org/agile101/practices-timeline/ (accessed 2 November 2017).

A survey jointly sponsored by CA Software and the Software Engineering Institute (SEI) at Carnegie Mellon University, of 50,000 agile teams ([17]), has found that for 90 percent of the respondents, using *Estimation Points* is better than a hybrid approach that still uses hours for *Sprint Backlog Item*s, which in turn is better than the "no estimates" technique, which in turn is better than estimating in hours.

The team can also use *Estimation Points* to estimate *Sprint Backlog Item*s on the *Sprint Backlog*. If the *Sprint Backlog* and *Product Backlog* use the same units for estimation, then the team can audit whether estimates for a given *PBI* are too optimistic or pessimistic by summing the estimates of the *SBI*s that the team must complete to bring the corresponding *PBI* to *Definition of Done*. Teams often find that original *PBI* estimates are optimistic because the process of design (of turning *PBI*s into *SBI*s) uncovers emergent work.

Estimation Points are just a technique. A team can regularly improve its use of this technique to avoid common pitfalls. The most important problematic pitfall is to not involve all the developers; the second most problematic pitfall is to allow undue influence from anyone else. There are more refined improvements to the technique that nonetheless can make a lot of difference; see *IEEE Software 30 [Jør13]*. The key points to remember here are that the pace of the schedule should be set by those carrying out the implementation work, and that people are very bad at reckoning estimates in absolute time units.

To the degree that *Development Team* members understand an item well enough to estimate it, they are likely to understand it well enough to implement it. Indeed, one of the main reasons to do estimation is to get the team thinking about the problem and solution early; when the time comes to implement a solution, it has already been rolling about in *Developers'* minds for a while. See ¶64 *Refined Product Backlog*.

---

17. "The impact of agile quantified." ProjectManagement.com, http://www.projectmanagement.com/pdf/469163_the-impact-of-agile-quantified.pdf, n.d. (accessed 13 November 2016).

¶61 Fixed-Date PBI

Alias: Due Date PBI

Confidence stars: *

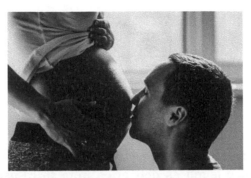

...your *¶54 Product Backlog* tracks the delivery order of value increments to the market. The *¶11 Product Owner* is accountable for value and orders the *Product Backlog*—not by priority—but to attain the highest overall value (usually long-term value). The *¶14 Development Team* has a reliable understanding of its velocity (see Notes on Velocity on page 320).

❖ ❖ ❖

Sometimes external dependencies block progress on a *¶55 Product Backlog Item (PBI)*. Some things happen on their own time, and the best laid plans of mice and men often go astray. Some events, developments, and deliveries are beyond the control of the *Development Team* or the *Product Owner*. However, in many cases we can still know when those developments and deliveries will take place. You can't control when an auto manufacturer will start selling a new line of trucks, but you usually can trust the manufacturer's announced availability date. The expected availability date is useful information for planning. It's good if the *Product Owner* can order deliveries according to their best fit to the market, and *only* according to their need to fit the market. However, suppliers tend to work on their own schedules. Some of them aren't agile and deliver on their own locally optimized schedules or on schedules constrained by parties beyond your control. And most of the time, when key personnel take family or scheduled medical leave, it's not under the *Product Owner*'s control or influence.

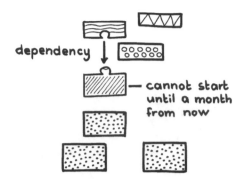

Therefore,

The *Product Owner* moves each *Product Backlog Item* blocked by a hard schedule dependency (such as deliveries from third-party partners) to a backlog position that corresponds to a date when it becomes ready for a ¶46 *Sprint* (e.g., the supplier's scheduled delivery date). The *Product Owner* marks the *PBI* with the expected resolution date for the dependency.

If another *PBI* depends on the fixed-date *PBI* such that the *Development Team* cannot start working on the dependent *PBI* until the fixed-date *PBI* is finished, then that *PBI* should be below the fixed-date *PBI* in the *Product Backlog*.

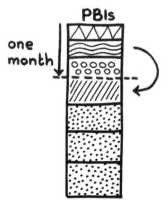

As is true with any manipulation of the *Product Backlog*, the ¶7 *Scrum Team* should frequently check relative position of the *PBI* and adjust it as necessary so it lands in the *Sprint* that will deliver by the target date.

Here is one illustrative anecdote:

> *A new telecom company appeared in the market. They promised to have the service available within six months; marketing campaigns and sales started. People started subscribing for their services. They needed a "good enough" call center. The telecom*

consulted third parties to provide the call center in time. The available market solutions offered more sophisticated solutions than what the telecom needed, and the cost was unreasonably high. The PO decided that the telecom instead would build its own call center in house (initial Fixed-Date PBI), with an availability date six months hence. They refined the initial PBI to specify a cheaper, lower-quality solution to meet the six-month deadline, with a longer-term plan to retire this interim system and replace it with a more robust and full-featured system.

Here is another:

An international agency's Scrum Teams required components from its infrastructure team. The infrastructure team's capacity was insufficient to provide all the required components in time for targeted deliveries. The Scrum Teams collaborated to identify their most important PBIs that could be resourced immediately by the infrastructure team. The Scrum Teams whose PBIs could not be resourced reorganized their Product Backlogs around their Fixed-Date PBIs (PBIs that the infrastructure teams could resource immediately).

❖ ❖ ❖

The *Fixed-Date PBI* stands out in the *Product Backlog* and its visibility enables the *Scrum Team* to replan.

The *Product Owner* is better able to forecast deliveries impacted by the *Fixed-Date PBI*. There is less likely to be inventory from prematurely available external components, or partially developed internal components awaiting delivery from an external source.

See Ackoff[18] about the pros and cons of contingency planning as an alternative to forecasts and probability.

Some uses of *Fixed-Date PBI* try to accommodate delays between relatively independent teams, one of whose work depends on the output of another. As a deeper solution, the development organization should eliminate such handoffs where possible. Toyota has reduced delay by locating most of its (often internal) suppliers within a 30-minute drive of where the goods are consumed.

See *¶62 Vacation PBI* as a variant on the idea of a *Fixed-Date PBI*.

---

18. Russel L. Ackoff. "Thinking about the future." Blogs.com, http://ackoffcenter.blogs.com/ackoff_center_weblog/files/ackoffstallbergtalk.pdf, 2005 (accessed 2 November 2017).

¶62 Vacation PBI

The team had been doing Scrum for a long time now and its velocity had stabilized around 100, running one-week Sprints. Summer was coming around and Sue, one of the five team members, was about to go on vacation. Sue was there for Sprint Planning on the last day before her vacation started. The team was trying to determine its forecast for the next Sprint. "Sue is going to be gone," said Dan Blooming, the ScrumMaster, "so we should reduce our velocity to 80." Everyone nodded in agreement. "But we should also try this new kaizen of pair programming."

A week later, when the team finished, they had completed 120 estimation points of work! They went ahead into the next Sprint and completed 100 estimation points of work.

On Friday, the last day of that Sprint, the team was doing Sprint planning, knowing that Sue would be returning Monday. Another team member, Jim, asked: "What should the team use as its velocity for forecasting the next Sprint's delivery?"

...your *¶54 Product Backlog* tracks the delivery order of value increments to the market. *¶24 Sprint Planning* has to accommodate vacation, family leave, anticipated medical leave, and even team outings, all of which take time away from development but are traditionally respected by corporate human resources culture. These activities affect delivered value directly and costs indirectly. Unlike work on Product Increments, for which *¶11 Product Owner*s can schedule the *¶14 Development Team* solely with respect to business considerations, vacations and other "personal" events are sometimes beyond their control (see *¶61 Fixed-Date PBI*). Medical leave and long-term competence development often fit in this same category.

The *¶7 Scrum Team* must be working in a Community of Trust (see *¶95 Community of Trust* on page 466).

❖ ❖ ❖

Most corporations honor vacation time and other planned time off for employees, and in that sense, allowing employees to take a break from work is a part of the corporate value system. However, they don't create market value in the same way that product increments do: the value lies outside traditional value streams. Therefore, it is common for Project Managers who become *¶19 ScrumMasters* or *Product Owners* to view vacations and other planned off time as impediments, as contributing negative value, or as "special cases" outside financial business value. For example, some teams may view vacation as a human resources concern outside the scope of development scheduling. Of course, that's unrealistic from a scheduling perspective, so it becomes necessary to plan staffing around planned absences. Many *Development Teams* adjust their forecast velocity (see Notes on Velocity on page 320) downward to compensate for anticipated absences, only to restore it on the individuals' return.

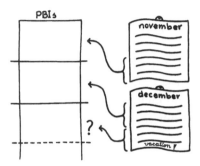

A team can use Scrum to optimize any value. Hall (*A Methodology for Systems Engineering [Hal62]*) broadens value to encompass the economic, casuistic, and psychological theories of value. The *Scrum Team* usually ignores vacation and training as contributors to the casuistic theory of value when making the *Product Backlog*. Usually, only items from the economic theory of value make it onto the *Product Backlog*. Workers in particular respond at least as strongly to the casuistic theory of value as to monetary rewards (*Drive: The Surprising Truth About What Motivates Us [Pin11]*) and, of course, the psychological theory of value is crucial in a work environment. Some of the most highly valued items on professional *Scrum Teams* lack representation on the major organ of value.

The *Development Team* wants to meet its forecast regularly, and you want the *Development Team* to regularly stay on a kaizen path that sees both predictability and capacity for work increase over time. The team uses velocity for both of these. And while velocity is not a strict predictor either of value (see *Value and ROI*) or of efficiency, it is the central empirical measure of the *Development Team*'s capacity both to predict and complete work.

Being shorthanded reduces what the team can deliver in a *¶46 Sprint*. While vacation absence is a small fraction of the year in the United States, the U.S. is also the only country in the world without a single legally required paid holiday (*USA Today [Hes13]*). Austrians take 35 paid days off each year: about 15 percent of the work year. If you combine these absences with conference attendance, continuing education, and other activities that don't contribute directly to the product, as much as 20 percent of the budget goes to activities that the business funds only "in the margins." ("Twenty percent" is a hypothetical figure based on 35 paid days off and about 12 days for training, conferences, corporate social activities, travel, medical leave, and so forth.) And during the summer or around winter holidays, the majority of the *Development Team* may disappear *together* for up to a month. It's important to give visibility to how that effects deliverables.

Scrum is an empirical framework that derives velocity empirically according to ¶66 *Yesterday's Weather*. A good *Development Team* tracks its velocity over time, focusing first on reducing its variance and secondly on occasionally increasing it through kaizen. Adjusting the velocity downward to compensate for an absence destroys the empirical nature of velocity, and can lead to complex, arbitrary compensations for scheduling as often found in Project Management. Scrum has no facility for "remembering" adjustments to velocity, and has no need to "remember" velocity: one can always derive it from empirical data. So a manual velocity adjustment would add a new Scrum artifact. The arbitrariness of a calculated velocity leaves the *Development Team* without any sense of responsibility to meet their forecast.

Therefore:

Track *planned Development Team* **member absences as ¶55 Product Backlog Items (PBIs)**. Let the *Development Team* estimate the cost of the *PBI* depending on the specifics of the absence and of the ¶46 *Sprint* in which it will occur. The *Product Owner* may choose to ascribe a corresponding value (ROI or other) to the *PBI* as well, corresponding to the value to the enterprise of giving people paid leave from work.

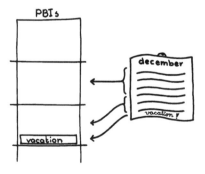

As is true with any manipulation of the *Product Backlog*, the *Product Owner* should frequently adjust the relative position of the *Vacation PBI* in the backlog so it falls in the *Sprint* commensurate with the fixed date (see *Fixed-Date PBI*).

❖   ❖   ❖

This will cause the *¶72 Sprint Backlog* content to more accurately reflect the expenditure of *Development Team* members' time during the *Sprint*.

One could analytically ascribe a cost to such *PBI*s based on the *Development Team* size, its velocity, and the absence duration. However, *Development Team* performance is rarely linear in the number of available team members. Different team members perform differently, but more important, an effective team works as a *gestalt* whose members multiply each other's effectiveness rather than just linearly adding to each others' contributions. This is why we let the *Development Team* estimate instead of using typical Project Management calculations. The common practice of letting the *Product Owner* (or even the team) adjust the velocity mechanically falls into this trap. There are further subtleties that the team estimation can accommodate. For example, adjusting merely for the absence of a *Development Team* member doesn't acknowledge the effort of reintegrating a member into the team on return: he or she must catch up with changes in the implementation, organization, market, and requirements that have transpired in the mean time.

Given these realities, the pattern has limitations in how it affects the accuracy of the *Sprint* forecast. Nonetheless, first, it directly supports the following Scrum principles:

- The effect of the vacation both on the forecast and on the *Sprint* results lies in the hands of those who can control the consequences: the *Development Team*.

- Velocity continues to be an empirical measure instead of being subject to special case adjustments or sophisticated calculations.

- We honor the value of transparency: one need only look at the *Product Backlog* to understand why an unchanged velocity will result in a smaller product increment in a given *Sprint*.

- This pattern ascribes explicit value to the planned absences that are germane to human beings in a work setting, in a way that honors the value to the individual on a par with the value accorded product increments.

Second, it is better than nothing: the situation is no better if the *Product Owner* or *Development Team* adjusts the velocity downward for absences. In the end, the *Development Team* owns the estimates: putting the velocity figure in the hands of someone other than a Pig takes away the *Development Team*'s sense of commitment (see *¶57 Pigs Estimate*).

This pattern is of course a two-edged sword, and each culture will modulate the boundaries of application of this pattern. It's important to ponder the stipulation that the *Product Owner* can neither schedule nor refuse personal absences that are traditionally matters of personal employee choice and discretion. Some cultures may give *Product Owner*s leeway in allowing or disallowing activities such as conference attendance (though vacation in particular is outside the *Product Owner*'s purview.) We use vacation as the exemplary case in this pattern to emphasize the Scrum principles above.

Another challenge exposed by this pattern is the awkwardness of publicly estimating individual contribution. It may insult Jim if Sue's vacation reduces velocity by 30, and Jim's vacation reduces velocity by 20. In practice the identity of the individual isn't the only factor in sizing such cost; for example, different technology mixes in a *Sprint* lead to variance in the cost of different individuals' absences, as do other variations. In any case, the *Development Team* will realize a change in velocity during a team member absence, and that will lead to the same issue of quantifying the value of the individual to the team. The fact is that the natural variance in velocity is likely to overshadow variances in the identity of the person absent, and it is unlikely that there are enough data to make any statistically significant judgment about such costs. Perception is everything; however, the *ScrumMaster* must educate the *Scrum Team* that variance in the estimation of a *Vacation PBI* is natural.

Some have argued that this is a complicated or overly long pattern. While the arguments are intricate, the solution is not. The traditions against such common-sense approaches are strong, which is why the forces here are sometimes hard.

These arguments and adjustments aside, the ceremonial inclusion of such absences on the *Product Backlog* makes visible that care for the personal well-being of team members (through vacation, medical care, etc.) is indeed part of the corporate value proposition. It shows that management cares. Management sympathy or empathy has empirically increased productivity[19] while disdain for such personal concerns can demotivate the team or build resentment. This is all within the Scrum spirit of extending the notion of value beyond the product, into concern for the team and its people, as exemplified in the mission statement of Toyota's NUMMI plant: (*The Toyota Way: 14 Management Principles from the World's Greatest Manufacturer [Lik04]*, p. 80)

---

19. "Hawthorne Effect: interpretation and criticism." Wikipedia, http://en.wikipedia.org/wiki/Hawthorne_effect#Interpretation_and_criticism, May, 2018 (accessed 8 June 2018).

1. As an American company, contribute to the economic growth of the **community** and the United States.

2. As an independent company, contribute to the **stability and well-being of team members**.

3. As a Toyota group company, contribute to the overall growth of Toyota by adding **value to our customers**.

Regarding transparency, the *Product Backlog* is an established information radiator and organ of transparency in the Scrum culture. Making extraordinary absences into *PBI*s takes away their extraordinariness; all necessary information is transparent. Any local adaptation of a *Sprint* velocity complicates the bookkeeping of velocity because it means keeping a history ("undo stack") of such adjustments that someone must process when the absence is over.

This approach is one example of using the *Product Backlog* for value concerns beyond what product increments yield for the corporation. Treating such absences as *PBI*s also makes visible on the *Product Backlog* approximately when and how the absence will affect the inclusion of individual product increments in projected releases. If the *Development Team* adjusts the *Sprint* velocity instead, then each *Sprint* has a custom velocity, and that seriously complicates the predictions provided by simple, manual tools as well as by more sophisticated computer-aided tools. These complications make the *Product Backlog*s unwieldy to interpret.

Note that this pattern does not apply to *unplanned Sprint* interruptions such as incidental sickness or unanticipated business-condition changes. Those are stochastic quantities that fall within the concept of *drag* (activities that displace time working on the product, thus causing the real velocity to decrease). In the worst case, the team addresses such interruptions with ¶32 *Emergency Procedure*.

> *After learning the Vacation PBI pattern, time came around for Asaf to go on vacation. While the team was striving to become more cross-functional, Asaf did most of the database work when it came up. There wasn't going to be much database work this Sprint, so the "bus factor" of Asaf being away wasn't very severe. Asaf and the rest of the team agreed to assess the cost of Asaf's absence at 15 points, so they created a 15-point PBI. During the Sprint, they burned down a proportional amount each day. The team missed their forecast by five points—well within the statistical norm of a healthy team's velocity. So the team didn't adjust their velocity, and carried on without any Vacation PBIs when Asaf returned.*

¶63 Enabling Specification

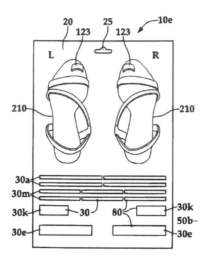

Enabling specification for U.S. Patent 7,329,448: Adhesive Pads for Footwear.

...the *¶54 Product Backlog* is in place and the *¶11 Product Owner* is working on *¶55 Product Backlog Item*s (*PBI*s).

❖ ❖ ❖

Unexplored requirements cause unpleasant surprises.

The agile tradition holds that user stories suffice as requirements artifacts, and early agile practice often blindly believed in deferring decisions and in having a ready, at-hand, on-site customer who could compensate for requirements shortfalls discovered during development. Given this background, it's easy for the *Product Owner* to throw ideas into the *Product Backlog* and think "that's good enough." Scrum can even support the *Product Owner* doing this because the *Product Backlog* is the *Product Owner*'s artifact, so we assume he or she can call the shots. We also welcome emergent requirements in Scrum, assuming the *Product Backlog* will change as everyone connected with the product learns more, and this may also lead us to having poorly considered *PBI*s. Having the *Product Owner* collocated with the team is often assumed to obviate this problem, but a half-baked idea is still a half-baked idea even if we socialize and review it.

Because Scrum acknowledges emergent requirements, it's easy for the business to claim that the real requirements will come out only when pushing on them during design. On the other hand, full-blown development is a heavy-handed way to elicit requirements. Sometimes all it takes is a bit of dialog between the *Product Owner* and the developers, or between the end users and the *Product Owner*. Testers are notoriously good at sniffing out requirements lapses—lapses that are often easy to fill in (by talking to end users or other stakeholders) once they are discovered. And the further you get into development, the more difficult it becomes to engage end users.

So it's good to do some up-front discovery, exploration, and planning, and to socialize proposals and open issues across all stakeholders. Scrum's roots in Japanese manufacturing also bear out this focus on engagement and planning. But how much should be communicated from the *Product Owner* to the *¶14 Development Team*, and how? A user story isn't even a full requirement: it is just a statement of some stakeholders' identities and their motivation behind some parts of what the system provides. They're just one small part of "the requirements." And while requirements help articulate a *PBI*'s contribution to the *¶39 Vision*, a requirement is not a definition of a product increment—it is only one insight on how that increment meets some isolated want or need. After all, it's a *Product Backlog* and not a "requirements backlog."

Most schedule surprises come from misunderstandings with roots in poor or poorly communicated analysis. Much of Scrum depends on the team having a stable Notes on Velocity on page 320. Once a system is designed, implementation effort usually can be predicted with a high degree of confidence. Once analysis is complete, design and implementation can often proceed without too many surprises. Since estimation focuses on what happens within the *¶46 Sprint*, it's important to move the uncertainty of analysis outside the *Sprint*—into the *Product Owner* process. If you don't do this, at least part of the task of analysis will fall to the developers. That greatly slows velocity, and because the team is not expert in analysis or end-user and market perspectives, the requirements suffer as well:

Therefore: **The *Product Owner* should deliver *Enabling Specification*s as a sign that he or she has done due diligence in exploring the requirements space.** An *Enabling Specification* is a specification rich enough that someone reasonably skilled in the discipline can implement a solution without substantial subsequent clarification with people outside the ¶7 *Scrum Team.* The *Scrum Guide*[20] says that part of the job of the *Product Owner* is "[e]nsuring the Development Team understands items in the Product Backlog to the level needed."

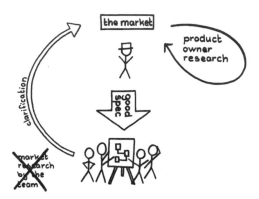

The *Product Owner* and *Development Team* work diligently together to bring the top of the *Product Backlog* to *Ready* (see ¶65 *Definition of Ready*) in the weeks leading up to ¶24 *Sprint Planning*, exploring all opportunities to create mutual understanding. But in the end, the *Product Owner* is responsible for bringing the *Development Team* enough information so it has a clear understanding of what to build. The *Development Team* members have the final say over whether they will take a *PBI* into the *Sprint* for implementation, based on whether they are confident in their understanding of the *PBI*.

❖ ❖ ❖

Enabling Specification in hand, the *Development Team* is prepared to create a ¶72 *Sprint Backlog* based on a deep understanding of the upcoming delivery stream. If the *Development Team* collectively do not believe that the *Product Owner* has communicated enough information to enable them to succeed in delivering the item, the *Development Team* will not pull the *Product Backlog Item* into a *Sprint*.

Establishing this understanding before the ¶75 *Production Episode* starts helps the *Development Team* stay in "flow" without having to interrupt development with the distraction of a meeting with the *Product Owner*. In the

---

20. Jeff Sutherland and Ken Schwaber. *The Scrum Guide*. ScrumGuides.org, http://www.scrumguides.org (accessed 5 January 2017).

end, the specification must live in the collective mind of the *Development Team*; that something in a document meets some criteria of completeness is almost immaterial. The specification in the developers' minds becomes enabling through interaction, explanation, prototypes, examples, and an exchange of questions and answers. A great *Enabling Specification* includes written test criteria so that test development is straightforward, and so there are objective criteria to support a ship/no-ship decision at the end of the *Sprint*. If the *Enabling Specification* isn't good enough to specify how the product increment will be tested, it isn't good enough to give the team honest confidence in how to build it.[21]

Of course, there are limits to perfection. If the *Development Team* finds itself in doubt about a *Product Backlog Item* while working on it during the *Production Episode*, then the *Development Team* and *Product Owner* should strive to resolve the gap at the earliest opportunity. The same applies if emergent requirements arise.

It is less important that the specifications be written down beforehand than it is that the *Product Owner* has done his or her homework and that the team has thoroughly discussed the new item. A written *Product Backlog Item* can memorialize and testify to the extent of that research. In fact, much of this research perhaps entailed discussions with the *Development Team*, suppliers, and partners, as well as market research, customers, and of course, end users.

A single, passionate message and written *Product Backlog Item*s alone aren't enough. Research shows that managers are better respected and get their message across more effectively if they deliver it multiple times, often through different media, relying on redundancy to drive the message home. A good *Product Owner* will mix informal descriptions, user stories that underscore the user motivation, use cases that explore edge cases (*Lean Architecture for Agile Software Development [BC10]*, pp. 167–169), visuals that preview the user experience, prototypes that encode major expectations, and anything else that may open its own path to understanding, complementing the others. *Harvard Business Review 89 [NL11]* The *Product Owner* should socialize new items with the team as soon as they arise, at the earliest opportunity when they and the team are working toward a *¶64 Refined Product Backlog*. Each *PBI* can become more and more enabling at each backlog refinement effort and at each *Sprint Planning* event.

---

21. Jeff Sutherland. "Enabling Specifications: The Key to Building Agile Systems." ScrumInc.com, https://www.scruminc.com/enabling-specifications-key-to-building/, 2 June 2012 (accessed 5 January 2017).

The phrase *enabling specification* is a term of law, applied as a standard for valid patents:

> "A patent specification is enabling if it allows a person of ordinary skill in the art to practice the invention without undue experimentation." *Intellectual Property Law: Commercial [DM91]*

A valid patent must serve to enable anyone reasonably skilled in the general area of the patent to be able to reproduce the invention from information in the patent alone without consulting the inventor. Analogously, the information that the *Product Owner* conveys to the team (whether in writing or not is immaterial) before the start of the *Sprint* should carry them through the *Sprint* in most instances, without need for further face-to-face consultation.

¶64 Refined Product Backlog

Alias: Backlog Refinement Meeting

Confidence stars: **

Careful arrangement.

...you have a *¶54 Product Backlog* and the *¶7 Scrum Team* needs to look ahead in its planning.

❖ ❖ ❖

Agile enterprises must be poised to respond quickly to capitalize on opportunities to create value, and should avoid working—or planning—too far ahead. To respond quickly to a market opportunity, the team needs to understand the stakeholder needs, and all of the ducks must be lined up to enable work to proceed on the items at hand. The *¶11 Product Owner* must have communicated how *¶85 Regular Product Increment* supports the vision. The *Product Owner* has time-ordered the deployment of *Product Increments* to meet peak market responsiveness, to create the highest value. When opportunity knocks, one wants to be ready for it. There may be a "last responsible moment" for market decisions; if it passes, the march of time and the resulting changing circumstances can take away your options or your ability to exercise them.

However, it's also important to defer work that won't generate value for a long time. Working prematurely on a long-term deliverable can have a high opportunity cost if it moves other viable product offerings out of their prime market window.

Further complicating this is the fact that some deliverables have hard dependencies on others. Some *¶55 Product Backlog Item* (*PBI*) may build on an earlier product increment; it's important to plan ahead so the right foundations are in place when the opportunity for the big market win presents itself. This may imply that you deliver some *PBI* earlier than you otherwise would. Although an early release may generate lower value for that item, it may set up a *Regular Product Increment* with even greater Value and ROI on page 246.

As time goes on, the team learns more about the market and about dependencies. However, at the same time, people inside the organization make development and market decisions, or the market itself moves in directions that may demand or provoke changes to existing plans. Every new decision is a constraint that could limit future product and market possibilities. For example, one may lose the opportunity to be first in a market by deferring the introduction of some feature in that market. The team may order *PBI*s to gain the highest value given today's understanding of the team and the market, but tomorrow may bring a window of opportunity that could create even higher value with a different backlog ordering. It is often difficult for the team to foresee these problems far in advance.

Therefore:

The *Scrum Team* (particularly the *Product Owner* and ¶14 *Development Team*) should meet frequently to properly order the *Product Backlog* and to break down the most imminent large *PBI*s into smaller ones. The *Development Team* should maintain current estimates for the *Product Backlog Item*s that it will eventually implement (¶57 *Pigs Estimate*).

The team should focus particularly on items near the top of the *Product Backlog*. Pay particular attention to dependencies between *PBI*s as well as to dependencies of *PBI*s on external market factors (e.g., holiday sales seasons) and to dates when resources may become available to make it possible to build the *PBI* (e.g., taking delivery of raw materials or enabling technology from a supplier). The *Scrum Team* should annotate *PBI*s on the backlog with estimates and value attributions.

*PBI*s near the top of the backlog (those for the next two to three ¶46 *Sprint*s) should be small enough so that no single one will require more work than 10 percent of the *Sprint* development effort. See ¶58 *Small Items*.

❖ ❖ ❖

Refinement includes detailed requirements analysis; working toward a ¶59 *Granularity Gradient* in the *Product Backlog*'s structure; bringing estimates up to date; reordering items to reflect dependencies between them or constraints related to the timing of a *PBI* release; and, in general, updating the *Product Backlog* to reflect any new information available to the team.

Keep in mind that the main purpose of bringing the team together to refine the backlog may be to get the team to start thinking about how to implement the envisioned features. Refinement is part of a learning process. Whether processing the envisioned need in their subconscious, or whether through informally discussing upcoming work over lunch, such advance mental processing of upcoming features fuels the breakthroughs that reduce visions to designs. Isaac Asimov proposed that creativity blossoms in the solitude away from collective activities and in the informal jovial exchanges outside structured professional settings (*On Creativity [Asi15]*). Steve Johnson points to "the slow hunch" as a major factor in creativity; backlog refinement and estimation plant the seeds that kindle this process in the minds of the team members. Seeing an item well ahead of its deployment gives time for this process to unfold (see "The Slow Hunch" in *Where Good Ideas Come From [Joh11]*).

One good first-cut ordering technique from the lean canon is the Design Structure Matrix[22] (see *Design Structure Matrix Methods and Applications [EB12a]*). Make a matrix each of whose axes are labeled with the *PBIs*, putting an "X" in the cells where there is a dependency between items:

	cellar	inside walls	floors	roof	doors	wiring	wall framing
cellar							
inside walls			X			X	X
floors	X						
roof							X
doors		X					
wiring							X
wall framing	X						

Then sort the matrix so that it is a lower-left diagonal matrix. That is, you pull the last responsible moments forward—you never defer them. Such was the original, pre-XP sense of the phrase "last responsible moment" (see "Positive versus Negative Iteration in Design" in *Proceedings of the 8th Annual Conference on the International Group for Lean Construction [Bal00]*). If it is a lower-left diagonal matrix, then every item will come after all of those on which it depends. Further, pulling these decisions forward leads the team to dive into the associated work, which will flush out emergent requirements and increase the level of insight into the problem at hand. The passage of time alone is no guarantee that any new insights will come along: the team must

22. "Design structure matrix." Wikipedia, https://en.wikipedia.org/wiki/Design_structure_matrix, 17 February 2016 (accessed 2 November 2017).

actively take an item into design and implementation to make emergent requirements appear.

	cellar	wall framing	roof	wiring	floors	inside walls	doors
cellar	░						
wall framing	X	░					
roof		X	░				
wiring		X		░			
floors	X				░		
inside walls		X		X	X	░	
doors						X	░

Deal with hard external dates using common sense. If it is impossible to sort the matrix, then there is a circular dependency and the team should review the items with more scrutiny. In the worst case, the team may combine two mutually dependent items into a single, larger item.

With the fundamental dependency constraints in hand, use the remaining ordering freedom to optimize market alignment and value opportunities. Knowing the *Development Team*'s forecasts of relative costs and the anticipated value the item will generate at the time of delivery, you can adjust the ordering of items to optimize value. Just changing the order of a given set of items can often double the realized value.

Work as diligently as possible to bring each *PBI* (near the top of the backlog) in line with the *¶65 Definition of Ready*.

Temper the refinement with *Granularity Gradient*. Focus on refining the *PBI*s for the upcoming two or three *Sprints* and work on the rest if time permits— and if you have the information to make informed, responsible decisions.

In the early days of Scrum, this activity took place during *¶24 Sprint Planning*. As history progressed, teams started to spread the work between *Sprint Planning* and a weekly meeting sometimes called "The Wednesday Afternoon Meeting" or "The Product Backlog Refinement Meeting." In contemporary practice it is common to spread the work even further in short, daily meetings. Each team can adjust the frequency and duration of these activities as necessary, but the total amount of face time that the *Product Owner* requires from the *Development Team* should not in general be more than 10 percent of the working time. The *Scrum Team* should schedule all such activities in advance: it is not work the *Product Owner* may request on demand.

As in *Sprint Planning*, the team makes adjustments to the backlog not only to strive for the *¶93 Greatest Value* but out of sheer *¶38 Product Pride*.

For more on estimates, see *¶60 Estimation Points*.

Backlog Refinement is not a proper event in *The Scrum Guide*.[23] One argument that has been given for this irregularity is that there is nothing in the *Scrum Guide* that pertains beyond the current *Sprint*. However, that argument is mistaken, as *The Scrum Guide* says, "Product Backlog items that will occupy the Development Team for the upcoming Sprint are refined so that any one item can reasonably be 'Done' within the Sprint time-box," and "The result of the Sprint Review is a revised Product Backlog that defines the probable Product Backlog items for the next Sprint."[24] A more common interpretation is that the activity need not be held on cadence nor conducted as a "meeting," giving the *Scrum Team* the freedom to carry out the activity as they best see fit.

Pulling planning activities for future *Sprint*s into the current *Sprint* is inspired in part by the overlapping *Sprint*s of "type B" production in the classic Harvard Business Review article by Takeuchi and Nonaka (*The New New Product Development Game [TN86]*).

23. Jeff Sutherland and Ken Schwaber. *The Scrum Guide*. ScrumGuides.org, http://www.scrumguides.org (accessed 5 January 2017).
24. Jeff Sutherland and Ken Schwaber. *The Scrum Guide*. ScrumGuides.org, http://www.scrumguides.org (accessed 5 January 2017).

¶65 Definition of Ready

Alias: Ready-Ready

Confidence stars: *

Ready to go.

...you have a *¶54 Product Backlog* that is a *¶64 Refined Product Backlog*, or nearly so, and you are beginning to plan a *¶46 Sprint*. Out of necessity, some items on the *Product Backlog* are still too nebulous for the *¶14 Development Team* to be able to implement then. Yet the *¶72 Sprint Backlog* embodies the work necessary to achieve the *¶71 Sprint Goal*, as well as guides development. Therefore, the items on the *Sprint Backlog* must be concrete; they cannot be nebulous. But how much "concreteness" does the *Development Team* need to do its job?

❖ ❖ ❖

If the *Development Team* does not precisely understand *¶55 Product Backlog Item*s (*PBI*), development effort and time tend to balloon, which in turn cause the *Sprint* to miss the *Sprint Goal* or to not deliver what stakeholders expect.

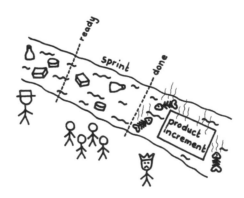

The challenge of development is taking new ideas and making them real—actually developing them. This is a fundamental change in thinking: the idea starts out quite abstract, but development demands that the idea become concrete in every particular. This change in thinking ultimately happens fully only in the moments of development. However, if you expect to do any detailed planning at all (and you need detailed short-term planning to inject some sanity into your process), the development ideas need to be concrete enough to make it possible to answer design questions. How concrete? Enough to enable detailed planning in which the team can have confidence.

> *I once did some mercenary programming for a small company. At one point, the CEO asked me to write some software, and proposed a fixed price. "Are we agreed?" he asked. "No," I said. "The software is not defined precisely enough for me to know how long it will take."*

Said another way: there is a shearing layer between the market world and the design world. The realizations they produce evolve at different scales: market understanding comes slowly, while design usually converges quickly (under *¶63 Enabling Specifications*). You need an organizational boundary between them; otherwise you dilute the focus both of the market effort and of the engineering effort. In theory you could achieve this separation with a process boundary. But people membership cuts across process, thus you are still faced with the problem that individuals may be torn between focusing on the business and value landscape and the product and technology landscape. You in turn could solve that problem by time-slicing individuals' focus between these two domains, but that leads to context switching, which is known to decrease efficiency. Scrum separates these concerns into the organizational realms of the *¶11 Product Owner* and *Development Team*, respectively. It is crucial for success that there be a touchpoint where these two realms meet.

When you are in the throes of planning, there is a strong temptation to make quick assumptions and defer hard questions (such as detailed estimation) until later. When a group does planning together there is often implicit peer pressure to defer hard questions so that the planning process can proceed. To combat this, the team needs to agree to face the most difficult issues first. To avoid starting work on shaky footing, the team needs to adhere to an objective standard of shared clarity about the end point.

Variability is one source of waste in lean thinking. If the *Development Team* insufficiently understands what some *Product Backlog Item* really means, or how to develop it or estimate it, there is increased variation in possible *Sprint* outcomes and the effort is likely to incur increased cost, risk, and uncertainty.

Therefore:

Each *Product Backlog Item* must meet at least the following criteria before the *Development Team* can take it as a candidate for the work on the *Sprint Backlog* during *¶24 Sprint Planning*:

1. The work is immediately actionable by the team.
2. The planned deliverable has value.
3. The *Product Owner* and the *Development Team* have discussed it.
4. The *Development Team* has estimated it.
5. It is testable, and the *Product Owner* has specified tests for it.
6. The *¶7 Scrum Team* has sized the pieces appropriately (see *¶58 Small Items*).

A *Product Backlog* is "Ready" if it has enough *Product Backlog Item*s at its top, meeting these criteria, to fill a *Sprint*.

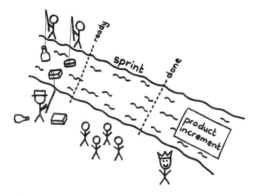

A good *Definition of Ready* can help guide the team to handle external dependencies. If an item depends on something outside the team's control, putting it on the *Sprint Backlog* can greatly increase the risk of not having a potentially releasable *¶85 Regular Product Increment* at the end of the *Sprint*, and you can't do anything about it! Take dependency analysis all the way down to the level of *Product Backlog Item*s instead of just managing gross dependencies at the level of *Regular Product Increment*; the team will ultimately need to understand dependencies at that level to order work during the *¶75 Production Episode*. Consider including criteria concerning external dependencies as part of the *Definition of Ready*.

There is important interplay between this pattern and *Enabling Specifications*. The candidate *Product Backlog Item*s for the upcoming *Sprint* must become *Ready* during *Sprint Planning* at the latest. Coming out of *Sprint Planning*, *Product Backlog Item*s—together with the *Product Owner*'s explanation and clarification—must *Enable* the team to start implementation undaunted.

❖ ❖ ❖

The goal is for the *Scrum Team* to meet all the *Ready* criteria as it works towards a *Refined Product Backlog* and strives to develop *Enabling Specifications* before *Sprint Planning*. The goal is that *PBI*s pass through the "Ready gate" without pause or delay, subject only to adherence to a short checklist. While the list is important for undeveloped teams to be able to "stop the line," the greater good comes from anticipating the stipulations and arranging ahead of time for the *PBI*s to be fully *Ready* by the time the *Sprint* starts, so that flow is unimpeded.

Note that *all PBI* in the *Product Backlog* do not have to be *Ready*, though as they move up the *Product Backlog*, they should progress toward becoming *Ready*.

Contrast the *Definition of Ready*, which applies to *PBI*s going into a *Sprint*, with the ¶82 *Definition of Done*, which is a criterion applied to a *PBI* for delivery during or at the end of a *Sprint*.

What happens if a *PBI* is not *Ready*? Though the entire team works on *PBI*s, the *Product Owner* is responsible to come to *Sprint Planning* fully prepared to enable the team to proceed unimpeded to develop the candidate *PBI*s for the current *Sprint*. Most of the time, being not *Ready* is a sign that the *Product Owner* has to go back and do more analysis and bring the *PBI* to the team again at a later date. The Scrum tradition is that if the *Product Backlog* is not *Ready* at *Sprint Planning*, the *Development Team* has the right to "go to the beach," as Jeff Sutherland describes in *Scrum: The Art of Doing Twice the Work in Half the Time [SS14]* ("Be Ready to be Done," p. 137). This makes it visible that the *Product Owner*s have not done their job to make the backlog *Ready*. If you end up at the beach a lot you are probably in the wrong line of work. What is *your* contribution to the backlog not being *Ready*? How can the team help the *Product Owner*?

To differentiate the Scrum notion of *Ready* as a term of the trade distinct from the vernacular sense of "ready," Scrum folk will sometimes use the phrase "Ready-Ready" instead of the single word "Ready." Richard Kronfält apparently published the first formal description of *Definition of Ready* in 2008.[25]

Thanks much to Peter Gfader for comments!

---

25. Richard Kronfält. "Ready-ready: the Definition of Ready for User Stories going into Sprint Planning." Blogspot.dk, Oct. 2008, http://scrumftw.blogspot.nl/2008/10/ready-ready-definition-of-ready-for.html (accessed 1 November 2017).

Notes on Velocity

Velocity is a much-misunderstood concept, and the purpose of this note is to help clarify what it is. *The Scrum Guide*[26] does not mention velocity but we know it plays an important role in helping most *¶7 Scrum Team*s to keep process variance in check and to create a basis for short-term forecasting. We have six patterns that discuss velocity in a focused way:

- *¶58 Small Items*, described earlier in the book;
- *¶60 Estimation Points*, also described earlier in the book;
- *¶66 Yesterday's Weather*;
- *¶67 Running Average Velocity*;
- *¶68 Aggregate Velocity*, and;
- *¶70 Updated Velocity*.

Velocity also plays a strong supporting role in many other patterns, such as *¶48 Release Plan*, *¶26 Kaizen Pulse* and *¶74 Teams That Finish Early Accelerate Faster*. Velocity in itself is not a pattern (it doesn't really build anything, but rather is a property of the *¶46 Sprint* and the team) and this note is here to help you understand the term as the patterns use it and to understand how you should use it with your team.

A *¶14 Development Team*'s velocity is a (usually unitless) number that indicates the team's capacity to complete potentially shippable work in a given *Sprint*. Velocity is intended to be a measure of the team's efficiency: how much work the team completes per unit time, where *Sprint*s are the units of time (e.g., two weeks).

Velocity is not a measure of effort: the effort that *¶15 Stable Teams* expend during a *Sprint* is constant because the *Sprint* duration is constant. It represents the total amount of work *Done* (see *¶82 Definition of Done*) during a *Sprint* as a sum of the estimates that the team created for the *¶55 Product Backlog Item*s (PBIs) at the beginning of the *Sprint*. Each of those estimates forecasts merely how much work it will take to complete a given *Product Backlog Item* relative to the amount of work for other *Product Backlog Items* (as with *Estimation Points*). The velocity varies from *Sprint* to *Sprint* as a consequence of natural variance and of many factors affecting efficiency such as loss of a team member, manufacturing equipment problems, variance in requirements quality, etc.

---

26. Jeff Sutherland and Ken Schwaber. *The Scrum Guide*. ScrumGuides.org, http://www.scrumguides.org (accessed 5 January 2017).

The velocity is the *Development Team*'s number. The team derives the number from historic data, based on recent *Sprint*s. The items that add up to the team's velocity—the *Product Backlog Item*s or ¶73 *Sprint Backlog Item*s (SBIs) the team forecasts that they will deliver—the team calls its *forecast* for the given *Sprint*. In the same sense that yesterday's weather is a good predictor of today's weather, so the performance in recent *Sprint*s is a good indicator of what the team will achieve in the *Sprint* at hand. The team can use velocity as a forecast of the work it will complete, but it is not a target or a guarantee for stakeholders. By analogy, if you forecast tomorrow's weather as reaching 77°F and sunny, that isn't the target for the weather, but only an informed guess of what the weather may be.

It is good practice to use recent history to inform the forecast for the upcoming *Sprint*: that is the essence of the pattern *Yesterday's Weather*. At any given time, the team's velocity is a reasonable forecast of the team's future performance based on an average of the team's recent velocities. Because there is variance in any process, some *Sprint*s will exhibit a higher-than-average velocity and some a lower-than-average velocity. When the *Development Team* uses velocity to size the amount of work to take into a *Sprint* (the ¶72 *Sprint Backlog*)—a recommended practice—then the team should expect to finish all items on that backlog only 50 percent of the time. Note that the *Scrum Team* commits to the ¶71 *Sprint Goal* and not their forecast delivery.

Velocity has a mean and a variance, and both are important to forecasting. A velocity with low variance leads to more precise forecasts, and makes it possible to assess whether a given kaizen (see Kaizen and Kaikaku on page 101) improved (or diminished) the team's performance in the *Sprint*s where they applied it.

Teams can reduce their velocity's variance through attentiveness to sound Scrum practices. Here are a few of the core practices that are rooted in *Development Team* autonomy:

- The whole *Development Team* estimates together as a unit (¶57 *Pigs Estimate*).

- The whole *Development Team* works together as a team rather than splitting deliverables among team members (¶25 *Swarming: One-Piece Continuous Flow*).

- The *Development Team* maintains its focus on the *Sprint Goal*, and on its *own* work plan, refusing outside requests to expand the *Sprint* scope during the ¶75 *Production Episode*.

- The *Development Team* refuses requests or pressure to reduce or otherwise manipulate its own work estimates.

Current broad practice bases velocity on the *Development Team*'s estimates rather than on either measured effort or measured results. In theory, we could somehow make the velocity more precise by reestimating the actual amount of work (in relative units) each *Product Backlog Item* took after the *Sprint* is over, and summing those estimates into a velocity. It's rarely worth the trouble. Estimates tend to converge over time, and the pessimism for one estimate usually offsets the optimism of another. If the team is using *Estimation Points*, it's impossible for the average to be overly optimistic or pessimistic because the time estimates are unitless. Feedback and *Yesterday's Weather* (as just described) drive both optimism and pessimism out of the forecast. In practice, teams find they can regularly use their velocity to predict what they will deliver in the upcoming *Sprint* with a precision of plus or minus 20 percent or even greater confidence.

Many teams (even Scrum teams) measure velocity in terms of absolute time. However, most people can't even tell you how many hours they "work" a day (work on actual *Product Backlog Item*s) let alone tell how much time they spend on a given item. We recommend relative estimation instead—and velocity is hence unitless.

Other teams use sizing instead of estimation: for example, partitioning the *Sprint Backlog* into tasks of equal size and using the number of *Done* tasks as the velocity. The conversion to the ¶54 *Product Backlog* estimates is unclear.

Many managers we have worked with believe they can increase a team's output by impressing on them the need to "work harder." But lack of developer effort is rarely the problem. Velocity isn't so much an indicator of how many coffee breaks the team is or isn't taking, but rather about how smart and effectively the team is working. We want to put our focus on efficiency rather than brute force.

We offer these other guidelines for proper interpretation of velocity:

- The focus of *Scrum Team*s should be on increasing value such as return on investment (ROI; see Value and ROI on page 246) over increasing velocity. While there is some benefit in increasing the team velocity, there's no guarantee that doing so will increase the value the team delivers.

- It is more important to reduce the variance in velocity than to increase its magnitude. A low-variance velocity aids medium-term prediction.

- Velocity is always a property of the *Development Team* as a whole and never of an individual team member. This usually implies that when the team estimates, they estimate as a team (see *Pigs Estimate*). *Development Team* members estimate each item without knowing ahead of time which of them will be working on it. This also suggests that the team creates a *¶85 Regular Product Increment* as a team, rather than carving out tasks for individuals.

The term *velocity* started becoming au courant in the year 2000. This replaced *load factor* which was too complex, as discussed by Kent Beck, Don Wells, and Robert C. Martin.[27]

---

27. "Velocity vs [sic.] Load Factor." C2.com, http://wiki.c2.com/?VelocityVsLoadFactor, 16 Feb. 2000 (accessed 19 June 2017).

¶66 Yesterday's Weather

Confidence stars: *

...a team is progressing with its historical staff and a stable *¶46 Sprint* length, and the time has come to forecast the team's delivery for the next *¶75 Production Episode*.

❖ ❖ ❖

It's human nature that individuals and teams with self-esteem set increasingly higher goals for themselves (*European Psychologist 12 [LL07]*). And it's also human nature for teams to be overly ambitious, which can result either in their taking shortcuts to avoid disappointing themselves and stakeholders, or in failing to deliver what they expected (*Academy of Management Perspectives 23 [OSGB09]*). By trying to achieve these goals, teams learn. Sometimes such strivings lead to immediate improvement, particularly when the team challenges itself to improve through use of a newfound technique or technology. Sometimes, however, the new technique doesn't pan out and the team's performance remains the same or even gets worse.

Sometimes, the team raises the bar just to raise the bar, either to test the limits or to (perhaps unconsciously) publish its bravado. These self-set performance challenges can pay off, especially in the short term. It is more common that these higher levels are unsustainable in the long term and performance reverts to original levels.

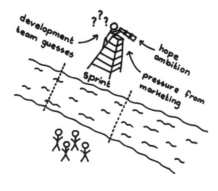

In some organizations there is pressure on teams to deliver more work than the team thinks they can commit to. The phrase "stretch goal" or perhaps "BHAG" (Big Hairy Audacious Goal) is the phrase used to make the amount of work seem exciting or challenging. Prescribing these targets on the team will crush autonomy and ignores the kaizen approach of the team (see Kaizen and Kaikaku on page 101) that leads to greater work efficiency.

Therefore: In most cases, the number of *¶60 Estimation Points* completed in the last *Sprint* is a reliable predictor of how many *Estimation Points* of work the team will complete in the next *Sprint*.

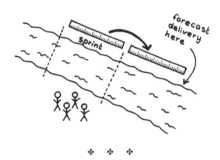

❖ ❖ ❖

The team can help manage stakeholder expectations by selecting work that is a good fit for the duration and conditions of the upcoming *Production Episode*. We define the short-term average of the summed estimation points per *Sprint* as the *¶14 Development Team*'s *velocity* (see Notes on Velocity on page 320). Since velocity is a statistical quantity with a mean and standard deviation, the team should expect about half of the *Sprint*s to fall short of achieving *Yesterday's Weather*, and about half to exceed it. The goal is to improve the process to reduce the variance in the velocity by reducing outside interference of the team, ensuring that the *¶11 Product Owner* provides *¶63 Enabling Specification*s, and that the team adopts good core practices.

Use *¶67 Running Average Velocity* to smooth out variance, and *¶68 Aggregate Velocity* when multiple teams are working together on one product.

If the velocity actually goes up for a given *Sprint*, consider *¶70 Updated Velocity*.

Armstrong (*Interfaces 14 [Arm91]*, p. 12) already recommended that teams "use yesterday's values" for prediction in the early 1980s. His paper, in turn, referred to the forecasting research done by Spyros Makridakis and Michèle Hibon. This research is also known as the M-Competitions or Makridakis Competitions.

¶67 Running Average Velocity

...a team has established its initial velocity (see Notes on Velocity on page 320). Velocity is likely to change over successive *¶46 Sprint*s. It is essential to maintain a reliable *Sprint* forecast.

❖ ❖ ❖

You want the velocity to reflect the team's current capacity, but it takes time for the velocity to stabilize after a change.

In most cases, a team's velocity mirrors its past performance (see *¶66 Yesterday's Weather*). One-time situations may cause a surprisingly large change in velocity. The velocity will probably return to its previous level in the next *Sprint*.

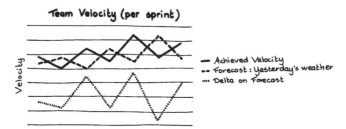

On the other hand, there is no such thing as a "stable velocity." There is natural variance in the work, in people's behavior, and in the requirements for any complex development. If the velocity were the same from Sprint to Sprint we would call it predictable manufacturing. *Yesterday's Weather* is a good way to get started.

If the team implemented a process change and the velocity went up, it isn't immediately clear whether the process change caused the velocity increase. It could be a coincidence. (*Hawthorne Revisited: Management and the worker:*

its critics, and developments in human relations in industry [Lan58]) So it would be premature to adjust the expected capacity.

On the other hand, the process change may well have caused the velocity to increase. If this is the case, it would be more accurate to increase the expected capacity. Likewise, a dip in velocity may be a one-time event, in which case you might be tempted to ignore it. But a different "one-time event" may actually recur more often, so ignoring these might be fooling yourself. Yet we must not get overly excited about possible catastrophes.

Velocity is a motivating factor for teams—they like to see velocity increase. This can lead to unhealthy behavior: people might overreact when faced with sudden changes in velocity. For example, a sudden drop may provoke panic and emergency measures, while an incidental increase may become the next *Sprint*'s "required" velocity.

In summary, while an accurate picture of the team's velocity is a crucial metric for both forecasting and for improvement, many things conspire against applying *Yesterday's Weather* too simply.

Therefore:

Use a running average of the most recent *Sprint*s to calculate the velocity of the next *Sprint*.

To get a meaningful running average (*Agile Estimating and Planning, 1st Edition [Coh05], Essential Scrum: A Practical Guide to the Most Popular Agile Process [Rub12]*), one should use at least three *Sprint*s. Teams will often run three initial *Sprint*s to establish the team's velocity. Velocity is empirical, you can measure it but not assuredly predict it.

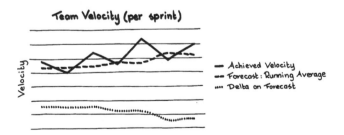

One might also use more than three sprints for the moving average. A larger number decreases the impact of a single anomalous velocity.

In release planning, the best teams apply a range of velocities rather than a single velocity. (*Succeeding with Agile: Software Development Using Scrum [Coh09]*)

How to use velocity is outside the scope of this pattern; here, we focus only on how to calculate it. But one can easily use a running average together with a rough notion of variance that the team can derive from recent *Sprint*s.

Changing the team composition perturbs its velocity, and you might reset the moving average at this time. However, even if you don't, the moving average will correct itself over a few *Sprint*s.

❖ ❖ ❖

A good velocity in hand, the *¶14 Development Team* properly can size the *¶72 Sprint Backlog*, and can roughly forecast the content of the next few *Sprint*s.

Velocity measures how much work the team gets *Done* within a *Sprint*, therefore the team needs a *¶82 Definition of Done*.

There is a close relationship between velocity and estimation. Using a running average increases the reliability of a team's estimation of how much work they will complete in a *Sprint*.

The effect is that any deviation in performance, either improvement or deterioration, has some impact on the velocity. This can encourage teams to improve velocity and to avoid things that reduce velocity.

An alternative approach is simply to keep an average of the velocity of all *Sprint*s, and not bother with a moving average. Compared to a moving average, it dilutes the impact of recent performance, and retains the influence of old velocities from *Sprint*s that may have followed different practices. Because teams should get better over time, you want to weight velocity in favor of recent activity. Therefore, a moving average is more accurate than a cumulative average.

One downside to using a moving average is that an anomalous *Sprint* has some impact on the velocity for the next several *Sprint*s. If its impact is large, it creates a one-time artificial opposite effect on the velocity when it leaves the moving window.

Note that the team must couple a *Running Average Velocity* with a culture of sustainable improvement. There is natural pressure from managers and from the team itself to continually improve. Too much pressure can burn out the team, and impel them work long hours and even fake the numbers. Any of these factors can compromise velocity—as well as trust and pride.

This pattern is related to *¶70 Updated Velocity*. This pattern describes the calculation of velocity to smooth out anomalies; *Updated Velocity* describes when to raise the bar.

¶68 Aggregate Velocity

...your product has grown to multiple *¶14 Development Team*s. These teams all split off from a single original team with a stable velocity (see Notes on Velocity on page 320), but now each team has its own velocity. Each *Development Team* estimates its own work items. The *¶11 Product Owner* wants to establish a new velocity to create a *¶48 Release Plan* from the *¶54 Product Backlog*.

❖　❖　❖

You need to know the development velocity to establish release schedules and to estimate delivery ranges for *¶55 Product Backlog Items* (*PBI*s). In a single-team Scrum you can use that team's velocity, but what do you do in a multi-team Scrum?

Each team has its own velocity, and there is no trivial way to average them together or to otherwise normalize them with each other. Just as there is a gestalt effect between team members that contributes to the high velocity of a team, so there are nonlinear influences between multiple coordinated teams that can either increase or decrease their collective effectiveness. Thus a multi-team Scrum has its own emergent velocity, and the *Product Owner* should use that collective velocity, rather than individual team velocities, when making the *Release Plan*.

During *¶24 Sprint Planning*, team members collectively estimate *PBI*s on the *Product Backlog* based on their intuition and past experience as a team. In a multi-team Scrum, each team can choose its own *PBI*s to take into a *¶46 Sprint* and can estimate them in isolation. If the team knows its velocity then it can forecast delivery of some set of *PBI*s. Even in a multi-team environment, an individual team could establish its velocity through experience over time. That would enable each team to select a set of *PBI*s that the team is very likely to complete at the end of the *Sprint*. The *Product Owner* can be confident in the possibility that the teams will meet their forecasts.

However, the *Product Owner* also predicts completion ranges for future releases and for specific *PBIs*. In a single-team environment the *Product Owner* can use the teams' *PBI* estimates and the team's velocity (as a range) for this calculation. However, multi-team efforts complicate the problem by raising the question of who estimates the *PBIs* and of how to calculate velocity.

Teams start estimating *PBIs* several *Sprints* before they come to the top of the *Product Backlog*. Assume that only a single team estimates each *PBI*. Either a team will implement the *PBIs* that it estimates, or some other team will. If teams implement only the *PBIs* that they themselves estimate, then it constrains the ownership of a *PBI* to teams long before development actually starts. There is a good chance that the *PBIs* will move up or down the *Product Backlog* in that interval. Consider that Team 1 estimates *PBIs* A, E, and F, and that Team 2 estimates *PBIs* B, C, and D. The *PBIs* have the order A - B - C - D - E - F as set by the *Product Owner*:

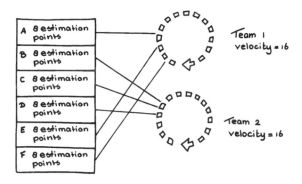

If both teams have a velocity of 20, and if teams must work on the items they themselves estimated, then it is impossible both for each team to fill its ¶72 *Sprint Backlog*, and to honor the *Product Owner*'s desired ordering. If you combine this constraint with the additional constraints of dependencies between *PBIs*, or of marketing scheduling constraints, this becomes a hopelessly frustrating problem. Note that this is true even if you have cross-functional teams.

We can conclude that if only a single team estimates each *PBI*, then the estimate isn't accurate enough for the *Product Owner* to calculate a range of release dates for it or for any *PBI* with a later delivery date—no matter who implements the *PBI*.

We could let multiple teams take turns estimating the *PBI*. Because teams use different baselines and have different talents, these numbers are likely to differ for different teams. You might imagine that you could make a running average over these numbers, but it doesn't make sense to average a set of numbers from different scales. It's like averaging miles per hour with kilometers per hour without any reference to the conversion factor between them. Note that this problem, too, arises even if you have cross-functional teams.

If, on the other hand, we reassign a *PBI* estimated by one team to another team to break it down into tasks for a *Sprint*, then the original estimate bears no correlation to the actual time or cost of the *PBI*. We should be concerned about that, because it was the original estimate that the *Product Owner* used to place this item in the *Product Backlog*. If we allow such reassignment for any *PBI*, then the *PBI* estimates are largely meaningless.

If there were some kind of conversion factor for velocities between teams, then we could normalize each *PBI*'s estimate by the ratio of the velocity of team that estimated the *PBI* to that of the team that will implement it. However, no such conversion factors exist: it makes no sense to compare team velocities because each team has its own baseline and range. Even if it were possible to compare them, the cost of implementing any particular *PBI* depends on the collective talents of the team that estimates those costs (because they anticipate implementing the *PBI*), and the difference in talents across teams can significantly skew such estimates. And what's worse, and even more basic, a team does not feel committed to an estimate defined by someone else, even if each team is actually cross-functional.

When a team takes a *PBI* into a *Sprint*, it can throw away an estimate provided by another team and use its own estimate for its forecast. But that means that the estimates on the backlog are arbitrary except those going into the current *Sprint*.

And beyond this is the more obvious problem that if each team estimates "its own" *PBI*s based on its own baseline and estimation range, it is in general impossible to compare the cost of two items on a *Product Backlog*: it's apples and oranges. You can't compare velocities between teams, even if each team is cross-functional. This makes it impossible for the *Product Owner* to make an informed ordering of the *Product Backlog* based on relative cost of items, all other things being equal.

You could give each team its own *Product Backlog*, populating each one from the Chief Product Owner's *Product Backlog* for the product. This might work if each team actually builds its own product with its own ¶41 *Value Stream* and ROI (see *Value and ROI*). Then, it makes sense to have multiple *Product Backlog*s and to do away with the overarching one. But if all teams contribute their own part of an integrated product, this approach reduces to the problem described above, of assigning *PBI*s to teams too early:

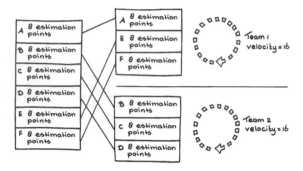

Furthermore, it complicates the *Product Owner*'s ability to reorder *PBI*s.

Therefore: **Have all teams estimate all *PBI*s together, to extend the scope of consensus to all *Development Team* members. Derive the ¶60 *Estimation Points* baseline and scale from all teams together. The aggregate velocity is simply the sum of all teams' velocities together.**

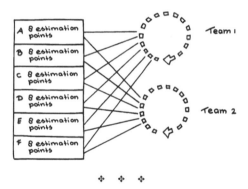

❖ ❖ ❖

This approach makes it possible for teams to estimate the *Product Backlog* in a way that does not limit how to assign any *PBI* to any team.

Each *Development Team* knows its own velocity and can properly size its *Sprint Backlog* for each *Sprint*.

There are many ways to implement this pattern. One might have each team estimate all *PBI*s in isolation before taking a second pass to reconcile the teams' individual estimates. Alternatively, one can just let the teams reform themselves into estimation groups that are both cross-functional and which represent the constituency of all the *Development Team*s. An additional benefit from of this approach is that team members bring back knowledge of the *Product Backlog*—a "whole-product purpose"—back to the team. The two mandatory building blocks of this pattern are that all teams contribute to the estimation of each *PBI*, and that all members of each *Development Team* participate in some estimation.

If you have specialized teams (e.g., *¶89 Value Areas*), you can use *¶69 Specialized Velocities*. The *Specialized Velocities* pattern more easily scales to a large number of teams than *Aggregate Velocity* does, while losing none of the "whole team" estimation one sacrifices when using the common practice of estimation by team representatives. It may also compensate for the impediment of multisite developments.

If all teams collectively estimate each *PBI* together, it could dilute the sense of each teams' commitment to its velocity.

Reflect carefully when faced with the temptation to compare velocities among teams that one might feel this pattern facilitates. If you do conclude to compare teams, please reflect again.

¶69 Specialized Velocities

A department store has different areas for different departments, with each department serving its own market. Each department has its own team that works at its own pace, independent of the pace in other departments.

...your product has grown to multiple teams, and some teams have developed along lines of specialization. The *¶11 Product Owner* wants to maintain one velocity for the *¶54 Product Backlog*.

❖ ❖ ❖

It is difficult and wasteful for a team to estimate *¶55 Product Backlog Item*s (*PBI*) outside its line of specialization. For example, you probably don't need a team working on the infotainment system for a car to also estimate the *PBI*s for (the specialized area of) the brake system, so involving it in such estimation would be wasteful. On the other hand, we want to recognize the ability of individuals to contribute from their perspectives. In fact, key insights sometimes come from the most unlikely places. As human beings we all have insights into all human phenomena. However, that isn't reason enough to drag all of humanity into an estimation exercise. A good approximation is enough. Estimation is waste in the *¶41 Value Stream* and we should minimize its cost.

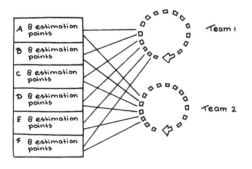

Teams naturally tend to specialize over time, given the opportunity. There is no fundamental problem with specialized teams as long as there is no a priori partitioning of product development that precludes any team from working on some part of the system outside of its usual purview. For example, when there is coupling between the infotainment system and the brake system, that may create a security leak. A design shortcoming allows a hacker to commandeer the car by first seizing control of the infotainment system, and then using the security flaw to take over the brake or accelerator. Either the infotainment or brake system teams should be able to work outside their area to deal with the issue from the market perspective, rather than from any single technology perspective. Teams estimate with the knowledge that they will freely work with each other during implementation. And though specialization can bring focus, it cannot be an excuse for any team or individual to refuse a *PBI* for inclusion in a *¶46 Sprint*.

The *¶68 Aggregate Velocity* approach does not depend on specialization and handles the fully general case, albeit at a cost of convening a large meeting. Individual voices tend to get lost in these large meetings, or the meetings bog down because of their size, or time-boxing and other expediencies cut off discussion prematurely. If more voices yearn to be heard, and if you believe there is value in hearing them, it will take more time to collect key insights from a large group than from a small group. And though the time spent eliciting input goes up, the amount of unique insights increases at a disproportionately smaller rate.

Therefore: **Each specialized team estimates and develops items within its realm of specialization.** Other *PBI* stakeholders will inform these estimates as necessary with their input. For example, you can elicit these stakeholders' input by first asking the specialized team to make an initial estimation pass and then subsequently refining the estimates in areas outside the team's experience, inviting external stakeholders as necessary. Many alternative approaches work just as well.

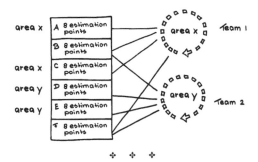

❖　❖　❖

The team will feel committed to the estimates in the end and will be able to size its *¶72 Sprint Backlog* appropriately and with confidence.

Teams should not specialize along the lines of engineering technique; that is, there should be no testing team or coding team or architecture team. This pattern addresses specialization along the gradient of the *Value Stream*. You might consider writing and socializing patterns such as *Market Team* (which develops products for a given market) or *Localization Team* (which adapts a product to an ethnic market segment). See *¶89 Value Areas* and *¶90 Value Stream Fork*.

Specialization creates stovepipes that could suffer from demand starvation in a given *Sprint*. If automobile software team A specializes on the infotainment system and team B specializes on the brake system, and if the candidate *Product Backlog* for the current *Sprint* doesn't contain enough items for team B, then either team A will eventually begin working on items outside its specialization—or we should reduce the number of estimation points taken into the *Sprint*. Solve this by avoiding lines of specialization when you have only a few teams. You will move more towards *¶10 Cross-Functional Team*s, expanding each team's ability to do competent work in a broad number of areas (*Scaling Lean & Agile Development [LV09]*, pp. 176–187).

This specialization was a contributor to the success of the oft-cited Borland QPW project (*Dr. Dobb's Journal of Software Tools 19 [CE94]*), though it is important to note that QPW did not meet the team's anticipated schedule.

See also *¶105 Team per Task* on page 467.

¶70 Updated Velocity

Confidence stars: *

Shift gears only after you've established the ability to cruise at a new level.

...you've started calibrating your velocity (see Notes on Velocity on page 320) by using *¶67 Running Average Velocity*, but find that it is still difficult to achieve good *¶46 Sprint* production forecasts.

❖ ❖ ❖

An average of recent past velocities isn't necessarily a predictable velocity.

You want the velocity to reflect the team's current abilities, yet it takes time to know whether process improvements actually worked. *¶66 Yesterday's Weather* works in a system that has settled into the rhythms of a given season, but the early days of an agile team are very much like the transition from winter to summer in Chicago, where the weather changes from hour to hour.

Good teams experience plateaus of normative stability between rockier episodes of change (see *¶26 Kaizen Pulse*). A *Running Average Velocity* takes no account of variance, so it is a particularly dubious predictor of system behavior in a *¶14 Development Team*'s early *Sprint*s. One can't extrapolate the historic velocity of a system into the future until the system has *normative* behavior.

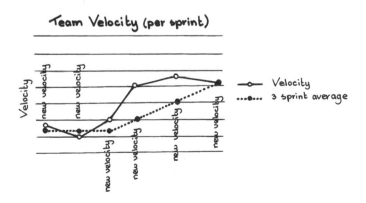

Further, good Scrum teams should have kaizen mind (see Kaizen and Kaikaku on page 101). Teams that have longstanding low variance in their velocity are dead teams: they are not growing in their practice and are likely not improving. So while *Running Average Velocity* works for these teams, it does not work for teams undergoing regular kaizen: the average of the past three *Sprint*s is, by definition, a non-normative predictor of values in a monotonically increasing series.

Therefore:

Recognize an updated velocity only if the team sustains a new level for three *Sprint*s in a row.

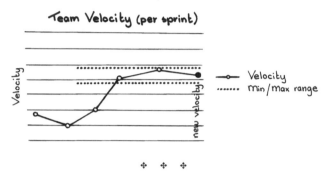

❖   ❖   ❖

Now the team is more likely to meet delivery expectations in the upcoming *¶75 Production Episode*. The velocity hopefully exhibits a long-term trend of improvement, but there is no law of nature preventing velocity from decreasing over time, either.

A great Scrum team runs in two modes: calibration mode and kaizen transition. During calibration mode, the team strives to normalize its velocity by reducing its variance. There are, in fact, good kaizens to this end: ensuring that the whole *Development Team* is involved in estimation; making sure that the *¶11 Product Owner* is not; making sure that all developer work comes from the *¶54 Product Backlog*; and so forth. Once the team establishes a new stable velocity, it can affect a kaizen with the aspiration of achieving a new plateau.

This pattern is an example of the Satir cycle of organizational change. The Satir cycle describes how outside changes ("foreign elements") temporarily disorient an individual or organization (*The Satir Model: Family Therapy and Beyond [Sat91]*, Chapter 5, "The Process of Change"). A kaizen is tantamount to a "foreign element" that invalidates the formerly invariant assumptions on which the old status quo depended. The organization must latch onto a *transforming idea* that brings it out of chaos into new normative work patterns. Good organizations wait out the inevitable chaotic stage and wait for a new normalcy to prevail before pronouncing a new velocity.

Perhaps the most important factor contributing to normalcy is to stabilize team membership. See *¶15 Stable Teams*.

Toyota, in fact, works in this way (*Extreme Toyota: Radical Contradictions That Drive Success at the World's Best Manufacturer [OSTD08 TOS08]*, pp. 84–85). After a kaizen, the teams stay the course with Mary Poppendieck's notion of Deliberate Practice, described by Jon Jagger in *97 Things Every Programmer Should Know [Hen10]* (pp. 44–45), to make sure the team integrates the kaizen into routine practice and that the improvement holds.

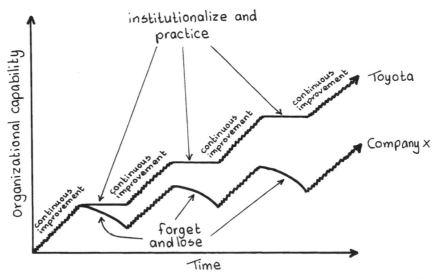

From Takeuchi et al., *Extreme Toyota: Radical Contradictions That Drive Success at the World's Best Manufacturer [OSTD08 TOS08]*, p. 84.

¶71 Sprint Goal

Confidence stars: **

...you are ready to embark on a *¶46 Sprint*, and you are planning it in *¶24 Sprint Planning*.

❖   ❖   ❖

The objective of a *Sprint* is to deliver value to the stakeholders. However, simply following a list of *¶73 Sprint Backlog Items* (SBIs; e.g., tasks) does not necessarily result in the creation of the greatest value possible.

Because the team lays out its work plan in terms of individual tasks or deliverables, it's easy for it to pick up an individual item and work on the item in isolation during the *¶75 Production Episode*. However, that dilutes the innovation that comes from the interactions between individuals who bring different perspectives to the work. Cubicle walls can become barriers to continuously communicating insights that are important to not only one developer, but rather to many developers (*¶14 Development Team* members) or to the entire team. Teamwork suffers.

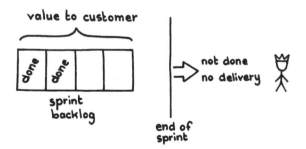

The team may need to partially replan a *Sprint* in progress to ensure that the team delivers value to the stakeholders at the *Sprint*'s end. New work may emerge from the team's latest insights, and the team should update its plan accordingly. If the team would instead follow the original work plan, it might not create the greatest value possible. Another common occurrence is that partway through the *Sprint*, it becomes clear that the team will not complete every *SBI* in the *¶72 Sprint Backlog*. This is often because the work required to complete *SBI*s expands. The team still wants to deliver value if at all possible, and it may take replanning to do so. Replanning the work for the *Sprint* requires forethought and time.

Another scenario is that the team needs important technical knowledge about how to implement a *¶55 Product Backlog Item* (*PBI*) to know how to develop it with confidence. The developers (or even the *¶11 Product Owner*) may need a technical prototype to validate a proposed architecture or to learn performance characteristics of some technology. While a *PBI* should identify such work, its uncertain nature requires that the team focus on obtaining the knowledge rather than completing all planned work. The technical prototype becomes a critical-path item for *Sprint* success.

In some cases, the greatest value might not be an explicit *Product Backlog Item*. To give one example, the greatest value for the team was to increase revenue per *Sprint*, and the team devoted a *Product Backlog Item* to this effort. On the other hand, sometimes the bulk of the *Sprint*'s value derives largely from one critical *PBI* out of many.

Therefore:

The *¶7 Scrum Team* commits to a short statement of the value it intends to create during the *Sprint*. This becomes the focus of all work in the *Sprint*.

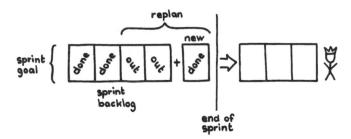

The entire *Scrum Team* jointly creates the *Sprint Goal*. The *Product Owner* will naturally guide the creation of the *Sprint Goal* because he or she has the best view on the next step toward the *¶39 Vision* and on how to create the *¶93 Greatest Value*. The *Scrum Team* should commit to the *Sprint Goal* as something always within reach.

The *Development Team* creates one *¶85 Regular Product Increment* to meet the *Sprint Goal* of each *Sprint*.

❖ ❖ ❖

The *Scrum Team* can use the *Sprint Goal* to frame the selection of *PBI*s for the *Sprint* but in some sense the *Sprint Goal* is more important even than the sum of the individual *PBI*s. The *Sprint Goal* creates coherence in the *PBI*s, helping to create a valuable *Regular Product Increment*. One good initial approach to a *¶54 Product Backlog* is to express it as a list of *Sprint Goals*, which the *Product Owner* and *Development Team* together elaborate into *PBI*s.

The members of *¶16 Autonomous Teams* must be able to manage themselves to accomplish their goals, and *¶76 Developer-Ordered Work Plan* states that *Development Teams* must be free to order their *Production Episode* work however they see fit. The *Sprint Goal* is the sole mechanism by which the *Product Owner* can influence the potential order in which the *Development Team* carries out its work (by inferring urgency from the importance conveyed by the *Sprint Goal*)—but, again, only with the *Development Team*'s consent.

During *Sprint Planning*, the *Scrum Team* determines *what* they aspire to achieve by the end of the *Sprint*; that, in short, is what the *Sprint Goal* is for. The *Development Team* defines the details on *how* to accomplish this *Sprint Goal* by creating a *Sprint Backlog*. If the *Development Team* concludes that they cannot accomplish the *Sprint Goal*, it should refine the *Sprint Goal* with the *Product Owner*. A key output of *Sprint Planning* is that the *Development Team* should be able to explain how it can accomplish the *Sprint Goal* and how to know it has achieved the goal. The ability to explain comes through a thorough understanding of the work ahead, which raises the probability that the team actually can achieve the *Sprint Goal* within the *Sprint*.

The *Development Team* commits to the *Sprint Goal*. This *Sprint Goal* can help unify the *Development Team* (see *¶117 Unity of Purpose* on page 468), and it serves to build stakeholders' trust in the team.

The *Sprint Goal* should be visible to the team; for example, put it on the Scrum Board or other *¶56 Information Radiator*.

The *Development Team* keeps the *Sprint Backlog* current during the *Sprint* to support meeting the *Sprint Goal*. Progress on the *Sprint Backlog* (such as indicated on a *¶43 Sprint Burndown Chart*) is like progress down the soccer field during a *Sprint*: though each yard of progress brings the ball closer to the end, the value comes in the goal. But it is sometimes possible to complete the *Sprint Goal* (in some way) without completing all *SBI*s. This helps teams handle contingencies and gives *Development Teams* flexibility in changing their work plan each day during the *¶29 Daily Scrum*. As an example: emergent impediments can threaten the *Development Team*'s delivery of the complete

Sprint Backlog. In that case, the team automatically resorts to the *Sprint Goal* as "Plan B" without expending long hours replanning. A study performed by Carnegie Mellon University *Gray Matter [ST13]* reports that teams that prepare ahead of time for interrupts handle them 14 percent better than teams that don't prepare. Teams that prepare for interrupts complete an uninterrupted task interval 43 percent faster than teams that don't prepare. It's a mindset to prepare for unplanned things: when they happen, teams can pivot to a new configuration to handle them, without external coaching.

It is theoretically possible to repeatedly achieve the *Sprint Goal* while completing only a fraction of the *PBI*s each *Sprint*. This should be uncommon because the *Sprint Backlog* should align with the *Sprint Goal*; if not, there is a serious problem with the *¶41 Value Stream*.

Velocity (see Notes on Velocity on page 320) helps teams understand if they are doing things right (given the assumption that doing things right increases your velocity). The *Sprint Goal* helps teams ensure that they are doing the right things. It is about understanding the "why" of what the team is doing so that it can keep focus when things change.

Jeff Sutherland adds that in addition to keeping the team focused, the *Sprint Goal* encourages swarming (see *¶25 Swarming: One-Piece Continuous Flow*): Can we get everyone working on one thing together? He relates:

> In Silicon Valley in 2007, Palm was working on a Web OS that was later acquired by Hewlett-Packard. Sprint to sprint the teams were doing well until they appeared to hit a wall in a couple of Sprints. PBIs were not getting finished. Developers were demotivated and going home early. I was brought in and got the Product Owners and ScrumMasters to spend an hour interviewing team members on why they were demotivated. **We found that they did not understand the reason they were working hard on low-level PBIs.**

> We spent an afternoon cleaning up the Product Backlog showing a clear linkage between high-level stories and the decomposition hierarchy. As soon as the developers understood that the *Sprint Goal* was to improve performance of the Web OS by 10%, they were motivated to complete the low-level stories and velocity went back up to normal.

> Understanding why the PBIs are being implemented is critical for developers, particularly for expert developers who would prefer to go surfing if they don't see the reason for their work.

The *Sprint Goal* usually relates to product value. The team can alternatively define *Sprint Goal*s in terms of process goals—for example, doing all programming through pair programming, or showing up ontime for the *Daily Scrum* every day.

Repeatedly driving to the *Sprint Goal* motivates the team to a higher level of engagement; conversely, the *¶91 Happiness Metric* can be an effective tool to define or suggest *Sprint Goal*s.

In 2001, Ken Schwaber and Mike Beedle were the first to describe the *Sprint Goal* (*Agile Software Development with Scrum (Series in Agile Software Development)* [SB01], p. 48).

¶72 Sprint Backlog

Alias: Sprint Plan

Confidence stars: **

...the *¶7 Scrum Team* has a well-defined *¶54 Product Backlog* and is convening *¶24 Sprint Planning* to define the current *¶46 Sprint*. The *¶14 Development Team* gives a forecast of the anticipated delivered *¶55 Product Backlog Item*s (*PBI*s) to the *¶11 Product Owner*, but the team members must define how they plan to develop them.

✢ ✢ ✢

In order to manage its progress during the *Sprint*, the *Development Team* needs to have a clear understanding of work remaining to achieve the *¶71 Sprint Goal*.

In order to understand whether the team can complete a *PBI* in the *Sprint*, it needs to understand the *PBI* in detail. Breaking a *PBI* down into *¶58 Small Items* helps the team more deeply understand the work necessary to bring a *PBI* to *Done* (see *¶82 Definition of Done*). This is design work that flows into the Scrum itself. You can't afford to shed any of this design work. But the team has only incomplete understanding of the work necessary at the beginning of the *Sprint*, and the work is likely to grow as more insight emerges.

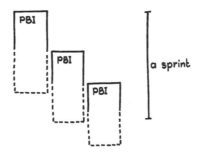

The *Development Team* needs a basis upon which to self-organize to accomplish the *Sprint Goal*. Frequent and accurate feedback at the *¶29 Daily Scrum* on the work remaining are essential for the *Development Team* to manage the dynamics of development.

The *Development Team* needs a starting point for measuring progress against the *Sprint Goal*. Of course, the *¶19 ScrumMaster* and *Product Owner* are interested too. But it's the *Development Team* that actually creates the *¶85 Regular Product Increment*.

Therefore:

Create a work plan for everything that the team must accomplish to meet the *Sprint Goal*. The team usually subdivides this work into *¶73 Sprint Backlog Items* (SBIs). These items may represent tasks that the team must complete, intermediate building blocks that combine into a deliverable, or any other unit of work that helps the team understand how to achieve the *Sprint Goal* within the *Sprint*.

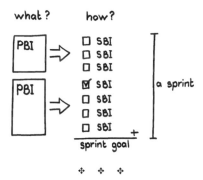

❖ ❖ ❖

The *Development Team* creates and owns the *Sprint Backlog* and only the members collectively can change it (*Agile Project Management with Scrum [Sch01]*, p. 50; see also *¶76 Developer-Ordered Work Plan*). The essence of creating the *Sprint Backlog* is the detailed design of the *PBIs* so that anyone in the *Development Team* can explain how they will accomplish the *Sprint Goal* (*Software in 30 Days: How Agile Managers Beat the Odds, Delight Their Customers, and Leave Competitors in the Dust [SS12]*). The *Sprint Backlog* helps provide a mechanism to express the *how* of development, and helps the *Development Team* remember its design decisions. But a *Sprint* is by definition time-boxed. Therefore, the *Development Team* must consider its velocity (see Notes on Velocity on page 320) to create a *Sprint Backlog* it thinks it can finish within the *Sprint*, in service of the *Sprint Goal*. Using patterns of velocity, such as *¶66 Yesterday's Weather* and *¶70 Updated Velocity*, will help the team determine how much it can put in the *Sprint Backlog*.

A precise *Sprint Backlog* helps the *Development Team* to remember all detailed work it needs to do. The *Development Team* decides the order of the *Sprint Backlog* and should keep it ordered to optimize the chances of meeting the *Sprint Goal*. The contents of the *Sprint Backlog* can change during the *Sprint*. As the *Development Team* learns more about the difficulty of the work, it might add or change *SBIs*. The team might remove *SBIs*, or even split or combine them. The dynamic nature of the *Sprint Backlog* makes it necessary to do incremental replanning as a major activity of the *Daily Scrum*.

The *Sprint Backlog* provides the basis for tracking progress[28] (*¶43 Sprint Burndown Chart*) and for making status visible (*¶78 Visible Status*). At the *Daily Scrum*, the *Sprint Backlog* helps the *Development Team* members decide what they will work on next. While there is no formal ordering of the *Sprint Backlog*, there is an ordering in the sense that certain *SBIs* depend on the completion of others. The *Development Team* swarming on *PBIs* (see *¶25 Swarming: One-Piece Continuous Flow*) also affects the ordering, but it's up to the *Development Team* how to manage it. However it is managed, the *Development Team* must understand the dependencies among the *SBIs* so it can order the work and have an accurate picture of status; see *¶79 Dependencies First*.

The *Development Team* should make the *Sprint Backlog* transparent to all stakeholders with an *¶56 Information Radiator* such as a *¶44 Scrum Board*, to increase transparency. One must be careful that people outside of the *Development Team* will not use this transparency to micromanage the team; the *ScrumMaster* should monitor for such abuse of any *Information Radiator*. The *Sprint Burndown Chart* and *Scrum Board* digest *Sprint Backlog* progress into more visual *Information Radiator*s.

---

28. Jeff Sutherland and Ken Schwaber. *The Scrum Guide*. ScrumGuides.org, http://www.scrumguides.org (accessed 5 January 2017).

¶73 Sprint Backlog Item

Confidence stars: *

...the *¶7 Scrum Team* has ordered the *¶55 Product Backlog Item*s. The team is in *¶24 Sprint Planning* and is ready to start planning the work for the *¶75 Production Episode* of the current *¶46 Sprint*.

❖ ❖ ❖

A *Product Backlog Item* (PBI) does not define how to arrive at a solution or implementation, or how to deploy the solution.

A *Product Backlog Item* represents the *¶63 Enabling Specification* for some product update that the *¶14 Development Team* will develop. A *PBI* clarifies *what* to build but does not specify *how* to build it.

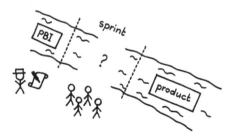

Scrum helps the team to manage risk. A *PBI* gives the *Scrum Team* enough information to assess outward-facing risk. However, it offers no insight into the risks associated with complex development. Development work is, by nature, emergent. *PBI*s describe deliverables in business (end-user and market) terms, while the *Development Team* works and estimates in production terms.

The two key elements of risk management are feasibility and time. In order to understand and reduce risk, you must understand the *PBI* in sufficient detail to have confidence that it is technically feasible, and can reach a state of *Done* (see *¶82 Definition of Done*) within the *Production Episode*. Even then, you can't have 100 percent confidence in feasibility up front. Even though you can mitigate most risks during *Sprint Planning*, you need to accept emergent requirements that arise during the *Production Episode* itself. We do not want to handle them in the margins or treat them as second-class citizens. Yet, they are not *PBIs* in their own right.

You could also reduce risk by taking a feature all the way into implementation; in fact, a good *¶11 Product Owner* might support the team with a working prototype of the feature. However, it is risky to take a *PBI* into a *Production Episode* after considering only commercial criteria while ignoring engineering, development, and deployment costs. If that top *PBI* takes an entire *Production Episode* by itself, then nothing else will get *Done* during the *Sprint*.

You could launch into the work on a given *PBI* and put it on the shelf upon discovering that it will put the *Sprint* delivery at risk. But then, work in progress may grow arbitrarily large.

Coarse granularity estimates are imprecise, unreliable, and unpredictable: you need *¶58 Small Items* to estimate.

You can get more development efficiency by viewing a *PBI* differently. A *PBI* entails a collection of complementary tasks that build on teamwork and parallel development. The team could self-organize to start working on it, but it needs some direction. What is to prevent all team members from launching into just one of the five things that they need to do to finish this *PBI*? If the team is going to swarm on a *PBI* (see *¶25 Swarming: One-Piece Continuous Flow*), they better have talked about it first.

Therefore:

Break down *Product Backlog Items* into work items and assemble them into a plan called a *¶72 Sprint Backlog*. Each work item is a *Sprint Backlog Item* (*SBI*). No *Sprint Backlog Item* typically should be any larger than a single *Development Team* member can complete in a single work day.

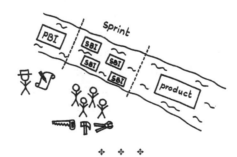

❖ ❖ ❖

The *Development Team* commonly expresses work items as tasks, but the team can instead represent them as internal artifacts or as the result of any other breakdown that gives the *Development Team* confidence about meeting its ¶71 *Sprint Goal* with the work items. The team takes all work items that it must complete during the *Sprint* and combines them into a plan called the *Sprint Backlog*. The *Sprint Backlog* becomes the *Development Team*'s view of the product increment development.

The process of design (either during *Sprint Planning* or during the *Sprint*) offers insight into the work. This design process reduces risks such as realizing the cost of unknown additional work, or delaying the delivery by finding large chunks of latent work too late into the *Sprint*. Design clarifies the *PBI*, and uncovers unknown work.

The team can use *SBIs* as units of progress measurement during a *Production Episode*. The ¶43 *Sprint Burndown Chart* reflects the progress at the granularity of the work items on the *Sprint Backlog*. This granularity supports rapid feedback. It also improves the fidelity of estimation by creating *Small Items* to estimate.

The collection of *SBIs* is dynamic and changes as we learn more about the product. *SBIs* can emerge as discovered work (e.g., more design and development are needed) or alternatively can die during the course of a *Production Episode*. So discuss them at the ¶29 *Daily Scrum* and replan the *Sprint*. The team should estimate new *SBIs* as they emerge and should assign ¶60 *Estimation Points* to each one. The team should also update the *Sprint Burndown Chart* accordingly.

The *Development Team* collectively remains responsible for all the *SBIs* on the *Sprint Backlog*.

It is a common practice to write *SBIs* on sticky notes and put them on the ¶44 *Scrum Board* to make progress on work completion visible. Keep the writing to a minimum: the written text for an *SBI* should be just enough to remind the *Development Team* of the outcome of accumulated work plan discussions to date. Another common practice is to also write the *Estimation Points* on the sticky notes, which enables easy updating of the *Sprint Burndown Chart* when the team moves the work item to Done. Teams use sticky notes in all manner of creative ways (e.g., colors, rotation, adding marks, etc.) to accommodate a good visualization of *Sprint Backlog* status. No prescriptive guidance is necessary on this usage: it is up to the *Development Team* to find out what works best.

¶74 Teams That Finish Early Accelerate Faster

...the *¶14 Development Team* may work together well but struggles every *¶46 Sprint* to attain the *¶71 Sprint Goal*. In the worst case, the team is feeling demoralized and velocity is low (see Notes on Velocity on page 320).

❖ ❖ ❖

Teams often take too much work into a *Sprint* and cannot finish it. Failure to attain the *Sprint Goal* prevents the team from improving.

*Development Team*s can be optimistic about their ability to finish *¶55 Product Backlog Item*s. But in doing so, they fail to give themselves time to reduce technical debt and sharpen their saws. Thus they are doomed to a persistently slow pace.

Market pressure and low velocity may make the *¶11 Product Owner* desperate, and the *Development Team* will accept larger and larger *Sprint Goal*s. This compounds the problem and they decelerate.

Individuals on a team may be working on other things subversively. *Development Team* members hide such work on teams that persistently overreach their ability or overestimate their capacity.

If the team takes on too much work, it feels overburdened and under pressure. When team members cannot get the work *Done* (see *¶82 Definition of Done*) by the end of the *Sprint*, everyone is unhappy—the *Development Team*, the *¶19 ScrumMaster*, the *Product Owner*, and management. Furthermore, the team does not have time to think clearly about how to improve its work and will probably enter the next *Sprint* with work that is only partially *Done*.

A lack of basic understanding of lean practices is often a cause of management pressure on teams. Taiichi Ohno's taxonomy of waste has the category of "Absurdity"—stress due to excessive scope (see *The Toyota Way: 14 Management Principles from the World's Greatest Manufacturer [Lik04]*, Figure 10–1). This can cause massive slowdown.

> *Muri* (無理) *is a Japanese word meaning "unreasonableness; impossible; beyond one's power; too difficult; by force; perforce; forcibly; compulsorily; excessiveness; immoderation," and is a key concept in the Toyota Production System (TPS) as one of the three types of waste (muda, mura, muri) (see articles for respective terms in Wikipedia).*

Therefore:

Take less work into a *Sprint* (than the previous *Sprint*) and aim for a less ambitious *Sprint Goal*. Note that the level of ambition of the *Sprint Goal* (outcome) may not be proportional to the volume, cost, or duration of the work.

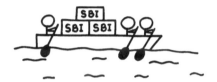

¶66 *Yesterday's Weather* will maximize your probability of success. Then you can implement ¶33 *Illegitimus Non Interruptus*, which will systematically deal with any interruptions that would prevent you from finishing early. On early completion of the *Sprint Goal*, pull forward from the next *Sprint*'s backlog, which will increase *Yesterday's Weather* for future *Sprint*s. To increase the probability of acceleration, apply ¶92 *Scrumming the Scrum* to identify your kaizen (see Kaizen and Kaikaku on page 101) in the ¶36 *Sprint Retrospective*. Put the kaizen in the ¶72 *Sprint Backlog* with acceptance tests (see ¶87 *Testable Improvements*) for the next *Sprint* as top priority.

❖   ❖   ❖

OpenView Venture Partners noticed this pattern after analyzing data from dozens of sprints with multiple teams. The teams that finished their *Sprint* early accelerated faster (*Proceedings of Agile 2009 [SA09]*). The common denominator was finishing early. It allowed teams to think more clearly about what they were doing—to remove impediments, to pull forward backlog from the next *Sprint*, to develop a winning attitude, and to increase *Yesterday's Weather*.

An earlier version of this pattern was published at HICCS 2014 (*Proceedings of 47th Hawaii International Conference on System Sciences [SHR14]*).

¶75 Production Episode

Confidence stars: **

...the team is done with *¶24 Sprint Planning*, and you have a *¶72 Sprint Backlog* that defines the work plan. You are striving to deliver the *¶85 Regular Product Increment* and are aiming for the *¶71 Sprint Goal*.

❖   ❖   ❖

Team members do the best work, and most efficiently complete planned work, when they can work together without distractions.

On one hand, it's good to feed development with just-in-time understanding about the work at hand. On the other hand, constant interruption brings certain disruption at some cost. Being in flow is good, and even a well-intentioned disruption to deliver a helpful requirements update may cost the *¶14 Development Team* some time to restore flow. It isn't clear whether the increased market value from a disruptive requirements correction will ever offset the impact to development cost. In any case, constantly disrupting a *Development Team* to "help" it with clarifying input takes the team out of flow and substantially reduces the value of each *¶46 Sprint* outcome.

Things rarely go well if the team receives both a list of work to do and a deadline by which it must be completed: motivation, quality, and efficiency all suffer (*Journal of Personality and Social Psychology 34 [ADL76]*). But to work with no sense of urgency or knowledge of the time available also leads to underachievement.[29]

---

29. This simulation was a predecessor of: John Sterman, David Miller, and Joe Hsueh, "CleanStart: Simulating a Clean Energy Startup." MIT Management, Sloan School, Leading Edge, https://mitsloan.mit.edu/LearningEdge/simulations/cleanstart/Pages/default.aspx, accessed 1 April 2019.

Agile says that we should respond to change, but a system that reacts to every small external change can become a system that is out of control. Flexibility may be a business goal, but constancy and stability are enablers of effective work.

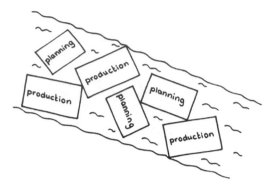

When the date to deliver work is not in the near future, people tend to have less focus and postpone important activities. (Just remember when you had to prepare for a test in high school, when you would start studying really hard the day before the exam.) In development, this could mean that in the early days you would focus on things that are easy or the most fun and you would not work on the most valuable *¶55 Product Backlog Item*s (PBIs). Parkinson's Law captures the end result that "work expands so as to fill the time available for its completion."[30]

Therefore:

Compartmentalize all market-facing product realization work in a time-boxed interval, with participation limited to the *Development Team*. This uninterrupted development interval falls between *Sprint Planning* and the *¶35 Sprint Review*. During this interval, the developers take a few short scheduled discussions with the *¶11 Product Owner* to work toward a *¶64 Refined Product Backlog*—but on the whole, this is otherwise uninterrupted time.

During the *Production Episode*, the team focuses on the *Sprint Goal* and strives to achieve its *forecast* to complete all work on the *Sprint Backlog*. There is an agreement between the *Product Owner* and the *Development Team* that the *Product Owner* may neither add nor change a *PBI* during the *Production Episode*. This ensures that the *Development Team* remains focused and committed so that there is enough stability to work on what is most important: the *Sprint Goal*. The *Product Owner* can change the long-term product direction by reordering the *¶54 Product Backlog*, but changes to the *Product Backlog* have no effect on

---

30. Parkinson's Law. Wikipedia, https://en.wikipedia.org/wiki/Parkinson's_law (accessed 2 November 2017).

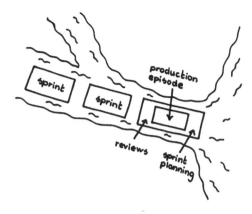

the *Development Team*'s work plan until it processes the *Product Backlog* content at the *Sprint Planning* event at the beginning of the following *Sprint*. This motivates the *Product Owner* to think carefully about what is most valuable to work on, and to not waste time and money developing less valuable *PBIs*.

All but the most disciplined *¶7 Scrum Teams* should disallow their delivery scope from changing during the *Production Episode* (except for continuing to pull from the top of the *Product Backlog* when finishing early). More advanced teams may find efficient ways to negotiate between the *Product Owner* and the *Development Team*, in ways that both still find positive and fair. Frequent changes in scope or interruption by management or the *Product Owner* can cause the team to lose motivation and can be a sign that the business is not faithful to the *¶39 Vision*.

During *Sprint Planning*, the *Development Team* members forecast (*not* "commit") the volume of work they feel they can complete during this *Sprint* and pull that amount of work into the work plan (*Sprint Backlog*), so the interval is a "gift from the project" rather than an externally imposed completion constraint. New work may emerge from unforeseen requirements or defects during the *Production Episode*, and the *Development Team* may update its *Sprint Backlog* accordingly. This emergent work tends to remain about the same in volume across *Sprints* and, while taken into account by the *Development Team* during the *Sprint*, there is no attempt to estimate it or account for it in advance. Such effort is absorbed into the team's estimates when using common estimation practices, such as described in *¶60 Estimation Points* and Notes on Velocity on page 320.

The duration of the *Production Episode* is the length of the *Sprint* less the time allotted to *Sprint Planning*, the *Sprint Review*, and the *¶36 Sprint Retrospective*. Four weeks is the upper bound on the length of a *Sprint*, and they typically last two weeks.

During the *Production Episode*, the *Development Team* assesses progress and replans the *Sprint* in the *¶29 Daily Scrum*. Every day, the *Development Team* updates the *Sprint Backlog* with a revised *¶76 Developer-Ordered Work Plan* optimized to achieve the *Sprint Goal*. Teams also maintain a discipline of *¶80 Good Housekeeping*.

❖ ❖ ❖

At the end of a successful *Production Episode*, the team reaches the *Sprint Goal* and realizes a new *Regular Product Increment* that is ready for the *Sprint Review*. Some *¶73 Sprint Backlog Item*s may remain in the *Sprint Backlog* at the end of the *Production Episode*, but the *Development Team* has completed enough of the backlog to have achieved the *Sprint Goal*. If the *Development Team* finishes early, it pulls additional work from the top of the *Product Backlog*, breaks the work down into a work plan, and continues with the *Sprint*. When a *Sprint* becomes in danger of not delivering the entire *Sprint Backlog*, the team should resort to the *Sprint Goal*. The team assesses this risk and responds accordingly every day at the *Daily Scrum*.

The *PBI*s that reach a state of *Done* (see *¶82 Definition of Done*) during a *Sprint* become delivery candidates for that *Sprint* or a subsequent *Sprint*. Scrum separates the decision of whether something is *Done* from the decision of whether to deploy; the *Product Owner* decides when to release a *PBI* to the market. The *Scrum Team* produces a *Regular Product Increment* at the end of the *Sprint* that is most often the key candidate for delivery, but more frequent delivery (e.g., of emergency repairs) is possible: see *¶84 Responsive Deployment*. Making *PBI*s small enough raises the chances that several of these become deliverable every *Sprint*.

A failed *Sprint* is one in which the *Scrum Team* does not achieve the *Sprint Goal*. Some practitioners avoid using the term *failed* and instead might say "A *Sprint* that did not achieve the *Sprint Goal*." It is possible (but unlikely) that the team nonetheless emptied the *Sprint Backlog*. Neither *The Scrum Guide*[31] nor any broad practice recognize any distinction in action that follows from failed and nonfailed *Sprint*s, but the distinction helps underscore the

---

31. Jeff Sutherland and Ken Schwaber. *The Scrum Guide*. ScrumGuides.org, http://www.scrumguides.org (accessed 5 January 2017).

importance of process improvement as the team discusses the *Sprint* during the *Sprint Retrospective*.

The team's *velocity* (see *Notes on Velocity*) is the amount of work that the team can complete in a single *Sprint*. It is a measure of the team's *demonstrated* capacity to complete work in a *Sprint* and is usually a measure of relative (or, sometimes, absolute) work per *Sprint*. The team establishes its velocity based on averaged recent historical performance; given *¶66 Yesterday's Weather*, the team's delivery should be in line with the expectations it sets when creating the *Sprint Backlog*. Because velocity is a stochastic value, about half of the *Sprint*s will finish all *Sprint Backlog Item*s early (before the *Sprint* is over) while half will miss the mark. Good teams learn to use *Yesterday's Weather* to avoid taking too much into the *Sprint* and thereby risking not delivering everything; good disciplines such as described in *¶74 Teams That Finish Early Accelerate Faster* will improve a team's delivery track record.

In exceptional cases, particularly when it becomes impossible to meet the *Sprint Goal*, the *Product Owner* may shorten a *Sprint*: see *¶32 Emergency Procedure*.

The pattern name honors Ward Cunningham's "Development Episode" pattern, which is also about framing of work.[32]

---

32. Ward Cunningham. "EPISODES: A Pattern Language of Competitive Development." http://c2.com/ppr/episodes.html, ca. 1995, accessed 17 April 2018.

¶76 Developer-Ordered Work Plan

Alias: Why Gantt Charts Don't Work

Confidence stars: **

Developers together decide the ordering of work items, day by day.

...the *¶14 Development Team* has created a work plan—a *¶72 Sprint Backlog* —from a *¶46 Sprint*'s worth of *¶55 Product Backlog Item*s pulled from the top of the *¶54 Product Backlog* in accordance with the team's velocity (see Notes on Velocity on page 320). It has started a *¶75 Production Episode*, and is seeking insight on how to start building the *¶85 Regular Product Increment* or to sustain yesterday's momentum by best ordering the work plan.

❖   ❖   ❖

There is only one time that Scrum demands an attitude of firm commitment to a specific objective: when the *Development Team* forecasts to deliver the *¶71 Sprint Goal* by the end of the current *Sprint*. And sound *¶7 Scrum Teams*, on the average, meet their forecasts for delivering the *Sprint Backlog*. The team plans in advance to create forecasts for the next two or three *Sprints*, but only the current *Sprint* is a unit of planned achievement. Of course, even this plan can miss the mark due to emergent requirements, but a well-run *Scrum Team* delivers regularly enough on its forecast that it can be depended upon to support the business.

Even Scrum practitioners sometimes have difficulty understanding *¶1 The Spirit of the Game*: that control of the *Sprint* lies in their hands. It's easy to lose sight of the autonomy that Scrum teams enjoy when they direct their focus toward stakeholders' expectations and to the team's commitments. The team commits to the *Sprint Goal* at the beginning of the *Sprint*. Some *Scrum Teams* argue that they should also create a work plan that follows the original ordering of the *Product Backlog Item*s (*PBIs*). If they do this, then argue that some *¶73 Sprint Backlog Item*s (*SBIs*) will be left unfinished at the end of a *Sprint*, they can have the satisfaction of at least having completed the most important items. But that mindset leads to complacency: the *Development Team* may lose its incentive to burn down the *Sprint Backlog* contents to zero. It leads to a practice of "we commit but…" that robs the term *forecast* of any attitude of commitment, and leaves the *¶11 Product Owner* insecure about his or her own ability to manage commitments to the market.

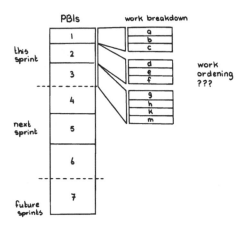

Optimally ordering the *Sprint Backlog* in advance is a challenge. If there are five *PBIs* and each has nine *SBIs*, then there are 45 factorial possible orderings (about 2×10^{56})! In addition to those original *SBIs*, emergent requirements cause the team to add new ones as the *Sprint* progresses (or, in some cases, to remove some). Some orderings enable really fast development while others are really slow, and that ordering changes every day. It's the essence of Scrum for the team to figure out what the fastest ordering is. That's what the *¶29 Daily Scrum* is for.

The *Product Owner* has no say over *how* the team achieves its forecast. Ken Schwaber, paraphrasing Nonaka (*The Knowledge-Creating Company: How Japanese Companies Create the Dynamics of Innovation [NT95]*, p. 85) says: "The team has full authority and is autonomous during the *Sprint*." The *Product Backlog* ordering reflects the *Product Owner*'s wishes. While *Product Owners* certainly have the final authority over the ordering of the *PBIs*, they have no authority over how the *Development Team* organizes its work. If the work plan follows the *PBI* ordering, it creates a leak in the firewall (see *¶114 Firewall* on page 468) between the *Product Owner* and the *Development Team*, letting the *Product Owner* tacitly direct or disrupt the *Development Team*'s organization of work.

If the Developer work plan follows the *Product Backlog* ordering, and market priorities change mid-*Sprint*, the *Product Owner* can argue to intervene in the delivery order. This amounts to the *Product Owner* meddling with the

Development Team mid-*Sprint*. If this happens and the *Development Team* fails to deliver at the end of the *Sprint*, it is easy to blame the *Product Owner*'s intervention, and it is difficult to believe that the same won't happen again in a subsequent *Sprint*. That saps the *Development Team*'s will to care at all about what it will or won't complete in a *Sprint*.

Such a forced work plan can over-constrain an immature *Development Team* that is not a *perfectly ¶10 Cross-Functional Team*. For example, if there are few database people on the *Development Team* and if the top *PBI*s are database-intensive, and if the *Development Team* is practicing *¶25 Swarming: One-Piece Continuous Flow*, then this keeps the team from making progress on *PBI*s that better fit the available skill set. On the other hand, the *Development Team* members may discover new opportunities to invest in learning and working outside their primary skill sets, which in the long term will increase multi-skilling team agility if it adjusts the work plan in that direction.

When impediments disrupt the *Sprint* flow, it lowers the value that the *Development Team* can deliver during a *Sprint*. It's important to keep development flowing when an impediment arises, yet pre-arranged work plans cannot foresee these exceptions. Furthermore, folks outside the *Development Team* have difficulty understanding how to navigate the myriad options at hand to deal with these impediments in a way that will preserve the greatest value.

The *Development Team* forecasts delivery of the entire *Sprint Backlog* to the *Product Owner*. The *Sprint Backlog* often represents a unit of market delivery; that is, at the level of the market campaigns, the *Product Owner* should be able to treat the entire contents of the *Sprint Backlog* as a minimal marketable feature: a *Regular Product Increment*. The *Product Owner* has a reasonable right to rely on the *Development Team*'s forecast to drive soft marketing plans. The *Development Team* becomes disincentivized if the *Product Owner* asks it to attack the most important work items first, while it is instead striving to complete everything. Sometimes the *Development Team* fails to deliver the entire *Sprint Backlog* as a natural consequence of emergent requirements. The team may be able to learn from an incomplete delivery, but it's unwise to externally impose even the best-intentioned work ordering constraints if the team sacrifices the self-organization that optimizes the chance of delivering the best long-term value.

Therefore: **Let the *Development Team* members decide the best ordering of tasks to reach their forecast of delivering the *Sprint Goal* and full *Sprint Backlog*.** The *Development Team* should self-organize to do work in the order it believes will incur the lowest cost or least time or, alternatively, to support the highest overall value. Let the *Product Backlog* ordering inform, but not drive, these decisions. The *Development Team* takes the initiative to create an informed and responsible ordering instead of an externally constrained ordering that is arbitrary with respect to emerging development requirements.

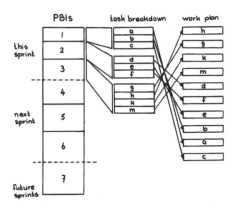

As items' granularity becomes finer and finer, the constraints on ordering items within a grouping (first, by *Sprint*; second, by *PBI*) becomes less and less stringent.

❖ ❖ ❖

The result is an ordered work plan that builds on flexibility and uses the *Development Team*'s collective insights to best support the business goals—embodied in the *Sprint Goal*—for the *Regular Product Increment*. The *Development Team* reviews the plan daily and may update it frequently in response to the team's progress, to changing market conditions, the *Sprint Goal*, and all other insights at the disposal of the *Development Team*. It's about the team being in charge: how can the *Development Team* members self-organize if someone tells them how to do things? It is the *¶19 ScrumMaster*'s job to motivate the team to this level of self-organization.

As with the weather, the amount of work the team anticipates completing during the *Sprint* is a forecast or estimate rather than a promise. The forecast is based in part on recent historical performance; see *¶66 Yesterday's Weather*. Further, the plan is dynamic: the team updates it every day at the *Daily Scrum*

If the *Development Team* creates its own work plan ordering, then it is better able to self-organize without undue influence from the *Product Owner*. The *Development Team* is free to find task orderings that build on its engineering strengths, and knowledge of how best to organize its work. This can be liberating, particularly for a team that has suffered being micromanaged, but it is also a call to responsibility, discipline, and a sense of ownership for the work plan. Growing into this sense of responsibility and ownership requires focus, and can often benefit from the guidance of the *ScrumMaster*, particularly as the team makes its journey out of micromanagement into the realm of *¶16 Autonomous Team*s.

Of course, any *Product Backlog* ordering dictated by foreseeable engineering dependencies between *PBI*s will also appear as a dependency between work plan items. The *Development Team* can use this information to properly order the work plan to satisfy technical dependencies.

Overly casual ordering of work plan items can lead to a large number of partially completed *PBI*s at the end of the *Sprint*. To remedy this, use *Swarming: One-Piece Continuous Flow*.

Some Scrum traditions honor an approach called "First Things First," which makes it incumbent on the team to deliver *Product Backlog Item*s in their order of appearance on the backlog. The idea is that the team doesn't have to waste time agreeing on an ordering, and that following the *PBI* ordering best honors the *Product Owner*'s wishes. We feel that this is an indirect way for the *Product Owner* to control the team and to dilute the team's ability to be self-managing. Such external constraints are likely to reduce the team's velocity, because they frustrate optimizations that the team can realize by reordering the work plan.

Teams should strive to resolve dependencies between items by mid-*Sprint*: see *¶79 Dependencies First*. If the *Product Owner*s feel that their inability to control the team work program puts crucial *PBI*s items at risk, they can mitigate the risk either with the *Sprint Goal* or by making a strategic adjustment to the *Sprint* length.

Consider the situation where the *Product Owner* must react to an unforeseen market shift by immediately delivering a *PBI* from the current *Sprint*. The *Product Owner* can reorder the deliverables—but only by making the exception visible and forcing the issue with *¶32 Emergency Procedure*. Only in the most experienced and mature *Scrum Team*s might it be acceptable for the *Product Owner* to negotiate the ordering of the *Development Team*'s work plan, but even then only with the *Development Team*'s consent.

In *The Scrum Handbook [Sut10]* (pp. 23–24), Jeff Sutherland writes, "The team chooses the ordering of Sprint Backlog tasks to maximize the velocity of production and quality of 'done' functionality." See *¶82 Definition of Done*.

Compare and contrast with *Swarming: One-Piece Continuous Flow* and *¶100 Informal Labor Plan* on page 467.

¶77 Follow the Moon

...you have *¶15 Stable Teams* that are also *¶8 Collocated Teams*.

❖ ❖ ❖

Every culture has rhythms, such as holidays, that have nothing to do with the Gregorian calendar, yet most business cycles are based on the latter. Religious holiday vacations tend to pop up at seemingly random dates, but in fact often follow a lunar calendar: Ramadan, Passover, Easter, and Hanukkah are typical examples. We as professionals tend to believe that time is uniform, that a day is a day and a week is a week, yet Project Managers learn that they should treat December as a month with only ten days of effective work. In the meantime, the reality of local holidays confounds the fixed, internal units of time that come from the Gregorian calendar and are the foundation of Scrum *¶46 Sprints*. And "local" differs from culture to culture and country to country. Denmark shuts down for the month of July; Germany tends to split its summer siesta across two months. Australia's holiday season is different yet again, and heaven help the poor enterprises that believe in multisite development and which have locations in *both* Europe and Australia. We won't even mention India, whose holidays follow the sun *and* the moon.

While we acknowledge the rhythm of the Sun in the *¶29 Daily Scrum*, we often ignore larger rhythms of life like the phases of the Moon and the local seasons. Human beings are not machines who can deliver the same every hour and day all time of year, just as European Project Managers deeply discount December. So we work in day time and sleep at night. We have weekends, holidays, and vacations. These create annoying irregularities for *¶24 Sprint Planning* and for the team's velocity.

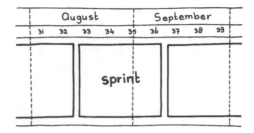

Early definitions of Scrum recommended that *Sprints* run on roughly monthly cycles; more specifically, on four-week cycles. In most cultures a Scrum "month" is not a calendar month. In monochronic cultures (*The Dance of Life* [Hal88]), we can define a day to be 86,400 seconds, and an "ideal month" is a collection of thirty such days. But these "months" are not the calendar months that vary in length: *Sprints* are always the same length. Scrum scheduling more closely follows the cultural rituals of the Scrum framework than it does any business calendar. (If you don't believe this, quickly answer how many business months you have in a year and then how many Sprints you have in a year, hopefully without having to do any math.) So we can define cadences in Scrum in terms of ceremonies, rituals, and benchmarks from the framework rather than from the calendar. And the recommended *Sprint* length from Scrum's early days was closer to the period-icity of our largest astral body than to the rhythms of the Gregorian calendar. (Today, two-week rather than four-week *Sprints* are the norm.)

Working outside natural rhythms upsets human subjects so badly as to suggest it has been the cause of numerous disasters such as Chernobyl, Three Mile Island, and the Exxon *Valdez* ship accident and oil spill (*Sync* [Str04], p. 85).

Therefore,

Define *Sprint*s with beginning and ending boundaries falling on the new moon and full moon. This creates a cadence that perfectly fits two-week and four-week *Sprints*. Use common sense when accommodating non-lunar local events such as Christmas, mid-summer, Thanksgiving, or other work pauses that are customary to the local culture. It can be a nice picture of incremental work.

Get the team involved in putting together a long-term *Sprint* calendar that accommodates holidays and traditional vacation times. For example, many European subcultures often take vacation together during the same two weeks or month.

Those cultures that follow the Hirji calendar (*altaqwim alhijriu*) or other lunar calendars are already halfway there. Many of the religious holidays that otherwise upset the normal Gregorian cadence also follow a lunar calendar, and the chances that they align well with *Sprint* boundaries is much higher if you *Follow the Moon*.

❖   ❖   ❖

This scheduling establishes a regular cadence, and universally sets expectations about when the next *Sprint* will end. The team can synchronize delivering *¶85 Regular Product Increment*s with broadly understood cultural rhythms. Team members' energy cycles will likely conflict less with naturally occurring cycles in the culture. This helps the team advance some of the deeper human nuances of *¶93 Greatest Value*.

This is a "Ha" (破—"break the rules") pattern, for advanced Scrum practice. For "Shu" (守—"by the book") use *¶61 Fixed-Date PBI*. In "Ri" (離—"expertly extemporaneous") we can playfully conjecture that you are enough harmonized with your cnvironment that you might follow the moon naturally.

Use common sense in dealing with holidays. One way to deal with the way that holiday seasons irregularly cut across the lunar calendar is to package them as *¶55 Product Backlog Item*s: see *¶62 Vacation PBI*.

Sally Helgesen (*Everyday Revolutionaries: Working Women and the Transformation of American Life* [Hel98], p. 140) writes about the importance of natural cycles to well-being:

> The sociologist Eviatar Zerubavel, in a fascinating study entitled *Hidden Rhythms*, observes that humans experience time in two entirely different ways: as the cyclical rhythms of nature, governed by recurrent seasons; and the repetitive rhythms of the machine, regulated by schedules, calendars, and clocks. He notes that being able to perceive time as cyclical is essential to our well-being, a crucial manifestation of our connection with nature in which time always moves in cycles.

See also *Sprint*.

¶78 Visible Status

Confidence stars: *

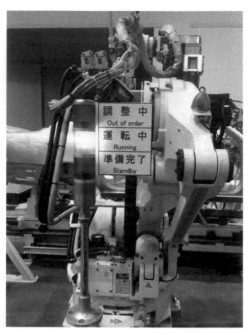

...the *¶7 Scrum Team* is using *¶56 Information Radiator*s to maintain transparency with all stakeholders.

❖ ❖ ❖

Without a frame of reference for your goals, you can unknowingly drift from them.

Our current goals strongly influence our behaviors, such as where we turn our attention (see *Journal of Applied Psychology 82 [vC97]*, and *American Psychologist 57 [LL99]*). Being focused on our work and direction actually dilutes our attention, as shown in a well-known video experiment where an observer is asked to count the number of ball passes between people, and totally misses someone in a gorilla suit walking through the scene; see *Perception 28 [SC99]*.

Scrum provides both direction and opportunities to focus on our work, but doing so may inherently prevent us from observing important changes in our work or work products. For example, members of the *¶14 Development Team* may be so focused on their current *¶73 Sprint Backlog Item*s so as to not notice an increase in defect rates—or equally the *¶11 Product Owner* may be so focused on the *¶54 Product Backlog* for the next *¶46 Sprint* that he or she misses important changes in sales results.

Although Scrum is a team sport, each person views the product and team's status through their own frame of reference. Some developers may view everything as going well whereas others may see a crisis coming, but without consensus the team will not change how it approaches its work.

Using *Information Radiator*s to maintain transparency is important for a functioning *Scrum Team*. Nonetheless, when the information does not create action, team members may passively accept whatever information that status boards and the environment provide. An example from our community: one of us was working with a company where at the end of the *¶29 Daily Scrum*, the *Development Team* members would look at the computer-generated *¶43 Sprint Burndown Chart*. No matter the shape of the burndown, the team did exactly what it had already agreed to during the *Daily Scrum*, even if the burndown was a straight, flat line. This is like a service message on the car dashboard that we ignore for months. This is different from the oil warning light that makes us stop the car straight away. We need both.

In spite of our best efforts at design and estimation at the beginning of a *Sprint*, we will be wrong. Finding out at the end of the *Sprint* that we were wrong does us no good.

Therefore:

Create a status overview that demands action when outside acceptable tolerance. *Information Radiator*s help to maintain the transparency for empirical process control but there is some information that cries out for immediate action. Use red lights, or emotive words like DANGER, or work environment lockouts on product and process state changes that need immediate attention and that disrupt the team's anticipated work plan or sequence of actions. Get people's attention and let them know something is not in a normal state. It is necessary for the team to discuss what "normal state" means. When the team finds itself no longer using a particular *Visible Status* for improvements, the team members should agree to remove it.

The status indicator must make it easy and fast to grasp the meaning of the measurements. The indicator must communicate whether a given property of the process is within an acceptable range of tolerance (and requires no immediate action) or is outside the range. In the latter case, the team needs to know what measures to apply (by an explicit notice on the indicator or from prior training) to bring the process back within tolerance. Keep things simple and clear by showing only the most important information. Visual information is best as it is easy to continuously transmit it to many collocated people. To avoid unnecessary distractions, the *Scrum Team* should maintain the least number of status indicators as possible.

Posting status is all about transparency, information sharing, and motivation.

❖   ❖   ❖

If the team maintains *Visible Status*, it ensures that there are no surprises that come in the way of delivering a ¶*85 Regular Product Increment*.

Use monitoring tools to gather data on all of the important metrics for your product and process and make them visible to the whole *Scrum Team*. Note that some metrics can be generated directly and automatically from the product or from related processes. There are many toolkits available for this, but you may also have to build something yourself. In either case, the final presentation to the team should be simple and obvious. Some examples out in the wild include:

- A traffic light to display whether the process is currently flowing smoothly.
- A lava lamp which signals that all is well when illuminated.
- A Homer Simpson statue that says "Mmmmm, donuts!" when a software engineer breaks the build, indicating that its now their turn to bring donuts for the whole team in the morning!

The call to action must be unambiguous. The change from no-action to action must also be clearly shared. This avoids losing time when the team is trying to make the decision, or worse, is not taking action because it is so used to ignoring the status.

Whatever you choose, it is important that the team clearly understand (from context, from a display on the status indicator itself, or from training) how much time it has to respond. For example, the traffic light could turn yellow if 24 hours is fast enough, or it could turn red when things need immediate attention. If high reliability is crucial to the business, the monitoring system may contact team members directly via their mobile phones (by analogy to ¶*21 Small Red Phone*).

The action needed can also be predefined. For example, product defects require the team to *¶81 Whack the Mole*. Or, when the reality of the *Sprint* has drifted too far from the *¶72 Sprint Backlog*, the team executes *¶32 Emergency Procedure*. Use the *Daily Scrum* to replan and respond effectively as a team.

The *Scrum Team* needs to collaboratively develop the *Visible Status*. This will help to build greater understanding of the status indicators and the cross-functional work of the team.

Product health has many components, including the ongoing operations of the current system. There are many service-level indicators that developers may want to monitor continuously—CPU load, memory utilization, network utilization, application errors—far more than they can see at a glance. Google's Site Reliability Engineer recommends alerting the team only when problems affect end users, and then making details available for easy drill-down for further investigation, as described in Chapter 6 ("Sharding the Monitoring Hierarchy") of *Site Reliability Engineering: How Google Runs Production Systems* *[MBJP16]*. Note that monitoring ongoing operations of the deployed system itself is not part of Scrum.

How widely should the team share information from the *Visible Status*? There is no call to hide anything in Scrum. Use common sense: share as much as possible but don't bother everyone with something that affects people only locally. If you walk the gemba (factory floor) and see an indicator that is active, then find out if you can be of any assistance. Reflect carefully if you feel this pattern facilitates comparing indicators between teams, and you become tempted to use the information to identify "the better team." If you do conclude you should compare teams, please reflect again.

Of course, make sure that you collect and display only accurate and relevant status data.

When the *Development Team* members can access accurate, up-to-date data, they get a better idea of where they are. They are in a position to make in-course corrections during a *Sprint* to help them achieve the *¶71 Sprint Goal*. They often do this of themselves, with little or no overt prodding from the *¶19 ScrumMaster*.

This pattern has origins in the Toyota Production System (TPS). TPS has *Information Radiator*s, such as a large overhead board that tracks production measures in the factory. These are the system metrics. But more importantly, the TPS factory floor also uses indicators that flag the need for immediate attention. An engineer can signal that a defect has arisen in a product or in the process by pulling a clothesline-like cord called the *andon cord* (literally, "lamp cord"). This sets a small flashing lamp into action and initiates background music to draw attention to the problem. The Chief Engineer and others may come to help resolve the problem; they resolve most problems in seconds, and the lamp turns off and the music stops. If the car starts to cross the line into the next work cell, it activates a more global factory indicator and the line stops because the defect now threatens the production of that car and the entire line. It is a signal that begs immediate human intervention. The idea in turn took inspiration from an invention by Sakichi Toyoda, who ran the loom manufacturing company from which Toyota Motor Corporation would spring. His invention caused a loom to shut down and ring a bell when it detected that either the warp or weft thread had broken so a person could intervene, fix the problem, and set the machine back into motion. He sold the invention to the British for £300,000, and with the money, started the Toyota Motor Corporation.

Isao Endo states in his book about *mieruka* (visualization) that there is a need to make people aware of situations and change their behaviors and actions. *Mieruka* also must show how the situation changes after people take action. As Endo writes in *Mieruka [End05]*, *mieruka* is the core concept of gemba power.

¶79 Dependencies First

Confidence stars: *

...your *¶54 Product Backlog* meets the *¶65 Definition of Ready*, and you have started into the *¶75 Production Episode*. The team is *¶25 Swarming: One-Piece Continuous Flow*, managing the delivery of the *¶73 Sprint Backlog Item*s for one *¶55 Product Backlog Item* at a time. However, there are dependencies between some of these work items.

❖　❖　❖

If critical dependencies remain halfway through the *¶46 Sprint* and the team is still discovering more, you risk failing the *Sprint*.

Significant risks can come from dependencies between *Product Backlog Item*s, and the separate but related dependencies between the corresponding *Sprint Backlog Item*s. Emergent requirements or unforeseen events may force the team to change the ordering of its work items. For example, a team may have to wait for a deliverable from a supplier or partner, or wait for promised but late lab resources to become available. Or a critical-path *Product Backlog Item* may become reordered to be later in the *Sprint*, when the team discovers that the item has a dependency on other *Sprint* work. When the team otherwise defers work, it is in the interest of overall progress (*¶104 Someone Always Makes Progress* on page 467).

You want to make sure that the team has flexibility in its work ordering, yet too much churn in the work plan creates uncertainty and raises the risk of not delivering what stakeholders expect. You want to line up work to avoid doing setup and administrative tasks twice, but it's hard to foresee all of this at the beginning of the *Sprint*. Foreseen dependencies become clearer as the *Sprint* progresses and new dependencies arise, and new knowledge leads the team to reorder the work plan at each *¶29 Daily Scrum*. However, leaving the dependencies until the "last responsible moment" leads to inefficiencies that show up as rework, balking, and blocking: you often don't know when the "last responsible moment" will arrive until it has passed. *Proceedings of the 8th Annual Conference on the International Group for Lean Construction [Bal00]*

Therefore:

Make sure that all known dependencies are under control by mid-*Sprint*.

You want to force emergent items to arise as early in the *Sprint* as possible. You do this by first tackling the most difficult items and going into the work where dependencies are most likely to arise. This suggests a risk management strategy based on handling the most difficult tasks first. Move mutually dependent *Sprint Backlog Item*s to the top of the *Sprint* work plan while still maintaining their grouping into *Product Backlog Item*s (*Swarming: One-Piece Continuous Flow*).

The *¶7 Scrum Team* can make a rough cut at properly ordering *Product Backlog Item*s as it works toward a *¶64 Refined Product Backlog* before the *Production Episode*. However, the *¶14 Development Team* does the bulk of this analysis and reordering during the *Daily Scrum*s in the first half of the *Sprint*—a *¶76 Developer-Ordered Work Plan*.

Occasionally this strategy won't work and dependencies are not under control. Invoke *¶32 Emergency Procedure*: abort the *Sprint*, stop, replan, and start up a new *Sprint* with newfound direction. Another alternative is to revert to the *¶71 Sprint Goal*.

❖   ❖   ❖

Properly lining up dependencies raises the chances of meeting the *Production Episode* delivery targets.

Using 5S techniques (*seiri, seiton, seiso, seiketsu, shutsuke*: sort, set in order, shine, standardize, and sustain; see *The Toyota Way Fieldbook: A Practical Guide for Implementing Toyota's 4Ps [LM05]*, p. 64) to scrub the *¶72 Sprint Backlog* is one way to drill down to the latent dependencies. Because 5S can be time consuming, the team should use it only when latent dependencies pose potentially high risk.

Jeff Sutherland relates a case study from OpenView where they needed to remove dependencies by mid-*Sprint*; if they didn't, they pulled out the *Product Backlog Item*. This pattern makes the problem visible with abnormal *Sprint* termination, rather than abrogating the team's commitment by small cuts.

This same pattern applies at the scope of the *Product Backlog*. The *Development Team* and ¶11 *Product Owner* should jointly consider development and deployment dependencies, respectively, as they work together toward a *Refined Product Backlog*. Insight into long-term technical dependencies can sometimes contribute to a more efficiently ordered *Product Backlog*.

See also *Emergency Procedure*.

¶80 Good Housekeeping

Alias: Daily Clean Code

Confidence stars: *

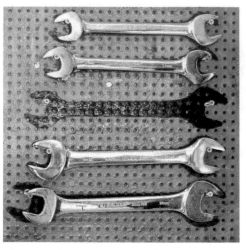

Someone borrowed a tool from the work environment and didn't return it. As a consequence the Team needs to search for it when they need the tool. Even worse, the Team might send an email to all the employees, which will distract them from current work and waste their time. As a last resort the Team might purchase a new tool.

...the *¶14 Development Team* wants to make progress toward the *¶71 Sprint Goal.*

❖ ❖ ❖

Where there's a mess you lose time and energy finding where and what to start on.

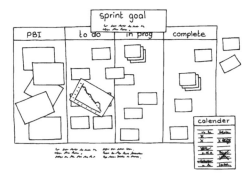

If a team member has to ask where to start working, *it's a waste of that team member's time.* If the team member needs to clean up a mess before starting work, *it's a waste of time*. If the team member builds on a mess and needs to rework what a previous team member has done, *it's a waste of time*. If the team member is unaware of the work state, the team member ends up repeating the work that another team member has already done; *it's a waste of time and energy*. If the team member needs to ask what to do next, *it's a waste of time*.

Too much information on an *¶56 Information Radiator* makes it hard for team members to separate signal from noise. This wastes the team's time.

Cleanup work accumulates to stagnate progress if the team defers cleanup until the end of the *¶46 Sprint*. The team may not clean up the work space at all, as there may be too much "real work" near the end of the *Sprint*. The mess will sharply decrease the velocity (see Notes on Velocity on page 320) or product quality in the upcoming *Sprint*.

Waste stems from working in the context of an unknown state.

Therefore:

Maintain a completely clean product and work environment continuously, or clean at the end of each day.

❖   ❖   ❖

It will be more obvious to team members what to work on when the work environment is clean. Tasks flow more smoothly in a clean work environment.

The *Development Team* needs to continuously focus on maintaining the product in a state where anyone in the team can safely start working. It will also need to continuously ensure the information in its environment is useful for the team. Continuously keeping the product in shape raises confidence about the quality of the *¶85 Regular Product Increment* produced at the end of the *Sprint*.

The product must be in a *Done* (see *¶82 Definition of Done*) state every day (or more often). The team will not necessarily create a *Regular Product Increment* as the product is in a transitional state toward attaining the *Sprint Goal*, but what the team creates must adhere to standards.

A work environment that is messy hinders team members from seeing the actual situation. Equally, a work environment that is sterile obscures the actual situation via invisibility (e.g., a clean desk policy). The *Development Team* needs to throw away only the excess and useless information, and no more. The team should maintain a continuous focus on the balance between too little and too much information.

Good Housekeeping is in line with 5S methodology of Toyota Production System. (5S has its origins in the disciplines of keeping a good Japanese house.) The 5S in Japanese stands for *seiri, seiton, seiso, seiketsu,* and *shitsuke* (sort, set in order, shine, standardize, and sustain). This methodology is about developing disciplined work habits which among other things results in a clean work area (*The Toyota Way Fieldbook: A Practical Guide for Implementing Toyota's 4Ps [LM05]*).

Good Housekeeping is not only cleaning up your own mess but also that of others. Robert Stephenson Smyth Baden-Powell, the father of the Boy Scouts, stated: "Try and leave this world a little better than you found it." Today, Scouts say, "Leave the campground cleaner than when you found it."[33] The same applies to leaving the product and shop floor cleaner than they were when you started. This approach is a significant part of the continuous attention to technical excellence that is a principle for agile teams.[34]

Good Housekeeping fosters commitment and discipline from the team. When starting with *Good Housekeeping*, the *Development Team* might feel that the effort is too great and eats into the *¶75 Production Episode*. This may be a sign that some processes/tools are too slow, and the team should address them as impediments. If a *Development Team* cannot leave the product in a clean state every day, then that may indicate a serious problem with the product, design, or work environment. Use *¶36 Sprint Retrospective*s for further inspection of what is holding you back. Create an *¶40 Impediment List* when there are more obstacles than you can handle. The rules for maintaining *Good Housekeeping* need to be part of *¶31 Norms of Conduct.*

¶81 Whack the Mole helps with *Good Housekeeping*. Whereas *Whack the Mole* is responsive, *Good Housekeeping* requires intention.

33. Lord Baden-Powell. BiographyOnline.net, http://www.biographyonline.net/humanitarian/baden-powell.html (accessed 9 June 2018).
34. *Manifesto for Agile Software Development: Principles.* Agilemanifesto.org, http://agilemanifesto.org/principles.html, 2001, accessed 23 January 2017.

¶81 Whack the Mole

Confidence stars: *

I once worked on a very large software project. Over time, our bug list grew larger and larger, until everyone realized that we had to do something. Management dispatched a team to clean up the bug list; to either fix the bugs or remove them from the list. A couple of months later, management announced with great fanfare that developers had reduced the bug list from around a thousand bugs to some six hundred, thus reducing the number of bugs from astronomical to merely unmanageable.

...the *¶14 Development Team* is in the throes of the *¶75 Production Episode*, adding new functionality to the code. You have, perhaps, committed to *¶80 Good Housekeeping* so you can sleep at night. As a *¶10 Cross-Functional Team* development, it feels like five steps forward and one step back: problems and emergent requirements interrupt progress and cause the team to lose focus. The team has a *¶82 Definition of Done* that encourages the team to leave no work undone, and to leave no known problem unresolved, at the end of the *¶46 Sprint*.

❖   ❖   ❖

There is always a tension between advancing product functionality and raising product quality.

Business pressures tend to make us view engineering problems, software bugs, and manufacturing line irregularities as necessary evils. We see them as distractions that lie outside the *Sprint*. And because developers really like to do new stuff, they often smooth over current product problems, or they postpone resolving them until the tomorrow that never comes. In software, such "small" issues often live under the radar of the tests that enforce *Good Housekeeping*. And even if one has the discipline to do *Good Housekeeping* comprehensively, one can't afford to defer resolving issues until the end of the day: it's hard to know how much time to set aside.

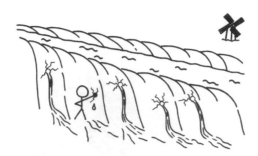

Fixing issues takes time, so we often defer such work. We believe that the market benefit is not worth the effort to fix them, or that they displace the "more important," revenue-generating work. However, McConnell (*Software Development 4 [McC96]*) has shown that bugs in software slow down the *Development Team* because they cause "stumbling" and work-arounds that create a drag on development. These impediments actually slow down other development that isn't directly related to fixing bugs.

We could administratively define issue repair as "real work" to incentivize the *Development Team* to turn its energies to ongoing repair instead of focusing only on new things. However, developers in a healthy development context find intrinsic motivation to repair issues. And we want to avoid the administrative overhead of tracking issues: the tracking sometimes costs more than the repair itself.

Collecting all issues to a "cleanup *Sprint*" leaves the product in a broken state until that *Sprint* arrives. And even when completing such a *Sprint*, it doesn't move the team along its ¶45 *Product Roadmap*. It only makes it visible that the team members should feel guilty about where they believe they stand on the *Product Roadmap*: previously delivered ¶55 *Product Backlog Item*s (*PBI*) were in fact not properly delivered.

There is some cost of switching context from *PBI* development to issue mitigation. However, when developers see an issue, they are motivated to fix it *now* while the issue is fresh in their mind, in touch within the context. The more the team postpones the change (until later in the day, or until a subsequent *Sprint*), the more expensive it becomes. Subsequent changes in the environment or in the product may make it challenging to reproduce the issue later.

Issues that the team doesn't fix **now** tend to accumulate, or become forgotten or lost in a defect-tracking system. Some issues may become legacy components of the product as technical debt grows—maintainability suffers and quality drops. Keeping an inventory is bad enough: keeping an inventory of defect descriptions is very un-lean. And keeping an issue work backlog separate from the backlog of value-generating work items makes it impossible for the team to know the total ordering of all work (issue-repairing and new value-generating). This situation can lead to one of two extremes: either issue resolution becomes a second-class citizen or the team becomes a firefighting team.

> Bob Martin relates a story of once fixing a spelling error in an application. However, many customers had built screen capture scripts that depended on the misspelled word. Management ordered him to "unfix" the misspelled word.

One of our clients found that they awoke one morning to 2000 Category 1 (highest-priority) bugs in their bug-tracking system and decided to launch a quality *Sprint* to reduce that number by 60 percent. Incentivized by the corporate reward structure, the teams met their goal—by reclassifying about 60 percent of those bugs as Category 2 bugs.

Therefore:

Immediately resolve product problems, big and small, as they arise. Don't pause to create and review a *Product Backlog Item*, but rather fix defects as they become evident. The team should hold it to be a higher priority to fix a broken product or a product that does the wrong thing than to enhance the product. After all, the presence of any issue means the team has not or cannot deliver some aspect of product value. What it held to be *Done* was not *Done*. If it's not clear whether the problem should be fixed, then the lack of clarity is itself a problem worth redressing immediately.

It doesn't matter whether the team introduced the problem in the current *Sprint* or in a previous *Sprint*: to the market, an issue is an issue. And it doesn't matter whether the issue was found in development or in the field: an issue is still an issue. Ensure that you have a good reporting path for issues up and down the *¶41 Value Stream* to give immediate visibility to all issues.

Developers should drop what they are doing and address product issues when they come to the attention of the *Development Team*. Developers should start by spending an agreed maximum number of hours (e.g., four hours) on the issue. Work should normally start on the issue without any significant engagement with the *¶11 Product Owner*. The *Development Team* should use its own judgment about whether a particular anomaly is actually a defect, but the *Product Owner* is available as an oracle if there is any doubt. The involved developers should in any case make the effort visible to the rest of the team through information radiators and the *¶29 Daily Scrum*. It is also good practice to make the work visible on the *¶72 Sprint Backlog*; keep this administration lightweight, as with sticky notes on a wall (see *¶56 Information Radiator*).

If the *Development Team* cannot remove the cause of the issue in the agreed time box, the team escalates it to the *Product Owner*. The *Product Owner quickly* decides whether to continue work on the issue at the potential expense of failing to complete all remaining *PBI*s in the *Sprint*, or alternatively creates a *PBI* for the issue and puts it visibly on the *¶54 Product Backlog*. If the *¶71 Sprint Goal* is at stake, the team may go into *¶32 Emergency Procedure*.

❖　❖　❖

One or two team members start work on the issue so that the rest of the team can continue making progress on a product increment that will generate new value; this helps better manage overall risk. See *¶105 Team per Task* on page 467.

Good discipline in use of this pattern will enable *Good Housekeeping* at the end of the day, and will demonstrate how serious the team is about *Good Housekeeping*. The end result is a heightened focus on the integrity of the *¶85 Regular Product Increment*. Also, this pattern has a close relationship to *Definition of Done*. A good *Definition of Done* will limit discussions about whether an issue is really an issue or not. The *¶7 Scrum Team* should continuously extend the definition to improve the immediacy of product repair during production. And it's important that the fix itself meet the *Definition of Done*. Just as importantly, the fix should not be a temporary patch that contributes to long-term technical debt.

This approach means you can do away with much issue administration, including the management of dependencies related to issues or issue prioritization.

This pattern can't retire existing technical debt. The team can slowly retire technical debt by refactoring, or the *Product Owner* can raise refactoring or redesign to the business level with *Product Backlog Item*s. Software refactoring is a form of this pattern at the micro level.

If this pattern causes the *Development Team* to do nothing but fix issues during the *Sprint*—which means unendingly deferring *PBI* development—this points to a serious quality problem that should probably cause the *Product Owner* to escalate *Emergency Procedure* all the way to Abnormal Sprint Termination. It should also result in serious head-holding during the *¶36 Sprint Retrospective*. See *¶33 Illegitimus Non Interruptus* as a high-discipline interim measure. *Illegitimus Non Interruptus* also helps moderate the effort put into emergent issue repair during the *Production Episode*. It does this by giving the *Product Owner* the option to consciously and visibly defer the resolution of a given issue until a later *Sprint*.

There are two distinct steps: fixing the issue, and fixing the process. The *Scrum Team* can address process changes after a calming period that follows the flurries of *Sprint* activity. The team can deal with the issues itself rather directly: each problem gets a fix. However, the corresponding process changes must consider broader context and subtle issues of organization, history, culture, and so forth. Process changes usually require more deliberation and focus than the team can muster in the middle of a *Sprint*, and team members often require *Product Owner* intervention—something we want to minimize during the *Sprint*. Except in obvious cases, leave process changes to the *Sprint Retrospective*, with consideration for implementation in subsequent *Sprint*s. One good process fix might avoid hundreds of subsequent product fixes.

There are many supporting patterns that deal with competing priorities along the *Value Stream*. *Daily Scrum* orders the work items on this particular area of the *Value Stream* to give priority to plugging holes in the dike. *Good Housekeeping* ensures that the workspace itself doesn't become flooded. *Illegitimus Non Interruptus* prevents the dike from ending up with so many holes that it collapses. *Emergency Procedure* flushes work in progress and redirects the flow.

See also *¶106 Sacrifice One Person* on page 467 and *¶108 Interrupts Unjam Blocking* on page 468.

¶82 Definition of Done

Alias: Done-Done

Confidence stars: **

...a member of the team demonstrates to the *¶11 Product Owner* a *¶55 Product Backlog Item* that has just been "completed." When the *Product Owner* asks the *¶14 Development Team* when the feature will be ready for users, the *Development Team* tells her that everything is done but that more testing is needed, and to just migrate the system to the client environment, which in turn depends on another task. Continuing the discussion, another team member says that because the item is an essential piece of the system, the *Development Team* and *Product Owner* should review it before release. "So when is it completed?" asks the desperate *Product Owner*. "You just demonstrated it, but there are still things that should be done."

❖   ❖   ❖

Each team member may have a different understanding of "work completed" for the team's deliverables.

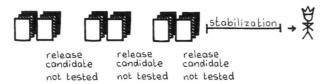

During the *¶35 Sprint Review*, the *Product Owner* needs to understand where development stands in terms of progress to be able to make informed decisions about what to work on in the next *¶46 Sprint*. *Product Owner*s need to know which issues need attention, and need input to support them in their responsibility to keep stakeholders informed. The more transparent the *¶85 Regular Product Increment* is to the *Product Owner*, the better the *Product Owner* and stakeholders can inspect it and make appropriate decisions (*Agile Project Management with Scrum [Sch01]*, p. 71).

For one person, "complete" may be when work is documented, reviewed, and having zero known bugs—for another, it may be "complete" when it does not break during light exploratory testing. This discrepancy may cause varying degrees of quality in delivered work.

The teams should be able to deliver a *Regular Product Increment* at the end of the *Sprint*. If the quality is lower than the stakeholders expect, the team should not view the increment as being releasable. Consequently, the team might require more time to stabilize, debug, and test the system. But if the *Sprint* is over, time is up.

Uneven work quality and unexpected delays may draw blame toward the team and also create tension within the team. For developers to be a team, they must be aligned with respect to quality so they all work in the same direction.

It's not just about stuff that's externally visible, but rather about anything that could be of value to any stakeholder, including the *Development Team* itself. For example, software source code that follows coding standards will cause developers less frustration and even increase efficiency when they work with it in the future.

It's easy for the team to unconsciously (or even consciously) hide the fact that it has skipped conventions of consistency or quality. Doing so creates technical debt: they owe the system some work, and payback comes sooner or later. However, these work items are absent from all the backlogs. While external product attributes will become visible in the *Sprint Review*, these remain hidden. It's important to have a standard for these internal items, even if you trust the team to do its best.

Therefore:

All work done by the *¶7 Scrum Team* must adhere to criteria, agreed upon by the *Development Team* and the *Product Owner*, which collectively form the *Definition of Done*. *Done* means the *Development Team* has verified there is no known remaining work with respect to these criteria. If the work does not conform to *Definition of Done*, the work is then by definition not *Done*, and the team may not deliver the corresponding *Product Backlog Item* (*PBI*).

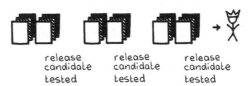

release
candidate
tested

release
candidate
tested

release
candidate
tested

It is wasteful to include items in the *Definition of Done* that fail to increase value for any stakeholder—remembering that *Development Team* members, too, are stakeholders.

The perfect *Definition of Done* includes all work that the team must complete to release the product into the hands of the customer. *Scrum Teams* start with a *Definition of Done* that is within their current capability and then strengthen it over time. A more complete *Definition of Done* gives the team more accurate insight into development progress, makes development more effective, and ensures that the team experiences fewer surprises as development continues.

The *Definition of Done* often captures small, repetitive work items that are too small for the *¶54 Product Backlog*. They are often just good habits of good professional behavior: checking in all the version management branches after programming a software module; updating engineering documents with design changes; updating inventory records for parts used; cleaning the shop floor or desktop, or measuring a component's compliance to manufacturing standards. The team can start by putting some of these items on the *Product Backlog*, but that approach tends to bloat the backlog with many instances of the same tasks. If these tasks appear neither on the backlog nor in the *Definition of Done*, the product's reaching *Done* is at the mercy of developers' attentiveness, professionalism, and good memory. It is best to create the *Definition of Done* with known internal tasks from the actual current process, and to grow it as the team discovers missing items.

*¶36 Sprint Retrospective*s are a great time to review and enhance *Done*, but the team can revisit the definition at any time. The *¶19 ScrumMaster* should challenge the team to periodically tighten up *Done*; see *¶26 Kaizen Pulse*. This facilitates team growth as it raises the bar for itself.

The *Scrum Team* owns its *Definition of Done*, and the standards of *Done* are always within the *Development Team*'s capability and control. The *ScrumMaster* enforces adherence to the *Definition of Done*—usually by making it visible if the team is about to deliver undone work. *Scrum Teams* generally create their initial *Definition of Done* based on how they currently operate, with a careful review of what demonstrably adds value.

An understandable, clear and enforced *Definition of Done* creates a shared understanding and common agreement between the *Product Owner* and the *Development Team*. This reduces the risk of conflict between the *Development Team* and the *Product Owner*. The *Development Team* can assure the *Product Owner* that it needs do no additional work to deliver work at the end of the

Sprint (such as an additional stabilization period.) The *Scrum Team* should occasionally explore whether it should add some kinds of hidden work to the *Definition of Done*.

Each criterion in the *Definition of Done* should be objective and testable. Every parent knows the following story. A father asks a child, "Did you clean your room?" The child answers, "Yes." Then the father continues, "Are the toys put away, clothes hung up, bed made, and floor vacuumed?" The child says, "No." So, do not test for activity but rather for concrete result state. This makes it also easy to formulate *Definition of Done* as a checklist—a commendable practice. Contrast this with *¶87 Testable Improvements*, which applies more to *process* Kaizen and Kaikaku on page 101; most elements of *Done* are properties of the *product*.

The *Development Team* should remove or reduce technical debt when it encounters old work that does not adhere to the current *Definition of Done*. Typically, the team cleans up only the area near the modification to limit the scope of change to a reasonable size. In the long run, *Definition of Done* helps to remove technical debt.

In larger organizations, a shared *Definition of Done* across all teams might establish a common quality level. Balance the idea of a shared *Definition of Done* against the need for team autonomy. In case multiple *Development Team*s work on a single product they all share the same *Definition of Done* as they deliver a single integrated *Regular Product Increment* at the end of a *Sprint*.

The team does not create a custom *Definition of Done* for each *PBI*, but rather applies a general set of criteria. However, a single set of general criteria may not always match all work items well. For example, criteria for documentation, calculations, and code could be different. If you have a wide range of varying types of work items that a single set does not cover adequately, you might have separate a *Definition of Done* for each type of work item. This is quite common.

❖ ❖ ❖

With a discipline regularly of achieving *Done*, the *Scrum Team* is in a position to deliver *Regular Product Increment*s of known quality. Just practicing *¶80 Good Housekeeping* can keep a team from getting in trouble with technical debt. As a consequence of each *PBI* being *Done* each *Sprint*, there are no "quality *PBI*s," "quality *Sprint*s," or "hardening *Sprint*s." Focusing on *Done* reduces the possibility of unpleasant surprises during later development, and knowing that previous work is *Done* makes progress forecasts more reliable. Having a hard *Definition of Done* eliminates the need for, as an example, development operations (DevOps) teams that configure releases for clients, which eliminates handoffs in a way that is in line with good lean practice. The ultimate in *Done* is readiness for end-user consumption or application.

A good *Definition of Done* captures the recurring required tasks that appear in multiple *PBIs* in multiple *Sprints*. Having one fixed, common list avoids having to repeat these items as *PBI* expectations or *¶73 Sprint Backlog Item* activities.

With a good *Definition of Done*, the team will avoid technical debt. Add the *Definition of Done* to the criteria the *Product Owner* uses to approve a *Product Backlog Item* in the *Sprint Review*. Good *ScrumMasters* challenge the *Development Team* to adhere to the agreed-upon *Definition of Done*; the *Product Owner* enforces compliance with externally facing requirements, communicated in *Product Backlog Items* as *¶63 Enabling Specifications*. The *Product Owner* will allow the organization to deliver only *Done PBIs* and should choose to let only *Done PBIs* into the *Sprint Review*. There are some gray areas, such as user-interface guidelines (think Apple Human Interface Guidelines), which are outward facing but which can be automated and potentially put under the purview of the *Development Team*.

¶83 Team Sprint

Alias: Hack Sprint

Let the Developers propose work every few Sprints.

...you have a *¶11 Product Owner* and *¶54 Product Backlog*. The *¶14 Development Team* is coming up with new ideas, features, or innovations that the *Product Owner* puts on the *Product Backlog* as *¶55 Product Backlog Item*s (*PBIs*). The organization is probably not yet *¶92 Scrumming the Scrum*.

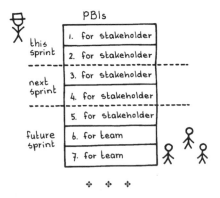

❖   ❖   ❖

Development Team members come up with ideas for *PBIs* that never make it into the *¶46 Sprint* as new higher-value items are constantly pouring in from the other stakeholders. The team gets frustrated as its *PBIs* won't ever make it into a *Sprint*. *¶14 Development Team* members can do much within their own sphere to increase their quality of work life and of the product by adding increments to the product, by creating or refining tools, or by improving their work environment. Yet these changes rarely make it to the boardroom-level discussions that usually guide the strategic development direction, so they never make it onto the *Product Backlog* and never influence the *Development Team*'s work. This might also lead to a situation where the team neglects redesign as the *Product Owner* sees no value in it.

PBIs elicited by the *Development Team* can be important from their own perspective, but new items from other stakeholders prevent the team's items from getting into a *Sprint*. Ideally the working relationship and trust between the *Development Team* and the *Product Owner* will be such that team's proposals can be accommodated among those that the *Product Owner* has developed. Unfortunately, the team often cannot convince the *Product Owner* to include technical items in a *Sprint* because the *Product Owner* may not understand neither technical debt nor the merits of good design.

It is demotivating to the *Development Team* if it has no say in what to work on. The team members want to work on items in which they have vested interests and for which they feel ownership (*Drive: The Surprising Truth About What Motivates Us [Pin11]*). For example, Google and Atlassian let their employees work on ideas of their own initiative on a regular basis.

Items that may be motivating for the *Development Team* may have lower value than those that come from the business. Therefore, the *Development Team* can't work solely on those *PBIs* it finds interesting. However, in the long term, it is a good idea to also work on those items suggested by the *Development Team*.

Getting to work on something else is refreshing and might even prevent burnouts.

Because *Development Team* members have less direct exposure to market constraints than the *Product Owner*, they are more able to propose ideas that are outside near-term business concerns. So some potential valuable innovations may be left unexplored or unimplemented if the *Product Owner* sees value only for items that are "safe." Furthermore, sometimes ideas might lie far outside the box and it is hard for anyone to see their value until the team actually implements them.

Therefore: **The *Product Owner* organizes a *Team Sprint* every fifth or tenth *Sprint* or as best suits the organization. In this *Sprint*, the *Development Team* can choose whatever *PBIs* it wants to include in the *Sprint*.**

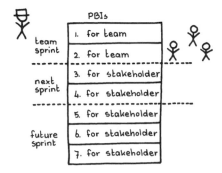

The work items (*PBIs*) should still go through the *Product Owner* to the backlog, otherwise it is not Scrum, and transparency may suffer.

❖   ❖   ❖

The *Development Team* can choose items it wants from the *Product Backlog*, to define its own *¶72 Sprint Backlog* and *¶71 Sprint Goal*, to shape its own *¶85 Regular Product Increment*, without respect to the usual practice of honoring the *Product Owner*'s ordering. In this way, the *Development Team* members really get to do what they want, and it will keep them motivated. If there is something more important coming up from the *Product Backlog*, then the *Team Sprint* can wait for a suitable moment. However, the team should not postpone the *Team Sprint* indefinitely, but instead agree on a concrete target date.

Having a *Team Sprint* helps reinforce the *Development Team*'s sense of being an *¶16 Autonomous Team*.

This approach also solves the issue of when the *Product Owner* does not invest time understanding the value of the *PBIs* that the team has proposed for the *Product Backlog*. The *Product Owner* might order the *Product Backlog* according to the perceived low market value of the team's proposals so they end up near the bottom of the backlog. Often, their weighted view of value is a function of overestimating or underestimating technical or implementation risk. But if the *Development Team* occasionally or periodically gets to decide freely which items it will take into the *Sprint*, the team's own *PBIs* will also eventually get attention. So this approach can open the door to potentially higher payoff from taking increased risk, while managing the risk by modulating the frequency of *Team Sprint*s.

As team members get to work once in a while on their own priorities, they are more motivated to also work on other *PBIs*. The idea is to tap into the team's passion and enthusiasm; see *¶91 Happiness Metric*. Avoid, at all costs, using this opportunity to retire technical debt or to "catch up." There should be no "quality *Sprint*s," "refactoring *Sprint*s," or other *Sprint*s to retire technical debt, as they dilute the discipline of *¶82 Definition of Done* to which a team should attend *every Sprint*. In the extreme case that the *Sprint Goal* is to retire past accumulated technical debt, the *Product Owner* should legitimize the effort with one or more *PBIs*.

The whole *Sprint* should be dedicated for the *Team Sprint*, so that there is enough time for the team to achieve some meaningful *Sprint Goal*. If the team needs new ideas to fill up a *Team Sprint*, one might consider hackathons or some other creativity event. The team can use the *Team Sprint* to come up with bug fixes, new features, or even developing tools. The team incorporates these items in its work plan as usual in *¶24 Sprint Planning*.

The *Product Owner* should balance between optimizing external value and keeping the team motivated.

An example is one of Google's most famous management philosophies called "Google Fridays." Some products that came out of this activity are: Google News, Gmail, and even AdSense. Gabrielle Benefield relates a story about introducing this idea at Yahoo!

> In 2003 I came up with the idea of Hack Sprints, as some teams were complaining that the pace was relentless with Scrum, and that they never had time to draw breath and just think. The idea was to have the entire team decide what they wanted to work on for that *Sprint*. It's like the idea of using 20% of one's time for undirected work ("Google Fridays"), but more focused. They did it about every 6th sprint as I recall.
>
> The team members included the *Product Owner* & *¶19 ScrumMaster*. Everyone had equal sway and you had to lobby and get others to agree to work on things together and to prioritize the backlog for the upcoming *Sprint*. Designers often wanted to look at the clouds and think up ideas, devs to fix annoying bugs, but often people came up with great ideas and got the whole team on board to build them.
>
> Not many teams tried this but for the ones that did they said it paid off in spades. The ideas were excellent and people felt motivated and that they weren't just "sprinting" with no end in sight.

Skype conducted between two and four *Hack Sprint*s per year, aligned across all teams, which gave rise to innovations such as mobile video image stabilization, in-call emoticons and screen-sharing among other heavily used features. — *[Gil19]*

¶84 Responsive Deployment

Fred Brooks said, "Faire de la bonne cuisine demande un certain temps" (to make great food requires a certain amount of time), but that's no reason to let food sit around and get cold or, worse, spoiled. It's lean to deliver when ready. But, remember, it's aggravating to have food forced on you when you're not hungry.

...*¶46 Sprint*s are flowing well and the team has demonstrated the discipline to manage its velocity and to predict its deliveries well. The customer base is manageably small, and there is an intimate trust connection between the *¶7 Scrum Team* and the market, as well as between the *¶11 Product Owner* and the *¶14 Development Team*. *Sprint*s are as short as practical given business forces, the need for a sustainable rhythm, and the need to balance the trade-off between planning overhead and production time. Business surprises may arise that require attention to market products on time frames as short as a day.

❖ ❖ ❖

Working in rhythm is good, but so is smoothing out flow (elimination of *mura* (斑)), and reducing the inventory of items waiting for the team to deliver them to the market. Having a good *Sprint* rhythm is key to the success of Scrum's short-term planning, but sometimes even a *Sprint* can seem too long given market urgencies. And the rhythm itself can lead to subtle lapses on the part of the team, which may postpone testing, quality assurance, or other tasks to the "last responsible moment" right before delivery. This, of course, violates *¶25 Swarming: One-Piece Continuous Flow*. Furthermore, the *Development Team* may believe that it's important to test everything together that will be delivered together. (While there's a bit of truth to that, it's more important to test what you can as early as you can.) That may cause the team to push testing to the end of the *Sprint*. That gets in the way of the team thinking like a true team that takes each item to *Done* (see *¶82 Definition of Done*) before moving on to the next. It leaves many *¶55 Product Backlog Item*s (*PBI*s)—and the product as a whole—in an uncertain state.

On one hand, it's nice to be able to give the market a generously sized package of product or functionality at the end of a *Sprint*. After all, it makes the *Development Team* look good if the deliverable is large. Development rhythms help the enterprise gain economies of scope by packaging the administrative procedures to deliver a set of features together, rather than administering each one separately. On the other hand, the team could have delivered much of the same business value piecemeal to the market much earlier. An early delivery can provide more timely value to the market and more timely feedback to a feedback-hungry team seeking to fine-tune the feature in the next *Sprint*. If you truly wait until the end of the *Sprint* to deliver a feature, it will take at least another *Sprint* to evaluate how it plays in the market, and a third *Sprint* to respond to customer feedback. Part of smoothing out flow (eliminating 斑) means reevaluating how frequently to deliver. Worse, product that sits in the warehouse waiting for deployment at the end of the *Sprint* is inventory, and inventory leads to waste.

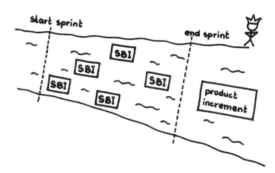

¶81 *Whack the Mole* says to deal with bugs when they arise. Yet, if the team can't deliver product until the end of the *Sprint*, the market will continue to suffer with the corresponding product defect until delivery takes place. There can be a high opportunity cost in delaying the delivery of bug fixes to coincide with unrelated feature deliveries; yet, there are administrative costs associated with delivering outside the normal product cadence.

Therefore: **Release selected *Product Backlog Item*s to the market as they become *Done* and as the *Product Owner* approves them in the course of the ¶75 *Production Episode*.** All usual Scrum quality standards such as *Definition of Done* still hold. Ensure that the cost and overhead of piecemeal delivery doesn't exceed the benefit. Keep as much of the administrative processing (such as invoicing for deliverables, updating the roadmap) on the *Sprint* cadence as possible.

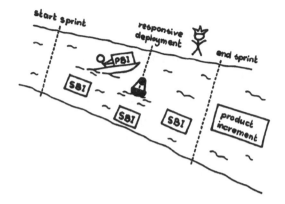

The *Scrum Team* can deploy a partial product increment to consumers as soon as it meets the *Definition of Done*. This can reduce the amount of time that a defect stays live in a deployed product. Most of the time, this technique complements normal Scrum rhythms that support the natural cadence of ¶77 *Follow the Moon*, and the team should continue to attend to other important rhythms of the Scrum cycle through patterns such as ¶96 *Named Stable Bases* on page 467. In a normal Scrum, reserve *Responsive Deployment* for urgent and exceptional cases. In more advanced situations where the market has a close relationship with the *Scrum Team*, the team can use this approach more extensively to break the normal Scrum rhythms by spreading release administration effort across days of the *Sprint* instead of compartmentalizing it in the ¶35 *Sprint Review*. This eliminates some *mura*.

For each partial product increment, the team (or, more likely, the *Product Owner* and some subset of the *Development Team*) does a mini-*Sprint Review*. This short and simple review focuses on the tactical issues of the partial product increment and leaves the strategic issues to the *Sprint Review* at the end of the *Production Episode*. These reviews need to be short and focused to not consume too much of the *Development Team*'s time. The *Product Owner* team can help this situation by taking on as many of the review tasks as possible.

❖ ❖ ❖

The team still delivers a ¶85 *Regular Product Increment* but smooths out the delivery to minimize the inventory of deliverables that are *Done* but awaiting deployment, and puts urgent deployments immediately in effect.

AT&T used to ship its main software content (called a *generic release*) on a periodic basis. The company deployed emergency fixes on demand as *broadcast warning messages* (BWMs) that comprised incremental patches. According to a 2012 article, Facebook ships at least daily, and often twice daily (*Ars*

Technica [Pau12]). More recent articles note that they ship every few hours.[35] The Finnish legalized gambling company Ålands Penningautomatförening (PAF) has an aggressive and disciplined release structure that can turn around changes in hours to respond to market changes (related to Jim Coplien by Ari Tanninen, 18 April 2011).

Key to the success of all of these approaches was that they incurred low per-delivery cost. In all of these cases, the enterprise minimized the overhead of incremental delivery cost with relentless improvement (see Kaizen and Kaikaku on page 101) over time. When transitioning to ad hoc delivery schedules, pay attention to velocity (see Notes on Velocity on page 320) and other indicators of value such as absence of defects or customer satisfaction, and manage the trade-offs between uninterrupted development flow and immediacy of feature delivery.

Delivering to the market during the *Production Episode* opens the door for feedback about that partial increment. End users and customers may come to expect the same attentiveness for a *Responsive Delivery* as they do for a regular delivery at the end of the *Sprint.* That raises the specter of a full-blown *Sprint Review* for each partial increment, with prospects for compounded feedback in response to every interim change. Giving priority to such changes takes ever-increasing time away from working on the original ¶72 *Sprint Backlog* and ¶71 *Sprint Goal.* It may place either in jeopardy. The *Product Owner* should intercept these interactions and protect the rest of the team from disruption. In most cases, the team should defer discussions about feedback on partial increments to the *Sprint Review.* The only potential exception to this rule is a business-affecting defect in a previously delivered *Regular Product Increment* that affects the end user's day-to-day operations. If an emergent requirement becomes apparent as a result of delivering a partial increment, the *Product Owner* might consider invoking ¶32 *Emergency Procedure.*

Emergency Procedure employs this pattern under more extreme circumstances than one finds in textbook Scrum. In *Emergency Procedure*, the team can deliver a product in response to an emergent request from the *Product Owner*, before the end of the *Sprint*, usually in some highly urgent context that escalates to top management as a "bet the company" high-risk issue. Not all invocations of *Emergency Procedure* entail abnormal *Sprint* termination. *Responsive Deployment* turns the exception into the rule: every day the *Development Team* works to finish what it can deliver soonest. The team manages itself to these deliveries, often without any particularly urgent

---

35. Chuck Rossi. "Rapid release at massive scale." In *Facebook Code*, https://code.fb.com/developer-tools/rapid-release-at-massive-scale/, 31 August 2017 (accessed 4 October 2018).

interaction with the *Product Owner*. Often, the team can deliver in the order that best suits planning constraints inside the *Development Team*. And often, there is enough trust between the *Development Team* and the *Product Owner* that even the *Product Owner* can add solid guidance to the ordering of *PBI* work within the *Sprint*. Such trust is necessary for this pattern to work; otherwise, the *Product Owner* will be seen as disrupting an *¶16 Autonomous Team*. To run a *Scrum Team* this way—with daily *Product Owner* engagement—requires a high degree of team maturity.

Product Owner engagement aside: To employ this pattern at all requires that the team have enough discipline to plan well, and that its market and development process be mature and regular enough that delivery before the end of the *Sprint* doesn't turn into ad hoc development. The team should have a strong *Definition of Done* and, perhaps even more so, a strong *¶65 Definition of Ready*. Lastly, the pause to assess the partial product increment prior to delivering it disrupts flow. Good flow is a prominent enabler of team throughput.

For these three previous reasons, this is a "Ha" (破—"break the rules") pattern in the Shu-Ha-Ri progression: it is outside the normal rules and only mature, disciplined teams should apply it. The pattern should be applied selectively, either in the case where there is a seamless interface between the *Scrum Team* and the market, or as an infrequent exception to handle urgent situations such as on-demand customer site visits that require the intervention of the team. The point is that the delivery should *respond* to something, and that delivery should be based on pull rather than push. The overall value proposition—including client comfort—should always be foremost in these decisions. Much development operations (DevOps) hype in software development tilts toward encouraging this behavior to help the development side keep a clean plate. It's worth exploring the consequences that might arise from a more casual use of *Responsive Deployment*.

To call this pattern "Continuous Delivery" would be a bit of a misnomer, but it remains the term of fashion. Delivery is rarely truly *continuous*; good product development depends on the deliberation tied to discrete steps. That is why a culture of *Named Stable Bases* on page 467 looms important. The vendor and market together must understand where they stand on delivery; the team must be able to step, rather than slide, towards a demarcated *Sprint* completion. Compare *¶88 One Step at a Time*. Development should proceed in discrete *¶103 Programming Episodes* on page 467 that are still best managed with *Swarming: One-Piece Continuous Flow*.

Responsive Deployment presumes that the market will absorb and use the product immediately when delivered: otherwise, it is simply a way of removing the product warehousing from the producer to the consumer premise. The lean principle of "just in time" is driven by an expectation deadline, where completing the product early may be just as bad as completing it late (for example, because of client-side inventory costs or because of possibly reduced test coverage).

Most product development reduces the negotiation overhead between developer and consumer by chunking deliveries around agreed-upon delivery schedules; that is much of the rationale behind *Sprints* in the first place. As noted above, pausing for a review during the *Production Episode* disrupts flow. In the way of metaphor, *Responsive Deployment* is like fast food: it is responsive to individual clients, with the potential downside that it may introduce queuing delays while one set of customers waits for the completion of other customers' orders. *Sprints* run more like a banquet house that can predictably deliver to a large market on a regular basis, though such cadence cannot achieve the time scales of fast food. These forces tend to relegate *Responsive Deployment* to a place more within the delivery of solutions to emergent requirements than for the normal *¶41 Value Stream* flow. Alternatively, *Responsive Deployment* might work between a single development organization and single consumer: it may be too difficult to align the schedules of multiple *Value Streams* to avoid both the delay before an anticipated delivery and the inventory waste of premature deployment.

One of the more unexplored areas of *Responsive Deployment* is its market impact. Nothing frustrates users like having their functionality changed out from under them, or to be forced to take hours to download and install the latest release. So while it's touted as a good thing, in fact, the majority of the time it's a bad *policy* to do *Responsive Deployment*. Instead, *Responsive Deployment* should be a set of *mechanisms* that apply selectively according to business mandates. In the spirit of *Whack the Mole*, a team should still always drop what it is doing to fix a product defect when it arises; whether one interrupts the client's daily life to deliver that fix is a matter of policy and, as described above, dependent on the urgency of the fix and the relationship to the client. *Responsive Deployment* of features usually makes better sense when a team is serving a single customer that they can easily bring into the *¶95 Community of Trust* on page 466. In a high-performing team, *Responsive Deployment* of defect repairs should be standard operating procedure.

Responsive Deployment sucks with multiple development threads. If you're continuously deploying software to multiple markets with multiple needs, sharing a common code base, the chances are high for unintentional contamination across them. *Responsive Deployment* is more likely to work in simple setups.

¶85 Regular Product Increment

Alias: Product Increment; Potentially Shippable Increment

Confidence stars: **

An ideal hen would lay one egg per day, and in fact their production rate is regular: once every 26 hours.

...the *¶11 Product Owner* is managing the *¶54 Product Backlog* and the *¶14 Development Team* is working toward the *¶71 Sprint Goal* in the current *¶75 Production Episode*.

❖   ❖   ❖

It is often very difficult to validate if the team has created value in every *¶46 Sprint*. However, the *Product Owner* wants to be sure that the product increases value, *Sprint* after *Sprint*.

The *Product Owner* wants to build a valuable product in the right way. The market has real needs and there is always the chance for a mismatch between these needs and the *Product Owner*'s intentions. So the *Product Owner* must regularly verify that the developed *¶55 Product Backlog Item*s (*PBIs*) are on track to create the value that he or she envisioned. Many practices, such as "Earned Value," use abstractions of the product for this verification. But such measures are decoupled from properties of the product itself, thus they may not reflect the customer's perspective on value.

To create a valuable product, the *¶7 Scrum Team* created a *Sprint Goal* in *¶24 Sprint Planning*, and used the goal to drive its work forward during the *Sprint*. At the end of the *Sprint*, the team should check the intended value described in the *Sprint Goal* against reality.

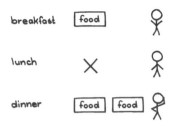

Stakeholders expect the *Development Team* to deliver something concrete at the end of the *Sprint*—something of value to them. A *Development Team* of specialists from several organizational silos, or indeed multiple *Development Teams* working together, may believe they have a real product when these specialists complete their work. But, due to lacking a shared team perspective, they may have produced nothing beyond isolated components. The whole product is more valuable than the sum of these components, and real value comes from integrating these components into a cohesive whole. The market is unlikely to care about how the team partitioned the product for development convenience.

Therefore: **Every Sprint, the *Scrum Team* strives to deliver a *Product Increment* that is *Done* (see ¶82 *Definition of Done*), usable, and potentially releasable. The team uses the *Product Increment* to validate if it has increased the value of the product, and to understand how the product actually performs in the market.** In the long term, the end users will be happier, and current use can hone foresight that can help the team head off many future risks.

The main value of Scrum is to produce a product for use by stakeholders, one assessable increment at a time, and to increase the knowledge that comes from experience using and building the product. That knowledge can help the team learn to incrementally improve both the process and the product; see Kaizen and Kaikaku on page 101. The *Sprint* can be seen as a gate between the *Scrum Team*'s intentions for the product and reality.

✦ ✦ ✦

The *Development Team* will deliver a *Product Increment* of value on a regular, recurring basis, that supports the *¶39 Vision*, reflects the *Product Owner*'s roadmap (see Product Roadmap on page 220), and meets the team's *Definition of Done*.

There is a close relationship between the increment and the *Sprint Goal*. The best *Product Increments* comprise cohesive *PBIs* that together at least achieve the *Sprint Goal*. One fundamental reason we use *Sprints* in Scrum is to deliver a cohesive increment of the product.

A Scrum product is an administrative unit that the *Product Owner* defines, owns, and manages. The *Product Owner* is accountable for product value (see Value and ROI on page 246). Scrum is silent on how cohesive a product is; we could define a bicycle and airplane as together constituting a product, or a browser and an operating system. A product supports one or more *¶41 Value Streams*: one for the end users, and one for the *Scrum Team* who are themselves stakeholders in the success of the product. The best Scrum products enable good market focus by supporting a single market (end user) *Value Stream*. Any given *Product Increment* creates value along one or more of these *Value Streams*.

To deliver the *Product Increment*, the *Development Team* should be a *¶10 Cross-Functional Team*, supporting the delivery of the increment across its organizational or role silos during the *Sprint*(s). This is a challenge for organizations adopting Scrum. Individuals in the organization will demonstrate the actual values of the organization (in contrast with the espoused values) through their local work practices. Having individual performance measures that reinforce local silo-based behaviors will fight against this cross-functional work and stop the *Development Team* from creating the *Product Increment*.

When a team or an organization is capable of delivering *Product Increments*, there will be new forces on the organization, including:

- Changes to the "triple constraint" or the "iron triangle." Time is fixed because the *Sprint* length is fixed, so scope and cost must vary to support this change.

- Though time is fixed, so is the delivery interval; there is no late delivery.

- It becomes simpler to report on delivery: the increment is *Done* or it is not.

- Internal silos that hinder *Product Increment* development will start to break down as teams work cross-functionally. This will change the roles for silo management from resource allocation to staff development (often a sidelined activity) and thought leadership.

After the end of the development time box for each *Sprint*, the team should convene a *¶35 Sprint Review* where, among other actions, it reviews the *Product Increment*. Yet additional feedback will inevitably come from the market after release; in the interest of eliciting this feedback as early as possible, the team should deploy (not just ship or release) every *Product Increment* to some constituency that actually uses it. The team can deliver the approved *Product Increment* to an ever-wider market scope over time, perhaps starting with a beta release to reduce risk and then widening to close partners and eventually the entire market; see *¶86 Release Staging Layers*. During its lifetime, the product's contribution to its users' quality of life, to the community that builds it, and to as large a community as possible, should rise to the *¶93 Greatest Value* possible.

At the end of the *Sprint*, the team should also hold a *¶36 Sprint Retrospective* to review the product development process.

The enterprise may consider splitting the product up if the products' *Value Stream*s become differentiated in their respective markets; see *¶90 Value Stream Fork*.

¶86 Release Staging Layers

...the *¶7 Scrum Team* is producing potentially shippable increments every *¶46 Sprint*.

Stakeholder feedback is crucial to agile development and to ongoing improvement and growth of the product, but it may be costly and risky to ship every release to the whole market. Testing and quality gates are one way to generate incremental, internal feedback, but internal evaluations don't really measure whether the product is generating real value in the environment of its targeted use. Such evaluations also risk creating an inventory of finished goods rather than putting those goods to work in the market.

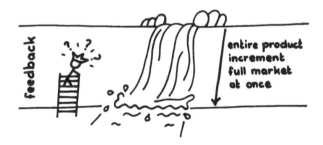

Though it would be ideal if most products were perfect out of the gate, most complex products improve over time with use and experience. Some features may become useful early in the development life cycle of a product, but some markets may need to aggregate the work of several *Sprint*s together to be able to realize any value from the product.

One can never test enough, but you can't wait to complete an eternal test suite before shipping. The market will always exercise your product much more than most enterprises can afford to complete in-house. Still, you want to avoid using customers as your primary source of feedback about whether the product does as agreed and expected.

All customers would of course rather have a full product in hand sooner than later, but premature revisions of the product may still miss conveniences that come with market experience. Though a feature may be on the right track the first time the team pronounces it *Done* (see *¶82 Definition of Done*), agile tells us that we are unlikely to get it right the first time and that market feedback helps steer the product in the right direction. There is a spectrum of customers—ranging from zero tolerance for such inconveniences to those with a higher appetite for early product availability, even at the cost of some awkwardness.

For example, a vendor may produce a Java compiler (a *compiler* is a computer tool that takes a programmer's instructions for how a computer should behave and turns it into a computer program that a third party can use.) The compiler vendor's client may use that compiler to in turn produce its own product such as a spreadsheet program. Even if the compiler isn't perfect or complete, it may be good enough for the spreadsheet company to start framing out a new product even before the vendor implements all features of the dark corners of Java. An aerospace manufacturer that uses Java to update its flight-control software in the field, on the other hand, will insist on a fully featured, high-quality Java compiler out-of-the-box from the vendor.

You could just delay releasing product for several *Sprint*s with the hope that the quality will be good enough at the time you release it. But fitness for use in the real world is unlikely to improve without real feedback, and you won't really know when the quality reaches a given threshold of acceptability unless it's in real use.

On the other hand, some customers are eager to capitalize on whatever partial benefit they can glean, as early as possible, even though the product isn't complete, or refined to popular taste, or ready for general use.

Different customers tolerate different rates of change. Customer readiness for a new release may not be bounded by functional product completeness alone, but also by the cost or risk of change. As in the compiler example above, some customers may want to be on the bleeding edge of technology while others want a more shaken-down version that reflects the corrections and removal of defects the vendor has introduced in response to market feedback. Sometimes major product changes require substantial training or adaptation efforts, and different market segments may tolerate such under-takings more often than others.

Therefore:

Identify a gradient of markets for releases, ranging from beta testers to full public release, and release every *Sprint* to some constituency suitable to the product increment maturity and to market conditions.

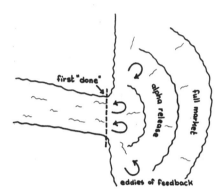

This does *not* mean that the teams assembling the product "release" it to the testers. Product release should be downstream from quality assurance efforts in the *¶41 Value Stream*. Though there will still likely be feedback to the *Scrum Team* from every consumer downstream in the *Value Stream*, the *Scrum Team* should maintain a "zero defects" mentality leading up to any release to any downstream stakeholder. Early engagement with (as opposed to release to) downstream stakeholders can help a lot, starting with their input to a *¶64 Refined Product Backlog* and ending with the feedback they provide in *¶35 Sprint Review* and the kind of engagement described in this pattern. The best arrangement is a *¶13 Development Partnership* between the *Scrum Team* and the client that engenders enough trust so that "release" becomes a low-ceremony formality, instead of a high-ceremony quality gate that triggers some large set of quality-control activities.

❖ ❖ ❖

You can deliver a *¶85 Regular Product Increment* to *someone* every *Sprint* to elicit feedback; if not, it's hard to claim that the team is agile. Perhaps start with a beta release, followed by a release to close partners and eventually to the entire market. "Close partners" might be individual or corporate clients who have a higher risk appetite than the market average, and who can benefit from early and even partial use of your product. In return for that benefit, you request that these partners provide feedback on problems, and you as a vendor can promise to do your best to resolve reported issues using the *¶84*

Responsive Deployment mechanisms already in place. Try to develop a partner relationship with a nearby circle of clients as described in *Development Partnership*. You can ship less frequently to the general market after feedback solidifies the product, and there may be a small number of intermediary layers between these two extremes. You still get feedback from some constituency every *Sprint*, but you don't put primary stakeholders at risk of receiving a product they don't like.

Over time this strategy helps to provide the ¶93 *Greatest Value* to the most stakeholders.

Good *Value Streams* operate on cadence so that expectations of all stakeholders can align along *Sprint* boundaries. Run these feedback cycles on a *Sprint* cadence. On both the possibility and possible futility of continuous deployment, see *Responsive Deployment*.

The longstanding practice of beta product releases is a common example of this pattern. Facebook always releases first to its in-house employees, who all will be served by the most recent Facebook build when using their own product. Then Facebook releases new capabilities to "the a2 tier" by populating a small subset of their servers so that the new release is exposed to a rather random group of users. The company eventually finishes with a full release (*Ars Technica [Pau12]*). Skype maintained a similar release structure.

Google maintains beta, Developer and "Canary" deployment channels that trade off risk with new features. The Canary channel "refers to the practice of using canaries in coal mines, so if a change 'kills' Chrome Canary, it will be blocked from migrating down to the Developer channel, at least until fixed in a subsequent Canary build."[36]

Telecommunications vendors usually deploy software provisionally (called "soak") so they can quickly roll back a deployment in the event that it is faulty. They may also introduce features in relatively low-risk markets prior to full release (e.g., if a new release has many changes to features large businesses commonly use, the telecom may first deploy the new release in a small town with a modest commercial customer base).

There is a risk that this strategy can reduce the attentiveness to kaizen mind (see Kaizen and Kaikaku on page 101). The ¶19 *ScrumMaster* should guard against this mentality by leading the team to an increasingly aggressive *Definition of Done*.

---

36. "Google Chrome." Wikipedia, https://en.wikipedia.org/wiki/Google_Chrome#Pre-releases, 6 June 2018 (accessed 9 June 2018).

¶87 Testable Improvements

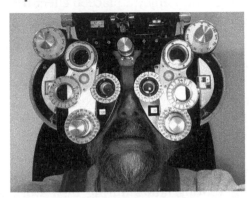

...the *¶7 Scrum Team* has completed a *¶46 Sprint* and wishes to improve in the next *Sprint*. Team members have collected information on their current performance, and are doing a *¶36 Sprint Retrospective* to determine what they should do to improve. Naturally, a team wants to take actions that have a real, lasting effect on performance.

❖   ❖   ❖

Self-improvement efforts are typically abstract platitudes. If a performance boost follows a planned change, it may simply be a coincidence.

It's easy to decide to do something in the hope that it will improve team performance. The success of a good kaizen (incremental improvement; see Kaizen and Kaikaku on page 101) depends first on agreeing on a plan of attack, second on adhering to that plan, and third on testing whether the plan worked. To change the plan without testing the consequences is an arbitrary behavior. Not following the plan of attack may mean that different team members have interpreted the plan differently and that people are following their own interpretation. It will be a waste of effort if the team blindly follows its plan without heeding data that suggest that the team is headed in the wrong direction. It feels good to focus on improvement, and it's easy to confuse how hard the team is trying with the degree the team is remaining faithful to the new discipline. Without feedback about results, it is as likely that a change can wreak havoc as create improvement. If the team is not conscious about what it is doing and the degree it is faithful to the agreed kaizen, it will be difficult to ascribe any change in performance to the planned kaizen itself. This leaves the team in a position of not knowing whether to continue a given behavior in the long term, or not.

When we take action to improve results, we expect to *see* improved results. Without specific objective measurement, we might just imagine improvement.

For example, people who buy a dietary supplement designed to make them feel healthier and stronger may enjoy a placebo effect that leads them to feel healthier and stronger, regardless of any physiological improvement.

Similarly, when we take some action to improve results, we may subconsciously change other behaviors because we are watching ourselves. For example, a person who buys a fuel efficiency device will probably see an improvement in gas mileage—not from the device but because he or she subconsciously changes driving habits to drive more efficiently. Who knows if the fuel efficiency device is even operating? A kaizen proposing that inspections might increase the fault detection rate brings as much focus to fault density as to the inspections themselves. Team members are likely to unconsciously be more circumspect about preventing faults during their work leading up to the inspection. It's an evil form of the old adage that you will get the results for which you measure, and the fault lies in measuring results alone.

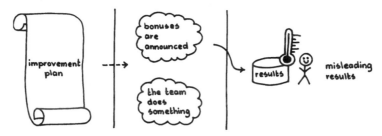

Some actions sound good, but without measurement we may invest considerable time and effort, but with no objective understanding of their impact. One of the authors worked in a large company when his division worked to obtain ISO 9001 certification. He asked the process coordinator whether he thought the actions required by certification would really result in any team improvement. The process coordinator was fully confident that ISO certification would spark considerable improvement. However, this author never saw any studies to determine whether quality or productivity had improved after ISO certification. The unspoken goal had become the certification rather than the culture of improvement it might have introduced. Furthermore, the certification evaluation is by nature somewhat subjective, and entails personal judgment about the degree of compliance.

Therefore:

Write improvement plans in terms of specific concrete actions (not goals) that the team can measure objectively to assess whether the team is applying the process change. First, measure to see if the team is following

the planned action. Second, measure the change in performance to evaluate whether the kaizen had the desired results.

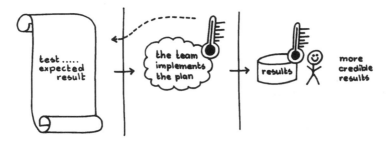

In short: say what you will do, and do what you say.

❖ ❖ ❖

If the team knows it has been following a planned set of improvement actions, then its members can assess results to know whether to continue on that path or rather to try something else.

In a *¶95 Community of Trust* on page 466, such as a good *Scrum Team*, there is no independent or external testing agent to scrutinize adherence to a plan of action. While Scrum follows the Toyota Production System in promoting transparency, research shows that decreasing employee monitoring can actually *increase* net transparency ("The Transparency Paradox" in *Administrative Science Quarterly 57 [Ber12]*). The *¶19 ScrumMaster* should encourage team members to assess themselves with checklists and reflection.

Important: This pattern is as much about knowing whether people are taking the agreed-upon actions as it is about measuring to see whether the team has improved (e.g., did your velocity increase?) First, we want to find out if the team is actually adhering to the planned action. Second, we measure whether the desired improvement actually came to pass.

This is all about getting away from wishing and hoping we will get better, moving to actually doing something concrete to get better, and understanding whether actions really had the desired results.

Examples:

- *Everyone attends all the ¶29 Daily Scrum meetings in the Sprint.*
- *Follow the ¶80 Good Housekeeping pattern completely (at the end of each day, there are no outstanding known faults in the product) to ensure we have a Done product increment at the end of the Sprint.*

> • *To ensure we keep focus on the ¶71 Sprint Goal, we will identify the three highest-priority work items at every Daily Scrum, and make sure that a team member has taken responsibility for each of them.*

Avoid measures that are hard to quantify, such as:

- Communicate more
- Work harder
- Define requirements more clearly
- Eliminate distractions
- Complete the entire Sprint backlog by the end of the Sprint (a goal that may not be a specific improvement)

Note that if the actions are not testable, it's usually really hard to know how to do them. For example, exactly how do you go about "communicating better?" So the natural reaction is to not bother trying. And you end up with retrospectives that are only window dressing, and the sense that this may be true becomes the elephant in the room.[37] Such pro forma actions lead people to view Scrum as an arbitrarily imposed set of hoops through which everyone must jump. That feeling can fuel apathy and cynicism.

Most Scrum traditions measure success in terms of ROI, some other impact on financials, or some other value proposition (see Value and ROI on page 246). Chris Matts[38] suggests that the business hold the ¶11 Product Owners accountable to some direct, measurable outcome of their ¶41 Value Stream management, within their purview of influence. For example, instead of measuring ROI, we might measure the market engagement with the product; a financial group or management can convert that to ROI if needed.

In order to implement *Testable Improvements*, you must have regular *Sprint Retrospectives*. Within a *Sprint Retrospective*, do the following:

1. Examine the previous *Testable Improvements* to see whether the team actually did them, and whether they had positive impact.

2. For each proposed improvement, ask how the team will validate the improvement (how you know whether the team took the planned action, and to what extent.) If you can't validate the proposed improvement, don't accept it.

---

37. Wikipedia: Elephant in the room. https://en.wikipedia.org/wiki/Elephant_in_the_room (accessed 28 January 2019).
38. Chris Matts. "Why business cases are toxic." The Risk Manager, https://theitriskmanager.word-press.com/2017/08/20/why-business-cases-are-toxic/, 20 August 2017, accessed 7 April 2018.

Note that some improvements require that the team "stop doing" something (e.g., "Stop picking your nose!"). Such improvements are generally easy to measure (e.g., video record you, and count the number of times you picked your nose).

To measure whether an improvement action actually works, you need a meter, a scale, and a baseline of the current performance. The team uses the scale to quantify the improvement, such as *percentage of Daily Scrum meetings nobody missed*. The meter indicates the process to establish a location on the scale, for example, *counting the Daily Scrum meetings nobody missed and calculating the percentage at the end of the Sprint*. As with other measures such as *velocity*, they are owned by the team and are for the team's use, though these measures remain transparent to all stakeholders. They should not be used for any external assessment of the team's performance.

You will be able to test whether you are moving toward *¶93 Greatest Value*.

Regarding objectivity and subjectivity: Jerry Weinberg says, "You can turn anything into a number." (Jerry has long said this, and confirmed it again in a conversation with Jim Coplien on December 15, 2017.) This is a two-edged sword. On one hand, you can come up with numbers that are meaningless, and people view them with far more statistical significance than they deserve. On the other hand, you can take deeply meaningful "subjective" concepts such as team engagement and quantify its trend as improving (+1), getting worse (-1), or staying the same (0). These measures provide a foundation for discussion and powerful discovery, particularly as one explores the *why* behind them. See *¶91 Happiness Metric*.

Contrast this pattern with *¶82 Definition of Done*, which is more about the result than the process used to obtain it. To a rough approximation, *Testable Improvements* is best when the *process* is the primary focus, and *Definition of Done* when the focus is on improving the *product*.

This is loosely related to the Japanese concept of *kamashibai*, which is a record of observations of conformance to standard work. The term kamashibai usually applies to management activities. Here, we intend that every team member self-monitor and that, in addition, the *ScrumMaster* continuously assesses the team members' faithfulness to their charted kaizen direction.

See also *Toyota Kata: Managing People for Improvement, Adaptiveness and Superior Results [Rot10]*, pp. 73–128.

¶88 One Step at a Time

Confidence stars: *

During a climb, you move only one hand or foot at a time. You can then explore a range of new handholds or footholds while maximizing safety with three points of control.

...a person or a team (any team) is trying to change for the better, either in what they build or how they do things.

✣ ✣ ✣

If you change multiple things at once, it's hard to know which one led to an improvement.

Reflections of any kind generally lead people to propose many possible *kaizen*s (incremental improvements; see Kaizen and Kaikaku on page 101). After all, every team has many challenges. Some may owe to lapses in execution or understanding, while some relate to constraints that frustrate straightforward progress. It is natural to want to fix all problems; we all strive for perfection.

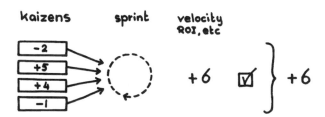

However, we can't always fix everything. It takes too much energy, and if we try to improve everything, we will improve nothing very well. In addition, trying to solve multiple problems at once often gives disproportionate focus to process concepts like priority ordering and scheduling. Every minute focusing on administration is a minute not spent improving the product and process. If we try to improve many things at once, our context will continuously be shifting from one concern to another. Most people do not do that very well (*Quality Software Management: Volume 1, Systems Thinking [Wei92]*).

Candidate improvements are often interdependent. Any change is highly likely to invalidate any current baseline. Making one improvement may change the team's dynamics such that another improvement is superfluous or even counterproductive. Making multiple changes may cause unneeded work or work at cross-purposes.

Therefore: **Attempt one improvement at a time, incrementally.** "Improvement" can be a change to the product itself, to the assembly line and tools, to the team's development, or to the development process.

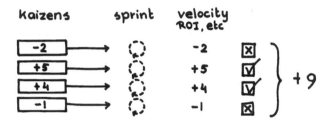

Make sure that the work queue (*¶54 Product Backlog*, *¶40 Impediment List*) is ordered (1, 2, 3) rather than categorized ("must have," "should have," "want"). Categorized lists give management and other stakeholders the expectation that the team might attack the work items in parallel. Let management artifacts clarify that the entire team will attack one item at a time. However, use common sense. If there are small items on the list that don't require the attention of the entire team together, and the items are independent, then it may be reasonable to tolerate a modicum of parallelism.

If the work queue is fundamentally unordered, as the *¶72 Sprint Backlog* might be, the team should still work on a single cohesive change at a time. In the case of the *Sprint Backlog*, the team works together on all *¶73 Sprint Backlog Item*s that contribute to a common, single *¶55 Product Backlog Item*. The associated product changes should normally attain the state of *Done* (see *¶82 Definition of Done*) before the team moves on to the next *Product Backlog Item (PBI)*. See *¶25 Swarming: One-Piece Continuous Flow*.

With care, the team can pursue a change from each of several decoupled domains in parallel. For example, there is unlikely to be confusion from pursuing a process change in parallel with a product change. "Unlikely" does not, however, mean "none," and the team should keep its eyes open if such entanglement threatens the measures one will use to gauge the success of one, the other, or both.

The team should size changes so they quickly can be enacted and, in the best cases, so the team can quickly assess their contribution (see ¶58 *Small Items*). If a given development or initiative will accumulate value only over a protracted period of time, inspect and adapt—but do commit to objectively evaluating the results of the effort at an appropriate, specific date and time. A *Product Backlog Item* annotation is a good place to record this commitment that the team makes to itself.

In the phrase "improvements to the product," the team should interpret the term *improvement* in the narrowest sense. If the product currently helps its user a certain way and the provider changes the product to make it more convenient to achieve the same result, or if the provider improves the result, that is an "improvement." Adding a new feature is informally said to be "improving" the product, but customers can just ignore additions above their ability to absorb. That doesn't harm the market but does mean that the vendor is producing product that no one ever uses. This is not a true improvement: it adds little or no value. The Toyota culture holds that overproduction is the number one cause of waste.

❖   ❖   ❖

Completing one thing at a time tends to reduce the amount of almost-*Done* work. It also helps the team—and the stakeholders—better understand the current status (as in "deliverable" or "fixed" or "operational") of production. It also helps manage expectations about work not yet completed (that all work is in progress hardly means that the team will complete everything by some deadline).

Focusing on one thing at a time and doing it well, taking it all the way to completion, bodes much better for success than trying to do several things at once. It takes discipline to intentionally decide to *not* do something that you think will be of benefit, even if another improvement effort is already committed. Short iterations help. For example, a ¶46 *Sprint* is a short iteration that provides opportunities for one process improvement at a time.

See ¶87 *Testable Improvements* for additional information about selecting improvements.

This is also about being safe from the effects of multiple changes. For an example, think about rock climbing: when you make a move, you change only one hand or foot position at a time, leaving the other three points on the rock. You can then explore a range of new handholds or footholds while maximizing safety with three points of control. So it is with development: we maintain a base of a product that works, or a base of practices that are known to work, while exploring the next product development or process improvement.

That the team focuses on only a single item at a time lies at the very foundation of Scrum; it is the basis for all continuous improvement. It is at the heart of teamwork. Contrast this approach with alternatives that micromanage work in progress, to optimize "resource" expenditure.

Some constituency should review every change with an eye to whether it needs additional work, or whether the team can move on. This responsibility typically falls either to the *¶14 Development Team* or the *¶11 Product Owner*, but the decision may involve other stakeholders such as management or customers. Use common sense, as long as the *Product Owner* maintains final authority over product content decisions and over the ordering of feature rollout. Process improvements should enjoy all the scrutiny normally accorded them at a *¶36 Sprint Retrospective*, striving for objective value-related measures where possible. Because of the risk of not being able to separate out the specific cause of a given improvement in value, interval, or quality, a team should normally undertake a single process improvement per *Sprint*. The *Sprint* provides the associated review cadence. If the *Development Team* takes two process improvements into a *Sprint*, it should normally undertake only one at a time, scrutinizing and reviewing results from each one carefully before moving on to the next. See *¶26 Kaizen Pulse* for more in-depth consideration of this issue.

One Step at a Time isn't so much a pattern you apply as it is a way to apply patterns. Christopher Alexander explained that the journey through a pattern language happens one pattern at a time. Select one pattern and apply it. If it works, move on to other patterns that may make the system better. If not, back it out and apply another pattern (*The Nature of Order: An Essay on the Art of Building and the Nature of the Universe—Book 2, The Process of Creating Life* [Ale04a], p. 216).

This principle pervades many other Scrum patterns and practices. *¶81 Whack the Mole* suggests fixing problems as they arise, which implies fixing them one at a time. In software projects, the discipline of continuous integration encourages rebuilding and testing the software for each change, rather than batching changes together. This not only reduces the magnitude of changes that affect other developers, but also isolates emergent problems to the single change in progress. It smooths out flow. In *¶80 Good Housekeeping*, the "step" of *One Step at a Time* is a single day. The end of each day should bring some sense of closure. *¶92 Scrumming the Scrum* also suggests a single process change at a time.

This pattern works well when the team can enact each change independently, or when the team can serialize their enactment. While the approach can work in complex systems, it cannot work well, or at all, when the respective changes have complex cause-and-effect relationships between them. There are important areas where it does *not* make sense to do *One Step at a Time* but rather to work in several areas at once, as a team, while continuously monitoring feedback between the changes. The Scrum tradition is to delineate the separable items as *Product Backlog Items*, and the necessarily concurrent items as *Sprint Backlog Items*. For example, the human interface of an object-oriented program and its underlying object model both reflect the same fuzzily understood end-user mental model. The design of a new feature in an interactive, object-oriented system might be a *PBI*, but the work on the code for the objects, and the screen design, and the business logic might be concurrent tasks broken down from the *PBI* as *Sprint Backlog Items*. Each evolves in response to requirements that emerge from work on the others. So while Scrum advocates the development of a single small feature at a time (at the level of *PBIs*), it nonetheless advocates that design, implementation, and testing (of any single deliverable) should be concurrent activities (at the level of *Sprint Backlog Items*). This is the main rationale behind ¶10 *Cross-Functional Teams* and *Swarming: One-Piece Continuous Flow*.

¶89 Value Areas

Trinity Cathedral/Charlie Comella Community Garden uses different garden beds to divide their work. Each bed grows one or more types of plant that are combined to produce the meals for the community.

...your product is a success in the market and more and more people are using it. New customer segments arise with a demand for new features. The *¶7 Scrum Team* still needs to deliver the product at market cadence. All teams strive to be able to deliver any *¶55 Product Backlog Item* (*PBI*) that comes along, but the teams are about to infuse a new domain and are starting to approach the boundaries of what a team can master.

❖   ❖   ❖

When the business cannot serve a growing number of customer segments with separate products, but rather needs to develop a single product that serves all markets, in many cases a single *Scrum Team* cannot quickly develop the necessary deep understanding of all those customer segments.

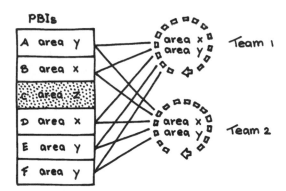

A *Scrum Team* should be able to add customer value on its own. Now that there are many customer segments, you might want to add more people who bring enough domain knowledge to the team so that all segments remain understood. Bigger teams are known to be slower because the team dynamics suffer. Also, the challenge of understanding multiple product parts in detail can result in demotivation.

Each product part creates value for a customer segment. Each component team needs specific detailed knowledge about the domain of its part. The classical solution is *divide et imperā*: treat the product as a collection of multiple products, one for each customer segment and each with its own *¶11 Product Owner*s and *¶54 Product Backlog*, so that each organization can deal autonomously with its own customer segment. But, the *Product Owner*s and their *Scrum Team*s will then locally optimize, each for their own parts, instead of optimizing for the whole product ("Requirement Areas" in *Scaling Lean & Agile Development [LV09]*). It is crucial to optimize the design for economies of scope.

When you develop one product with multiple *Product Owner*s, each working from a separate *Product Backlog*, it becomes harder to coordinate changes that cut across them and harder to give priority to the highest-value *PBI*s. This is because (1) the *¶14 Development Team*s specialize by customer segment so each team is likely not to be able to relate to needs in other areas, and (2) different specializations dominate the work cross section in different *¶46 Sprint*s. Therefore, a strategy based on doing the highest-value *PBI*s first will overload some teams while leaving other teams with spare capacity. As a side effect, not all the highest-value *PBI*s can be staffed in a given *Sprint*, forcing the *Product Owner* to select lower-value *PBI*s to keep the teams with spare capacity busy.

Organizing *Scrum Team*s around architectural components might seem a good solution, but a customer feature often requires an end-to-end slice across components, rather than just a component in isolation. A component team structure leads to sequential development, all kinds of delay, working on low-value *PBI*s, an opaque view on development progress, and unnecessary coordination roles (*Practices for Scaling Lean & Agile Development [LV10]*, "Requirements & PBIs," p. 215). The same kind of issues arise when you organize your teams around single functions like testing, architecture or analysis. See *¶10 Cross-Functional Team*.

Every *Sprint*, the *Scrum Team*s need to produce a *¶85 Regular Product Increment*. Therefore, the *Scrum Team*s need to integrate their work and handle their dependencies. Managing dependencies across architectural components is hard with many teams. Often, the product introduces an otherwise unnecessary role like a project manager or external feature owner to manage, coordinate, and plan multi-team dependencies.

Therefore: **Scale your product along *Value Areas*. A *Value Area* is a valuable product part that addresses the needs of a customer segment but which**

has no useful value or identity apart from its inclusion in the product. With this organization, each set of *Development Teams* needs to understand only a subset of customer segments while each team is still capable of delivering valuable *PBIs* into the *Regular Product Increment*.

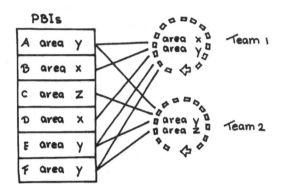

A large product can end up with many of *Value Areas*; when this happens, the *Product Owner* is not able to manage the *Product Backlog* on his or her own because of the vast amount of work and required to detail customer-segment understanding. In this situation, the *Product Owner* forms a ¶*12 Product Owner Team* to manage the *Product Backlog* across *Value Areas* (see "Scaling Scrum" in *Succeeding with Agile: Software Development Using Scrum [Coh09]*, "Scaling Scrum," p. 331). A *Product Owner Team* member typically specializes and assists the *Product Owner* in one *Value Area*. A *Product Owner Team* member does not own the product in any sense; the one owning the product is sometimes called the Chief Product Owner.

> A large energy company has the following *Value Areas*: I-Join, I-Pay, and We-Support. Each *Value Area* exists because it specifically addresses an area of customer value and requires specific detailed knowledge.
>
> The I-Join area is about finding and adding new customers. The I-Pay area handles all the billing functionality and the We-Support area takes care of everything related to helpdesk and complaints.
>
> Each *Value Area* consists of four to six *Development Teams* working together in a single *Sprint* to add customer features to the overall product.

Each *Value Area* has one or more *Development Teams* that work together in a single *Sprint*. A *Development Team* usually works within one *Value Area*. The *Development Teams* organize and coordinate their work themselves without any special coordination roles. All the *Development Teams* work from the same *Product Backlog*, and have one and the same *Product Owner*. Each team individually integrates valuable *PBI*s into a single *Regular Product Increment* each *Sprint*.

❖   ❖   ❖

Organizing into *Value Areas* reduces functional dependencies between *Development Team*s when most customer segments encapsulate coupled closures of functionality. The remaining dependencies are pushed to the implementation level, and the teams must be attentive to the risk that this pattern might worsen technical dependencies between teams. Code management tools can help resolve implementation dependencies, as can continuous integration and other agile engineering practices (not tools that support or coordinate team interactions). The *Development Team*s also need to address crosscutting concerns like architectural integrity or a common user experience of the product. Members from the *Development Team*s can form into communities to handle these concerns and create knowledge across all *Value Areas*: see ¶5 *Birds of a Feather*.

Because the *Development Team*s start to specialize in a single *Value Area*, they lose deep understanding about all *Value Areas*. But the *Development Team*s still work on valuable (from the customers perspective) *PBI*s while maintaining focus on the whole product.

The *Development Team*s in a *Value Area* need to coordinate their work. You want the teams to notice when there is a need to coordinate, and then coordinate in time with the right people. Therefore, decentralized and informal coordination mechanisms are better than centrally organized meetings (see "Requirement Areas," Chapter 9, in *Scaling Lean & Agile Development [LV09]*.) You can start with the ¶34 *Scrum of Scrums*, a common approach to team coordination.

When a new business opportunity arises that you expect will require significant capacity in the near future, add an existing high-performing *Development Team* to work on the business opportunity. The *Development Team* learns fast about the opportunity's development risks and business potential. When the business opportunity turns out to be successful, the new team becomes a grounding team that helps the other teams get up to speed in this new domain. The drawback is that it is difficult to find an existing team that is available, that has a track record of high performance, and which has competence in the domain of the new business.

Value Areas are an interim response to unanticipated spikes in demand for expertise. One can help avoid such surprises with regular use of ¶42 *Set-Based Design*. In the long term, the teams should strive to again become *Cross-Functional Team*s across all areas.

¶90 Value Stream Fork

Confidence stars: *

Sometimes you need to break an egg to make an omelet.

...your product has become a success in the market, and there are frequent requests for changes and extensions. The product starts to take on a new face that is increasingly distant from the initial *¶39 Vision*, or finds itself needing to serve two or more markets with divergent needs, economies, or release cycles. Market data suggest that consumer identities have a strong link to product identity; diluting product uniqueness or identity may reduce product attractiveness. The broadening scope of work dilutes the focus of a single *¶7 Scrum Team* so it is unlikely to meet the demands of all markets in a timely fashion. The question arises as to whether this is feature creep or a business opportunity. In light of the potential for increased value, the Scrum organization ponders how best to meet the demand.

❖   ❖   ❖

There is some correlation between feature richness and profitability, but development costs can grow disproportionately large relative to casually adopted increases in product scope. Stories abound about the percentage of developed features that are rarely or never used. Systems nonetheless evolve to keep pace with changing end-user demands, and agile development helps to lubricate that process. We often think of these changes in terms of tweaking existing functionality, but it's probably more common that products grow in capabilities. Such changes are sometimes large enough that a product can start to take on a new identity. Habit formation is a strong force in product use, and when the product changes enough to confound end-user expectations and habits, sales can get disrupted (as happened when New Coke replaced Coke, or when Windows Vista® broke much compatibility with the Windows NT® and Windows XP® traditions). However, the pressure to distinguish one's self against the competition is strong in a market where novelty reigns—as is true in most agile businesses today, for better or worse. So products grow.

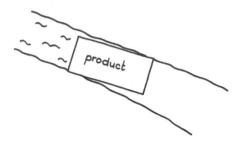

If you start by defining a product too broadly, the product lacks focus and direction, and users may have difficulty identifying with it. The same can happen over time if a product suffers scope creep. If, on the other hand, you start with a narrow product definition, you can broaden the product as the *¶11 Product Owner* assesses the market's ability to absorb new features and the enterprise's ability to manage the growth. It's noteworthy that great products grow from small products that work. The product's creator should ever be mindful that the product meet market demand and remain competitive against new features from the competition. But, he or she should also be mindful that the product not lose any valuable identity it has gained through market exposure or use. There is an essential tension between market breadth and product identity. Research establishes that consistency in product identity is one of the greatest indicators of profitability (*Research on Product Identity by analyzing the examples of Mobile Phones [Ahn07]*). The same research suggests that "being agile" by following fashion hampers long-term profitability. However, clinging to a single identity to the extent that the enterprise ignores the market can lead to results as extreme as the death of the product or even the enterprise—as happened to one of the subject corporations in the source just cited. There is broad research showing that consumers make their choices out of a need to differentiate themselves from others based on product properties (*Journal of Abnormal Psychology 86 [SF77]*), but that the need for such differentiation varies according to the degree that individual identities are entangled in the product identity. That need varies from product to product (*Journal of Consumer Research 34 [BH07]*). We don't wrap our identity around products that we think of as commodities, such as eggs or paper towels. But our identity is in gear for high-tech products. For example, 76 percent of iPhone users cannot imagine owning any other kind of phone, and the rationalization is wrapped up in the owners' identity: "The first driver behind why we buy a particular product is self-identity."[39]

The product may evolve beyond the bounds of the initial *Vision*. The *Scrum Team* may consider process improvements that would increase its velocity enough that the *Product Owner* can deliver to each market as needed. However, the nature of these improvements may differ for different markets. The team loses focus trying to serve both the original *Vision* and alternative, emergent *Vision*s as well. This lack of focus lowers the team's velocity (see Notes on Velocity on page 320).

You could grow the *¶14 Development Team* to increase capacity, yet we know *¶9 Small Teams* are most effective. Scrum builds on team autonomy, and the addition of every new team on a complex product reduces the autonomy of existing teams. If the product is complex, then the vendor cannot easily partition it into independent parts, which suggests that individual teams are unlikely to sustain autonomy over their development. Research shows that if we compare the output of a five-person teams with that of twenty-person teams, the outputs are about the same: there is a schedule gain of about one week over eight or nine months. What distinguishes the larger teams are their higher defect rates and a factor of four lower rate of efficiency.[40, 41]

Even when these *Small Teams* can work independently, *¶4 Conway's Law* says that the product taxonomy should also reflect small, independent chunks, because these products are "most important concerns for the creation of value" for the enterprise as a whole. Or we could increase capacity by adding a *Development Team* to the existing product, but that detracts from each team's autonomy and adds coordination cost. A common rule of thumb is that, all other things being equal, going from one team to two adds about 40 percent overhead.

Growth often takes place by a broadening of the product into multiple *¶41 Value Stream*s, sometimes with the appearance that each stream delivers a distinct product. One can indeed feed multiple *Value Stream*s with a single

39. David Glance. "The psychology behind Apple's fans. Blind loyalty or just wanting to belong?" The Conversation, https://theconversation.com/the-psychology-behind-apples-fans-blind-loyalty-or-just-wanting-to-belong-31671, 14 September 2014 (accessed 9 July 2019).
40. "Haste Makes Waste: When You Over-Staff to Achieve Schedule." Compression Quantitative Software Management, n.d. (before 2012), http://www.qsm.com/risk_02.html (accessed 12 April 2017).
41. Carl Erickson. "Small Teams Are Dramatically More Efficient than Large Teams." https://spin.atomicobject.com/2012/01/11/small-teams-are-dramatically-more-efficient-than-large-teams/, 11 January 2012 (accessed 13 April 2017).

development effort from a single *Scrum Team* if that team has the capacity to deliver to all streams in a timely fashion; see *¶89 Value Areas*. For example, much of the differentiation between the iPhone® and iPad® is in the skin and packaging, while the bulk of development is shared. If a single *¶54 Product Backlog* drives all *Value Stream*s, the *Product Owner* must interleave product release sequencing from several *Value Stream*s, making it more difficult to develop a release vision for any single *Value Stream*. Because a single product construction strategy may not optimally fit each of multiple release strategies for different markets, it is difficult for a single backlog to simultaneously reflect all these perspectives.

A large product can realize economies of scope. However, uniformly marketing all of a large product's features to a single market is likely to confuse the consumer. That suggests that ultra-feature-rich products still need multiple *Value Stream*s and multiple market outlets. On the other hand, differentiating a single product for each of several *Value Stream*s makes the product more complex. While the *Product Owner* and *Development Team* for a mega-product can act autonomously (see *¶16 Autonomous Team*), the marketing and sales efforts cannot. Simple, conceptually integral products grow in complexity as they incorporate new features while still retaining their identities as single products. Just about anyone who has tried to support multiple markets that share a complex, evolving component can attest to the challenges that come along with this approach. In the worst case (or often, over time, in the end) it drives the product to a "one size fits all" mentality to retain development economies of scale.

There may even be legal forces for splitting a product into multiple products, such as those that caused Microsoft to unbundle Internet Explorer from Windows®. We become limited in our ability to tailor existing products to add market differentiation.

The usual reasons to keep a single product come from production concerns such as maintaining a small parts catalog, interoperability, and code sharing in software. However, experience shows that the cost of sharing non-commodity code can outweigh the benefit because of the need to coordinate the corresponding development efforts; having a small "parts catalog" overly constrains the ability of production to support innovation. Additional motivations might include political forces such as broadening the span of control of a powerful manager, or giving in to a tradition of command-and-control management, or a fear that individual products will locally optimize instead of developing a portfolio that delivers the *¶93 Greatest Value*. These are often anxieties that come with agile transitions.

Therefore: Grow a product's functionality—along with its supporting development organization—to the point where at least two of the product's *Value Streams* have distinct delivery cadences, rates of feature change, market ergonomics, or business contexts that suggest that there should be more than one product identity. Split the product into multiple products corresponding to the dominant *Value Streams*. Each product will have its own *Product Backlog* and *Product Owner*.

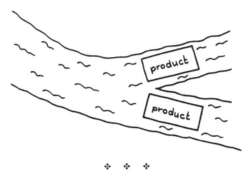

❖ ❖ ❖

No product development team needs to coordinate how it develops any component with any other product. The remaining external dependencies are mostly commodities.

The teams can now evolve each product independently to serve its market and *Value Stream*. If there are common commodity components across the new products, then yet a third organization can produce them (but *only* in the case that they are commodities—otherwise you have increased the number of handoffs). Non-commodity common parts can have an identity (e.g., domains from software to automobile manufacturing have parameterized platforms) but the responsibility for developing such shared parts should remain a shared, coordinated effort. The *Product Owners* should oversee the coordination of such efforts where possible.

In the meantime, this product organization supports market freedom and flexibility. The browser is no longer packaged with the operating system (as in the above example of Explorer and Windows), because each market *Value Stream* has its own product identity so users can purchase each separately. As a consequence, products are more likely to evolve along the lines of standard external interfaces rather than building on proprietary technology.

This raises the decision of major functionality growth to a business decision, handled within the *business* framework of Scrum (i.e., by explicitly identifying a new *Product Owner*) instead of evolving into "feature creep" at the individual product level.

So the iPhone becomes the iPhone and the iPad—almost identical products with largely shared development, but in different packaging. Coke becomes Coke Classic and New Coke. Each *Product Owner* now has greater autonomy to tailor a product to a particular market, rather than having to compromise, commoditize, or deal with complexity in terms of development coordination. Further and perhaps more important, each *Product Owner* has freedom to direct his or her *Development Teams*. Each *Scrum Team* has autonomy in ordering its ¶55 *Product Backlog Item*s for release of its product, without undue concern for weaving in releases for another *Value Stream*.

Multiple products can of course still share common commoditized parts, much as many car models share the same chassis and engine. As an example, Skoda Octavias serve one market while Volkswagen Golfs serve another—but they share most of the same infrastructure. Product line architectures and business organizations can emerge.

The Apple product ecosystem is a good example of this kind of differentiation. Building on a common base that started with a music player, Apple differentiated it into a phone product while still retaining the music player (and though the phone probably contained much of the music player software, the hardware packaging was completely new). Apple later further differentiated the phone product into the iPad tablet, and finally further differentiated both the phones and the tablets. While all products shared many sales channels, the products represented rather independent *Value Stream*s whose products Apple marketed quite differently.

Value Areas is an alternative pattern that applies when the organization can realize economies of scope by coordinating all *Value Stream*s with a single *Product Backlog*. It is a matter both of the coupling between "latent *Value Stream*s" (and therefore, of the communication overhead between their teams) and of the ability or willingness of the producing organizations to cooperate. *Value Stream Fork* is based on the assumption that all *Product Owner*s work together as a team, perhaps under the auspices of a forum such as the ¶37 *MetaScrum*. For example, the enterprise may decide to run one of the products as a loss leader, and the corresponding *Product Owner* makes that a central consideration of the product value proposition. *Value Areas* balances the forces that arise when *Product Owner*s are unable or unwilling to do this, but need to have their control consolidated under a *Product Owner* with a broader span of control. This limits individual *Value Areas*' autonomy and may be well-suited to product lines that do not need agile decision-making at the "latent *Value Stream*" level. *Value Stream Fork* maximizes product autonomy. It raises the number of autonomous entities but reduces the overall amount of control in the system (*The Social Psychology of Organizations [KK66]*, p. 314). It is a cooperative work environment based on trust (see *¶95 Community of Trust* on page 466). It tends to produce more entities that inter-work according to standards, which is a major lean foundation. So *Value Stream Fork* suits Spotify,[42] which has largely autonomous teams and a flat management structure, and *Value Areas* suits hierarchical organizations such as one commonly finds in military and public-sector contracting, where there is often a legacy of top-down product integration.[43]

Consider also *Conway's Law*.

42. Henrik Kniberg. "Spotify Engineering Culture Part 1 (Agile Enterprise Transition with Scrum and Kanban)." YouTube.com, https://www.youtube.com/watch?v=4GK1NDTWbkY (accessed 28 January 2019).
43. Cesário Ramos and Sandra Roijakkers. "Thales Surface Radar Case Study." Less.works, https://less.works/case-studies/thales-surface-radar.html, 2015 (accessed 2 November 2017).

¶91 Happiness Metric

...you have a *¶95 Community of Trust* on page 466 that shares a common *¶39 Vision*. The team is a mature team with a shared sense of *value*. The *¶7 Scrum Team* is an *¶16 Autonomous Team*. You are holding regular *¶36 Sprint Retrospective*s to increase *velocity* and other traditional measures of *value* and of the potential to generate *value*. (See Value and ROI on page 246 and Notes on Velocity on page 320.)

❖ ❖ ❖

In reflection and other self-improvement activities, there are generally many ideas for improvement. The heart of Scrum is incremental improvement— what in Scrum's Japanese roots is called *kaizen* (see Kaizen and Kaikaku on page 101). But you often don't know in advance which improvement activities will produce great benefits, and which will not.

The pattern *¶88 One Step at a Time* recommends focusing on a single improvement so the effects of an improvement activity are clear. But there are many opportunities for improvement, and you need a way to work on the things that are most likely to have the most positive benefit.

It is natural to come up with long lists of things that are supposed to help improve velocity. Because there are so many, it's possible that you are working on the wrong thing; the improvement selected will not actually improve velocity at all, and if it does, it is likely not the biggest or most important improvement.

People often feel disconnected to these long lists because most people can't manage more than a handful of ideas at a time. Having many options to choose from actually changes the emotional state, pushing it towards "negative emotions" (*Scientific American 290 [Sch04]*). People lose motivation to make the items work.

So you need to work on the right improvement, and the team must feel some passion about the improvement.

We commonly believe that people derive great satisfaction from doing their jobs well. But more importantly, they are often in a good position to understand what things can make them more effective, and what things are standing in their way. Associated with this, most people have a strong sense of responsibility toward their jobs, particularly if they are in an *Autonomous Team*.

Therefore:

Drive the improvement process with a single, small improvement at a time, chosen through team consensus. Pose a question to the team that helps it reflect on which of the alternatives on the table will best tap into the collective passion or sense of engagement, and use the answer to choose the kaizen that will most energize the team. The team commits (to itself) to work on that item in the next *¶46 Sprint*.

It's important to drive to consensus, rather than using majority voting or a pronouncement by the *¶19 ScrumMaster* or *¶11 Product Owner*, to arrive at the decision. Make the selection in some consensus forum such as the *Sprint Retrospective*. Voting and decision by fiat are both forms of control. The operative mechanism here is that the team feels it has control, and anything that dilutes that sense cuts to the core of what makes the pattern work. In the end, this is about tapping into and amplifying the team's sense of autonomy. The decision must tap into the team's passion rather than individuals' willingness to defer to any a priori "decision process" or even to objective value- or business-based indicators alone.

Affective measures such as happiness can and should be an end in themselves, but one also must pay the bills. Most "temperature readings" (affective assessments) of a team's state attempt to align other values that are indicators of business success. One of the most common is *engagement*, and there are others as well (*The measurement of engagement and burnout and: A confirmative analytic approach [SSGB02]*):

> [Work] engagement is a positive, fulfilling, work-related state of mind that is characterized by vigor, dedication, and absorption. Rather than a momentary and specific state, engagement refers to a more persistent and pervasive affective-cognitive state that is not focused on any particular object, event, individual, or behavior. Vigor is characterized by high levels of energy and mental resilience while working, the willingness to invest effort in one's work, and persistence even in the face of difficulties. Dedication refers to being strongly involved in one's work and experiencing a sense of significance, enthusiasm, inspiration, pride, and challenge. Absorption, is characterized by being fully concentrated and happily engrossed in one's work, whereby time passes quickly and one has difficulties with detaching oneself from work.

That is, the team will put its highest level of energy behind an improvement whose implementation engages them the most. This level of dedication in turn benefits both team well-being and business improvement—which are ostensibly the reasons behind the team's motivation to work on them.

There are various ways to measure the team's sense of engagement in each kaizen, but teams popularly use a simple subjective five-point scale for the sense of engagement that will increase happiness over time. You don't need to be fancy. We believe that a happy team strives to make things even better, and of course a team where nothing is working can't be entirely happy. Happiness is a measurement of overall long-term climate, expectations, and environment, and is a sum of incremental happiness improvements, (*Harvard Business Review 90 [Gil12]*, p. 88). Happiness may be a measure of engagement but, more importantly, letting the team decide what will improve its happiness sends a message that the team is autonomous, and autonomy has well-established links to a state of emotional well-being. However, even more important than happiness may be autonomy itself, team morale, and, above all else, passion. Support of autonomy in workplaces has consistently been related to workplace engagement, productivity, organizational citizenship, and generally a full list of pro-social behaviors. Edward L. Deci and Richard M. Ryan's research into self-determination theory (*Canadian Psychology/Psychologie Canadienne 49 [DR08]*) has shown this to be the case across time and cultures.

The pattern is called *Happiness Metric* for historical reasons, in line with early attempts to identify a reliable emotional predictor of success. While *overall* happiness correlates to good future performance, modern research shows that ascribing happiness (or disappointment) to any *specific* change is problematic. And though the evidence is strong that a correlation exists between current happiness and future performance, the arguments for causality are scarce, particularly with respect to individual contributing factors. Measuring (merely) happiness sometimes works—not because anticipation of happiness is causal, but rather because people are exercising autonomy. Henrik Kniberg of Crisp, the company that pioneered the metric in the agile software development space, notes that one of the main benefits of measuring happiness is to turn an organization's attention to awareness of itself; independent of any numbers, the fact that an organization measures happiness at all reinforces Crisp's value proposition to all involved (*Personal exchange between Henrik Kniberg and James Coplien [Kni17]*). As described in the work of Deci and Ryan, positive emotional and personal outcomes are the focus, rather than quantitative measures that are often politically manipulated. Such measures are nonetheless obviously empirical. In practice, teams have been inclined to measure happiness because they feel there is likely a two-way back and forth effect between happiness and improvement efforts. This is partly true, but more importantly, happiness can never stand alone (see the discussion below).

What probably attracts organizations to measuring happiness is the tacit argument that "no one can argue with happiness." Business and commercial practice have long promised a pot of happiness at the end of every rainbow. Even a short period of happiness that is just around the corner is sold like it were a Happy Hour. Though the roots of Happy Hour go way back, it is really just a technique that plays on people's desire to save a little money and to draw a few more people into the establishment.

Happiness is not the key to the Happiness Metric.

We critically revisit this premise below and implicitly explore what might lie behind any expectations for a development binge. We can better formulate the question to tap into a broad sense of value and an emotional spectrum beyond happiness, such as in:

> What can we do next Sprint that will both improve our team as an even greater place for us all to work, and improve our product so that the market realizes even greater value from it?

The team should balance the efforts they put into product quality and quality of work life. A simpler variant that builds on passion (see below) is:

> What are we most excited about, as a team, to do next Sprint to improve our process?

While tapping into the team's shared energy for an idea, temper the consideration with sober feasibility. The team should make testing criteria clear and should estimate the work necessary to achieve this kaizen. As in *¶92 Scrumming the Scrum*, account for the estimate by packaging the kaizen as an estimated *¶55 Product Backlog Item* at the top of the *¶54 Product Backlog*.

❖ ❖ ❖

The team's kaizen efforts will move in a direction that reflects the passion of the team, instead of deferring to business measures or objective criteria alone. In healthy teams, the collective notion of ¶93 *Greatest Value* that precipitates from the *Vision* drives this passion. To tap into that passion means shifting focus from the rationally dominated to the affectively dominated: the realm of feelings. There is a chorus of voices speaking to the fidelity of emotional measures, among them Jerry Weinberg and his timeless saying "Feelings are facts," (Chapter 21 in *Exploring Requirements 2: First Steps Into Design [GW11]*), and there is a good body of medical research substantiating this (see "Feelings are Facts" in *Respiratory Medicine 106 [HNWC12]*). Emotional cues telegraph the deeper concerns that matter. Dan Pink proposes that the triad of autonomy, mastery, and purpose is fundamental to the engagement that fuels business success (*Drive: The Surprising Truth About What Motivates Us [Pin11]*). Coincidentally (with no reference to Pink), Jeff Sutherland notes that autonomy, mastery, and purpose are not only the foundations of great teams, but are also at the root of happiness (*Scrum: The Art of Doing Twice the Work in Half the Time [SS14]*, p. 153). He offers anticipated *happiness* as his chosen emotional indicator.

Another key to this pattern's success: framing the chosen kaizen in terms of what the team thinks will be beneficial affirms to the team that it really is an *Autonomous Team*. If one measures the success of a team by how it makes itself feel better, the team will likely gain a sense of control over its fate and a heightened sense of *autonomy*. This tacit benefit alone may contribute as much to the emotional state of the team as do the prospects for the improvement results themselves.

The desired improvement might become part of the ¶71 *Sprint Goal*, in which case this pattern can help create the *Sprint Goal*. A series of *Sprint Goal*s line up with Pink's broader notion of *purpose. Purpose* links to affirmation and a sense of morality; Etzioni (*Society 53 [Etz16]*) puts happiness in conflict with affirmation or doing that which is in line with the team's moral commitments, with a proper sense of purpose reflecting that the team is doing something morally profound.

In Japanese culture, and particularly in Okinawa, the term *ikigai* (生き甲斐) represents what gives you a reason for getting out of bed in the morning. It is about having a sense of purpose, and research has borne out that purpose is central to happiness (*Ikigai: The Japanese secret to a long and happy life [GM17]*).

Happiness Metric is quite a bit longer than other patterns because of the follow-ing extended rationale. We have included this rationale because of our concern that there are broad misconceptions about how this pattern works and even what it means. The following discussion, based on experience and authoritative references, helps set the record straight.

Is happiness the right metric? The research shows that happiness does indeed measure *something*, and the literature broadly suggests that happiness links to engagement, which most references correlate to good team performance. It turns out that focusing on the happiness of the team indeed helps the team uncover issues standing in the way not only of happiness as an end in its own right, but of effectiveness as well. The argument for the *Happiness Metric* is that people feel more personally connected to and committed to the improvement (engagement), and team performance correspondingly improves. The common stereotype holds that this is because people derive great satis-faction from doing their jobs well. However, the research shows that in fact the opposite is more often true: established happiness leads to good perfor-mance more than good performance makes employees happy. In a Korn Ferry Institute article, the authors discuss the oft-cited Gallup study that suggests a correlation between happiness and good performance, but note that the causality is reversed from how we usually see it:

> The effort to use happiness as a measure of a society's productivity on a macro scale is paralleled and bolstered by research on the micro level, which shows that **being happy at work actually makes individuals more productive**. In a recent study done for Gallup using a longitudinal database of 2,178 business units in 10 large organizations, the researcher James Harter "found evidence supporting the causal impact of employee perceptions on bottom-line measures" like customer loyalty, employee retention, revenue, sales and profit. In a related finding, the Gallup-Healthways well-being index showed earlier this year that Americans of all ages and income levels felt less happy at work and more disengaged from what they do than ever before. Gallup found that this disengagement correlated with lower productivity and poorer health outcomes and cost companies an estimated $300 billion annually. (Emphasis ours)[44]

So, again, the common stereotype holds that happiness is a leading *indicator* of good performance. This is sometimes true, yet correlation is not causality. The passion and engagement that bode for good performance can evidence themselves in a number of emotions: excitement, confidence, self-assuredness, anticipation, determination, optimism, and sometimes happiness. But they may also trigger other emotions for which we do not hold a positive association,

---

44. Korn Ferry Institute. "The Happiness Metric." *Briefings Magazine*, 11 May 2012, http://www.kornferry.com/institute/423-the-happiness-metric (accessed 17 February 2017).

such as desperation or righteous anger. Weinberg notes that there is no such thing as a "bad emotion," and the broad research shows that "negative emotions" are key to well-being (see *Scientific American Mind 24 [Rod13]*). In one HBR article, we find that *grumpiness*, rather than happiness, bodes for good performance and that, again, the causality is not what one might think it is (*Harvard Business Review 87 [Cou09]*):

> ...in a study we conducted on symphonies, we actually found that grumpy orchestras played together slightly better than orchestras in which all the musicians were really quite happy.

> That's because the cause-and-effect is the reverse of what people believe: When we're productive and we've done everything good together (and are recognized for it), we feel satisfied, not the other way around. In other words, the mood of the orchestra members after a performance says more about how well they did than the mood beforehand.

So not only is happiness insufficient for success, it is also unnecessary. Happiness is not always a leading indicator of success, which strongly suggests that anticipated happiness is even less so. The Danes—one of the most efficient economies in the world—were ranked as the happiest people on Earth for years, and much of the theory prognosticates that it's because their expectations for the future were so low (*Why are some people happier than others? [Lyu01]*). (In fact, the Danes would not say that they are happy, but would use the untranslatable word *tilfreds*—which might best be translated as "content.")

In the publication of a study done at Deloitte,[45] the authors attempt to typify the emotional roots of great performance through a quote from Theodore Roosevelt, (*The man in the arena: the selected writings of Theodore Roosevelt; a reader [RT03]*) who suggests that the path to achievement is hardly one of happiness:

> The credit belongs to the man who is actually in the arena, whose face is marred...; who strives valiantly; who errs, who comes short again and again, because there is no effort without error and shortcoming; but who does actually strive to do the deeds; who knows great enthusiasms, the great devotions; who spends himself in a worthy cause; who at the best knows in the end the triumph of high achievement, and who at the worst, if he fails, at least fails while daring greatly, so that his place shall never be with those cold and timid souls who neither know victory nor defeat.

---

45. John Hagel, John Seely Brown, Alok Ranjan, and Daniel Byler. "Passion at work: Cultivating worker passion as a cornerstone of talent development." Deloitte.Com, Deloitte University Press, https://www2.deloitte.com/insights/us/en/topics/talent/worker-passion-employee-behavior.html, 7 October 2014 (accessed 2 November 2017).

Sutherland, by coincidence, has also used this quote, in the emotive context of a team that was "frantic" and "nervous" with "tremendous time pressure" and "skeptical" stakeholders who expected yet another in a series of failures —with "happy" conspicuous by its absence (*Scrum: The Art of Doing Twice the Work in Half the Time [SS14]*, pp. 17–18). Sutherland apparently chose this quote to communicate this demeanor of the team. But one can sense drive, passion, and a sense of team identity in both the quote and in the example Sutherland relates.

Focusing on happiness may paradoxically lead to a self-fulfilling prophecy and a "happy bubble" (see *¶28 Pop the Happy Bubble*). Peter N. Stearns notes: (*Harvard Business Review 90 [Ste12]*, p. 109)

> [A]lthough the most obvious drawback of the emphasis on happiness involves the gaps with reality that can, paradoxically, create their own discontents, there's also the risk that people will fail to explore reasons for dissatisfaction because of pressure to exhibit good cheer... Those risks suggest the need to cut through the pervasive happiness rhetoric at certain points.

Happiness, therefore, may be the wrong metric, also because it fails to predict well and works at the wrong level of granularity (i.e., while being a broad indicator, it doesn't appear to correlate to individual results in isolation). One can be temporarily encouraged or excited about the prospects of some improvement succeeding, but happiness comes from less situational drivers. A host of research (summarized in *Why are some people happier than others? [Lyu01]*, p. 240) suggests that "objective circumstances, ... and life events" contribute to no more than about eight percent and certainly no more than 15 percent of the variance in happiness. Further, "people are not very good at predicting what will make them happy and how long that happiness will last." (*Harvard Business Review 90 [Gil12]*, p. 86). Nobel laureate Daniel Kahneman has done research that shows our happiness with a given environment relies on memory, and memory is usually faulty. A person's memory of happiness focuses on the highest level or emotional culmination of an experience, rather than on any sustained feeling over the interval of the entire experience. So, the answer to: "Were you happy in your last job?" is likely to be a selective remembrance of how the job ended, or might crystalize the high point of the job experience though the overall experience was terrible (*Thinking, Fast and Slow [Kah13]*, ff. 380). These results imply that it doesn't work to tie the benefit of potential improvement to an anticipated sense of happiness. In no case does the literature offer evidence that any gradient of happiness is useful for selecting the best from among alternative improvements or mitigations.

In *The Four-Hour Work Week: Escape the 9–5, Live Anywhere and Join the New Rich [Fer07]* (p. 51, "What do you want?"), the author Ferriss properly dissects popular axes of emotion:

> Let's assume we have 10 goals and we achieve them—what is the desired outcome that makes all the effort worthwhile? The most common response is what I also would have suggested five years ago: happiness. I no longer believe this is a good answer. Happiness can be bought with a bottle of wine and has become ambiguous through overuse. There is a more precise alternative that reflects what I believe the actual objective is.
>
> Bear with me. What is the opposite of happiness? Sadness? No. Just as love and hate are two sides of the same coin, so are happiness and sadness. Crying out of happiness is a perfect illustration of this. The opposite of love is indifference, and the opposite of happiness is—here's the clincher—boredom.
>
> Excitement is the more practical synonym for happiness, and it is precisely what you should strive to chase. It is the cure-all. When people suggest you follow your "passion" or your "bliss," I propose that they are, in fact, referring to the same singular concept: excitement.

Lastly, happiness is more the result of an integration over many successive, small improvements than of any single change, and we can rarely tie increased happiness to any specific, single change (*Harvard Business Review 90 [Gil12]*, p. 88). Henrik Kniberg notes (*Personal exchange between Henrik Kniberg and James Coplien [Kni17]*):

> We've seen many examples of the metric influencing our actions, and our actions influencing the metric (but not on a day-by-day basis, more like a few times per year)... Interestingly enough our average happiness is very stable and boring, it hovers around 4.0 (+/- 0.2) most of the time. And in that sense the average happiness is pretty useless data, there are no interesting trends to follow, except some things like that the happiness tends to gradually degrade and then make a jump back up after our unconferences. The ROI of getting everyone together was directly measurable :)

Some even argue that happiness is genetically linked, and that "urging a person to become happier is like insisting she become taller." (*Harvard Business Review 90 [Ste12]*, p. 108) These insights suggest that the use of happiness at all is an unreliable indicator of any property, emotional or otherwise, of any single change.

Putting the team's fate in its own hands gives the team a stronger sense of autonomy, but autonomy alone won't carry the day. Therefore, the measure needs a connection to some purpose that transcends the individual. The team members must share some sense of value and be focused on the whole, and on an outwardly directed sense of *Greatest Value*. Consider this case study contributed by John Hayes for one of his teams. The team members ranked happiness along a spectrum that ranged from loving their job and not wanting to look elsewhere, to desperately seeking alternative employment. They started doing Scrum and started moving toward a *¶8 Collocated Team*. The team was measurably unhappy with this, as each team member valued being able to work from home. Happiness drove to an all-time low. So in one *Sprint*, people were allowed to work individually, at home, in silos. (The gap in the data comes from two *Sprints* that weren't measured, because the team abandoned their faith in the *Happiness Metric* while their impatience with collocation grew.)

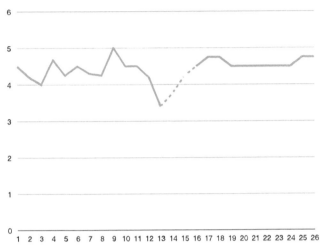

Team Happiness (Likelihood to stay working at the same job)

Velocity went up for a short period, but then curiously returned about to the level it had achieved before the change. Note, however, that happiness sustained a high level and even increased slightly over time.

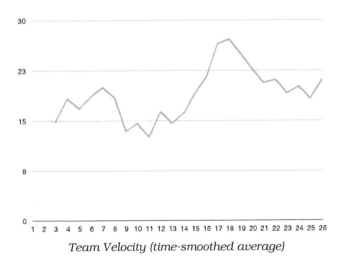

Team Velocity (time-smoothed average)

The team measured happiness as an end in its own right, with no consideration for engagement or transcendent purpose, which made it a bad choice from a business perspective. So while happiness seems to have a high correlation with performance, it is not sufficient to support any non-emotive business goal. It is important to formulate the question to the team in terms of what we often call the two products of a Scrum effort: the team itself, and the product that the team delivers to the market. The broad research bears out the danger of measuring happiness alone:[46]

> Many companies are using misleading data to define how good their culture is. If they only ask their employees to rate their happiness on a scale from 1–10, they are leaving a lot of missed opportunities on the table.

We have explored Pink's admonishment for autonomy and mastery—what about purpose? Etzioni (*Society 53 [Etz16]*) warns us that happiness is hedonistic, and that to be attentive to the kind of transcendent value (as in *Greatest Value*) and vision that goes beyond the individual, we must instead attend to what is morally profound. He notes: "Subjective well-being is surely a much more meaningful and richer concept than that of happiness." That begs a different metric:

> This views the person as being subject to an irreconcilable conflict between the quest for happiness (of one kind or another) and the quest to live up to their moral values, with the completion of the latter resulting in a sense of *affirmation*.

This *affirmation* is much more in line with the pursuit of *Greatest Value* than happiness is, exemplified in the mission statement of Toyota USA when they set up the NUMMI (New United Motor Manufacturing, Inc.) truck assembly plant in California (*The Toyota Way: 14 Management Principles from the World's Greatest Manufacturer [Lik04]*, p. 80):

- As an American company, contribute to the economic growth of the *community* and the United States.

- As an independent company, *contribute to the stability* and *well-being of team members*.

- As a Toyota group company, contribute to the *overall growth of Toyota* by adding value to our customers.

It has always been a puzzle when doing Scrum interventions in companies whose products are bad, or that the law has put under administrative oversight

---

46. Jacob Shriar. "Why Measuring Employee Happiness Is A Huge Mistake." OfficeVibe.com, https://www.officevibe.com/blog/measuring-employee-happiness-huge-mistake#fn-5054781-1, 2 August 2015 (accessed 17 February 2017).

because of poor performance, about what motivates people to stay there. We started asking, and found that it's because people "enjoy the challenge," or because the pay is good relative to other companies in the same business sector. Surprisingly few felt trapped in their jobs. The people are happy enough not to switch jobs. Yet their products are buggy and late and the business continuously interferes in development's affairs. The workers are often out of touch with their end users and feel no daily consequences from lack of improvement. It begs the questions: What's important to measure? What does happiness really indicate? The answer in these environments is often, "I like the challenge"—which indeed contributes to satisfaction and maybe even happiness, which benefits only the individual and which falls far short of affirmation, certainly at the team level.

Christiaan Verwijs observes:[47]

> I strongly believe that in a cohesive, well-running team, people are willing to go the extra mile even if it makes them (a bit) unhappy for the duration of the task. They will accept this for the greater good.

Happiness can be an indicator of moving towards *Greatest Value* if the team is circumspect and honest with itself. But, by the reasoning of the Gallup study, happiness is more an enabler for future results than an indicator of process or product qualities of intrinsic value in the current work setting. Happiness is good for its own sake. Google knows this and has a whole organization supporting a mindfulness program for its employees. The book describing this program starts with a description of "the happiest man in the world" (*Search Inside Yourself: The Unexpected Path to Achieving Success, Happiness (and World Peace) [TGK14]*). Its author, Chade-Meng Tan, is Google's "jolly good fellow." Popular culture credits the book as the source of no small part of Google's success. The author supports its techniques with impressive scientifically validated results. Create the happiness first, *then* select from potential alternative courses of action. The fact that the team is set up to chart a direction that optimizes their happiness may, in itself, be enough to engender a sense of happiness. It may remove the threat of willful business decisions trading off business benefits against quality of work life. These are the threats behind fear in the workplace. Deming says that the first thing to do is drive out fear (see "Disease and Obstacles," Chapter 3 in *Out of the Crisis [Dem00]*). Letting a team decide what it is going to do to increase its

---

47. Christiaan Verwijs. "Agile Teams: Don't use happiness metrics, measure Team Morale." Agilistic.nl, http://blog.agilistic.nl/agile-teams-dont-use-happiness-metrics-measure-team-morale/, April 2014 (accessed 2 November 2017).

assuredness and confidence (perhaps instead of happiness—i.e., autonomous decision-making) may be one key to this first step advocated by Deming.

While happiness and engagement (which may be closely linked) are important, the notion of *passion* in the work place drives even deeper. The Deloitte study concluded that increased engagement (as measured by happiness) leads to only single spurts of improvement rather than sustained improvement. Furthermore, they hold that engagement is not sufficient (and may not be necessary) to improve performance levels:[48]

> The concept of worker passion, which we describe as the "passion of the Explorer," is different from engagement. Employee **engagement** is typically defined by how **happy** workers are with their work setting, coworkers, organization-wide programs, and their overall treatment by their employer. Employee engagement is important, and improving it typically will give a firm a bump in performance. But engagement is often a one-time bump; employees move from unhappy to happy, bring a better attitude to work, and possibly take fewer sick days. However, **workers who are merely engaged won't actively seek to achieve higher performance levels**, to the benefit of self and firm; passionate workers will, though. (Emphasis ours.).

Note that the example from John Hayes above evidenced exactly what the Deloitte study found: that an improvement linking happiness to the team's engagement in the improvement led to a single bump in performance. This property of *passion* recurs in several other studies. Spreitzer and Porath call it *vitality* (*Harvard Business Review 90 [SP12]*), which they complement with continuous learning. They describe how the two together lead to a *sustainable* luster in performance.

Christiaan Verwijs offers *team morale* as an alternative to happiness and pointedly describes why it is better than happiness. It is team-oriented, less susceptible to mood, and not as biased as happiness. His research is based on data from over 10,000 subjects and over 2,300 teams. He draws his arguments from research in military psychology texts on team cohesion and effectiveness, which define team morale as follows:

> (Team) Morale is the enthusiasm and persistence with which a member of a team engages in the prescribed activities of that group. (*Handbook of Military Psychology [Man01]*)

This definition closely matches the findings of the Deloitte study. If teams are autonomous (as most modern militaries have been striving for the past forty

---

48. John Hagel, John Seely Brown, Alok Ranjan, and Daniel Byler. "Passion at work: Cultivating worker passion as a cornerstone of talent development." Deloitte.Com, Deloitte University Press, https://www2.deloitte.com/insights/us/en/topics/talent/worker-passion-employee-behavior.html, 7 October 2014 (accessed 2 November 2017).

years) then this approach supports the effectiveness of measuring happiness, to the degree that such measurement suggests that the team is able to navigate its own way to improvement.

The research by van Boxmeer et al. (*International Military Testing Association [BVBD08]*) strongly suggests that morale correlates with autonomy and purpose.

The *Happiness Metric* can help prevent burnout. Burnout occurs when people work long hours or spend much mental energy over an extended period without any respite. They just get tired of the pace. Burnout can kill productivity by reducing the team's capacity to sustain the current pace ("...there will be more or less an hour of undertime for every hour of overtime"—Tom DeMarco and Tim Lister, *Peopleware [DL99]*, p. 15) or by people leaving to find a saner environment. If burnout is threatening, someone will likely request to "stop the insane work hours" as the upcoming kaizen.

Some people (such as stereotypical old-time managers) may fear that the team members could game the system; deciding that they could best improve their happiness by taking every Friday off, for example. Of course this is possible. Like all aspects of team autonomy, one must trust the team to follow ¶1 *The Spirit of the Game*. Trust the team, but verify: the *ScrumMaster* should ensure that the goals are within the value proposition. (And if you don't trust the team, or if the team violates *The Spirit of the Game*, you have much bigger problems on your hands!)

¶92 Scrumming the Scrum

...you are using Scrum as a process improvement. The *¶7 Scrum Team* must have effective *¶36 Sprint Retrospective*s and be willing to *¶28 Pop the Happy Bubble*. The basic Scrum mechanisms are in place, and you want to leverage Scrum to fulfill its vision of kaizen (see also Kaizen and Kaikaku on page 101):

> **kai-zen** (カイゼン) n. a Japanese business philosophy of continuous improvement of working practices, personal efficiency, etc. <ORIGIN> Japanese, literally 'improvement'. *New Oxford American Dictionary, 3rd ed. [SLJA17]*

Also see Toyota Kata. *Toyota Kata: Managing People for Improvement, Adaptiveness and Superior Results [Rot10]*

❖ ❖ ❖

Only a small minority of Scrum teams make the paradigm shift to a radical new level of performance and ability to create value. This is because most teams fail to identify and remove impediments. Their work is not *Done* (see *¶82 Definition of Done*), their backlog is not *Ready* (see *¶65 Definition of Ready*), and the team does not self-organize to improve performance.

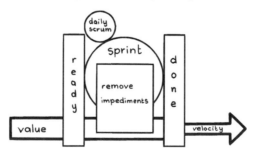

Difficult impediments may require extremely focused efforts to remove. Working on many impediments at once often leads to a lot of work with little gain and can demoralize the team.

Therefore:

Identify the single most important impediment at the *Sprint Retrospective* and remove it before the end of the next ¶46 *Sprint*. To remove the top priority impediment, put it in the ¶72 *Sprint Backlog* as a task with acceptance tests (see ¶87 *Testable Improvements*) that will determine when it is Done. Then evaluate the state of the task in the ¶35 *Sprint Review* like any other task.

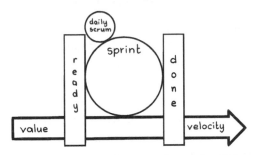

Focusing attention on the top priority impediment will have the side effect of the team self-organizing to remove other high-priority impediments as well, without losing focus on the highest-priority impediment.

❖ ❖ ❖

This pattern assures continually increasing efficiency or sustainable high-level work capacity, perhaps as measured by velocity (see Notes on Velocity on page 320). If you are not continually improving, your throughput will flatline or decrease over time. Lean expert Hugo Heitz (*Personal communication between Jeff Sutherland and Hugo Heitz, Paris, France [Hei10]*) emphasized that Scrum teams do not put enough focus on process improvement: "They need to put the kaizen in the backlog. They need to Scrum the Scrum. They need to use Scrum to make Scrum better."

While the ¶19 *ScrumMaster* owns the process for creating and prioritizing the impediment list, the whole *Scrum Team* owns eliminating the impediments. Team members can resolve many impediments themselves. In other cases, the team may need management help (see ¶6 *Involve the Managers*).

Removing the top priority impediment should yield immediate improvement in the team's performance. If not, the *Scrum Team* has not properly analyzed system dynamics and understood the root cause of the primary dysfunction.

When the team is successful in increasing its throughput or becoming more efficient, the system will re-stabilize after impediment removal. Yet, the next most important impediment may be in an unexpected place. So it is likely wasteful for the team to work on multiple impediments or constraints at once. Focus on the top priority impediment.

Scrum is a framework for inspecting and adapting to achieve continual improvement by removing impediments. Continual improvement can dramatically increase performance, even by integral factors of throughput. Beedle et al. established the perspective early on (see "Scrum: A Pattern Language for Hyperproductive Software Development" in *Pattern Languages of Program Design 4 [BDSS99]*, pp. 637–651) that Scrum is a pattern language for highly responsive and productive software development.

Past work in both highly disciplined organizations (*Proceedings of Agile 2009 [JS09]*) and dysfunctional organizations suggests that any team can achieve an uncharacteristically high state of effectiveness by implementing specific Scrum practices. For example, Systematic, a CMMI maturity level 5 company in Denmark, demonstrated that all teams could double the amount of work done by having software tested at the feature level and bug-free at the end of a *Sprint*. A second doubling resulted from a high ready state of the *¶54 Product Backlog* at the beginning of a *Sprint*.

Example:

A team used the *¶91 Happiness Metric* as a way to identify and prioritize process improvements. On a scale of 1–5 they asked: (1) How do you feel about your role in the company? (2) How do you feel about the company? Then, the team shared what would make the members feel better and used planning poker to estimate the value of things that would make team members feel better. The team estimated the value (as opposed to effort) of backlog items as well. The team estimated the entire *Product Backlog* to sum up to 50 points of value.

"Better user stories" was the top priority improvement for the team. The team estimated that removing this impediment would yield over 60 points of value. The Chief Product Owner of the *¶12 Product Owner Team* wondered if removing that impediment might double velocity as the impediment value was higher than the entire *Product Backlog* value for the *Sprint*.

The *¶11 Product Owner* put "Improve User Stories" into the *Product Backlog* and the developers pulled it into the next *Sprint* with a *Definition of Done*. The team defined this *Definition of Done* as acceptance tests that had metrics that they calculated at the next *Sprint Review*. The metrics included:

1. How many stories got into the Sprint that did not meet the *INVEST* criteria (immediately actionable, negotiable, valuable, estimable, sized to fit, and testable)? There should be none.

2. How many times did Developers have to go back to the Product Owner to clarify a PBI during a Sprint?

3. How many times did dependencies force a PBI into a hold state during a Sprint?

4. How many stories had process efficiency of over 50 percent? (Process efficiency = actual work time/calendar time)

5. How many stories were not clear to Developers? Measure by number of team members that complained about a PBI.

6. How many stories implied technical implementation rather than clarifying desired user experience?

7. For how many stories did Developers understand the linkage between the PBI, the theme that produced the PBI, the epic that generated the theme, and the business need that generated the epic? Measured by number of team members complaining that they did not understand why they were doing a PBI.

While improving the quality of user stories is never ending, the *Sprint Review* demonstrated significant improvement on this backlog item as measured by the acceptance tests. Significant improvement resulted in an increase in velocity after several *Sprint*s. After velocity had doubled this impediment fell off the top of the impediment list and another impediment took its place.

The following graph[49] shows the velocity of the team doing weekly Sprints. In Sprint 86 (around December 27, 2010) the team doubled in size. By Sprint 89, "Improve User Stories" became a backlog item in each *Sprint*. Within three *Sprint*s velocity more than doubled. The team realized an average 10 percent increase in velocity per *Sprint* in subsequent *Sprint*s by Scrumming the Scrum.

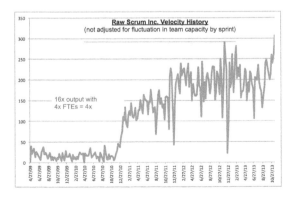

---

49. "*The Scrum Guide*: An interview with Jeff Sutherland." StickyMinds.com, https://www.stickyminds.com/interview/scrum-guide-interview-jeff-sutherland, 21 October 2014 (accessed 2 November 2017).

Some teams prefer to explicitly put the process improvement item at the top of the *Product Backlog* instead of immediately just putting it on the *Sprint Backlog*. This emphasizes that working impediments is real work rather than something done by the developers in the margins. It is also a formal acknowledgment that the *Product Owner* has accounted the cost and value of the work.

Credits to Hugo Heitz for suggesting this pattern.

¶93 Greatest Value

Confidence stars: **

...you have a vision of changing the world. The team assesses its value as the sum of individual sub-values: of the value generated by individual teams, or individual value systems, or individual products or organizations.

❖ ❖ ❖

The team finds itself not being able to rise above local optimizations and short-term thinking. When teams assess overall value by adding the value from relatively independent contributing efforts, they can too easily to optimize the parts at the expense of the whole.

A *¶7 Scrum Team* exists to create and sustain value. If you don't contemplate beyond your navel, your impact is likely to be local and of relatively inconsequential value. It doesn't take much effort to work in isolation, either as an individual or a team, and managers feel that they easily can reward individual contributions. However, that can lead to being blindsided. Acting from the perspective of an imagined isolation can do great harm rather than serve the greater good. On the other hand, if you strive immediately for world peace, you are unlikely to succeed.

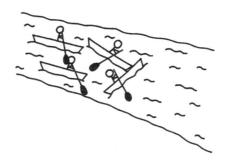

Therefore:

Create the greatest overall value at the greatest scale and scope within the enterprise's span of influence, and continuously strive to expand that scope. Manage work locally with a view to the Whole, using effective engagement and feedback, to eliminate local optimizations. If the team is successful, the individual doesn't matter. If the product is successful, the team doesn't matter. If the company is successful, the product doesn't matter. If the country is successful, the company doesn't matter.

A good *¶39 Vision* points beyond itself: ensure that your *Vision* does so. Use ceremony and celebration to reinforce relationships in the organization and the cooperation it fosters, so that organizational Wholeness doesn't remain an abstraction. Extend this consideration beyond the enterprise to the broader community of value.

❖ ❖ ❖

Jeff Sutherland relates a story from his days at the medical software company IDX.[50] Mary Rettig, the *¶19 ScrumMaster*, asked him how she could achieve a perfect rating of ten on the corporate performance appraisal. Jeff responded that if she met all of the corporate reviewers' expectations, that she would achieve a rating of five. Exceeding the expectations resulted in a rating of six. If Mary's own team, together with the *¶11 Product Owner*, agreed that Mary's work exceeded expectations, she would get a seven. If the CEO said that the corporate direction and success owed directly to Mary's contribution, she would achieve an eight. If customers were writing rave reviews about Mary's work in particular, she could get a nine. To get a ten, she had to appear on the cover of the likes of *Business Week* or *Harvard Business Review*.

The next year, Mary's team earned a ten with her support as ScrumMaster.

---

50. Jeff Sutherland. "Agile Performance Reviews." JeffSutherland.com, http://jeffsutherland.com/2006/11/agile-performance-reviews.html (accessed 27 January 2019).

The principle works at all scales. Mary's example was a win-win between an individual and a team; the same principle applies between teams. At a European company that makes telecommunications software, one of the products needed to split the first column in the Person relation of the database into two columns, for the Surname and Given Name. Another product, which uses the same database, could live with that but would have preferred to keep the single column and to avoid the costly database conversion. The *Product Owners* together decided that it was in the best long-term interest of the value proposition to go to the two-column format. That caused one product to absorb a short-term loss that owed to the conversion cost, but which was more than compensated by increases in overall corporate-wide results made possible by the conversion.

At Powerhouse (Almere, Netherlands) in 2015, two teams both needed to create the same interface to the workflow system for their *¶55 Product Backlog Items*. The teams agreed to add the interface work to the *¶72 Sprint Backlog* of just one of the teams to avoid duplicated work. During the *¶46 Sprint*, other work delayed that team's progress and the other team picked up the work instead.

And the pattern extends beyond team boundaries. Remember the Toyota USA mission statement (*The Toyota Way: 14 Management Principles from the World's Greatest Manufacturer [Lik04]*, p. 80):

- As an American company, contribute to the economic growth of the *community* and the United States.

- As an independent company, *contribute to the stability* and *well-being of team members*.

- As a Toyota group company, contribute to the *overall growth of Toyota* by adding value to our customers.

Patterns like *¶106 Sacrifice One Person* on page 467 and *¶107 Day Care* on page 468 are exemplary of this non-local thinking.

A great *Vision* aspires at least in part to this *Greatest Value*.

At the end of its life, when a product ceases to provide value, the stakeholders should celebrate its life in a *¶94 Product Wake*.

¶94 Product Wake

All good things must come to an end.

…your product has striven to succeed and may even have enjoyed a long life —or perhaps not—but in any case, the *¶7 Scrum Team* has achieved the *¶39 Vision* or its relevance is past, or it becomes obvious that the product will not achieve its *Vision*, or people agree that the *Vision* is so misplaced as not to further pursue it.

❖ ❖ ❖

Killing off products is often what organizations are worst at. Few living things are immortal, and the cycles of nature ultimately bring great works back to the dust from which they arose.

People become invested in their creations, almost as if they were their children, born out of love and noble aspirations. This happens at the level of individual visionaries (like *¶11 Product Owner*s) but also at the level of entire enterprises or communities (like the Saturn automobile, or the Philadelphia Giants, or Nokia, or the Lisp programming language). It's always possible to put enough energy into a system to fight entropy, but at some point, the energy and cost expended aren't worth the limited harmony that the product contributes to the environment.

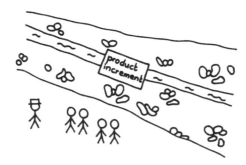

You'd like products to last forever, but growth leads to clutter, and humanity learns in jumps and stages that usually leave the creations of human endeavor obsolete. You could perpetuate them into the future but the benefit and utility sometimes don't cover the pain and effort to sustain them.

And endings can be painful. To end a product is to bring an end to the livelihood of many. The demise of a product can leave the bereaved in a state of denial, and closure comes hard. Yet to heroically strive to keep the product afloat is usually futile and results in repeated increments of layoffs and death by a thousand cuts.

Often, when ¶89 *Value Areas* diversify within a product or as the result of a ¶90 *Value Stream Fork*, a product's demise might give rise to its own successor. Even though the product may disappear along with its old identity, the market need may persist.

Therefore: **At the end of its life, give a product a decent burial.** Bring development efforts to closure with finality and dignity. Keep everything transparent so that the demise unfolds in line with stakeholders' expectations. Create a transition of good grief.

Hold a retrospective to reflect on the product's place in history and to archive key learnings. One wonders if NeXT (a company founded by Steve Jobs in 1985) consciously archived the technology that would pop up in Apple a few months later. If there are bright spots in the product's history worth celebrating, by all means celebrate them.

❖ ❖ ❖

Scrum doesn't say when to kill a product's development, but it does tell us that the *Product Owner* is accountable for value. The *Product Owner* should be the final decision point, though the need here is strong for as broad a consensus as possible. ROI is one consideration. And timing is everything: it's good to kill a product before it ends a slide into negative value from which there is no return. Data, forecasts, and analytics can help, but it is not easy to dismiss the valid place of feeling and experience in these decisions.

Google in particular has been good at killing off low-value lines of business, such as Google Video, Google Desktop, Wave—no fewer than thirty-seven products at this writing. This is not to say that they maintain only a nose-to-the-grindstone, near-term profitability focus—they continue to explore self-driving cars, energy-producing kites, and a host of other high-risk ventures.

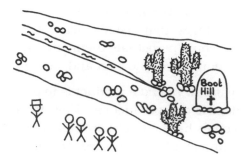

Death isn't always about killing: in the norm, it's an everyday part of life. Sometimes what were once good products simply come to the end of their useful life. Customized software to support a town festival is retired after the festival is over. Such ends-of-the-road are particularly worth celebrating and reflecting upon.

Try to bring finality to the demise. Be done and move on. This pattern is named for the ceremony that the team might hold to bring the demise to closure, and such a ceremony can help a team and its people move on. Look for opportunities to apply the talent in new or existing products—both the *Product Owner* and *¶19 ScrumMaster* have responsibilities here, to support the individuals on the team and help them to their transition to a new station in life.

That a product comes to its end doesn't necessarily imply that its *Scrum Team* will split up. Teams often stick together across product developments within a corporation and sometimes across companies. See *¶15 Stable Teams*.

¶53 Money for Nothing has much in common with this pattern, because it might bring development to a "premature" end in light of optimizing overall value. See also *¶125 Failed Project Wake* on page 469.

CHAPTER 4

Composing Your Own Pattern Language

The pattern languages described in this book are generic. They describe patterns as general forms from which individual teams can choose to build a foundation for their own work. Yet every product is different and every team is different. While your team should take to heart many of the patterns in this book, your insight (and experience) will lead you to leave some out. And, what's more, you will find some of your own.

Alexander recommends that you should get started with a pattern language by selecting the patterns that speak to you. You can do that with each of the two pattern languages in this book (the Product Organization Pattern Language on page 11 and the Value Stream Pattern Language on page 185). You are using the patterns to build a one-off Scrum instance as an open-ended project in its own right. Hiroshi Nakano, a colleague of Christopher Alexander, uses the term *project language* for the set of patterns with which you are working at any given moment.

After you have started, you may discover other patterns that you want to try. Some of them may be Scrum patterns that are beyond the scope of this initial work, while others may relate to specific practices such as pair development or budget-less development. And you may discover variation in how you apply different patterns to different teams within your development effort or your organization. You may want to tailor some of the patterns to your own environment. Alexander recommends that a community take ownership of the patterns in its pattern language, and that the community meet annually to formally delete and add patterns. As this set of patterns matures it becomes a self-standing pattern language in its own right. Alexander subtly uses the phrase "*a* pattern language" to describe the generic patterns that one can find in a book, and "*the* pattern language" to describe the version which you have tailored to your organization.

Project Languages

There are no projects in Scrum. The term as used in project management usually refers to a work program that has a beginning, an end, and an expected objective. As such, projects have fixed scope and fixed budget. In Scrum, you always get another chance in the next Sprint, as is necessary on any complex development with unforeseeable requirements. So, in that sense, we do not use the term "project" in Scrum.

The pattern community, however, has adopted the term *project* in a different way. Christopher Alexander humbly called his original pattern collection "*A* Pattern Language" rather than "*The* Pattern Language." His intent was that people pick and choose patterns from his book, add some of their own, and create their *own* language that communicated the vision of what to build. In the same way, you can choose patterns in this book that together will help you build the Scrum team that you envision. There is no single right path.

Hiroshi Nakano, an architect (and now professor) who worked with Alexander on the Eishen school project, calls these derived languages *project languages*. An organization starts to create a project language by going through the pattern book and putting yellow sticky notes on the patterns that "feel right." Then the group arranges those in order to create a sequence to follow as they build their dream organization. Each pattern guides an act of growth or repair to your organization and its development process at successive steps of improvement. Adopt one pattern at a time: try one, and if it works, keep it; otherwise, discard it, and try another. You are likely to add your own patterns along the way. Revisit your sequence frequently so you are always applying a pattern that best increases the wholeness of the entire organization.

Others have gone before you and done the same. In the next section we'll look at one example from the co-creator of Scrum, Jeff Sutherland.

A Project Language of Highly Effective Teams

Jeff Sutherland describes a project language that he believes can get teams off to a good start and can help make even the best teams even better. These patterns unfold over time as a sequence that the team follows to improve its Scrum team, *¶88 One Step at a Time*.

Jeff's project language unfolds like this:

1. First, just get started. Start with *¶15 Stable Teams*.

2. Next, decide how you are going to size your releases every ¶46 *Sprint*. Start developing and establish a velocity (see Notes on Velocity on page 320) and bring it into statistical control: use ¶66 *Yesterday's Weather*.

3. Next, work on getting stuff *Done* (see ¶82 *Definition of Done*) instead of foundering in rework. It takes teamwork to do that. Use the pattern ¶25 *Swarming: One-Piece Continuous Flow*.

4. Interruptions are one of the largest potential killers of velocity. You need to know how to deal with interruptions during the *Sprint*. We presume you have a ¶19 *ScrumMaster*, but you need a more finessed technique that suggests a framework of discipline to make interruptions visible and structure how you deal with them. Try ¶33 *Illegitimus Non Interruptus*.

5. Focus on quality from the beginning, *every day*. Early on, strive for ¶80 *Good Housekeeping*.

6. Stuff happens, and dealing with emergencies is a discipline. Align the organization to deal with emergencies using the disciplined replanning of ¶32 *Emergency Procedure*.

7. The heart of Scrum is process improvement. Get into a rhythm of improving your process every *Sprint* with ¶92 *Scrumming the Scrum*.

8. Part of improving is to measure—but measure more with heart than with raw numbers. Drive forward with the ¶91 *Happiness Metric*.

9. Revisit how you are sizing your *Sprint*s. Instead of pushing the team to take more and more into the *Sprint*, refocus on *Yesterday's Weather* and give yourself room to improve. Try ¶74 *Teams That Finish Early Accelerate Faster*.

Your Own Pattern Language

Maybe you used this book to build and grow a sequence for your first Scrum organization. Maybe it worked well and you learned some things and you found an opportunity to repeat the experience with a new product, a new ¶7 *Scrum Team*, and a new ¶41 *Value Stream*. The sequences may have been different for each one. Maybe you even added new patterns that applied only to some of the developments and not to others.

As described earlier, this book describes *a* (not *the*) pattern language for value streams and *a* (not *the*) pattern language for product organizations. You started with those and created *your* particular sequences for *your* particular value streams and organizations. Maybe all of these were within the same organization, or perhaps just the same industry, such that most of the patterns were common to all of them but some of the patterns customized the value stream and organization for a particular context. It might be that you have *your* own pattern language that is a unification of the sequences you have discovered.

After all, when we wrote this book, all we had was a sea of patterns and the sequences people used to weave them together. Looking at the possible combinations of patterns in the sequences, we then created the languages in this book. You can do the same thing for your own organization or industry, starting with the patterns you used in your sequences and combining them into a single language that all your *Scrum Teams* can share. For example, let's say that you discovered these sequences:

$$A \rightarrow B \rightarrow D \rightarrow C$$
$$A \rightarrow B \rightarrow C \rightarrow D \rightarrow F$$
$$A \rightarrow E \rightarrow F$$

Maybe A, B, and C are from this book and the rest are patterns that you have discovered. You might express a language that will generate all of these sequences this way:

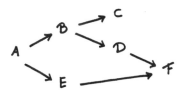

You don't have to factor all of your patterns into the common language. Individual Scrums can just maintain their own local variant patterns if they have unique, local needs. All of the Scrums, along with management and potentially other stakeholders, should meet about once a year to review new patterns, retire outdated ones, and to otherwise update the pattern languages. This becomes a powerful way for organizations to manage their process knowledge and to share ideas about how to make Scrum work in different parts of your organization or industry. You might organize one of your first ¶5 *Birds of a Feather* to develop the sequence for rolling out Scrum in your organization. That same *Birds of a Feather* or another one like it might be the body that meets annually to evolve your shared pattern languages.

With regard to adding your own patterns to your project language, we send our cautious encouragement. One does not decide to create a new pattern lightly. A pattern earns its wings by building on multiple known examples (we use a rule of thumb that there must be three independently discovered prior examples) by being able to let forces resolve themselves, and by adding to the Quality. Remember that patterns are not just techniques and are much more than just a way of documenting how you do things. Alexander tells us repeatedly that each pattern has a moral grounding, and that a good pattern is morally profound (*IEEE Software 16 [Ale99]*). Further, he writes:

> And there is an imperative aspect to the pattern. The pattern solves a problem. It is not merely "a" pattern, which one might or might not use on a hillside. It is a *desirable* pattern; and for a person who wants to farm a hillside, and prevent it from erosion, he *must* create this pattern, in order to maintain a stable and healthy world. In this sense, the pattern not only tells him how to create the pattern of terracing, if he wants to; it also tells him that it is essential for him to do so, in certain particular contexts, and that he must create this pattern there. (*The Timeless Way of Building [Ale79]*, p. 183.)

In short, be guided by what may be the two most important patterns in this book: the first one, and one of the last ones—¶1 *The Spirit of the Game* and ¶93 *Greatest Value*, respectively. Patterns are not a tool that helps one set of people control another. They are a way for a community to celebrate and leverage the small, selfless, daily acts that add up to a great team, environment, and product, and which weave into the core moral fabric of a community—of your community. Not all of your patterns will be morally profound, but you should nonetheless set that before yourself as a goal. Tirelessly refine your patterns to add new insights and to ever make them more literary, more human, and more profound.

Patlets

This appendix of *patlets*—pattern summaries—might help you find a pattern that addresses some particular problem or context in your Scrum team, or might help you find a pattern you vaguely recall having heard of. The patlets are simple problem/solution pairs that summarize the core of each pattern. We encourage you to go back and read the original pattern to pick up important subtleties not covered here.

Patterns in the Product Organization Pattern Language

¶1 *The Spirit of the Game* If team members believe they can "implement Scrum" by following its rules instead of acting on the deeper rationales behind them, then explicitly emphasize the spirit, not the rules of Scrum, as a foundation for the culture.

¶2 *The Mist* Great works start with a vague longing across some community. Therefore, an individual, or a collective mind of several individuals, conceives a vision of how to improve quality-of-life.

¶3 *Fertile Soil* Personal interaction qualities both reflect and define organization qualities. Therefore, demonstrate the values of Commitment, Focus, Openness, Respect, and Courage in your day-to-day behaviors and interactions.

¶4 *Conway's Law* An organization should partition itself to maximize its communication effectiveness. Therefore, structure the organization into Small Teams, each attuned to concerns that create the most value to the enterprise.

¶5 *Birds of a Feather* Empowered teams that self-organize tend to isolate themselves from the enterprise, but people best develop core competencies across boundaries of diverse work. Therefore, form an ad hoc group for sharing expertise in each core competency.

¶6 *Involve the Managers* If development efforts are languishing for lack of coordination across products or because administrative tasks displace development efforts, then enlist a small management staff as "über ScrumMasters" who can initiate radical change, remove impediments, provide administration and coordinate from a "big picture" position.

¶7 *Scrum Team* Division of labor is inefficient at producing complex products. Therefore, form a team of people: Development Team, a Product Owner, and a ScrumMaster.

¶8 *Collocated Team* If the complexity of collaborative development demands high-fidelity communication, then locate the team together within talking distance.

¶9 *Small Teams* Having many people working on the same thing inflates communication overhead. Therefore, use small teams of people working on serialized work rather than striving for false parallelism.

¶10 *Cross-Functional Team* Organizations often organize around areas of competence, but it is too slow to coordinate across these boundaries. Therefore, the team as a whole should embody all the talent necessary to deliver product.

¶11 *Product Owner* You need a single, ordered Product Backlog. Therefore, get a Product Owner with deep business experience and domain knowledge to create the backlog.

¶12 *Product Owner Team* For a large product, the Product Owner can get overwhelmed. Therefore, several people form a team to bridge the business concerns with development, led by the Chief Product Owner.

¶13 *Development Partnership* Arbitrary organizational or political boundaries obstruct communication between the vendor and the client. This leads to requirement handoffs, distrust, and eventually failure. Therefore, break down the barriers with a mutual agreement to collaborate frequently.

¶14 *Development Team* Many hands make light work. Therefore, build a stable team to deliver successive increments of the Product Owner's vision.

¶15 *Stable Teams* If you need predictability, then keep teams stable and avoid shuffling people around between teams.

¶16 *Autonomous Team* If policies and procedures applied across multiple contexts are dysfunctional, then the Scrum Team governs its work free from external control, and the Development Team manages its own work.

¶17 *Self-Organizing Team* Specialized skills can't accomplish work without coordination. Therefore, the Development Team organizes itself to get its work Done.

¶18 *Mitosis* A Scrum Team should grow in an incremental, piecemeal fashion; but eventually, the team just becomes too large to be efficient. Therefore, after it gradually grows to the point of inefficiency (about seven people), split one large Development Team into two small ones.

¶19 *ScrumMaster* A self-organizing team cannot objectively see itself. Therefore, select one member to be the ScrumMaster, who helps the team improve its effectiveness.

¶20 *Oyatsu Jinja (Snack Shrine)* Interruptions take focus away from product development. Therefore, create a snack shrine (Oyatsu Jinja) with snacks and drinks, where developers can entertain requests from the rest of the organization without interrupting their periods of flow.

¶21 *Small Red Phone* If the whole team is dependent on select key members, then issue a cellular hotline to the key members, only for critical use.

¶22 *Scrum (Master) Coach* If the ScrumMaster's own shortcomings are limiting the team's growth, then the ScrumMaster should periodically seek opportunities for reflection with a coach.

¶23 *Fixed Work* The Product Owner must account for all work to use team velocity for release planning, yet not all development work can be time-boxed. Therefore, leave the fixed work of standard, recurring Scrum events out of the Production Episode time budget.

¶24 *Sprint Planning* A Sprint aims to produce a potentially shippable product increment within a fixed time box. If the Scrum Team agrees on the Sprint Goal at the beginning of each Sprint, then they plan which PBIs to complete and how to do the work.

¶25 *Swarming: One-Piece Continuous Flow* Working on too many things at once reduces velocity and the quality of work. Therefore, have the whole Development Team work together on one Product Backlog Item at a time.

¶26 *Kaizen Pulse* It's difficult to absorb improvement lessons continuously without careful observation. Therefore, alternate process improvement with periods of controlled velocity.

¶27 *Remove the Shade* If a hero in a team starts to overshadow other members, then remove the hero so that the rest of the team can grow.

¶28 *Pop the Happy Bubble* If teams get complacent when things go well, then burst the team's bubble by making them confront their deficiencies.

¶29 *Daily Scrum* When delays and blockages happen in a Sprint, team dynamics require reshaping. But too much replanning wastes time. Therefore, have a short meeting every day to replan the Sprint.

¶30 *ScrumMaster Incognito* At the Daily Scrum, the Development Team members report status to the ScrumMaster instead of interacting with each other. Therefore, the team addresses each other instead, with the ScrumMaster taking on a silent role.

¶31 *Norms of Conduct* Members of a new Scrum Team bring different norms that could lead to misunderstanding and distrust. Therefore, establish norms of conduct to facilitate accountability and allow positive conflict.

¶32 *Emergency Procedure* Inevitably, unanticipated problems arise and cause the Sprint Goal to slip out of reach, but waiting until the Sprint Review derails the whole Sprint. Therefore, reevaluate the work plan mid-Sprint and escalate the solution with a predefined procedure.

¶33 *Illegitimus Non Interruptus* If various stakeholders and emergent requirements interrupt the team, crippling its progress, then explicitly allot time for interrupts and time-box unplanned work to that budget.

¶34 *Scrum of Scrums* The Product Owner specifies goals that may be common across multiple Development Teams. Therefore, give the Development Teams the right and responsibility to coordinate their efforts to realize these common goals, jointly collaborating as a group of workers called the Scrum of Scrums.

¶35 *Sprint Review* Business stakeholders do not intervene during the Production Episode time box, but they need to stay in sync with product development. Therefore, hold a meeting for the Product Owner and other stakeholders to discuss what the Development Team has produced.

¶36 *Sprint Retrospective* Over time, without explicit attention, processes and discipline tend to decay. Therefore, hold a meeting at the end of each Sprint to reflect on the development process.

¶37 *MetaScrum* Scrum Teams are in place in an enterprise, but legacy management interferes by trying to exercise control over products.

Therefore, create a forum (the Meta Scrum) for the whole enterprise to give management a say in Product Owners' portfolio decisions.

¶38 *Product Pride* If team members need to know their work matters and to have a say in how it's done, then create a climate that enables Autonomy, Mastery, and Purpose.

Patterns in the Value Stream Pattern Language

¶39 *Vision* Overly specific constraints can turn contributors into subservient robots. Therefore, stakeholders and potential future coworkers rally to articulate and to refine together the Product Owner's Vision.

¶40 *Impediment List* Impediments to progress surface all the time, but addressing them immediately may not be practical. Therefore, make them visible on a list.

¶41 *Value Stream* The development process and the path from conception to market are as important to product success as the product idea itself. Therefore, create an ecosystem to deliver ever-increasing value in an evolving product.

¶42 *Set-Based Design* If tackling a problem with many dimensions, then explore multiple potential solutions where each one probes different regions of each dimension, so the team develops a broad intuition of the problem, leading to the best feasible current option.

¶43 *Sprint Burndown Chart* Progress should be immediately visible to Development Team members. Therefore, publicly post a graph that plots estimated work remaining in the Sprint against the remaining time.

¶44 *Scrum Board* There's a danger that the Development Team will lose its focus on the Sprint Goal. Therefore, create a Scrum Board that visualizes the Sprint Backlog and the current status of the work.

¶45 *Product Roadmap* When the vision is clear and the market is ready, the team needs concrete steps to act on the opportunity. But a list cannot express the uncertainty ahead. Therefore, the Product Owner should lay out alternative paths, making the uncertainty visible. Only then a Product Backlog can take shape.

¶46 *Sprint* The team needs to deliver Product Increments often enough to correct its course based on frequent feedback from the end user. Therefore: Organize development around recurring, frequent, fixed-length time-boxed intervals called Sprints.

¶47 *Organizational Sprint Pulse* The Scrum Team and the rest of the organization are out-of-step, causing waiting time or interruptions. Therefore, synchronize the teams' Sprints to the organization's rhythm at least once a month.

¶48 *Release Plan* If the stakeholders need to know which product increments are coming out and when, then create an ordered list of deliverables and forecast dates from the Product Backlog.

¶49 *Release Range* Release dates inherently lack precision, but stakeholders tend to treat an estimated delivery date as a commitment. Therefore, make pessimistic and optimistic estimates for release dates based on Product Backlog Item estimates and a range of historic team velocities.

¶50 *ROI-Ordered Backlog* The Product Backlog needs some order to drive the order of delivery. Therefore, Order PBIs in a way that generates the largest long-term ROI.

¶51 *High Value First* Some PBIs are critical, while others are just nice to have. Therefore, deliver the highest-value product increment first.

¶52 *Change for Free* The Scrum Team wants to respond to new client requirements while avoiding scope creep. Therefore, offer clients the option of exchanging an emergent requirement for any existing PBI that is of equal or lower value to them, as long as the development cost of the new item is no more than the cost of the original.

¶53 *Money for Nothing* Spending time building a product increment that costs more than it's worth is waste. Therefore, stop work when the product's development costs begin to exceed its expected value.

¶54 *Product Backlog* Even when everyone agrees to what product increments to deliver, the Development Team doesn't know what it should deliver first. Therefore, create an ordered list of product increments arranged by their delivery date.

¶55 *Product Backlog Item* The Product Backlog is composed of large, monolithic parts that impose unnecessary risk. Therefore, create Product Backlog Items (PBIs), distinct specifications of changes and additions to the product.

¶56 *Information Radiator* Information flow is critical to the organization, but sharing through reports and meetings wastes effort, often discouraging communication. This results in sharing too little. Therefore, display information on a physical wall and keep it frequently updated.

¶57 *Pigs Estimate* Estimates of effort should be based on what is known rather than on wrong assumptions and wishful thinking. Therefore, let the Development Team, whose members are committed to working on the product, estimate the work.

¶58 *Small Items* When work items are too big, they become hard to understand and estimate. Therefore, decompose large items into smaller items that Developers can easily understand and build.

¶59 *Granularity Gradient* Small Items are easiest to estimate, but breaking down larger work items is work in itself. Therefore, break down only the earliest Product Backlog Items into Small Items.

¶60 *Estimation Points* It is important to easily make estimates that are reliable enough to confidently forecast the amount of work that the team can complete in a Sprint. Therefore, use unitless relative numbers for effort estimation.

¶61 *Fixed-Date PBI* Dependencies for the product often appear on their own time and cannot be scheduled by the Development Team—but the team must account for how it shifts the schedule.

¶62 *Vacation PBI* Most corporate value systems honor vacations. But while they don't create market value in the way that product increments do, the Product Owner should make their cost and value visible. Therefore, track the time and value of team members' absences as PBIs.

¶63 *Enabling Specification* If the Development Team is uncertain about the product vision and the development process, then the Product Owner should specify the PBI for the Development Team in enough detail to leave no question unanswered.

¶64 *Refined Product Backlog* Market volatility changes the relative value of PBIs. Therefore, the Scrum Team meets regularly to properly order, break down, and estimate the Product Backlog.

¶65 *Definition of Ready* Improperly defined PBIs lead to waste in development effort in a Sprint, causing it to fail. But a common understanding of PBIs leads to focus in the team. Therefore, create an objective "Ready" standard before placing a PBI in a Sprint (i.e., estimated, testable, small items, discussed, and has customer value).

¶66 *Yesterday's Weather* If courage emboldens the team to set overoptimistic goals, then refer to the work Done in the last Sprint to forecast the work for the upcoming Sprint.

¶67 *Running Average Velocity* The velocity should reflect the team's current capacity, but velocity takes time to stabilize after a change. Therefore, use a running average of the most recent Sprints to estimate the velocity.

¶68 *Aggregate Velocity* Multiple Scrum Teams working towards a single release date should estimate when they will deliver, but it makes no sense to sum unitless velocities from different teams. Therefore, estimate PBIs together so there is a single velocity scale across teams.

¶69 *Specialized Velocities* If the product grows to multiple teams, then each team estimating and delivering the product increments for the whole product is waste.

¶70 *Updated Velocity* You want the velocity to reflect the team's current abilities, yet it takes time to monitor your improvements. Therefore, update the velocity only if the team sustains a new level for three Sprints in a row.

¶71 *Sprint Goal* A Sprint that consists only of tasks is not enough to relate the team's effort to Greatest Value. Therefore, create a concise goal to unify the team's achievements throughout the Sprint.

¶72 *Sprint Backlog* The Development Team should understand the work needed for achieving the Sprint Goal. Therefore, create a work plan at the Sprint Planning Meeting for everything that the Development Team needs to do in that Sprint.

¶73 *Sprint Backlog Item* A PBI clarifies what to build but does not specify how to build it. Therefore, during Sprint Planning, break down PBIs into smaller work items for the development plan.

¶74 *Teams That Finish Early Accelerate Faster* Teams often take too much work into a Sprint and cannot finish it. Failure to attain the Sprint Goal prevents the team from improving. Therefore, take less work into a Sprint.

¶75 *Production Episode* The collective flow of the team demands fewer disruptions and a sense of urgency. Therefore, time-box all development efforts, with participation limited to the Development Team.

¶76 *Developer-Ordered Work Plan* The Scrum Team commits to a Sprint Goal, and there are multiple ways to achieve it. Therefore, let the developers decide the best ordering of the work in the Sprint Backlog to achieve the Sprint Goal.

¶77 *Follow the Moon* Every culture acts in cadence to natural events, yet business cycles track the Gregorian calendar. Therefore, define Sprints with beginning and ending boundaries on the New Moon and the Full Moon.

¶178 *Visible Status* Without a frame of reference, you can unknowingly drift. Therefore, create a status overview that demands action when statuses are outside acceptable tolerance.

¶179 *Dependencies First* If dependencies remain halfway through the sprint, they may bring the rest of the Sprint to a halt. Therefore, make sure that all known dependencies are under control by mid-Sprint.

¶180 *Good Housekeeping* Where there's a mess, you lose time and energy finding where and what to start on. Therefore, maintain a completely clean product and work environment continuously, or clean at the end of each day.

¶181 *Whack the Mole* Defects arise while adding new functionality. Postponing work on defects causes them to pile up, which further impedes development. Therefore, as soon as the team discovers defects, developers should drop what they are doing and mitigate them immediately.

¶182 *Definition of Done* Mismatched understanding of *Done* in the team will produce varying quality in tasks. *Done* means that there's no more work left for that task. Therefore, the Development Team agrees on what *Done* means beforehand.

¶183 *Team Sprint* PBIs with smaller value never make it to a Sprint, even if the team cares deeply about them and they may contribute to long-term cost reduction. Therefore, on occasion, let the team choose which PBIs they want to include in the Sprint.

¶184 *Responsive Deployment* If some PBI development finishes in the middle of a Sprint, then instead of waiting until the end of the Sprint, the Product Owner releases PBIs as soon as they're Done.

¶185 *Regular Product Increment* It's important to measure development progress by checking off completed work, but outcomes are more important than output. Therefore, mark progress every Sprint as a delivered Product Increment, and elicit feedback on how it matches end-user needs.

¶186 *Release Staging Layers* We would like to receive stakeholder feedback as frequently as possible, but it is too risky to deploy to the whole market at once. Therefore, partition the market into multiple release groups, from beta testers to the whole market. Release every Sprint to the appropriate groups.

¶187 *Testable Improvements* If you are working on a complex product, measures of value may vary for both planned and unplanned reasons, and it may be difficult to tie an increase to a planned kaizen. Therefore, monitor both the actions that a team takes to realize a kaizen, and the corresponding change in value.

¶88 *One Step at a Time* If changing multiple things at once obscures which change led to an improvement, then make one process improvement at a time.

¶89 *Value Areas* If teams work across more and more customer domains and start to approach the boundaries of what they can master, then organize the teams around areas of customer value.

¶90 *Value Stream Fork* Product success needs a crisp market identity, but a growing product with divergent features dilutes the focus of a single Scrum Team. Therefore, split a large product and its Value Stream into multiple Value Streams, each with its own Product Backlog and Product Owner.

¶91 *Happiness Metric* If a growing list of improvement activities dampens the team's passion for the work, then prioritize the items on the impediment list in order of the team's passion to solve them.

¶92 *Scrumming the Scrum* Scrum is more than just doing work; it's also about improving the way we work. Therefore, resolve the most important impediment by putting one in the Product Backlog every Sprint.

¶93 *Greatest Value* The team works to contribute to overall value, but short-term thinking leads to improving just the small things. Therefore, let the Vision direct the team's attention to the greater scope.

¶94 *Product Wake* Products can't last forever, and the organization shouldn't tie up talent to feed a dead Value Stream. Therefore, at the end of a product's life, give it a decent burial.

Patterns from the Organizational Patterns Book

The following patlets describe patterns from the *Organizational Patterns* book, *Organizational Patterns of Agile Software Development [CH04]* and the section number refers to the section number in that reference.

¶95 *Community of Trust* If you are building any human organization, then you must have a foundation of trust and respect for effective communication at levels deep enough to sustain growth. (Section 4.1.1.)

¶96 *Named Stable Bases* If you want to balance stability with progress, then have a hierarchy of named stable basis that people can work against. (Section 4.1.4.)

¶97 *Take No Small Slips* If you are getting behind schedule and you need additional time resources, then take one large planned slip instead of creating project instability and low team morale with small, unanticipated slips. (Section 4.1.9.)

¶98 *Completion Headroom* If work is progressing against a set of hard dates, then make sure there is Completion Headroom between the completion dates of the largest task and the hard delivery date. (Section 4.1.10.)

¶99 *Recommitment Meeting* If the schedule can't be met with simple adjustments to the work queue and staffing, then assemble Developers and interested managers to recommit to a new strategy based on doing the minimal amount of work to reach a satisfactory conclusion. (Section 4.1.12.)

¶100 *Informal Labor Plan* If development needs are fluid, then instead of master planning, let Developers negotiate among themselves to develop short-term plans. (Section 4.1.14.)

¶101 *Developer Controls Process* If you need to orchestrate the activities of a given location or feature, then put the Developer role in control of the succession of activities. (Section 4.1.17.)

¶102 *Work Flows Inward* If you want information to flow to the producing roles in an organization, then put the Developer at the center and see that information flows *toward* the center, not *from* the center.

¶103 *Programming Episodes* If you need to split up work across time, then do the work in discrete episodes that combine to create concrete deliverables. (Section 4.1.19.)

¶104 *Someone Always Makes Progress* If distractions constantly interrupt your team's progress, then whatever happens, ensure someone keeps moving toward your primary goal. (Section 4.1.20.)

¶105 *Team per Task* If a big diversion hits your team, then let a subteam handle the diversion so the main team can keep going. (Section 4.1.21.)

¶106 *Sacrifice One Person* If a smaller diversion hits your team, then assign just one person to resolve it. (Section 4.1.22.)

¶*107 Day Care* If your experts are spending all their time mentoring novices, then put one expert in charge of all the novices and let the other experts develop the system. (Section 4.1.23.)

¶*108 Interrupts Unjam Blocking* If you need to schedule urgent development activities according to some reasonable priority scheme, then use an interrupt scheme to keep individual problems from blocking the entire project. (Section 4.1.25.)

¶*109 Don't Interrupt an Interrupt* If a new urgent need arises while you're already in the middle of handling an interrupt to keep the project from getting stuck, then continue handling the current issue before moving on to the new one. (Section 4.1.26.)

¶*110 Size the Organization* If an organization is too large, communications break down. If it is too small, it can't achieve its goals or easily overcome the difficulties of adding more people. Therefore, start projects with a critical mass of about 10 people. (Section 4.2.2.)

¶*111 Apprenticeship* If you have difficulty retaining expertise, then grow expertise internally from existing employees or even new hires. (Section 4.2.4.)

¶*112 Solo Virtuoso* If a project is intellectually small, then overstaffing it is a waste of time and money. Therefore, staff small projects with Solo Virtuosi. (Section 4.2.5.)

¶*113 Surrogate Customer* If you need answers from your customer, but no customer is available to answer your questions, then use scenarios to define the problem. (Section 4.2.7.)

¶*114 Firewall* If you want to keep your Developers from being interrupted by extraneous influences and special interest groups, then impose a Firewall, such as a manager, to "keep the pests away." (Section 4.2.9.)

¶*115 Gatekeeper* If a team walls itself in and becomes overly incestuous, then use a Gatekeeper role to tie development to other projects, research, and the outside world. (Section 4.2.10.)

¶*116 Self-Selecting Team* If you appoint people to a team, the people don't come together as a team. People who share similar outside interests make the best team members. Therefore, teams should be largely self-selecting, performing limited screening of candidates based on their track record and outside interests. (Section 4.2.11.)

¶*117 Unity of Purpose* If a team is beginning to work together, then make sure all members agree on the purpose of the team. (Section 4.2.12.)

¶1118 *Team Pride* If a team needs to perform above and beyond the call of duty, then instill a well-grounded sense of elitism in its members. (Section 4.2.13.)

¶1119 *Patron Role* If you need to insulate Developers so Developers Control the Process, and you must support organizational inertia at a strategic level, then identify a Patron accessible to the project who can champion the cause of the project. (Section 4.2.15.)

¶1120 *Matron Role* If your team needs ongoing care and feeding, then include a Matron Role on the team who will naturally attend to the team's social needs. (Section 4.2.18.)

¶1121 *Wise Fool* If critical issues do not get aired easily, then nurture a Wise Fool to say the things nobody else dares say. (Section 4.2.21.)

¶1122 *Domain Expertise in Roles* If you need to staff all roles, it's difficult to determine how to match people to roles in order to optimize communication. Therefore, match people to roles based on domain expertise, and emphasize that people play those roles in the organization. (Section 4.2.22.)

¶1123 *Moderate Truck Number* If you can't eliminate having a single point of failure in allocating expertise to roles, then spread that expertise around as far as possible, but not more so. (Section 4.2.24.)

¶1124 *Compensate Success* If enterprises are to succeed, they must reward the behaviors that lead to success; however, these behaviors are varied, and success is difficult to measure. Therefore, establish a spectrum of reward mechanisms for both teams and individuals. (Section 4.2.25.)

¶1125 *Failed Project Wake* If people have put their hearts and souls into a project that subsequently is canceled, then celebrate the project's demise and hold a "wake" for it. (Section 4.2.26.)

¶1126 *Developing in Pairs* If you want to improve the effectiveness of individual Developers, then have people develop in pairs. (Section 4.2.28.)

¶1127 *Engage Quality Assurance* If Developers can't be counted on to test beyond what they already anticipate going wrong, then engage QA as an important function. (Section 4.2.29.)

¶1128 *Producer Roles* If your organization has too many roles, but does not know which to eliminate, then identify roles as Producers, Supporters, or Deadbeats and reduce the number of roles to sixteen or fewer. (Section 5.1.3.)

¶*129 Organization Follows Market*   If there is no clear organizational accountability to a market, then make some organization accountable for each market to ensure that the market's needs will be met. (Section 5.1.9.)

¶*130 Face-to-Face Before Working Remotely* If a project is divided geographically, then begin the project by inviting everyone to a meeting at a single place. (Section 5.1.10.)

¶*131 Distribute Work Evenly* If you want to optimize team effectiveness and productivity, then alleviate overload on specific groups and individuals in your organization by Distributing Work Evenly. (Section 5.1.13.)

¶*132 The Water Cooler* If you need more communication between institutionalized organizations, then leave space for everyday human activities that can provide more complete and informal communication. (Section 5.1.20.)

¶*133 Smoke-Filled Room*   If you need to make a decision quickly and you need both authoritative backing for the decision as well as expediency, then make the decision in the absence of broad engagement, publicizing the decision only afterwards. (Section 5.2.6.)

¶*134 Stand-Up Meeting*   If there are pockets of misinformation or if people are out of the loop, then hold short daily meetings to socialize emerging developments. (Section 5.2.7.)

Patterns from Fearless Change

This patlet describes a pattern from *Fearless Change [RM05]* by Linda Rising and Mary Lynn Manns.

¶*135 Do Food* If you want to draw people to an event in which they otherwise might hold only a neutral interest, then entice them with food and refreshments.

Picture Credits

Picture on page xvii Original painting by Kaku-an Shu-en; this rendition by Tokuriki Tomikichiro, 1902–1999.

Sketch on page xx Esther Vervloed.

Picture on page 3 Cover of The Spirit of the Game, by Rob Smyth, published by Elliot & Thompson, 5 June 2010.

Picture on page 17 Shutterstock.com, https://www.shutterstock.com, Stonehenge, United Kingdom.

Sketch on page 17 Esther Vervloed.

Sketch on page 18 Esther Vervloed.

Picture on page 20 Shutterstock.com, https://www.shutterstock.com.

Picture on page 23 Images provided by PresenterMedia.com.

Sketch on page 24 Esther Vervloed.

Sketch on page 26 Esther Vervloed.

Picture on page 31 Shutterstock.com, https://www.shutterstock.com, Michoacan, Mexico.

Sketch on page 32 Esther Vervloed.

Sketch on page 32 Esther Vervloed.

Picture on page 35 Shutterstock.com, https://www.shutterstock.com.

Sketch on page 36 Esther Vervloed.

Sketch on page 38 Esther Vervloed.

Picture on page 45 Dirk Hansen, https://www.flickr.com/photos/dirkhansen/3235465927/, 24 January 2009.

Sketch on page 46 Esther Vervloed.

Sketch on page 47 Esther Vervloed.

Picture on page 50 NASA, S116-E-05983, https://spaceflight.nasa.gov/gallery/images/shuttle/sts-116/html/s116e05983.html, 12 December 2006.

Picture on page 51 Alistair Cockburn. Communicating, Cooperating Teams. In Agile Software Development. Boston: Addison-Wesley Longman Publishing Co., 2006, pp. 90–100.

Picture on page 52 Thomas J. Allen. Managing the Flow of Technology. Boston: Massachusetts Institute of Technology, 1977.

Sketch on page 50 Esther Vervloed.

Sketch on page 53 Esther Vervloed.

Picture on page 55 The Scrum Patterns Group (Lachlan Heasman). Neil Harrison's kitchen, Utah, USA, 17 October 2014.

Sketch on page 56 Esther Vervloed.

Sketch on page 57 Esther Vervloed.

Picture on page 60 Shutterstock.com, https://www.shutterstock.com.

Sketch on page 60 Esther Vervloed.

Sketch on page 62 Esther Vervloed.

Picture on page 65 Henry Ford Hitting Soybean Plastic Trunk with an Axe, Image from the Collections of The Henry Ford. Gift of Ford Motor Company, 02 November 1940, image-id: P.188.28273, https://www.thehenryford.org/collections-and-research/digital-collections/artifact/220805#slide=gs-223214.

Sketch on page 65 Esther Vervloed.

Sketch on page 67 Esther Vervloed.

Picture on page 70 Masatoshi Okauchi/Shutterstock.com, https://www.shutterstock.com, Motor Corporation president Akio Toyoda with the new Toyota GR sports car, Tokyo, Japan, 19 September 2017.

Sketch on page 70 Esther Vervloed.

Sketch on page 71 Esther Vervloed.

Picture on page 73 Two Mules Learn Cooperation Donkeys Postcard (Los Angeles, CA, August 1941).

Sketch on page 74 Esther Vervloed.

Sketch on page 75 Esther Vervloed.

Picture on page 78 Shutterstock.com, https://www.shutterstock.com.

Sketch on page 79 Esther Vervloed.

Sketch on page 80 Esther Vervloed.

Picture on page 82 Shutterstock.com, https://www.shutterstock.com.

Sketch on page 82 Esther Vervloed.

Sketch on page 83 Esther Vervloed.

Picture on page 86 U.S. Department of Defense, Joel Rogers, ID: 636681-E-PBD16-814, https://dod.defense.gov/Photos/Photo-Gallery/igphoto/2001084205/. Milan, Italy, 2003.

Sketch on page 87 Esther Vervloed.

Sketch on page 87 Esther Vervloed.

Picture on page 91 Gerard Mak/Pixabay, https://pixabay.com/photos/migration-bird-clouds-2792834/, Arcen, Netherlands, November 2011.

Sketch on page 92 Esther Vervloed.

Sketch on page 92 Esther Vervloed.

Picture on page 97 The Scrum Patterns Group (Mark den Hollander). Created with Blender 2.79, Blender.org, https://www.blender.org, October 2017.

Sketch on page 98 Esther Vervloed.

Sketch on page 99 Esther Vervloed.

Picture on page 104 Sir Edmund Hillary, 1953.

Sketch on page 104 Esther Vervloed.

Sketch on page 107 Esther Vervloed.

Picture on page 110 The Scrum Patterns Group (James Coplien). Scrum class Oyatsu Jinja, Tokyo, Japan, 30 Oct. 2013.

Sketch on page 110 Esther Vervloed.

Sketch on page 111 Esther Vervloed.

Picture on page 113 Shutterstock.com, https://www.shutterstock.com.

Sketch on page 113 Esther Vervloed.

Sketch on page 114 Esther Vervloed.

Picture on page 115 Giuseppe Maria Crespi, Sacramento della confessione ovvero la regina di Boemia si confessa da S. Giovanni Nepomuceno, Pinacoteca, Torino, 1742.

Sketch on page 116 Esther Vervloed.

Sketch on page 116 Esther Vervloed.

Picture on page 119 Shutterstock.com, https://www.shutterstock.com.

Sketch on page 119 Esther Vervloed.

Sketch on page 121 Esther Vervloed.

Picture on page 123 Image Provided by PresenterMedia.com.

Sketch on page 123 Esther Vervloed.

Sketch on page 124 Esther Vervloed.

Picture on page 127 Shutterstock.com, https://www.shutterstock.com.

Picture on page 128 Gerald Weinberg. Quality Software Management: Volume 1, Systems Thinking: New York: Dorset House, 1992, p. 284.

Picture on page 129 Figure from Liker, The Toyota Way: 14 Management Principles from the World's Greatest Manufacturer, 2004, Chapter 8, Figure 8-4.

Picture on page 132 Scrum Patterns Group (Esther Vervloed). Steensel, Netherlands, May 2018.

Picture on page 133 Hirotaka Takeuchi et al. Extreme Toyota. Wiley, May 2011.

Picture on page 136 Pixabay, https://pixabay.com/en/flowers-growing-winter-grow-plant-1911205/, 6 February 2016.

Sketch on page 136 Esther Vervloed.

Sketch on page 137 Esther Vervloed.

Picture on page 139 Richard Heeks, https://www.flickr.com/photos/11164709@N06/3673992165, 30 June 2009.

Picture on page 143 Photograph by Walker Lewis, 1944, Library of Congress, Prints & Photographs Division, FSA/OWI Collection, LC-USW3-055963-D.

Sketch on page 144 Esther Vervloed.

Sketch on page 145 Esther Vervloed.

Picture on page 148 The Scrum Patterns Group (Lachlan Heasman). Kuala Lumpur, Malaysia, 7 July 2011.

Sketch on page 148 Esther Vervloed.

Sketch on page 149 Esther Vervloed.

Picture on page 150 Shutterstock.com, https://www.shutterstock.com.

Picture on page 152 National Museum of the U.S. Air Force, photo 090605-F-1234P-021, http://www.nationalmuseum.af.mil/Upcoming/Photos.aspx?igphoto=2000558698. Near Hanoi, North Vietnam, 12 August 1967.

Picture on page 155 NAVAIR 01-F14AAp-1B, NATOPS Pocket Checklist, F-14B Aircraft, U.S. Army, 1 August 2001, p. 26.

Picture on page 157 Shutterstock.com, https://www.shutterstock.com, Cows grazing on open land in Gower, United Kingdom.

Sketch on page 157 Esther Vervloed.

Sketch on page 159 Esther Vervloed.

Picture on page 161 Greg Neate, http://www.flickr.com/photos/neate_photos/3522905573/in/album-72157617918428883, https://www.flickr.com/photos/neate_photos/3522905573/in/album-72157617918428883. Prince Regent Swimming Pool, Brighton, United Kingdom, 9 May 2009.

Sketch on page 161 Esther Vervloed.

Sketch on page 163 Esther Vervloed.

Picture on page 165 Members of the Women's Royal Naval Service sampling the Christmas pudding at Greenock in Scotland, 19 December 1942, Imperial War Museum (A 13392).

Sketch on page 165 Esther Vervloed.

Sketch on page 167 Esther Vervloed.

Picture on page 170 Image from: M.C. Escher's "Hand with Reflecting Sphere." The M.C. Escher Company—The Netherlands, All rights reserved. http://www.mcescher.com, 1935.

Sketch on page 170 Esther Vervloed.

Sketch on page 172 Esther Vervloed.

Picture on page 176 NASA, GPN-2000-001705, https://archive.org/details/GPN-2000-001705. Washington D.C., USA, 1 January 1921.

Sketch on page 177 Esther Vervloed.

Sketch on page 177 Esther Vervloed.

Picture on page 181 r.nagy/Shutterstock.com, https://www.shutterstock.com, Barcelona, Spain.

Sketch on page 181 Esther Vervloed.

Sketch on page 182 Esther Vervloed.

Picture on page 191 NASA, ID: 9260665, https://images.nasa.gov/details-9260665.html, 25 May 1961.

Sketch on page 192 Esther Vervloed.

Sketch on page 192 Esther Vervloed.

Picture on page 195 Damian Dovarganes, AP – Associated Press/Scanpix. Topanga Caynon Road, California, USA, 10 January 2005.

Sketch on page 195 Esther Vervloed.

Sketch on page 196 Esther Vervloed.

Picture on page 198 Shutterstock.com, https://www.shutterstock.com.

Sketch on page 198 Esther Vervloed.

Sketch on page 199 Esther Vervloed.

Picture on page 203 Shutterstock.com, https://www.shutterstock.com.

Picture on page 204 Interface quality as a function of the number of design iterations: Measured usability will normally go up for each additional iteration, until the design potentially reaches a point where it plateaus, Jakob Nielsen. Iterative User Interface Design. In IEEE Computer 26(11), 1993, pp. 32–41, https://www.nngroup.com/articles/iterative-design/.

Picture on page 205 David J. Singer, Norbert Doerry, and Michael E. Buckley. What is set-based design? In Naval Engineers Journal 121(4), 2009, pp. 31–43, Intentional phases of convergence and divergence.

Sketch on page 205 Esther Vervloed.

Picture on page 206 Allen Ward, Jeffrey K. Liker, John J. Cristiano, and Durward K. Sobek, II. The Second Toyota Paradox: How Delaying Decisions can Make Better Cars Faster. In Sloan Management Review 36(3), January 1, 1995, p. 43, Converging interdependent components over time.

Picture on page 207 David N. Ford and Durward K. Sobeck, II. Adapting Real Options to New Product Development by Modeling the Second Toyota Paradox. In David N. Ford, and Durward K. Sobek, II, eds., IEEE Transactions on Engineering Management 52(2), May 2005, pp. 175–185, Expected quality of point-based and set-based development projects.

Picture on page 207 David N. Ford and Durward K. Sobeck, II. Adapting Real Options to New Product Development by Modeling the Second Toyota Paradox. In David N. Ford, and Durward K. Sobek, II, eds., IEEE Transactions on Engineering Management 52(2), May 2005, pp. 175–185, Expected values of flexibility in set-based development relative to point-based development.

Picture on page 210 U.S. Navy photo by Erik Hildebrandt, 170728-N-UZ648-093, https://www.navy.mil/view_image.asp?id=242661. Atlantic Ocean, 28 July 2017.

Sketch on page 211 Esther Vervloed.

Sketch on page 212 Esther Vervloed.

Picture on page 215 The Scrum Patterns Group (Mark den Hollander).

Sketch on page 216 Esther Vervloed.

Sketch on page 216 Esther Vervloed.

Picture on page 220 Image Provided by PresenterMedia.com.

Sketch on page 221 Esther Vervloed.

Picture on page 222 Photo credit: Todd Herman Associates, 2016, https://www.toddherman.com/improve-business/client-roadmap. Reconstructed by Mark den Hollander and Esther Vervloed (April 2019).

Sketch on page 223 Esther Vervloed.

Picture on page 228 Morzaszum/Pixabay, https://pixabay.com/photos/spot-runs-start-la-stadion-862274/, 29 July 2015.

Sketch on page 230 Esther Vervloed.

Sketch on page 231 Esther Vervloed.

Picture on page 234 Cicero Castro/Shutterstock.com, https://www.shutterstock.com, Group of folklore of Madeira island perfoming at â 24 horas a bailarâ festival in Santana city, Madeira Island, Portugal, July 2017.

Sketch on page 234 Esther Vervloed.

Sketch on page 235 Esther Vervloed.

Sketch on page 235 Esther Vervloed.

Picture on page 237 Sgt. Neil Bryden, Royal Air Force, https://www.flickr.com/photos/ 14214150@N02/16669707664. Nepal, 27 April 2015.

Sketch on page 238 Esther Vervloed.

Sketch on page 238 An Esther Vervloed rendering of a slide from Mike Cohn.

Picture on page 241 Scrum Patterns Group (James O. Coplien), Shinjuku Gyoen National Garden, Sendagaya, Tokyo, Japan, 24 March 2018.

Sketch on page 242 Esther Vervloed.

Sketch on page 243 Esther Vervloed; original from Mike Cohn.

Picture on page 248 Amateur007/Shutterstock.com, https://www.shutterstock.com, Orienteering race. Traditional annual orienteering game Partisan Spark Cup 2018, Yuzhnoukrainsk, Ukraine, 26 May 2018.

Sketch on page 249 Esther Vervloed.

Sketch on page 249 Esther Vervloed.

Picture on page 251 Photo by JTV, Jackson, Michigan, USA. The event was the American 1 Supermarket Sweep, benefiting the Food Bank of South Central Michigan. https://jtv.tv/supermarket-sweep/, 7 April 2014.

Sketch on page 252 Esther Vervloed.

Picture on page 255 Shutterstock.com, https://www.shutterstock.com.

Sketch on page 256 Esther Vervloed; original from Geir Amsjø.

Picture on page 258 Shutterstock.com, https://www.shutterstock.com.

Sketch on page 260 Esther Vervloed; original from Geir Amsjø.

Picture on page 263 Tomatin Distillery Co., Ltd.

Sketch on page 263 Esther Vervloed.

Sketch on page 265 Esther Vervloed.

Picture on page 268 Shutterstock.com, https://www.shutterstock.com.

Sketch on page 269 Esther Vervloed.

Sketch on page 269 Esther Vervloed.

Picture on page 274 The Scrum Patterns Group (Kiro Harada). VAL Research, Kōenji, Japan, May 2018.

Sketch on page 274 Esther Vervloed.

Sketch on page 276 Esther Vervloed.

Picture on page 277 The Scrum Patterns Group (Cesário Ramos). Netherlands, 2008 (reconstructed by Mark den Hollander, April 2019).

Picture on page 280 http://www.antiquegamblingchips.com/CelebritiesPlayingPoker.htm.

Sketch on page 280 Esther Vervloed.

Sketch on page 281 Esther Vervloed.

Picture on page 283 Shutterstock.com, https://www.shutterstock.com.

Sketch on page 285 Esther Vervloed.

Sketch on page 286 Esther Vervloed.

Picture on page 288 The Scrum Patterns Group (Mark den Hollander). Gerbeaud Kávéház, Budapest, Hungary, 25 July 2017.

Sketch on page 288 Esther Vervloed.

Sketch on page 289 Esther Vervloed.

Sketch on page 290 Esther Vervloed.

Picture on page 292 Planning Poker® Cards, Mountain Goat Software.

Sketch on page 294 Esther Vervloed.

Sketch on page 294 Esther Vervloed.

Picture on page 297 Shutterstock.com, https://www.shutterstock.com.

Sketch on page 298 Esther Vervloed.

Sketch on page 298 Esther Vervloed.

Picture on page 300 Image Provided by PresenterMedia.com.

Sketch on page 301 Esther Vervloed.

Sketch on page 302 Esther Vervloed.

Picture on page 306 Adhesive Pads for Footwear (2008), United States Patent and Trademark Office, http://patft.uspto.gov/. Many thanks to Richard Beem, patent attorney.

Sketch on page 307 Esther Vervloed.

Sketch on page 308 Esther Vervloed.

Picture on page 311 Shutterstock.com, https://www.shutterstock.com.

Sketch on page 313 Esther Vervloed.

Sketch on page 314 Esther Vervloed.

Picture on page 316 Rawpixel Ltd., https://www.rawpixel.com/image/8657/hands-holding-bangkok-thailand-travel-guide-book-map-floor.

Sketch on page 316 Esther Vervloed.

Sketch on page 318 Esther Vervloed.

Picture on page 324 Image Provided by PresenterMedia.com.

Sketch on page 324 Esther Vervloed.

Sketch on page 325 Esther Vervloed.

Picture on page 326 Shutterstock.com, https://www.shutterstock.com.

Sketch on page 326 Esther Vervloed.

Sketch on page 327 Esther Vervloed.

Picture on page 329 Image Provided by PresenterMedia.com.

Sketch on page 330 Esther Vervloed.

Sketch on page 332 Esther Vervloed.

Sketch on page 332 Esther Vervloed.

Picture on page 334 Wei Huang/Shutterstock.com, https://www.shutterstock.com, Display windows of Harrods, an upmarket department store, London, United Kingdom, 19 October 2016.

Sketch on page 334 Esther Vervloed.

Sketch on page 335 Esther Vervloed.

Picture on page 337 Engin Akyurt, https://pixabay.com/en/shift-gear-knob-vehicle-parts-1838138/, 1 March 2008.

Sketch on page 337 Esther Vervloed.

Sketch on page 338 Esther Vervloed.

Picture on page 339 From Hirotaka Takeuchi, et al. Extreme Toyota: Radical Contradictions That Drive Success at the World's Best Manufacturer. Chichester, U.K.: Wiley, 2008, pp. 84–85.

Picture on page 340 Shutterstock.com, https://www.shutterstock.com.

Sketch on page 340 Esther Vervloed.

Sketch on page 341 Esther Vervloed.

Picture on page 345 Shutterstock.com, https://www.shutterstock.com.

Sketch on page 345 Esther Vervloed.

Sketch on page 346 Esther Vervloed.

Picture on page 348 Image Provided by PresenterMedia.com.

Sketch on page 348 Esther Vervloed.

Sketch on page 349 Esther Vervloed.

Picture on page 351 Gaie Uchel / Shutterstock.com, https://www.shutterstock.com, Japan athlete's in action during 38th Asian Track Championships 2018 at National Velodrome in Nilai, Malaysia, 16 February 2018.

Sketch on page 351 Esther Vervloed.

Sketch on page 352 Esther Vervloed.

Picture on page 353 Shutterstock.com, https://www.shutterstock.com.

Sketch on page 354 Esther Vervloed.

Sketch on page 355 Esther Vervloed.

Picture on page 358 Shutterstock.com, https://www.shutterstock.com.

Sketch on page 359 Esther Vervloed.

Sketch on page 361 Esther Vervloed.

Picture on page 363 Shutterstock.com, https://www.shutterstock.com.

Sketch on page 364 Esther Vervloed.

Sketch on page 365 Esther Vervloed.

Picture on page 366 Scrum Patterns Group (James O. Coplien), Toyota Commemorative Museum of Industry and Technology, Nagoya, Japan, 27 October 2015.

Sketch on page 366 Esther Vervloed.

Sketch on page 367 Esther Vervloed.

Picture on page 371 Shutterstock.com, https://www.shutterstock.com.

Sketch on page 371 Esther Vervloed.

Sketch on page 372 Esther Vervloed.

Picture on page 374 Pixabay, https://pixabay.com/en/labour-day-tools-work-1393864/, 13 May 2016.

Sketch on page 374 Esther Vervloed.

Sketch on page 375 Esther Vervloed.

Picture on page 377 Shutterstock.com, https://www.shutterstock.com.

Sketch on page 378 Esther Vervloed.

Sketch on page 379 Esther Vervloed.

Picture on page 382 The Scrum Patterns Group (Ville Reijonen). Dirty dishes in Ville Reijonen's kitchen, Helsinki, Finland, 2012.

Sketch on page 382 Esther Vervloed.

Sketch on page 383 Esther Vervloed.

Picture on page 387 U.S. Air Force, Airman 1st Class Samuel Taylor, 120625-F-MN676-097, https://www.dover.af.mil/News/Photos/igphoto/2000139408/. Dover, United Kingdom, 22 June 2012.

Sketch on page 387 Esther Vervloed.

Sketch on page 388 Esther Vervloed.

Picture on page 391 winterbee/Shutterstock.com, https://www.shutterstock.com, Cambridge, United Kingdom, 18 July 2011.

Sketch on page 392 Esther Vervloed.

Sketch on page 393 Esther Vervloed.

Picture on page 397 Shutterstock.com, https://www.shutterstock.com.

Sketch on page 398 Esther Vervloed.

Sketch on page 398 Esther Vervloed.

Picture on page 401 Image Provided by PresenterMedia.com.

Sketch on page 401 Esther Vervloed.

Sketch on page 403 Esther Vervloed.

Picture on page 405 The Scrum Patterns Group (James O. Coplien). Rungsted Kyst, Denmark, 1 April 2019.

Sketch on page 406 Esther Vervloed.

Sketch on page 407 Esther Vervloed.

Picture on page 410 Heinz Hummel, Pixabay.com, https://pixabay.com/en/climb-free-climbing-sun-rock-2296308/.

Sketch on page 410 Esther Vervloed.

Sketch on page 411 Esther Vervloed.

Picture on page 415 Jeff Schuler, https://www.flickr.com/photos/88127747@N00/1353039387. Cleveland, Ohio, USA, 9 September 2007.

Sketch on page 415 Esther Vervloed.

Sketch on page 417 Esther Vervloed.

Picture on page 419 Image Provided by PresenterMedia.com.

Sketch on page 420 Esther Vervloed.

Sketch on page 423 Esther Vervloed.

Picture on page 426 U.S. Air Force, Tech. Sgt. Rey Ramon, ID: 090307-F-5435R-131, http://www.kadena.af.mil/News/Photos/igphoto/2000611358/. The Rotary Plaza, Okinawa, Japan, 7 March 2009.

Sketch on page 430 Esther Vervloed.

Picture on page 429 Shutterstock.com, https://www.shutterstock.com.

Picture on page 435 John Hayes.

Picture on page 435 John Hayes.

Picture on page 440 Shutterstock.com, https://www.shutterstock.com.

Sketch on page 440 Esther Vervloed.

Sketch on page 441 Esther Vervloed.

Picture on page 443 The Scrum Guide: An interview with Jeff Sutherland. StickyMinds.com, https://www.stickyminds.com/interview/scrum-guide-interview-jeff-sutherland, 21 October 2014 (accessed 2 November 2017).

Picture on page 445 Pixabay, Alexander Lesnitsky, https://pixabay.com/en/planet-earth-cosmos-continents-1457453, 15 June 2016.

Sketch on page 445 Esther Vervloed.

Sketch on page 446 Esther Vervloed.

Picture on page 448 Shutterstock.com, https://www.shutterstock.com.

Sketch on page 448 Esther Vervloed.

Sketch on page 450 Esther Vervloed.

Bibliography

[AB07]   Deborah Ancona and Henrick Bresman. *X-teams: How to Build Teams that Lead, Innovate and Succeed.* Harper Business, New York, NY, 2007.

[ADL76]   Teresa M. Amabile, William DeJong, and Mark R. Lepper. Effects of externally imposed deadlines on subsequent intrinsic motivation. *Journal of Personality and Social Psychology.* 34[1]:92–98, 1976.

[Ahn07]   Hyeshin Ahn. Research on Product Identity by analyzing the examples of Mobile Phones. *Ph.D. Thesis, Universität Duisburg-Essen.* 2007.

[AIS77]   Christopher Alexander, Sara Ishikawa, and Murray Silverstein. *A Pattern Language.* Oxford University Press, New York, NY, 1977.

[Ale04]   Christopher Alexander. *The Nature of Order: An Essay on the Art of Building and the Nature of the Universe—Book 1, The Phenomenon of Life.* Routledge, New York NY, USA, 2004, July.

[Ale04a]   Christopher Alexander. *The Nature of Order: An Essay on the Art of Building and the Nature of the Universe—Book 2, The Process of Creating Life.* Routledge, New York NY, USA, 2004.

[Ale04b]   Christopher Alexander. *The Nature of Order: An Essay on the Art of Building and the Nature of the Universe—Book 3, A Vision of a Living World.* Routledge, New York NY, USA, 2004.

[Ale04c]   Christopher Alexander. *The Nature of Order: An Essay on the Art of Building and the Nature of the Universe—Book 4, The Luminous Ground.* Routledge, New York NY, USA, 2004.

[Ale79]   Christopher Alexander. *The Timeless Way of Building.* Oxford University Press, New York, NY, 1st edition, 1979.

[Ale99]   Christopher Alexander. The Origins of Pattern Theory: The Future of the
            Theory, and the Generation of a Living World. *IEEE Software.* 16[5]:72–82,
            1999, September/October.

[All77]   Thomas J. Allen. *Managing the Flow of Technology.* MIT Press, Cambridge,
            MA, 1977.

[And10]   David J. Anderson. *Kanban: Successful Evolutionary Change for Your
            Technology Business.* Blue Hole Press, http://www.e-junkie.com/129573,
            2010.

[Arg10]   Michael Argyle. *Bodily Communication.* Routledge and Kegan Paul, London,
            2, 2010.

[Arg91]   Chris Argyris. Teaching smart people how to learn. *Reflections.* 4[2], 1991.

[Arm91]   J. Scott Armstrong. Forecasting by Extrapolation: Conclusions from
            Twenty-five Years of Research. *Interfaces.* 14[6], 1991.

[Asi15]   Isaac Asimov. On Creativity. *MIT Technology Review.* 118[1]:12–13, 2015.

[AWP10]   Neal M. Ashkanasy, Celeste P M Wilderom, and Mark F. Peterson. *The
            Handbook of Organizational Culture and Climate.* SAGE Publications,
            Thousand Oaks, California, USA, 2010.

[Bal00]   Glenn Ballard. Positive versus negtive iteration in design. *In Proceedings
            of the 8th Annual Conference on the International Group for Lean Construction
            (IGLC-8).* 2000, June.

[BC10]   Gertrud Bjørnvig and James Coplien. *Lean Architecture for Agile Software
            Development.* John Wiley & Sons, New York, NY, 2010, July.

[BDSS99]   Mike Beedle, Martine Devos, Yonat Sharon, Ken Schwaber, and Jeff
            Sutherland. *Scrum: An extension pattern language for hyperproductive
            software development. In Brian Foote and Hans Rohnert, eds., Pattern
            Languages of Program Design - 4.* Addison-Wesley, Boston, MA, 1999.

[Bec04]   Kent Beck. *Extreme Programming Explained: Embrace Change.* Addison-
            Wesley, Boston, MA, 2, 2004.

[Ber12]   Ethan S. Bernstein. The Transparency Paradox: A Role for Privacy in
            Organizational Learning and Operational Control. *Administrative Science
            Quarterly.* 57[2]:181–216, 2012, June.

[Ber13]   Joe Bergin. *Agile Software: Patterns of Practice.* Software Tools, New York,
            New York, USA, 2013, March.

[BH07]   Jonah Berger and Chip Heath. Where Consumers Diverge from Others:
            Identity-Signaling and Product Domains. *Journal of Consumer Research.*
            34[2]:121–134, 2007, August.

[Bir51]   Peter Birch. Pride in Work. *The Irish Monthly.* 79[933]:101–104, 1951.

[Boe81]   Barry Boehm. *Software Engineering Economics.* Prentice Hall, Englewood Cliffs, NJ, 1981, October.

[Bra95]   Stewart Brandt. *How Buildings Learn: What Happens After They're Built.* Penguin, New York, NY, 1995.

[Bro95]   Frederick P. Brooks Jr. *The Mythical Man-Month: Essays on Software Engineering.* Addison-Wesley, Boston, MA, Anniversary, 1995.

[Bur94]   Thomas F. Burgess. Making the Leap to Agility: Defining and Achieving Agile Manufacturing through Business Process Redesign and Business Network Redesign. *International Journal of Operations and Production Management.* 14[11]:23–24, 1994.

[BVBD08]   L. E. L. M. van Boxmeer, Christian Verwijs, Robert de Bruin, Jacco Duel, and Martin C. Euwema. *The Netherlands' armed forces morale survey: empirical evidence for the morale models' main propositions. In International Military Testing Association (IMTA 2008) Congress edition 50.* International Military Testing Association, http://www.imta.info, 2008, October.

[CE94]   James O. Coplien and John Erickson. Examining the Software Development Process. *Dr. Dobb's Journal of Software Tools.* 19[1]:88–97, 1994, October.

[CH04]   James O. Coplien and Neil B. Harrison. *Organizational Patterns of Agile Software Development.* Addison-Wesley, Boston, MA, 2004.

[CL83]   Neil C. Churchill and Virginia L. Lewis. The Five Stages of Small Business Growth. *Harvard Business Review.* 61[3]:30–50, 1983, May-June.

[Coc06]   Alistair Cockburn. *Agile Software Development: The Cooperative Game.* Addison-Wesley, Boston, MA, 2006.

[Coh04]   Mike Cohn. *User stories applied: For agile software development.* Addison-Wesley, Boston, MA, 2004.

[Coh05]   Mike Cohn. *Agile Estimating and Planning.* Addison-Wesley, Boston, MA, 2005, November.

[Coh09]   Mike Cohn. *Succeeding with Agile: Software Development Using Scrum.* Addison-Wesley, Boston, MA, 2009, October.

[Con68]   Melvin E. Conway. How do committees invent?. *Datamation.* 14[4]:28–31, 1968, April. Note: The punctuation error in this entry is an artifact of the publication tools and is beyond author control.

[Cop17]   James O. Coplien. Kaikaku Mind. *Lean Magazine.* 15:21–23, 2017, November.

[Cou09]   Diane Coutu. Why Teams Don't Work. *Harvard Business Review.* 87[5], 2009, May.

[Cov94]   Stephen R. Covey. *The 7 Habits of Highly Effective People.* The Free Press, New York, NY, 1994.

[Dem00]   W. Edwards Deming. *Out of the Crisis.* MIT Press, Cambridge, MA, Paperback, 2000.

[DL06]   Esther Derby and Diana Larsen. *Agile Retrospectives: Making Good Teams Great.* The Pragmatic Bookshelf, Raleigh, NC, 2006.

[DL99]   Tom Demarco and Timothy Lister. *Peopleware: Productive Projects and Teams.* Dorset House, New York, NY, Second edition, 1999.

[DLP97]   Claude R. Duguay, Sylvain Landry, and Frederico Pasin. From Mass Production to Flexible/Agile Production. *International Journal of Operations and Production Management.* 17[12]:1183–1195, 1997.

[DM91]   Jay Dratler and Stephen M. McJohn. Obtaining Patent Rights. *Intellectual Property Law: Commercial, Creative, and Industrial Property.* 1:2–231 § 2.07[6], 1991.

[DR08]   Edward L. Deci and Richard M. Ryan. Self-determination Theory: A Macrotheory of Human Motivation, Development, and Health. *Canadian Psychology/Psychologie Canadienne.* 49[3]:182–185, 2008.

[EB12]   Ulrik Ecklund and Jan Bosch II. Applying Agile Development in Mass-Produced Embedded Systems. *Proceedings of XP 2012.* 31–46, 2012.

[EB12a]   Steven D. Eppinger and Tyson R. Browning. *Design Structure Matrix Methods and Applications.* MIT Press, Cambridge, MA, 2012.

[End05]   Isao Endo. *Visualization [Mieruka].* Toyo-Keizai-Shinbun-Sha, Tokyo, Japan, 2005.

[Etz16]   Amitai Etzioni. Happiness Is the Wrong Metric. *Society.* 53[3]:246–257, 2016.

[Fer07]   Timothy Ferries. *The Four-Hour Work Week: Escape the 9–5, Live Anywhere and Join the New Rich.* Crown Business, New York, NY, 2007.

[FFKP17]   M. Lance Frazier, Stav Fainshmidt, Ryan L. Klinger, Amir Pezeshkan, and Veselina Vracheva. Psychological Safety: A Meta-Analytic Review and Extension. *Personnel Psychology.* 70:113–165, 2017.

[FHR00]   Brian Foote, Neil Harrison, and Hans Rohnert. *Pattern Languages of Program Design 4.* Addison-Wesley, Boston, MA, 2000.

[FS05]   David N. Ford and Durward K. Sobeck II. Adapting Real Options to New Product Development by Modeling the Second Toyota Paradox. *IEEE Transactions on Engineering Management*. 52[2]:175–185, 2005, May.

[Fuj99]   Terunobu Fujino. Federation Pattern. *JapanPLoP*. 1999.

[Gal85]   John Gallant. Software Pricing Strategies: Tough Times bring Independents to the Table. *Computerworld*. XIX[52]:50–52, 1985, December.

[Gar13]   David A. Garvan. How Google Sold Its Engineers on Management. *Harvard Business Review*. 91[12]:74–82, 2013, December.

[GB10]   W. James Greville and Marc J. Buehner. Temporal Predictability Facilitates Causal Learning. *Journal of Experimental Psychology*. 139[4]:756–771, 2010.

[Ger89]   Connie J. Gersick. Marking time: Predictable transitions in task groups. *Academy of Management Journal*. 32:274–309, 1989.

[Gig08]   Gerd Gigerenzer. *Gut Feelings: The Intelligence of the Unconscious*. Penguin, New York, NY, Reprint, 2008, June.

[Gig14]   Gerd Gigerenzer. *Risk Savvy: How to Make Good Decisions*. Viking Press, New York, NY, 2014, March.

[Gil12]   Daniel Gilbert. The science behind the smile. *Harvard Business Review*. 90[1-2]:85–90, 2012, January-February.

[Gil19]   Mark Gillett. —. *Personal discussion with James Coplien*. 2019, February.

[GM17]   Héctor Garcia and Francesc Miralles. *Ikigai: The Japanese secret to a long and happy life*. Hutchinson, London, England, 2017.

[Gre10]   Daniel Greening. Enterprise Scrum: Scaling Scrum to the Executive Level. *Proceedings of 43rd Hawaii International Conference on System Sciences*. 1–10, 2010.

[GS05]   Douglas Griffin and Ralph D. Stacey. *Complexity and the Experience of Leading Organizations*. Routledge and Kegan Paul, London, 2005.

[GW11]   Donald C. Gause and Gerald M. Weinberg. *Exploring Requirements 2: First Steps Into Design*. Weinberg & Weinberg, Lincoln, Nebraska, USA, Kindle, 2011.

[Gün15]   Stefan T. Güntert. The impact of work design, autonomy support, and strategy on employee outcomes: A differentiated perspective on self-determination at work. *Motivation and Emotion*. 39:74–87, 2015, December.

[Hac02]   Richard Hackman. *Leading Teams: Setting the Stage for Great Performances*. Harper Business, New York, NY, 1, 2002.

[Hal62]   Arthur David Hall III. *A Methodology for Systems Engineering.* Van Nostrand Reinhold, New York, New York, 1962.

[Hal88]   Edward T. Hall. *The Dance of Life.* Doubleday, New York, NY, 1988.

[Ham03]   Keith H. Hammonds. How Google Grows... and Grows... and Grows. *Fast Company.* 69:74–81, 2003, April.

[Hea09]   Ralph Heath. *Celebrating Failure: The Power of Taking Risks, Making Mistakes, and Thinking Big.* The Career Press, 220 West Parkway, Unit 12, Pompton Plains, NJ 07444 USA, 2009, July.

[Hec95]   Charles Heckscher. The Limits of Participatory Management. *Across the Board.* 54:16–21, 1995, November/December.

[Hei10]   Hugo Heitz. Scrumming the Scrum. *Personal communication between Jeff Sutherland and Hugo Heitz, Paris, France.* 2010, December.

[Hel98]   Sally Helgesen. *Everyday Revolutionaries: Working Women and the Transformation of American Life.* Doubleday, New York, NY, 1998, January.

[Hen10]   Kevlin Henney. *97 Things Every Programmer Should Know.* O'Reilly & Associates, Inc., Sebastopol, CA, 2010.

[Hes13]   Alexander E. M. Hess. USA Today. 24/7 Wall St. On holiday: Countries With the Most Vacation Days. *USA Today.* 54, 2013, June.

[HM96]   Sir Lonsdale August Hale Col. (ret) and Aldershot Military Society. *The Fog of War.* Edward Stanford, 26 and 27, Cockspur Street, Charing Cross, S.W., London, England, 1896.

[HNWC12]   Marie-Astrid Hoogerwerf, Maarten K. Ninaber, Luuk N. A. Willems, and Adrian A. Captein. "Feelings are facts": Illness perceptions in patients with lung cancer. *Respiratory Medicine.* 106[8]:1170–1176, 2012.

[Joh11]   Steven Johnson. *Where Good Ideas Come From: The Natural History of Innovation.* Riverhead Books, New York, NY, 2011, September.

[JS09]   Carsten Ruseng Jakobsen and Jeff Sutherland. Scrum and CMMI—Going from Good to Great: are you ready-ready to be done-done?. *Proceedings of Agile 2009.* 2009, August. Note: The punctuation error in this entry is an artifact of the publication tools and is beyond author control.

[JTAL16]   Marie-Ève Jobidon, Isabelle Turcotte, Caroline Aubé, Alexandre Labrecque, Shelly Kelsey, and Sébastien Tremblay. Role Variability in Self-Organizing Teams Working in Crisis Management. *Small Group Research.* 48[1]:62–92, 2016.

[JWBL13]   Daniel T. Jones, James P. Womack, David Brunt, and Matthew Lovejoy. *Seeing the Whole Value Stream.* Lean Enterprise Institute, One Cambridge Center Cambridge, MA 02142 USA, 2, 2013, November.

[Jør13]   Magne Jørgensen. Relative Estimation of Software Development Effort: It Matters with What and How You Compare. *IEEE Software.* 30[2]:74–79, 2013, March-April.

[Jør14]   Magne Jørgensen. Top-down and bottom-up expert estimation of software development effort. *Information Software Technology.* 46[1]:3–16, 2014.

[Jør14a]   Magne Jørgensen. What we Know about Software Development Effort Estimation. *IEEE Software.* 31[2]:37–40, 2014.

[Kah13]   Daniel Kahneman. *Thinking, Fast and Slow.* Farrar, Straus and Giroux, New York, NY, 2013.

[Kan84]   Rosabeth Moss Kanter. *Change Masters: Innovation and Entrepreneurship in the American Corporation.* Touchstone, New York, NY, 1984.

[Kee09]   Gerard Keegan. *Higher Psychology: Approaches and Methods.* Hodder Gibson, 2a Christie Street, Paisley PA1 1NB, UK, 2, 2009, September.

[Ker01]   Norm Kerth. *Project Retrospectives: A Handbook for Team Reviews.* Dorset House, New York, NY, 2001, February.

[KI06]   Steve W. J. Kozlowski and Daniel R. Ilgen. Enhancing the Effectiveness of Work Groups and Teams. *Psychological Science in the Public Interest.* 7[3]:77–124, 2006.

[KK66]   Daniel Katz and Robert Luis Kahn. *The Social Psychology of Organizations.* John Wiley & Sons, New York, NY, 1966.

[Kni17]   Henrik Kniberg. —. *Personal exchange between Henrik Kniberg and James Coplien.* 2017, June.

[Kol15]   John Kolko. Design Thinking Comes of Age. *Harvard Business Review.* 93[9]:ff. 66, 2015.

[KSDP92]   Tatsuya Kameda, Mark F. Stasson, James H. Davis, Craig D. Parks, and Suzi K. Zimmerman. Social Dilemmas, Subgroups, and Motivation Loss in Task-Oriented Groups: In Search of an 'Optimal' Team Size in Division of Work. *Social Psychology Quarterly.* 55[1]:47–56, 1992, November/December.

[Kuh04]   Patricia K. Kuhl. Early Language acquisition: Cracking the speech code. *Nature Reviews Neuroscience.* 5:831–843, 2004, November/December.

[LA68]   Gardner Lindzey and Elliot Aronson. *The Handbook of Social Psychology.* Addison-Wesley, Boston, MA, 2, 1968.

[Lan58]   Henry A. Landsberger. *Hawthorne Revisited: Management and the worker: its critics, and developments in human relations in industry.* Cornell University Press, Ithaca, NY, USA, 1958.

[LHSB06]   Patricia R. Laughlin, Eric C. Hatch, Jonathan S. Silver, and Lee Boh. Groups Perform Better Than the Best Individuals on Letters-to-Numbers Problems: Effects of Group Size. *Journal of Personality and Social Psychology.* 90[4]:644–651, 2006, November/December.

[Lik04]   Jeffrey K. Liker. *The Toyota Way: 14 Management Principles from the World's Greatest Manufacturer.* McGraw-Hill, Emeryville, CA, 2004.

[LL07]   Gary P. Latham and Edward A. Locke. New developments in and directions for goal-setting research. *European Psychologist.* 12[4]:290–300, 2007, November/December.

[LL16]   John Lunney and Sue Lueder. *Postmortem Culture: Learning from Failure.* In Betsey Beyer et al., eds., *Site Reliability Engineering: How Google Runs Production Systems.* O'Reilly & Associates, Inc., Sebastopol, CA, 2016.

[LL99]   Edwin A. Locke and Larry P. Latham. Building a practically useful theory of goal setting and task motivation: A 35-year odyssey. *American Psychologist.* 57[9]:705–717, 1999.

[LM05]   Jeffrey Liker and David Meier. *The Toyota Way Fieldbook: A Practical Guide for Implementing Toyota's 4Ps.* McGraw-Hill, Emeryville, CA, 2005.

[LM90]   John M. Levine and Richard L. Moreland. Progress in Small Group Research. *Annual Review of Psychology.* 41:585–634, 1990.

[LV09]   Craig Larman and Bas Vodde. *Scaling Lean & Agile Development.* Addison-Wesley, Boston, MA, 2009.

[LV10]   Craig Larman and Bas Vodde. *Practices for Scaling Lean & Agile Development: Large, Multisite, and Offshore Product Development with Large-Scale Scrum.* Addison-Wesley, Boston, MA, 2010.

[Lyu01]   Sonja Lyubomirsky. Why are some people happier than others? The role of cognitive and motivational process in well-being. *American Psychologist.* 56:239–249, 2001.

[Man01]   Frederick J. Manning. *In Reuven Gal and A. David Mangelsdorff, eds., Handbook of Military Psychology.* John Wiley & Sons, New York, NY, 2001.

[MBJP16]   Niall Murphy, Betsey Beyer, Chris Jones, and Jennifer Petoff. *Sharding the Monitoring Hierarchy.* In Betsey Beyer et al., eds., *Site Reliability Engineering: How Google Runs Production Systems.* O'Reilly & Associates, Inc., Sebastopol, CA, 2016.

[MBN04]   Angela Martin, Robert Biddle, and James Noble. The XP Customer Role in Practice: Three Studies. *Proceedings of the Agile Development Conference (ADC'04)*. 42–54, 2004, November/December.

[McC06]   Steve McConnell. *Software Estimation: Demystifying the black art*. Microsoft Press, Redmond, WA, 2006.

[McC96]   Steve McConnell. The XP Customer Role in Practice: Three Studies. *Software Development*. 4[8]:38–42, 1996, August.

[MSNG99] Thomas P. Moran, Eric Saund, William van Nelle, Anjur U. Gujar, Kenneth P. Fishkin, and Beverly L. Harrison. Design and Technology for Collaborage: Collaborative Collages of Information on Physical Walls. *Proceedings of the 12th annual ACM symposium on User interface software and technology*. 197–206, 1999.

[Nie93]   Jakob Nielsen. Iterative User Interface Design. *IEEE Computer*. 26[11]:32–41, 1993.

[NL11]   Tsedal Neeley and Paul M. Leonardi. Defend Your Research: Effective Managers Say the Same Thing Twice (or More). *Harvard Business Review*. 89[5], 2011, May.

[NT95]   Ikujiro Nonaka and Hirotaka Takeuchi. *The Knowledge-Creating Company: How Japanese Companies Create the Dynamics of Innovation*. Oxford University Press, New York, NY, 1995.

[OC13]   Sean O'Connor and Michael Cavanagh. The coaching ripple effect: The effects of developmental coaching on wellbeing across organizational networks. *Psychology of Well-Being: Theory, Research and Practice*. 3[1]:2, 2013, June.

[Ohn88]   Taichi Ohno. *Toyota Production System: Beyond Large-Scale Production*. Productivity Press, New York, NY, 1988.

[OSGB09] Lisa D. Ordóñez, Maurice E. Schweitzer, Adam D. Galinsky, and Max H. Bazerman. Goals gone wild: The systematic side effects of overprescribing goal setting. *Academy of Management Perspectives*. 23[1]:6–16, 2009, June.

[OSTD08] Emi Osono, Norihiko Shimizu, Hirotaka Takeuchi, and John Kyle Dorton. *Extreme Toyota: Radical Contradictions That Drive Success at the World's Best Manufacturer*. John Wiley & Sons, New York, NY, 2008.

[OW10]   Andy Oram and Greg Wilson. *What Does 10X Mean? In Making Software, by Steve McConnell*. O'Reilly & Associates, Inc., Sebastopol, CA, 2010.

[OWW93]   Brid O'Conaill, Steve J Whittaker, and Sylvia Wilbur. Conversations Over Video Conferences: An Evaluation of the Spoken Aspects of Video-Mediated

Communication. *Human-Computer Interaction.* 8[4]:389–428, 1993, November/December.

[Pau12]   Ryan Paul. Exclusive: A behind-the-scenes look at Facebook release engineering. *Ars Technica.* 2012, April.

[Pic10]   Roman Pichler. *Agile Product Management With Scrum: Creating Products That Customers Love.* Addison-Wesley, Boston, MA, 2010, March.

[Pin11]   Daniel Pink. *Drive: The Surprising Truth About What Motivates Us.* Riverhead Books, New York, NY, 2011.

[Rei09]   Donald Reinertsen. *The Principles of Product Development Flow: Second Generation Lean Product Development.* Celeritas Publishing, Redondo Beach, CA, 2009, May.

[Rei98]   Donald Reinertsen. *Managing the Design Factory: A Product Developer's Toolkit.* The Free Press, New York, NY, 1998, March.

[Rie11]   Eric Ries. *Lean Startup.* Penguin, New York, NY, 2011.

[RL07]   Darren Rowley and Manfred Lange. Forming to Performing: The Evolution of an Agile Team. *Proceedings of Agile 2007.* 408–414, 2007.

[RM05]   Linda Rising and Mary Lynn Manns. *Fearless Change.* Pearson, 75 Arlington Street, Suite 300, Boston, MA 02116 USA, 2005.

[Rod13]   Tori Rodríguez. Taking the Bad with the Good. *Scientific American Mind.* 24[2]:26–27, 2013, August, May.

[Rot10]   Mike Rother. *Toyota Kata: Managing People for Improvement, Adaptiveness and Superior Results.* McGraw-Hill, Emeryville, CA, 2010.

[Roy70]   Winston Royce. Managing the development of large software systems. *Proceedings of IEEE WESCON.* 1–9, 1970, August.

[RS11]   Dan Rawsthorne and Doug Shimp. *Exploring Scrum: The Fundamentals.* Create Space, Scotts Valley, CA, 2011.

[RSBH12]   Daniel Rodríguez, Miguel-Ángel Sicilia, Elena García Barriocanal, and Rachel Harrison. Empirical findings on team size and productivity in software development. *Journal of Systems and Software.* 85[3]:562–570, 2012, August.

[RT03]   Theodore Roosevelt and Brian Thomsen. *The man in the arena: the selected writings of Theodore Roosevelt; a reader.* Forge Publishing, Dartmouth, Nova Scotia, Canada, 2003, March.

[Rub12]   Kenneth S. Rubin. *Essential Scrum: A Practical Guide to the Most Popular Agile Process.* Addison-Wesley, Boston, MA, 2012.

[SA09]   Jeff Sutherland and Igor Altman. Take No Prisoners: How a Venture Capital Group Does Scrum. *Proceedings of Agile 2009*. 2009.

[Sat91]   Virginia Satir. *The Satir Model: Family Therapy and Beyond*. Science and Behavior Books, Palo Alto, CA, 1991, December.

[SB01]   Ken Schwaber and Mike Beedle. *Agile Software Development with Scrum (Series in Agile Software Development)*. Pearson, 75 Arlington Street, Suite 300, Boston, MA 02116 USA, 2001.

[SC99]   Daniel J. Simons and Christopher F. Chabris. Gorillas in Our Midst: Sustained Inattentional Blindness for Dynamic Events. *Perception*. 28[9]:1059–1074, 1999, September.

[Sch01]   Ken Schwaber. *Agile Project Management with Scrum*. Microsoft Press, Redmond, WA, 2001.

[Sch04]   Barry Schwartz. The Tyrrany of Choice. *Scientific American*. 290[4]:71–75, 2004, April.

[Sch06]   Edgar H Schein. *Organizational Culture and Leadership*. Jossey-Bass Publishers, San Francisco, CA, 3, 2006, March.

[SDB09]   David J. Singer, Norbert Doerry, and Michael E. Buckley. What Is Set-Based Design?. *Naval Engineers Journal*. 121[4]:63–68, 2009, October. Note: The punctuation error in this entry is an artifact of the publication tools and is beyond author control.

[Sen06]   Peter Senge. *The Fifth Discipline*. Doubleday, New York, NY, 2006.

[SF77]   Charles R. Snyder and Harold L. Fromkin. Abnormality as a Positive Characteristic: The Development and Validation of a Scale Measuring Need for Uniqueness. *Journal of Abnormal Psychology*. 86:518–527, 1977.

[Sho10]   John Shook. How to Change a Culture: Lessons from NUMMI. *MIT Sloan Management Review*. 51:63–68, 2010, Winter.

[SHR14]   Jeff Sutherland, Neil Harrison, and Joel Riddle. Teams That Finish Early Accelerate Faster: A Pattern Language for High Performing Scrum Teams. *Proceedings of 47th Hawaii International Conference on System Sciences*. 47, 2014.

[SJJ07]   Jeff Sutherland, Carsten Ruseng Jakobsen, and Kent Johnson. Scrum and CMMI Level 5: A Magic Potion for Code Warriors!. *Proceedings of Agile 2007*. 272–278, 2007.

[SLJA17]   Angus Stevenson, ed., Christine A. Lindberg, ed., Elizabeth J. Jewell, and Frank Abate. *The New Oxford American Dictionary*. Oxford University Press, New York, NY, 3, 2017.

[Smy10]   Rob Smyth. *The Spirit of Cricket: What makes cricket the greatest game on Earth.* Elliott & Thompson Limited, 27 John Street, London WC1N 2BX, 2010, May.

[SP12]   Gretchen Spreitzer and Christine Porath. Creating Sustainable Performance. *Harvard Business Review.* 90[1-2]:93–99, 2012, January/February.

[SS04]   John Storey and Graeme Salaman. *Managers of Innovation: Insights into Making Innovation Happen.* John Wiley & Sons, New York, NY, 2004, December.

[SS12]   Ken Schwaber and Jeff Sutherland. *Software in 30 Days: How Agile Managers Beat the Odds, Delight Their Customers, and Leave Competitors in the Dust.* John Wiley & Sons, New York, NY, 2012, April.

[SS14]   Jeff Sutherland and J. J. Sutherland. *Scrum: The Art of Doing Twice the Work in Half the Time.* Dorset House, New York, NY, 2014.

[SSGB02]   Wilmar B. Schaufeli, Marisa Salanova, Vincente González-Romá, and Arnold B. Bakker. The measurement of engagement and burnout: A two sample confirmatory factor analytic approach. *Journal of Happiness Studies.* 3[1]:71–92, 2002, March.

[ST13]   Bob Sullivan and Hugh Thompson. Gray Matter. Brain Interrupted. *New York Times.* SR12, 2013, May.

[Sta12]   Ralph D. Stacey. *Tools and Techniques of Leadership and Management: Meeting the Challenge of Complexity.* Routledge, New York NY, USA, 2012.

[Ste12]   Peter N. Stearns. The history of happiness. *Harvard Business Review.* 90[1-2]:104–109, 2012, January-February.

[Ste72]   Ivan Dale Steiner. *Group Process and Productivity.* Academy Chicago Publishers, Chicago, IL, 1972.

[Str04]   Steven H. Strogatz. *Sync.* Penguin, New York, NY, 2004.

[Str06]   Mark Striebeck. Ssh! We're Adding a Process .... *Proceedings of Agile 2006.* 193–201, 2006.

[Sut01]   Jeff Sutherland. Agile Can Scale: Inventing and Reinventing SCRUM in Five Companies. *Cutter IT Journal: The Great Methodology Debate, Part 1.* 5–11, 2001.

[Sut05]   Jeff Sutherland. Future of Scrum: Parallel Pipelining of Sprints in Complex Projects. *Proceedings of Agile Development Conference (ADC'05).* 2005.

[Sut10]   Jeff Sutherland. *The Scrum Handbook.* Scrum Training Institue Press, 32 Appleton Street Somerville, MA 02144, 2010.

[SW92]   Joop Swieringa and André F. M. Wierdsma. *Becoming a Learning Organization: Beyond the Learning Curve*. Addison-Wesley, Boston, MA, 1992.

[Tay4)]   Frederick Winslow Taylor. *Principles of Scientific Management*. Harper One, 201 California St, San Francisco, CA 94111, 1923 (2014).

[TGK14]   Chade-Meng Tan, Prof. Daniel Goleman Ph.D., and Jon Kabat-Zinn Ph.D.. *Search Inside Yourself: The Unexpected Path to Achieving Success, Happiness (and World Peace)*. John Wiley & Sons, New York, NY, Reprint, 2014, September.

[TJ14]   Adam Trendowicz and Ross Jeffery. *Software Project Effort Estimation: Foundations and Best Practice Guidelines for Success*. Springer, New York, NY, 2014, 2014.

[TN86]   Hirotaka Takeuchi and Ikujiro Nonaka. The New New Product Development Game. *Harvard Business Review*. 64[1]:137–146, 1986, January.

[TOS08]   Hirotaka Takeuchi, Emi Osono, and Norihiko Shimizu. The Contradictions that Drive Toyota's Success. *Harvard Business Review*. 86[6], 2008.

[vC97]   Don vandeWall and Larry L. Cummings. A test of the influence of goal orientation on the feedback-seeking process. *Journal of Applied Psychology*. 82[3]:390–400, 1997.

[Wei87]   Jiri Weiss. IBM Boosts Sales Force, Accents Client Support. *InfoWorld*. 9[8], 1987, February.

[Wei92]   Gerald M. Weinberg. *Quality Software Management: Volume 1, Systems Thinking*. Dorset House, New York, NY, 1992.

[Wis13]   Thomas P. Wise. *Trust in Virtual Teams: Organization, Strategies and Assurance for Successful Projects*. Routledge and Kegan Paul, London, 2013, May.

[WL68]   Arthur H. Walker and Jay W. Lorsch. Organizational Choice: Product vs. Function. *Harvard Business Review*. 46[6]:129–138, 1968, November.

[WLCS95]   Allen Ward, Jeffrey K. Liker, John J. Cristiano, and Durward K. Sobek II. The Second Toyota Paradox: How Delaying Decisions Can Make Better Cars Faster. *Sloan Management Review*. 36[3], 1995, January.

[WML14]   Ben Waber, Jennifer Magnolfi, and Greg Lindsay. Workspaces that move people. *Harvard Business Review*. 92[10], 2014, October.

Index

DIGITS

3M, 179
5S techniques, 372, 376

A

Abnormal Termination of
  Sprint Ceremony, 114, 154
absorption, engagement and,
  427
acceptance testing
  Sprint Review and, 167–
    168
  Teams That Finish Early
    Accelerate Faster and,
    352
accountability
  Autonomous Team and,
    88
  autonomy and, 162
  management and, 39
  Product Owner, 70, 408
Ackoff, Russell Lincoln, 103,
  299
adaptation, as central to
  Scrum, xxv
Aggregate Velocity
  patlet, 464
  vs. Specialized Velocities,
    335
  understanding, 320,
    325, 329–333
  uses, 295
Agile Manifesto, 5, 22, 173
Agile Retrospectives, 173
*Agile Software Development
  with Scrum*, 22

Aguiar, Ademar Manuel Teix-
  eira de, xxi
Ålands Penningautomatféren-
  ing (PAF), 393
alerts, Visible Status and,
  369
Alexander, Christopher
  on Small Teams, 57
  on moral grounding of
    patterns, 455
  on pattern languages,
    xxix, 413, 451–452
  on patterns, xxvi, xxxiv
  pattern numbers and,
    xxxvi
  A Place to Wait, 112
  Theory of Centers, 100
Allen Curve, 51–52
Allen, Paul Gardner, 194
Allen, Thomas J., 51
andon cord, 152, 370, *see also* Emergency Procedure
Apple, 421, 424
Apprenticeship
  Mitosis and, 100
  patlet, 468
Armstrong, J. Scott, 325
artifacts, in core patterns
  overview, 7–10
Asimov, Isaac (Айзек Азимов),
  313
AT&T, 36, 393
attention
  goals and, 366
  Visible Status and, 366–
    370
Atterbury, Ed, 152

authority
  Autonomous Team and,
    88
  Product Owner, 176,
    178, 180, 265
  ScrumMaster, 108
Autonomous Team, *see al-
  so* autonomy
  as Cross-Functional
    Team, 62
  Development Team as, 4,
    35, 80–81, 86–90, 95,
    99, 165, 210, 362, 389
  Happiness Metric and,
    430
  interconnections between
    teams, 40
  order in pattern se-
    quence, xxix
  patlet, 459
  Scrum Team as, 38, 48,
    86–90, 178, 181–182,
    234
  ScrumMaster Incognito
    and, 149
  as Self-Organizing Team,
    88–89
  The Spirit of the Game
    and, 4
  Sprint Goal and, 342
  structure and organiza-
    tion, 87–90
  Team Sprint and, 389
  understanding, 86–90
autonomy, *see also* Autonomy
  Team
  Birds of a Feather and,
    33
  Developer-Ordered Work
    Plan and, 358–362

Happiness Metric and, 428, 430, 434, 438
isolation from, 106
mastery and, 33
motivation and, 89
Product Pride and, 182
purpose and, 439
responsibility and, 162
scaling and, 89
autotracer.org, xxii

B

ba, 183
Bachmann, Philipp, xxi
Backer, M. Y. C. (Yvette), xxi
backlog, *see* Product Backlog; Refined Product Backlog; ROI-Ordered Backlog; Sprint Backlog; Sprint Backlog Item
Backlog Refinement Meeting, 267, *see also* Refined Product Backlog
Baden-Powell, Robert Stephenson Smyth, 376
baseline, Testable Improvements and, 409
Be Ready to be Done, 319
Beck, Kent, 323
Beedle, Mike, 344, 442
Benefield, Gabrielle, 390
Berczuk, Stephen Paul, xxi
Bergin, Joseph Anthony, xxii, 254
best practices
Autonomous Team and, 87
Self-Organizing Team and, 91
beta testers, Release Staging Layers and, 403–404
Beyond the Happy Bubble, *see* Pop the Happy Bubble
Big Hairy Audacious Goal (BHAG), 325
Birds of a Feather
Autonomous Team and, 88, 90
composing pattern languages and, 454
management role in, 39, 42
Mitosis and, 100
patlet, 458

in Product Organization sequence, 14
roles, 33
Scrum of Scrums and, 163
ScrumMaster and, 33
for ScrumMasters, 109, 117
Stable Teams and, 85
Team Pride and, 28, 33
team structure and organization, 27–28
understanding, 31–34
Value Areas and, 418
bit-planner.com, 278
Bjørnvig, Gertrud, xxi
blame
blameless culture, 208
Estimation Points and, 295
Information Radiator and, 277
quality and Definition of Done, 383
Boehm, Barry, 290
Borland, 147, 336
Bosch Software Innovations, 30
Boy Scouts, 376
branching, 253
broadcast warning messages (BWMs), 393
Brooks, Frederick Phillips Jr., 97, 391
Brooks' Law, 83, 94, 97–98, 211
bubbles, *see* Pop the Happy Bubble
Buddhism and Ten Bulls, xvii–xx
budget, MetaScrum and, 180
Buehner, Marc Jens, 233
bugs, *see* defects
burnout
Happiness Metric and, 439
ScrumMaster, 109
BWMs (broadcast warning messages), 393

C

cadence, *see also* Organizational Sprint Pulse; rhythms
learning and, 232

One Step at a Time and, 413
roles and, 79
Sprint, 229, 232
understanding, 225–227
calibration mode, 338
Canary deployment, 404
Captain, Swarming and, 129
career development, Birds of a Feather and, 33
casuistic theory of value, 247, 301
causal learning, 233
Cech, Petr, 153
Centers, Theory of, 100
Challenger, 274
change, *see also* Change for Free
MetaScrum and, 179
Satir cycle, 338
The Spirit of the Game and, 4–6
time for in Kaizen Pulse, 132–135
Whack the Mole and, 381
change fees, 256
Change for Free, *see also* changes
Development Partnership and, 76, 257
High Value First and, 252, 254
with Money for Nothing, 260
origins, 257, 260
patlet, 462
in Product Backlog Sequence, 261
ROI-Ordered Backlog and, 250
understanding, 255–257
Change for Free and Money for Nothing, 260
chapters, 34, 42
charters, 33
checklist, Definition of Done, 385
Chief Engineer, 49, 267, 370
Chief Product Owner
Development Partnership and, 75
role, 68, 71–72, 458
scaling and, 95
Value Areas and, 417
Citrix Online, 130

cleanup, *see* Good Housekeeping

clients, *see* Development Partnership

close partners, Release Staging Layers and, 403

coaching, *see* Scrum (Master) Coach

The coaching ripple effect, 118

Cockburn, Alistair Aidan, 52, 279

code ownership, team structure and organization, 29

Coke, 419, 424

collaboration
    Collocated Team and, 50–54
    large teams, 55–57
    Small Teams and, 55–59

Collins, Jamie, xxi

Collocated Team
    Development Partnership and, 75, 77
    Development Team as, 80
    identity, 54
    Mitosis and, 100
    patlet, 458
    Product Owner Team as, 72
    Scrum Team as, 15, 48
    as Self-Organizing Team, 93
    in simple pattern sequence, 8
    vs. Small Red Phone, 114
    structure and organization, 27, 52–54
    understanding, 50–54

commitment
    Fertile Soil and, 22
    as organizational value, 21

committees, disadvantages, 65–66

communication, *see also* Information Radiator
    Allen Curve, 51–52
    Chief Product Owner, 72
    Collocated Team and, 50–54
    large teams, 55–59
    nonverbal, 51
    online, 51, 54
    Oyatsu Jinja (Snack Shrine) and, 110–112
    ScrumMaster role, 109

Small Red Phone and, 113–114

Small Teams and, 55–59

team structure and organization, 23–24, 26

The Water Cooler and, 112

communities of practice, 33–34, *see also* Birds of a Feather

Community of Trust
    Autonomous Team and, 86
    Development Team and, 80
    Emergency Procedure and, 153
    Impediment List and, 196
    Information Radiator and, 277
    Norms of Conduct and, 151
    patlet, 466
    in Product Organization sequence, 14
    Responsive Deployment and, 396
    Sprint Planning and, 126
    Sprint Retrospective and, 174
    Sprint Review and, 166, 168
    Stable Teams, 83
    Testable Improvements and, 407
    Vacation PBI and, 300
    Value Stream Fork and, 425

Compensate Success patlet, 469

competencies
    business, 33
    Cross-Functional Team and, 61–64
    missing, 62
    organizing around, 27–34
    Set-Based Design and, 207

Completion Headroom, 160, 467

complexity
    Collocated Team and, 458
    One Step at a Time and, xxx
    of organizations, xxx, 20
    Scrum of Scrums and, 161

Self-Organizing Team and, 91

Value Stream Fork and, 421, 424

constraints
    creativity and, 191, 228, 233
    Set-Based Design and, 206
    triple constraint, 399

context switching, 317

continual improvement, Regular Product Increment and, 398

continuous delivery, *see* Responsive Deployment

continuous discontinuity, 102

continuous improvement, *see also* kaikaku; kaizen; Kaizen and Kaikaku; Kaizen Pulse; Sprint Retrospective; Testable Improvements
    One Step at a Time and, 410–414
    Pop the Happy Bubble and, 139–142
    Responsive Deployment and, 394
    Running Average Velocity and, 328
    Scrum Team and, 46–47, 49
    ScrumMaster role, 15
    Sprint Retrospective and, 16
    time for, 132–135

contracts, cross-functionality and, 61

convergence in Set-Based Design, 204–209

Conway's Law
    Autonomous Team and, 90
    Collocated Team and, 53
    feature growth and, 421
    Fertile Soil and, 22
    levels of, 27–28
    organizing around competencies, 27–30
    organizing around processes, 27
    origins, 28
    patlet, 457
    in Product Organization sequence, 14
    scaling and, 96

understanding, 23–30
Value Stream Fork and,
425
Coplien, James, 78
costs
change fees, 256
Change for Free and,
255–257
High Value First and,
251–254
Money for Nothing and,
258–260
Pigs Estimate and, 282
Product Backlog Item or-
dering, 273
Refined Product Backlog
and, 314
Responsive Deployment
and, 394
termination fees, 259
courage
Fertile Soil and, 22
Norms of Conduct and,
151
as organizational value,
21
creativity
constraints and, 191,
228, 233
solitude and, 313
cricket, 3, 6
Crisp, 428
cross-cutting structures,
team organization, 25–26
Cross-Functional Team
Autonomous Team as, 62
Collocated Team and, 53
concurrent activities and,
414
Developer-Ordered Work
Plan and, 360
Development Team as,
80, 96, 99, 200, 232,
399
kaikaku and, 103
multiple, 63
order in pattern se-
quence, xxix
Organizational Sprint
Pulse and, 236
patlet, 458
Scrum Team as, 15, 48,
57, 61, 182, 200
in simple pattern se-
quence, 8
Small Teams as, 58, 62

Specialized Velocities
and, 336
Stable Team and, 62, 84
structure and organiza-
tion, 28, 61–64
team size and, 57–58
understanding, 60–64
Value Areas and, 418
variance in velocity
kaizen, 134
cross-training, Small Teams
and, 58
Cuddicini, Carlo, 153
culture
Autonomous Team and,
88
blameless, 208
Development Partnership
and, 74–77
monochronic, 226, 364
Norms of Conduct and,
150–151
polychronic, 226
Cunningham, Ward, 357
customers, see also Development Partnership
Change for Free and,
255–257
vs. end users, 67
High Value First and,
251–254
lack of in Scrum, 67
Money for Nothing and,
258–260
Release Staging Layers
and, 401–404
Surrogate Customer pat-
let, 468
Value Stream and, 200–
201
Vision and, 193

D

Daily Clean Code, see Good
Housekeeping
Daily Scrum, see also Scrum
of Scrums
benefits, 146
defined, 8
Dependencies First and,
372
Developer-Ordered Work
Plan and, 361
duration, 144–145, 149
kaizen in, xxxi
misunderstandings, xxvii
ordering during, 359

Oyatsu Jinja (Snack
Shrine) after, 111
patlet, 460
in Product Organization
sequence, 13, 15
Production Episode and,
356
questions for, 145
rhythms and, 225–226
Scrum Board and, 217
ScrumMaster Incognito
and, 145, 148–149
ScrumMaster role, 107,
144–145, 149
in simple pattern se-
quence, 9
Small Items and, 285
Sprint and, 230
Sprint Backlog and, 347
Sprint Backlog Item and,
350
Sprint Goal and, 15, 144–
146, 149, 171, 342
Sprint Planning and, 125
vs. Sprint Retrospective,
171
Swarming and, 131
understanding, 81, 143–
147
in Value Stream Se-
quence, 189
Visible Status and, 369
Whack the Mole and,
380–381
Daily Standup, see Daily
Scrum
Day Care
Greatest Value and, 447
patlet, 468
de Liefde, Martin, xxi
deadlines
motivation and, 353
Production Episode and,
353
Release Range and, 244
Deci, Edward L., 428
decision-making
Autonomous Team and,
86–90
autonomy and responsi-
bility, 162
consumer, 420
Cross-Functional Team
and, 28
High Value First and, 259
last responsible moment,
240, 311, 313, 372
MetaScrum and, 179

Product Backlog as framework for decision-making, 240
Product Owner and, 39
speed of, 25–26
team identity and, 28
team structure and organization, 24–26, 28
dedication, engagement and, 427
defects
interruptions and, 159
Responsive Deployment and, 392–393, 396
tolerance for, 159
Visible Status and, 369
Whack the Mole and, 159, 369, 377–381, 392
Definition of Done
checklist, 385
criteria for, 385
Cross-Functional Team and, 60–62, 80
vs. Definition of Ready, 319
delivery and, 232
Development Team and, 80, 92, 382–386
documentation and, 272
Emergency Procedure and, 152
Estimation Points and, 294, 296
fixing issues and, 379–380
Good Housekeeping and, 375
internal tasks and, 384
One Step at a Time and, 411
patlet, 465
Product Backlog Item and, 232, 269, 273
Production Episode and, 356
in project language example, 453
Regular Product Increment and, 398
Release Plan and, 239
Release Staging Layers and, 402, 404
Responsive Deployment and, 391–392, 395
scaling and, 95–96
Scrum Board and, 218

Scrum of Scrums and, 163
ScrumMaster role, 43, 384–386, 404
Self-Organizing Team and, 92
Small Items and, 285
Sprint Backlog Item and, 350
Sprint Burndown Chart and, 213
Sprint Retrospective and, 174
Sprint Review and, 167, 189, 382–383, 386
Swarming and, 129–131
vs. Testable Improvements, 409
testing and, 385, 391
understanding, 382–386
velocity and, 320
Definition of Ready
criteria for, 318
vs. Definition of Done, 319
Development Team role, 308, 316–319
Fixed Work and, 119
Granularity Gradient and, 290
patlet, 463
Product Backlog and, 264, 267, 316–319
Product Backlog Item and, 188, 270
in Product Backlog Sequence, 262
Product Owner role, 308, 317–319
Product Owner Team role, 71
Responsive Deployment and, 395
Small Items and, 287
Sprint Planning and, 125
understanding, 316–319
Dekker, Maurice, 43
Deliberate Practice, 339, see also Intentional Practice
delivery
Definition of Done and, 232
feedback and, 232, 392
last responsible moment and, 391
Money for Nothing and, 258–260

organizing teams around deliverables, 26
Release Staging Layers and, 401–404
Responsive Deployment and, 391–396
Sprint schedule and, 231
Value Stream and, 200
in Value Stream Sequence, 189
Delivery Team, see Development Team
Delphi technique, 295
Deming, W. Edwards, 438
Dependencies First
decision-making and, 240
Developer-Ordered Work Plan and, 362
patlet, 465
Scrum of Scrums and, 164
Sprint Backlog and, 347
understanding, 371–373
deployment, Canary, 404, see also delivery; Responsive Deployment
design, see also pattern languages; Set-Based Design
clarification of Product Backlog Item, 350
Design Structure Matrix, 313–314
Design Sprint, 207
Developer Controls Process
Autonomous Team and, 88
patlet, 467
Developer-Ordered Work Plan
Dependencies First and, 372
vs. Informal Labor Plan, 362
patlet, 464
Product Backlog and, 266
Production Episode and, 356
Self-Organizing Team and, 93
Sprint and, 230
Sprint Goal and, 342
vs. Swarming, 362
Swarming and, 131, 362
understanding, 358–362
Developing in Pairs
autonomy and, 89
experience levels and, 116

patlet, 469
Remove the Shade and, 138
Development Episode pattern, 87, 357
Development Partnership
    Change for Free and, 76, 257
    customer concept and, 67
    Money for Nothing and, 260
    Norms of Conduct and, 151
    Organizational Sprint Pulse and, 236
    patlet, 458
    in Product Organization sequence, 15
    Release Staging Layers and, 403–404
    Scrum Team and, 49, 403
    understanding, 73–77
    Value and ROI and, 246
Development Team, *see also* Daily Scrum; Developer-Ordered Work Plan; Emergency Procedure; Pigs Estimate; Product Backlog; Product Backlog Item; Production Episode; Refined Product Backlog; Regular Product Increment; Sprint; Sprint Backlog; Sprint Backlog Item; Sprint Goal; Sprint Planning; Sprint Retrospective; Sprint Review; Swarming; Teams That Finish Early Accelerate Faster; velocity
    administrative duties, 105
    Aggregate Velocity and, 329–333
    as Autonomous Team, 4, 35, 80–81, 86–90, 95, 99, 165, 210, 362, 389
    boundaries, 28
    Change for Free and, 256
    Chief Product Owner role, 72
    as Collocated Team, 80
    coordination with other teams, 49
    creating, 80
    as Cross-Functional Team, 80, 96, 99, 200, 232, 399

defined, 7
Definition of Done and, 80, 92, 382–386
Definition of Ready and, 308, 316–319
Dependencies First and, 371–373
developer title, 80
Development Partnership and, 74–77
dividing work between multiple teams, 29
Enabling Specification and, 72, 307–310
Estimation Points and, 293–296
feature growth and, 421
Fixed Work and, 120–122
Fixed-Date PBI and, 297
Good Housekeeping and, 374–376
Granularity Gradient and, 289–291
hero culture and, 136–138
High Value First and, 251–254
identity, 28, 47, 80, 146
Impediment List and, 195–197
importance of, 78
Intentional Practice, 133
managers, working with, 44
Mitosis, 96–100
morale, 93
One Step at a Time and, 413
open environments and, 27
Organization Follows Market and, 27
Organizational Sprint Pulse and, 49
Oyatsu Jinja (Snack Shrine), 110–112
patlet, 458
performance, 78, 303, 321
Product Backlog creation, 68
in Product Backlog Sequence, 261–262
in Product Organization sequence, 13, 15
Product Owner role, 15, 48, 68, 72, 78–81
pulling Product Owner from, 69

Release Plan and, 237–240
Release Range and, 244
ROI-Ordered Backlog and, 248–249
Running Average Velocity and, 328
scaling and, 163
in Scaling Sequence, 94–96
Scrum (Master) Coach and, 117
Scrum Board and, 215–219
Scrum of Scrums and, 16, 163–164
in Scrum Team, 47–49
ScrumMaster Incognito and, 145, 148–149
ScrumMaster role, 15, 68, 81, 106–109
as Self-Organizing Team, 4, 92–93, 95, 165, 171, 361
Self-Organizing Team as, 81
Self-Selecting Team as, 80
Set-Based Design and, 204–206
in simple pattern sequence, 9
size, 47, 79, 81
Small Items and, 283–287
as Small Team, 80
Sprint Burndown Chart and, 210–214
stability and multiple teams, 85
as Stable Team, 48, 85
structure and organization, 23, 27–30, 79–81
Team Sprint and, 232, 387–390
understanding, 78–81
Vacation PBI and, 300–305
Value and ROI and, 246
Value Areas and, 416–418
Value Stream Fork and, 424
Value Stream Sequence and, 187
Visible Status and, 366
Whack the Mole and, 377–381

Dias, Sandra, xxi

differentiation, role, 45, 79

Distribute Work Evenly
Cross-Functional Team and, 62
patlet, 470

Do Food, 112, 470

Do Lots of Deliberate Practice, 339

documentation
Definition of Done and, 272
Product Backlog Item and, 271–272, 309

Domain Expertise in Roles
patlet, 469
team structure and organization, 27

domain experts
Cross-Functional Team and, 62
Development Partnership and, 75

Done-Done, *see* Definition of Done

Don't Interrupt an Interrupt, 468

double-loop learning, 175

drag, 120, 305

Drive, 233

drive, Happiness Metric and, 433

Due Date PBI, *see* Fixed-Date PBI

DuPuy, Paul, Jr., xxii

E

economic theory of value, 247

edge cases, 309

emergence, xxx

Emergency Procedure
Dependencies First and, 372
interruptions and, 152, 305
managers and, 152–153, 176
patlet, 460
in Product Organization sequence, 13, 16
Production Episode and, 357
in project language example, 453
Responsive Deployment and, 394–395

Scrum of Scrums and, 164
Scrum Team and, 49
Small Red Phone and, 114
understanding, 152–156
Visible Status and, 369
Whack the Mole and, 380–381

emergent requirements, *see also* Enabling Specification
Change for Free and, 255–257
Dependencies First and, 371–372
Developer-Ordered Work Plan and, 360
Emergency Procedure and, 152, 156
Release Range and, 244
Sprint Backlog Item and, 350
trading, 256

empowerment, 31, 40, 162

Enabling Specification
Change for Free and, 257
Definition of Done and, 386
Definition of Ready and, 317–318
Development Team and, 72, 307–310
patlet, 463
Product Backlog and, 266–267, 306–310
Product Backlog Item and, 271
in Product Backlog Sequence, 262
Product Owner Team and, 71–72
Small Items and, 283, 287
Sprint Review and, 168
term, 310
time and, 122
understanding, 306–310
Yesterday's Weather and, 325

end users
vs. customers, 67
focus on and team organization, 25

Endo, Isao (遠藤 功), 370

Engage Quality Assurance patlet, 469

engagement
Greatest Value and, 446
Happiness Metric and, 427–428, 430–431, 438
performance and, 431–432, 438

An Essay on the Art of Building and the Nature of the Universe, 100

estimating, *see also* Estimation Points; Granularity Gradient; Pigs Estimate
in absolute units, 293, 322
Aggregate Velocity and, 329–333
bottom-up, 286, 290
Change for Free and, 255–257
confidence in, 242
Definition of Ready and, 318
Enabling Specification and, 307
errors, 284, 288–289
Happiness Metric and, 429
High Value First and, 252–254
poker-planning, 292, 295
Product Backlog Item and, 270–271, 293–296
Product Owner and, 292–296
Product Roadmap and, 223
Refined Product Backlog and, 312
relationship to velocity, 328
in relative units, 293–296, 322
Release Plan and, 239
Release Range, 241–245
Running Average Velocity and, 326–328
with sizing, 322
Small Items and, 284–286, 288, 290
Specialized Velocities and, 334–336
Sprint Burndown Chart and, 212–213
top-down, 286, 290
Vacation PBI and, 300–305
velocity and, 293–295, 320–323, 334–336

waterfall organizations
and, 290
Wideband Delphi, 282
Yesterday's Weather and,
324–325
Estimation Points, *see also* estimating; Pigs Estimate
Aggregate Velocity and,
332
confidence in, 242
Granularity Gradient
and, 291
patlet, 463
Product Backlog Item
and, 271, 293–296
Production Episode and,
355
Refined Product Backlog
and, 296
Release Plan and, 239
ROI-Ordered Backlog
and, 250
Sprint Backlog Item and,
293–296, 350
Sprint Burndown Chart
and, 212
Stable Teams and, 85
understanding, 292–296
velocity and, 293–295,
320, 322
Yesterday's Weather and,
325
Etzioni, Amitai, 430
events, in core patterns
overview, 7–10
Extreme Toyota, 135

F

Face-to-Face Before Working
Remotely
Daily Scrum and, 146
Development Partnership
and, 77
patlet, 470
Facebook
Release Staging Layers
and, 404
Responsive Deployment
and, 393
Failed Project Wake, 450, 469
failsafes, 102, 155
Fair, Joe, xxi
fear, 438
Fearless Change, 470
features
growth and Conway's
Law, 425

growth and profitability,
419
Money for Nothing and,
258–260
organizing teams around,
26, 63
in Vision, 193
Federation Pattern, 77
feedback, *see also* Sprint
Retrospective; Sprint Review
Autonomous Team and,
88
as central to Scrum,
xxiii, xxv
in communication, 51, 53
delivery and, 232, 392
Greatest Value and, 446
patience for, 106
Pop the Happy Bubble
and, 140
Regular Product Increment and, 400
Release Staging Layers
and, 401–404
Responsive Deployment
and, 392, 394
Scrum Team and, 45–48
Small Items and, 284
in Sprint, 229, 231
Sprint duration and, 229
team structure and organization, 23
velocity and, 322
Ferries, Timothy, 434
Fertile Soil
The Mist and, 19
patlet, 457
in Product Organization
sequence, 14
Sprint Planning and and,
126
understanding, 20–22
Fibonacci series, 295
Fidelity Investments, 214
Firewall
managers as, 39
patlet, 468
ScrumMaster as, 88, 109
First Things First, 362
Fixed Work
Definition of Done and,
239
patlet, 459
Scrum Team and, 48,
120, 122
understanding, 119–122

Fixed-Date PBI
patlet, 463
as Shu pattern, 365
understanding, 271, 297–
299
Vacation PBI as, 299
focus
Fertile Soil and, 22
as organizational value,
21
focus groups, 168
fog of war, 215
Follow the Moon
Emergency Procedure
and, 154
patlet, 464
Responsive Deployment
and, 393
rhythms and, 225, 236,
363–365
Sprint duration and, 230
understanding, 363–365
in Value Stream Sequence, 188
food
Do Food, 112, 470
Oyatsu Jinja (Snack
Shrine), 110–112, 459
forces, xxviii
Ford, David N., 206
Ford, Henry, 65
forecasting, 321
formal team term, 97
free riding, 56
Fujino, Terunobu, 77
Funch, Rune, xxi

G

Gabriel, Richard Paul, xxii,
33, 114
games, *see also* The Spirit of
the Game
Cross-Functional Team
and, 64
paper airplane game, 64
Scrum as, 1
Gatekeeper
Autonomous Team and,
90
compared to Oyatsu Jinja
(Snack Shrine), 112
patlet, 468
ScrumMaster as, 109
Gates, William Henry III, 194
GE Healthcare, 164

generative pattern languages, 11

generativity and patterns, xxx

Gfader, Peter, xxi, 319

Gigerenzer, Gerd, 40

Gillett, Mark Alastair, xxi, 131

goals, *see also* Sprint Goal
  attention and, 366
  Fertile Soil and, 22
  impossible, 194
  MetaScrum and, 178
  Organizational Sprint Pulse and, 236
  overestimating, 324–325
  Scrum of Scrums and, 161–164
  stretch, 324–325
  Vision and, 192

Good Housekeeping
  One Step at a Time and, 413
  patlet, 465
  Product Backlog Item and, 272
  Production Episode and, 356, 376
  in project language example, 453
  team synchronization and, 232
  understanding, 374–376
  Whack the Mole and, 376–377, 380–381

Google
  blameless culture, 208
  Design Sprint, 207
  Fridays, 390
  kaikaku and, 102
  lack of branching, 253
  managers, 38, 41
  mindfulness program, 437
  Release Staging Layers and, 404
  Site Reliability Engineer, 369
  terminating products and, 449

Granularity Gradient
  patlet, 463
  Pigs Estimate and, 282
  Product Backlog and, 267
  Product Backlog Item and, 271, 289–291
  in Product Backlog Sequence, 261

Refined Product Backlog and, 312, 314
  Small Items and, 261, 287–291
  understanding, 288–291

Greatest Value
  Autonomous Team and, 86
  Change for Free and, 256
  Development Partnership and, 76
  feature growth and, 422
  Fertile Soil, 21
  Follow the Moon and, 365
  Happiness Metric and, 434, 436–437
  Kaizen and Kaikaku and, 101
  Kaizen Pulse and, 135
  management role and, 39
  Organizational Sprint Pulse and, 236
  patlet, 466
  pattern creation and, 455
  Product Backlog Sequence and, 261
  Product Pride and, 182
  Refined Product Backlog and, 315
  Regular Product Increment and, 400
  Release Staging Layers and, 404
  Sprint Goal and, 341
  Sprint Planning and, 123, 126
  Sprint Retrospective and, 172
  Sprint Review and, 166–169
  Testable Improvements and, 409
  understanding, 445–447
  Value and ROI and, 247
  Value Stream and, 200
  in Value Stream Sequence, 190
  Vision and, 194, 446–447
  as Whole, 446

Greening, Daniel Rex, xxii

Grenning, James, 295

Greville, W. James, 233

grumpiness and performance, 431

guilds, 33–34, *see also* Birds of a Feather

Gummi Bears, 295

H

Ha pattern, 365, 395

Hack Sprint, *see* Team Sprint

hackathons, 389

Hackman, Richard, 162

Hall, Edward Twitchell, 225–226, 232

hansei, 101, 172

Happiness Metric, xxii
  Norms of Conduct and, 151
  patlet, 466
  Product Pride and, 183
  in project language example, 453
  rationale, 431–439
  Scrumming the Scrum and, 442
  Self-Organizing Team and, 93
  Sprint Goal and, 344, 430
  Sprint Retrospective and, 173
  Team Sprint and, 389
  Testable Improvements and, 409
  understanding, 426–430

Happy Bubble, *see* Pop the Happy Bubble

Hardin, Garret, 158

Hayes, John, xxii, 434, 438

Heath, Robert, 208

Hegarty, Christine, xxi

Heitz, Hugo, 441, 444

Helenekilde Badhotel, xxi

Helgesen, Sarah James (Sally), 365

hero culture
  Remove the Shade and, 136–138
  Swarming and, 130

Hewlett-Packard, 343

Hibon, Michèle, 325

HICCS 2014, 352

hierarchies
  disadvantages, 24, 31, 161
  lack of in Development Team, 4
  shallow, 27

High Value First
  decision-making and, 259
  patlet, 462

Product Backlog and, 251–254
Product Backlog Item and, 273
in Product Backlog Sequence, 261
Release Plan and, 240
vs. ROI-Ordered Backlog, 252
ROI-Ordered Backlog and, 250–254
understanding, 251–254
Hillary, Edmund Percival, 104
Hillside Group, xxi
holidays
Follow the Moon and, 363
Vacation PBI and, 300–305
Holst, Nis, xxi
How Google Grows, 38
human resources, 42, 82, *see also* Vacation PBI

I

IBM, 37
ideas
Fertile Soil and, 20–22
The Mist and, 17–19
identity, *see also* team identity
product identity, 420, 423
self-identity and purchases, 420
IDX Systems, 164, 446
ikigai, 430
Illegitimus Non Interruptus
Emergency Procedure and, 152, 156
patlet, 460
in Product Organization sequence, 16
in project language example, 453
Teams That Finish Early Accelerate Faster and, 352
understanding, 157–160
Whack the Mole and, 381
Impediment Backlog, *see* Impediment List
Impediment List
Good Housekeeping and, 376
as Information Radiator, 279

MetaScrum and, 178
One Step at a Time and, 411
patlet, 461
Product Backlog Item and, 272
Product Pride and, 182
Scrumming the Scrum and, 440–444
Sprint Retrospective and, 173–174, 196
understanding, 195–197
impediments, *see* Impediment List; Scrumming the Scrum
improvement, *see* continuous improvement; kaikaku; kaizen; Kaizen and Kaikaku; Kaizen Pulse; Testable Improvements
Informal Labor Plan
vs. Developer-Ordered Work Plan, 362
patlet, 467
Self-Organizing Team and, 93
Information Radiator
Autonomous Team and, 88
Daily Scrum and, 146
examples, 279
Good Housekeeping and, 375
patlet, 462
Product Backlog as, 264
in Product Backlog Sequence, 261
Product Roadmap and, 223
Scrum Board as, 216, 218, 279
Sprint Backlog and, 347
Sprint Burndown Chart as, 212, 279
Sprint Goal as, 342
in Toyota Production System, 369
transparency and, 367
understanding, 274–279
vs. Visible Status, 279, 367
Whack the Mole and, 380
inkscape.org, xxii
innovation, historic, 17
instrumental team term, 97

Intentional Practice, *see also* Deliberate Practice
kaizen, 133
rhythms and, 226
interactions, Fertile Soil and, 20–22
interface quality, 204
Internet Explorer, 422
interruptions, *see also* Illegitimus Non Interruptus
Don't Interrupt an Interrupt, 468
Emergency Procedure and, 152, 305
Interrupts Unjam Blocking, 381, 468
Product Backlog Item and, 272
in project language example, 453
Sprint Goal and, 343
Teams That Finish Early Accelerate Faster and, 160, 352
Vacation PBI and, 305
Whack the Mole and, 159, 381
Interrupts Unjam Blocking
patlet, 468
Whack the Mole and, 381
Intimacy Gradient, 112
Involve the Managers, *see also* managers; MetaScrum
Birds of a Feather and, 33
Emergency Procedure and, 152
Kaizen and Kaikaku and, 102
patlet, 458
in Product Organization sequence, 15
Release Range and, 244
Scrumming the Scrum and, 441
team structure and organization, 30
understanding, 35–44
iPad, 421, 424
iPhone, 421, 424
iron triangle, 399
ISO 9001 certification, 406
Iterative User Interface Design, 204

J

Jagger, Jonathon Rodney Bull, 133, 339
Jan, Henk, 43
Jaquet, Mette, xxi
Järvelä, Jukka, 169
Jeffries, Ron, 295
job satisfaction, self-governing teams, 162, *see also* Happiness Metric
Jobs, Steve, 179
Johnson, Chris, xxi
Johnson, Steven Berlin, 17, 233, 313
Jørgensen, Magne, 286

K

Kahneman, Daniel, 433
kaikaku, *see also* continuous improvement; kaizen; Kaizen and Kaikaku
  defined, 101
  vs. Kaizen Pulse, 135
  managers and, 38, 41, 102
  Retrospective of Kerth and, 175
  ScrumMaster role, 43, 105
  understanding, 101–103
kaizen, *see also* continuous improvement; kaikaku; Kaizen and Kaikaku; Kaizen Pulse
  as central to Scrum, xxxi
  defined, 101, 440
  Definition of Done and, 384
  Emergency Procedure and, 155
  Happiness Metric and, 426–430
  Impediment List and, 196
  including in Product Backlog, 429
  Intentional Practice, 133
  learning in, 134
  One Step at a Time and, 410–414, 426
  Oyatsu Jinja (Snack Shrine) and, 111
  Release Range and, 244
  Release Staging Layers and, 404
  rhythms and, 226
  Scrum (Master) Coach and, 115–117
  ScrumMaster role, 105, 409
  Scrumming the Scrum and, 440–444
  Sprint and, 231
  Sprint duration, 125
  Sprint Retrospective and, 134, 174
  stretch goals and, 325
  Teams That Finish Early Accelerate Faster and, 352
  Testable Improvements and, 405–409
  transition mode, 338–339
  types of velocity kaizen, 134
  understanding, 101–103
  Updated Velocity and, 135, 338
  Value and ROI and, 134, 246
  velocity mean and, 321
Kaizen and Kaikaku
  Daily Scrum and, 144
  Fertile Soil and organizational values, 21
  management role in, 37–38, 41–42
  Responsive Deployment and, 394
  risk and, 37
  Scrum Team role in, 33, 37–38, 43
  ScrumMaster role, 43, 101, 105
  Teams That Finish Early Accelerate Faster and, 352
  understanding, 101–103
  Value and ROI and, 246
Kaizen Pulse
  learning in Sprint, 232
  One Step at a Time and, 413
  patlet, 459
  Product Pride and, 135, 182
  scaling and, 94
  Scrum Team and, 49, 133–135
  understanding, 132–135
  Value Stream and, 201
  velocity and, 132–135, 320

Kaku-an Shu-en (廓庵師遠), xvii
kamashibai, 409
Kanban Board, 218–219
Kanter, Rosabeth Moss, 162
Kawaguchi, Yasunobu (川口恭伸), xxii
Keeling, Michael, xxi
Kerth, Norm, 174–175
Kniberg, Henrik, 34, 428, 434
knowledge, Daily Scrum and, 146
knowledge relationships, 31
Kohler effect, 57
Koskinen, Johannes, xxi
Kronfält, Richard, 319

L

Lander, Adrian, xxii
last responsible moment
  Dependencies First and, 372
  Refined Product Backlog and, 311, 313
  Release Plan and, 240
  Responsive Deployment and, 391
layers, shearing, 25, 317
Leadership and Intuition, 40
Leading Teams, 162
Lean
  Design Structure Matrix, 313–314
  partnerships concept, 67
  process and, 187
Lean Startup, 42
learning
  cadence and, 232
  causal, 233
  Cross-Functional Team and, 61–64
  double-loop, 175
  kaizen and, 134, 232
  Scrum Team and, 46
  situated, 34
  in Sprint, 231–232
  in Sprint Retrospective, 231
  in Sprint Review, 168, 231
  triple-loop, 175
Leppänen, Marko Kristian, xxi
Let the Light In, *see* Remove the Shade

Liquid Networks, 17

load factor, 323, *see also* velocity

Lopez, Marcelo R., xxi

Lucid, 33

Lueder, Sue, 208

The Luminous Ground, xxxiv

lunar calendar, *see* Follow the Moon

Lunney, John, 208

M

M-Competitions, 325

MacDonald, Brian, xxii

Majdanac, Boško, xxi

Makridakis Competitions, 325

Makridakis, Spyros, 325

management tools, 89, 418

managers, *see also* Involve the Managers
    Autonomous Team and, 89
    Birds of a Feather and, 33, 39, 42
    Development Partnership and, 76
    Emergency Procedure and, 152–153, 176
    interruptions and, 159
    kaikaku and, 38, 41, 102
    Kaizen and Kaikaku role, 37–38, 41–42, 102
    lack of in Scrum, 35
    MetaScrum and, 16, 38–39, 42, 96, 176–180
    micromanagement and, 291, 347
    perception of meddling, 38
    Release Range and, 244
    Remove the Shade and, 137
    role of, 35–44
    Running Average Velocity and, 328
    scaling and, 42, 96
    Scrumming the Scrum and, 441
    status of, 36, 39
    stopping work, 41
    team structure and organization, 30
    Vacation PBI and, 304
    variance in velocity kaizen, 134

Managing the Flow of Technology, 51

Manns, Mary Lynn, 470

marginal gains, 102

Martin, Robert Cecil, 323, 379

mastery
    Birds of a Feather and, 33
    Happiness Metric and, 430
    Product Pride and, 182

Matron Role patlet, 469

Matts, Chris, 408

meet-ups, 34

meetings, *see* Backlog Refinement Meeting; Daily Scrum; MetaScrum; Scrum of Scrums; Sprint Review; Sprint Retrospective; stand-up meetings

Mei, Jowen, xxi

memory and happiness, 433

Merckens, Dary, xxi

MetaScrum
    management role in, 16, 38–39, 42, 96, 176–180
    patlet, 461
    in Product Organization sequence, 16
    scaling and, 96
    team structure and organization, 27
    understanding, 48, 176–180
    Value Stream Fork and, 424

MetaScrum Product Owner, 177

meter, Testable Improvements and, 409

micromanagement
    Granularity Gradient and, 291
    Sprint Backlog and, 347

Microsoft, 419, 422

mieruka, 370

Mikkelsen, Søren, xxii

The Mist
    patlet, 457
    in Product Organization sequence, 14
    understanding, 17–19
    in Value Stream Sequence, 187

Mitosis
    patlet, 459
    in Scaling Sequence, 94, 96
    Small Teams and, 59, 100
    understanding, 97–100

Mock, Paul Douglas, xxi

Moderate Truck Number
    Cross-Functional Team and, 62
    patlet, 469
    Remove the Shade and, 137–138
    Stable Teams and, 85

Money for Nothing
    Development Partnership and, 76
    origins, 257, 260
    patlet, 462
    in Product Backlog Sequence, 261
    Product Wake and, 450
    ROI-Ordered Backlog and, 250
    understanding, 258–260

monochronic cultures, 226, 364

Moon, *see* Follow the Moon

morale, 93, 438

motivation
    autonomy and, 89
    changes in scope and, 355
    control and, 92
    Daily Scrum and, 149
    deadlines and, 353
    Development Team sense of ownership, 388
    Happiness Metric and, 426
    intrinsic motivation, 233
    Kohler effect, 57
    Production Episode and, 355
    ScrumMaster Incognito and, 149
    Sprint Goal and, 344
    Swarming and, 130
    Team Sprint and, 389–390
    to self-organize, 361
    velocity and, 327
    Visible Status and, 368

muda
    Cross-Functional Team and, 63

handoffs as, 200
in taxonomy of waste, 352
multitasking, disadvantages, 127–129
Munck, Kenny, xxi, 114
mura
    Cross-Functional Team and, 63
    Organizational Sprint Pulse and, 236
    in taxonomy of waste, 352
muri
    Organizational Sprint Pulse and, 236
    in taxonomy of waste, 352
Musk, Elon Reeve, 194

N
Nakano, Hiroshi (中埜博), 451–452
Named Stable Bases
    patlet, 467
    Responsive Deployment and, 393, 395
names
    patterns, xxxvii
    Product Backlog Item, 269
NASA, 83, 274
National Advisory Committee for Aeronautics, 176
The Nature of Order, xxxiv
net present value (NPV)
    about, 246
    High Value First and, 252
    Product Backlog Item and, 268
    project managers and, 66
    ROI-Ordered Backlog and, 250
Nielsen, Jakob, 204
Nokia, 37
Nonaka, Ikujiro (野中 郁次郎), 315
Norgay, Tenzing, 104
Norms of Conduct
    Autonomous Team and, 88
    Good Housekeeping and, 376
    patlet, 460

Pop the Happy Bubble and, 141
    Scrum Team and, 48
    team identity and, 28
    understanding, 150–151
Northern Telecom, 36–37, 40, 42
NPV, see net present value (NPV)
NUMMI plant, 436, 447

O
objectivity, 409
Odawara Resort, xxi
Ohno, Taiichi (大野耐), 172, 352
One Step at a Time
    composing pattern languages, 452
    generativity and, xxx
    Happiness Metric and, 426
    patlet, 466
    pattern sequences and, xxxiii
    Responsive Deployment and, 395
    rhythms and, 226
    understanding, 410–414
One Team per Task
    patlet, 467
    Whack the Mole and, 380
one-by-one production, 131
openness, Norms of Conduct and, 151
OpenView Venture Partners, 352, 373
Organization Follows Market
    Autonomous Team and, 90
    Development Team and, 27
    patlet, 470
organizational patterns, see Product Organization Pattern Language
Organizational Patterns of Agile Software Development
    about, xxxii
    patlets, xxxvii, 466–470
Organizational Sprint Pulse
    Development Partnership and, 76
    Development Team and, 49

Emergency Procedure and, 154
    MetaScrum and, 178
    patlet, 462
    rhythms and, 226, 234–236
    scaling and, 96
    Scrum of Scrums and, 163, 236
    team synchronization and, 232
    terminating Sprint early, 154
    understanding, 234–236
organizational values, 20–22
orienteering, 248
Østergaard, Jen, 90
outsourcing, Scrum Team and, 49
overtime, 130, 439
overtime pay, 130
Oyatsu Jinja (Snack Shrine)
    patlet, 459
    ScrumMaster role, 88
    understanding, 110–112
Oyatsu Jinja (おやつ神社), 112

P
PAF (Ålands Penningautomat-förening), 393
Pagonis, John (Ioannis) (Ιωάννης Παγώνης), xxi
pair programming, see Developing in Pairs
Palm, 343
paper airplane game, 64
parallelism
    disadvantages of multi-tasking, 128
    One Step at a Time and, 411
    Set-Based Design and, 204
Parkinson's Law, 354
partnerships, see Development Partnership
passion
    Happiness Metric and, 433, 438
    performance and, 431–432, 438
patents, 310
PatientKeeper, 154, 178, 180
patlets, 457–470
    about, xxxvii

from *Fearless Change*, 470

notation, xxxviii

from *Organizational Patterns of Agile Software Development*, xxxvii, 466–470

Product Organization Pattern Language, 457–461

Value Stream Pattern Language, 461–466

Patron Role patlet, 469

pattern languages, *see also* Product Organization Pattern Language; Value Stream Pattern Language

composing, 451–455

creating, xxxiii

defined, xxx, 11, 13

generative, 11

as starting points, xxxi–xxxiii

Whole and, xxx

pattern sequences

about, xxvii, xxix, xxxiii

defined, 8

Product Backlog Sequence, xxxiii, 261–262

Product Organization Sequence, xxxiii, 12–16

Scaling Sequence, xxxiii, 94–96

simple example, 8

Value Stream Sequence, xxxiii, 187–190, 261

Whole and, xxxiii

patterns, *see also* patlets; pattern languages; pattern sequences

about, xv, xvii

as about people, xxx

context, xxviii

creating, xxv, xxvii, xxx, xxxiii, 454–455

defined, xxiv, xxvi, 12

form, xxviii

fundamental process of, xxxiv

Ha pattern, 365, 395

as interconnected, xxix, 11

largest, 13

methodology, xxiv, xxvii

moral grounds and, 455

names, xxxvii

notation, xxvii, xxix, xxxvi–xxxvii

order in book, xxxvi–xxxvii

overview of core, 7–10

Shu, 365

stars, xxix

uses, xxvi

PDCA (plan-do-check-act), xxxiv, 135

PDSA (plan-do-study-act), xxxiv, 135

Pelrine, Joesph, 295

people

emphasis on in Agile, 22

emphasis on in Toyota Way, 22, 304, 436, 447

patterns focus on, xxx

People Building Something Together, 1–2

performance, *see also* velocity

Development Team, 78, 303, 321

grumpiness and, 431

Happiness Metric and, 428, 431–433, 436, 438

individual assessment, 5

Norms of Conduct and, 150–151

passion and, 431–432, 438

Pop the Happy Bubble and, 139–142

Running Average Velocity and, 326–328

scaling and, 94

Scrumming the Scrum and, 440

Self-Organizing Team and, 93

Testable Improvements and, 405

Vacation PBI and, 303

The Phenomenon of Life, xxxiv

phone, *see* Small Red Phone

Pigs Estimate, *see also* estimating; Estimation Points

patlet, 463

Product Backlog Item and, 188, 271, 282

Refined Product Backlog and, 282, 312

Release Range and, 244

Stable Teams and, 85

understanding, 280–282

Vacation PBI and, 303

velocity and, 321, 323

Pink, Daniel H., 233, 430, 436

A Place to Wait, 112

plan-do-check-act (PDCA), xxxiv, 135

plan-do-study-act (PDSA), xxxiv, 135

poka-yoke, 102, 155

poker-planning, 292, 295

polychronic cultures, 226

Pop the Happy Bubble

Autonomous Team and, 88

Happiness Metric and, 433

Kaizen and Kaikaku and, 101

patlet, 460

ScrumMaster and, 108, 141

understanding, 139–142

Poppendieck, Mary Brust, 339

Porath, Christine, 438

Post-it Notes®, *see* sticky notes

Potentially Shippable Increment, *see* Regular Product Increment

Pover, Mary, 446

Powerhouse, 447

PowerPoint, 167

predictability

cadence and, 232

Stable Teams and, 84

pride, *see* Product Pride; Team Pride

privacy

autonomy and, 89

in work environment, 53

problem-solving

avoiding in Daily Scrum, 145

patterns and, xxvi

Whack the Mole and, 377–381

process loss, team size and, 49, 57

The Process of Creating Life, xxxiv

The Process of Repair, 100

processes

building right, 105, 187

organizing around, 27
process change and
  Whack the Mole, 381
Producer Roles
  patlet, 469
  ScrumMaster and, 108
Product Backlog, *see also* Definition of Done; Product
  Backlog Item; Refined
  Product Backlog; ROI-Ordered Backlog
  Aggregate Velocity and,
    329–333
  creation of, 68
  defined, 8
  Definition of Ready and,
    264, 267, 316–319
  Developer-Ordered Work
    Plan and, 358–362
  Enabling Specification
    and, 266–267, 306–310
  Fixed Work and, 119–122
  as framework for decision-making, 240
  High Value First and,
    251–254
  Impediment List and, 196
  interruptions and, 157–160
  kaizen in, 429
  MetaScrum and, 177–180
  Mitosis and, 100
  One Step at a Time and,
    411
  ordering, 68, 72, 107,
    244, 261, 359, 362
  patlet, 462
  Pigs Estimate and, 282
  Product Owner role, 15,
    65, 67–69, 107, 264–267
  Product Owner Team
    and, 68, 71–72, 269
  Product Pride and, 182
  vs. Product Roadmap,
    222, 224, 264
  Product Roadmap and,
    220–224
  Production Episode and,
    354–357
  Release Plan and, 223,
    238, 266
  Release Range and, 243–245
  Responsive Deployment
    and, 391–396
  scaling and, 95–96
  Scrum Board and, 216–219

Scrum Team and, 48,
  264–267
ScrumMaster and, 107
Scrumming the Scrum
  and, 266, 442–444
Sequence example,
  xxxiii, 261–262
Set-Based Design and,
  208
in simple pattern sequence, 8–9
Small Items and, 283–287, 289–291
Specialized Velocities
  and, 333–336
Sprint Burndown Chart
  and, 211–214
Sprint Goal and, 265,
  341–344
Sprint Planning and,
  123–126, 264, 266
Sprint Review and, 166,
  168
Swarming and, 129–131
Team Sprint and, 387–390
understanding, 263–267
Vacation PBI and, 300–305
Value and ROI and, 247,
  266
Value Areas and, 416–418, 424
Value Stream and, 185,
  200, 265
vs. Value Stream Fork,
  96
Value Stream Fork and,
  423–425
in Value Stream Sequence, 187–188
velocity and, 320–323
Visible Status and, 366
Vision and, 193, 264–265
Whack the Mole and, 380
as Whole, 261
Product Backlog Item, *see also* Definition of Done; Product Backlog; Refined Product Backlog; ROI-Ordered Backlog
  Aggregate Velocity and,
    329–333
  annotations, 412
  Change for Free and,
    255–257
  Cross-Functional Team
    and, 62–63

Definition of Done and
  delivery, 232
Definition of Ready and,
  188, 270, 316–319
Dependencies First and,
  371–373
Developer-Ordered Work
  Plan and, 358–362
documenting, 271, 309
Enabling Specification
  and, 271, 306–310
Estimation Points and,
  271, 293–296
Fixed Work and, 119–122
Fixed-Date PBI and, 271,
  297–299, 365
Granularity Gradient
  and, 271, 289–291
High Value First and,
  251–254, 273
last responsible moment,
  240
Mitosis and, 100
names, 269
One Step at a Time and,
  411, 414
ordering, 68, 72, 119,
  261, 273, 359, 362,
  372, 395
patlet, 462
Pigs Estimate and, 188,
  271, 282
in Product Backlog Sequence, 261
Product Owner role, 65,
  119, 269–273
Product Owner Team
  role, 71–72, 269
Product Roadmap and,
  222–224
Production Episode and,
  271, 354–357
Release Plan, 237–240
Release Range, 241–245
Responsive Deployment
  and, 391–396
risk and, 348–349
Scrum Board and, 216–219
Scrumming the Scrum
  and, 272, 443
Set-Based Design and,
  208
Small Items and, 283–287, 289–291, 345
Specialized Velocities
  and, 333–336
Sprint Burndown Chart
  and, 211–214

Sprint Goal and, 270, 341–344
Sprint Planning and, 123–126, 270
Sprint schedule and delivery, 231
Team Sprint and, 387–390
team structure and organization, 29
for technical debt, 389
understanding, 268–273
Vacation PBI, 246, 300–305, 365
Value and ROI and, 247, 268, 270, 273
Value Areas and, 416–418
Value Stream Fork and, 424
in Value Stream Sequence, 188–189
velocity and, 320–323
Whack the Mole and, 380
The Product Backlog Refinement Meeting, 314
Product Backlog Sequence, xxxiii, 261–262
product identity, 420, 423
Product Increment, *see* Regular Product Increment
Product Organization, *see also* Product Organization Pattern Language
Sequence, xxxiii, 12–16
Vision and, 192–193
as Whole, 1, 11
Product Organization Pattern Language
about, xxx–xxxi, xxxvi, 1
composing pattern languages and, 451
figure, 11
kaizen and, xxxi
patlets, 457–461
rhythms and, 225
Vision and, 193
Product Organization Sequence, xxxiii, 12–16
Product Owner, *see also* Product Owner Team
administrative duties, 105
Aggregate Velocity and, 329–333
authority, 176, 178, 180, 265

Birds of a Feather and, 33
Change for Free and, 256
Daily Scrum and, 145
defined, 7, 15
Definition of Done and, 382–384, 386
Definition of Ready and, 308, 317–319
Dependencies First and, 373
Developer-Ordered Work Plan and, 359–362
Development Partnership and, 74–76
Development Team role, 15, 48, 68, 72, 78–81
dividing work, 29
Emergency Procedure and, 152–155, 394–395
Enabling Specification and, 306–310
estimating and, 280, 282, 292–296
Estimation Points and, 292–296
feature growth and, 420–421
Fixed Work and, 119–122
Fixed-Date PBI and, 297–299
Granularity Gradient and, 289–291
High Value First and, 252
Impediment List and, 196
Intentional Practice, 133
interruptions and, 159
management role, 36–40, 42
managers, as separate from, 35, 41
managers, working with, 41, 44
MetaScrum and, 16, 96, 177–180
Mitosis and, 100
One Step at a Time and, 413
ordering Product Backlog, 107, 244, 261, 359
origins, 267
patlet, 458
Pop the Happy Bubble and, 141
Product Backlog Item role, 119, 269–273
Product Backlog role, 15, 65, 67–69, 107, 244, 264–267, 359

Product Backlog Sequence and, 261–262
in Product Organization sequence, 13, 15
Product Pride and, 67, 182–183
Product Roadmap role, 69, 220–224
Product Wake and, 449–450
Production Episode and, 354–357
Proxy Product Owner, 74
Refined Product Backlog role, 311–315
Regular Product Increment and, 189, 397
Release Plan and, 69, 237, 240
Release Range and, 244
Remove the Shade and, 137
research, 120–122
Responsive Deployment and, 392–395
ROI-Ordered Backlog and, 248–250, 261, 265
Scaling Sequence, 95–96
Scrum Team role, 15, 47–49, 65, 68, 200
ScrumMaster, relation to, 106–107
Scrumming the Scrum and, 442
Self-Organizing Team and, 93
Set-Based Design and, 204–205
in simple pattern sequence, 8
Small Items and, 283–287
Small Red Phone and, 113–114
The Spirit of the Game and, 6
Sprint Burndown Chart and, 210–211
Sprint costs and, 232
Sprint Goal and, 341–342
Sprint Planning role, 15
Sprint Retrospective and, 173
Sprint Review and, 16, 165–169, 171, 189, 230
Sprint role, 230

subcontracting arrangements, 41
Team Sprint and, 387–390
team structure and organization, 27, 29, 67–69
terminating Sprint early, 154, 159
Testable Improvements and, 408
tests and, 167
understanding, 65–69
Vacation PBI and, 301–302
Value and ROI role, 246–247
Value Areas and, 416–418
Value Stream and, 199–200, 408, 421
Value Stream Fork and, 423–425
Value Stream Sequence and, 187
velocity and, 119, 303–304
Visible Status and, 366
Vision role, 15, 67–69, 192–193
Whack the Mole and, 380–381
Yesterday's Weather and, 325
Product Owner Team, see also Product Owner
Chief Product Owner, 68, 71–72, 75, 417, 458
as Collocated Team, 72
Development Partnership and, 75
estimating and, 282
MetaScrum and, 176
patlet, 458
Product Backlog and, 68, 71–72
Product Backlog Item and, 269
research, 120
scaling and, 95
Scrum of Scrums and, 163
Set-Based Design and, 72, 208
Small Items and, 287
understanding, 70–72
Value Areas and, 417
when to use, 68
Product Pride
Collocated Team and, 54

Development Partnership and, 77
Emergency Procedure and, 156
interruptions and, 160
Kaizen Pulse and, 135, 182
Oyatsu Jinja (Snack Shrine) and, 112
patlet, 461
in Product Organization sequence, 13, 16
Product Owner and, 67, 182–183
Product Owner Team and, 72
Refined Product Backlog and, 315
Scrum of Scrums and, 164
Self-Organizing Team and, 93
Set-Based Design and, 209
Sprint Planning and, 126
Sprint Retrospective and, 174
Sprint Review and, 169
Stable Teams and, 85
Swarming and, 131
understanding, 181–183
Value Stream and, 200
Product Roadmap
patlet, 461
vs. Product Backlog, 222, 224, 264
Product Owner role, 69, 220–224
Regular Product Increment and, 220–221, 399
Release Plan and, 223, 239
Small Items and, 284
vs. Sprint Backlog, 224
Sprint Review and, 168
understanding, 220–224
Value Stream Sequence and, 188
Vision and, 193, 221–224
as Whole, 201
Product Vision, 193, see also Vision
Product Wake
Failed Project Wake, 450, 469
Greatest Value and, 447
management role in, 40

patlet, 466
understanding, 183, 448–450
in Value Stream Sequence, 190
Production Episode
Dependencies First and, 372
Development Team and, 189
duration, 356
Enabling Specification and, 308
Fixed Work and, 120
Good Housekeeping and, 356, 376
Information Radiator and, 278
patlet, 464
Product Backlog Item and, 271, 354–357
in Product Backlog Sequence, 262
Responsive Deployment and, 356, 392–395
rhythms and, 227
Sprint and, 230
Sprint Backlog Item and, 350
Sprint Planning and, 15, 355–356
Sprint Review and, 166–169
time-boxing, 121, 354–357
understanding, 353–357
Value Stream and, 200
in Value Stream Sequence, 189
velocity and, 232, 357
Whack the Mole and, 381
Yesterday's Weather and, 325
productivity
Small Teams and, 56–58
Swarming and, 130
profitability, feature growth and, 419
Programming Episodes
patlet, 467
Responsive Deployment and, 395
Progress Software, 34
project languages, composing, 451–455

project managers
  Development Partnership
    and, 75
  disadvantages, 66
Project Oxygen, 41
prototypes, 309
Proxy Product Owner, 74
psychological theory of value,
  247
pulse, *see* Kaizen Pulse; Organizational Sprint Pulse
purpose
  autonomy and, 439
  Happiness Metric and,
    430, 434–437
  Product Pride and, 182

Q

QPW (Quattro Pro for Win-
  dows), 147, 336
quality
  Definition of Done and,
    383, 385
  Engage Quality Assur-
    ance patlet, 469
  The Quality Without a
    Name, xxiv, xxvi
  Release Staging Layers
    and, 401–403
quality circles, 33, *see al-
  so* Birds of a Feather
The Quality Without a Name,
  xxiv, xxvi
Quattro Pro for Windows
  (QPW), 147, 336
quiet rooms, 53
Quinta da Pacheca, xxi
QWAN, *see* The Quality With-
  out a Name

R

Rauhamäki, Jari, xxi
Rawsthorne, Dan, 131
RBI, *see* Regular Product In-
  crement
Ready-Ready, *see* Definition
  of Ready
Recommitment Meeting, 467
red phone, *see* Small Red
  Phone
Refined Product Backlog, *see
  also* Product Backlog
  decision-making and, 240
  Dependencies First and,
    373

dividing work between
  multiple teams, 29
Enabling Specification
  and, 309
estimating, 312
Estimation Points and,
  296
Fixed Work and, 119, 121
Granularity Gradient
  and, 290, 312, 314
patlet, 463
Pigs Estimate and, 282,
  312
in Product Backlog Se-
  quence, 262
Product Owner Team
  and, 72
Production Episode and,
  354
Proxy Product Owner and
  Development Partner-
  ship, 74
Release Staging Layers
  and, 403
Scrum of Scrums and,
  163
Set-Based Design and,
  206
timing, 267
understanding, 311–315
reflection, change and, 133
Regular Product Increment
  Change for Free and,
    256, 260
  defined, 8
  Definition of Done and,
    382–383, 385
  Definition of Ready and,
    318
  Developer-Ordered Work
    Plan and, 360–361
  Development Team and,
    81, 323
  drop in value over time,
    259
  Emergency Procedure
    and, 156
  Follow the Moon and, 365
  Good Housekeeping and,
    375
  interruptions and, 158
  MetaScrum and, 176,
    179
  Mitosis and, 99
  Organizational Sprint
    Pulse and, 235
  patlet, 465
  Product Backlog and,
    264–267

Product Backlog Item
  and, 270, 272
Product Backlog Se-
  quence and, 261
Product Pride and, 182
Product Roadmap and,
  220–221, 399
Production Episode and,
  356
Release Plan, 237–240
Release Range and, 244
Release Staging Layers
  and, 403
Responsive Deployment
  and, 393–394
ROI-Ordered Backlog
  and, 249–250
scaling and, 96
Scrum Team and, 48,
  397–400
ScrumMaster role, 108
Set-Based Design and,
  208
in simple pattern se-
  quence, 9
Small Items and, 284
Small Teams and, 58
Sprint as representation
  of, 231
Sprint Goal and, 342,
  397, 399
Sprint Planning and,
  123–126
Sprint Review and, 165–
  169, 189, 230, 400
Team Sprint and, 389
understanding, 397–400
Value Areas and, 416–
  418
Value Stream and, 185,
  200, 399
in Value Stream Se-
  quence, 187, 189
velocity and, 238–240
Visible Status and, 368
as Whole, 201
Reinertsen, Donald, 53
Release Burndown, 242
Release Plan
  Aggregate Velocity and,
    329
  Information Radiator
    and, 278
  patlet, 462
  Product Backlog and,
    223, 238, 266
  Product Owner role, 69,
    237, 240

Product Roadmap and, 223, 239
Small Items and, 284, 286
understanding, 237–240
velocity and, 238–240, 320
in waterfall development, 221

Release Range
Estimation Points and, 295
patlet, 462
Release Plan and, 240
understanding, 241–245

Release Staging Layers
patlet, 465
Regular Product Increment and, 400
team synchronization and, 232
understanding, 401–404
in Value Stream Sequence, 189

Release Train, 274

releasing, *see also* Release Plan; Release Range; Release Staging Layers
Definition of Done and, 232
High Value First and, 254
Information Radiator and, 278
Product Owner role, 232
Release Burndown, 242
Responsive Deployment and, 391–396
Running Average Velocity and, 327

Remove the Shade
patlet, 460
ScrumMaster and, 108, 136, 138
understanding, 136–138

Requirement Areas, 418

research
Product Owner role, 120–122
time for, 120

resource management, 82

respect
Fertile Soil and, 22
Norms of Conduct and, 151
as organizational value, 21

responsibility
Autonomous Team and, 86, 88
autonomy and, 162
management and, 36, 38–39
Product Owner and, 37, 39–40, 67–70, 72
project managers and, 66
Self-Organizing Team and, 92–93
Sprint Retrospective and, 171

Responsive Deployment
market impact, 396
patlet, 465
Production Episode and, 356
Release Plan and, 240
Release Staging Layers and, 404
understanding, 391–396
Value Stream and, 200
in Value Stream Sequence, 189

Retrospective of Kerth, 175

Rettig, Mary, 446

Return on Equity (ROE), 250

rewards, limiting, 130

rhythms, *see also* cadence
Follow the Moon and, 225, 236, 363–365
Organizational Sprint Pulse and, 226, 234–236
Sprint, 226, 228, 230
understanding, 225–227

Ries, Eric, 42

Rising, Linda, 470

risk
Development Partnership and, 75–76
feasibility, 348
Kaizen and Kaikaku and, 37
management and, 37, 40
Money for Nothing and, 258
Product Backlog Item and, 348–349
Product Owner and, 37, 39
Release Plan and, 237
Release Range and, 244
Scrum Team and, 37
Small Items and, 283
Sprint and, 228

Sprint Backlog Item and, 348–349
Team Sprint and, 389

ROE (Return on Equity), 250

ROI, *see also* ROI-Ordered Backlog; value; Value and ROI
High Value First and, 252
kaizen and, 134
management role in, 40
project managers and, 66
terminating products and, 449

ROI-Ordered Backlog
vs. High Value First, 252
High Value First and, 250–254
kaizen and, 134
patlet, 462
Product Backlog Item and, 273
in Product Backlog Sequence, 261
understanding, 247–250, 265

Role Theory, 79

roles
cadences, 79
in core patterns overview, 7–10
differentiation, 45, 79
self-selection, 79
Wally Number, 57

Roosevelt, Theodore, 432

Rosing, Wayne, 38, 41

Rother, Mike, 201

Royal Air Force, 237

Running Average Velocity
patlet, 464
Stable Teams and, 85
understanding, 320, 325–328
as Updated Velocity, 328
vs. Updated Velocity, 337–338
uses, 295

Ryan, Richard M., 428

S

Saab Defense, 179

Sacrifice One Person
Greatest Value and, 447
patlet, 467
Whack the Mole and, 381

Sarni, Robert Allan, xxi

Satir cycle, 338

scale, Testable Improvements and, 409

scaling, *see also* Mitosis
  about, 94
  autonomy and, 89
  geographic, 95
  managers and, 42, 96
  MetaScrum and, 96
  Scaling Sequence, xxxiii, 94–96
  Scrum of Scrums and, 96, 163
  Specialized Velocities, 333
  Value Areas and, 95–96, 415–418
  Value Stream Fork and, 96, 419–425

Scaling Sequence, 94–96

Schwaber, Ken
  on Sprint Goal, 344
  on autonomy of team, 359
  Scrum of Scrums and, 164
  Sprint Burndown Chart and, 214

scope
  creep, 420
  Emergency Procedure and, 153
  feature growth and, 419, 422
  Production Episode and, 355
  Regular Product Increment and, 400
  Teams That Finish Early Accelerate Faster, 154
  waste and, 352

Scrum
  defined, xxiii
  Definition of Ready and, 319
  as framework, xxiii, xxv, xxviii, 4
  as game, 1
  as journey, xx
  as more than Daily Scrum, xxvii, 147
  as more than Scrum Board, 219
  as more than Sprint, xxvii
  as more than Sprint Goal, xxviii

need for understanding, 104–106
  origins, xvii, xxiv, 94, 172

Scrum (Master) Coach
  avoiding burnout with, 109
  patlet, 459
  Self-Organizing Team and, 93
  understanding, 115–118

Scrum Board
  as Information Radiator, 216, 218, 279
  patlet, 461
  Product Backlog and, 216–219
  Sprint Backlog and, 347
  Sprint Backlog Item and, 350
  Swarming and, 130
  understanding, 215–219
  Value Stream and, 200

The Scrum Guide, xxiii, xxv, 5, 226, 308, 315

The Scrum Handbook, 362

Scrum of Scrums, *see also* Scrumming the Scrum
  Autonomous Team and, 90
  coordination with other teams, 49
  management role in, 39
  Mitosis and, 100
  Organizational Sprint Pulse and, 163, 236
  patlet, 460
  in Product Organization sequence, 16
  regular events, 163
  scaling and, 96, 163
  Sprint Planning and, 126, 163
  team structure and organization, 27
  understanding, 161–164
  Value Areas and, 418

Scrum Patterns Group, xxv

Scrum Team, *see also* Daily Scrum; Emergency Procedure; MetaScrum; Scrum Board; Scrum of Scrums; Sprint Goal
  as Autonomous Team, 38, 48, 86–90, 178, 181–182, 234
  boundaries, 28
  Change for Free and, 256

as Collocated Team, 15, 48
  cross-cutting structures, 26
  as Cross-Functional Team, 15, 48, 57, 61, 182, 200
  defined, 7
  Definition of Done and, 382–384
  Definition of Ready and, 318
  Emergency Procedure and, 49
  feature growth and, 421
  feedback, 45–48
  Fixed Work and, 48, 120, 122
  Fixed-Date PBI and, 298–299
  Greatest Value and, 445
  High Value First and, 254
  identity, 28
  Impediment List and, 195–197
  interruptions and, 157–160
  Kaizen Pulse and, 49, 133–135
  kaizen role, 33, 37–38, 43, 49, 133–135
  as locus of learning, 46
  management role, 36–38
  managers, working with, 41–42
  multiple, 48
  Norms of Conduct and, 48, 150–151
  Organizational Sprint Pulse and, 49, 234–236
  patlet, 458
  Pigs Estimate and, 282
  Pop the Happy Bubble and, 140
  Product Backlog and, 48, 264–267
  Product Backlog Item and, 124, 188, 270
  Product Backlog Sequence and, 261
  in Product Organization sequence, 13, 15
  Product Owner role, 15, 47–49, 65, 68, 200
  Product Pride and, 181–183
  Product Roadmap and, 221–224
  Product Wake and, 450

Production Episode and, 355

Refined Product Backlog and, 312, 314

Regular Product Increment and, 48, 397–400

Release Range and, 242–245

Release Staging Layers and, 403

Responsive Deployment and, 393, 395

rhythms and, 226

Scaling Sequence, 95–96

Scrumming the Scrum and, 441

as Self-Organizing Team, 108

in simple pattern sequence, 8

size, 48–49, 57

Small Items and, 283–287

Small Red Phone, 114

as Small Team, 48

Sprint Burndown Chart and, 210–214

Sprint Goal and, 321, 340–344

Sprint Planning role, 15, 48, 124–126

Sprint Retrospective and, 16, 49, 171–175

Sprint Review and, 16, 49

Sprint role, 230

stability and multiple teams, 85

as Stable Team, 48, 85, 450

structure and organization, 24–25, 27–28, 47–49

understanding, 45–49

Vacation PBI and, 300

Value Areas and, 415–416

Value Stream and, 185, 199, 201, 234

Value Stream Fork and, 424

Value Stream Sequence and, 187

velocity and, 245, 320, 322

Visible Status and, 368

Vision and, 45, 47, 193

Whack the Mole and, 380–381

Scrum, Daily, see Daily Scrum

ScrumMaster, see also Scrum (Master) Coach
activities, 107
Autonomous Team role, 88–90
Birds of a Feather and, 33
Birds of a Feather for, 109, 117
as coach, 41, 106, 108
Collocated Team and, 53
Daily Scrum and, 107, 144–145, 149
defined, 7, 106
Definition of Done and, 43, 384–386, 404
Development Partnership and, 76
Development Team role, 15, 68, 81, 106–109
Emergency Procedure and, 153
as Firewall, 88, 109
as Gatekeeper, 109
Happiness Metric and, 439
Impediment List and, 196
Information Radiators and, 347
Intentional Practice, 133
Kaizen and Kaikaku role, 43, 101, 105, 409
management role, 38–39, 43–44
managers as, 15
managers, working with, 44, 76
Mitosis and, 100
origins, 267
Oyatsu Jinja (Snack Shrine) role, 88
patlet, 459
Pop the Happy Bubble and, 108, 141
in Product Organization sequence, 13, 15
Product Pride and, 182
Product Wake and, 450
in project language example, 453
pulling Product Owner from Development Team, 69
Release Range and, 244
Release Staging Layers and, 404

Remove the Shade and, 136, 138
removing, 108
Scaling Sequence, 95
Scrum Board and, 217
Scrum of Scrums and, 164
in Scrum Team, 47–49
ScrumMaster Incognito, 145, 148–149, 460
Scrumming the Scrum and, 441
selecting, 108
Self-Organizing Team and, 93, 361
in simple pattern sequence, 9
Small Red Phone and, 108, 113–114
The Spirit of the Game and, 6
Sprint Burndown Chart and, 213
Sprint Planning role, 15
Sprint Retrospective and, 174
Team Sprint and, 390
team structure and organization, 27
Testable Improvements and, 409
understanding, 104–109
Vacation PBI and, 301, 304
Value and ROI role, 246

ScrumMaster Incognito
Daily Scrum and, 145, 148–149
patlet, 460
understanding, 148–149

Scrumming the Scrum, see also Scrum of Scrum
hansei and, 172
vs. Kaizen Pulse, 135
One Step at a Time and, 413
patlet, 466
Pop the Happy Bubble and, 141
Product Backlog and, 266, 442–444
Product Backlog Item and, 272, 443
Product Pride and, 182
in project language example, 453
Self-Organizing Team and, 93, 441

Sprint Retrospective and, 173, 441–444
Teams That Finish Early Accelerate Faster and, 352
understanding, 440–444
Value Stream and, 201
in Value Stream Sequence, 189

Search Inside Yourself, 438

seiketsu, 372, 376

seiri, 372, 376

seiso, 372, 376

seiton, 372, 376

self-determination theory, 428

self-identity and purchases, 420

Self-Managing Team, *see* Autonomous Team

Self-Organizing Team
Autonomous Team as, 88–89
Birds of a Feather and, 31
as Development Team, 81
Development Team as, 4, 92–93, 95, 165, 171, 361
interruptions and, 158, 160
Norms of Conduct and, 150
Oyatsu Jinja (Snack Shrine) and, 111
patlet, 459
Scrum of Scrums and, 161–164
Scrum Team as, 108
Scrumming the Scrum and, 93, 441
as Stable Team, 84
Swarming and, 130
understanding, 91–93

Self-Selecting Team
as Development Team, 80
patlet, 468
Small Teams as, 58
as Stable Team, 84

Senge, Peter, 31

sequences, *see* pattern sequences

Set-Based Design
Cross-Functional Team and, 63
Mitosis and, 100

patlet, 461
Product Owner Team and, 72, 208
Product Roadmap and, 224
scaling and, 418
time and, 121–122
understanding, 203–209
Value Areas and, 418

shearing layers, 25, 317

Shimp, Douglas E., xxii

Shu pattern, 365

shutsuke, 372, 376

Siili Solutions, 34

Simons, Al J., xxi

Site Reliability Engineer, 369

Site Reliability Engineering, 208

situated learning, 34

Sival, Michiel, xxi

Size the Organization
Development Team and, 81
patlet, 468

sizing, 322

skills
coverage in teams, 61
Cross-Functional Team and, 61–64
Product Owners, 69
Scrum of Scrums and, 163
Swarming and, 130

Skype, 175, 390

The Slow Hunch, 119

slow hunch, 313

Small Items
Definition of Ready and, 318
Granularity Gradient and, 261, 287–291
One Step at a Time and, 412
patlet, 463
poker-planning and, 295
Product Backlog Item and, 271
Sprint Backlog and, 284–287, 345
understanding, 283–287
velocity and, 320

Small Red Phone
patlet, 459

ScrumMaster and, 108, 113–114
understanding, 113–114

Small Teams
Collocated Team and, 53
cross-cutting structures, 25
as Cross-Functional Team, 58, 62
Development Team as, 80
domain experts and, 63
feature growth and, 421
Mitosis and, 59, 100
patlet, 458
process loss and, 49
Scrum Team as, 48
as Self-Organizing Team, 93
as Self-Selecting Team, 58
as Stable Team, 59
structure and organization, 24–27, 57–59
understanding, 55–59

Smoke-Filled Room
management and, 44
patlet, 470

Snack Shrine, *see* Oyatsu Jinja (Snack Shrine)

soak, 404

Sobek, Durward K., 206

social loafing, team size and, 56–57

soil, fertile, *see* Fertile Soil

solitude
creativity and, 313
working spaces, 50, 53

Solo Virtuoso
patlet, 468
Remove the Shade and, 138
when to use, 81

solutions in pattern form, xxviii

Someone Always Makes Progress
Dependencies First and, 371
patlet, 467

Specialized Velocities
vs. Aggregate Velocity, 335
patlet, 464
scaling and, 333
understanding, 334–336

The Spirit of the Game
about, 1
decision-making and, 28
Developer-Ordered Work
Plan and, 358
Happiness Metric and,
439
Information Radiator
and, 277
The Mist and, 18
patlet, 457
pattern creation and, 455
in Product Organization
sequence, 13–14
ScrumMaster and, 109
as starting point, xxxvi
understanding, 3–6
Value and ROI and, 247

Spotify, 34, 42, 425

Spreitzer, Gretchen, 438

Sprint, *see also* Daily Scrum;
Emergency Procedure; Orga-
nizational Sprint Pulse;
Product Backlog; Product
Backlog Item; Production
Episode; Regular Product
Increment; Sprint Backlog;
Sprint Backlog Item; Sprint
Burndown Chart; Sprint
Goal; Sprint Planning;
Sprint Retrospective; Sprint
Review; Teams That Finish
Early Accelerate Faster; velocity
autonomy of, 90
corrective actions, 16
cost, 232
defined, 7, 188, 229
Dependencies First and,
371–373
duration of, 125, 225–
226, 229–230, 232,
234, 364
dysfunction causes, 152
Emergency Procedure, 16
failed, 356
feedback in, 229, 231
Fixed Work and, 119–122
interruptions and, 157–
160
kaizen and, 134
learning in, 231–232
management role in, 39
as measure of time, 230
misunderstandings, xxvii
patlet, 461
Product Backlog Se-
quence and, 261

Product Owner Team
role, 71
in project language exam-
ple, 453
as Regular Product Incre-
ment, 231
Release Range and, 242–
245
rhythms and, 226, 228,
230
Self-Organizing Team
and, 93
Set-Based Design and,
206, 208
in simple pattern se-
quence, 9
Small Items and, 283–
287
structure and organiza-
tion, 229–233
Team Sprint, 175, 232,
387–390, 465
terminating early, 153–
155, 158–159, 232,
357
understanding, 228–233
in Value Stream Se-
quence, 188
Visible Status and, 366
as Whole, 201

Sprint Backlog, *see also* Emergency Procedure; Regular
Product Increment; Sprint
Backlog Item
5S techniques, 372, 376
Daily Scrum and, 146
defined, 8
Developer-Ordered Work
Plan and, 358–361
Development Team and,
81, 188
Enabling Specification
and, 308
One Step at a Time and,
411
ordering, 347, 359
origins, 267
patlet, 464
Product Backlog Item
and, 270, 272
Product Backlog Se-
quence and, 261
vs. Product Roadmap,
224
Production Episode and,
354–357
Responsive Deployment
and, 394

Running Average Velocity
and, 328
Scrum Board and, 215–
219
Scrumming the Scrum
and, 441–444
in simple pattern se-
quence, 9
Small Items and, 284–
287, 345
Sprint Burndown Chart
and, 213, 347
Sprint Goal and, 341–342
Sprint Retrospective and,
173
Team Sprint and, 232
Teams That Finish Early
Accelerate Faster and,
352
understanding, 345–347
Vacation PBI and, 303
Value Stream and, 185,
200
in Value Stream Se-
quence, 187–188
Visible Status and, 369
Whack the Mole and, 380
as Whole, 201

Sprint Backlog Item, *see also* Emergency Procedure;
Regular Product Increment;
Sprint Backlog
Daily Scrum and, 144
defined, 346
Dependencies First and,
371–373
Developer-Ordered Work
Plan and, 358–361
duration, 285
Estimation Points and,
293–296, 350
Granularity Gradient
and, 290
One Step at a Time and,
411, 414
ordering, 286, 347, 359
patlet, 464
Small Items and, 284–
287
Sprint Burndown Chart
and, 213, 350
understanding, 348–350
Visible Status and, 366

Sprint Burndown Chart
as Information Radiator,
212, 279
patlet, 461
Product Backlog and,
211–214

Scrum Board and, 217–218

Sprint Backlog and, 213, 347

Sprint Backlog Item and, 213, 350

Sprint Goal and, 342

understanding, 210–214

updating, 213

Sprint Goal, *see also* Sprint Burndown Chart

ability to explain, 125

Autonomous Team and, 88

Daily Scrum and, 15, 144–146, 149, 171, 342

Dependencies First and, 372

Developer-Ordered Work Plan and, 358, 361

Emergency Procedure and, 152, 154

failed Sprints, 356

Fixed Work and, 120

focus on in Sprint, 230

Happiness Metric and, 344, 430

misunderstandings, xxviii

motivation and, 130

patlet, 464

Pop the Happy Bubble and, 140

Product Backlog and, 265, 341–344

Product Backlog Item and, 270, 341–344

Product Pride and, 182

Regular Product Increment and, 342, 397, 399

Responsive Deployment and, 394

ROI-Ordered Backlog and, 261

scaling and, 96

Scrum Board and, 216–219

Scrum of Scrums and, 16

Scrum Team and, 321

Small Items and, 285

Sprint Backlog Item and, 350

Sprint Planning and, 124–126, 342

in Sprint Review, 167

Swarming and, 131, 343

Team Sprint and, 389

Teams That Finish Early Accelerate Faster and, 351–352

understanding, 340–344

in Value Stream Sequence, 188

velocity and, 321, 343

Whack the Mole and, 380

The Sprint Guide, 357

Sprint Plan, *see* Sprint Backlog

Sprint Planning

acceptance testing and, 167

Autonomous Team and, 90

defined, 8

Definition of Ready and, 262

dividing work between multiple teams, 29

Emergency Procedure and, 154

Fixed Work and, 121

High Value First and, 251–254

Organizational Sprint Pulse and, 236

patlet, 459

Pigs Estimate and, 282

Product Backlog and, 123–126, 264, 266

Product Backlog Item and, 123–126, 270

in Product Organization sequence, 13, 15

Production Episode and, 15, 355–356

Proxy Product Owner and Development Partnership, 74

Refined Product Backlog and, 314

rhythms and, 226

Scrum of Scrums and, 126, 163

Scrum Team and, 48, 124–126

in simple pattern sequence, 9

Small Items and, 286

Sprint Goal and, 124–126, 342

Sprint Review and, 169

terminating Sprint early, 154

time for, 120

understanding, 123–126

Value Stream and, 124, 200

Sprint Pulse, *see* Organizational Sprint Pulse

Sprint Retrospective

Autonomous Team and, 88, 90

defined, 8

Definition of Done and, 384

Development Partnership and, 76

Emergency Procedure and, 154, 156

failed Sprints and, 357

Fixed Work and, 121

Good Housekeeping and, 376

Impediment List and, 173–174, 196

kaizen and, xxxi, 134, 174

learning in, 231

Norms of Conduct and, 151

One Step at a Time and, 413

Organizational Sprint Pulse and, 236

Oyatsu Jinja (Snack Shrine) after, 111

patlet, 460

Pop the Happy Bubble and, 139, 141

in Product Organization sequence, 16

Regular Product Increment and, 400

rhythms and, 226

Scrum Team and, 16, 49, 171–175

Scrumming the Scrum and, 173, 441–444

Self-Organizing Team and, 93

in simple pattern sequence, 10

Small Red Phone and, 114

Sprint Burndown Chart and, 214

vs. Sprint Review, 168, 171

Sprint Review and, 168–169

Team Sprint and, 175

terminating Sprint early, 154

Testable Improvements and, 173, 408
time for, 120
understanding, 170–175, 230
Value Stream and, 201
in Value Stream Sequence, 189
Whack the Mole and, 381
Sprint Review
activities, 167
Autonomous Team and, 88, 90
defined, 8
Definition of Done and, 167, 189, 382–383, 386
Fixed Work and, 121
kaizen and, 134
learning in, 168, 231
name example, xxxvii
Organizational Sprint Pulse and, 236
Oyatsu Jinja (Snack Shrine) after, 111
patlet, 460
in Product Organization sequence, 16
Product Owner and, 16, 165–169, 171, 189, 230
Regular Product Increment and, 165–169, 400
Release Staging Layers and, 403
Responsive Deployment and, 393–394
rhythms and, 226
Scrum of Scrums and, 163
Scrum Team and, 16, 49
Scrumming the Scrum and, 441, 443
in simple pattern sequence, 9
Small Items and, 284
vs. Sprint Retrospective, 168, 171
Sprint Retrospective and, 168–169
time for, 120
understanding, 165–169
Value Stream and, 200
in Value Stream Sequence, 189
Stable Teams
Change for Free and, 256

as Cross-Functional Team, 62
Cross-Functional Team as, 84
Development Partnership and, 76
Development Team as, 48, 85
identity, 85
importance of, 339
Organizational Sprint Pulse and, 236
patlet, 458
in project language example, 452
Scrum Team as, 48, 85, 450
Self-Organizing Team as, 84
Self-Selecting Team as, 84
Small Teams as, 59
structure and organization, 83–85
understanding, 82–85
velocity and, 84–85, 320
Stand-Up Meeting pattern, 147, 470
stand-up meetings, 144, 147, 470, see also Daily Scrum
standards, Autonomous Team and, 87
stars notation, xxix
Status, Visible, see Visible Status
Stearns, Peter N., 433
sticky notes
creating project languages, 452
for Estimation Points, 350
Information Radiator and, 278, 380
Product Roadmap and, 224
Scrum Board and, 217
for Sprint Backlog Items, 287, 350
using this book, xxxii, xxxix
Stop the Line, see Emergency Procedure
Stora Nyteboda, xv, xxi
stretch goals, 324–325
subcontractors, Value and ROI and, 246

subjectivity, 409
Suenson, Espen, xxi
Sun Microsystems, 37
Surrogate Customer patlet, 468
Sutherland, Jeff
Change for Free and, 257, 260
Money for Nothing and, 257, 260
on Definition of Ready, 319
on Dependencies First, 373
on Developer-Ordered Work Plan, 362
on Enabling Specification, 308
on Greatest Value, 446
on Happiness Metric, 430, 433
on Small Items, 287
on Sprint Goal, 343
on Sprint Planning, 125
on Sprint Retrospective, 174
on *The Scrum Guide*, xxv
on autonomy, 90
on reordering PBIs, 250
pattern language example, 452–453
Product Owner origins, 267
scaling and, 94
Scrum of Scrums and, 164
Scrum Team concept, 49
Swarming: One-Piece Continuous Flow
concurrent activities and, 414
Cross-Functional Team and, 62, 64
Dependencies First and, 372
vs. Developer-Ordered Work Plan, 362
Developer-Ordered Work Plan and, 131, 360, 362
last responsible moment and, 391
One Step at a Time and, 411
patlet, 459
Product Backlog Item and, 349

in Product Organization sequence, 15
in project language example, 453
Responsive Deployment and, 395
Sprint Backlog and, 347
Sprint Goal and, 131, 343
understanding, 127–131
in Value Stream Sequence, 189
velocity and, 321

Swieringa, Joop, 175

synergy, management role in, 38, 41

system engineers, 246

Systematic, 130, 179

Søltoft, Rune Funch, xxi

T

Take No Small Slips, 156, 467

Takeuchi, Hirotaka (竹内 弘高), 315

Tan, Chade-Meng, 438

Task Board, see Scrum Board

taxonomy of waste, 352

Taylorism, 161

team identity
Collocated Team and, 54
Daily Scrum and, 146
Development Team and, 47
Happiness Metric and, 433
Stable Teams and, 85
Swarming and, 130
Team Pride and, 28
Vision and, 80

Team per Task
patlet, 467
Whack the Mole and, 380

Team Pride
Birds of a Feather and, 28, 33
Collocated Team and, 54
Daily Scrum and, 146
Emergency Procedure and, 156
Mitosis and, 100
Norms of Conduct and, 151
patlet, 469
Pop the Happy Bubble and, 142

Product Organization sequence, 16
Remove the Shade and, 138
Scrum (Master) Coach and, 117
ScrumMaster Incognito and, 149
Self-Organizing Team and, 93
Stable Teams and, 85
team identity and, 28
team structure and organization, 27

Team Pulse, see Organizational Sprint Pulse

Team Sky, 102

Team Sprint
defined, 232
patlet, 465
Sprint Retrospective and, 175
understanding, 387–390

teams, see also Autonomy Team; Collocated Team; Conway's Law; Development Team; Mitosis; Scrum Team; Self-Organizing Team; Self-Selecting Team; Small Teams; team identity; Team Pride; Teams That Finish Early Accelerate Faster
diversity in perspectives, 191
empowerment, 31
formal vs. instrumental, 97
morale, 93, 438
self-managing, 31
status and size, 55
structure and organization, 23–30

Teams That Finish Early Accelerate Faster
Emergency Procedure and, 154
interruptions and, 160, 352
patlet, 464
Production Episode and, 357
in project language example, 453
understanding, 351–352
velocity and, 320, 351–352

technical debt
Definition of Done and, 385–386
retiring, 380
Sprint Review and, 168
Team Sprint and, 389
Teams That Finish Early Accelerate Faster and, 351
Whack the Mole and, 380

teleconferences, Collocated Team and, 54

Ten Bulls, xvii–xx

termination fees, 259

Terry, John, 153

Tesco, 199

Testable Improvements
vs. Definition of Done, 409
One Step at a Time and, 412
patlet, 466
Scrumming the Scrum and, 441
Sprint Retrospective and, 173, 408
vs. testing Done, 385
understanding, 405–409

testing, see also Testable Improvements
acceptance testing, 167–168, 352
Definition of Done and, 385, 391
Definition of Ready and, 318
delaying, 128
Enabling Specification and, 308
Happiness Metric and, 429
patience for, 106
requirement lapses and, 307
Responsive Deployment and, 391
Sprint Review and, 167–168

Theory of Centers, 100

Thiokol, Morton, 275

thrashing, 56, 266

time, see also time-boxing
Fixed Work and, 119–122
for interruptions, 158
for kaizen, 132–135
monochronic cultures, 226, 364

polychronic cultures, 226
for research, 120
rhythms of, 225–227
risk element, 348
Sprint as measure of, 230
Sprint duration, 125,
    225–226, 229–230,
    232, 234, 364
Value Stream and, 122,
    200
time-boxing
    as central to Scrum, xxiii
    Daily Scrum, 144–145,
        149
    Production Episode, 121,
        354–357
    rhythms and, 226
    Set-Based Design and,
        208
    Sprint, 229, 231–232
    Sprint Planning and, 125
    Sprint Retrospective,
        173–174
    Sprint Review and, 167
The Timeless Way of Building,
    xxvi
Tony's Chocolonely, 43, 194
Tornhill, Adam, xxi
Toyoda, Akio (豊田章男), 70
Toyoda, Sakichi (豊田 佐吉),
    370
Toyota
    autonomy and, 89
    Fixed-Date PBI and, 299
    GR sports car, 70
    impossible goals and, 194
    kaikaku and, 37
    kaizen and, 101
    mission statement, 436,
        447
    overproduction as waste,
        412
    poka-yoke, 102
    process route, 129–131
    production capacity, 130
    scaling and, 94
    Set-Based Design and,
        203, 206
    trust and, 22
    Updating Velocity and,
        339
    value of people, 22, 304,
        436, 447
    Value Stream and, 199
    work cell and Scrum
        Team concept, 49
Toyota Kata, 201, 409, 440

Toyota Product Development
    System, xxiv
Toyota Production System
    5S techniques, 376
    Information Radiator
        and, 369
    scaling and, 94
    Scrum origins in, xxiv,
        94, 172
    Sprint Retrospective and,
        172
    Value Stream and, 199
    Visible Status and, 369
    visual control, 279
    work cell and Scrum
        Team concept, 49
The Toyota Way Fieldbook, 22
TPS, see Toyota Production
    System
tragedy of the commons, 157
training, Vacation PBI and,
    301
transcendence
    Birds of a Feather and,
        33
    mastery and, 33
transparency
    Autonomous Team and,
        89
    Emergency Procedure
        and, 156
    employee monitoring and,
        407
    Fertile Soil and, 22
    Information Radiator
        and, 367
    as organizational value,
        21
    Product Wake and, 449
    Sprint Backlog and, 347
    Sprint Review and, 166
    Team Sprint and, 389
    trust and, 22
    Vacation PBI and, 303,
        305
    Visible Status and, 368–
        369
tribes, 33–34, see also Birds
    of a Feather
triple constraint, 399
triple-loop learning, 175
truck number, see Moderate
    Truck Number
trust, see also Community of
    Trust
    accountability and, 88

Autonomous Team and,
    88
change fees and, 256
Collocated Team and, 54
Daily Scrum and, 146
Release Plan and, 237
Scrum (Master) Coach
    and, 117
Sprint Goal and, 342
Sprint Review and, 166,
    168
transparency and, 22
Value Stream Fork and,
    425
Tulton, Adaobi Obi, xxii
Tung, Portia, xxi
type B production, 315

U
Uncle Bob, see Martin, Robert
    Cecil
Unity of Purpose
    patlet, 468
    Product Roadmap and,
        223
    Sprint Goal and, 342
    Sprint Planning and, 126
    Vision and, 193
Updated Velocity
    kaizen and, 135, 338
    patlet, 464
    Running Average Velocity
        and, 328, 337
    Sprint Backlog and, 346
    understanding, 320,
        325, 337–339
use cases, 309
user stories
    Enabling Specification
        and, 306–307
    Product Backlog Item
        and, 271
    Scrumming the Scrum
        and, 442

V
Vacation PBI
    as Fixed-Date PBI, 299
    Follow the Moon and, 365
    patlet, 463
    understanding, 300–305
    Value and ROI and, 246

value, *see also* Greatest Value; ROI; Value and ROI; Value Stream; Value Stream Fork; Value Stream Pattern Language
  annotations, 247–248
  casuistic theory of, 247, 301
  economic theory of, 247
  estimating and, 282
  net present value (NPV), 66, 246, 250, 252, 268
  organizational values, 20–22
  Product Backlog and, 266
  Product Owner and, 67–69
  project managers and values, 66
  psychological theory of, 247
  Regular Product Increment and, 397–400
  Return on Equity (ROE), 250
  Scrum Team and, 48
  Vacation PBI and, 302
Value and ROI
  kaizen and, 134, 246
  management role in, 40
  Product Backlog and, 247, 266
  Product Backlog Item and, 247, 268, 270, 273
  Product Pride and, 182
  Regular Product Increment and, 399
  Release Plan and, 240
  ROI-Ordered Backlog and, 249
  Small Items and, 285
  understanding, 246–247
  Vacation PBI and, 246
  velocity and, 322
Value Areas
  defined, 416
  feature growth and, 421
  Mitosis and, 100
  patlet, 466
  scaling and, 95–96, 415–418
  Specialized Velocities and, 336
  team structure and organization, 25
  understanding, 415–418

as Value Stream Fork, 424
  in Value Stream Sequence, 189
Value Stream, *see also* Value Stream Fork; Value Stream Pattern Language
  about, 185
  Autonomous Team role, 88–90
  defined, 187
  Development Team and, 79, 187
  Fertile Soil and, 22
  management role in, 41
  mapping, 201
  MetaScrum and, 179
  Money for Nothing and, 258–260
  patlet, 461
  Product Backlog and, 185, 200, 265
  Product Backlog Sequence and, 261
  Product Owner and, 199–200, 408, 421
  Product Roadmap and, 223
  Regular Product Increment and, 185, 200, 399
  Release Staging Layers and, 403
  Responsive Deployment and, 396
  ROI-Ordered Backlog and, 250
  Scrum Team and, 185, 199, 201, 234
  sequence example, 187–190, 261
  Sprint and, 230
  Sprint Goal and, 343
  Sprint Planning and, 124, 200
  team structure and organization, 25, 27
  time and, 122, 200
  understanding, 198–202
  Value Stream Sequence and, 188
  visibility of issues and, 379
  Vision and, 185, 193
  Whack the Mole and, 381
  as Whole, 1, 11, 200–201
Value Stream Fork, *see also* Value Stream
  Mitosis and, 100

patlet, 466
  vs. Product Backlog, 96
  Product Backlog and, 423–425
  Regular Product Increment and, 400
  scaling and, 96, 419–425
  Specialized Velocities and, 336
  understanding, 419–425
  as Value Areas, 424
  in Value Stream Sequence, 189
Value Stream Pattern Language
  about, xxx–xxxi, xxxvi, 1, 185
  composing pattern languages and, 451
  figure, 185
  kaizen and, xxxi
  patlets, 461–466
  rhythms and, 225
Value Stream Sequence, xxxiii, 187–190, 261
Value Streams
  Cross-Functional Team and, 63
  feature growth and, 421
  Product Owner Team and, 72
  Release Staging Layers and, 404
  Specialized Velocities and, 336
van Boxmeer, L.E.L.M., 439
van Steenbergen, Martien, xxii
velocity, *see also* Aggregate Velocity; Follow the Moon
  Autonomous Team and, 89
  baseline, 133, 135
  defects and, 159
  defined, 232, 320
  Enabling Specification and, 307
  estimating and, 293–295, 320–323, 328, 334–336
  Estimation Points and, 293–295, 320, 322
  feature growth and, 421
  Fixed Work and, 119
  individual contributions, 304
  interruptions buffer, 158–160

Kaizen Pulse and, 132–135, 320
mean, 321
Mitosis and, 100
as motivating factor, 327
One Step at a Time and, 410–411
ordering in Daily Scrum, 143
Product Owner and, 119, 303–304
Production Episode and, 232, 357
in project language example, 453
Regular Product Increment and, 238–240
Release Plan and, 238–245, 320
Remove the Shade and, 137
Responsive Deployment and, 394
Running Average Velocity, 85, 295, 320, 325–328, 337–338, 464
scaling and, 94
scatteredness and multitasking, 127
Scrumming the Scrum and, 441, 443
Specialized Velocities, 333–336, 464
Sprint Backlog and, 346
Sprint Goal and, 321, 343
Sprint Planning and, 125
Sprint Review and, 168
Stable Teams and, 84–85, 320
Swarming and, 130
Teams That Finish Early Accelerate Faster and, 320, 351–352
term, 323
types of velocity kaizen, 134
understanding, 320–323
Updated Velocity, 135, 320, 325, 328, 337–339, 346, 464
Vacation PBI and, 300–305
variance, 245, 321–322, 325–326, 338
Yesterday's Weather and, 302, 320–322, 324–326

vendors, *see also* Development Partnership
Money for Nothing and, 258–260
Responsive Deployment and, 395
Value and ROI and, 246
Vision and, 193
Verwijs, Christiaan, 437–438
videoconferences, Collocated Team and, 54
vigor, engagement and, 427
Visible Status
vs. Information Radiator, 279, 367
patlet, 465
Sprint Backlog and, 347, 369
understanding, 366–370
Vision
Autonomous Team and, 88
changes in scope and, 355
defined, 192
Development Team and, 15, 78–80
Enabling Specification and, 307
feature growth and, 421
forming teams and, 62
Greatest Value and, 194, 446–447
The Mist and, 18–19
patlet, 461
Product Backlog and, 193, 264–265
Product Backlog Item and, 270
Product Owner role, 15, 67–69, 192–193
Product Owner Team and, 72
Product Pride and, 182–183
Product Roadmap and, 193, 221–224
Production Episode and, 355
Regular Product Increment and, 399
Release Plan and, 237–240
scaling and, 95–96
Scrum of Scrums and, 163
Scrum Team and, 45, 47, 193

in simple pattern sequence, 8
Sprint Goal and, 341
understanding, 191–194
Value and ROI and, 247
Value Stream and, 185, 193
in Value Stream Sequence, 187–189
A Vision of a Living World, xxxiv
visuals, 309

W
wakes, *see* Failed Project Wake; Product Wake
Wally Number, 57
Warfield, Robert Walter, xiii, 147
waste
Good Housekeeping and, 374–376
overproduction as, 412
taxonomy of, 352
Watanabe, Katsuaki (渡辺 捷昭), 194
The Water Cooler, 112, 470
waterfall organizations
about, 29
estimating and, 290
release burndown charts and, 242
Release Plan and, 221
scaling and, 94
Watson, Jesse, 63
The Wednesday Afternoon Meeting, 314
Weinberg, Jerry, 128, 409, 430–431
Wells, Don, 323
Whack the Mole
Good Housekeeping and, 376–377, 380–381
interruptions and, 159, 381
One Step at a Time and, 413
patlet, 465
Responsive Deployment and, 392
understanding, 377–381
Value and ROI and, 246
Visible Status and, 369
whining, 174

Whole
as central concept, xx, xxxiv
continuous improvement and, 103
core patterns overview, 7–10
Development Team and, 80
in fundamental process of patterns, xxxiv
Greatest Value as, 1, 446
pattern form and, xxvi
pattern languages and, xxx
pattern sequences and, xxxiii
Product Backlog as, 261
Product Organization as, 1, 11
Product Roadmap as, 201
Regular Product Increment as, 201
Sprint as, 201
Sprint Backlog as, 201
Value Stream as, 11, 200–201
Value Stream Sequence and, 188

Why Gantt Charts Don't Work, *see* Developer-Ordered Work Plan
Wideband Delphi, 282
Wierdsma, André, 175
Windows, 419, 422
WIP (Work-In-Progress)
Kanban Board and, 218
minimizing, 127
Wise Fool patlet, 469
work environment, *see also* Collocated Team
Good Housekeeping and, 374–376
Information Radiator and, 278
open environments, 27
Oyatsu Jinja (Snack Shrine), 110–112
privacy in, 53
solitude in, 50, 53
Work Flows Inward
interruptions and, 158, 160
patlet, 467
Product Backlog and, 267
Work-In-Progress (WIP)
Kanban Board and, 218
minimizing, 127
working agreements, 151

Y
Yahoo!, 390
Yasui, Tsutomo (安井 力), xxii
Yesterday's Weather
Developer-Ordered Work Plan and, 361
Emergency Procedure and, 152
interruptions and, 160
patlet, 463
Production Episode and, 325, 357
in project language example, 453
Sprint Backlog and, 346
Teams That Finish Early Accelerate Faster and, 352
understanding, 320–322, 324–325
Vacation PBI and, 302
velocity and, 320–322, 324–326

Z
Zen Buddhism and Ten Bulls, xvii–xx
Zerubavel, Eviatar, 225, 365

Thank you!

How did you enjoy this book? Please let us know. Take a moment and email us at support@pragprog.com with your feedback. Tell us your story and you could win free ebooks. Please use the subject line "Book Feedback."

Ready for your next great Pragmatic Bookshelf book? Come on over to https://pragprog.com and use the coupon code BUYANOTHER2019 to save 30% on your next ebook.

Void where prohibited, restricted, or otherwise unwelcome. Do not use ebooks near water. If rash persists, see a doctor. Doesn't apply to *The Pragmatic Programmer* ebook because it's older than the Pragmatic Bookshelf itself. Side effects may include increased knowledge and skill, increased marketability, and deep satisfaction. Increase dosage regularly.

And thank you for your continued support,

Andy Hunt, Publisher

Pragmatic Bookshelf

SAVE 30%!
Use coupon code
BUYANOTHER2019

The Nature of Software Development

You need to get value from your software project. You need it "free, now, and perfect." We can't get you there, but we can help you get to "cheaper, sooner, and better." This book leads you from the desire for value down to the specific activities that help good Agile projects deliver better software sooner, and at a lower cost. Using simple sketches and a few words, the author invites you to follow his path of learning and understanding from a half century of software development and from his engagement with Agile methods from their very beginning.

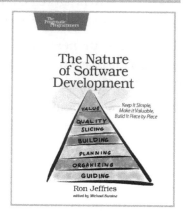

Ron Jeffries
(176 pages) ISBN: 9781941222379. $24
https://pragprog.com/book/rjnsd

Fixing Your Scrum

Broken Scrum practices limit your organization's ability to take full advantage of the agility Scrum should bring: The development team isn't cross-functional or self-organizing, the product owner doesn't get value for their investment, and stakeholders and customers are left wondering when something—anything—will get delivered. Learn how experienced Scrum masters balance the demands of these three levels of servant leadership, while removing organizational impediments and helping Scrum teams deliver real-world value. Discover how to visualize your work, resolve impediments, and empower your teams to self-organize and deliver using advanced coaching and facilitation techniques that honor and support the Scrum values and agile principles.

Ryan Ripley and Todd Miller
(200 pages) ISBN: 9781680506976. $45.95
https://pragprog.com/book/rrscrum

Code with the Wisdom of the Crowd

Build systems faster and more effectively with Mob Programming. Mob Programming is an approach to developing software that radically reduces defects and key-person dependencies by having a group of people work together at a single machine. See how to avoid the most common pitfalls that teams make when first starting out. Discover what it takes to create and support a successful mob. Take collaborative programming to the next level!

Mark Pearl
(122 pages) ISBN: 9781680506150. $26.95
https://pragprog.com/book/mpmob

Creating Great Teams

People are happiest and most productive if they can choose what they work on and who they work with. Self-selecting teams give people that choice. Build well-designed and efficient teams to get the most out of your organization, with step-by-step instructions on how to set up teams quickly and efficiently. You'll create a process that works for you, whether you need to form teams from scratch, improve the design of existing teams, or are on the verge of a big team re-shuffle.

Sandy Mamoli and David Mole
(102 pages) ISBN: 9781680501285. $17
https://pragprog.com/book/mmteams

The Pragmatic Bookshelf

The Pragmatic Bookshelf features books written by developers for developers. The titles continue the well-known Pragmatic Programmer style and continue to garner awards and rave reviews. As development gets more and more difficult, the Pragmatic Programmers will be there with more titles and products to help you stay on top of your game.

Visit Us Online

This Book's Home Page
https://pragprog.com/book/jcscrum
Source code from this book, errata, and other resources. Come give us feedback, too!

Keep Up to Date
https://pragprog.com
Join our announcement mailing list (low volume) or follow us on twitter @pragprog for new titles, sales, coupons, hot tips, and more.

New and Noteworthy
https://pragprog.com/news
Check out the latest pragmatic developments, new titles and other offerings.

Save on the eBook

Save on the eBook versions of this title. Owning the paper version of this book entitles you to purchase the electronic versions at a terrific discount.

PDFs are great for carrying around on your laptop—they are hyperlinked, have color, and are fully searchable. Most titles are also available for the iPhone and iPod touch, Amazon Kindle, and other popular e-book readers.

Buy now at *https://pragprog.com/coupon*

Contact Us

Online Orders:	*https://pragprog.com/catalog*
Customer Service:	*support@pragprog.com*
International Rights:	*translations@pragprog.com*
Academic Use:	*academic@pragprog.com*
Write for Us:	*http://write-for-us.pragprog.com*
Or Call:	+1 800-699-7764

Milton Keynes UK
Ingram Content Group UK Ltd.
UKHW051947241123
433080UK00010B/6